AF593549

REGARDING THE LAND

for Edith —
Now, for something
entirely different. Enjoy this tour
through 40 years of my work.

[illegible signature]

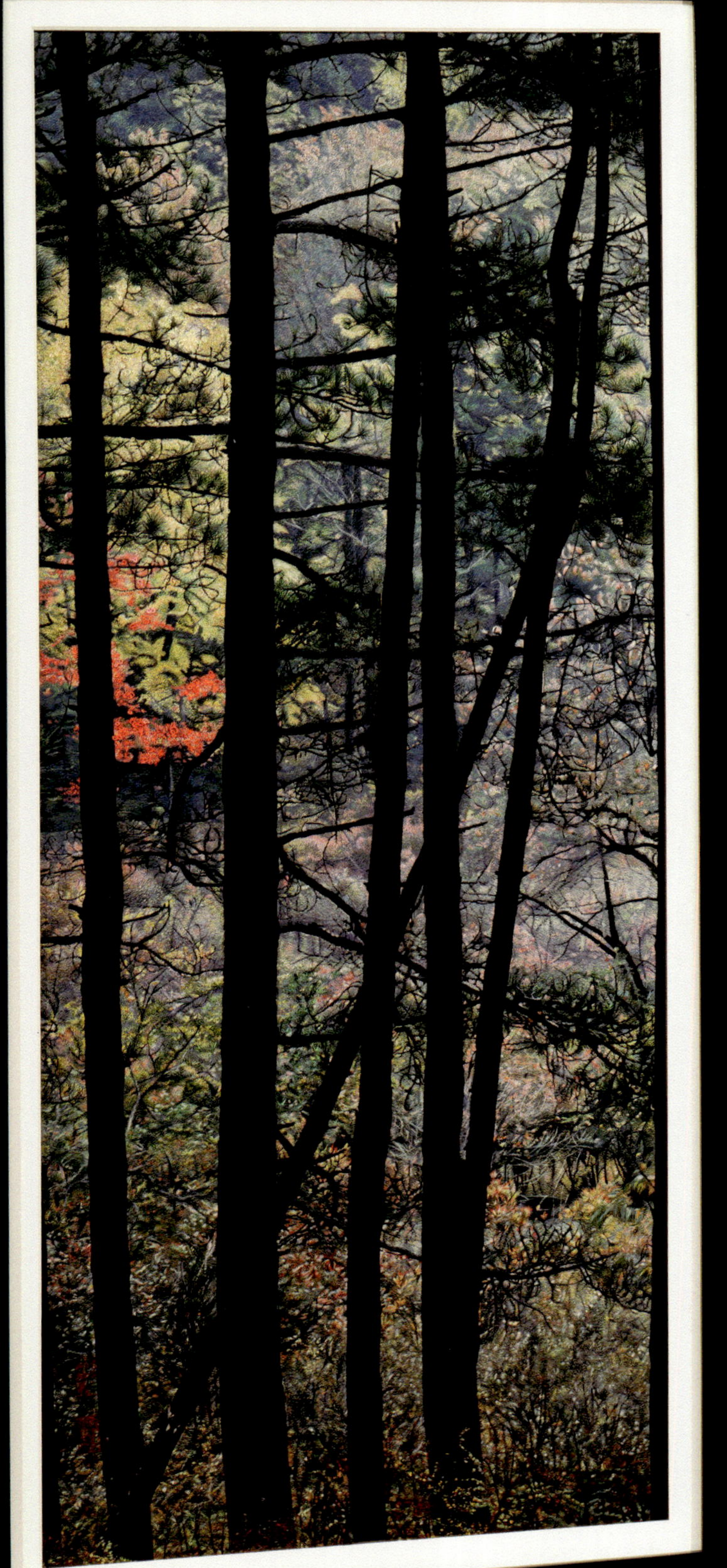
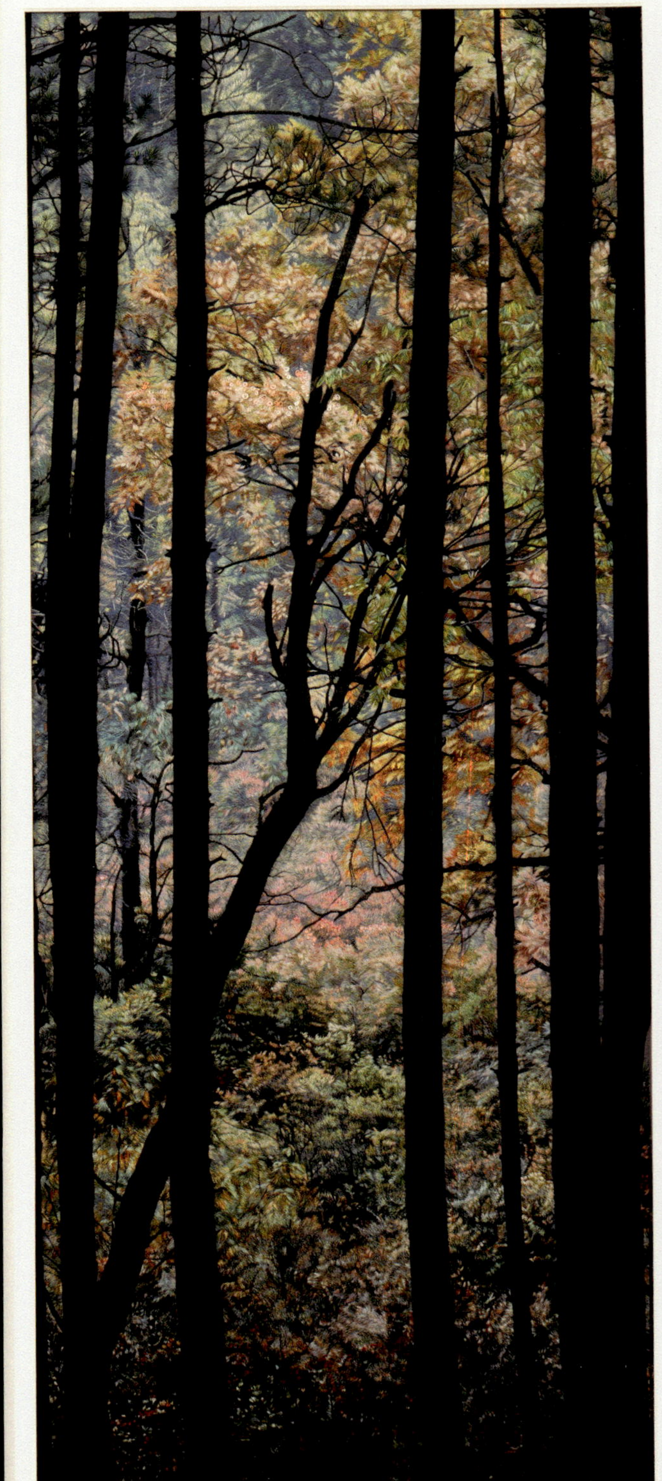

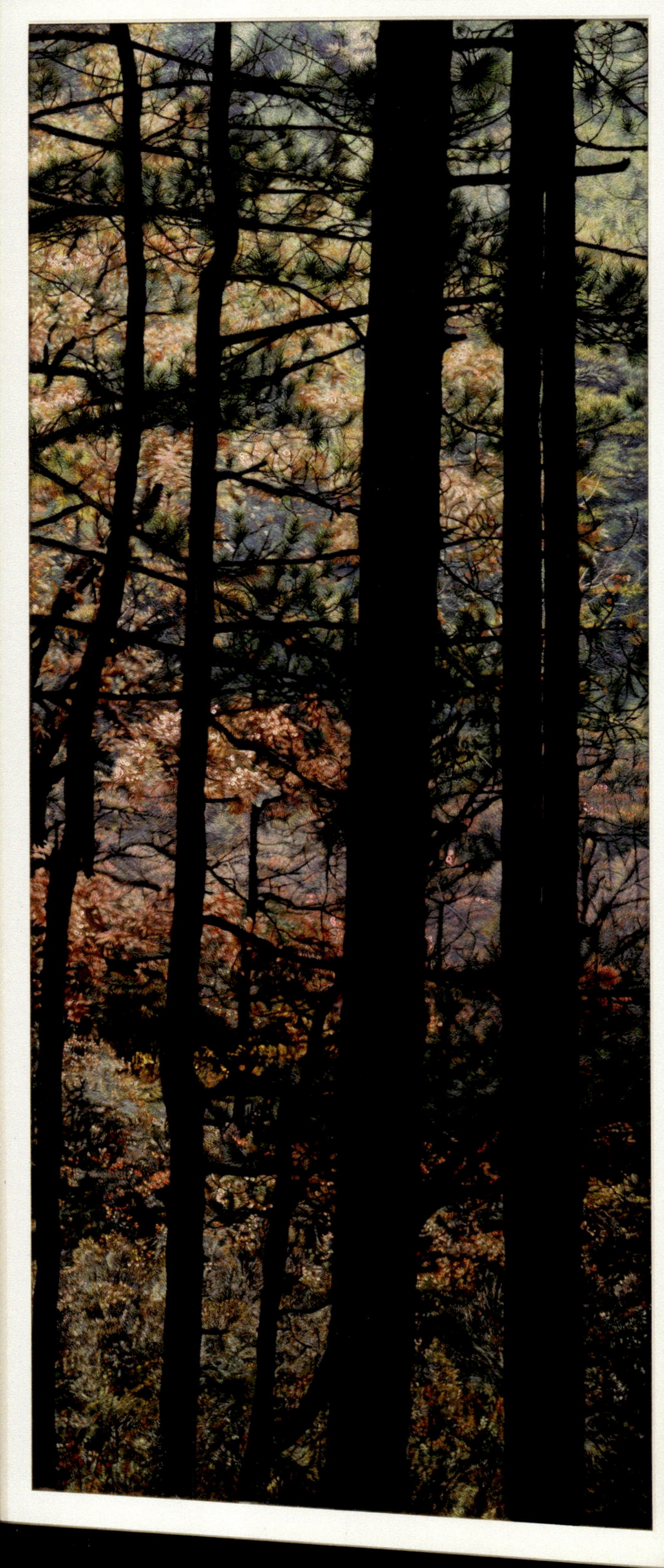

REGARDING THE LAND

ROBERT GLENN KETCHUM

AND THE LEGACY OF

ELIOT PORTER

BY JOHN ROHRBACH

WITH ROBERT GLENN KETCHUM

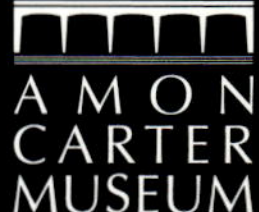

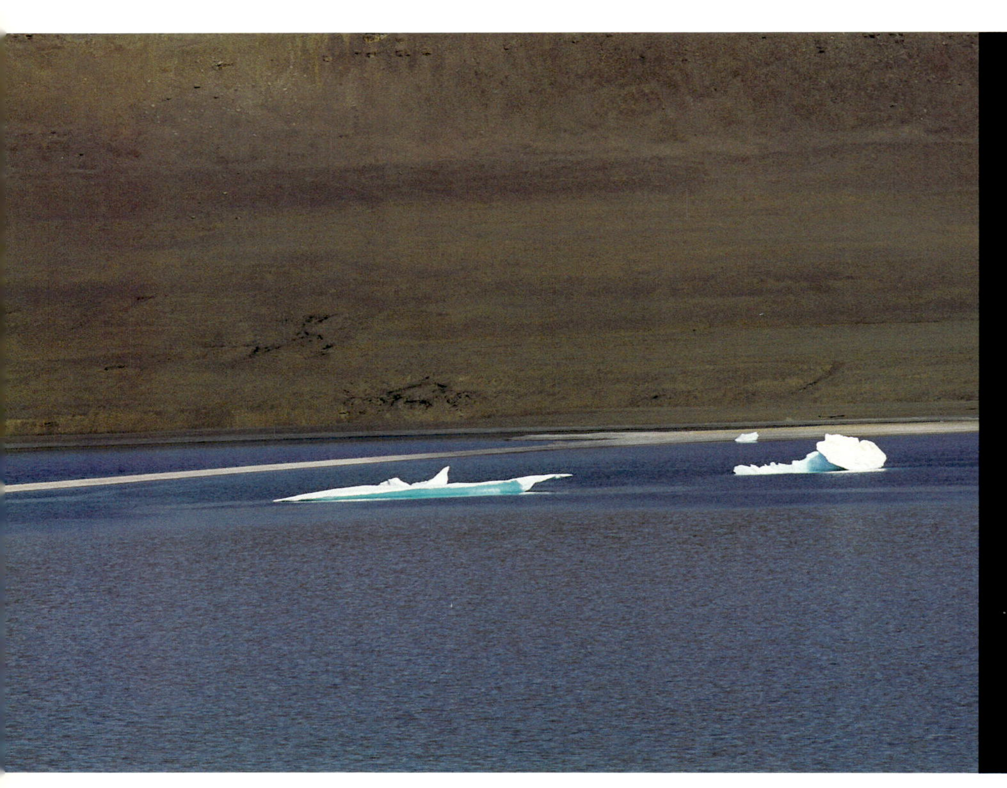

Look Again

JOHN ROHRBACH

ROBERT GLENN KETCHUM has a problem. His problem is Eliot Porter. Of course, Ketchum is not alone. Today, fifty years after Porter first began photographing eastern woodlands in color, most nature magazines come filled with his style of imagery. Eliot Porter's vision, quite simply, sets the standard for color landscape photography. It is not that Ketchum has acquiesced to walking in Porter's shadow, but he readily acknowledges how often he has looked to Porter for guidance and inspiration.

Eliot Porter (1901–1990) found an unimaginably broad and enthusiastic audience when he partnered with David Brower and the Sierra Club to publish books of his photographs. Their first volume, *"In Wildness Is the Preservation of the World," Selections & Photographs by Eliot Porter* (1962), transformed the club into an internationally respected advocate of environmental preservation and Porter into a household name.[1] That book's tremendous, if unexpected, commercial success led Porter and Brower to immediately assemble *The Place No One Knew: Glen Canyon on the Colorado* (1963) and subsequent books that together expanded the Sierra Club's reach to global lengths.[2]

Robert Glenn Ketchum (b. 1947) has built his audience in similar fashion by working with Michael E. Hoffman at the Aperture Foundation to produce finely printed books using his color landscape photographs to similarly address environmental issues. Their book *The Hudson River and the Highlands* (1985) argued for the economic potential of a cleaned-up Hudson River Valley. Their volume *The Tongass: Alaska's Vanishing Rain Forest* (1987) successfully brought national attention to the indiscriminate and massive logging in southeastern Alaska and contributed to congressional passage of significant timber-reform legislation. *Overlooked in America: The Success and Failure of Federal Land Management* (1991) drew equally persuasive attention to the beauty of less spectacular federally managed lands that were all too often becoming dumping grounds for society's detritus. *Rivers of Life: Southwest Alaska, The Last Great Salmon Fishery* (2001) and *Wood-Tikchik: Alaska's Largest State Park* (2003) revealed both the beauty and the ecological value of the river-laced tundra lands of southwestern Alaska that are today threatened by proposals for mining and oil development.

Despite the similarity of Porter's and Ketchum's ends, however, the underlying impetus of each artist's work is quite different. Porter was at heart a scientist, albeit one with a remarkably imaginative and poetic eye. His colleagues often dismissed and even ridiculed his photographs as lacking artistic foundation, in part because he generally talked about them in terms of their biological and geological subjects.[3] Ketchum, on the other hand, is at his core an artist. Where Porter's work comes grounded in a strongly scientific upbringing and academic concentration in biochemistry, Ketchum's art comes founded on the experimental formalism promulgated by his former teachers Edmund Teske and Robert Heinecken. For Ketchum, photographs do not merely describe the world; they are also tools for exploring how we see.

• • •

BY A RATHER CIRCUITOUS ROUTE, Robert Glenn Ketchum became what he is today. When he enrolled in 1966 as an undergraduate at his neighborhood school, the University of California, Los Angeles, he had more passion for surfing than for academic study. But he dutifully put that love aside to begin following the prelaw path advocated by his parents. He solidified his environmental sympathies almost by happenstance when, late in his freshmen year, he and his friends stopped to camp among the redwoods in Big Sur while returning to Los Angeles from the infamous Monterey Pop Festival where Jimi Hendrix burned his guitar onstage. Early the next morning, walking back into the forest, Ketchum had an epiphany: "The fog was burning off and big shafts of

Title page: Robert Glenn Ketchum, *Can't See the Trees for the Forest*, 2004 (embroidery)
Left: Robert Glenn Ketchum, *From the Franklin Expedition Gravesite, Beechey Island* (detail; p. 69)

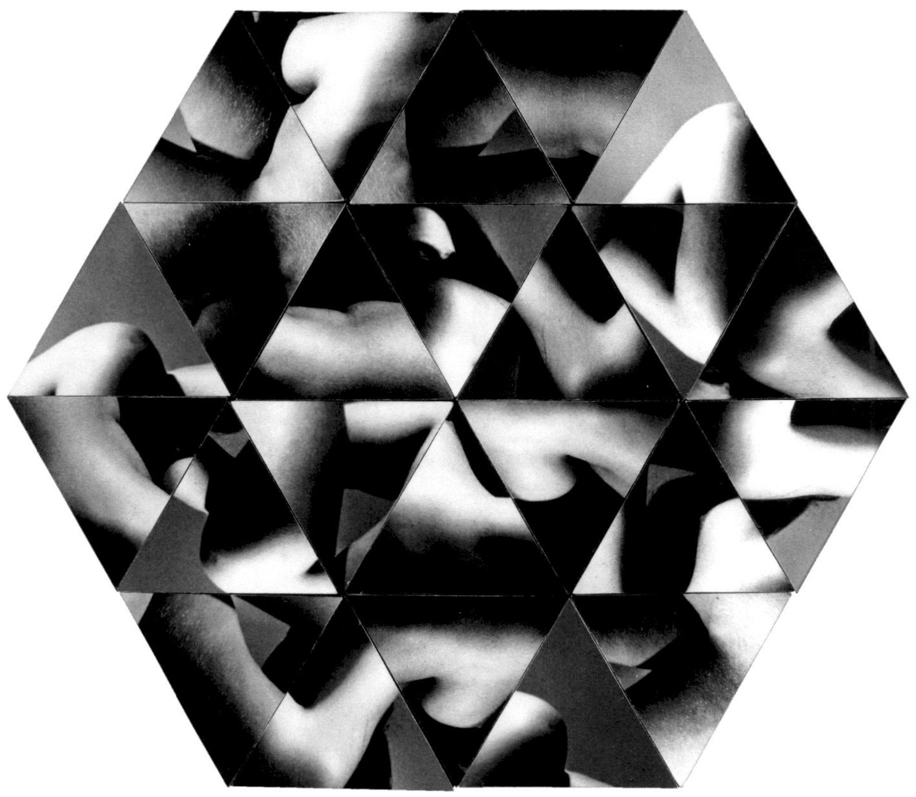

radiant light were coming down through the trees, and the insects were starting to wake up and fly around. All I could hear were water sounds . . . I put it all together in a way I never had before, and it changed everything forever and absolutely."[4] The experience brought Rachel Carson's *Silent Spring* (1962) and Aldo Leopold's *A Sand County Almanac and Sketches Here and There* (1949) to Ketchum's mind, leading him to ponder his place within the living world and humanity's moral obligation to take personal responsibility for actions that might pollute or poison it.

In school, Ketchum was just finishing several art and design courses. Although he had enrolled in these classes to fulfill degree requirements, he had discovered that he excelled at the subjects. Entering his sophomore year he changed his major to design. The new regimen led him to UCLA's photography program, which was run under the aegis of the fine arts department by Teske and Heinecken, two of the most experimental artist-photographers of their generation. Under their tutelage Ketchum was encouraged to investigate photography as an idea and a tool for experimentation. Besides learning about solarization, negative manipulation, and multiple printing, he made one-of-a-kind photographic books about the Sunset Boulevard rock scene, which was then seeing the emergence of bands like The Doors, Cream, and Buffalo Springfield. By this time he had joined the Sierra Club and Audubon Society, but he found most traditional fine art photography, and landscape photography in particular, boring.

During his last undergraduate semester at UCLA, Ketchum experienced another awakening. Heinecken

Robert Heinecken (b. 1931), *Refractive Hexagon*, 1965
Courtesy of Pace/MacGill Gallery, New York. © Robert Heinecken

gave his class an assignment to develop a formal slide lecture that would analyze the achievements of a photographer whose work was distinctly outside the domain of the student's own practice. So as not to repeat the standard accolade-filled presentations of his peers, Ketchum chose to report on Paul Caponigro, whose work he abhorred as irrelevant. But something unexpected happened. As he prepared for what he planned would be a flippant exposé, he found himself seduced by the photographer's images. Rather than presenting a sarcastic study of artistic solipsism, Ketchum found himself voicing admiration for Caponigro's subtle landscapes and tonally rich prints. In closing, he projected his favorite Caponigro photograph onto the screen (below, right). Explaining that it showed a star-filled expanse of night sky, he extolled the artist's new willingness to manipulate his prints, in this case by producing irregular edges. After an extended silence, one of Ketchum's friends spoke up. "What are you talking about?" he asked. "That photograph is of an apple lying on its side."[5] Ketchum realized he had been fooled by his own assumptions. Caponigro had taken a simple subject and through the power of personal vision had crafted a photograph with multiple realities. It was an apple on a plate, but it was also a night sky. (Caponigro confirmed that reading when Ketchum subsequently shared it with the photographer.)[6] This realization gave Ketchum new respect for photography's ability to use direct recording of the world as a means for exploring poetic vision. The experience transformed his approach, pushing him far closer to that kind of picture making.

Ketchum graduated from UCLA in 1970 with a design degree and a newfound interest in landscape photography. But rather than stay in Los Angeles, with the rock scene imploding into a world of drugs and violence, he took off for Sun Valley, Idaho, where he landed jobs photographing real estate holdings and ski activities, as

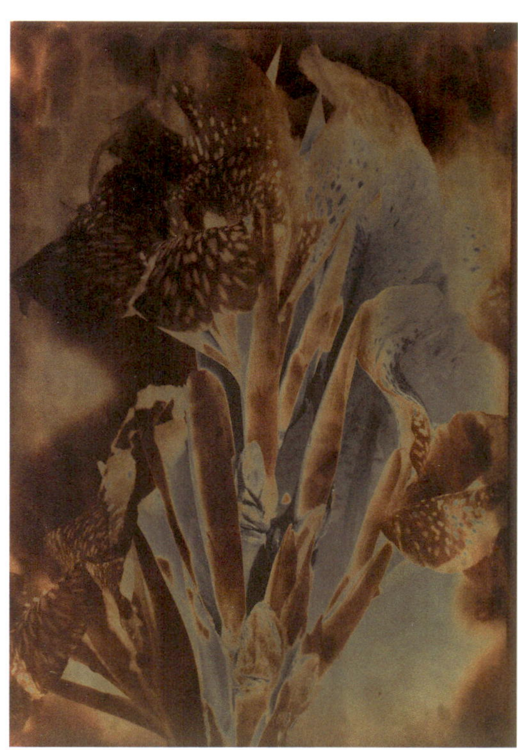

Edmund Teske (1911–1996), *Floral Study*, 1960
The J. Paul Getty Museum, Los Angeles. © Edmund Teske Archives/ Laurence Bump and Nils Vidstrand, 2001

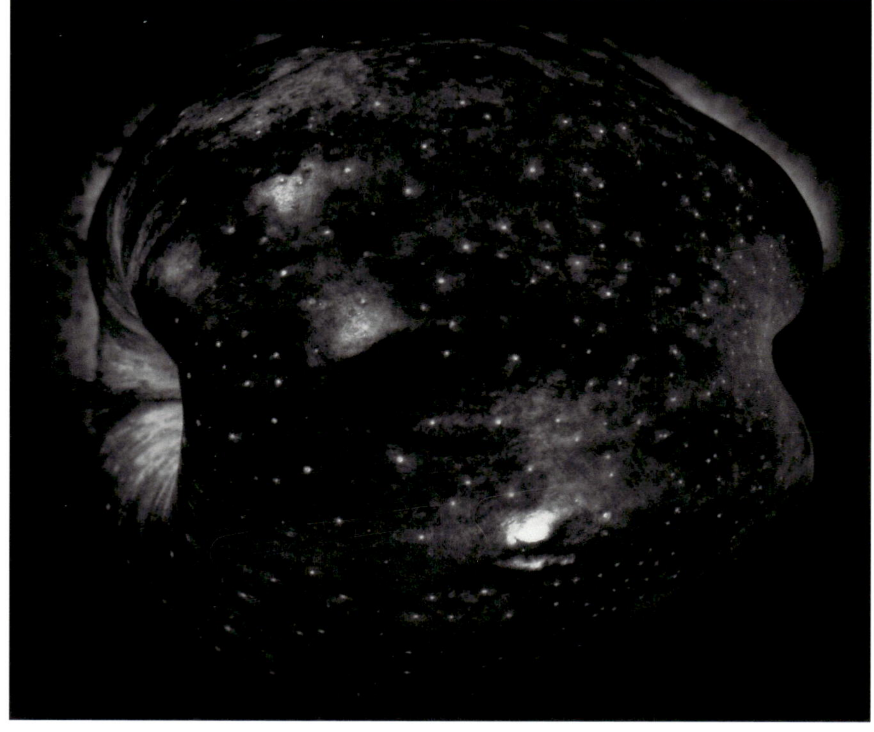

Paul Caponigro (b. 1932), *Apple, New York*, 1964
Courtesy Eric J. Keller, Director, www.soulcatcherstudio.com. © Paul Caponigro

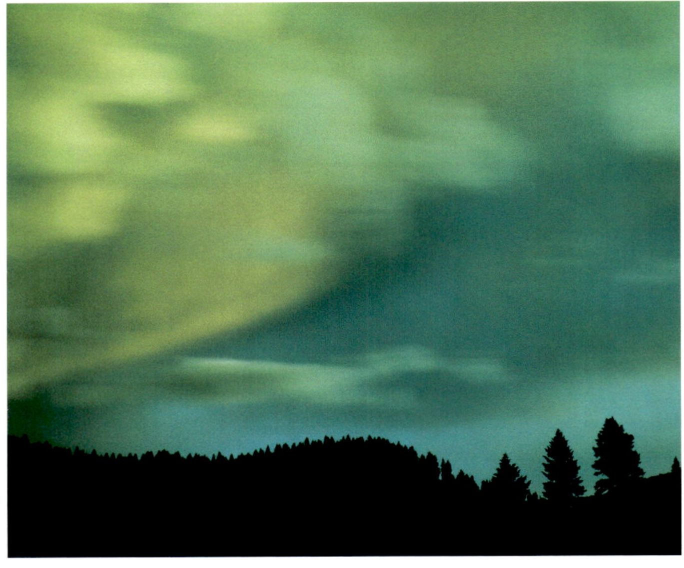

well as running light shows in a dance club. He worked for a short time on a photographic series he called *Twilight*, wherein he used monochromatic and bichromatic palettes to make the hues of his photographs take precedence over their subjects (above). Interested as well in black and white, he found an outlet for that form when he joined a small group of avid cross-country skiers who trekked for days at a time through the deep-powder backcountry. During those trips, in pauses of exhausted, hyperventilated rest grabbed between hours of pulling a heavy sled across steep ridgelines and ravines, he started making a series of 35mm photographs that played head-on with abstraction and scale (p. 20). These studies transformed white snow into a blanketlike backdrop. Out of that solidity emerged delicate grays of subtle shadow and line. Ghostly trees and feathery mountain escarpments floated in white. Ansel Adams this was not. By flattening the picture plane as in Japanese and Chinese painting, Ketchum was using photography not so much to record the world as to open conversations with other art traditions and media. Ultimately, he would self-publish this work as the portfolio *Winters, 1970–1980*.

Even as Ketchum continued to explore minimalism with his black-and-white winter views, he took up his 4-by-5-inch view camera and began to pursue a mode of seeing that was exactly the opposite of what he was finding in the mountains. Rather than match the grand, elegant emptiness of *Winters*, he sought out mundane subjects filled with extensive detail—nondescript thickets, dense forests, bushes, and grasses—and photographed them in color. While the resulting images, like *Cottonwood Thicket* (right), are rich with textural details and subtle tonal shifts, they lack a traditional sense of beauty. But as with his winter views, Ketchum's goal was not to mirror the world. Rather, it was to explore notions of sight and how we understand the world, in this case by subsuming subject to color and pattern.

Over the next few years, Ketchum gradually added photographs to both his *Winters* and prosaic landscape projects. He also solidified his technique in black and white and in color through a year of study at the Brooks Institute of Photography in Santa Barbara and two subsequent years earning an MFA from the newly established California Institute of the Arts in Valencia. CalArts was just then becoming a bastion of postmodernism. For the school's photographers this meant self-consciously dissecting their medium's structural and interpretive components as well as critically questioning intent, context, and the meaning of their photographs. Most of Ketchum's fellow students curtly dismissed his traditional predilections in much the same way he himself had done to others throughout most of his time at UCLA. Even so, after graduating from CalArts, Ketchum taught for a year there. He found more intellectual challenge, though, when he began assembling contemporary and historical exhibitions for the Los Angeles Center for Photographic Studies. There, he reintroduced the work of James Van Der Zee to West Coast audiences and rediscovered the photographs of Paul Outerbridge Jr. To make ends meet, he accepted commissions that ranged from creating Ansel Adams–inspired views of the ranches of wealthy clients to pro-

Robert Glenn Ketchum, *Madrugada*, 1972, from the series *Twilight*

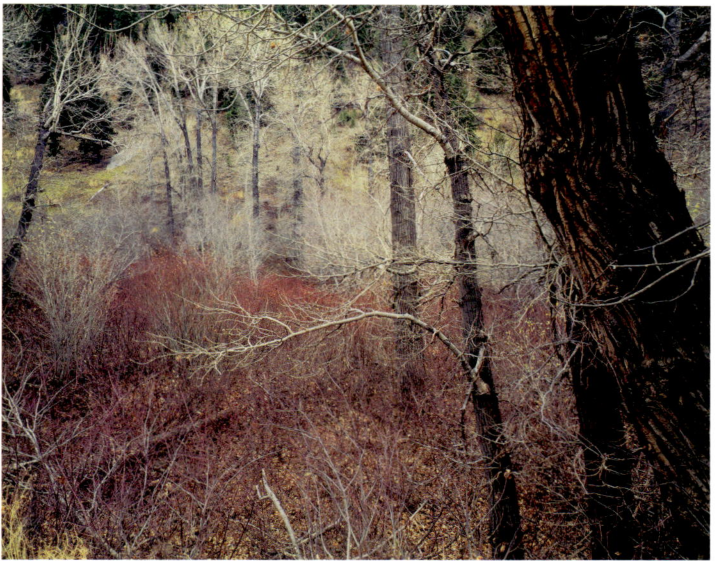

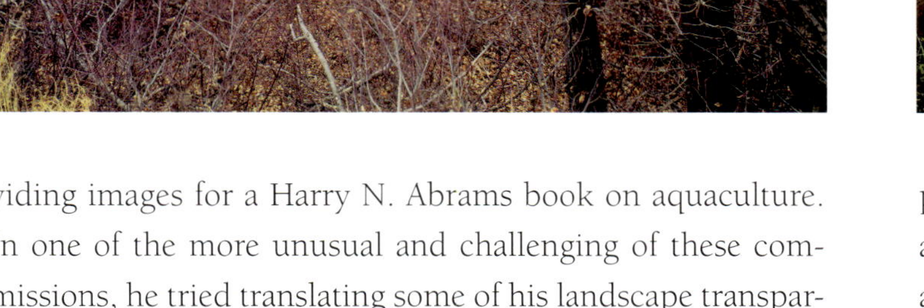

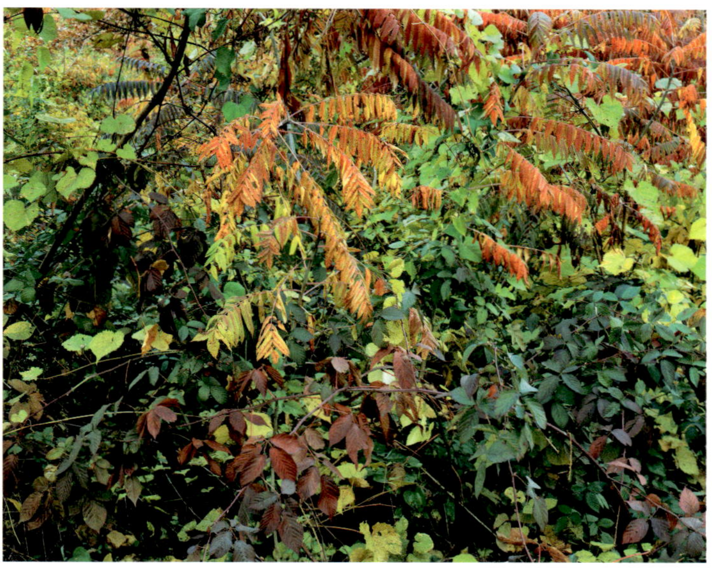

viding images for a Harry N. Abrams book on aquaculture. In one of the more unusual and challenging of these commissions, he tried translating some of his landscape transparencies into 7-by-9-foot fabric panels.[7]

With the assistance of one of his ranch clients, Ketchum also persuaded the National Park Foundation to fund an exhibition and catalogue celebrating the history of photography in America's national parks, from William Henry Jackson's views of Yellowstone to the present.[8] The project led to his being hired as the curator of photography for the National Park Foundation, to a move to Washington, D.C., and to a discovery of the answer to a problem that had been preoccupying him about the work of Eliot Porter. He had met Porter while collecting work for the national parks project, spending part of a day looking at prints in the older photographer's studio, and by this date owned numerous Porter books. He appreciated the tremendous variety and nuance of color projected by Porter's prints of eastern forests and understood that this nuance derived in part from Porter's expert command of the dye imbibition process. But never had he seen such diversity of color.[9]

Driving one fall day along a Maryland parkway shortly after arriving in the Washington area, Ketchum spied a patch of grape leaves that had taken on their brilliant autumn tones. He skidded to a stop, pulled out his camera, and made a photograph (above), much to the surprise and chagrin of a Maryland state trooper. In that photograph, which projects all of the drama and energy of a Jackson Pollock drip painting, he found an answer to his growing fascination and concurrent confusion over Porter's photographs. In these grape leaves, he had not merely discovered where Porter found such vibrant woodland color. He had matched, and even surpassed, Porter's expert ability to make the plants, which were the ostensible subject of his images, equally compelling as simple patterns of color, form, texture, and balance. Brilliant color and tangled pattern not only dominated the image—they became its subject. Here was the answer to all that Ketchum had been trying to achieve with color on the West Coast. Immediately, he started seeking similar tangles of visual cacophony in woodlands up and down the East Coast. He took to calling the results "anti-landscapes." In homage to Pollock, he named the developing series *Order from Chaos*.[10] Challenging his postmodernist colleagues' insistence on photography's inherent denotative character, he assigned playfully metaphoric titles to his prints, like *Brewster Boogie Woogie*.[11]

Robert Glenn Ketchum, *Cottonwood Thicket,* 1972, from the series *Order from Chaos/West Coast*

Robert Glenn Ketchum, *Transition,* 1981, from the series *Order from Chaos*

If painters like Piet Mondrian, Pollock, and Frank Stella could use such titles, why couldn't he?

Order from Chaos both affirms and negates Porter's approach to landscape. Following Porter's lead, Ketchum focused on uninhabited woodland scenery. But where Porter generally simplified woodland patterns to create pleasing compositions, Ketchum drew attention to and even exaggerated tangle, parodying traditional landscape practice. Rather than offering pleasing compositions of picturesque or sublime scenery, these photographs confront viewers with confusing snarls of tight space (p. 28). Porter had accepted and even reveled in photography's descriptive role. As a scientist he had thought it to be natural, even as the artist in him sought something more. Ketchum, on the other hand, was, in this new work, taking photography's descriptive vocabulary and turning it on its head. Pattern without hierarchy or organization had become his primary subject. In that leveling he removed both himself and the viewer from their usual positions of power and control. The *Order from Chaos* series also expanded on Porter's use of color. Ketchum had learned from Porter how overcast days made the colors of objects seem clearer and more vivid. Taking up the new Cibachrome process in collaboration with the master printer Michael Wilder, he pushed that characteristic to an extreme, making prints of such saturated color that they verge on artifice.[12] Porter had been well aware of color's emotional contribution to his photographs; he particularly had brought color to the fore in his work in the Glen Canyon in the early and mid-1960s. But he was too much of a scientist to make it the predominant force in most of his work, especially in his views of East Coast forests. Ketchum believed just the opposite. For him, the photograph, not the scene, was the subject, and color was not merely a descriptive device but also an emotional one. *Order from Chaos* challenges Porter's notions about size as well. Where Porter had remained largely committed to making photographic prints that approximated 11-by-9 inches, Wilder made Ketchum's prints on 30-by-40-inch photographic paper. The increased size dramatically deepens the photographs' illusion of spatial depth. Rather than looking comfortably at a forest scene from outside the image, the viewer is pulled inexorably into its thicket of branches.

By the time Ketchum began publishing and exhibiting his *Order from Chaos* series in 1983, he had recognized that he was heading toward a dead end. Formalism was interesting, but it did not serve his growing preoccupation with specific environmental issues. The previous fall he had taken a commission from the Lila Acheson Wallace Fund to photograph along the Hudson River. Although he was free to photograph whatever he liked, his resulting images would be used to build broad public support for cleaning up the Hudson River Valley.[13] The project led him to realize another distinct characteristic of the eastern woodlands. Whereas the western landscape is defined by dramatic vistas, the East, with its rolling hills and deciduous forests, offers a landscape characterized by constantly changing light. He had focused simply on composing the rectangle in creating his *Order from Chaos* photographs, but now he began focusing on moments in time to the point of incorporating the hour that he made each exposure into the titles of his images. He also began photographing in all kinds of weather; the worse the weather, the more he wanted to be out photographing in it.[14]

Perhaps the most significant evolution in Ketchum's work at this time was his conscious decision to resist editing out traditionally undesirable content. Porter had ignored human intrusion in his ecological studies published by the Sierra Club, but Ketchum decided that he now had to address the region's array of trash-inscribed rail yards, dilapidated town docks, interstate highways, and suburban development. One cold, smoggy winter day, driving down Route 9W from Garrison to Peekskill, he stopped at the Peekskill overlook to peer out at the Indian Point Nuclear Power Plant (p. 32). It was four o'clock in the afternoon, and the air had taken on a murky orange color—the refraction of the setting sun off a horrific pollution-laden haze. He realized that with just the right exposure, translated into Cibachrome's oversaturated metallic color palette, the scene would take on the disturbingly beautiful, even surreal, cast of a copper plate—a perfect blend of attraction, horror, subject, and print materials. The result of the photograph he made that afternoon empowered him to start looking for other urban and industrial subjects.

About three weeks later, as steady rains were transforming winter into spring, he stopped along an elevated walkway over the rail tracks in Beacon, the site of one of the first dockyards built north of Manhattan. By now he had realized that if the Hudson River project were going to have any effect, people living in the primarily blue-collar towns like Beacon would have to be motivated to participate in the cleanup; as it was, they feared the cost of investing in greenway development and were unsure that they would benefit from the outcome. As he crossed a pedestrian bridge over the tracks that parallel the shoreline of the Hudson, his attention was drawn to a subject that offered a perfect metaphor. Decades earlier, ferries from Manhattan had dropped passengers at this site. But now it had become a yard for storing winter road salt and discarded rail construction materials. Under a dull gray sky, Ketchum saw the sullen tones in harmony with the emotion of the view (p. 44). However, a telephone pole and its connecting cables kept bisecting his preferred viewpoint. Pondering this challenge, he remembered his colleague Stephen Shore's innovative willingness to eschew hierarchy and accept everything as pertinent in his photographs. Embracing that perspective, Ketchum placed the pole in the center of the view. Just as in the Indian Point photograph, compositional balance would combine with Cibachrome's hypersaturation of metallic color to create unnerving beauty, in this case communicated through intense hues of damp steely blue. When the Wallace Fund's director, Barnabas McHenry, saw these new images, he encouraged Ketchum to continue working in this vein and approached Michael Hoffman at Aperture about publishing the Hudson River works. The resulting volume, *The Hudson River and the Highlands* (1985), turned out to be central and highly persuasive in the Hudson River cleanup campaign.

The Hudson River project reinforced Ketchum's decision to do more with his art than simply have an academic discussion with his UCLA and CalArts peers. He still wanted to explore artistic possibilities, but he also wanted to use his art to contribute to broader political debates. He did just this in far more confrontational terms in his next two projects. In the first, he photographed the Tongass rain forest in southeastern Alaska to promote a timber-reform act for the region. The issues were complex. Ketchum and his allies were not opposed to logging in the region per se. Logging provided jobs. But they were opposed to large-scale corporate logging that depended heavily on government subsidy and that sent its entire product to Japan. After spending six and one-half months in the field, he realized that he had barely scratched the surface. With help from the Wallace Fund and the McIntosh Foundation, he returned for another eight months in 1986 to capture broader aerial views and, with the assistance of his wife, Carey, collect over one hundred hours of interviews with people living in the area. Only then did he feel that he had enough material to satisfactorily build his argument. The following year Aperture warily published the results in *The Tongass: Alaska's Vanishing Rain Forest*. (The last thing Michael Hoffman wanted to do was jeopardize Aperture's not-for-profit status by bringing the Reagan administration down on it.) Just as David Brower had done with Porter's book *The Place No One Knew*, Ketchum and his associates mailed copies of *The Tongass* to each member of Congress and anyone else involved in the debate. The press quickly picked up on the book, transforming Ketchum into a celebrity. Within two years of the book's publication, congressional support of the Tongass Reform Bill jumped from forty to ninety-six members. A year later Congress passed the legislation by an overwhelming margin, and President George H. W. Bush signed the bill establishing one million acres of protected old-growth forest and creating five new wilderness areas.

Impressed with the results of Ketchum's Tongass work, the Akron Art Museum, in a joint project with the National Park Service, commissioned him to work in the newly established Cuyahoga Valley National Recreation Area in northeastern Ohio.[15] Ketchum made this project a meditation on the valley's changing history, in particular its shifts from woodland to farmland to dumping ground and, finally, to preserve (pp. 46–53). When Aperture stepped in to produce the book, he again relied on words to highlight the disjunction between the project's many appealing woodland views and the broader reality of government treatment of its lands. In compiling his Hudson River book, Ketchum and Hoffman had followed Porter's model, mixing literary and historical quotes among his photographs. In his Tongass book, Ketchum had bracketed his images with a detailed, impassioned discussion of the effects of logging in that region. Now, he made that interplay between image and text even more integral, interspersing his images with sound bites gathered from his twenty years of collecting environmentally related newspaper clippings. Those extracts tell vivid tales of the federal government's widespread and ongoing mismanagement of the land in its control across the United States. Ketchum deliberately hid the locations of his images by refusing to identify the Cuyahoga Valley in the book's title and titling his images with only a negative number and the initials of the Recreation Area. He has suggested that it allows the titles to be read as numbers on a map or as license plates, for although the photographs depict the Cuyahoga Valley, he wanted them to symbolize sites across the United States. He even at times flipped expectations about beauty and ugliness. The book's cover image, for example, presents what seems to be an idyllic autumnal view of a woodland stream cascading down an embankment (p. 46). But in one of the book's few descriptive image titles, Ketchum reveals that this river is filled with chemicals. Back in Beacon, he had instilled ugliness with a touch of beauty. Here, he sabotages beauty by pointing out its underlying toxicity. In this context, the orange leaves framing the creek bed take on an unsettling and acrid acidity.

Even as Ketchum found himself ever more immersed in specific environmental causes, he retained his passion for more open-ended photographic experimentation. Shortly after starting the Cuyahoga Valley project, he also accepted Robert Redford's invitation to take up an extended residency at his Sundance Institute. That residency would provide a much-needed break. Whereas the Hudson River, Tongass, and Cuyahoga Valley projects had specific political agendas, the Sundance residency did not. Redford told him he did not even have to bring his camera. It was like returning home for Ketchum, back to the kind of terrain that he had found so captivating in Idaho's Sawtooth Mountains where he had assembled most of his *Winters* series. Visiting Sundance for the first time in fall 1987, the photographer found himself captivated by the light, color, and terrain: "I just sat back and looked at the amazing landscape around me and asked myself what is up here? And what was up there in particular was a fall like no other, just an unbelievable fall which gave me a place to play with color for a while, so I went crazy."[16]

Over parts of the next three years, Ketchum exposed some 1,000 transparencies at Sundance, 700 of them during autumn months. Out of that collection came the *Sundance Suite*, a group of photographs that stretch the boundaries of color and light. Working in the Glen Canyon, Porter had reveled in the unexpected reflections of light and color off rock faces and water. The Glen Canyon project was Ketchum's favorite of Porter's place studies (pp. 56–58).[17] Sundance allowed Ketchum to match Porter on these same terms. In *Cosmic Trees*, for example, the maple and aspen trunks filling the frame project an unexpected blue cast (p. 78). The ghostlike effect is eerily unreal. But like Porter's Glen Canyon imagery, even as the color of those tree trunks surprises, that color makes perfect sense in relation to the light and feel of the scene. Likewise, in *Predawn Glow, Elk Point,* a swatch of aspens cuts across the lower flank of a distant slope, projecting such bright red color that it seems lit from within (p. 75). The entire image is bathed in the distinctive pink-and-purple cast of sunrise. One feels immersed in color.[18]

• • •

LIKE PORTER BEFORE HIM, Ketchum had by the late 1980s become a leading environmental artist. In 1989 the Sierra Club recognized him with its Ansel Adams Award for Conservation Photography. Two years later he received the Global 500 Outstanding Environmental Achievement Award from the United Nations. He was conducting workshops for the Nature Conservancy and receiving commissions to photograph areas of ecological significance around Carmel Valley and on the outskirts of the national parks. But despite all of this success, his heart still lay with expanding the vocabulary of photographic vision. This endeavor led him back north to work further on a problem that he had encountered but had not fully resolved in the Tongass. Alaskan terrain had proved incredibly difficult to work in. Not only is its scale immense, it does not offer the visual variety found across much of the lower forty-eight states. Ketchum once explained: "There is a joke in Alaska that you can paddle for five hours and get out and everything still looks like the same place you were. In terms of walking, it is even more preposterous. It goes on forever."[19] During his second year there he had tried photographing from the air. The abstraction created by the frequent absence of horizon and tremendous scale of the land opened up a new order of dimension and space. But he had only had time to touch on the possibilities. Thus, when William E. Simon, former secretary of the treasury, invited him in 1994 to join a twenty-three-day voyage across the Northwest Passage from Alaska to Greenland, Ketchum jumped at the opportunity.[20] With no political agenda, the trip would give him a new opportunity to play with the flattening of space that he had started investigating in the Tongass. It also would take him into a landscape dominated by the same whites and blues that in 1974 had lured Porter to Antarctica.

Taking advantage of the expedition's helicopter to photograph extensively from the air, Ketchum now started shifting the horizon line more dramatically. At times horizons blend fluidly between ground and sky, as in *Dead-calm Sunset before the Storm, Larsen Sound* (p. 72). On other occasions, as in *From the Franklin Expedition Gravesite, Beechey Island*, sky becomes another flattened palette of interlocking color (p. 69). The effect evokes the emotional resonance of Barry Lopez's book *Arctic Dreams* (1986). Porter had similarly skirted abstraction when visiting Antarctica, but even when making aerials he had almost always kept the identity and dimensionality of his subjects clearly apparent. Ketchum now additionally played with the surreal displacement of scale to create images like *Vertical Shoreline, Bylot Island* (p. 73). Porter, with his penchant for description, had largely avoided doing this despite the immense scale of the Antarctic terrain (pp. 59–61). Ketchum may have been taking up a subject similar to one addressed by Porter, but rather than following Porter's commitment to describe, he was building on what he had learned with

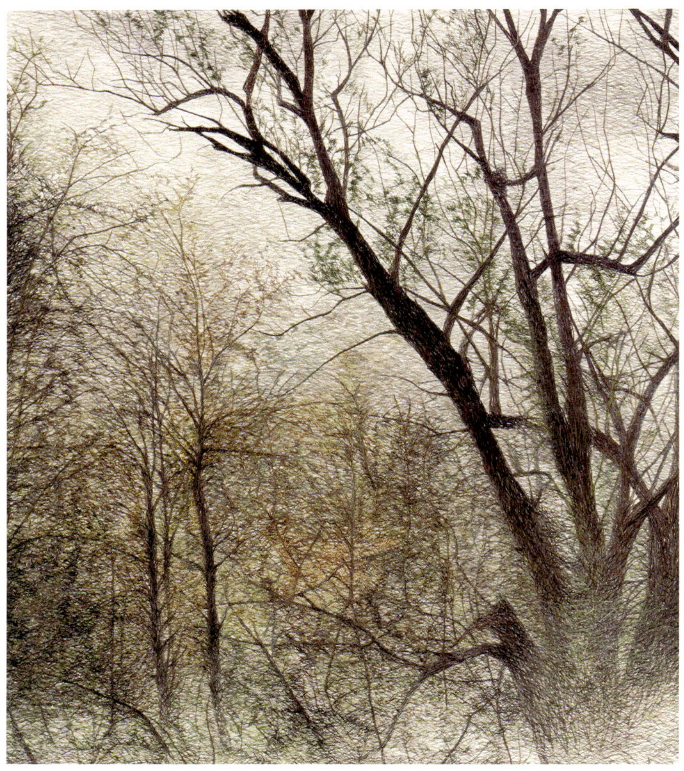

Caponigro's apple, fluidly blending pure description with abstraction and metaphor to reflect the landscape's emotional rather than structural character.

By the early 1990s Ketchum was also gaining momentum with a revolutionary means of photographic translation that had interested him for years—a form that Porter had never considered. He had tried translating his photographs into loom weavings and scanning them with a mural printer back in the 1970s, but the results had left him disappointed because they lacked photographic character and subtlety. Even so, he had never stopped considering the idea. In the late 1970s he had clipped a *Los Angeles Times* photograph of a political rally in Beijing featuring a gigantic embroidered portrait of Mao Zedong and filed it away for future reference. Noting the portrait's remarkable detail, he had concluded that the embroidery must have been derived from a photograph. In the early 1980s, when China opened to the West and UCLA set up an exchange program, he asked his alma mater to facilitate contact with the entity credited in the photograph as having made the banner, the Suzhou Embroidery Research Institute (SERI). UCLA was supportive, but the negotiations would take almost two years.

Not until 1986 did Ketchum receive an invitation to visit SERI. On his first night in Suzhou, the director of the embroidery institute, Zhang Meifang, made a point of testing her idealistic and self-confident young American guest, asking him whether he understood the significance of her city.[21] Luckily, Ketchum had studied its history: Suzhou, he replied, was where Marco Polo obtained the silk he brought to Venice, creating the Silk Road. In recognition of Suzhou's many canals, he explained, the Venetians called Suzhou the Venice of the East. Zhang responded that the Chinese viewed Venice as the Suzhou of the West. Thus began a remarkable twenty-five year relationship between Ketchum and SERI. Still, it would take another month of extended discussions with the institute staff before they would agree to take on the translation of any of his photographs. Finally, despite much apprehension that the task was too complex, the staff agreed to try translating Ketchum's *Winters* portfolio image *Snowfall* into a random-stitch silk embroidery. The Chinese liked the Asian foundations of the *Winters* portfolio, and translating a black-and-white image seemed like it would be easier (pp. 21, 104). To accomplish the feat, the institute's master embroiderers departed in several significant ways from their standard practices. Rather than build the work on a sheer, even-patterned silk back, they created a special loom-woven white silk background that showed vertical streaks mimicking falling snow. Instead of isolating a few key elements of natural beauty and eliminating the rest of the original photograph's details, they emphasized an overall effect without losing detail. Finally, to further reflect the movement of the snowflakes, they dropped their

Robert Glenn Ketchum, detail from the embroidery *The Beginning of Time* (p. 97)

standard tight weave and built the flakes out of combinations of knots and loops that at times draped across the embroidery surface. To everyone's surprise, save Ketchum's, the resulting 12-by-18-inch, double-sided table screen translated his photograph with remarkable fidelity and grace.

With that success, Ketchum began coaxing the institute to take on more complex photographs, both black and white and color. To address the challenges, the SERI staff developed new techniques and stitches. Creating the works soon became collaborative efforts that required Ketchum's intermittent presence and approval. By 1994, when the SERI embroiderers completed the spectacular three-panel double-sided room screen *The Beginning of Time*, an image based on Ketchum's Cuyahoga Valley photograph *CVNRA #412*, the tables had turned (pp. 96–97). Now the institute staff were asking to take on ever more elaborate works.

In recent years Ketchum has continued this double track of photography and embroidery, taking up extensive photographic projects describing the vast tundra landscape of southwest Alaska while continuing his work with SERI. He asserts that his photography and embroidery are two distinctly separate events.[22] Even so, his most recent Alaskan photographs play aggressively with the same investigations of texture found in the embroideries. Created primarily from the air above southwestern Alaska's vast bog-laden Wood-Tikchik State Park, many of the images offer maplike carpets of yellow and green intersected with blue lakes and rivers (p. 80). His attention to texture in these images is a by-product of his efforts to make clear the terrain's vastness and ecological variety. To adequately translate the almost abstract textures of one of these tundra aerials, Zhang suggested, much to the surprise of her staff, that it be completed as a loom weaving. To accomplish the task, they rebuilt their loom so that it could accommodate 3,000 rather than the standard 1,000 lines of weft and used it to create a 5-by-8-foot, four-panel piece that Ketchum calls *YK Delta from 1500* (p. 98). In designing that larger loom, Zhang told Ketchum that she was challenging 2,500 years of Chinese weaving tradition. Upon completion, SERI recognized the new benchmark of accomplishment that the embroidery represented for the institute and offered to buy the work back from Ketchum.

At the same time that they took up the *YK Delta from 1500* weaving, the institute returned to a challenge that they had refused to address years earlier. In the infancy of their collaboration, Ketchum had asked SERI to create a random-stitch embroidery interpretation of his Hudson River photograph *October 24, 1983/2:10 p.m.*, requesting that they leave the foreground trunks unembroidered as negative space (p. 43). But the suggestion had been too unorthodox. Why, they asked, would one want to leave the principal object out? But they had compromised. Ketchum would give up his request about the trunks, and SERI would commit to making its largest piece ever. In 1991, after more than two years of work, they completed the first version, building up layer after layer with more than twenty different kinds of stitches and hundreds of hand-dyed thread colors.[23] Everyone was happy with the results, which led the institute to reconsider Ketchum's original idea. To create *Can't See the Trees for the Forest*, Zhang was concerned that a dark background would suppress the brilliance of the embroidered colors to be added. So the designers hand dyed only that part of the silk where the tree trunks would be (title page). The resulting tones are so delicate that the trunks look black when illuminated from the front but almost transparent when lit from the back. To retain the illusion of a luminous forest, the SERI staff built texture through a variety of single layer knots, some so loosely sewn that light filters through from behind. Today, contemporary Chinese artists have started to take notice of what Ketchum and

SERI have achieved together and to approach SERI about translating their work in new ways.

• • •

ELIOT PORTER'S VISION may still set the model for most contemporary color landscape photography, but Robert Glenn Ketchum has clearly expanded on Porter's vocabulary in substantial ways by suggesting the new possibilities offered by the metallic saturation of Cibachrome color; by exploring how increased size affects one's reading of space and dimension; and through overt play with color, space, light, and texture. Porter's photographs induced Ketchum to look at the land more closely and encouraged him to explore his more intuitive responses to it. They taught him to think critically about color's broad spectrum and subtlety and helped him understand how various films and papers translated color differently. Porter's work also taught Ketchum to appreciate how finely designed and printed photography books could provide something beyond the capability of finely crafted photographs alone, and how texts might add expressive dimension to the images. Whereas Porter's photographs were founded on careful description, Ketchum's reveal how landscapes are ideas that can be shaped, even defined, by the imagination. Porter's photographs build understanding and appreciation for specific places. Ketchum's photographs do the same, even as they explore sight itself. They are not about discovering wilderness but exploring wildness, including the freedom to test boundaries of expectation. Choice and surprise are key to his success.

ENDNOTES

1. Porter's photographs seemed to provide eloquent visual ratification of Rachel Carson's arguments against DDT and Aldo Leopold's posits about ecological interconnectedness. See Rachel Carson, *Silent Spring* (New York: Houghton Mifflin, 1962) and Aldo Leopold, *A Sand County Almanac and Sketches Here and There* (New York: Oxford University Press, 1949).

2. *The Place No One Knew* is a paean to Utah's Glen Canyon. When Brower astutely sent it to every member of Congress, western dam building stopped almost instantly. In fact, the book probably saved the Grand Canyon from becoming a bathtub. Its success led Brower and Porter to produce *Baja California and the Geography of Hope* (1967) to reveal the subtle beauty of a terrain that most people had heretofore dismissed as desert wasteland. Their last book, *Galápagos: The Flow of Wildness* (1968), used Porter's photographs to celebrate global ecological diversity.

3. John Rohrbach, "Envisioning the World in Color," in *Eliot Porter: The Color of Wildness* (New York: Aperture, 2001), 93–100.

4. Robert Glenn Ketchum, interview with John Rohrbach, June 26, 2005, tape 1:1 transcript, 12–13, Amon Carter Museum Archives.

5. Robert Glenn Ketchum, e-mail message to author, November 14, 2005. See also Ketchum, interview, tape 1:1 transcript, 16.

6. Ketchum, interview, tape 1:1 transcript, 16.

7. Paul Dowdey, ed. *Threads of Light, Chinese Embroidery from Suzhou and the Photography of Robert Glenn Ketchum* (Los Angeles: UCLA Fowler Museum of Cultural History, 1999), 65–66; Ketchum, interview, tape 2:1 transcript, 2–8. To produce his Fluor Corporation piece in 1976, Ketchum used an early digital scanner-printer that airbrushed minute dot patterns directly onto the fabric. But he found that this method failed as well to adequately convey color nuance or detail. His experimentation with fabric translations of his photographs stemmed from his appreciation of the range of artists in the Los Angeles community who were blurring the boundaries between painting, sculpture,

photography, and performance. He was well aware of Heinecken's images printed on emulsion-coated canvases and similar works by Bea Nettles and Lou Brown Di Giulio. Di Giulio, a former UCLA colleague, had created sculptures by photographing each leaf of a head of lettuce, printing each of these photographs on a piece of fabric, and then sewing the fabric pieces together to reconstruct the head of lettuce. Ketchum also worked for a short time with loom weaving in San Miguel de Allende, Mexico, but was unhappy with the lack of resolution.

8. The project became *American Photographers in the National Parks*. On completion in 1981, it showcased forty photographers. The exhibition of 235 prints, accompanied by a catalogue, traveled for three years through nine cities to venues ranging from the Corcoran Gallery of Art in Washington, D.C., to the Amon Carter Museum in Fort Worth, Texas, and the Los Angeles County Museum of Art.

9. The dye imbibition process, often known through Kodak's trade term as the dye transfer process, offers the opportunity to closely control hue, saturation, and contrast because it requires one to separate the colors of the originating negative or transparency and then recombine their complementary colors in making a print.

10. The title led Ketchum to give a comparable suite he had assembled of twelve western photographs a similar title: *Order from Chaos/West Coast*.

11. The print was shot in Brewster, New York; its title references Piet Mondrian's painting *Broadway Boogie Woogie* (1942–43).

12. Cibachrome is the commercial name for the dye destruction process of photographic printing. Here, papers contain three layers of silver, each sensitized to a primary color (red, green, or blue) and each carrying that color's complementary dye. In development, the exposed silver and dyes are bleached away. In the resulting print the three dye layers are read as one. By the time Wilder finished making the *Order from Chaos* prints, he had become so proficient in chromatic masking that the makers of Cibachrome were consulting him on technique.

13. The commission, which also included photographers Stephen Shore and William Clift, sought to build local public support for the idea of transforming the Hudson River Valley into a greenway and a destination for international tourism. The Wallace Fund was working in tandem with New York State, which had become interested in providing grants to local communities along the river to clean up their waterfront areas and to help identify and mark historical buildings.

14. Ketchum, interview, tape 3:1 transcript, 4. Ketchum remembers being influenced by the phrase "In All Seasons and in Every Weather," used by John K. Howat, curator emeritus and former Lawrence A. Fleishman Chairman of the Department of American Art at the Metropolitan Museum of Art, in discussing Hudson River school painting.

15. In 1979 the Akron Art Museum had commissioned Lee Friedlander to photograph that region in a project that culminated in the exhibition and book *Factory Valleys* (New York: Callaway Editions, 1982).

16. Ketchum, interview, tape 3:2 transcript, 20.

17. The variety of light and reflection in the Glen Canyon transcended the capabilities of Porter's film. Rather than try to compensate for this problem by adding filters to his lenses, he allowed colors to land where they might.

18. For a portfolio of the Sundance photographs, see Robert Glenn Ketchum, *The Legacy of Wildness: The Photographs of Robert Glenn Ketchum* (New York: Aperture, 1993), 108–115.

19. Ketchum, interview, tape 3:2 transcript, 21.

20. The trip would culminate in Ketchum's publication of *Northwest Passage* (New York: Aperture, 1996).

21. Ketchum recounts his ongoing interaction with SERI in *Threads of Light*.

22. Ketchum, interview, tape 3:2 transcript, 27.

23. Ketchum discusses the production of this random-stitch embroidery in *Threads of Light*, 72–75.

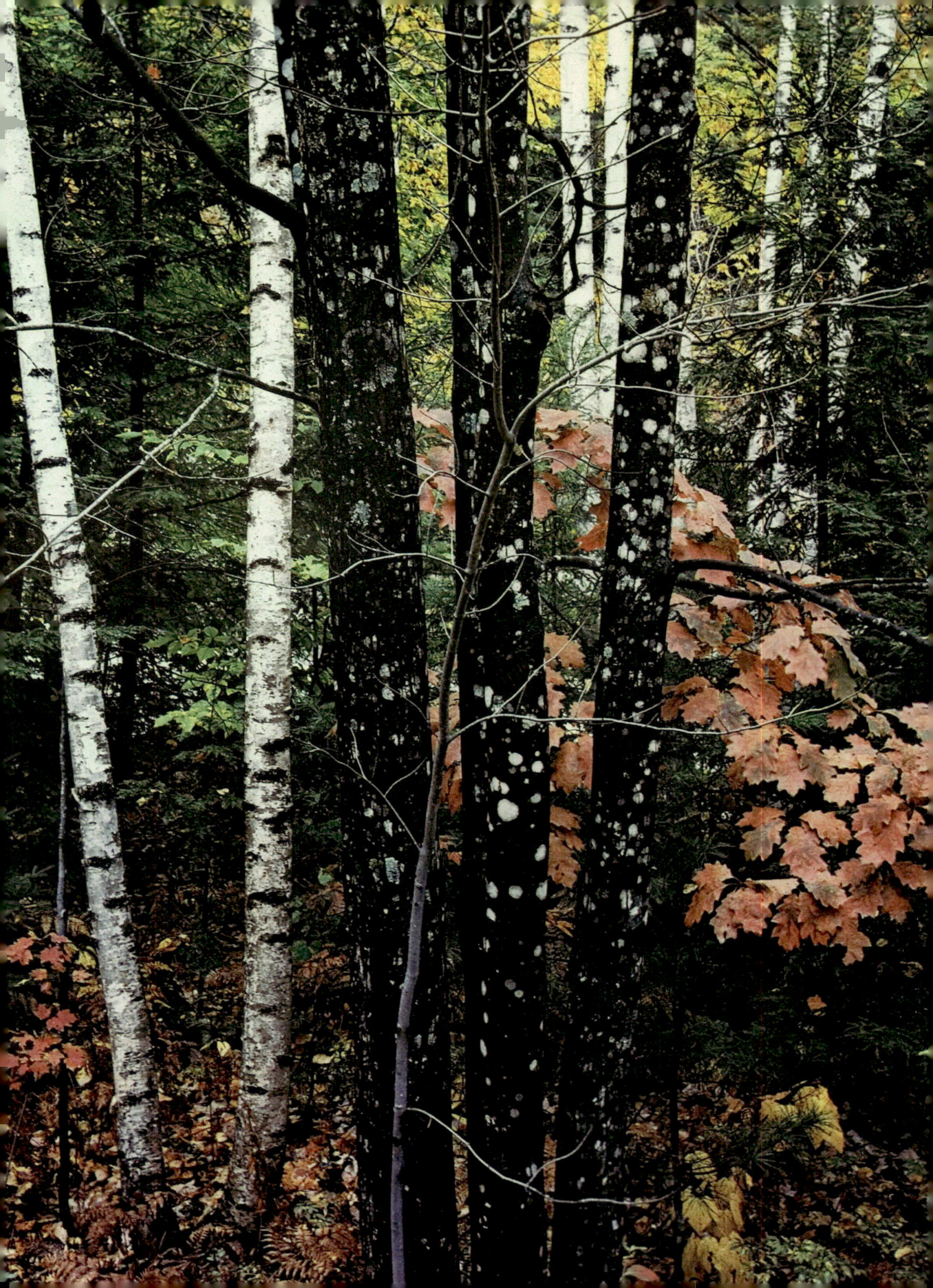

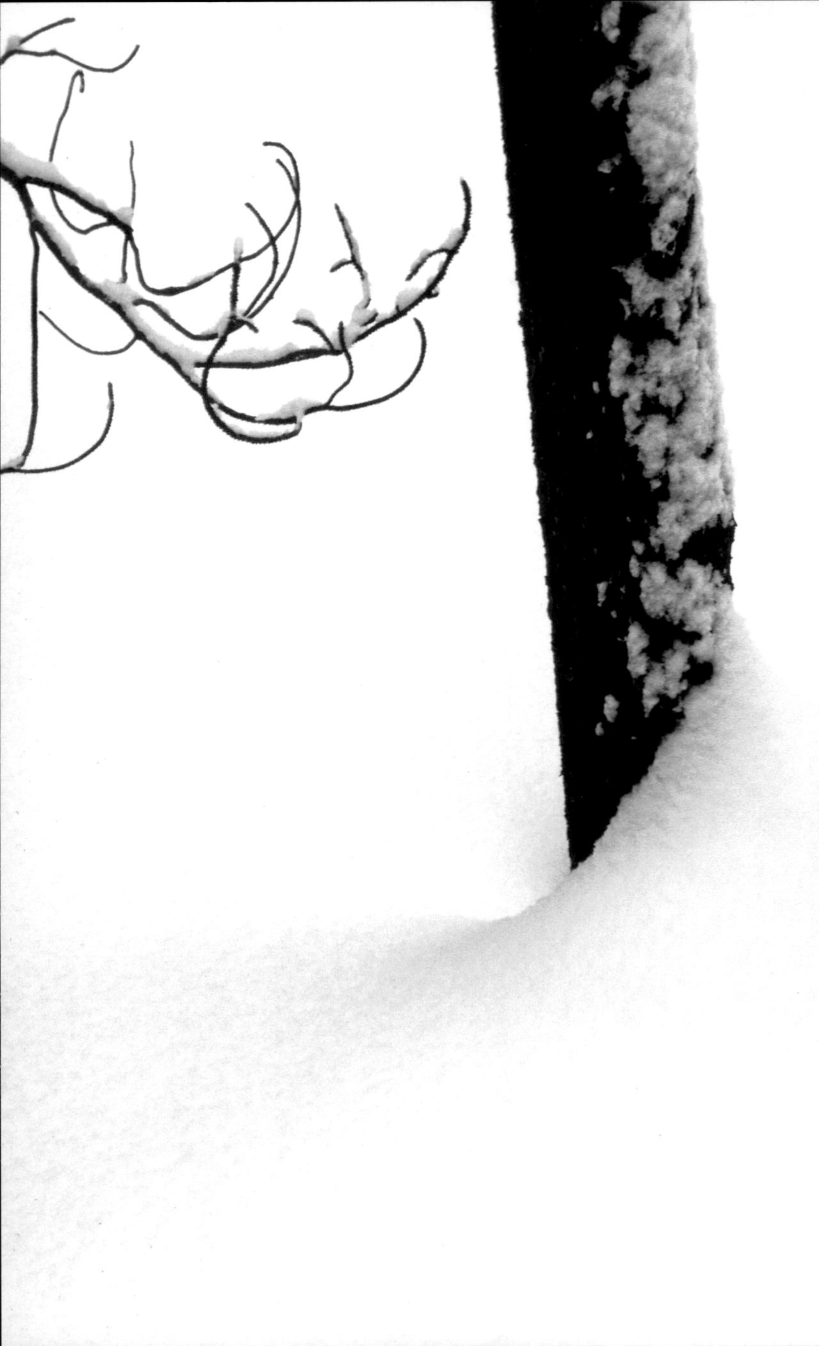

ANTI-LANDSCAPES

I see Porter being really descriptive of place. I don't want to describe places. I'm interested in the line and form and the rectangle. Remember, the view through the camera back is upside down and backward. This, to me, is the interesting aspect.

—Robert Glenn Ketchum

Robert Glenn Ketchum, *Peak, Above a Cloud*, 1973, from the portfolio *Winters: 1970–1980*

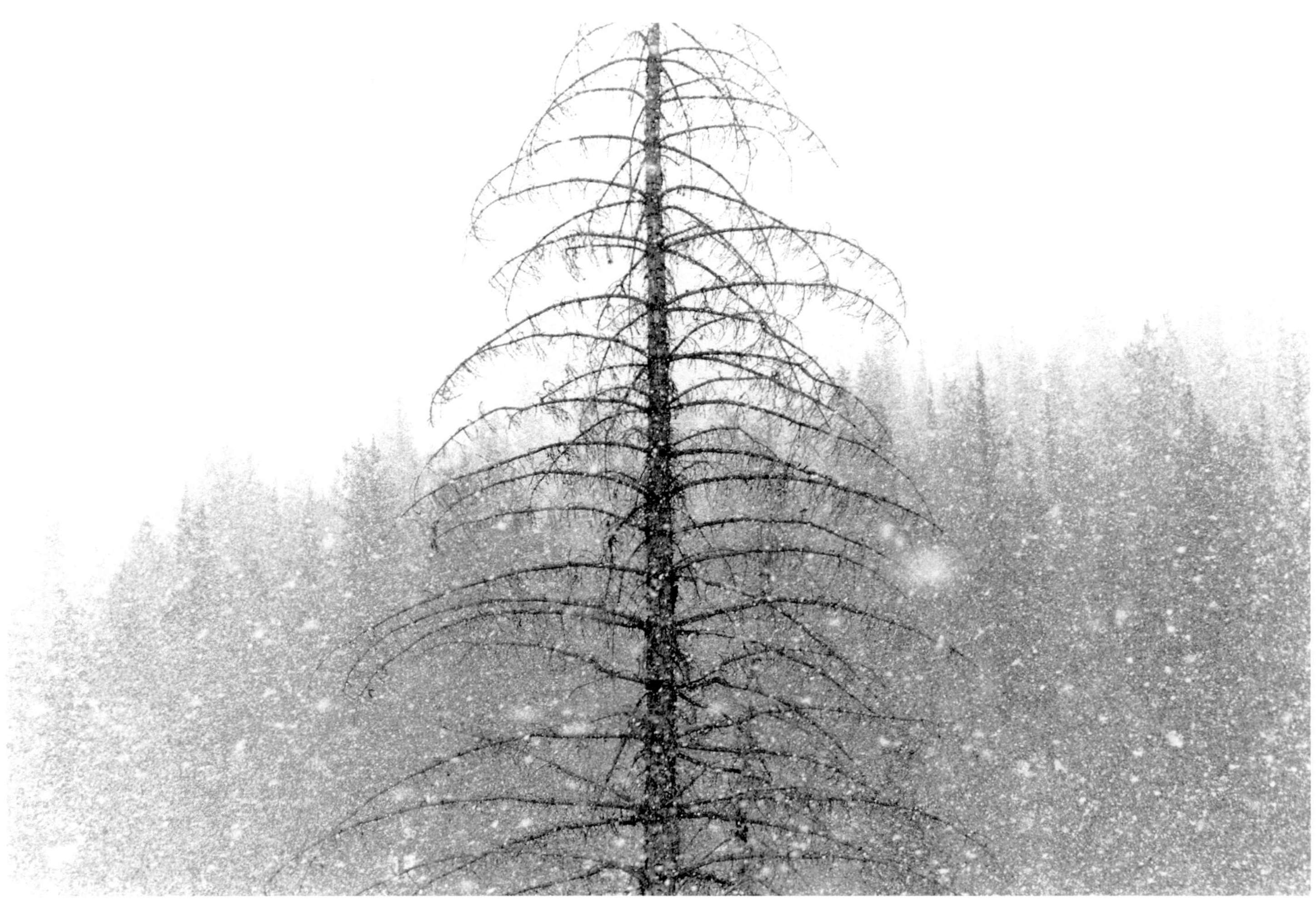

Robert Glenn Ketchum, *Snowfall,* 1979, from the portfolio *Winters: 1970–1980*

Robert Glenn Ketchum, *Snow Collapsing along a Creek Drainage,* 1978, from the portfolio *Winters: 1970–1980*

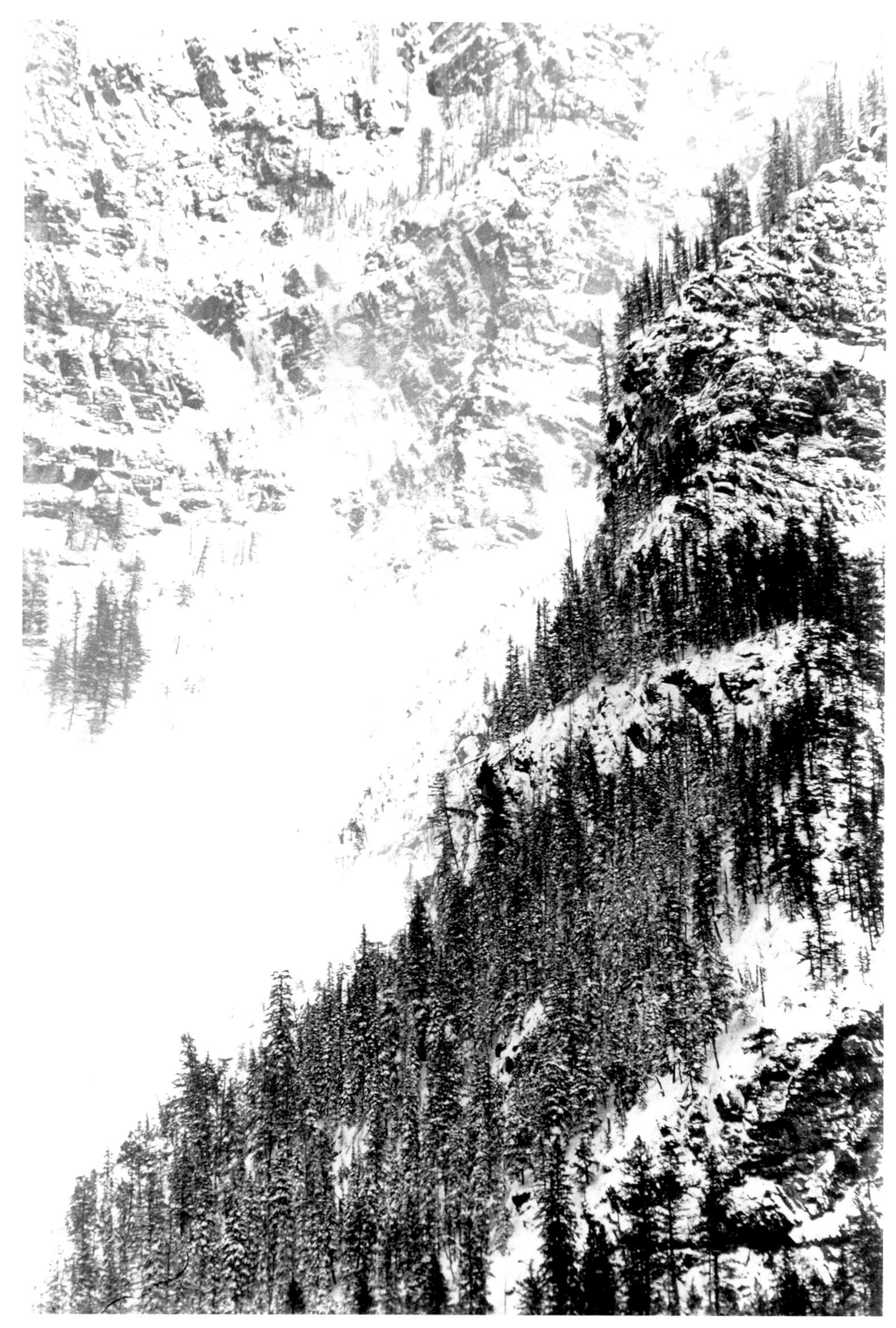

Robert Glenn Ketchum, *Chute Detail*, 1974, from the portfolio *Winters: 1970–1980*

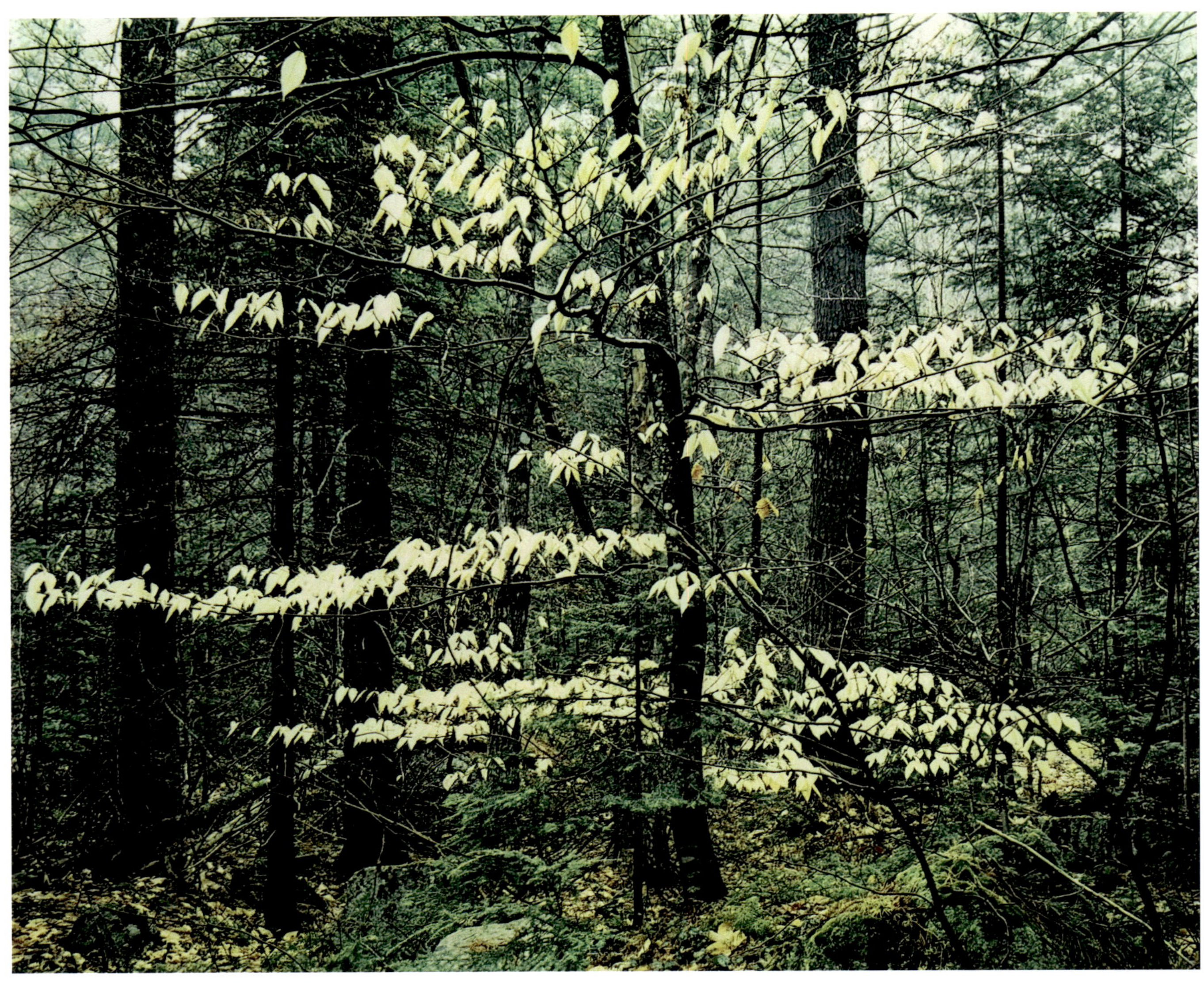

Eliot Porter, *Beech Seedling, Chocorua, New Hampshire, May 7, 1961*

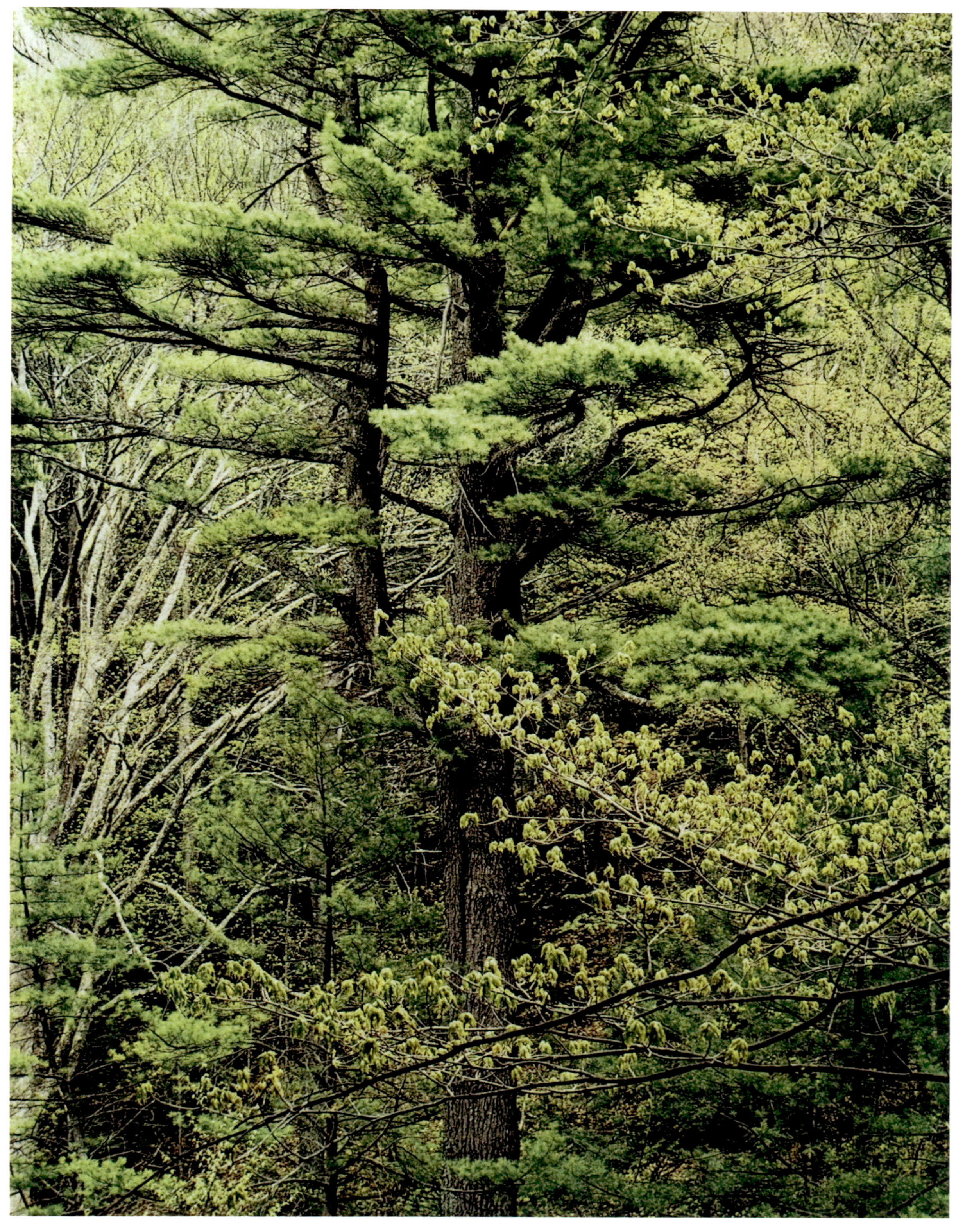

Eliot Porter, *Pine Tree, Bash Bish Falls, Massachusetts, May 19, 1961*

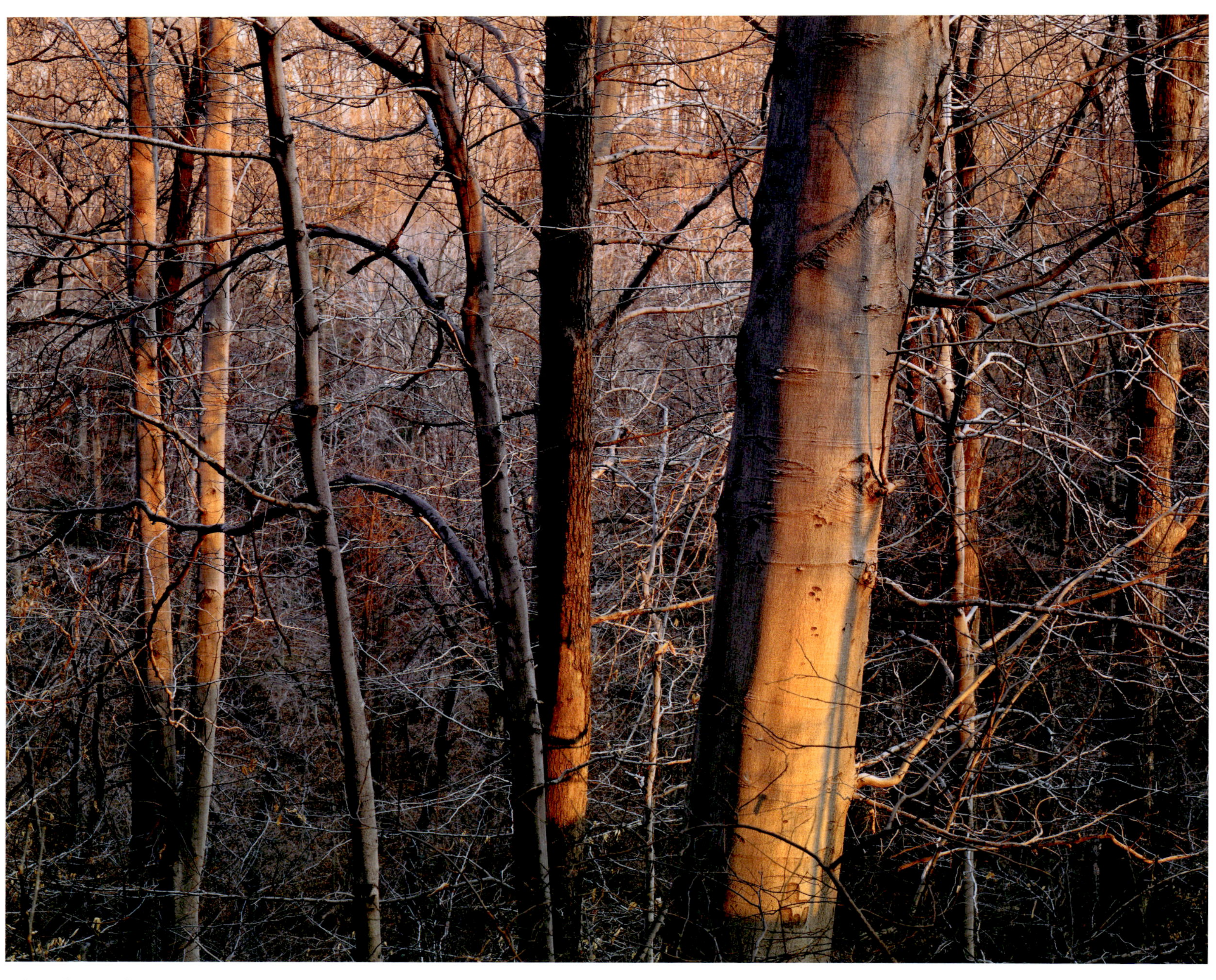

Robert Glenn Ketchum, *La Couleur de mon amour,* 1982, from the series *Order from Chaos*

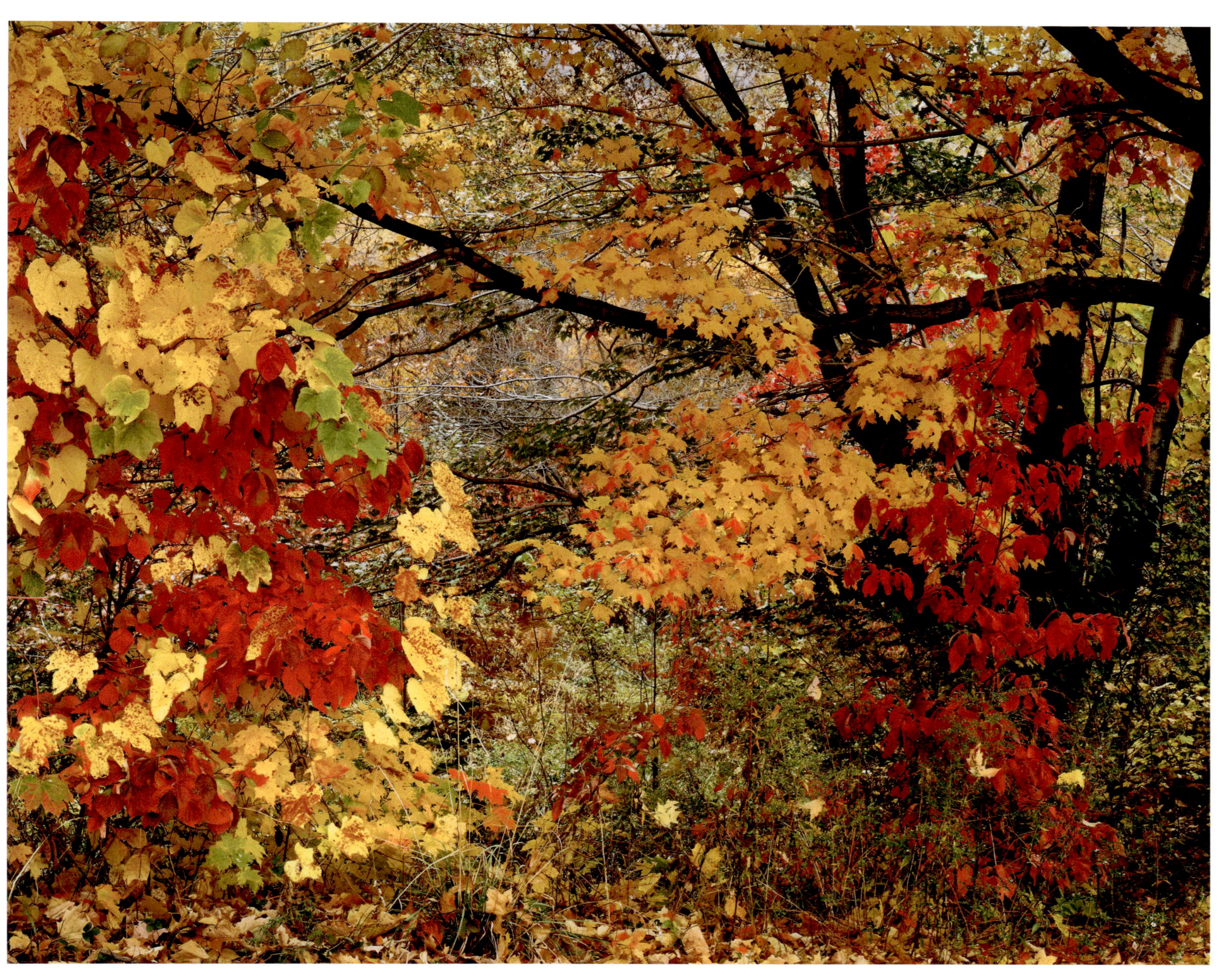

Robert Glenn Ketchum, *Brewster Boogie Woogie, 27*, 1979, from the series *Order from Chaos*

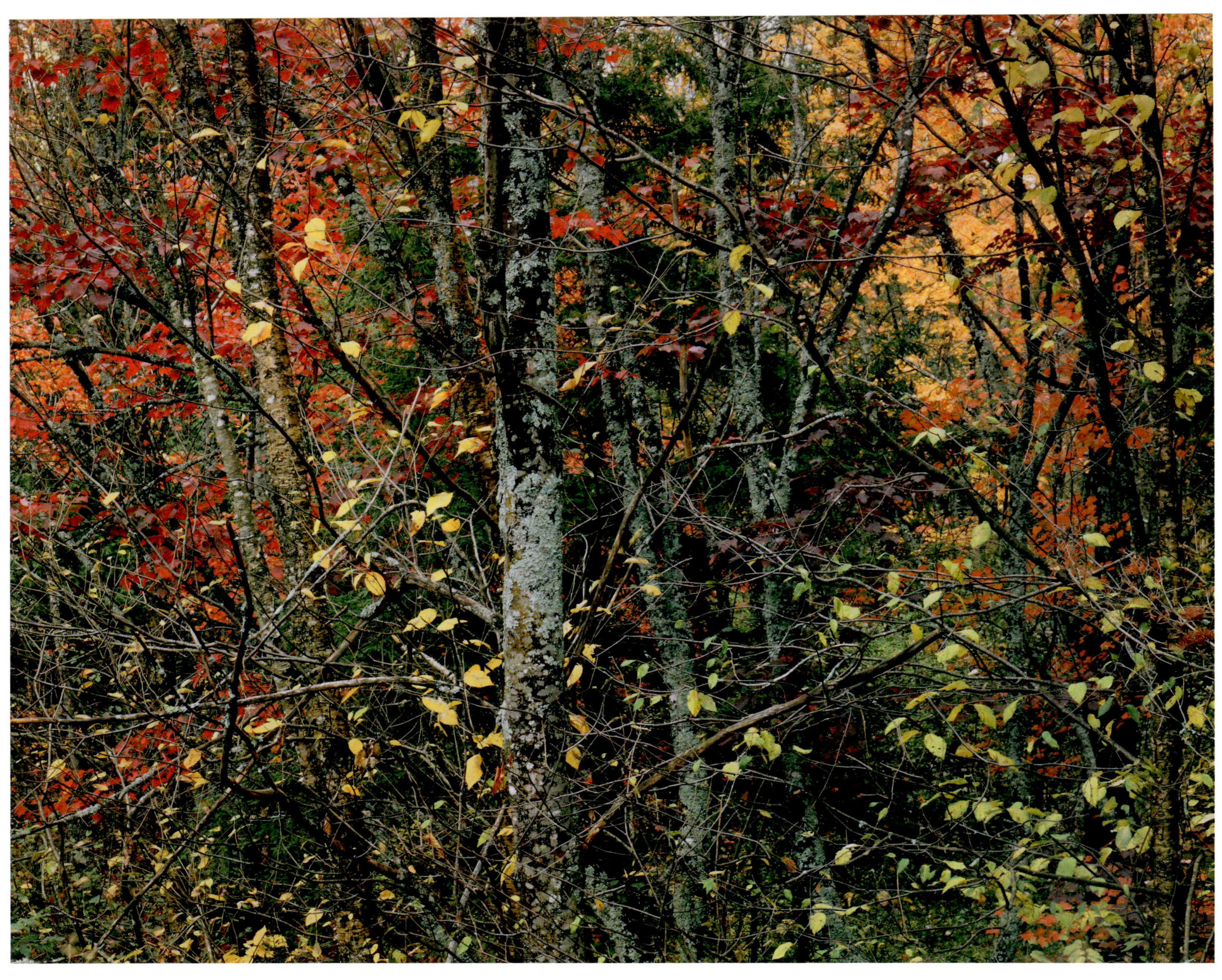

Robert Glenn Ketchum, *Autumnal Warp*, 1982, from the series *Order from Chaos*

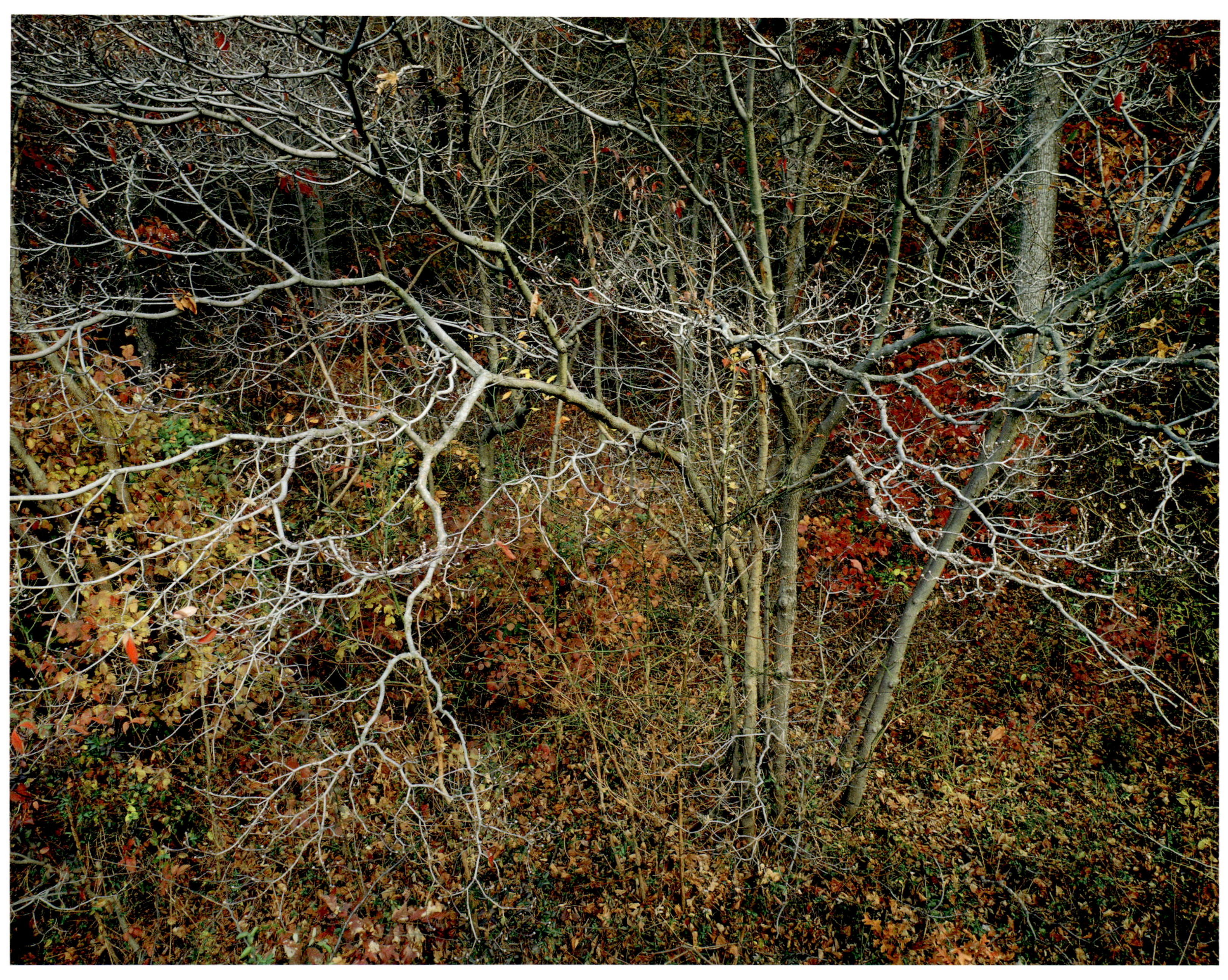

Robert Glenn Ketchum, *And Gravity Lets You Down,* 1981, from the series *Order from Chaos*

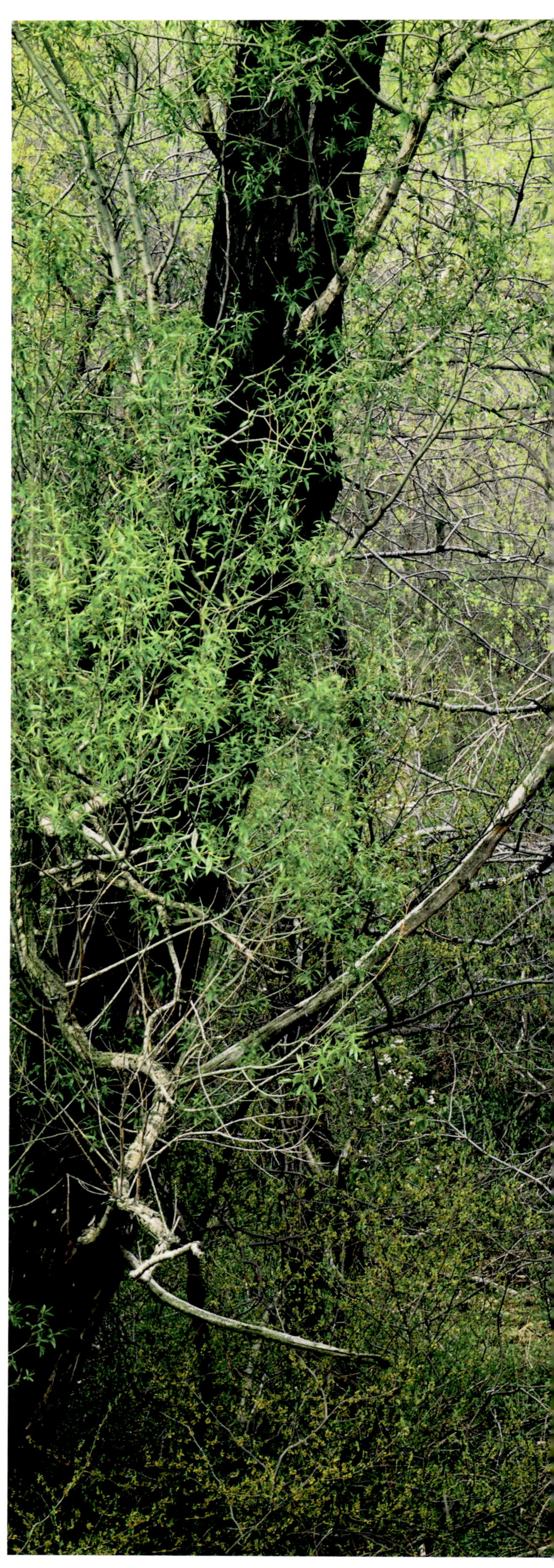

Robert Glenn Ketchum, *"The Voyage of Life"/Homage to Thomas Cole*, 1984, from the series *Order from Chaos*

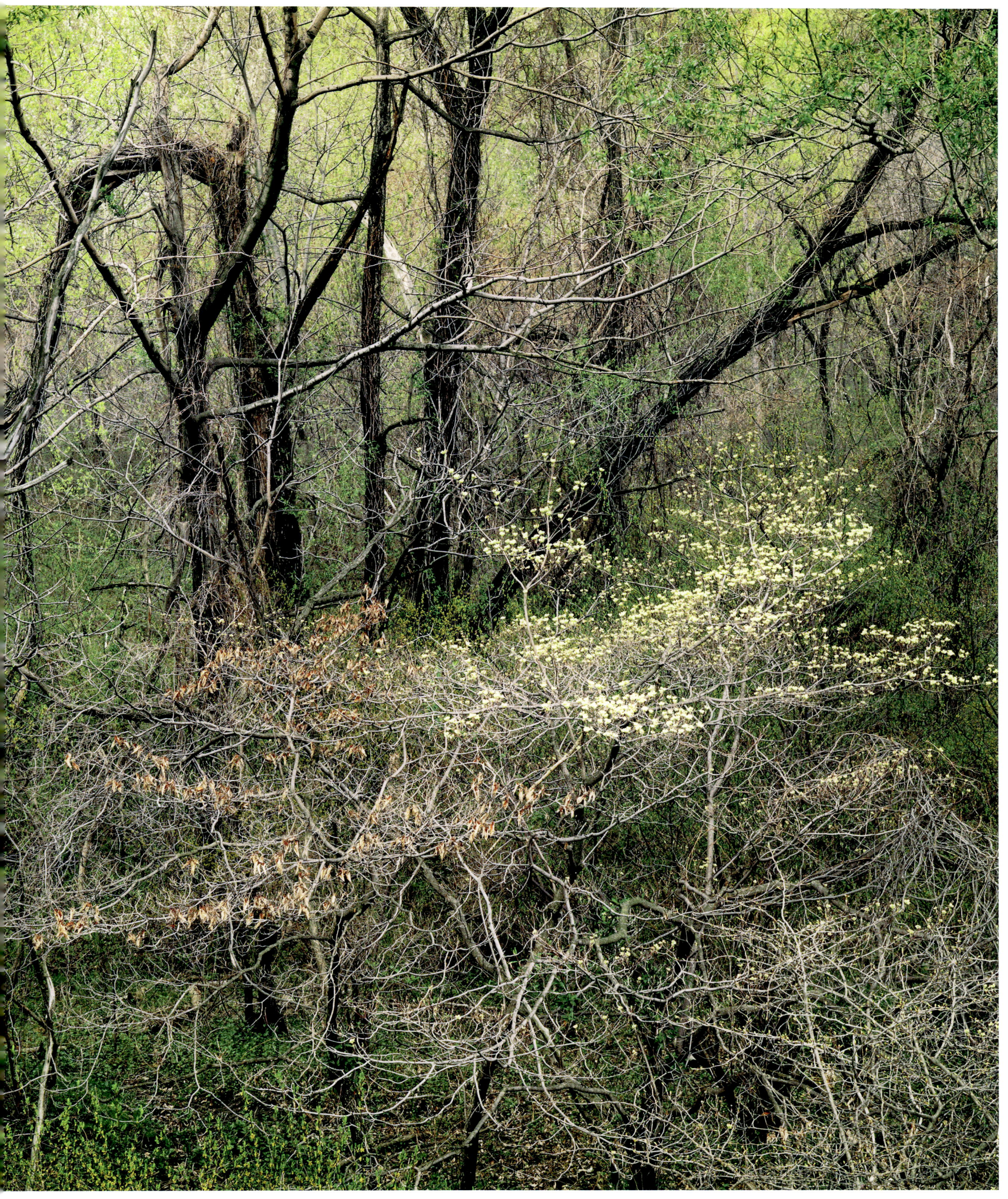

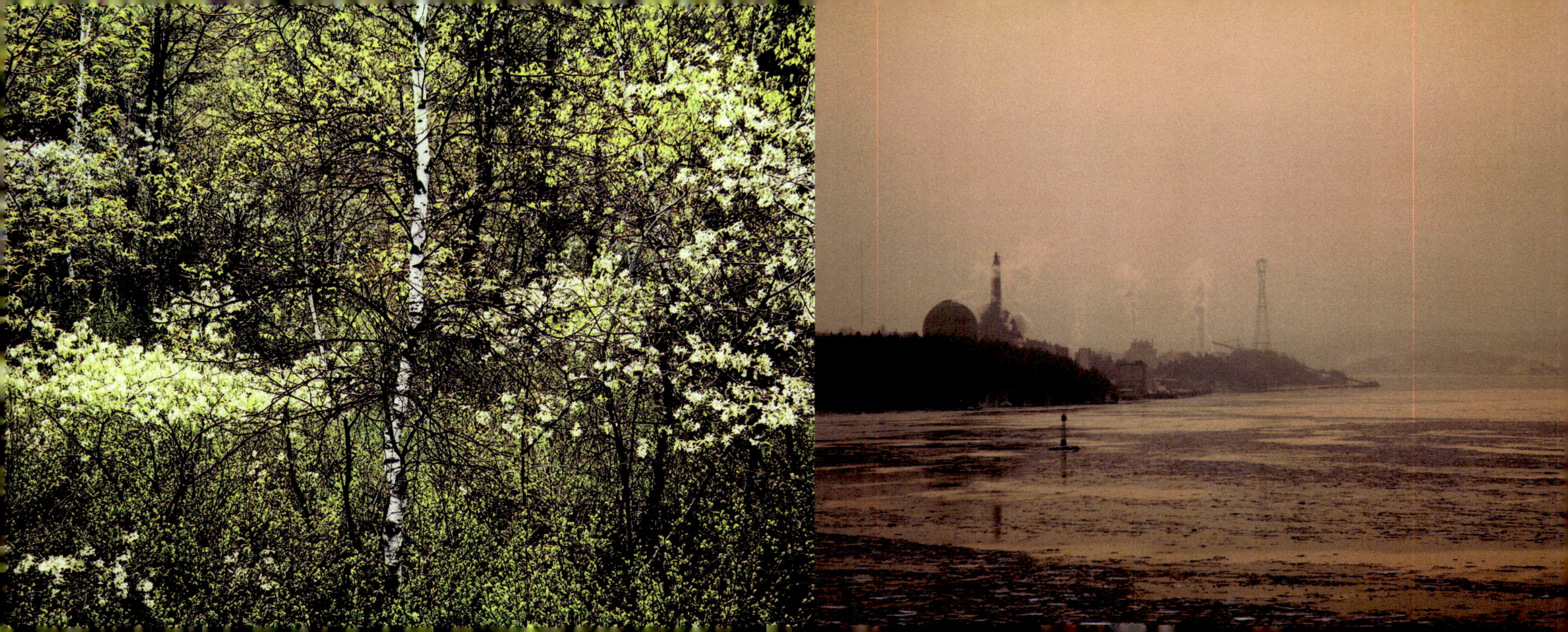

ART FOR ENVIRONMENTAL ADVOCACY

I had to ask myself, Am I still having a discussion with my peers about what is going on in postmodernist photography? Or am I having a discussion with the land and how these photographs explain it?

—Robert Glenn Ketchum

Eliot Porter, *Shad Bushes, Mount Washington, Massachusetts, May 21, 1961*

Robert Glenn Ketchum, *The Indian Point Atomic Power Plant from the Eastern Shore, Looking South across the Bay of Peekskill*, 1983, from the Hudson River project

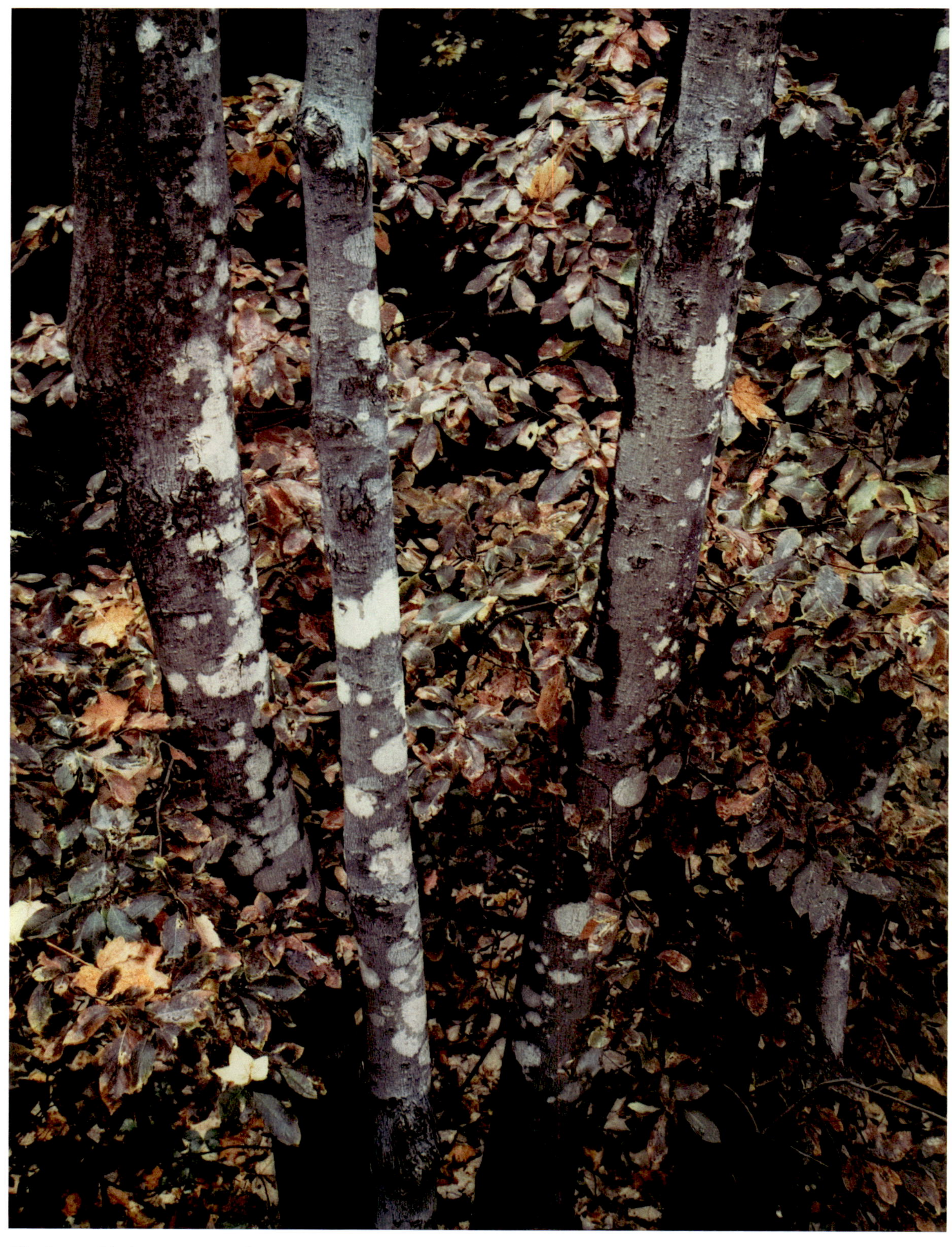

Eliot Porter, *Blueberry Leaves and Maple Trunks, Passaconaway, New Hampshire, October 7, 1952*

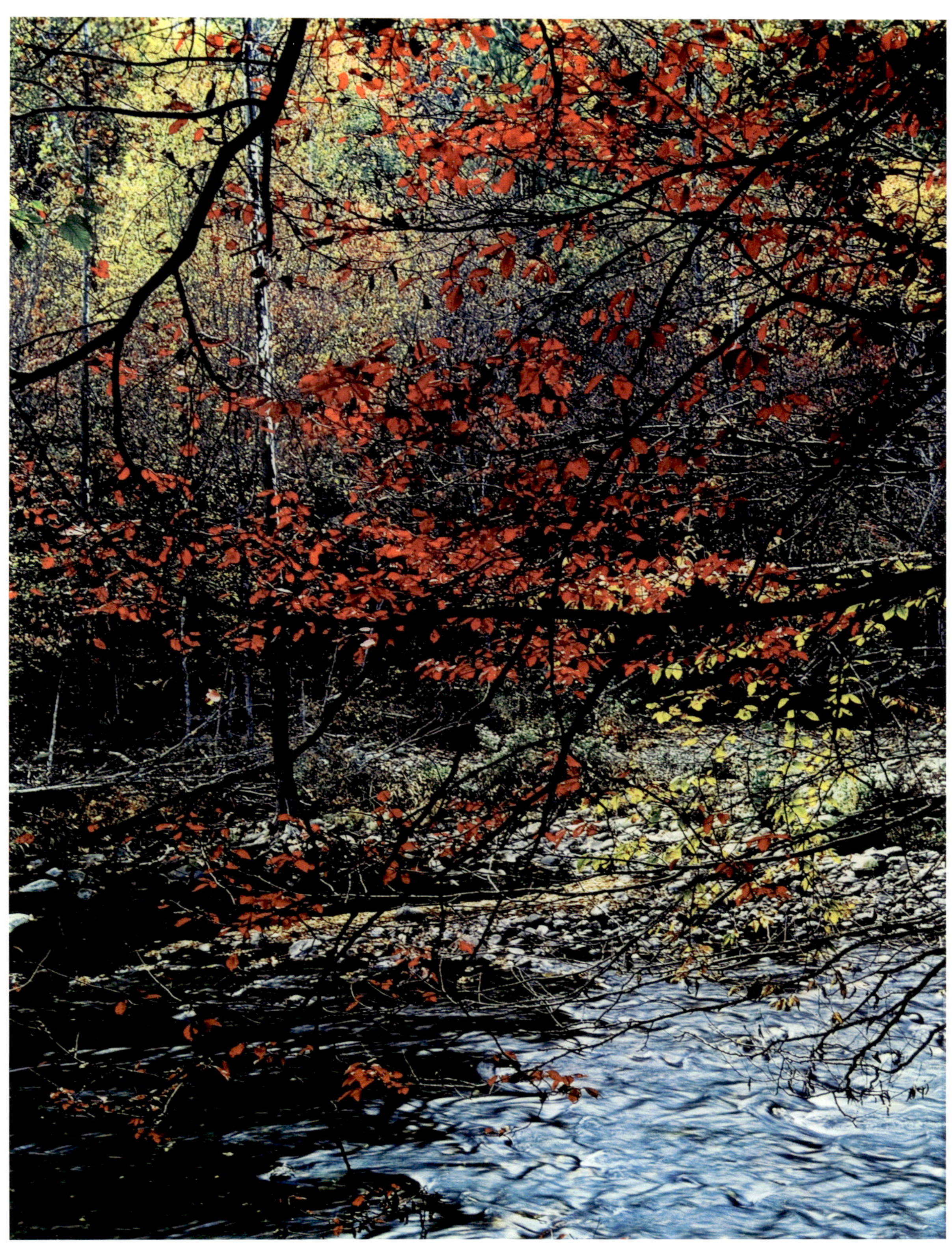

Eliot Porter, *Red Leaves Over Little River, on Road to Cades Cove, Great Smoky Mountains National Park, Tennessee, October 7, 1967*

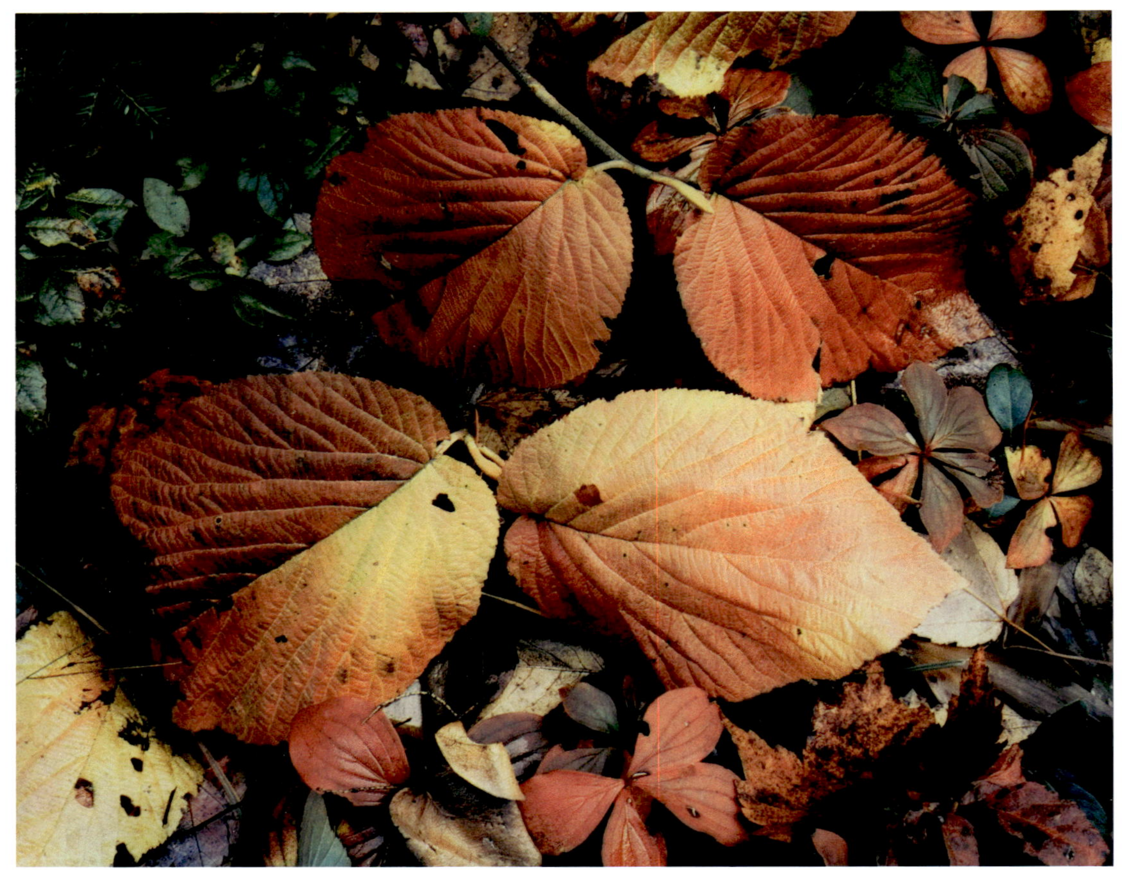

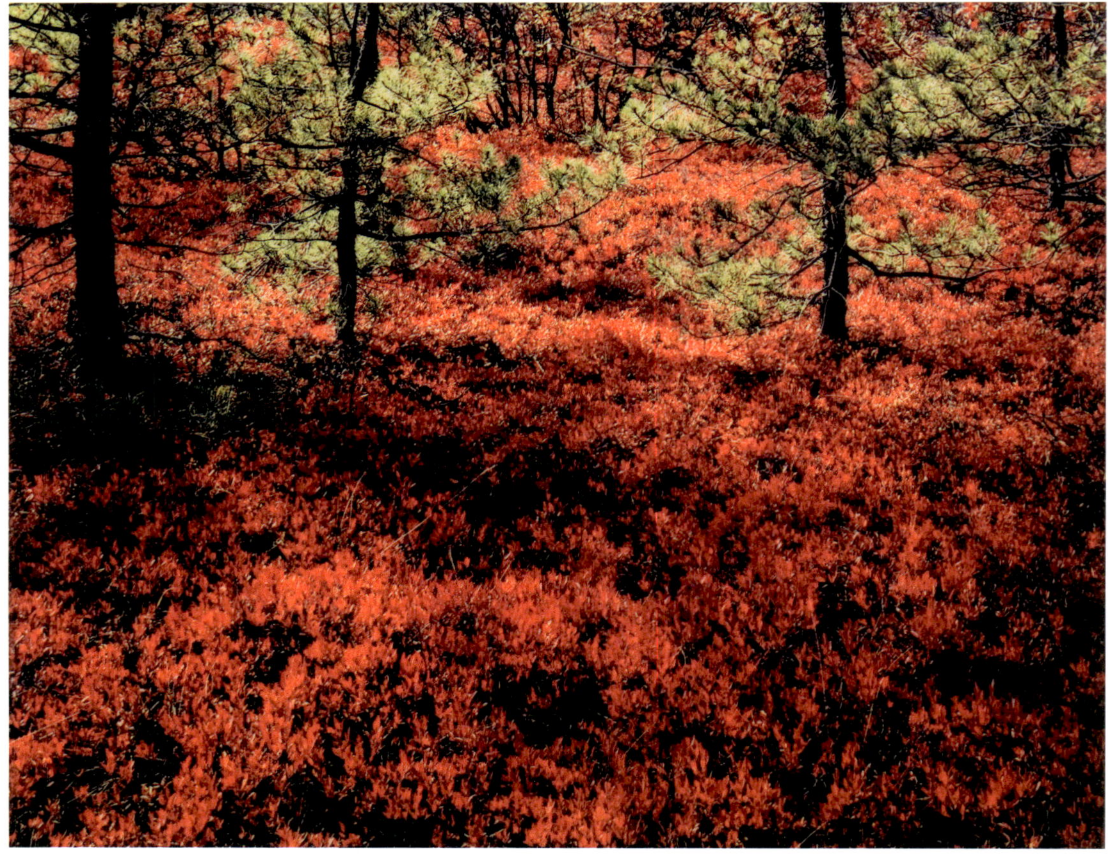

Eliot Porter, *Bunchberry and Hobble Bush Leaves, Passaconaway, New Hampshire, October 7, 1952*, and *Red Blueberries, Pitch Pine, Silver Lake, New Hampshire, October 15, 1953*

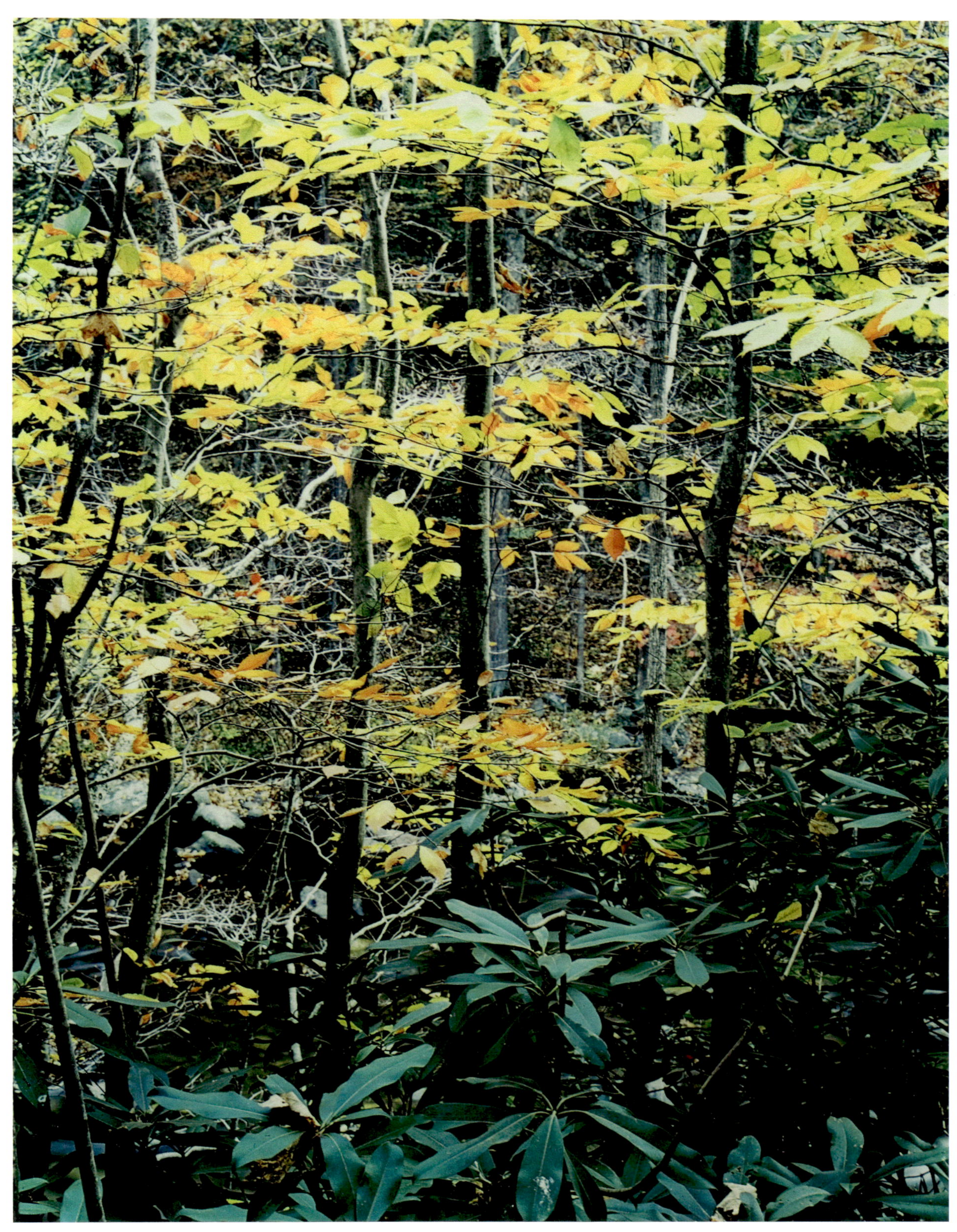

Eliot Porter, *Beech Seedlings, Cades Cove Road, Great Smoky Mountains National Park, Tennessee, October 15, 1967*

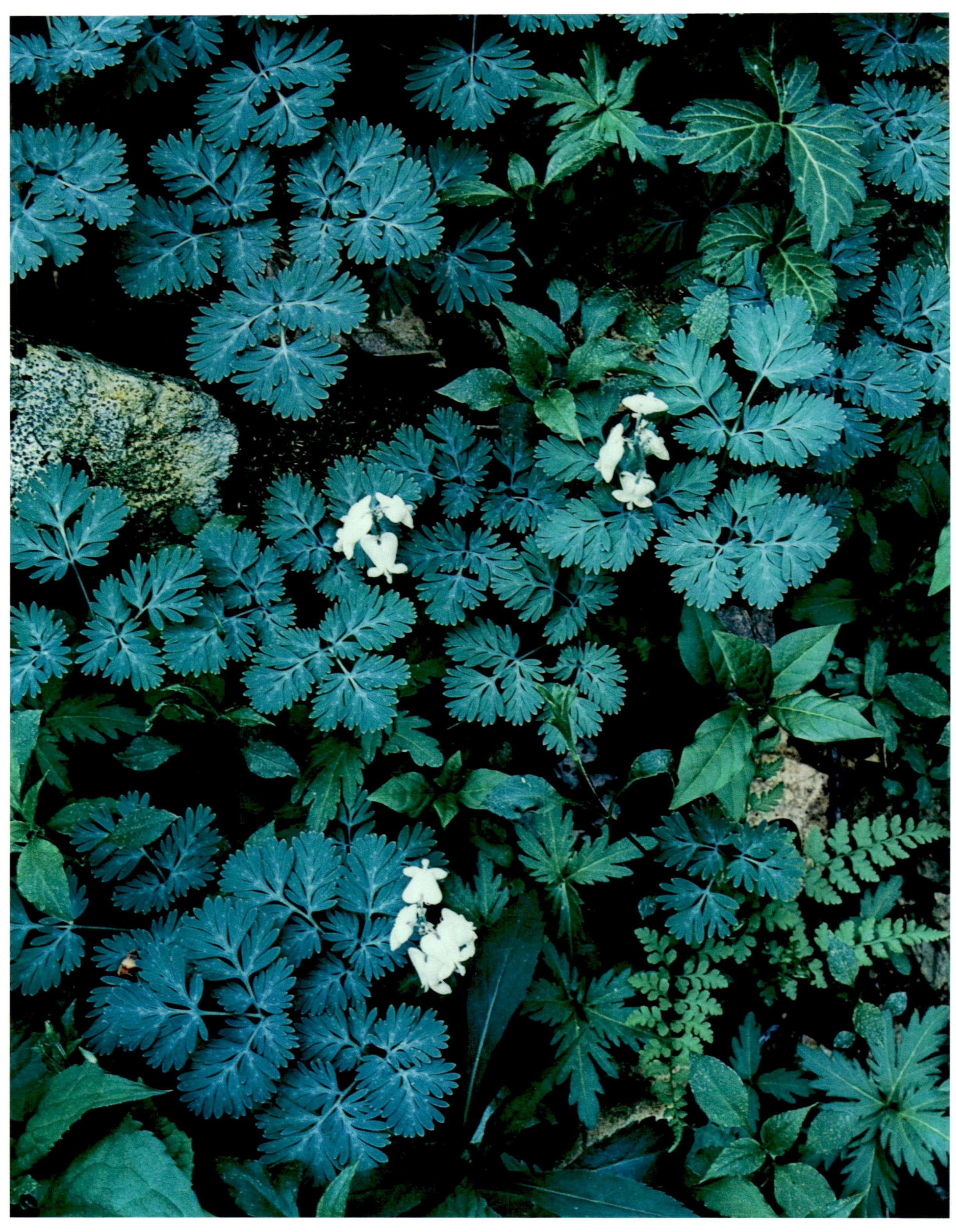

Eliot Porter, *Squirrel Corn, Walnut Bottoms, Great Smoky Mountains National Park, Tennessee, April 14, 1968*

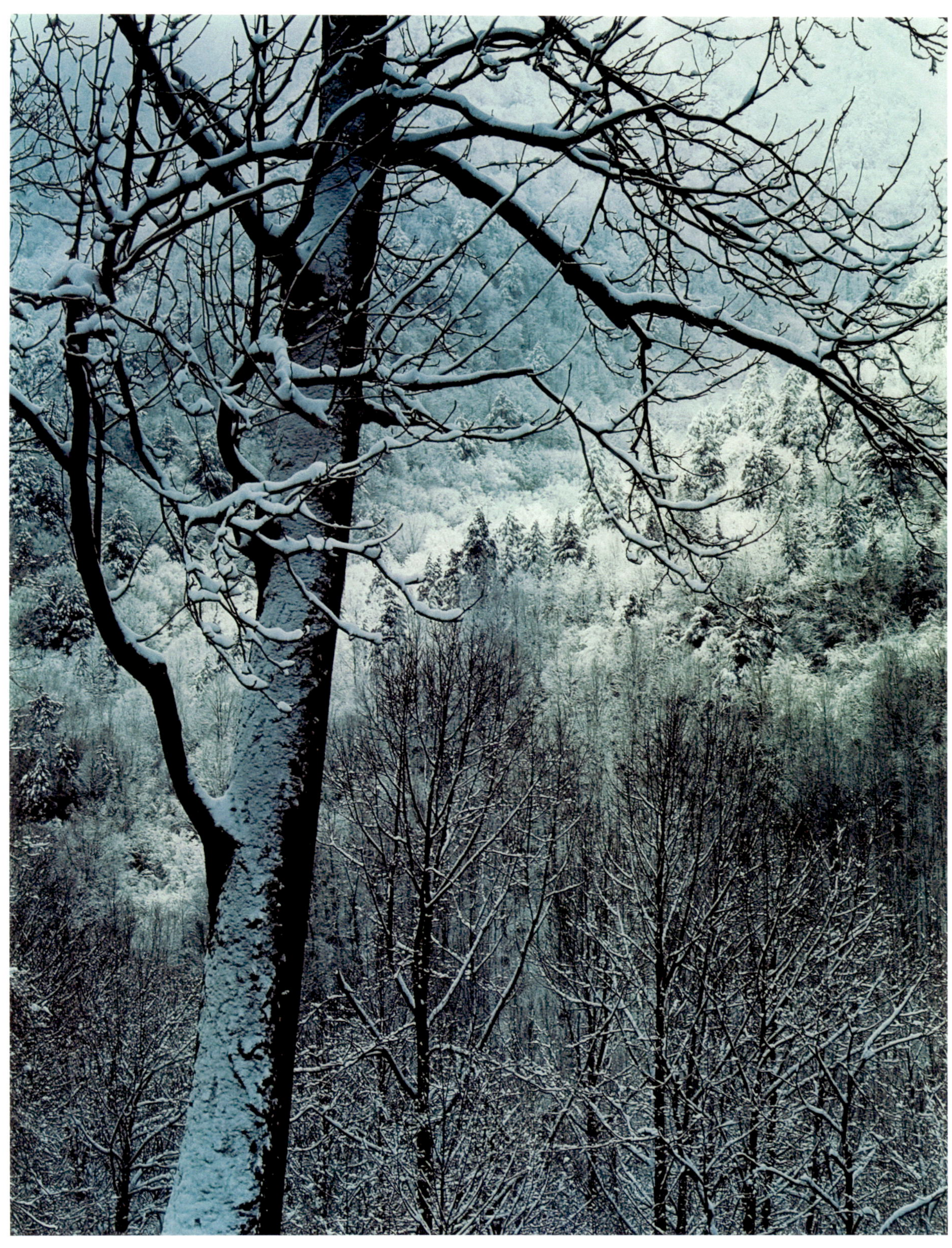

Eliot Porter, *Tree and Mountain Valley, Great Smoky Mountains National Park, Tennessee, March 11, 1969*

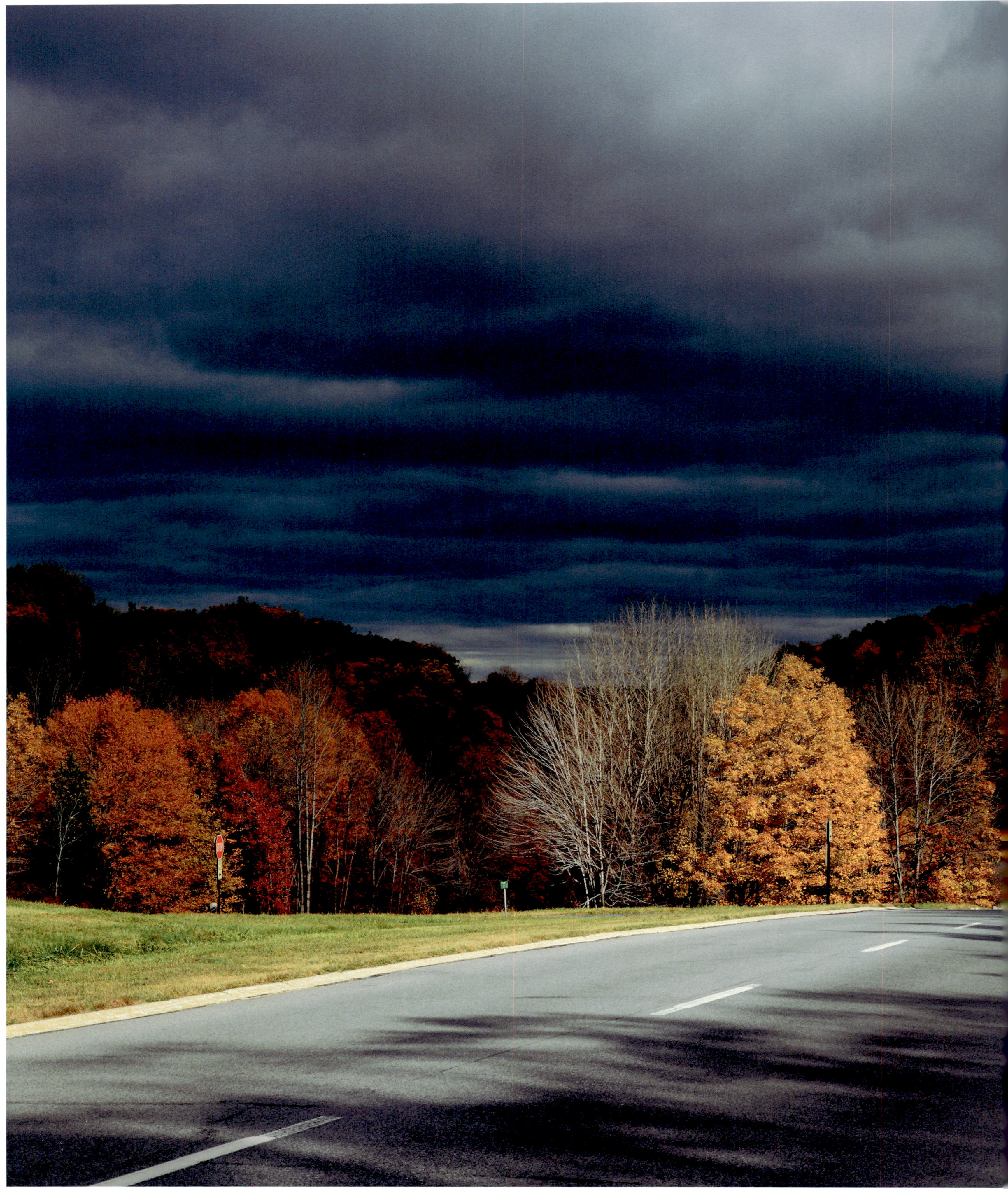

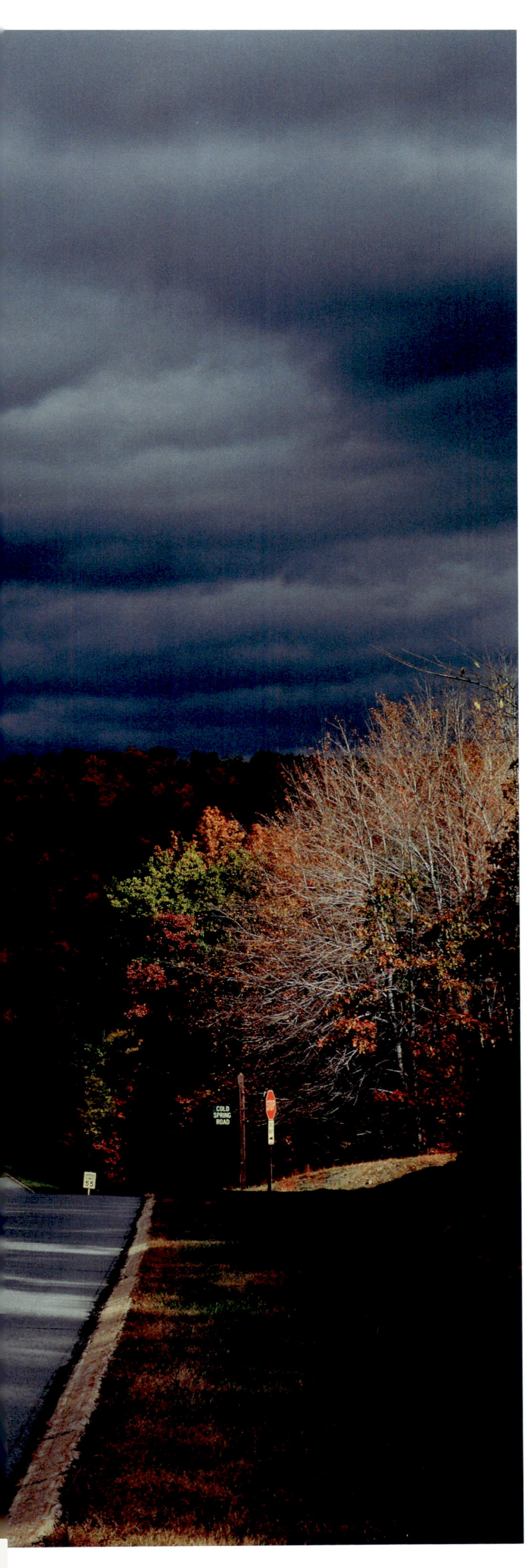

Robert Glenn Ketchum, *The Taconic Parkway, North to Albany*, 1983, from the Hudson River project

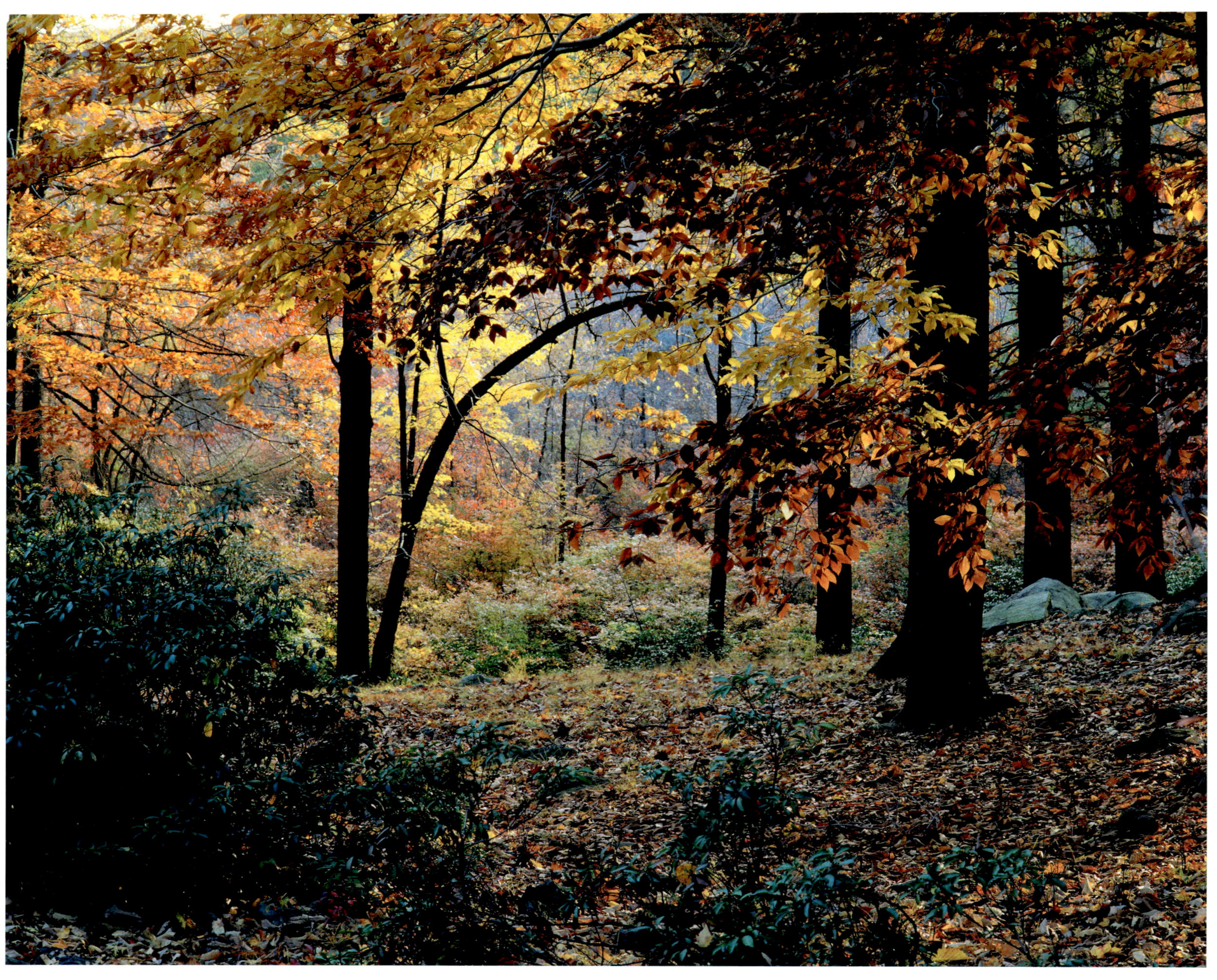

Robert Glenn Ketchum, *October 30, 1983/4:30 p.m.*, from the Hudson River project

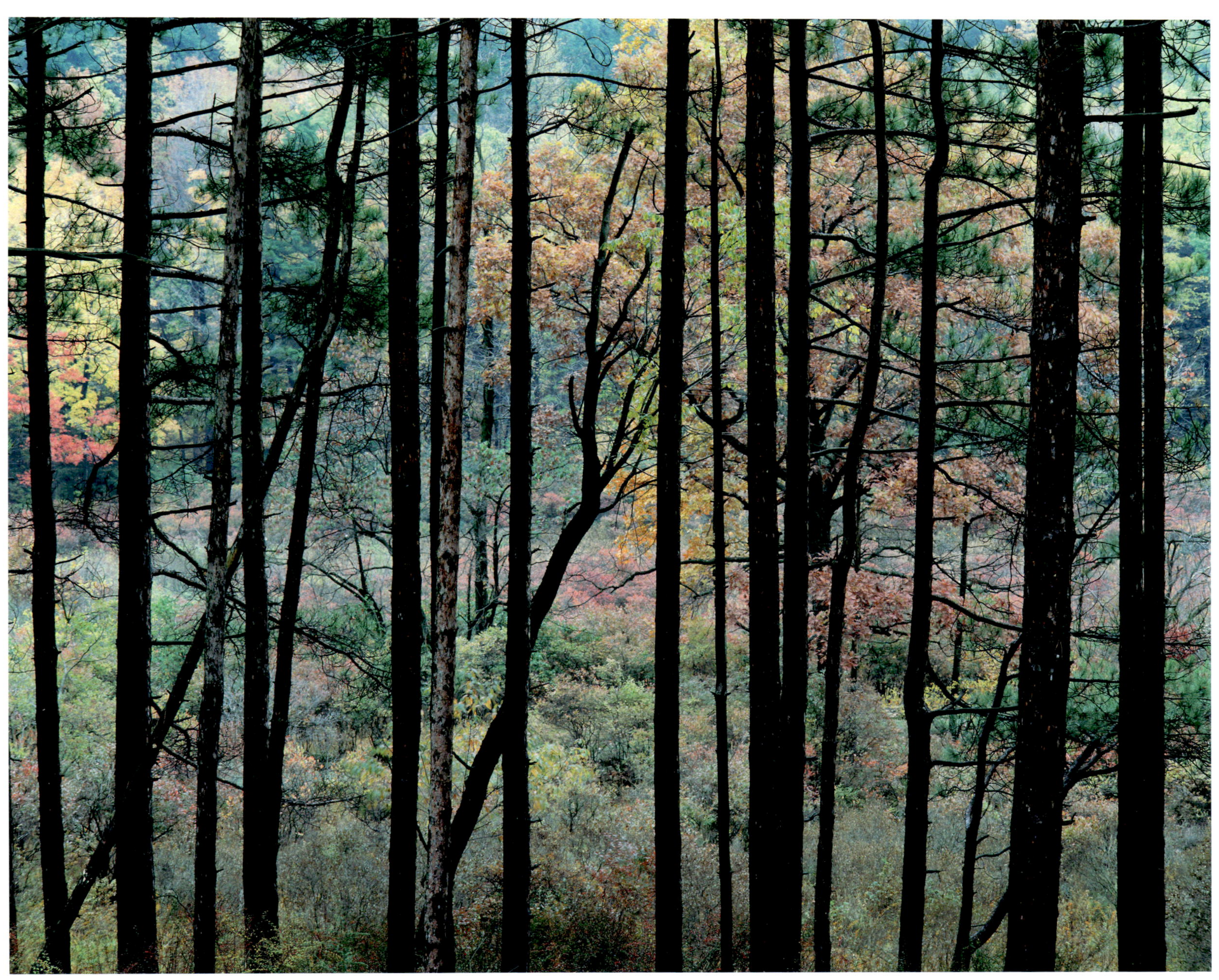

Robert Glenn Ketchum, *October 24, 1983/2:10 p.m.*, from the Hudson River project

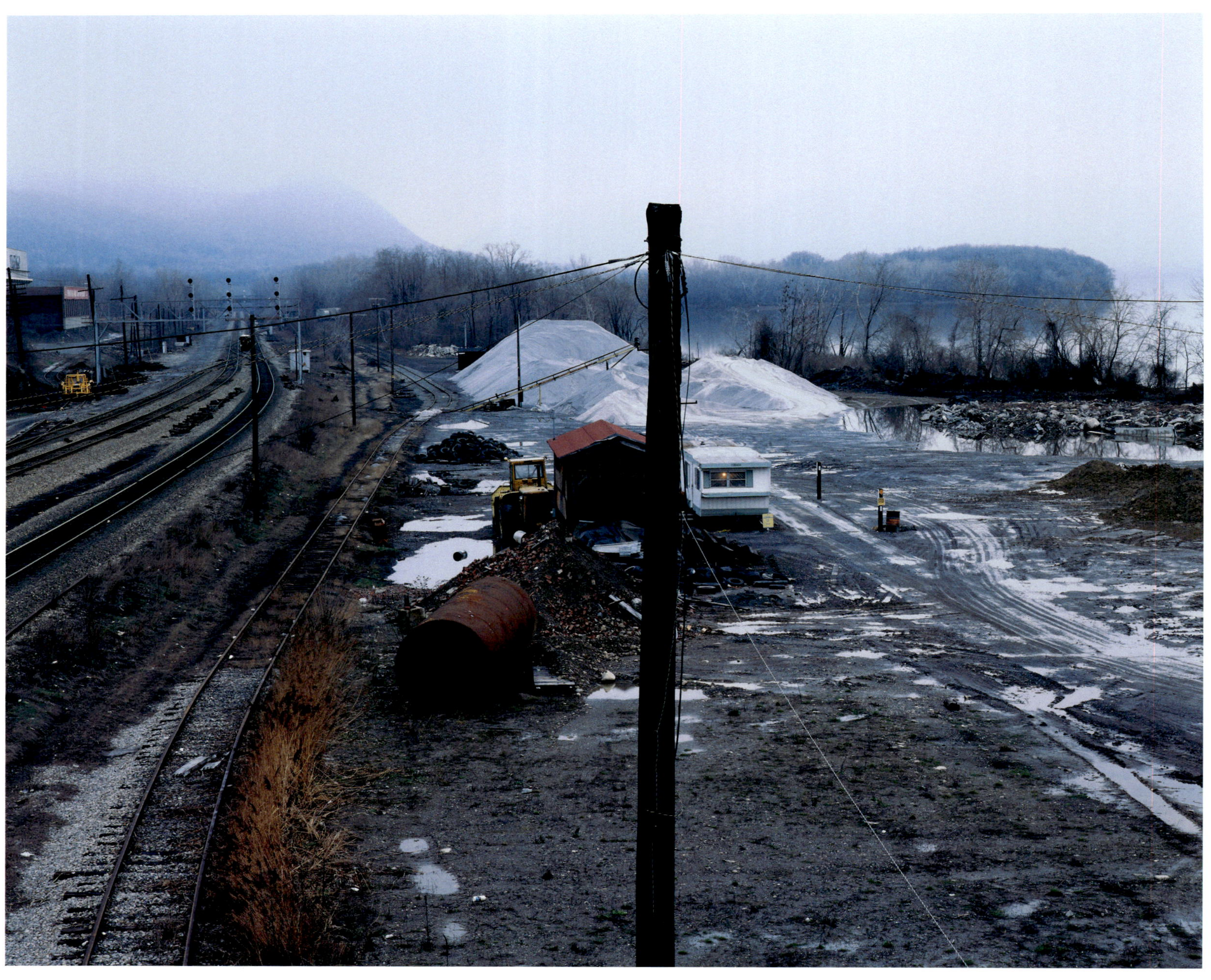

Robert Glenn Ketchum, *Railyard adjacent to the Beacon Landing*, 1984, from the Hudson River project

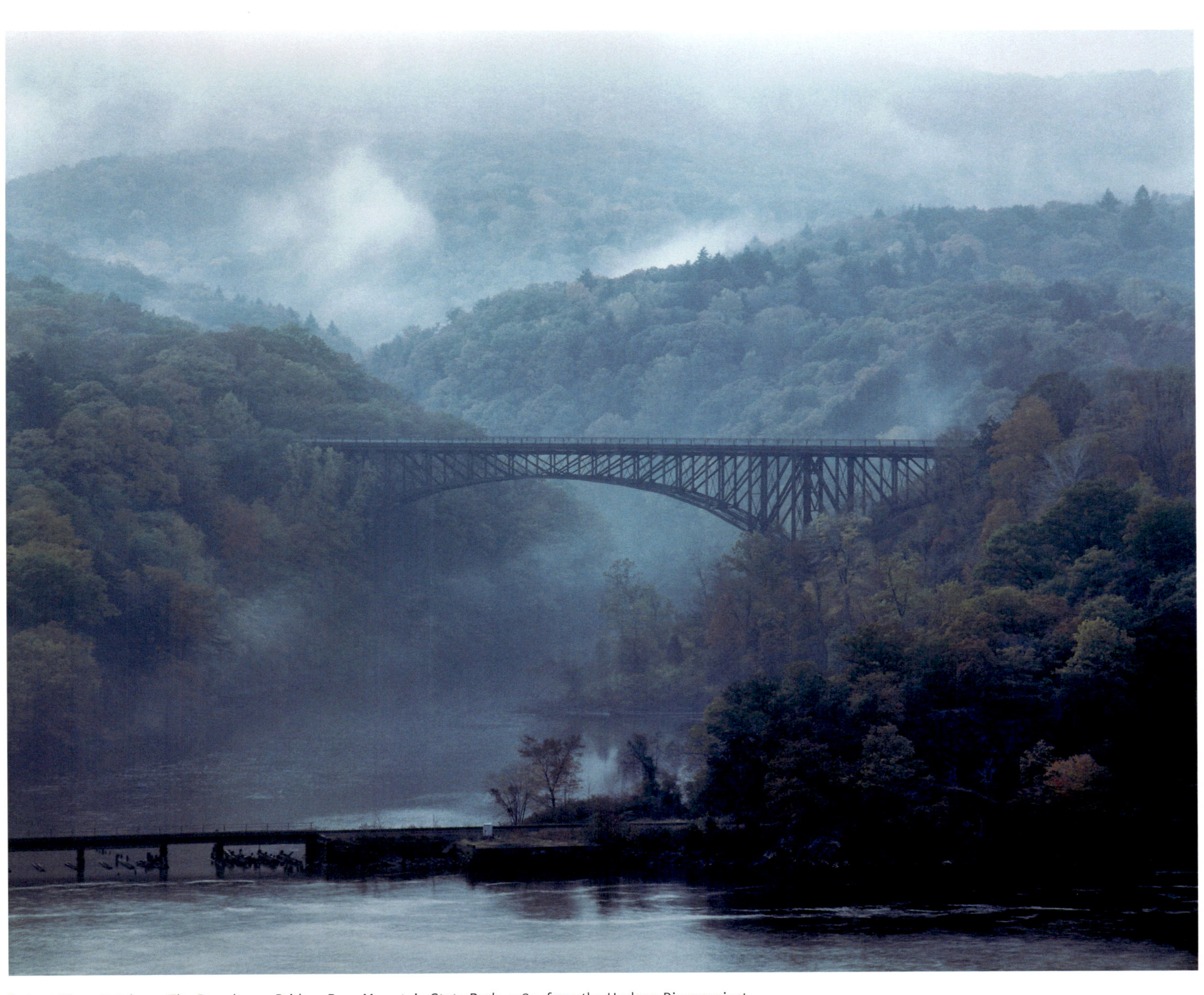

Robert Glenn Ketchum, *The Popolopen Bridge, Bear Mountain State Park,* 1983, from the Hudson River project

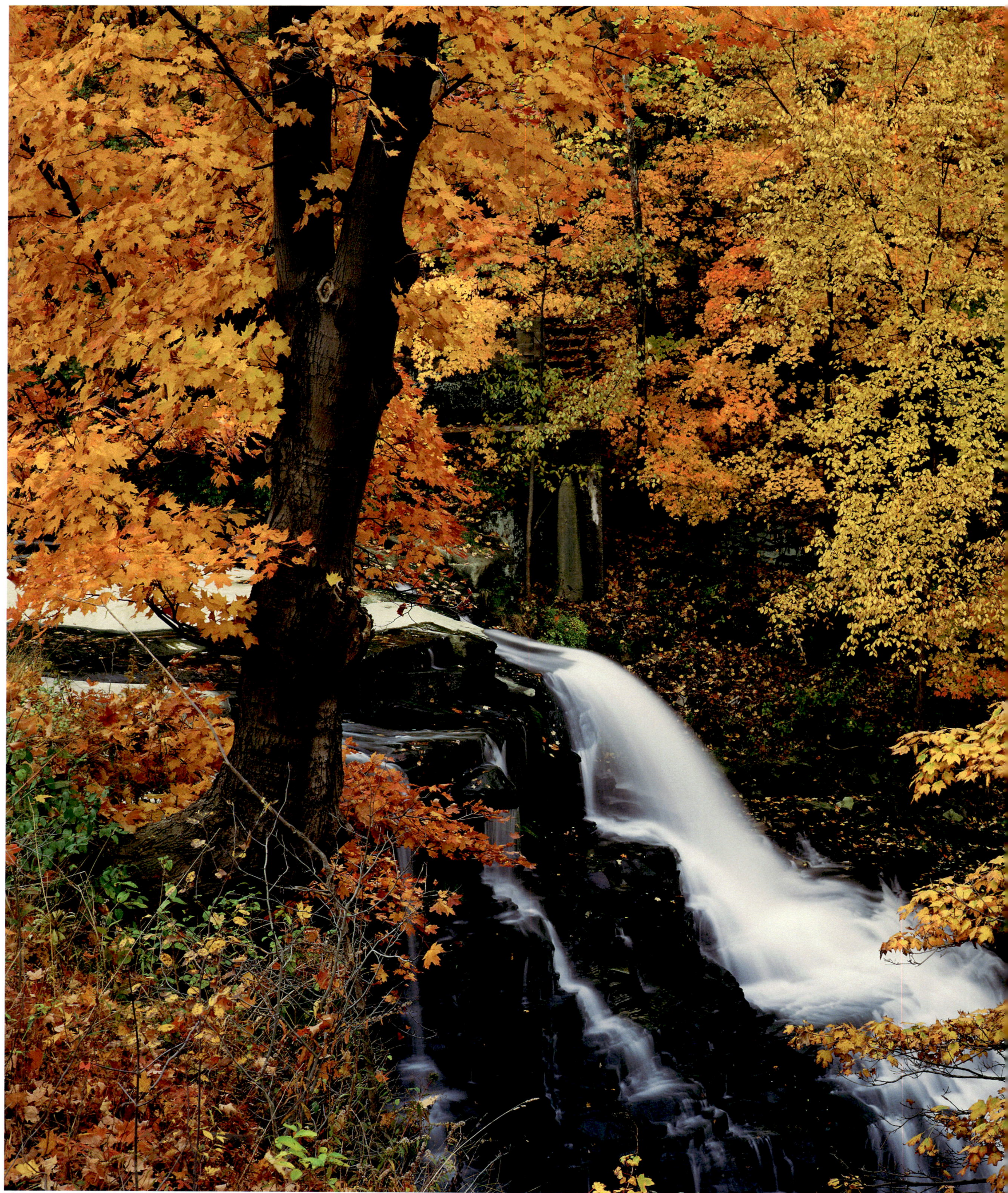

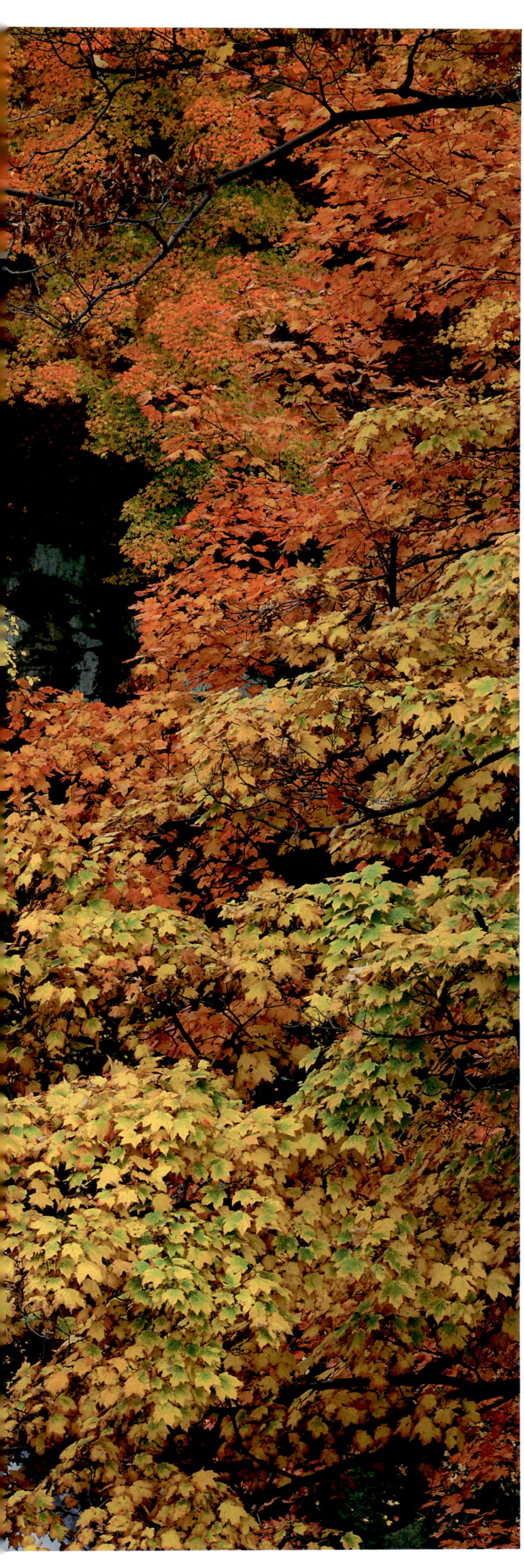

Robert Glenn Ketchum, *CVNRA #125 (a toxic waterfall in a national recreation area)*, 1986, from the Ohio/Federal Lands project

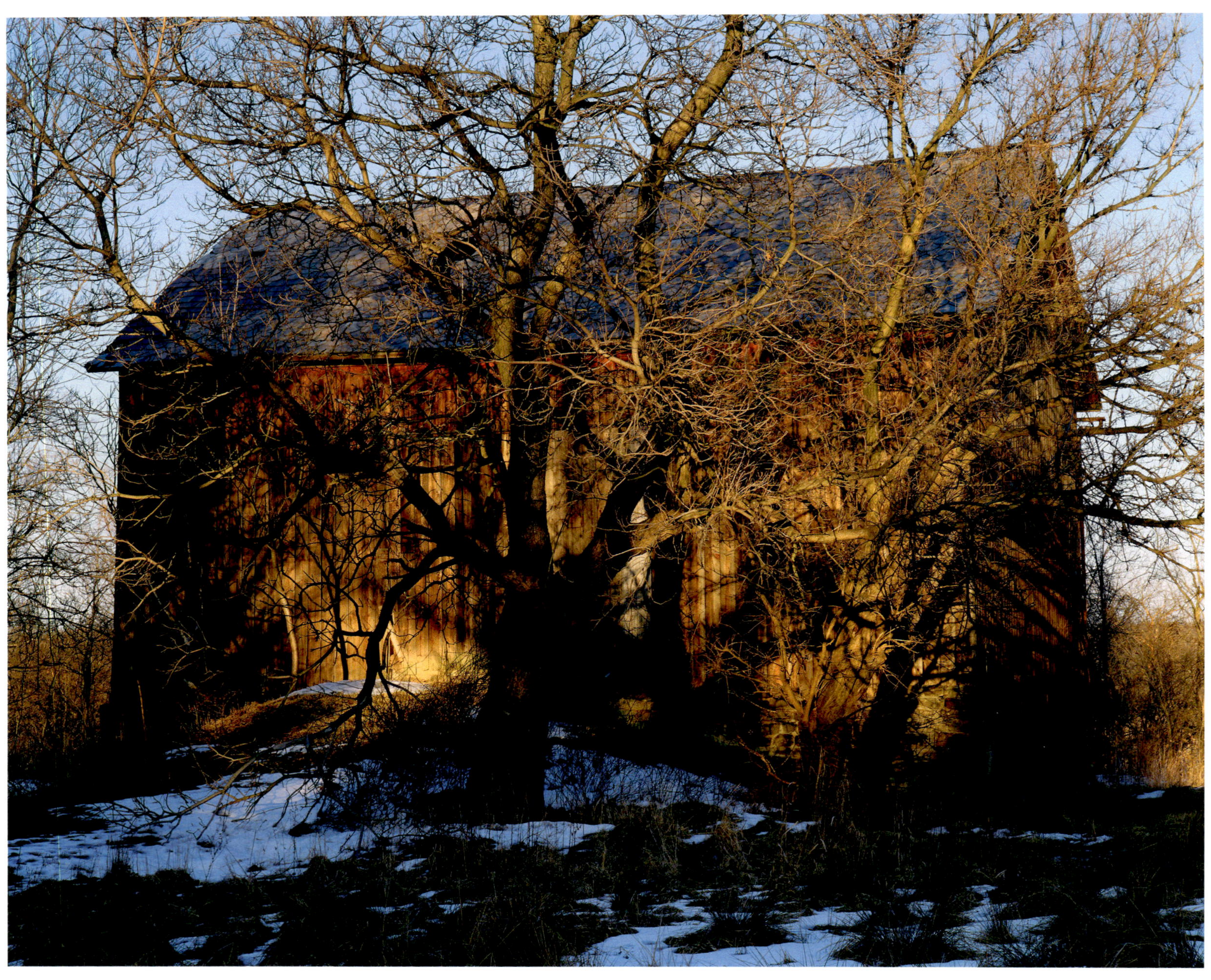

Robert Glenn Ketchum, *CVNRA #302*, 1988, from the Ohio/Federal Lands project

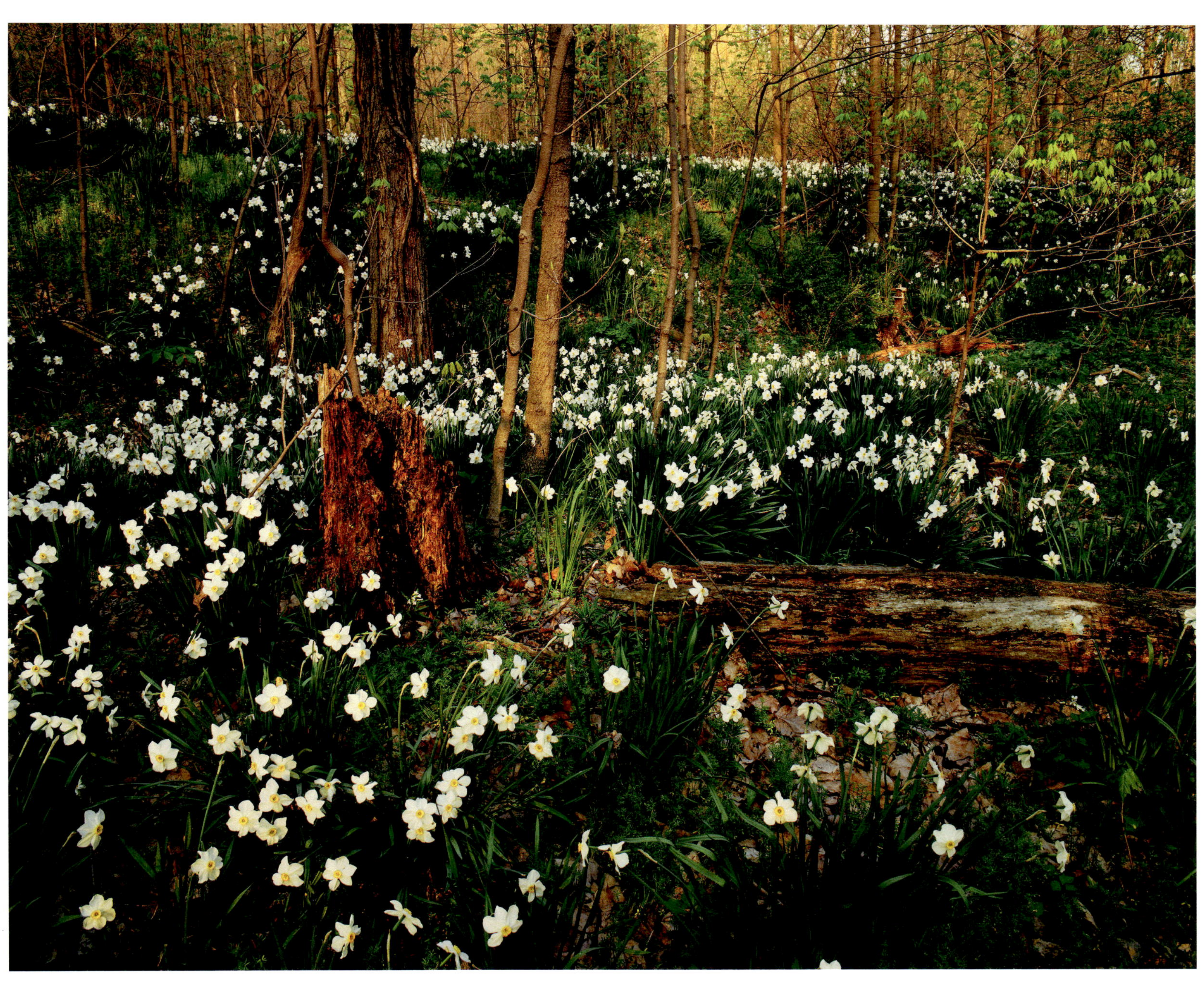

Robert Glenn Ketchum, *CVNRA #397*, 1986, from the Ohio/Federal Lands project

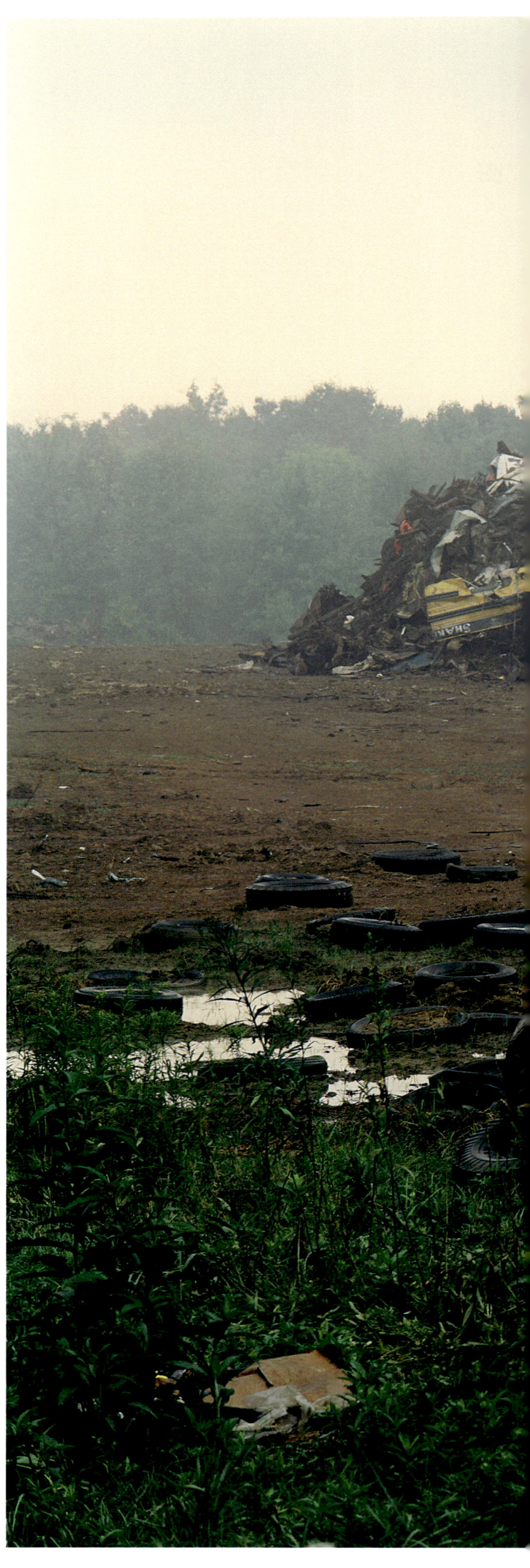

Robert Glenn Ketchum, *CVNRA #705*, 1988,
from the Ohio/Federal Lands project

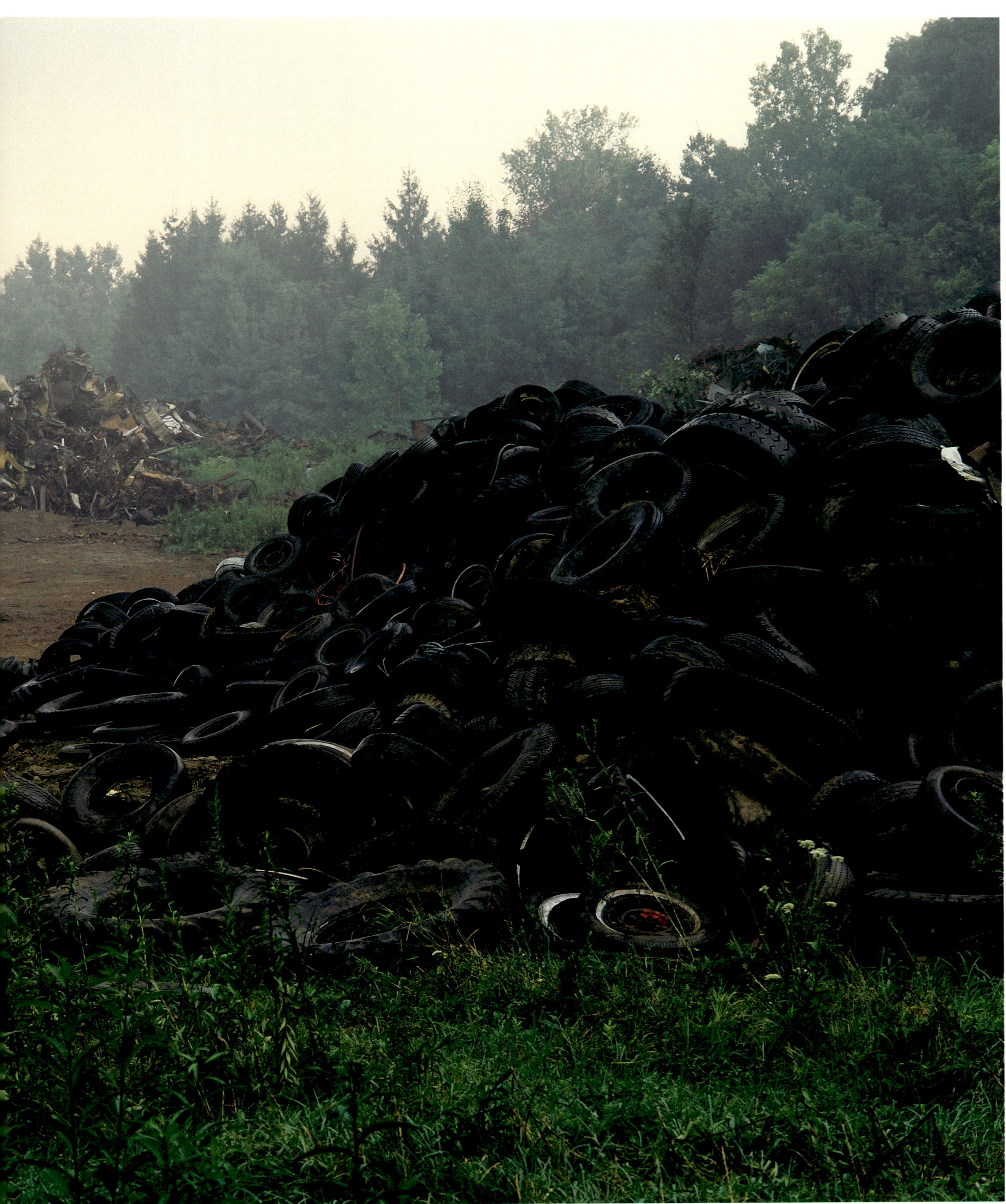

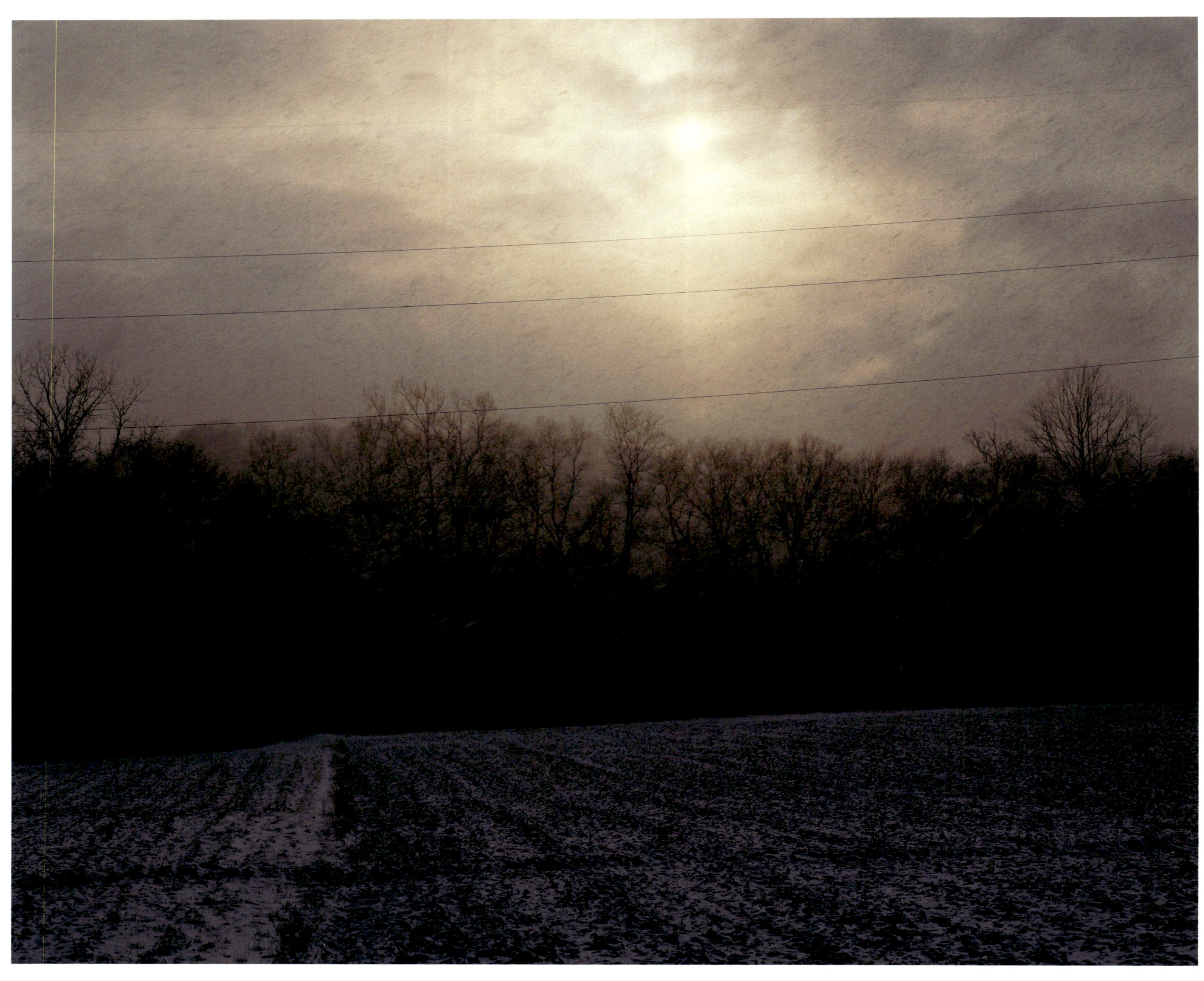

Robert Glenn Ketchum, *CVNRA #741*, 1988, from the Ohio/Federal Lands project

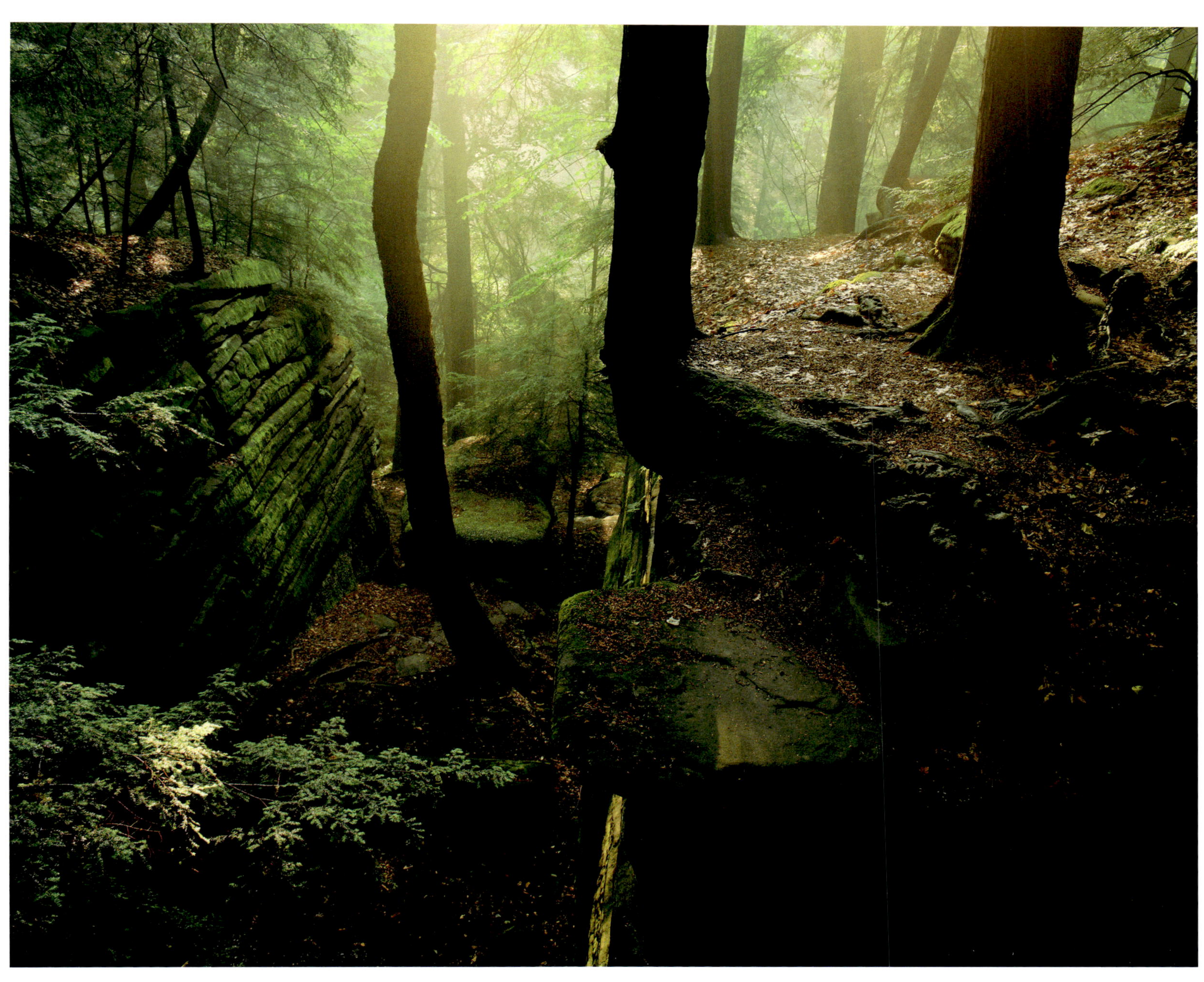

Robert Glenn Ketchum, *CVNRA #866*, 1988, from the Ohio/Federal Lands project

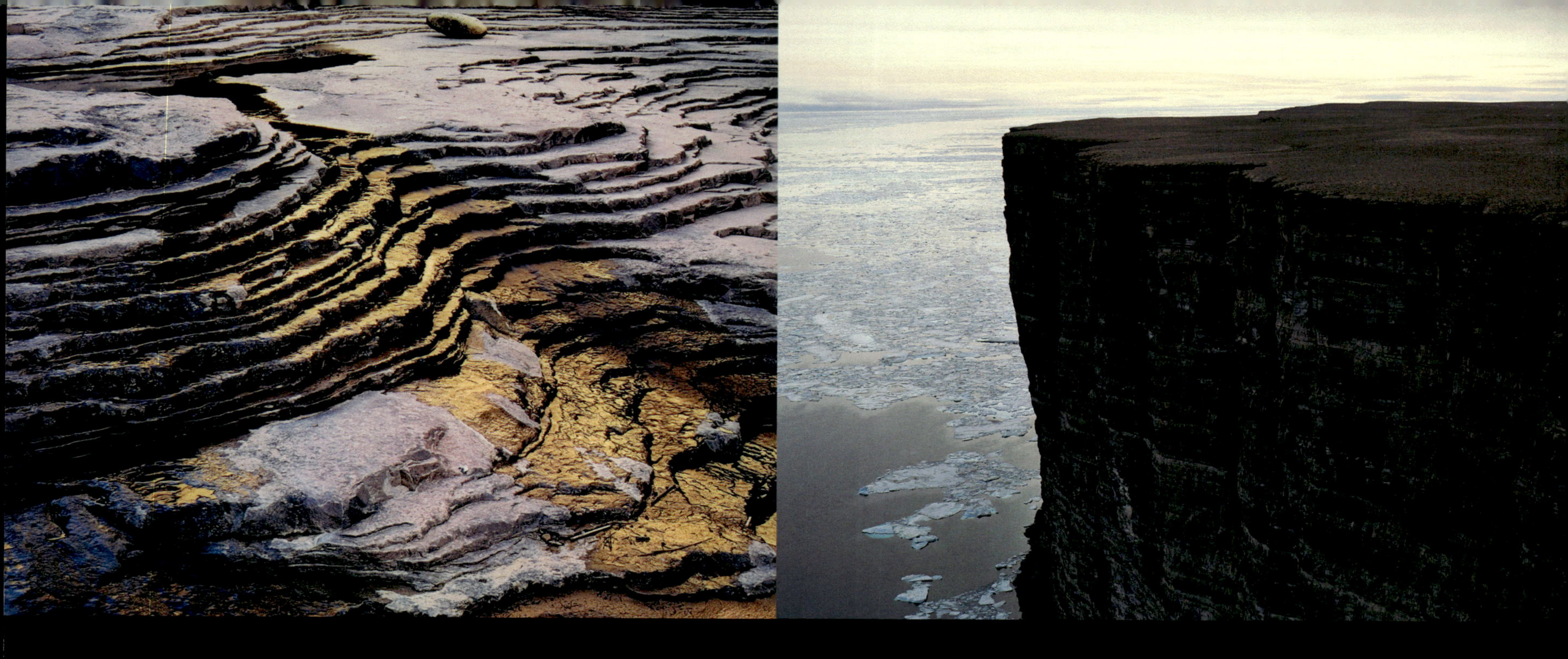

EXPLORING SIGHT

To me, Glen Canyon is the pinnacle of Porter's work, perhaps his Sundance. He was free in those canyons to give service to his science and his documentation and still be in abstraction heaven.

—Robert Glenn Ketchum

Eliot Porter, *Terraces in Brook, Aztec Creek, Forbidden Canyon, Utah, August 28, 1961*

Robert Glenn Ketchum, *Rookery Cliffs at the Edge of Lancaster Sound*, 1994, from the ARCTIC project

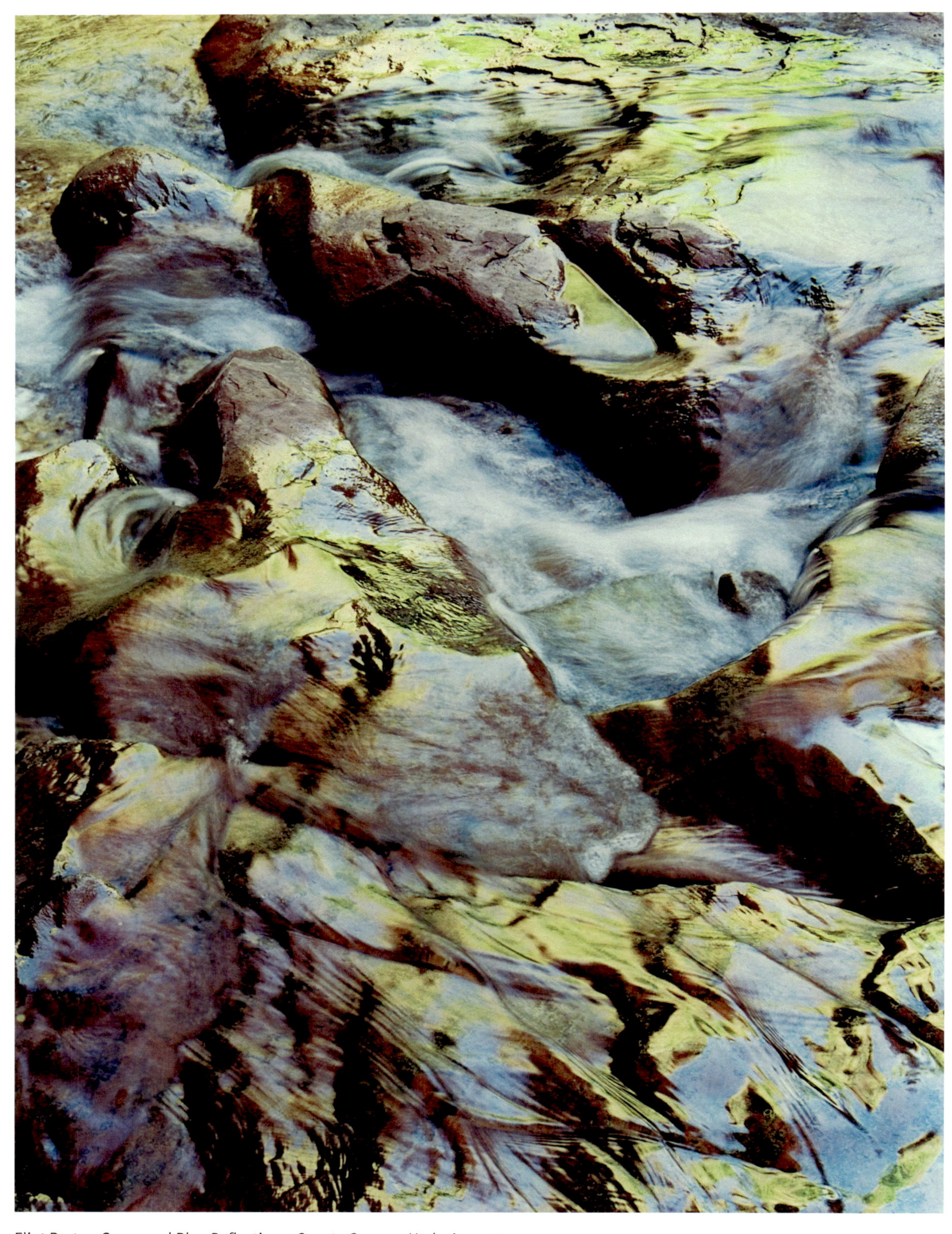

Eliot Porter, *Green and Blue Reflections, Coyote Canyon, Utah, August 14, 1971*

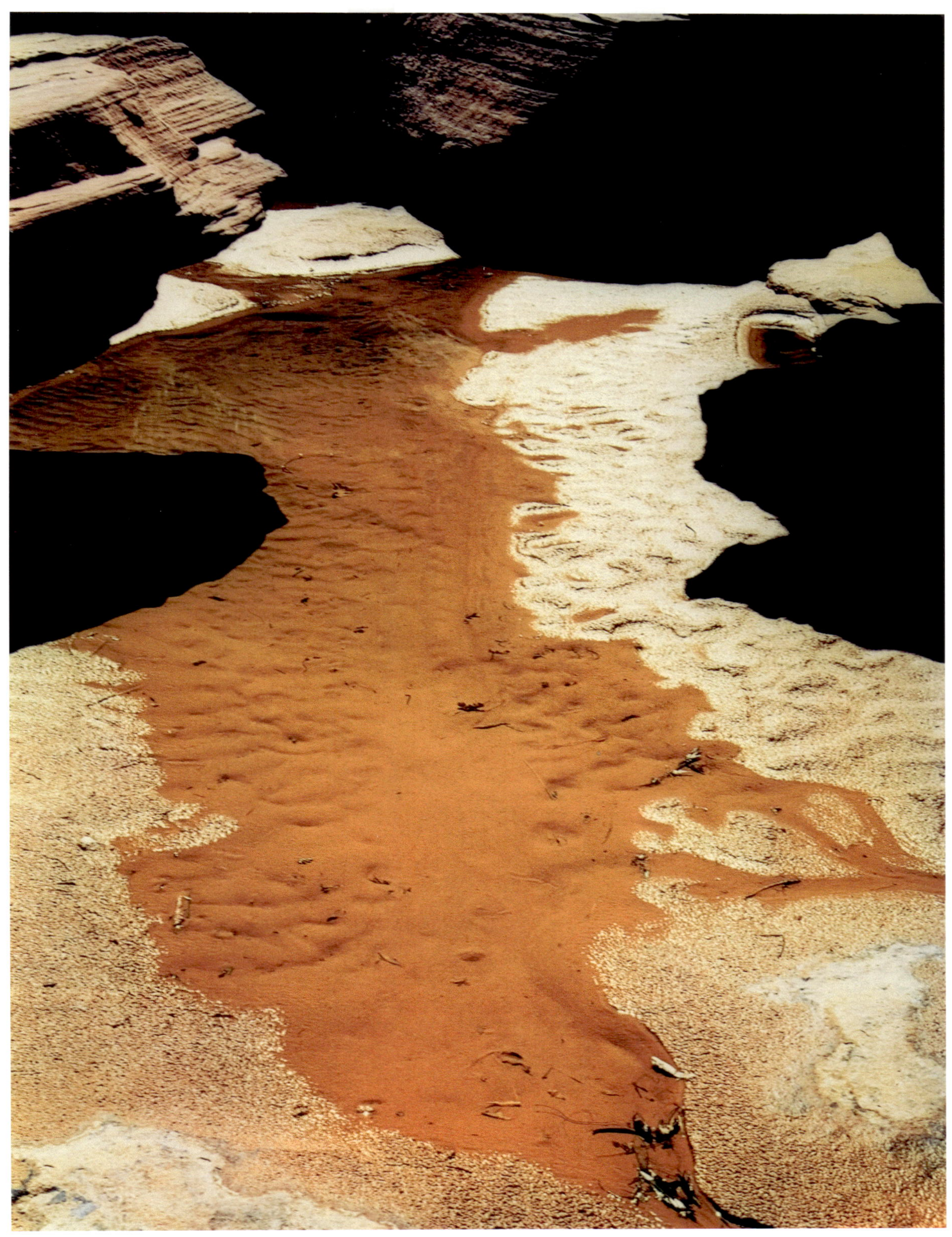

Eliot Porter, *Pool and Rocks, Music Temple, Glen Canyon, Utah, September 23, 1961*

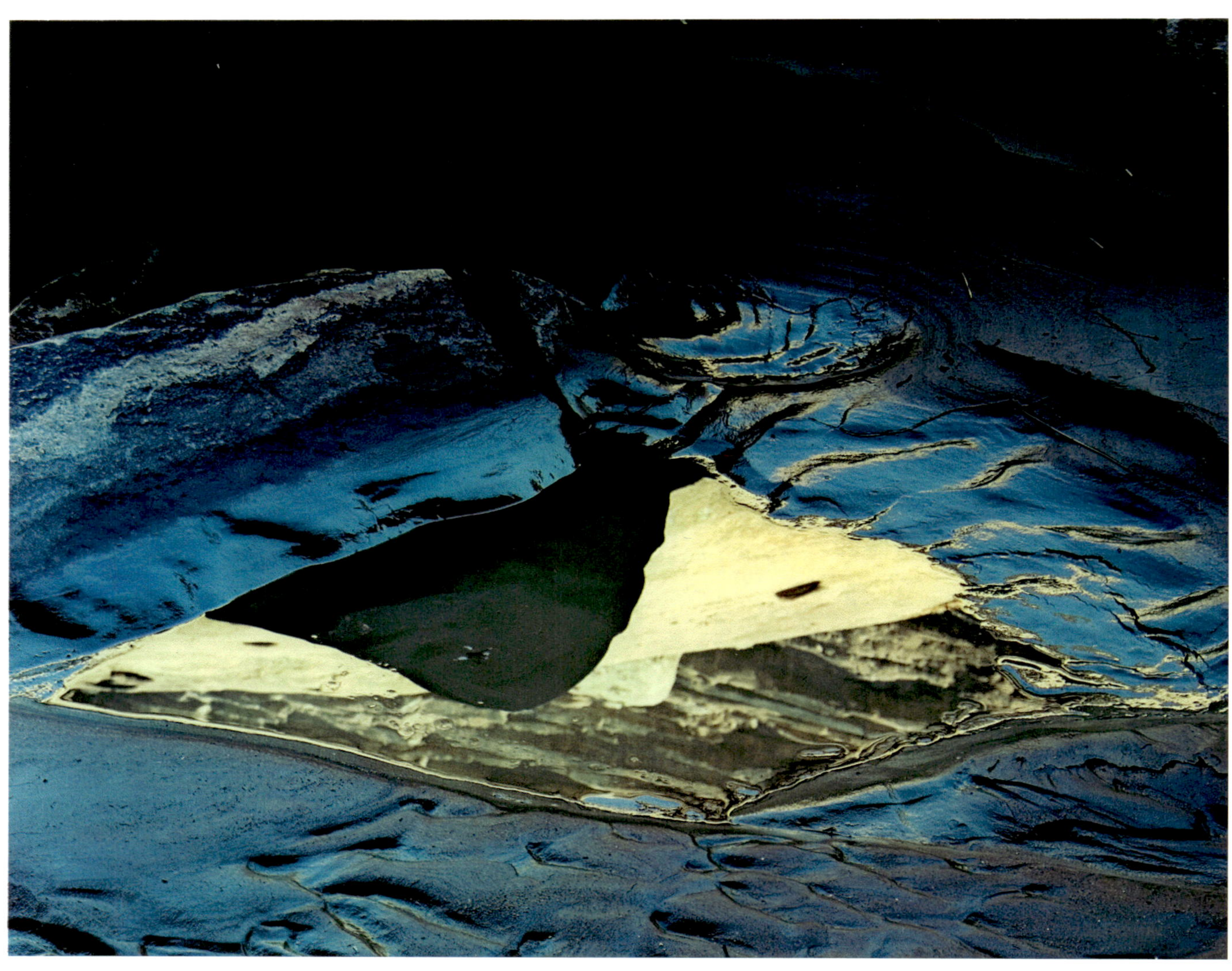

Eliot Porter, *Pool and Sand, Coyote Canyon, Utah, August 17, 1971*

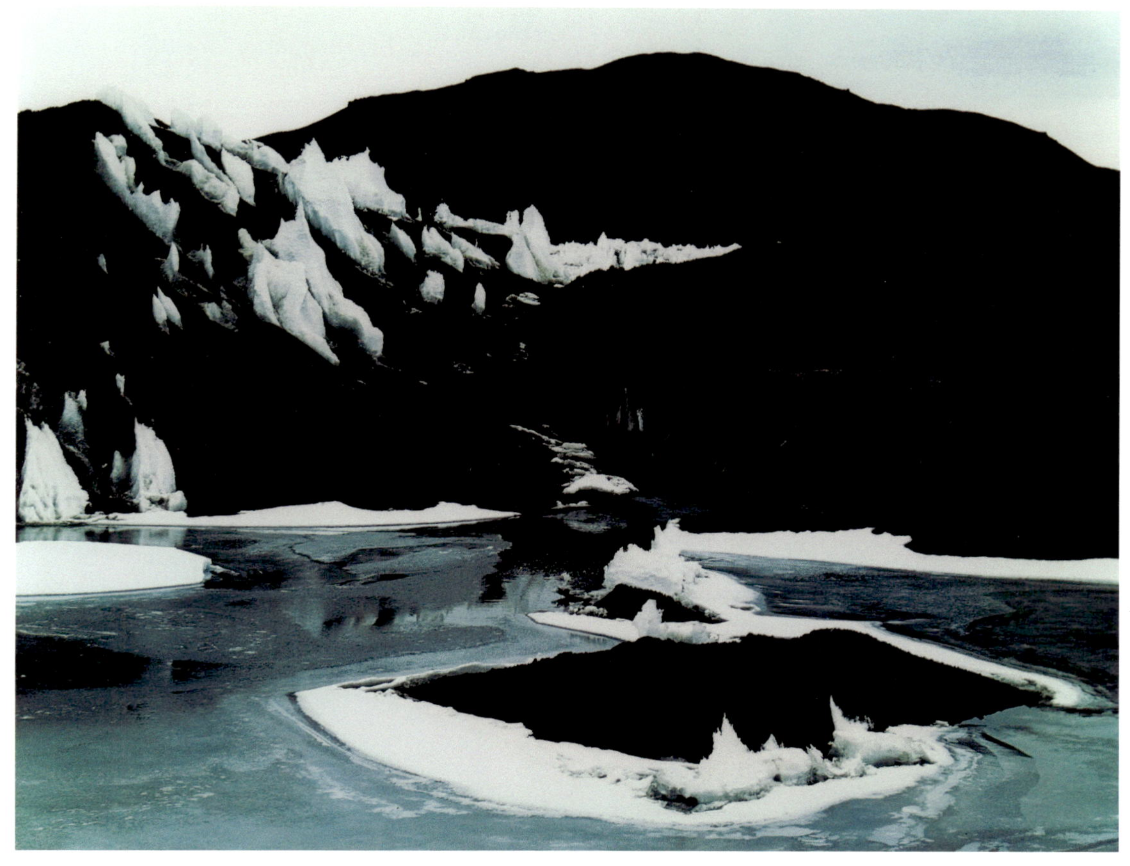

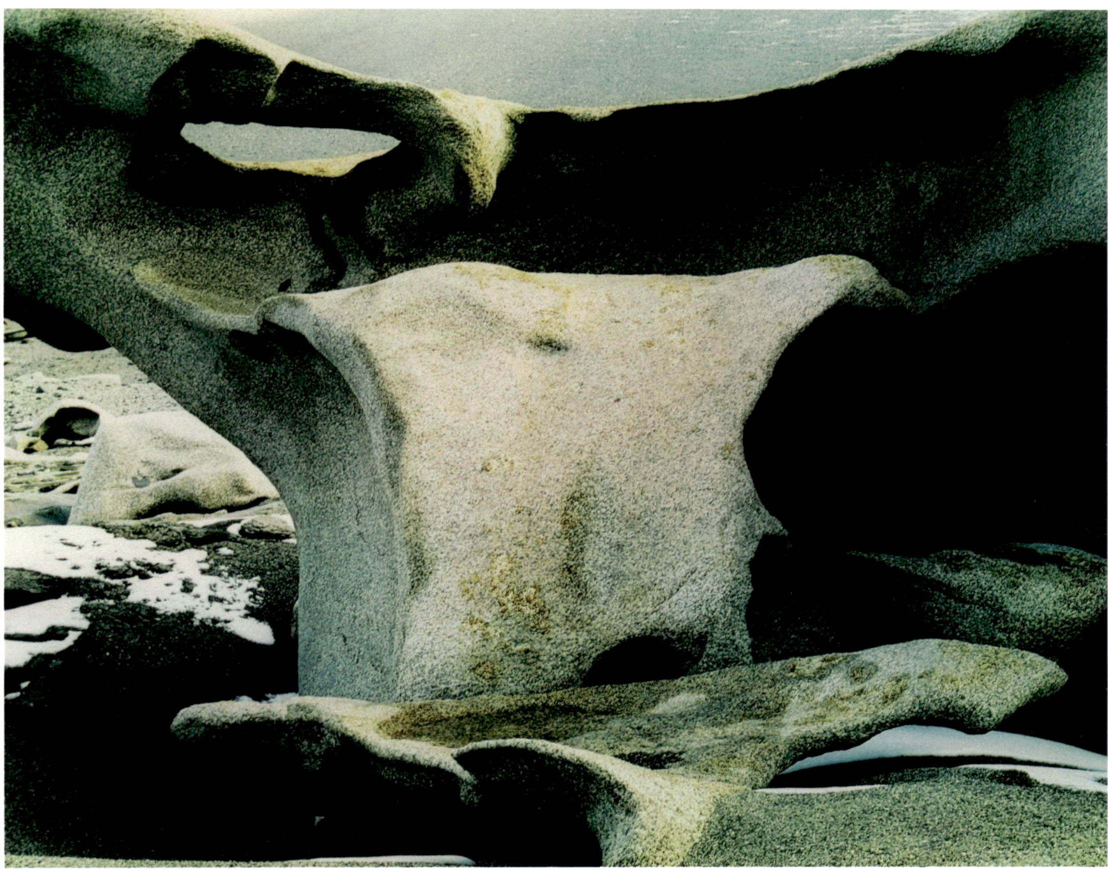

Eliot Porter, *Frozen Pond and Cinder Cone, Dailey Islands, McMurdo Sound, Antarctica, December 30, 1975*, and *Cove Erosion, Bull Pass, Antarctica, December 27, 1975*

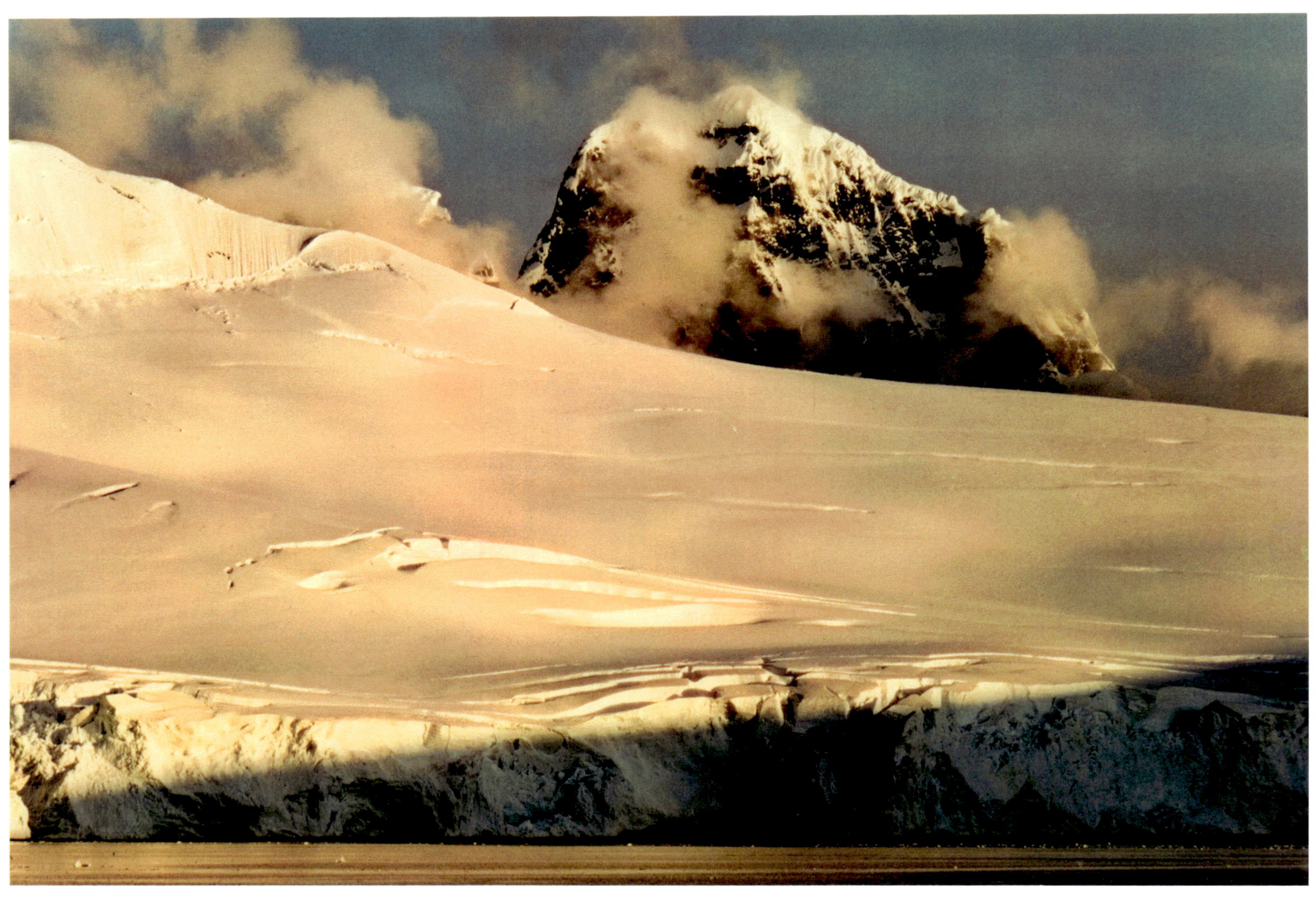

Eliot Porter, *Wiencke Island, Bismarck Strait, Antarctica, February 1976*

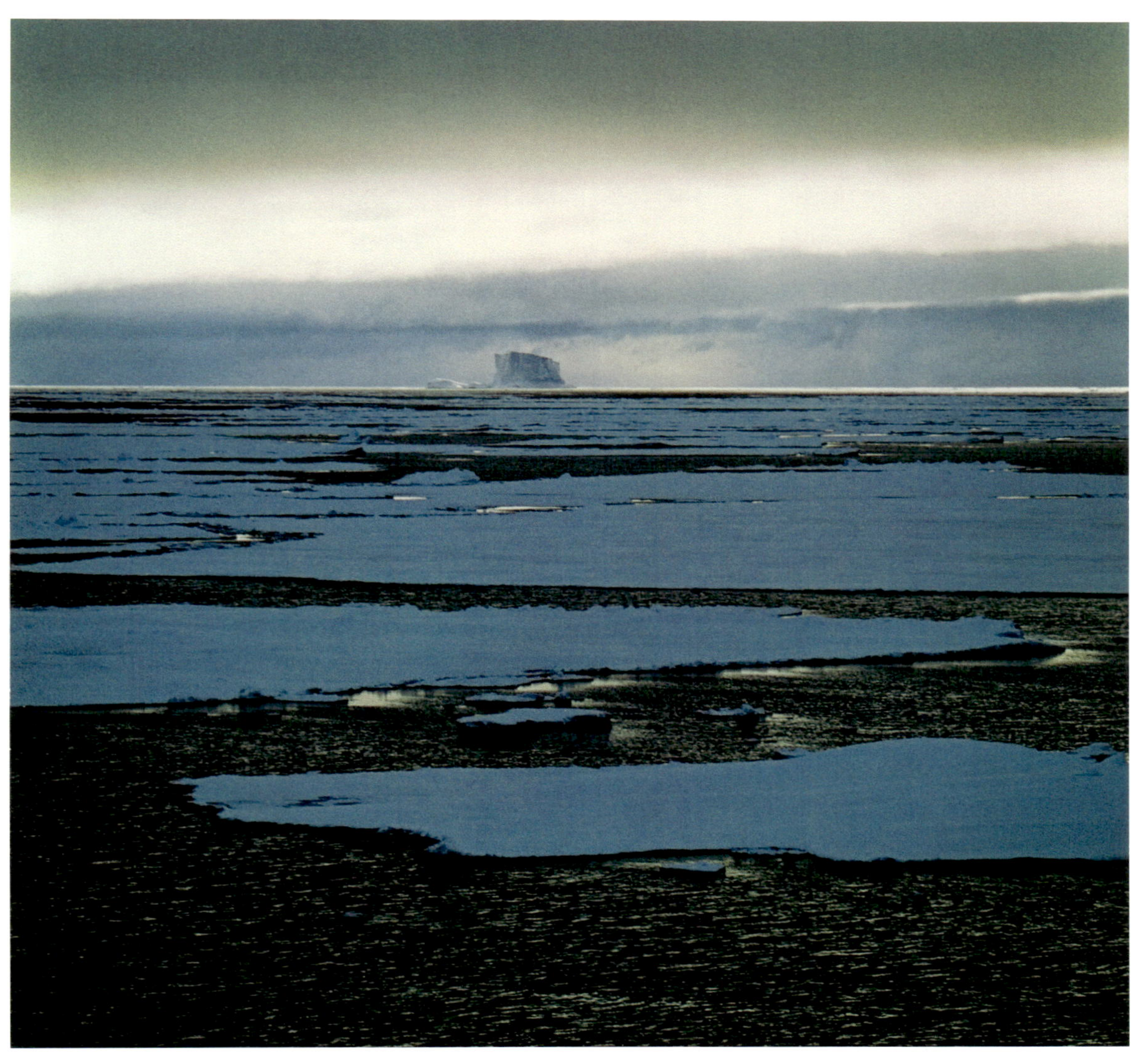

Eliot Porter, *Arthur's Harbor, Palmer Station, Antarctica, January 1976*

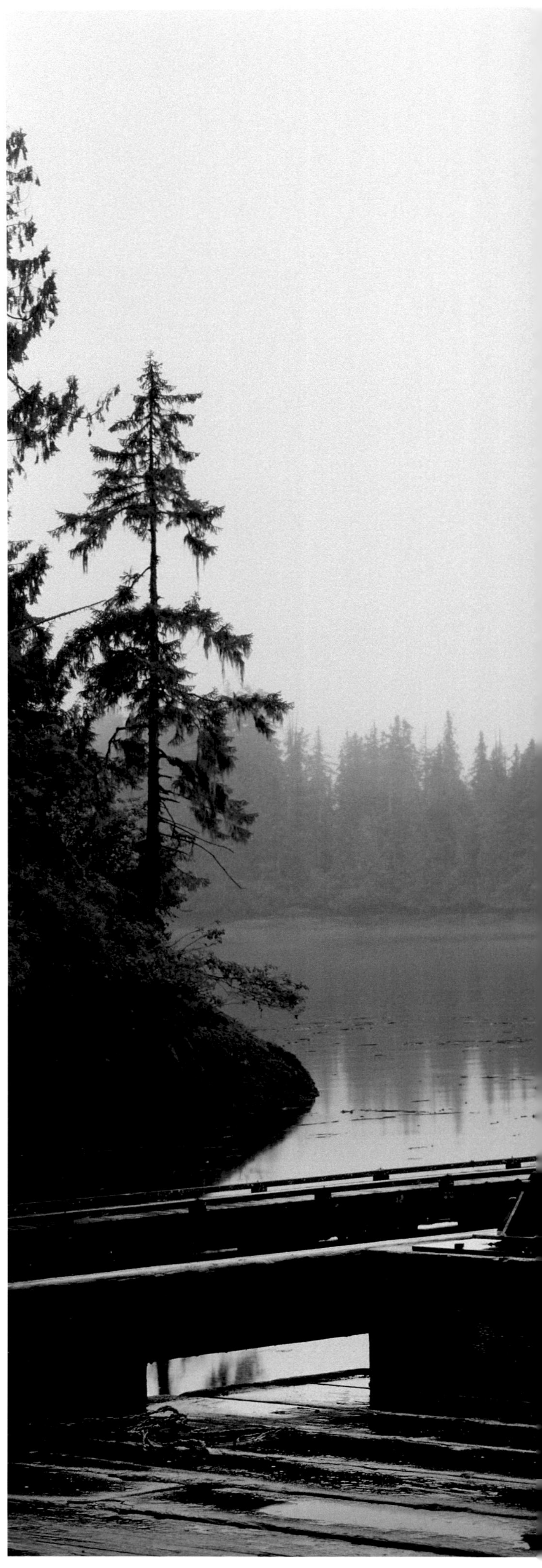

Robert Glenn Ketchum, *Sylvia's Tokeen*, 1986, from the Tongass project

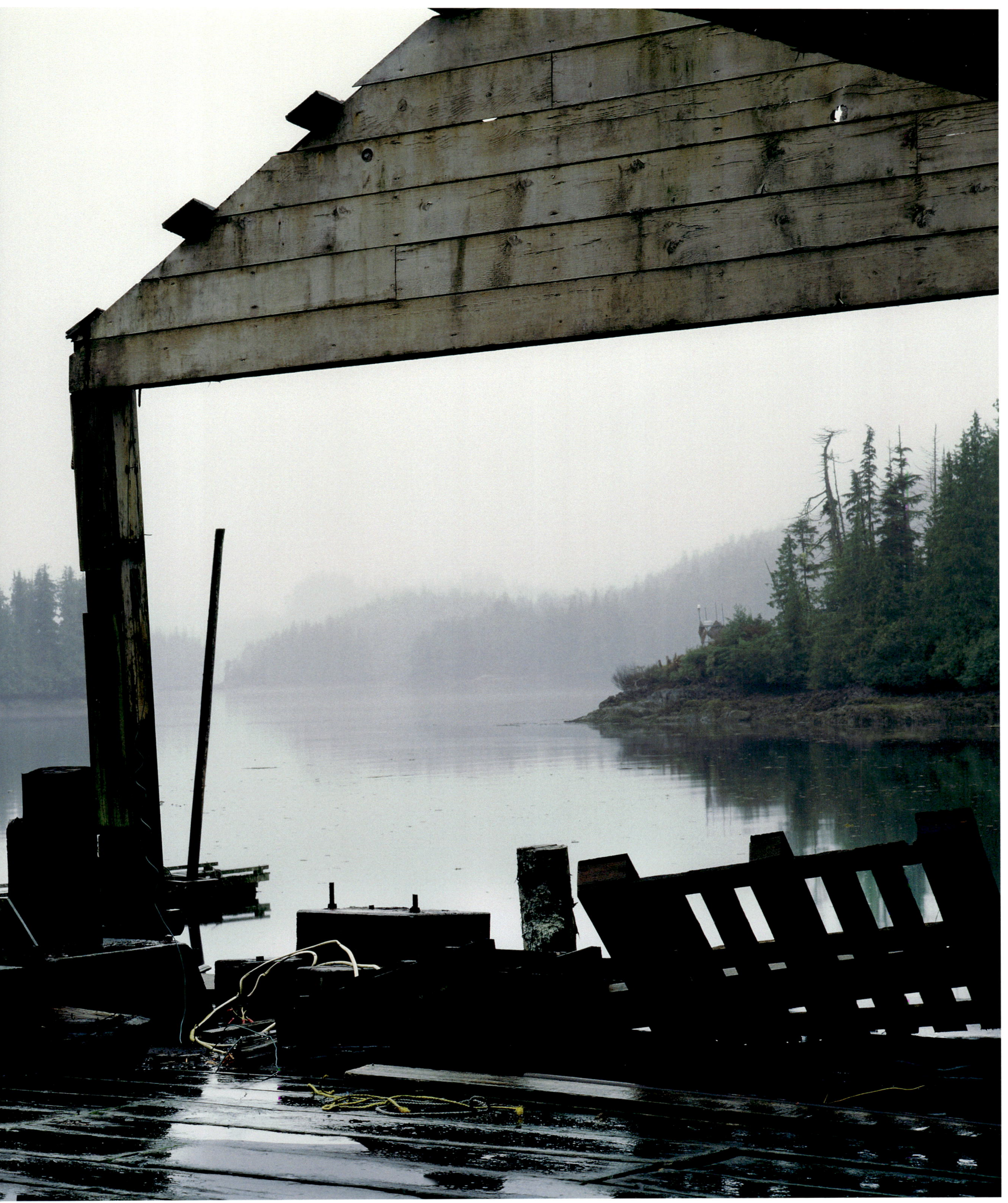

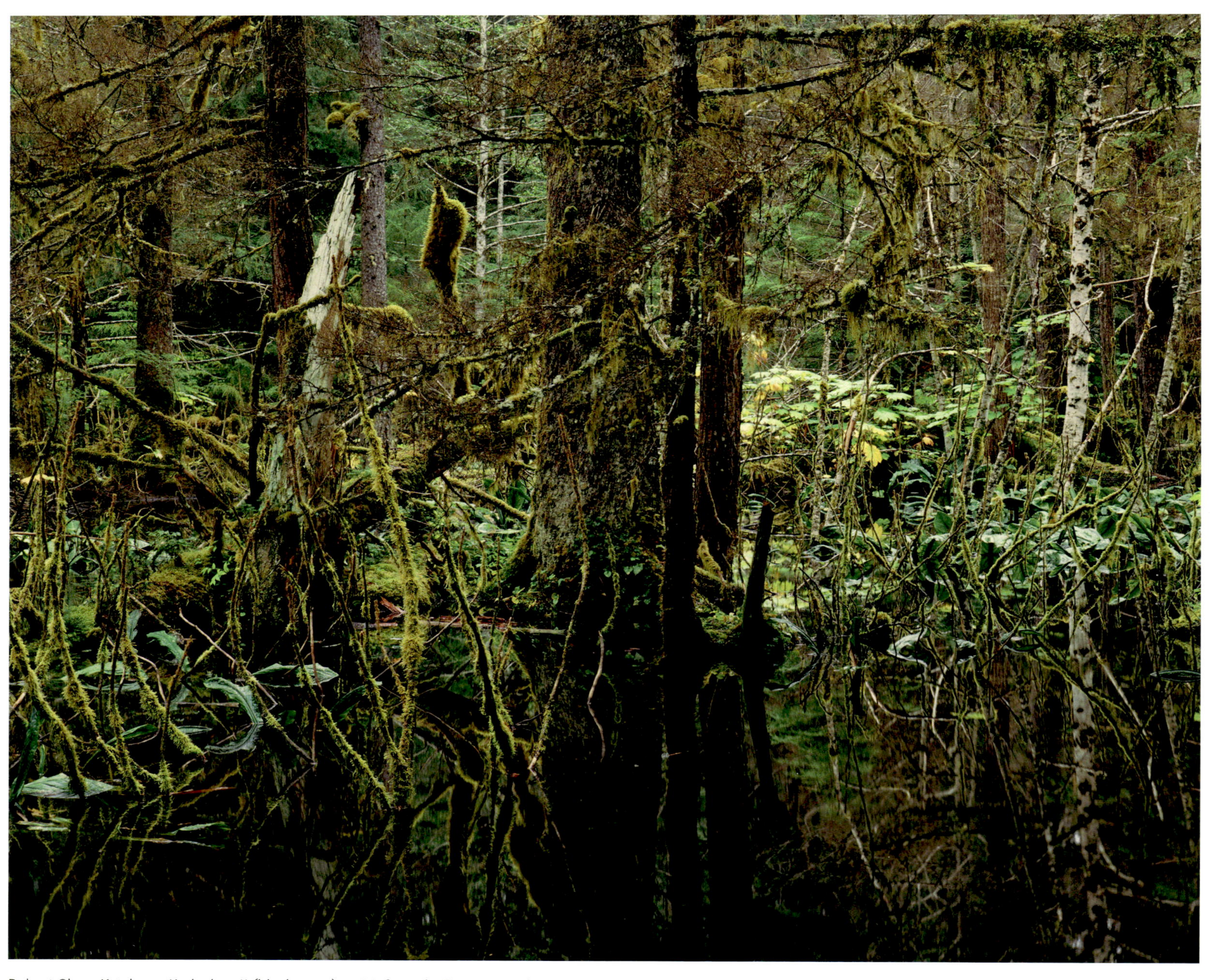

Robert Glenn Ketchum, *Kadashan II (blackwater)*, 1986, from the Tongass project

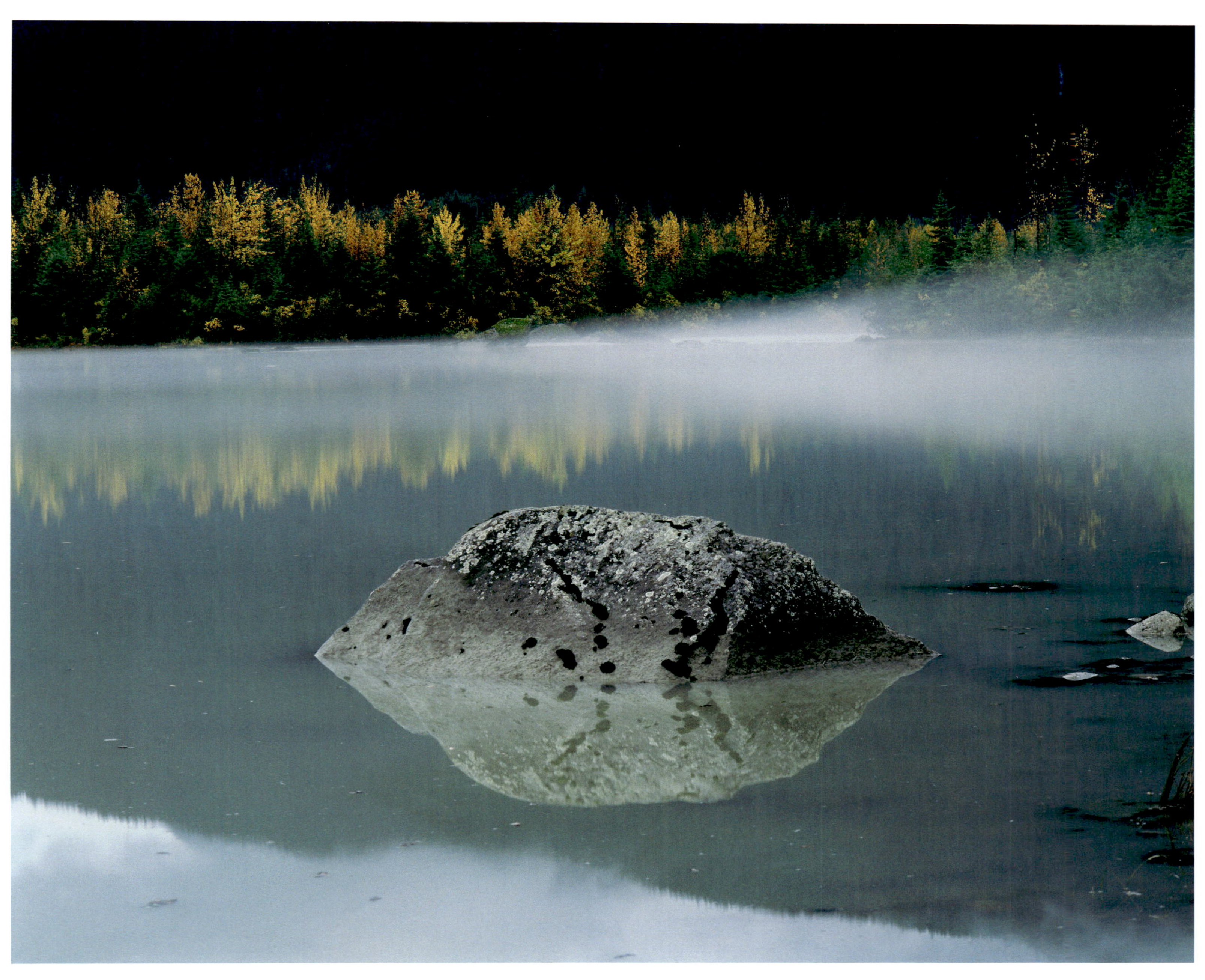

Robert Glenn Ketchum, *Mendenhall Lake,* 1986, from the Tongass project

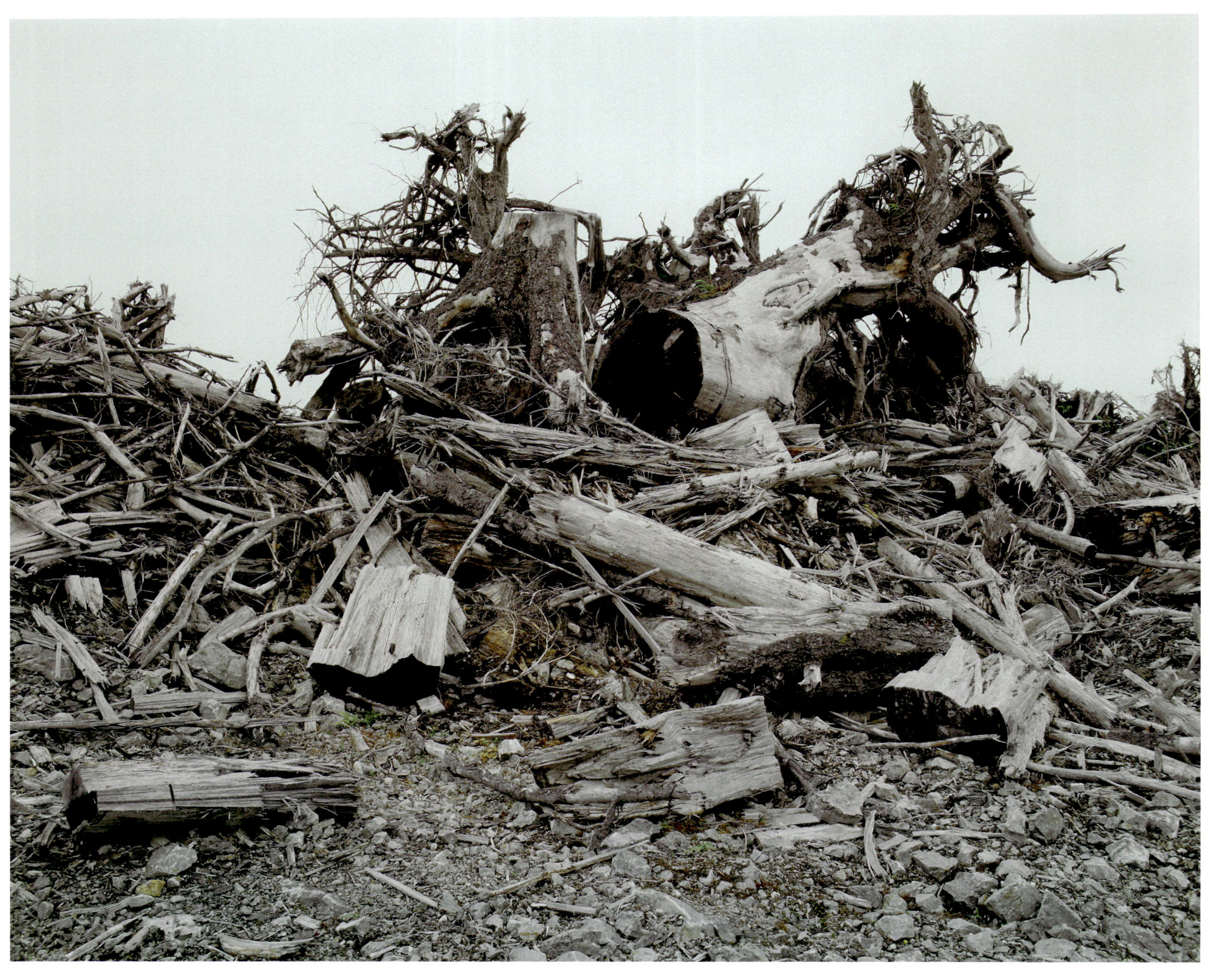

Robert Glenn Ketchum, *Rootwads and Slash/Ode to Woodie*, 1986, from the Tongass project

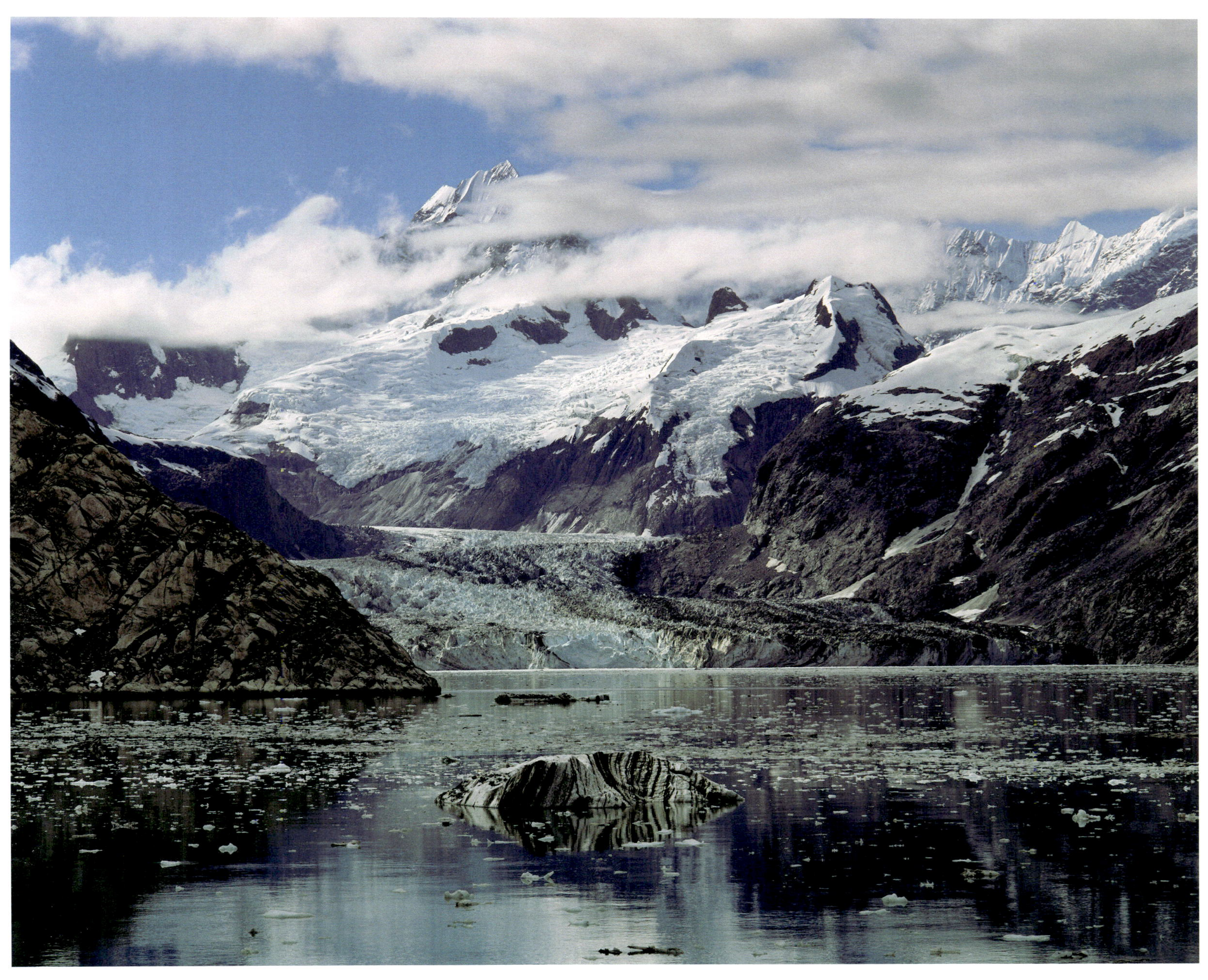

Robert Glenn Ketchum, *Johns Hopkins Inlet, Glacier Bay,* 1988, from the Tongass project

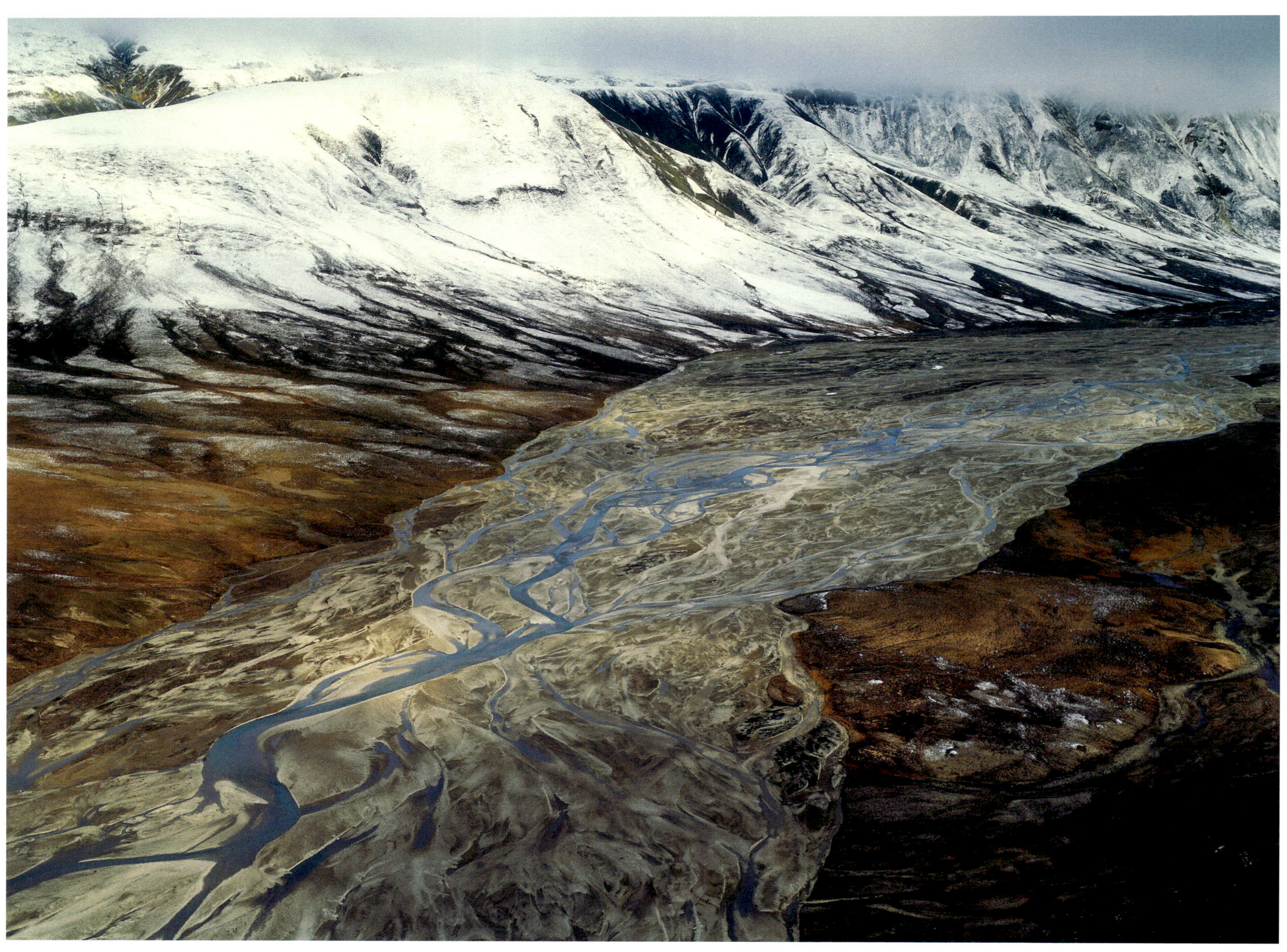

Robert Glenn Ketchum, *Glacial Outflow, Otto Fjord*, 1994, from the ARCTIC project

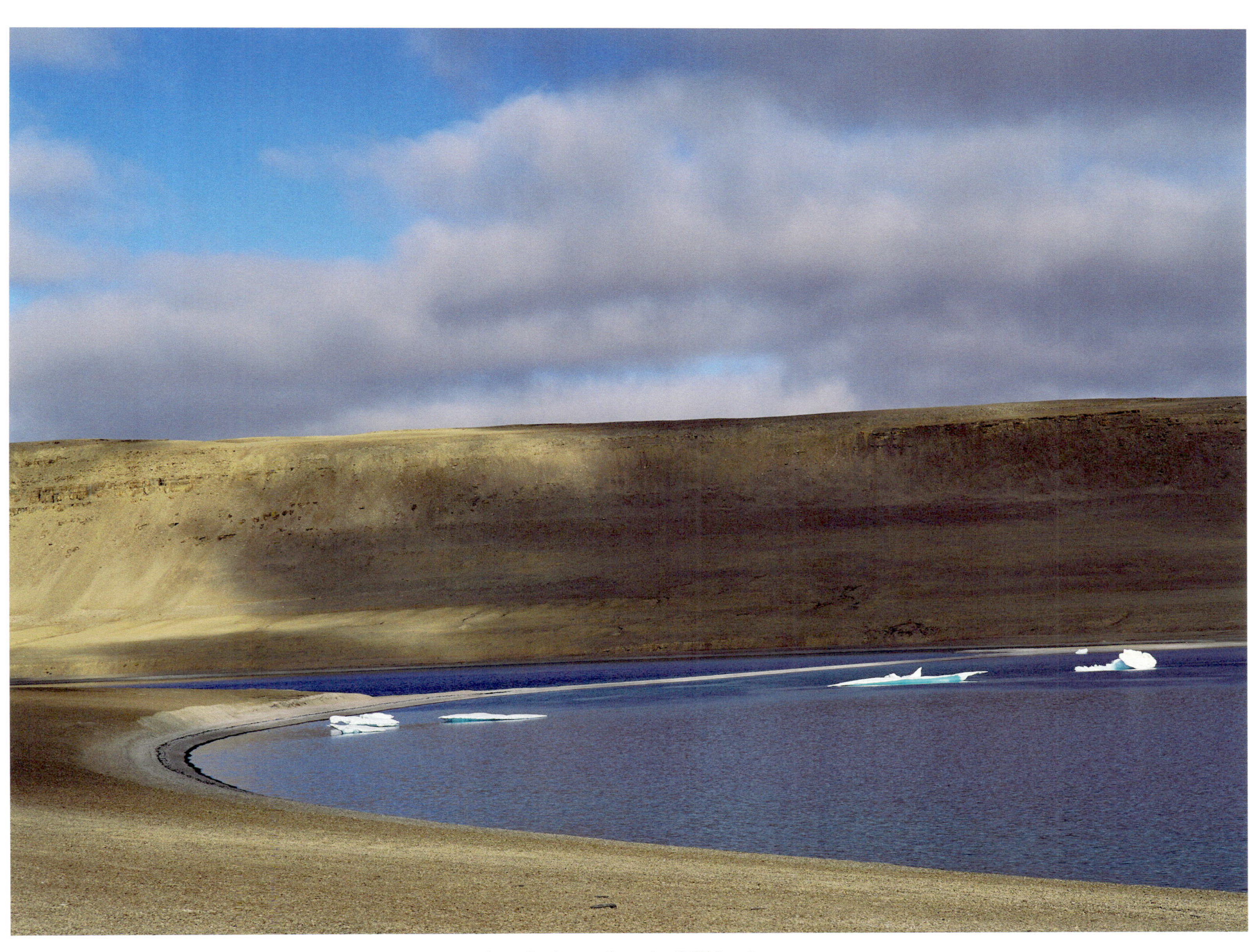

Robert Glenn Ketchum, *From the Franklin Expedition Gravesite, Beechey Island,* 1994, from the ARCTIC project

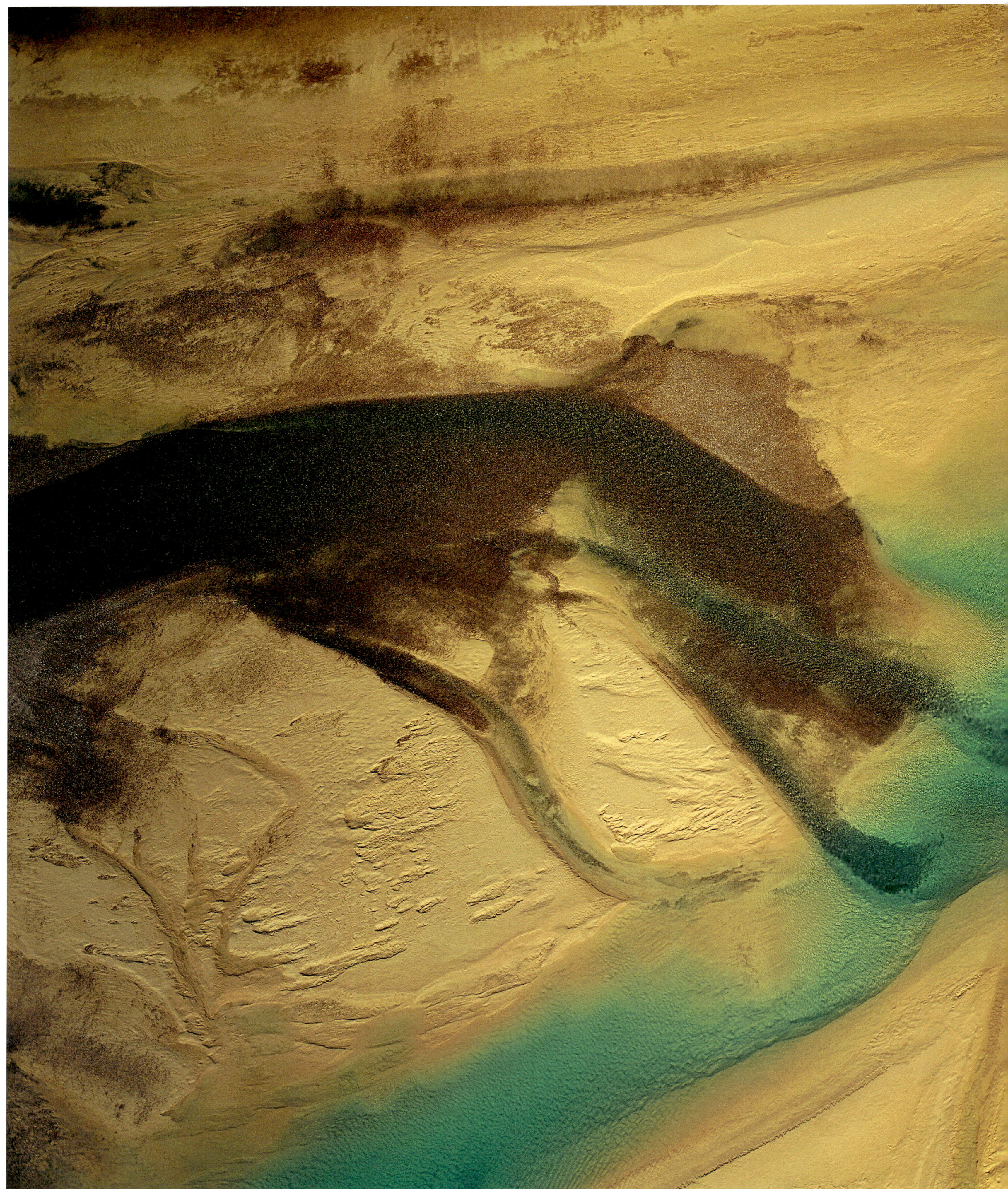

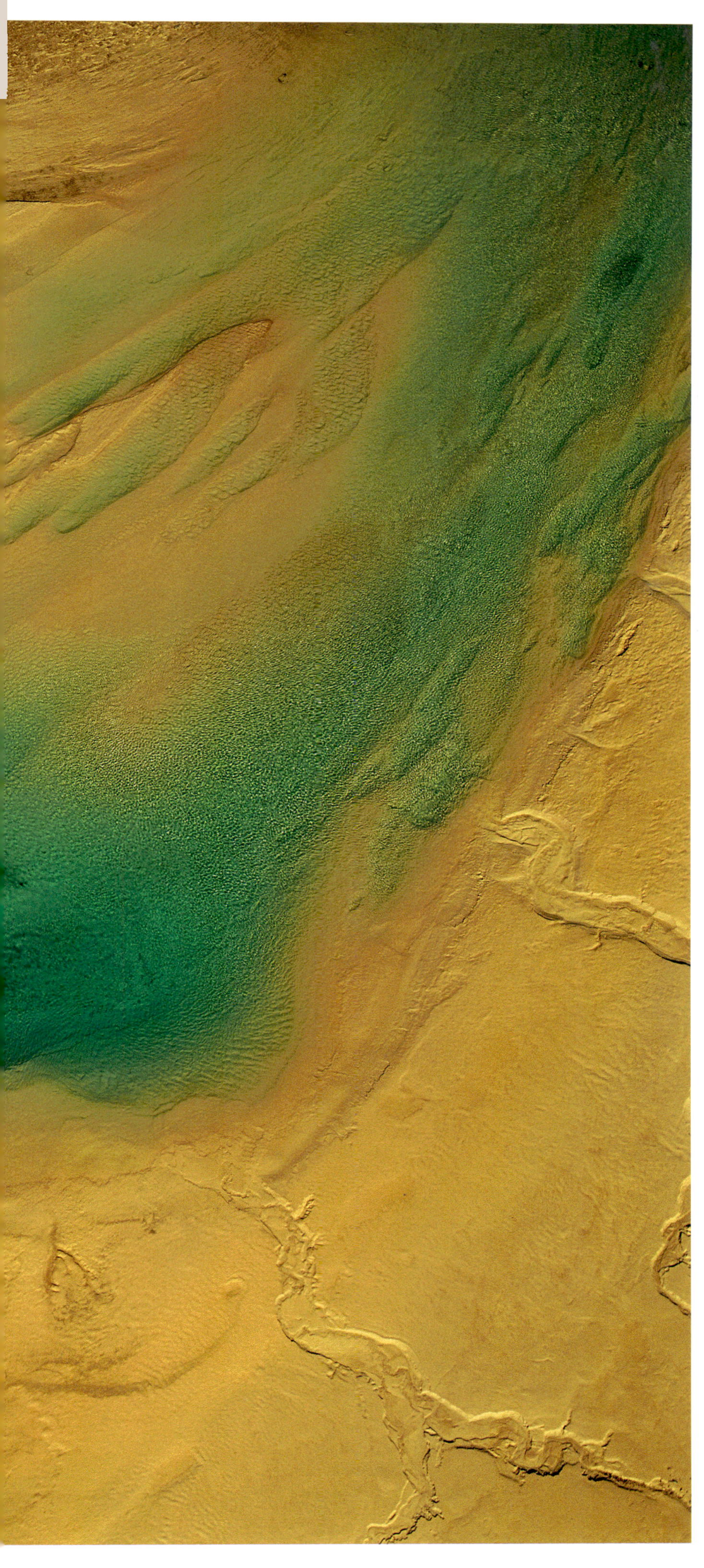

Robert Glenn Ketchum, *Meltwater Flowing over Golden Silt and Sand Bars, Baffin Island*, 1994, from the ARCTIC project

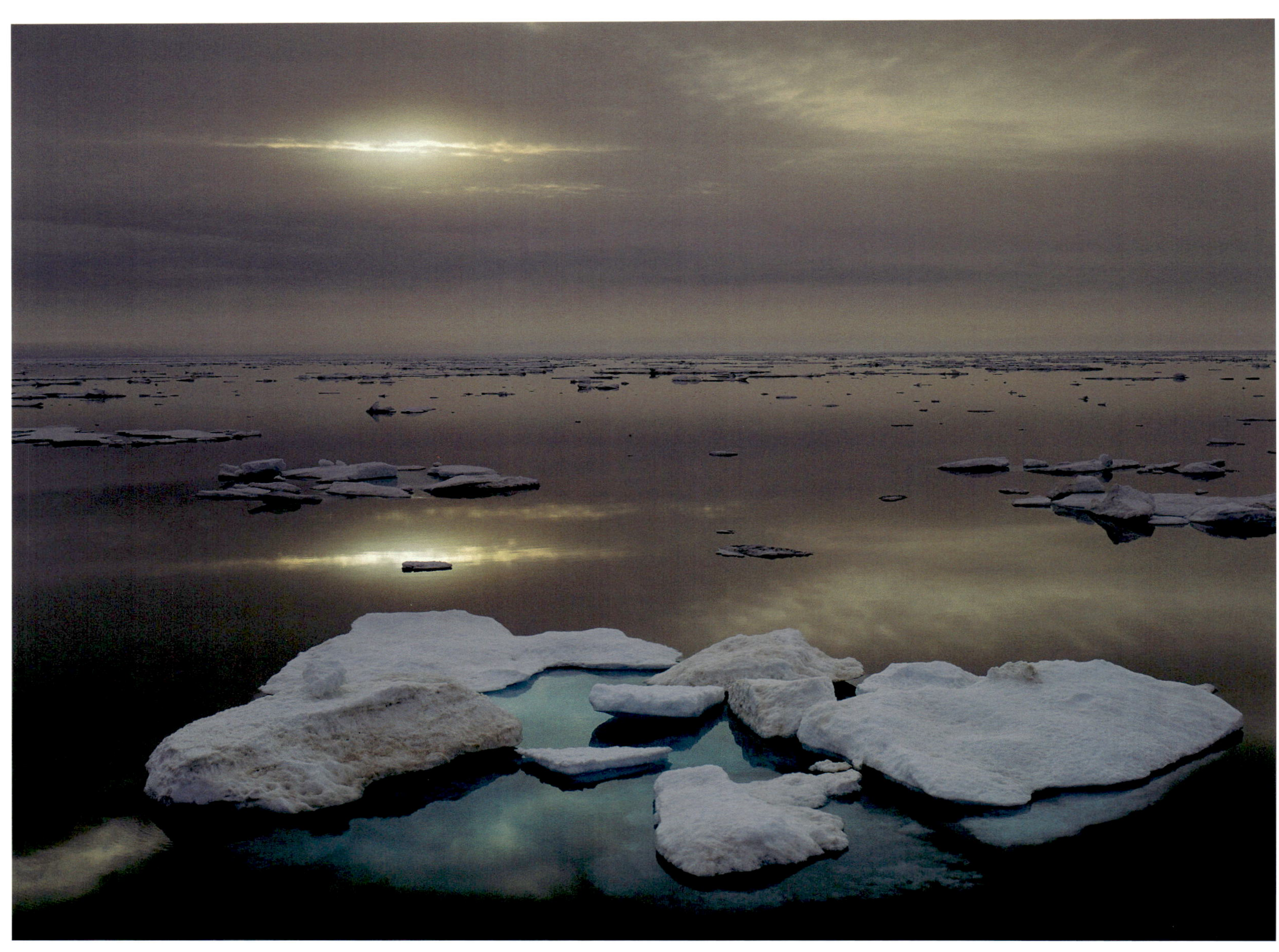

Robert Glenn Ketchum, *Dead-calm Sunset before the Storm, Larsen Sound*, 1994, from the ARCTIC project

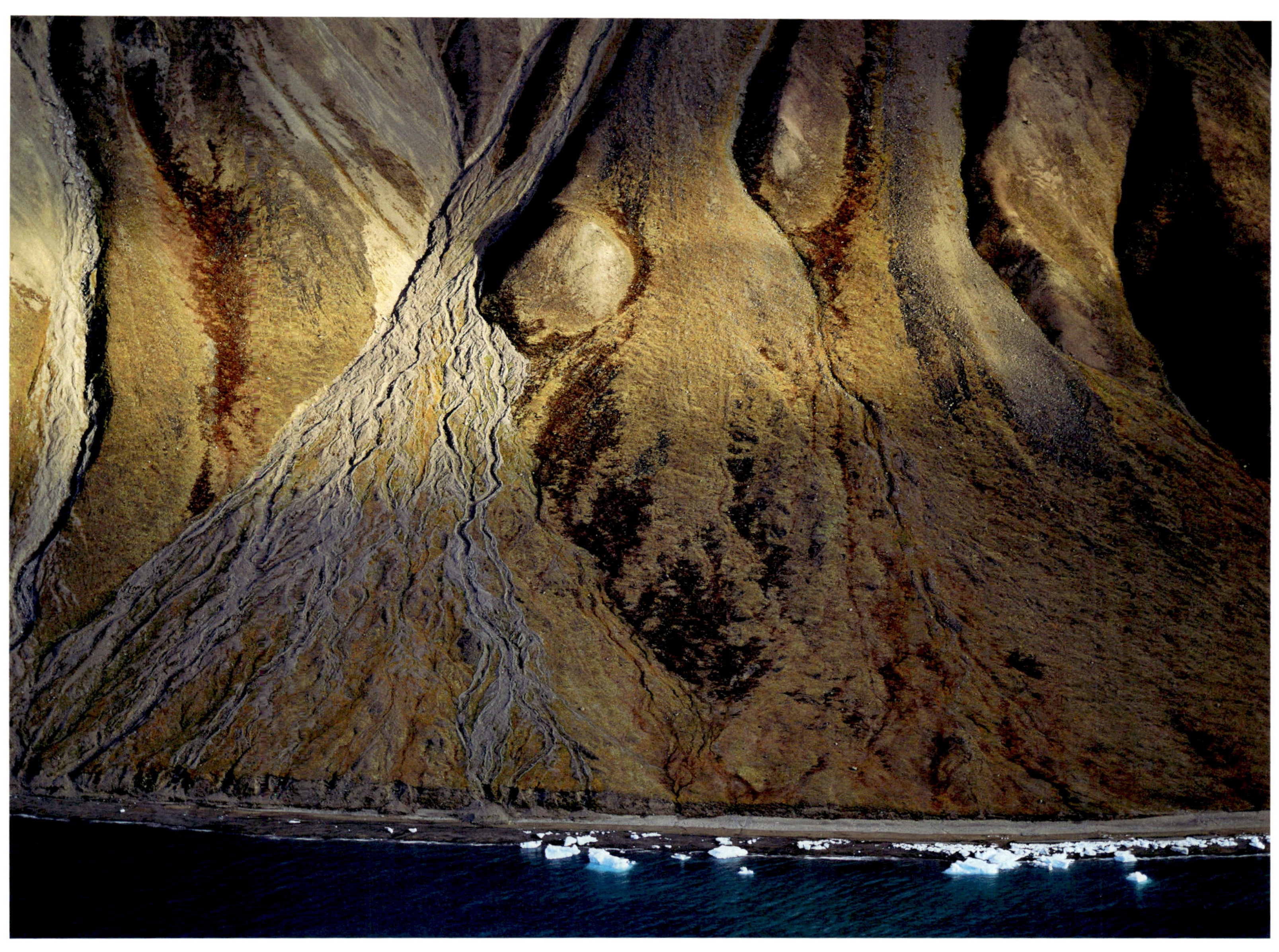

Robert Glenn Ketchum, *Vertical Shoreline, Bylot Island,* 1994, from the ARCTIC project

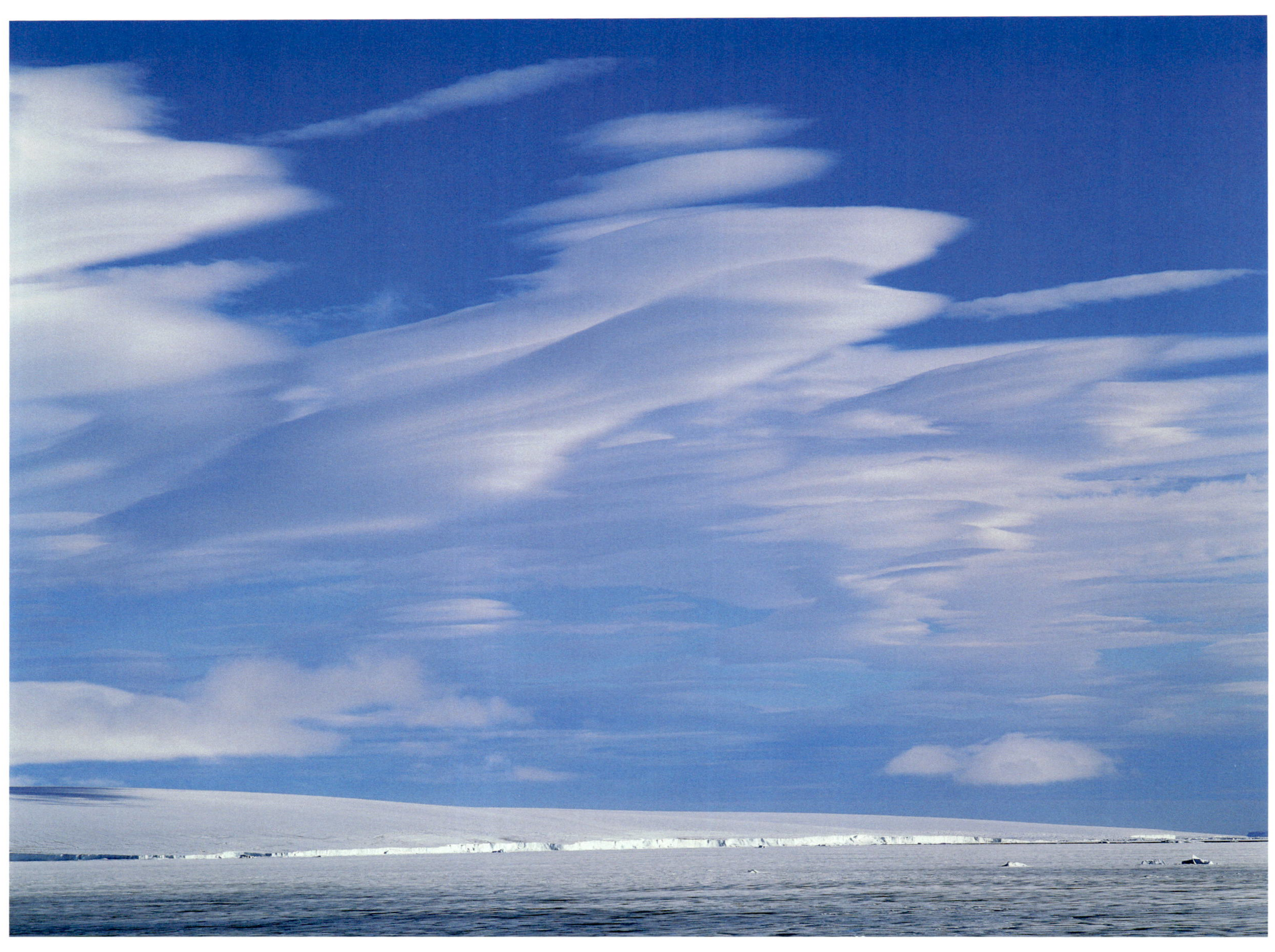

Robert Glenn Ketchum, *Franz Josephland*, 1998, from the ARCTIC project
Opposite: *Predawn Glow, Elk Point*, 1988, from the Sundance residency

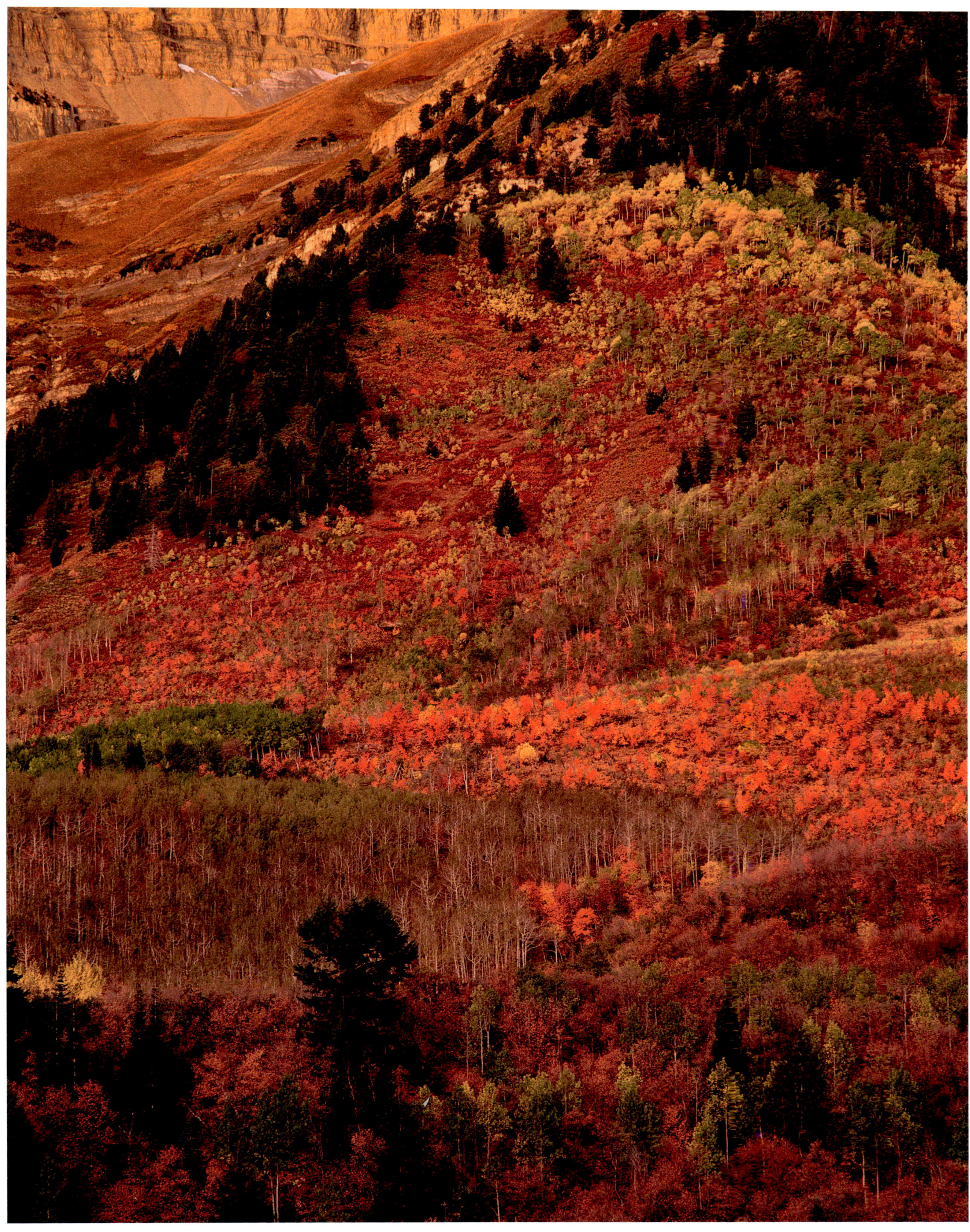

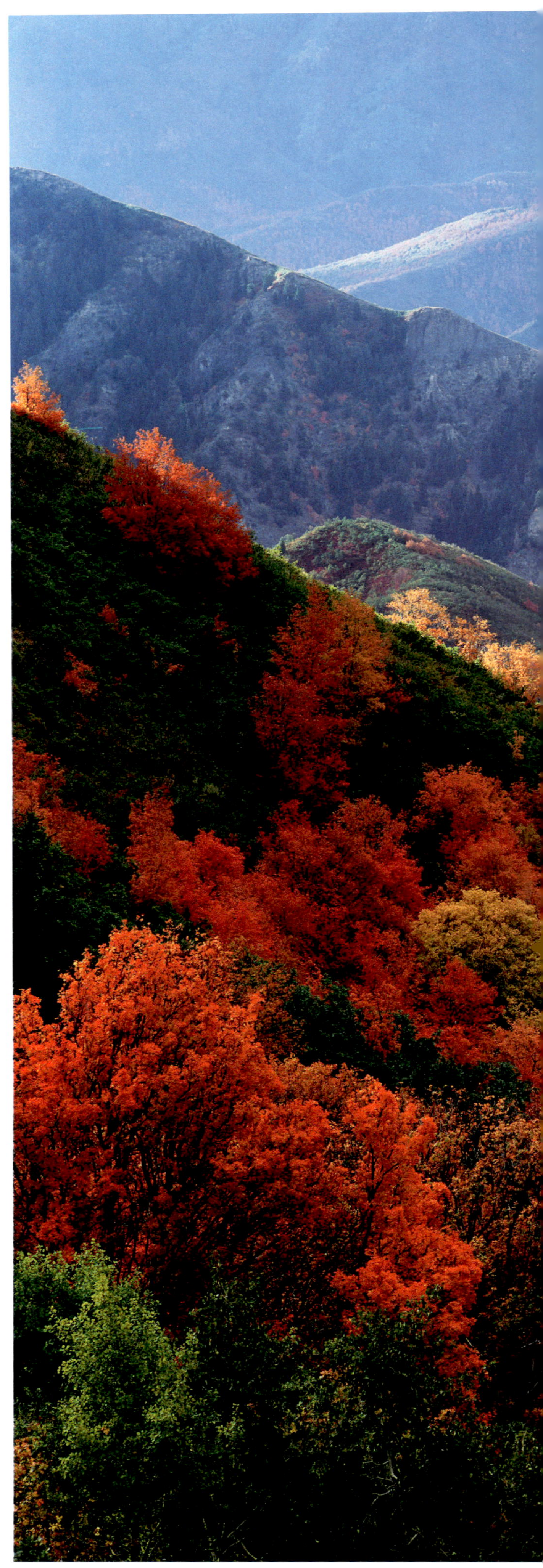

Robert Glenn Ketchum, *Sun Dance*, 1989, from the Sundance residency

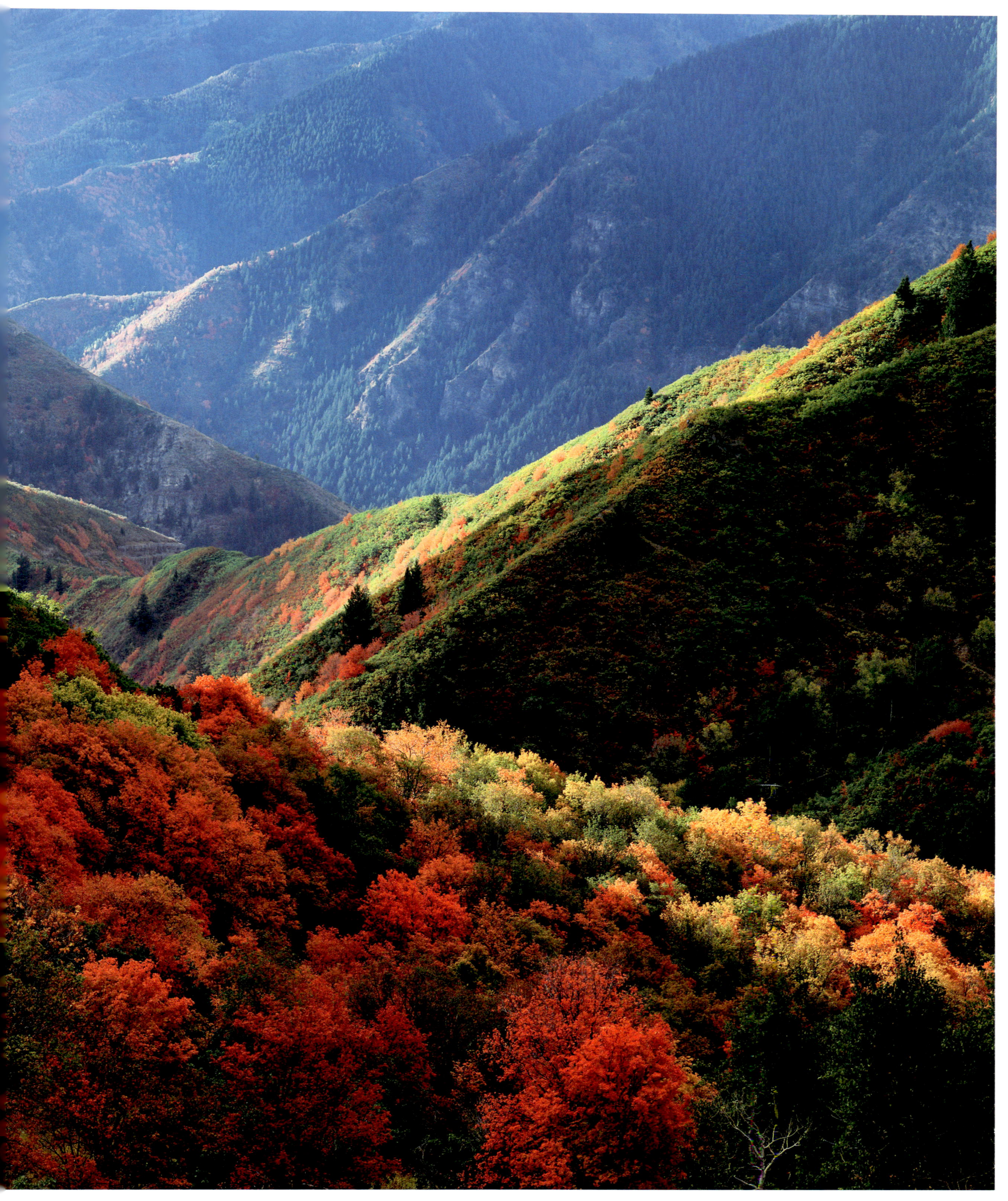

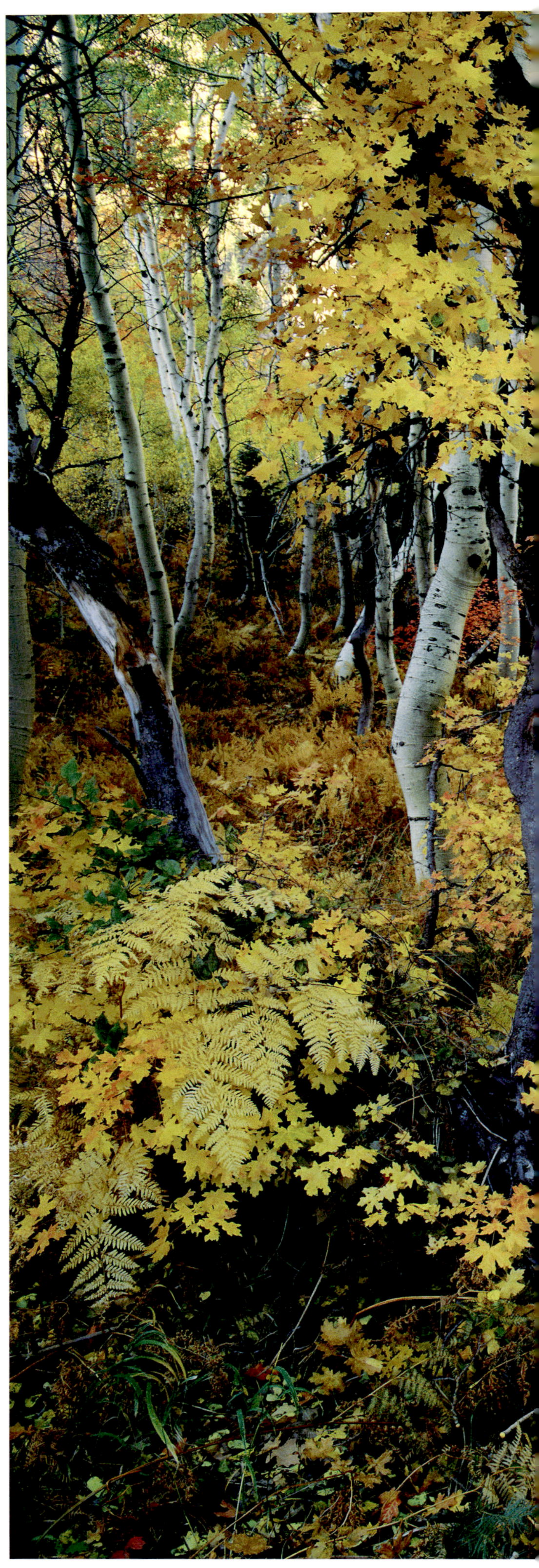

Robert Glenn Ketchum, *Cosmic Trees*, 1988, from the Sundance residency

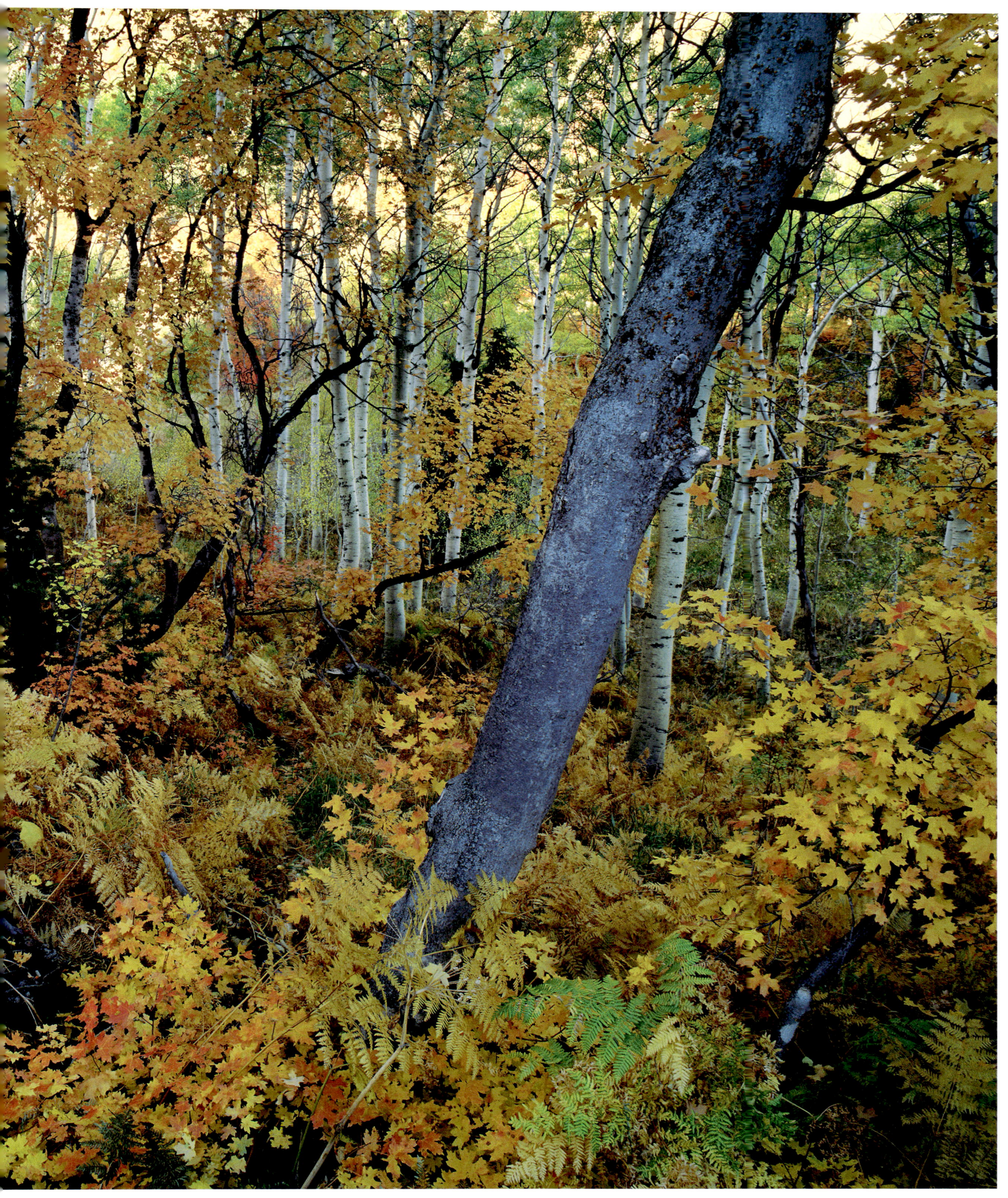

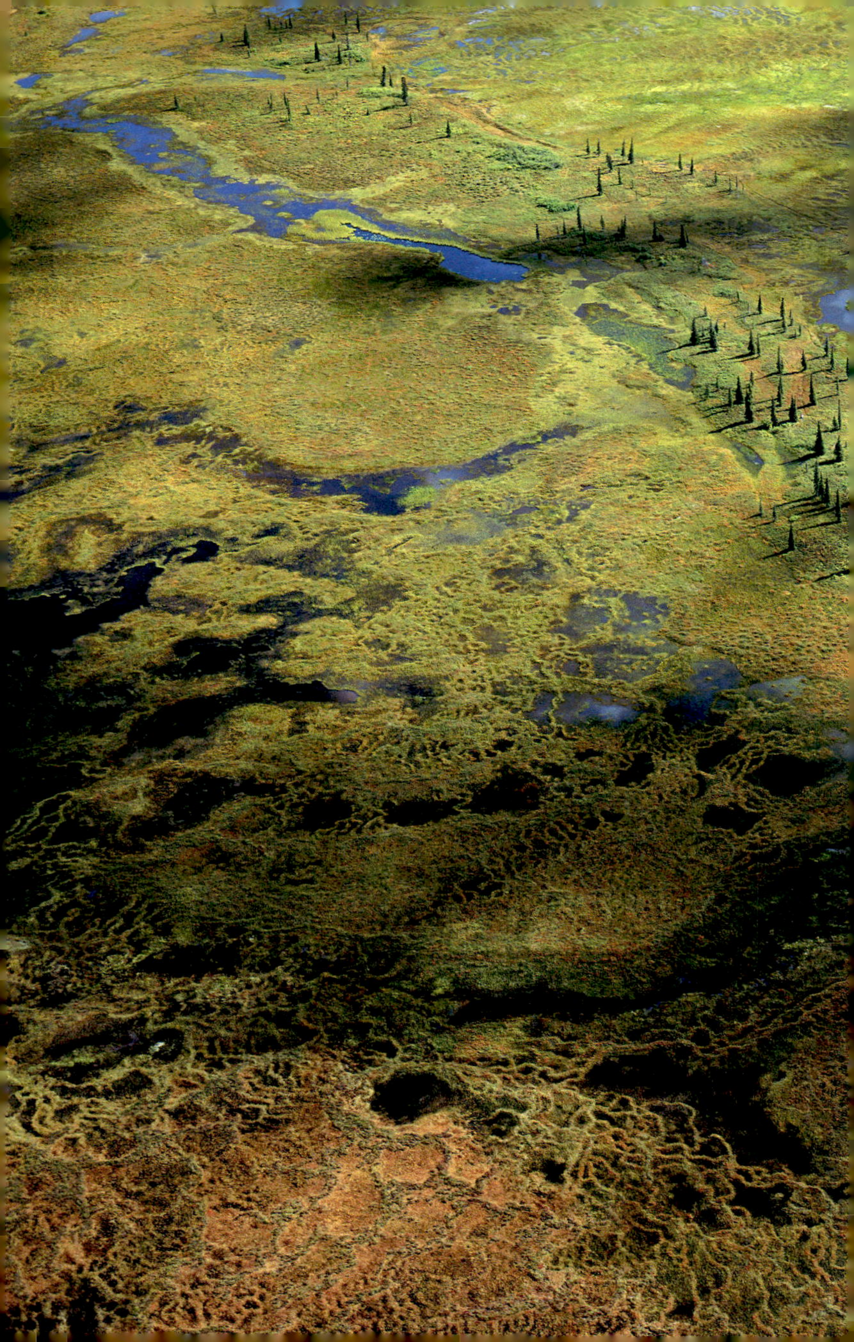

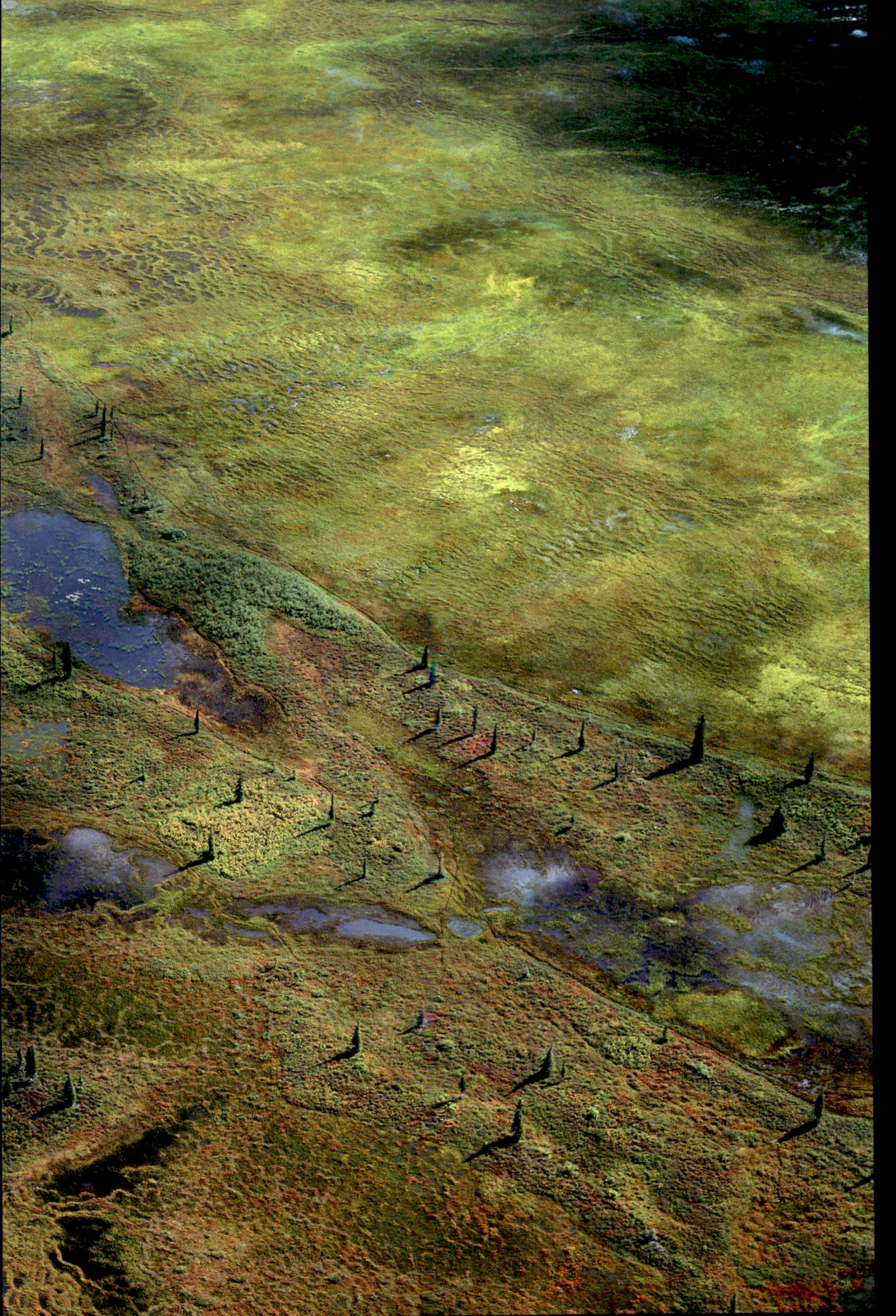

EXPANDING SIGHT

The embroiderers didn't understand why you would do a piece that had tree trunks as its principal design element, but then not embroider the trunks of those trees. . . . I asked for it for ten years before they finally agreed to do it.

—Robert Glenn Ketchum

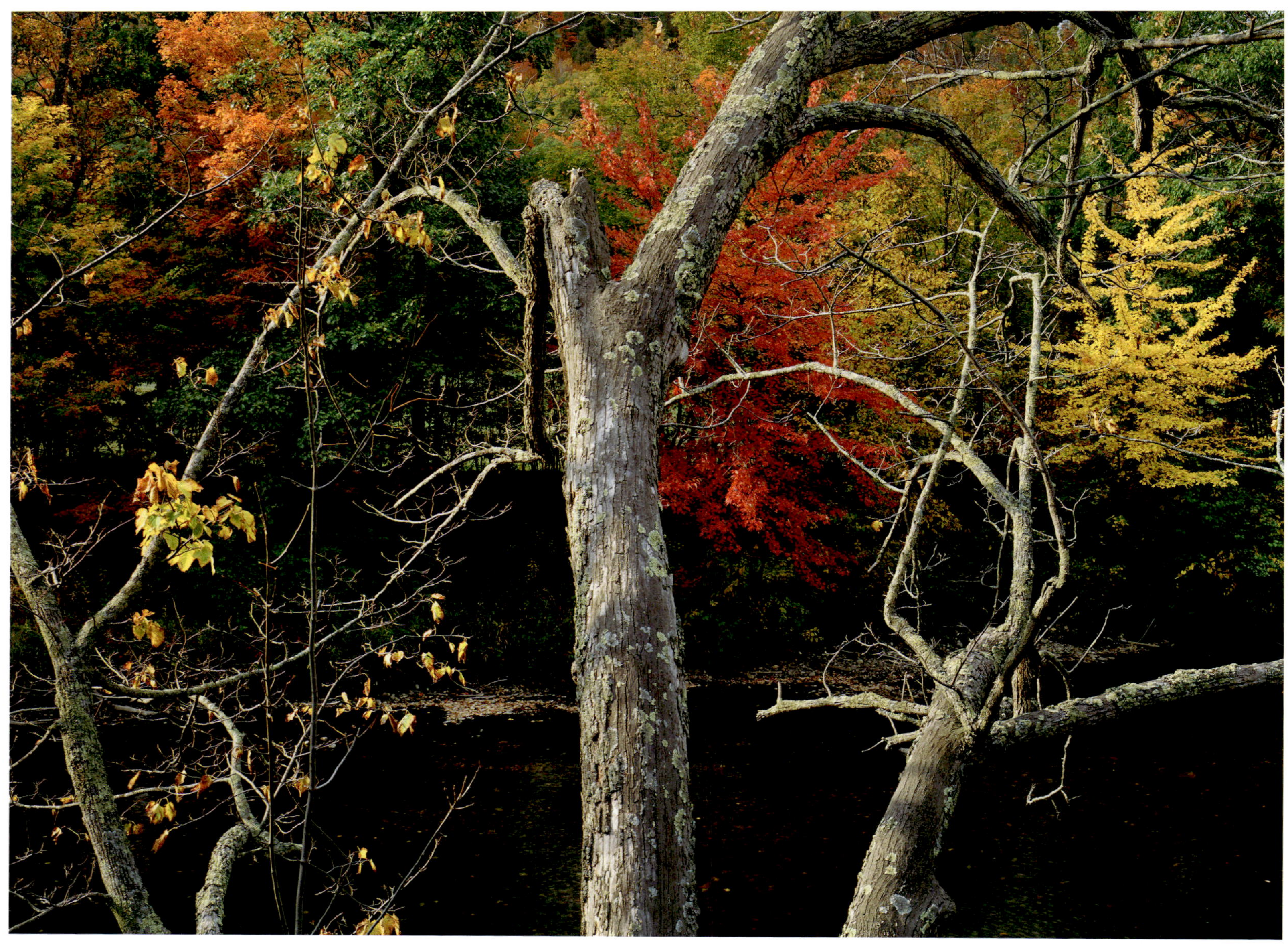

Robert Glenn Ketchum, *Untitled*, n.d.

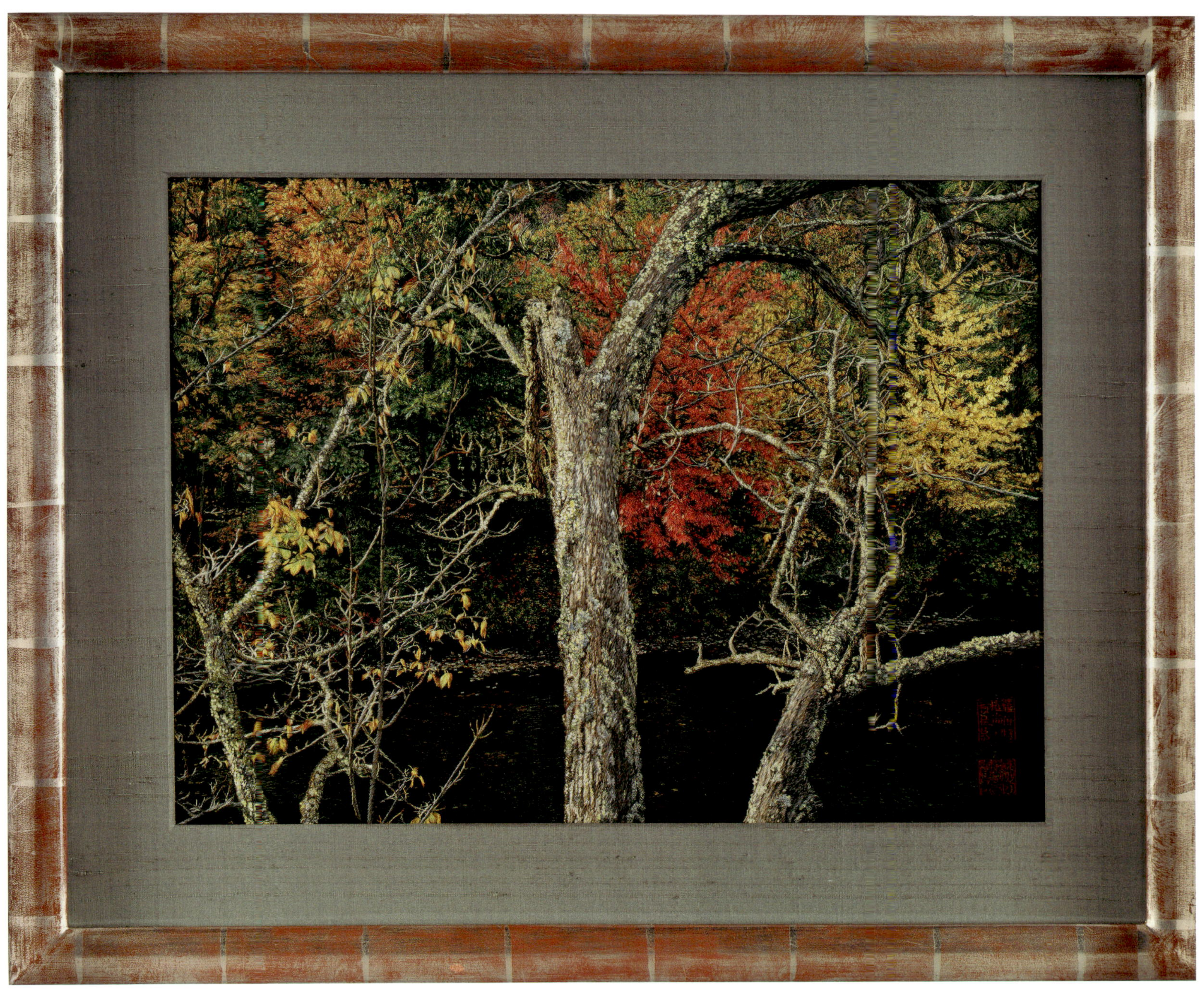

Robert Glenn Ketchum, *Old Tree in Autumn Forest*, 2004 (embroidery)

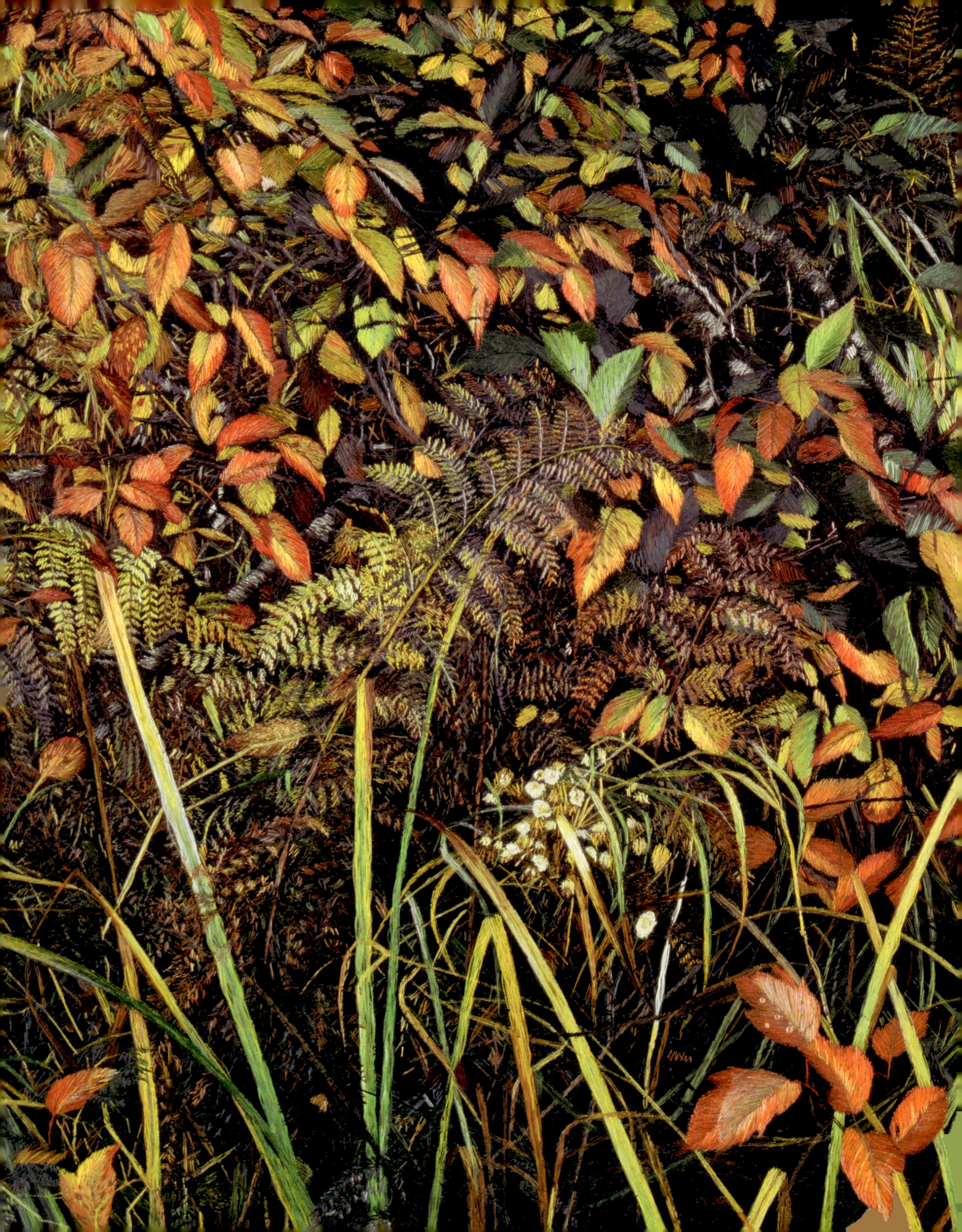

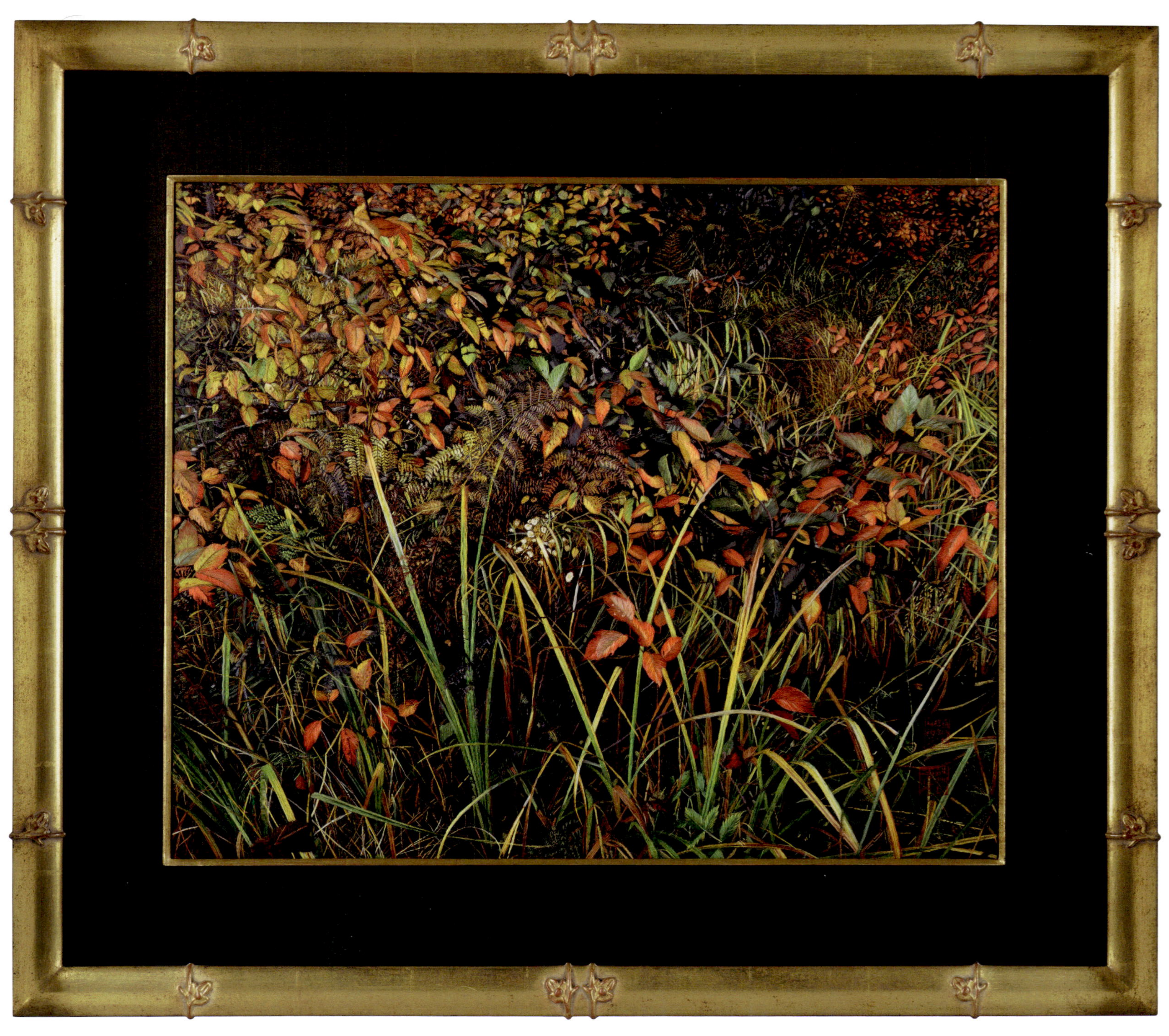

Robert Glenn Ketchum, *Colorful Leaves and Grasses*, 2003 (embroidery; detail at left)

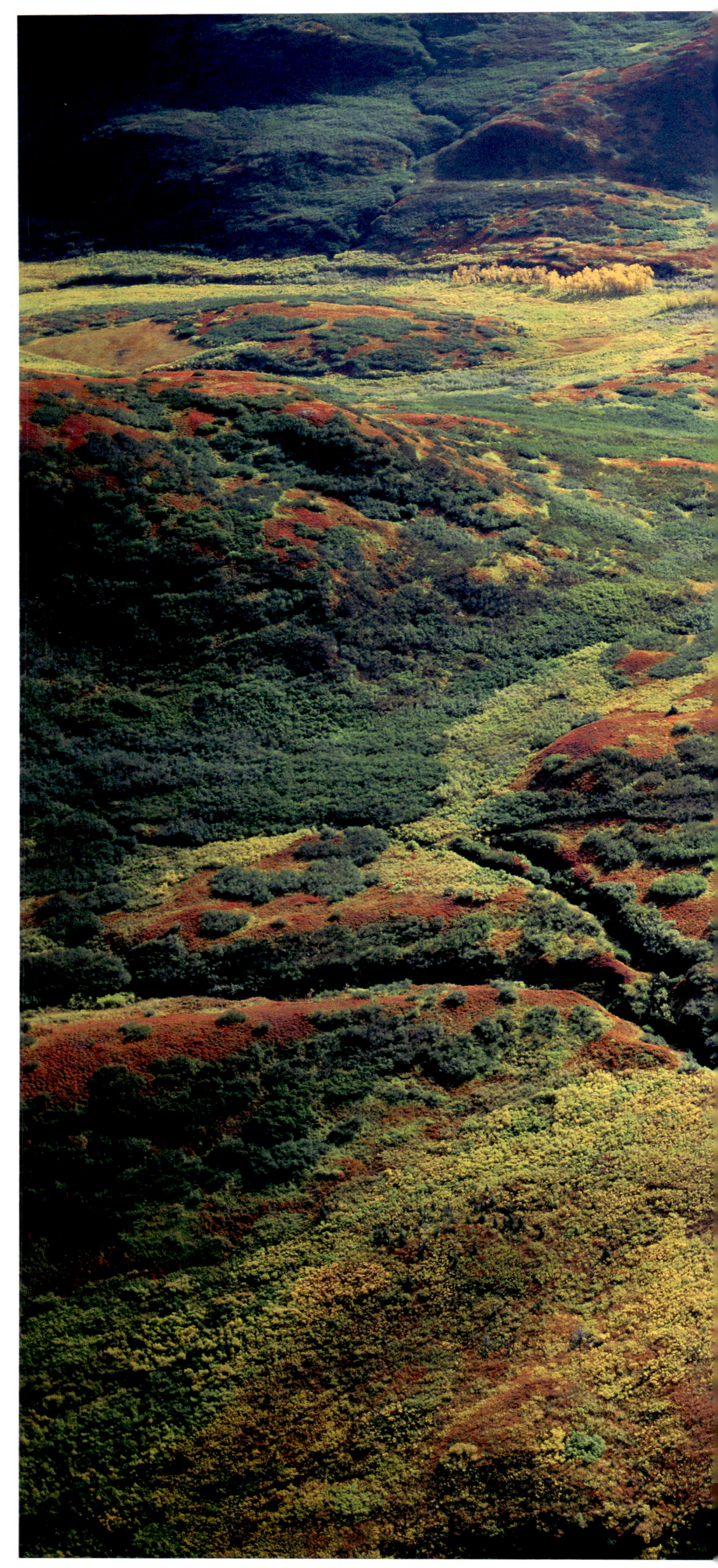

Robert Glenn Ketchum, *Everything Has Its Place*, 2001, from the Southwest Alaska project

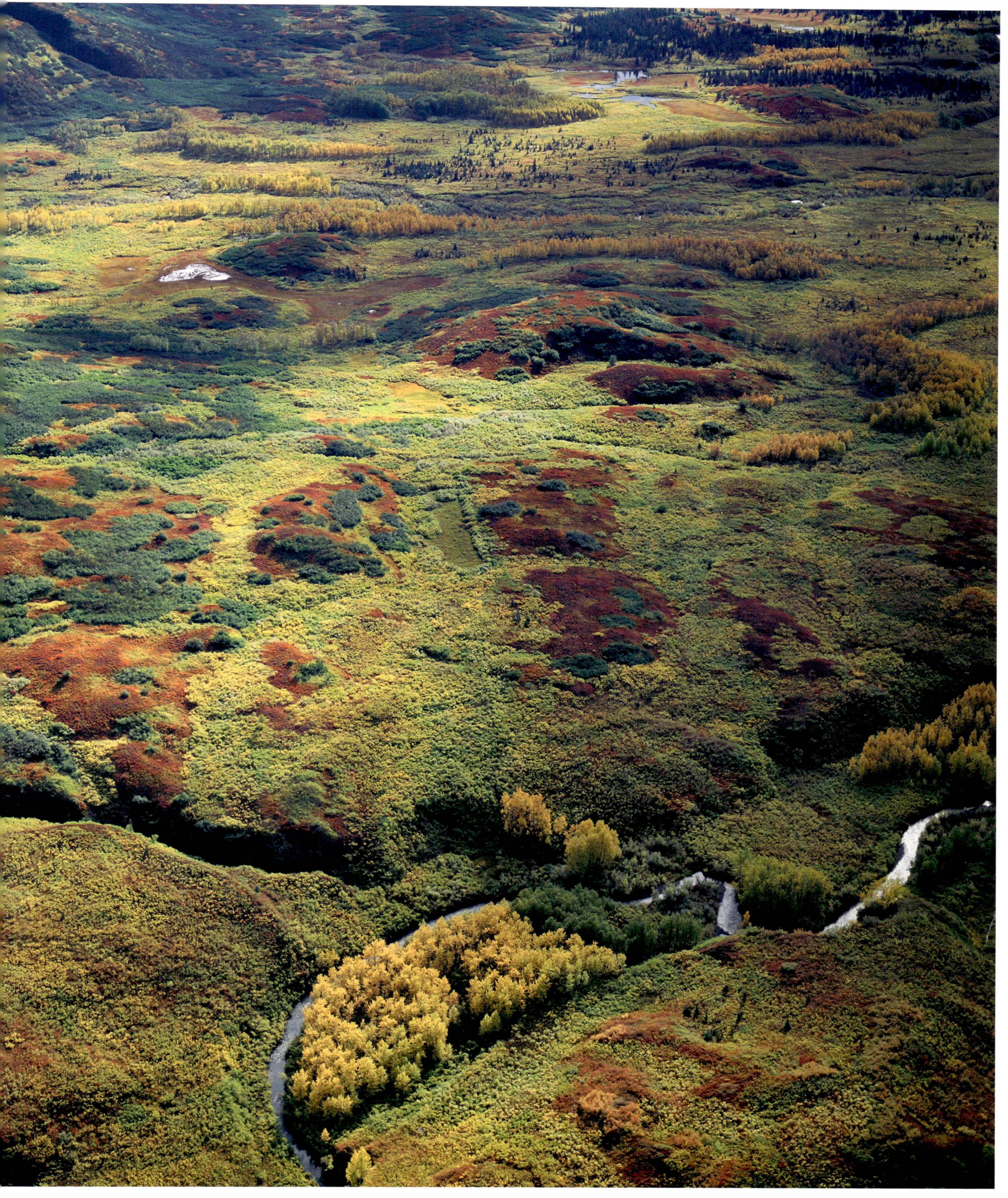

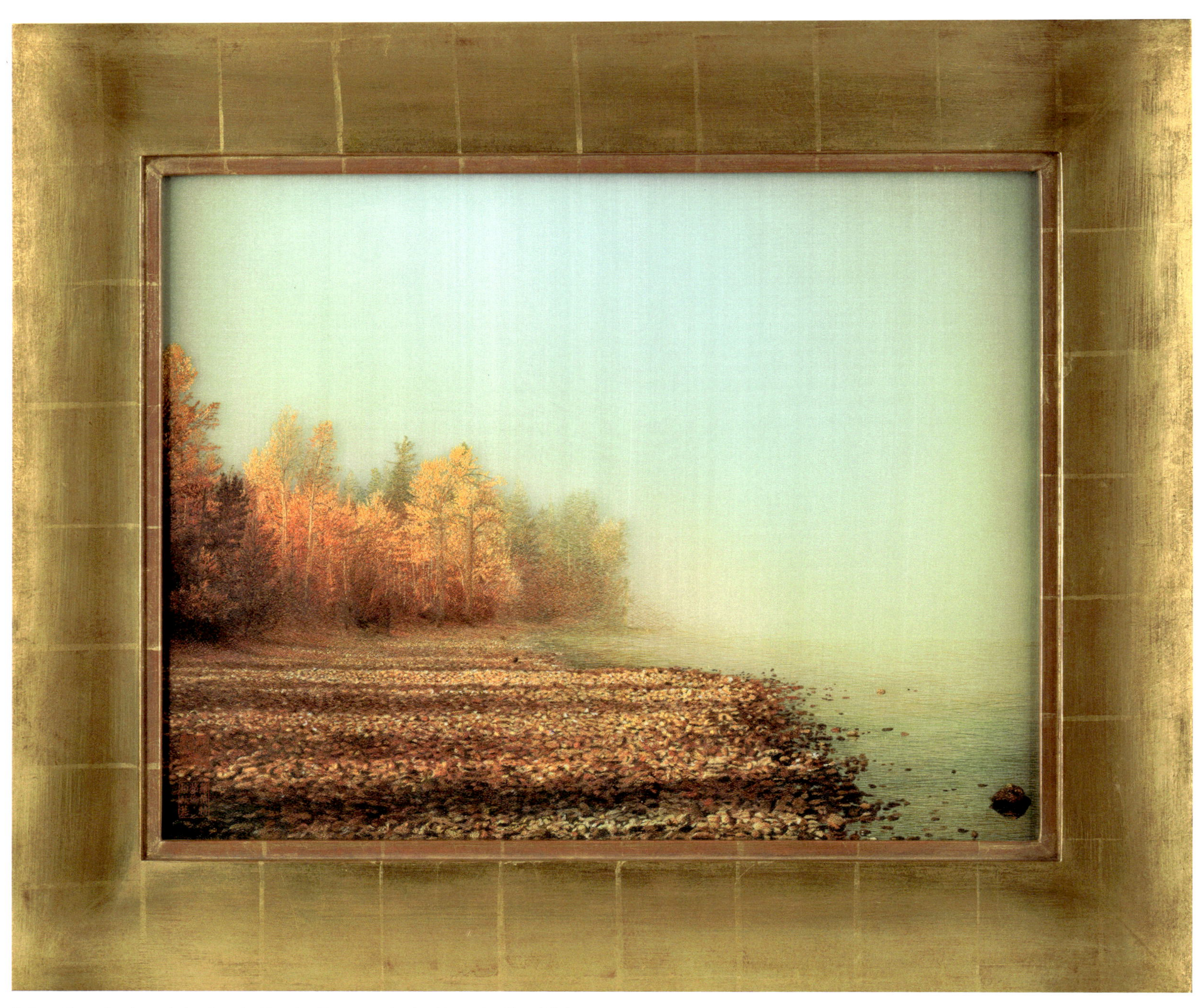

Robert Glenn Ketchum, *Lakeshore in Morning Fog*, 2000 (embroidery; detail at right)

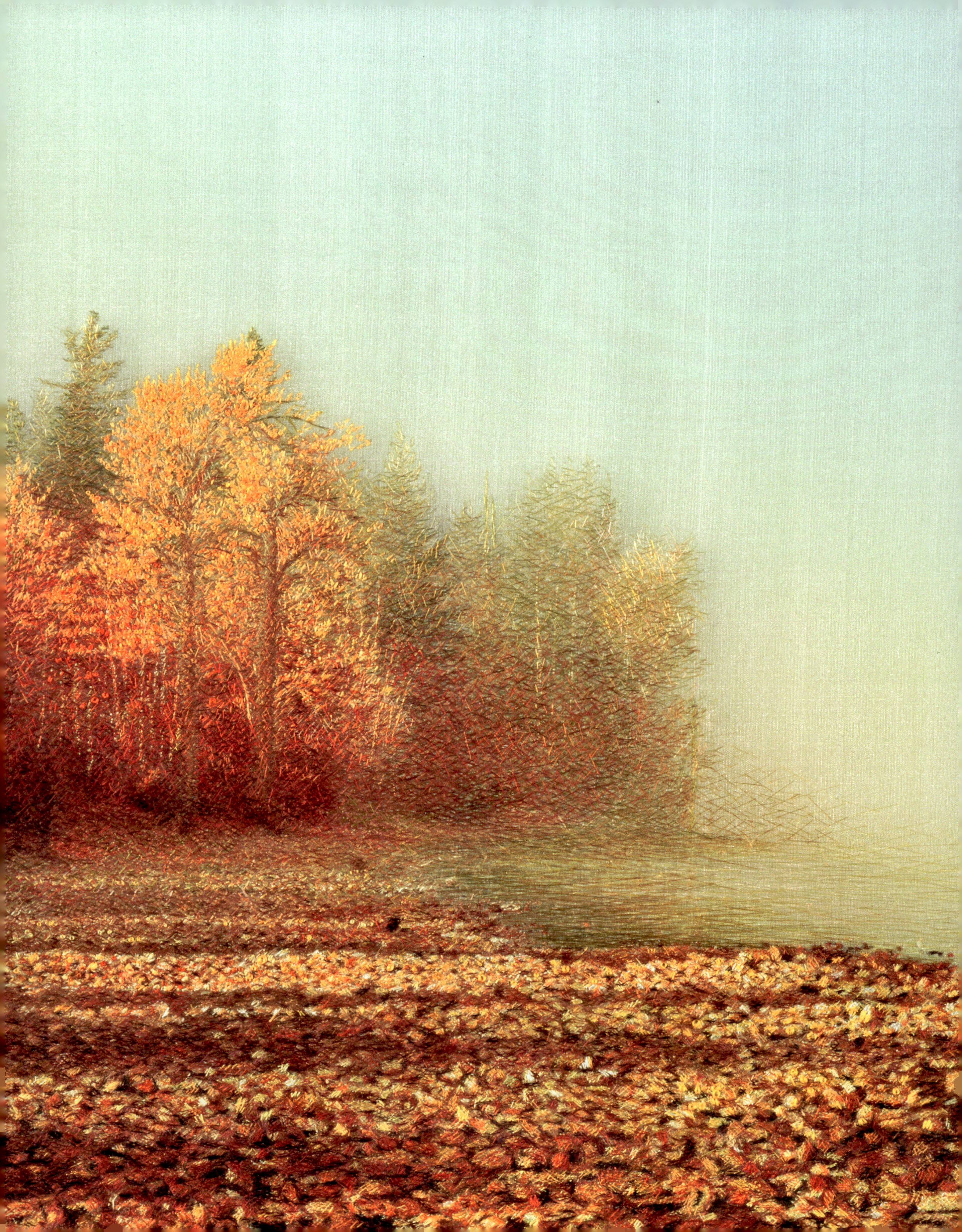

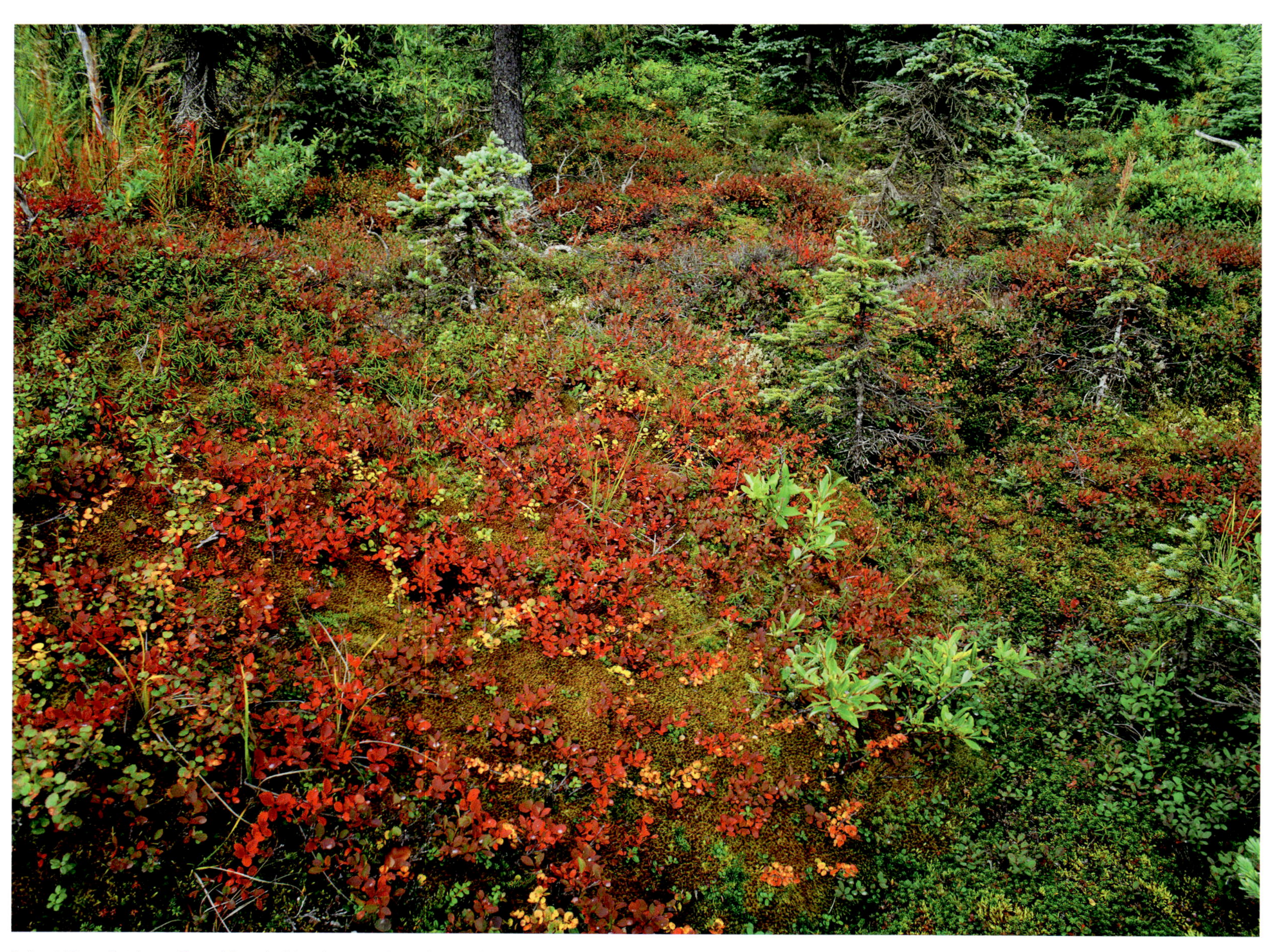

Robert Glenn Ketchum, *Boreal Boogie Woogie*, 1998, from the Southwest Alaska project

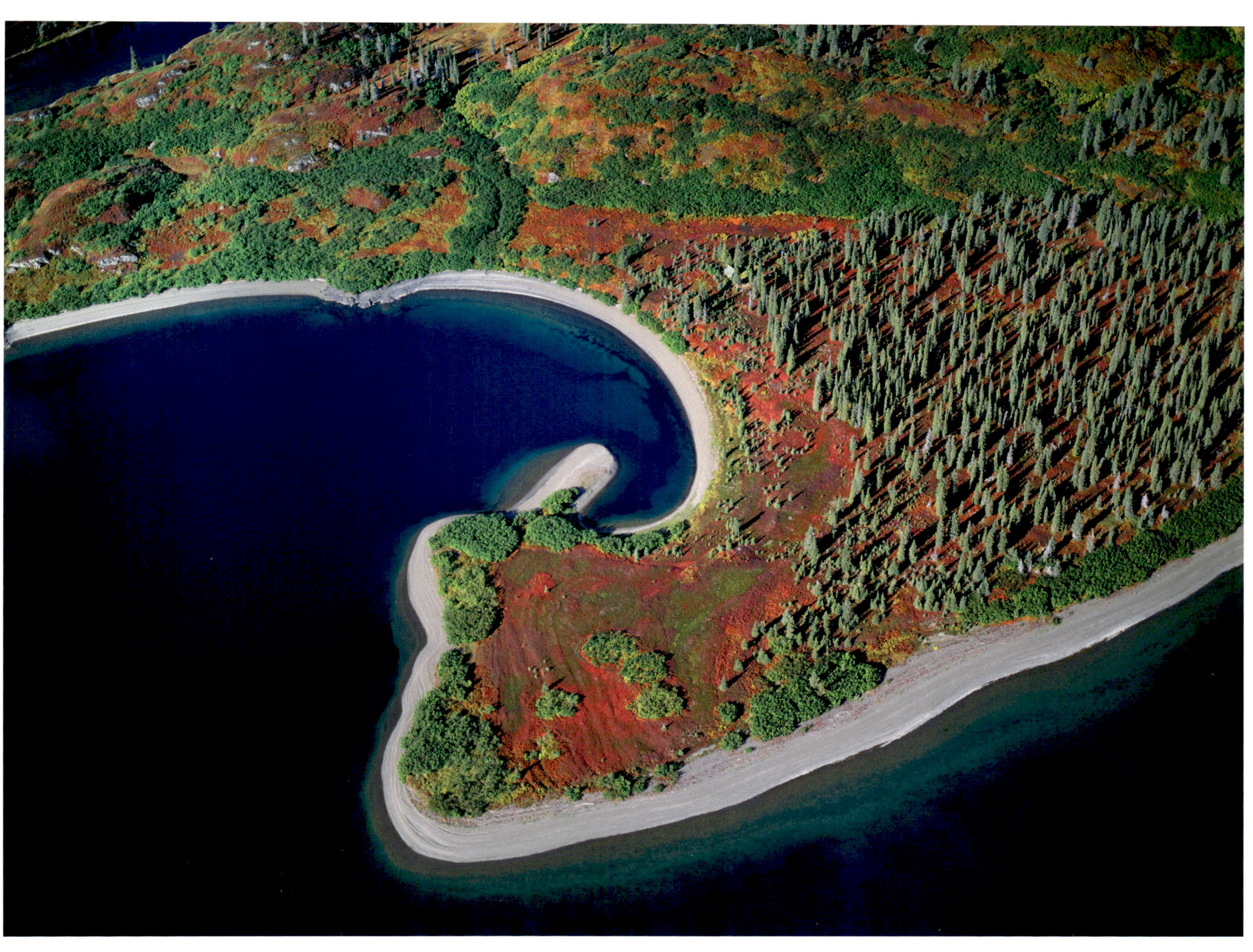

Robert Glenn Ketchum, *Fall Spit, Nuyakyk*, 2001, from the Southwest Alaska project

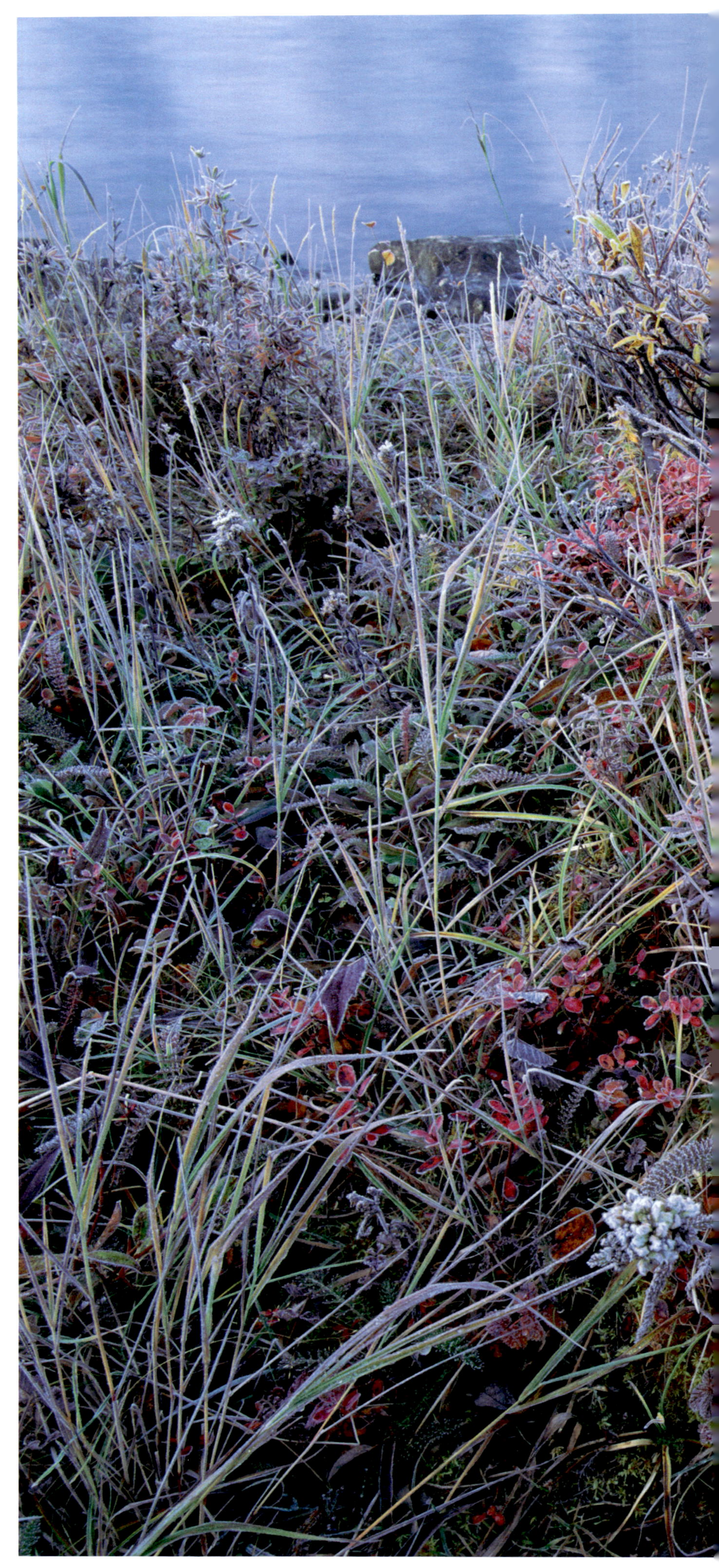

Robert Glenn Ketchum, *Fall Frost at the River's Edge*, 1999, from the Southwest Alaska project

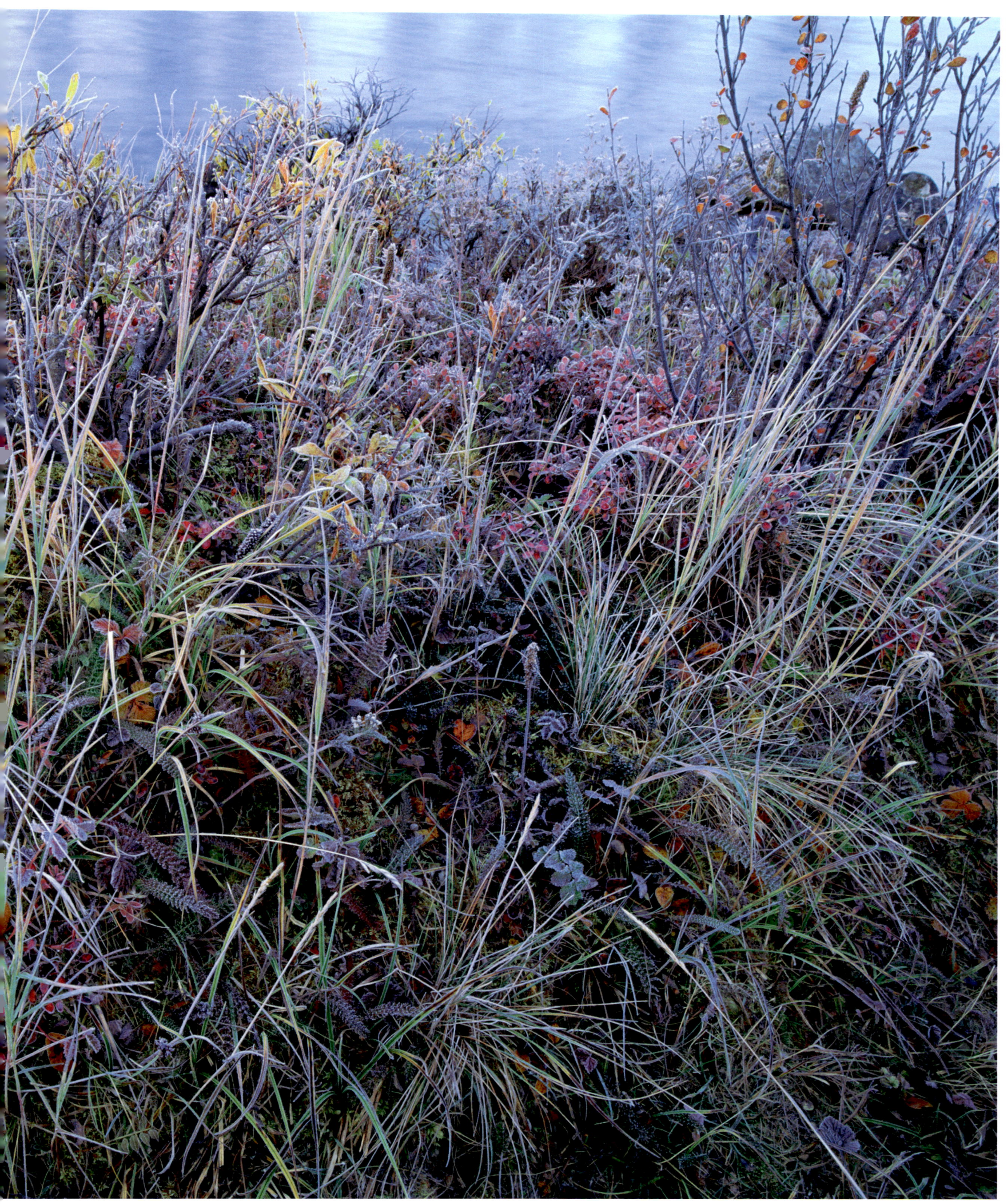

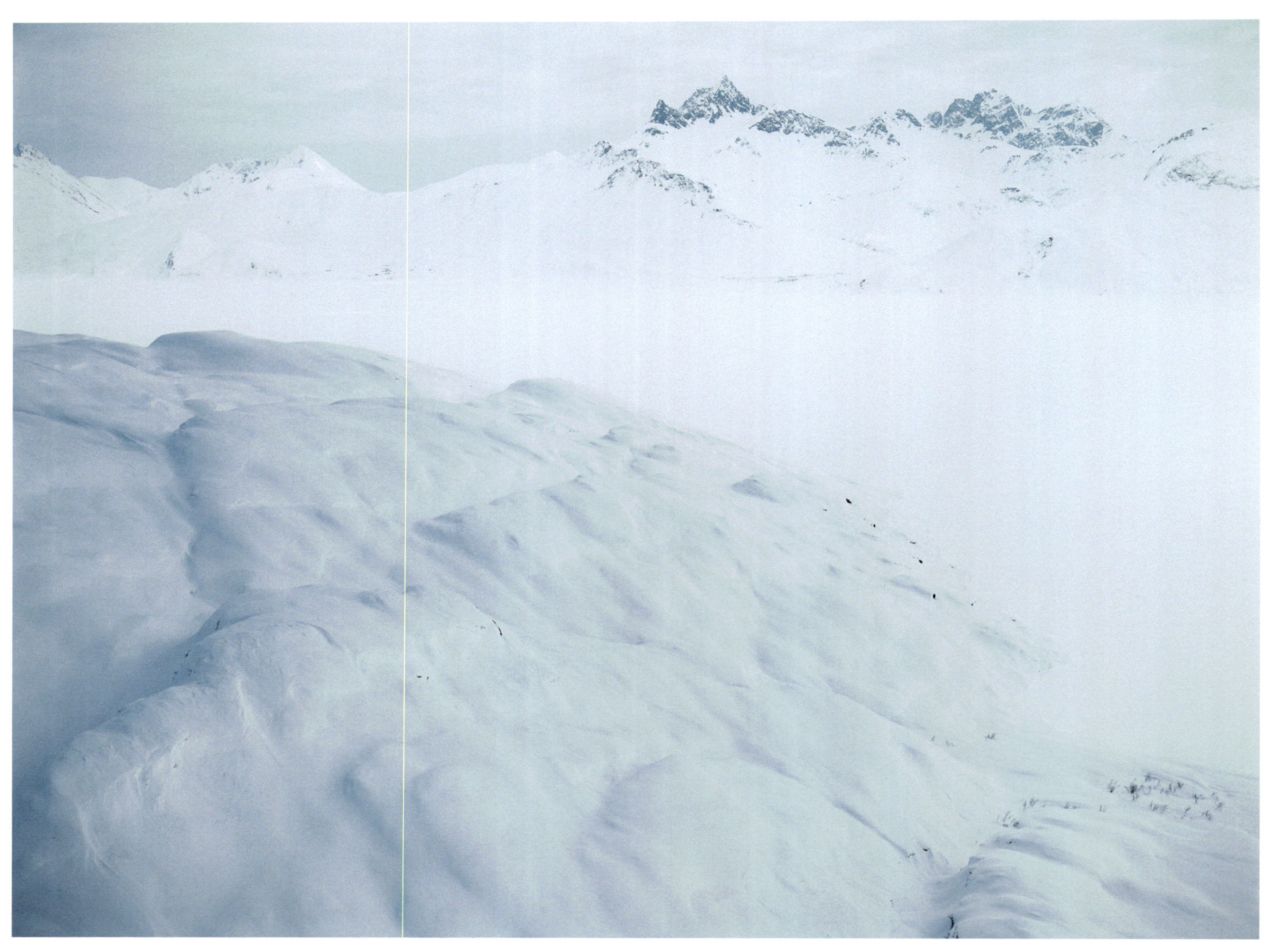

Robert Glenn Ketchum, *Twilight and Frozen Lake, Wood River Mountains*, 2002, from the Southwest Alaska project

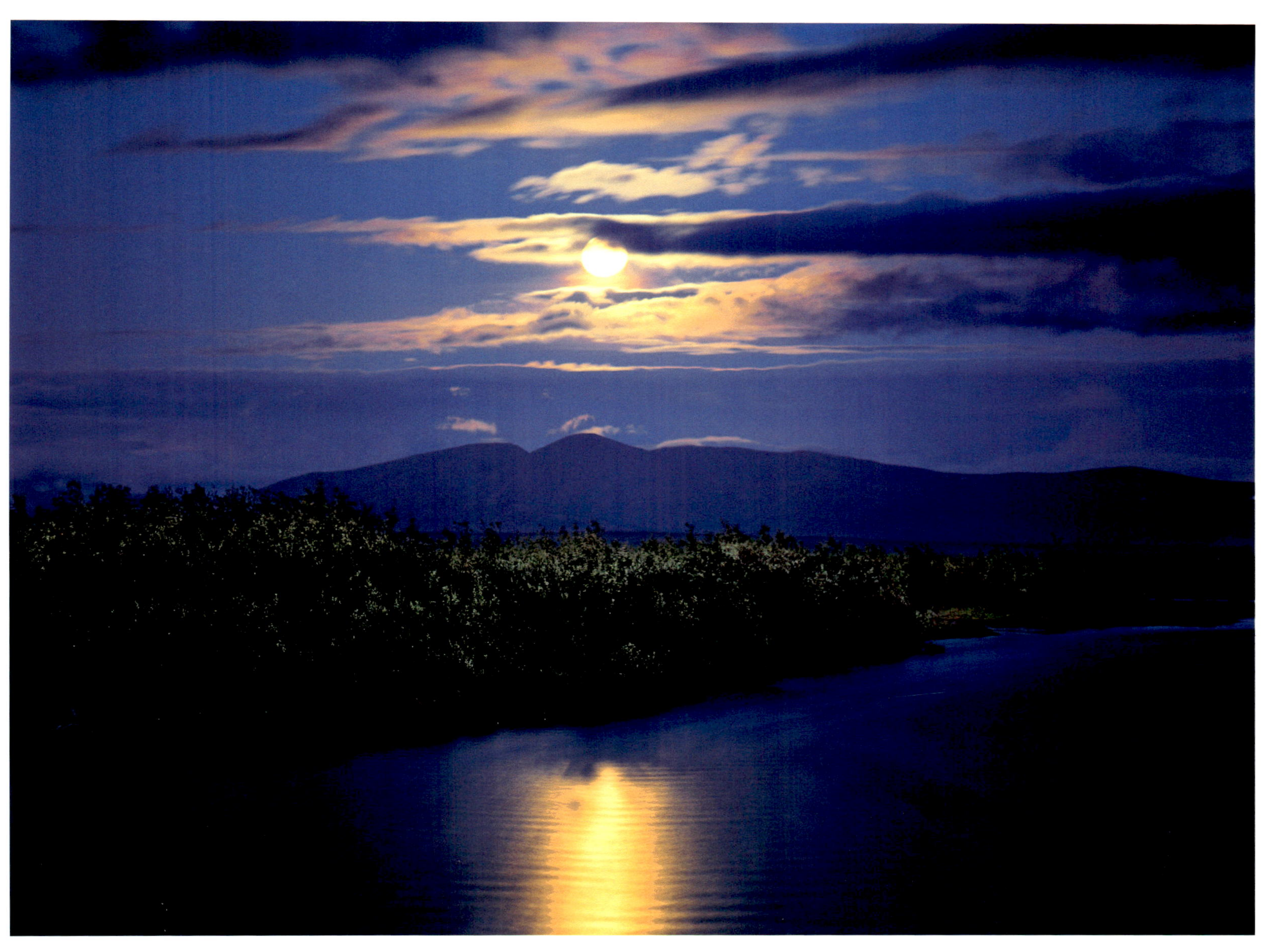

Robert Glenn Ketchum, *Full Moon Rising, Kanektok*, 1999, from the Southwest Alaska project

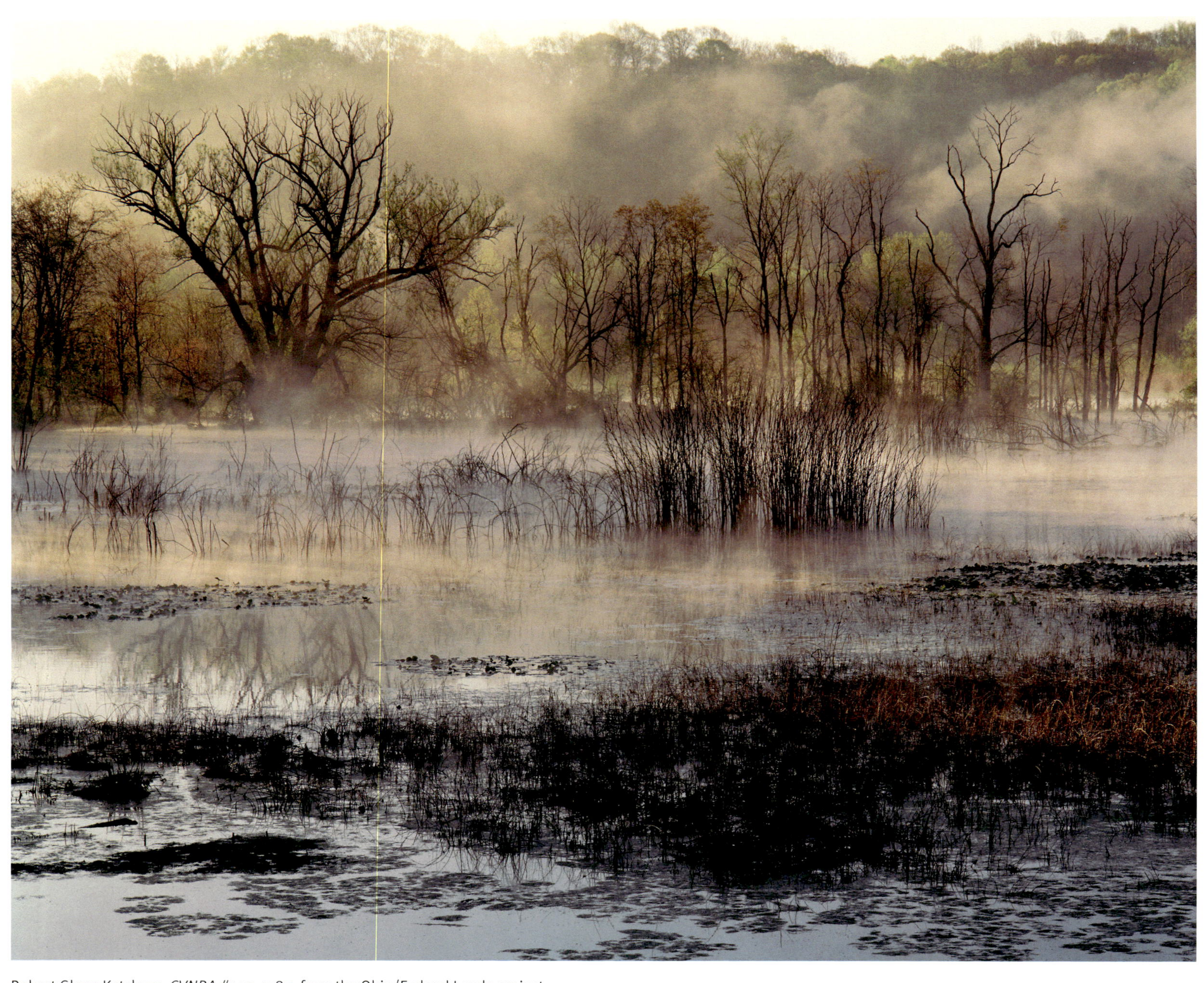

Robert Glenn Ketchum, *CVNRA #412*, 1987, from the Ohio/Federal Lands project

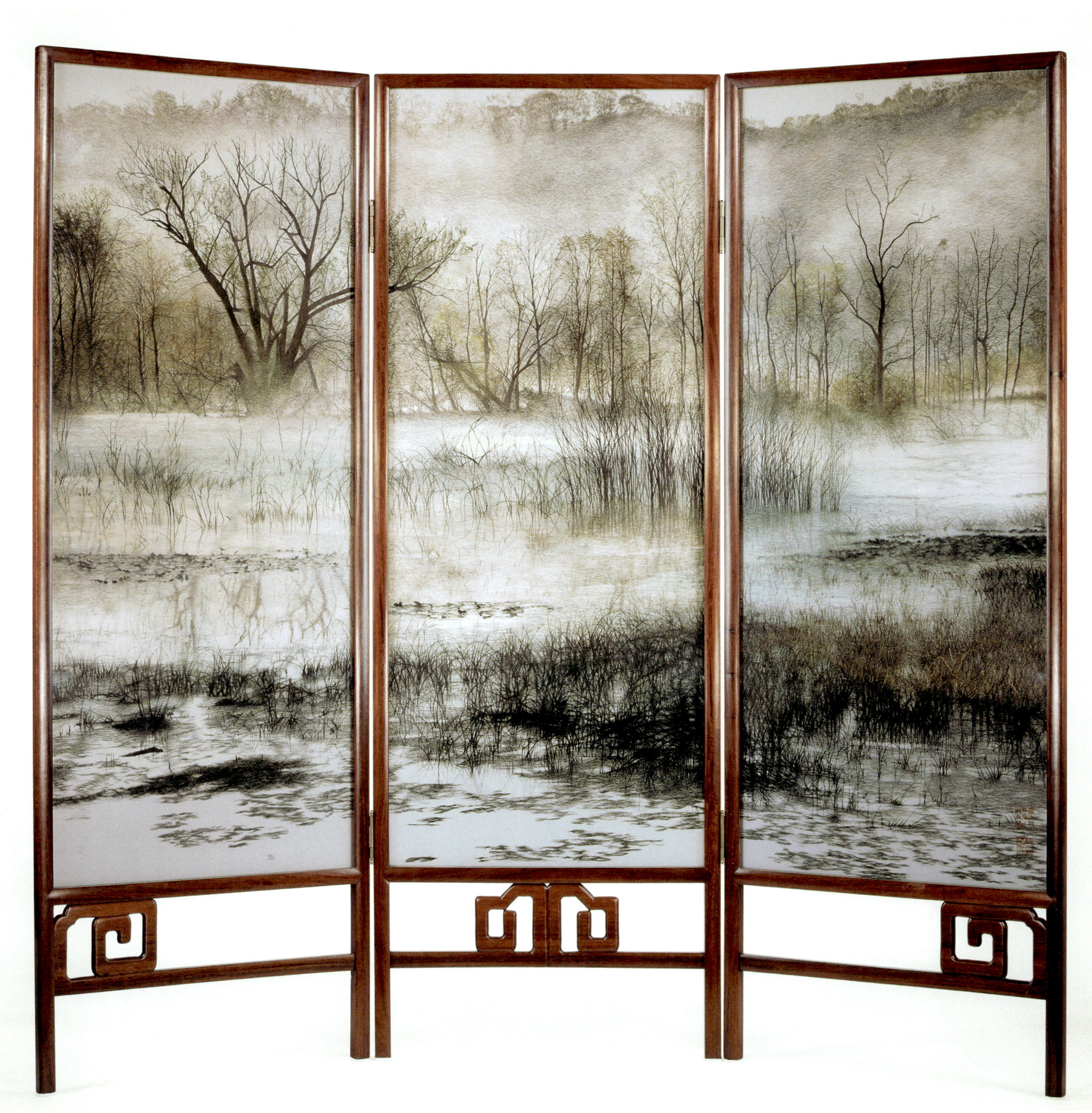

Robert Glenn Ketchum, *The Beginning of Time*, 1994 (embroidery)

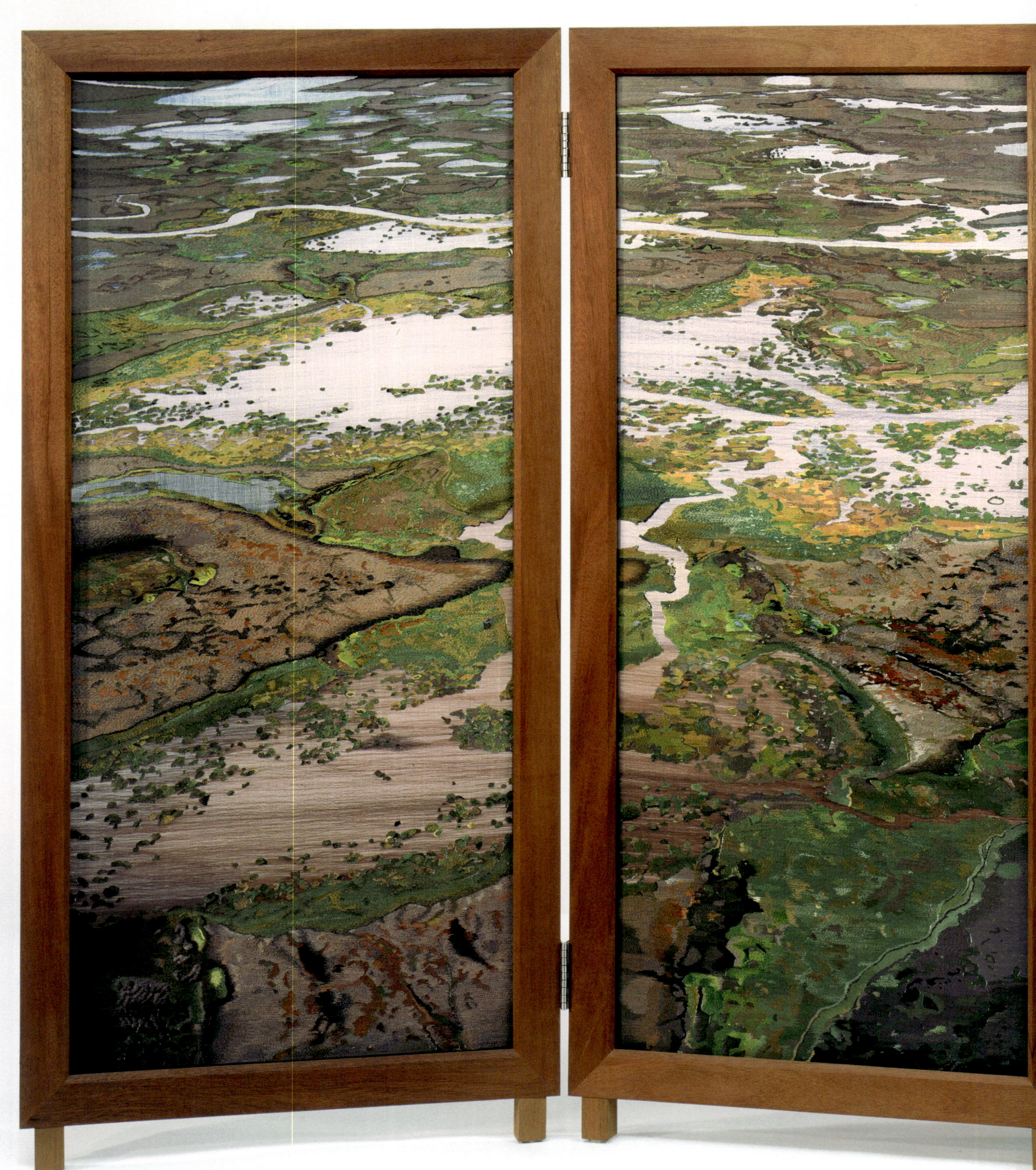

 Robert Glenn Ketchum, *YK Delta from 1500*, 2003 (loom weaving; details pp. 100–101)

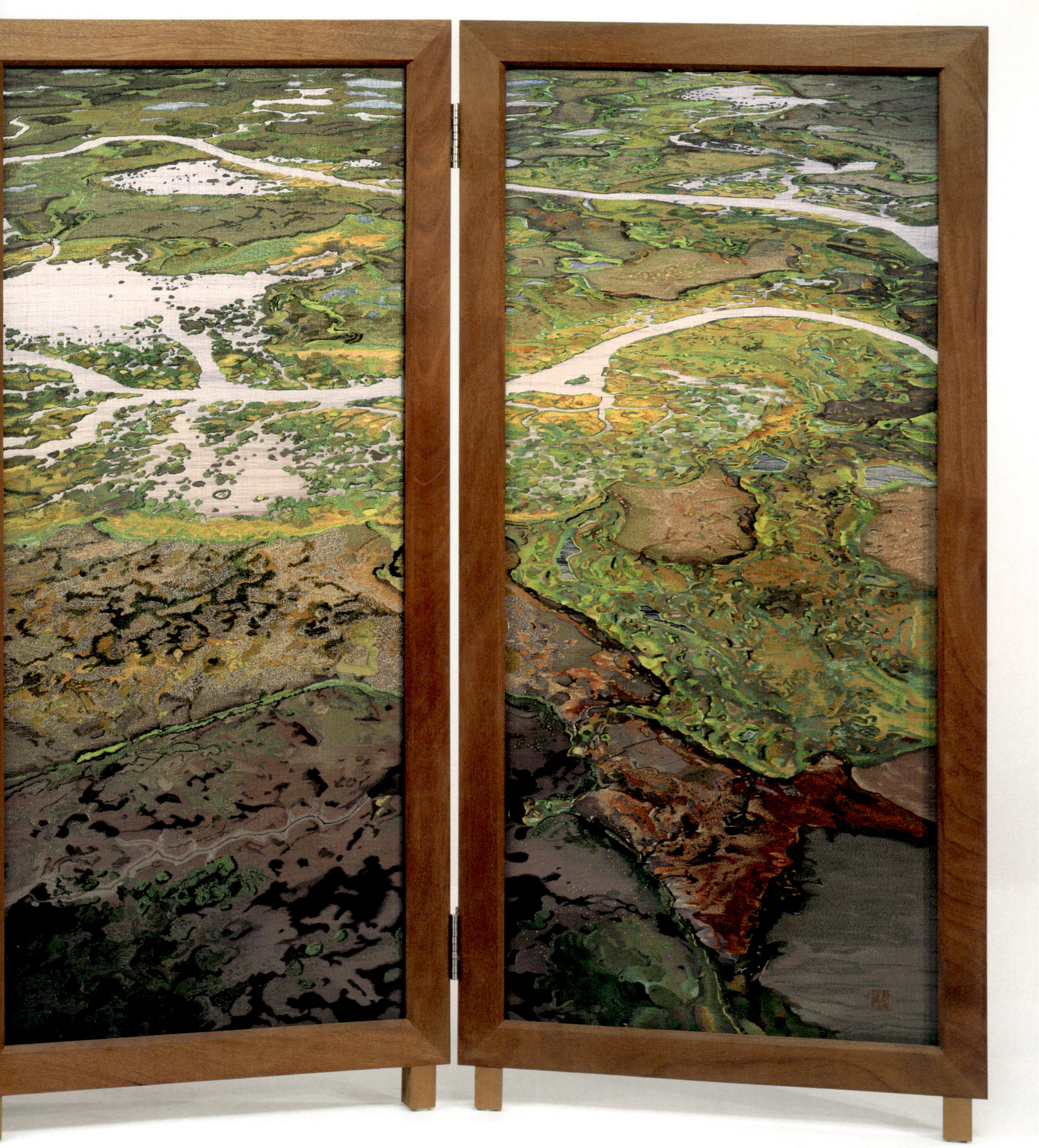

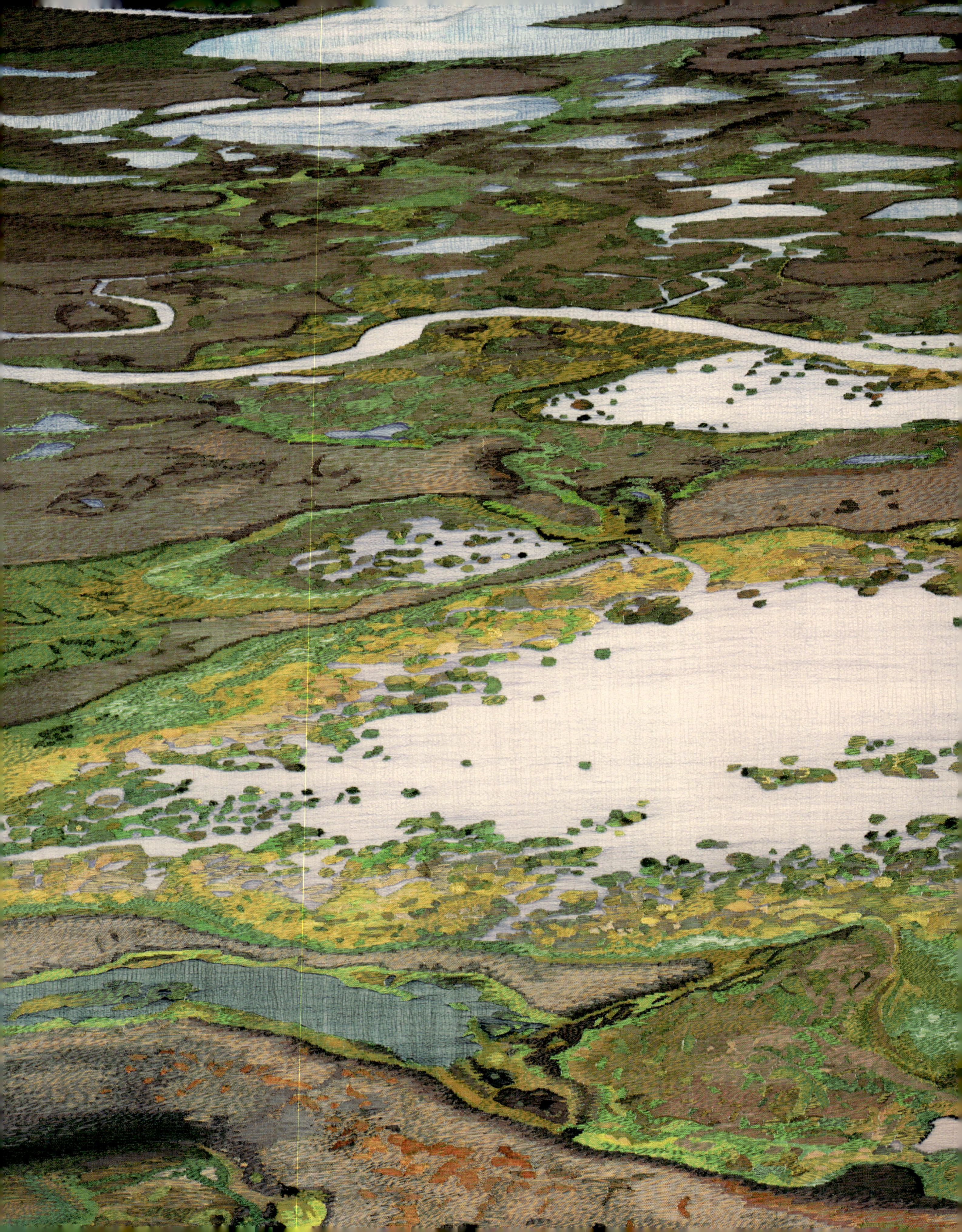

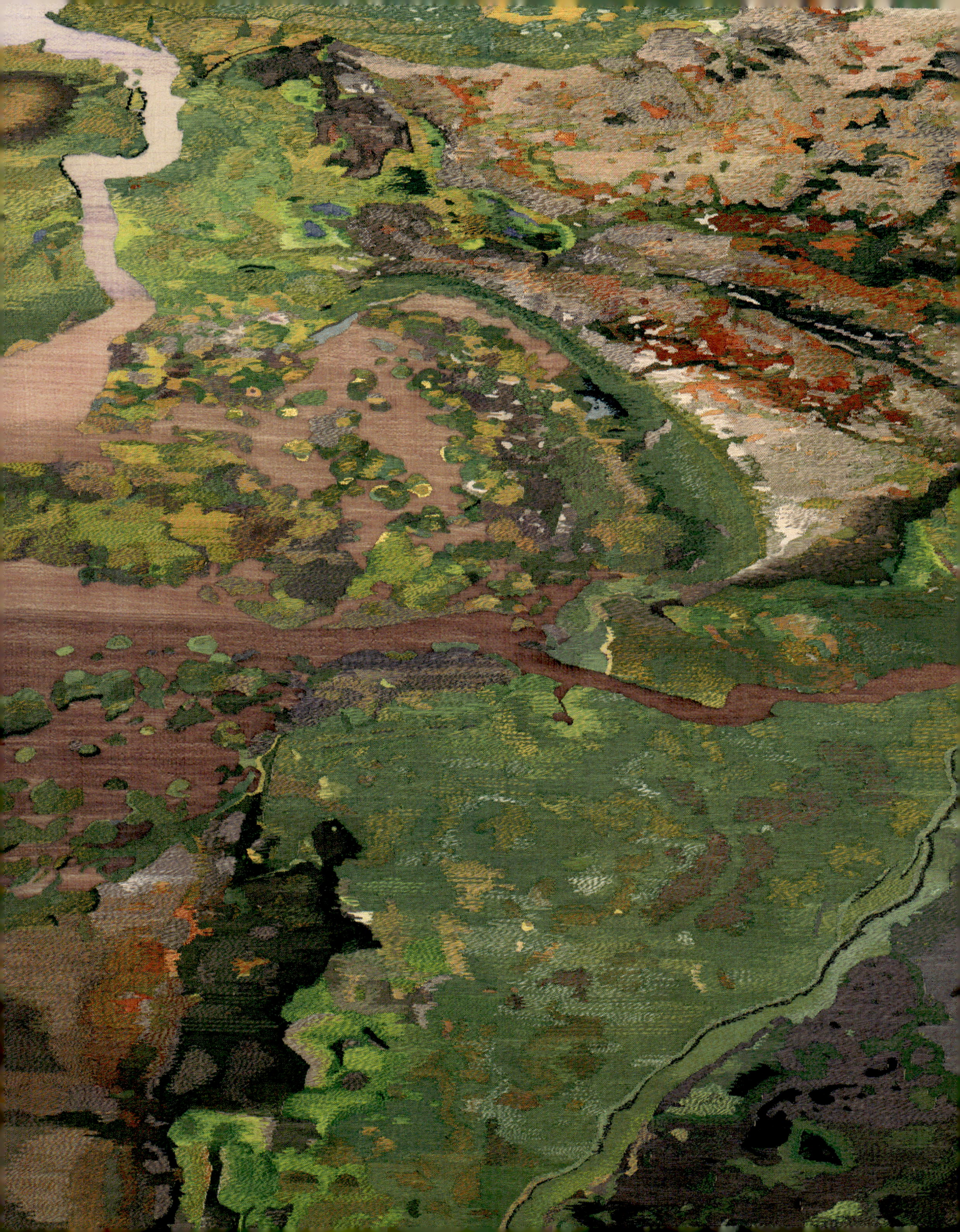

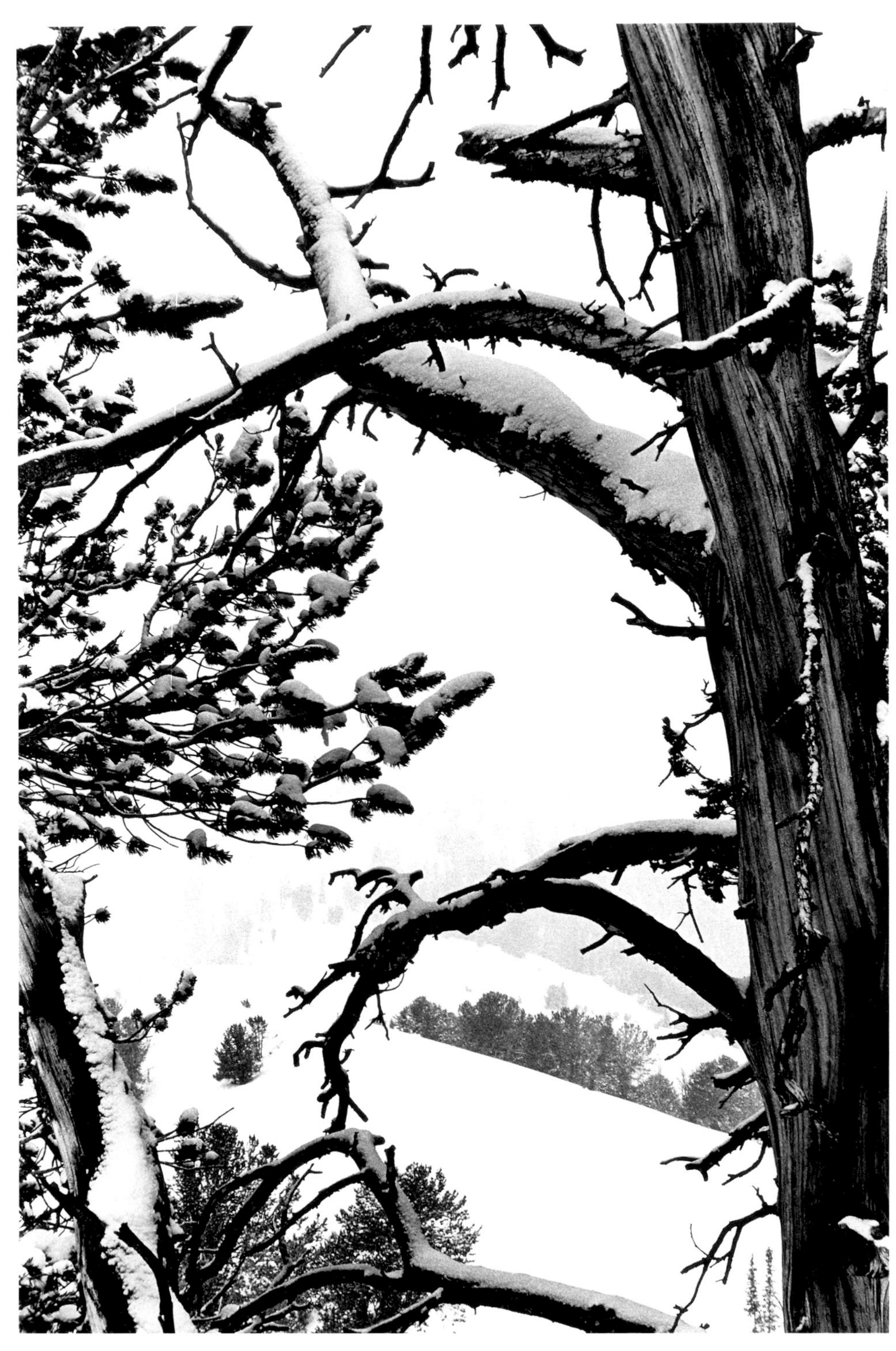

Robert Glenn Ketchum, *View in a Storm*, 1973, from the portfolio *Winters: 1970–1980*
Opposite: *Distant Trees through Falling Snow*, 1999 (embroidery)

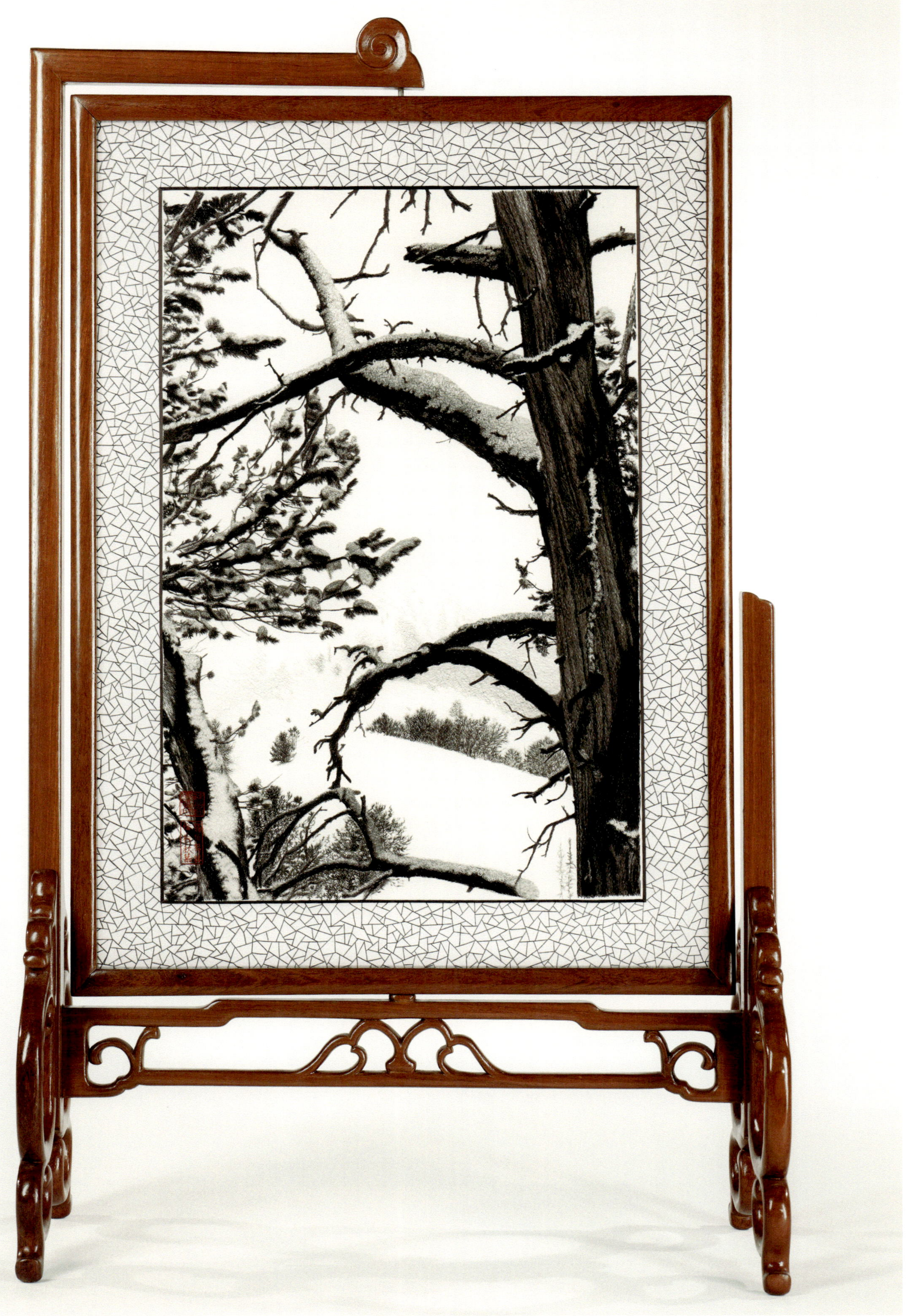

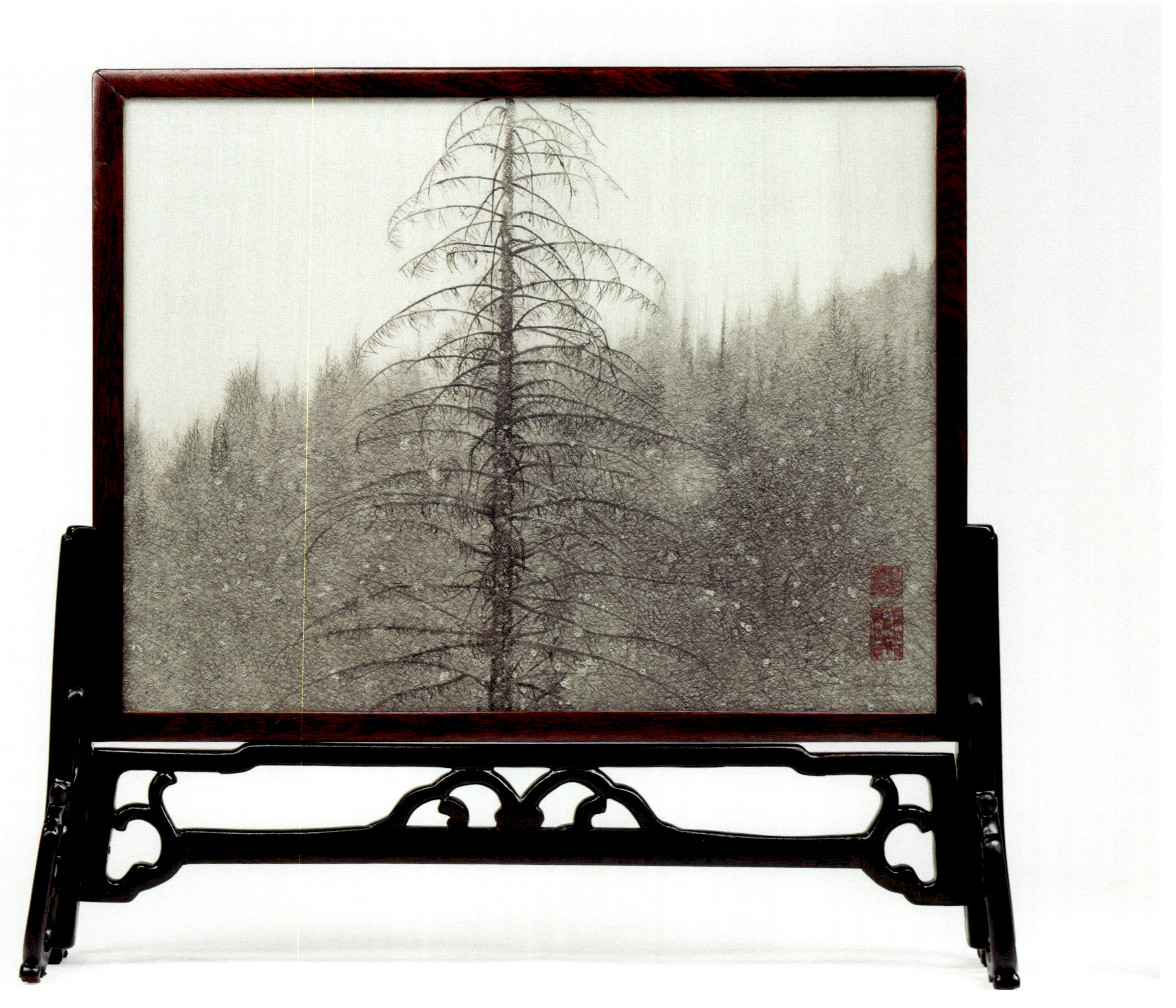

Robert Glenn Ketchum, *Snowfall,* 1986 (embroidery)

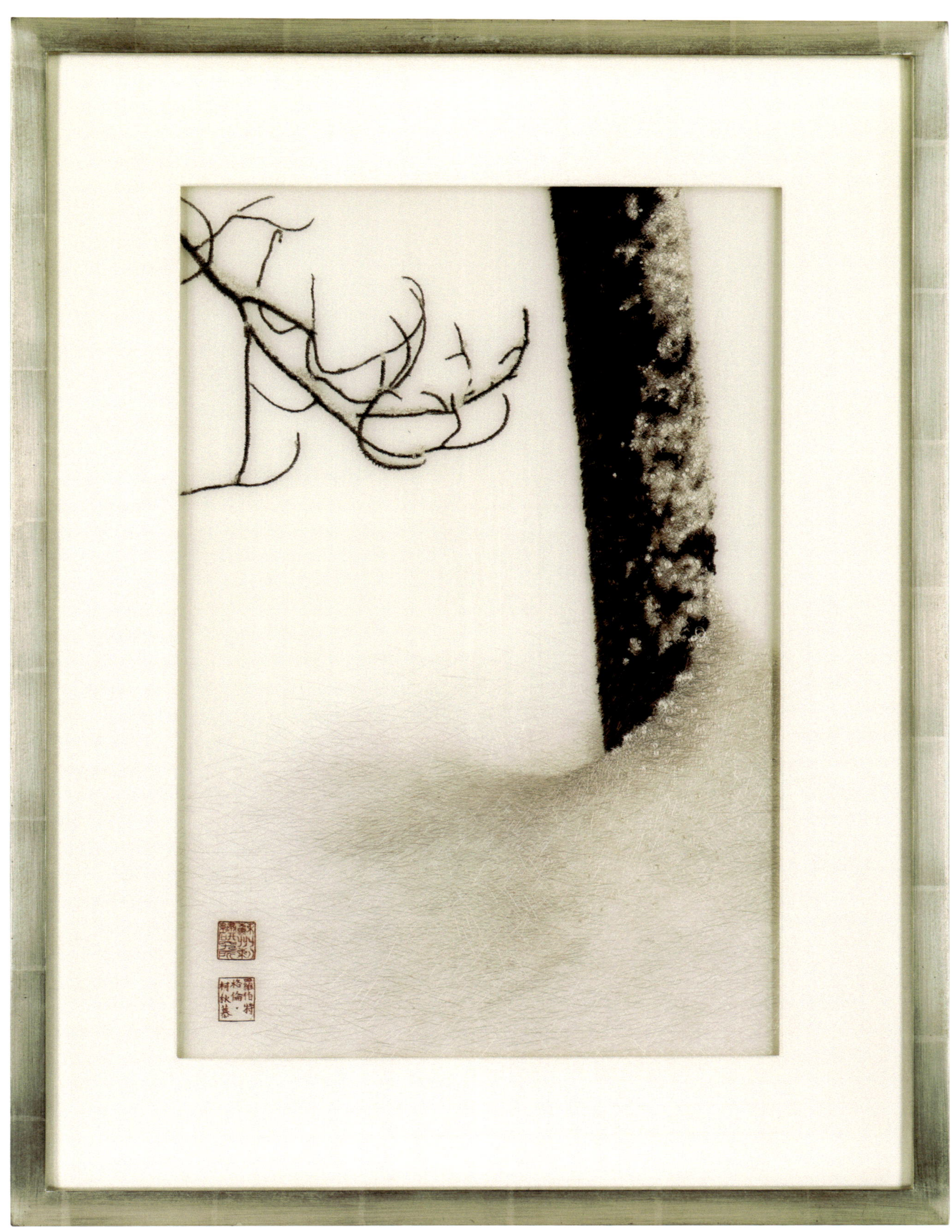

Robert Glenn Ketchum, *Tree and Branch in Deep Snow*, 1996 (embroidery)

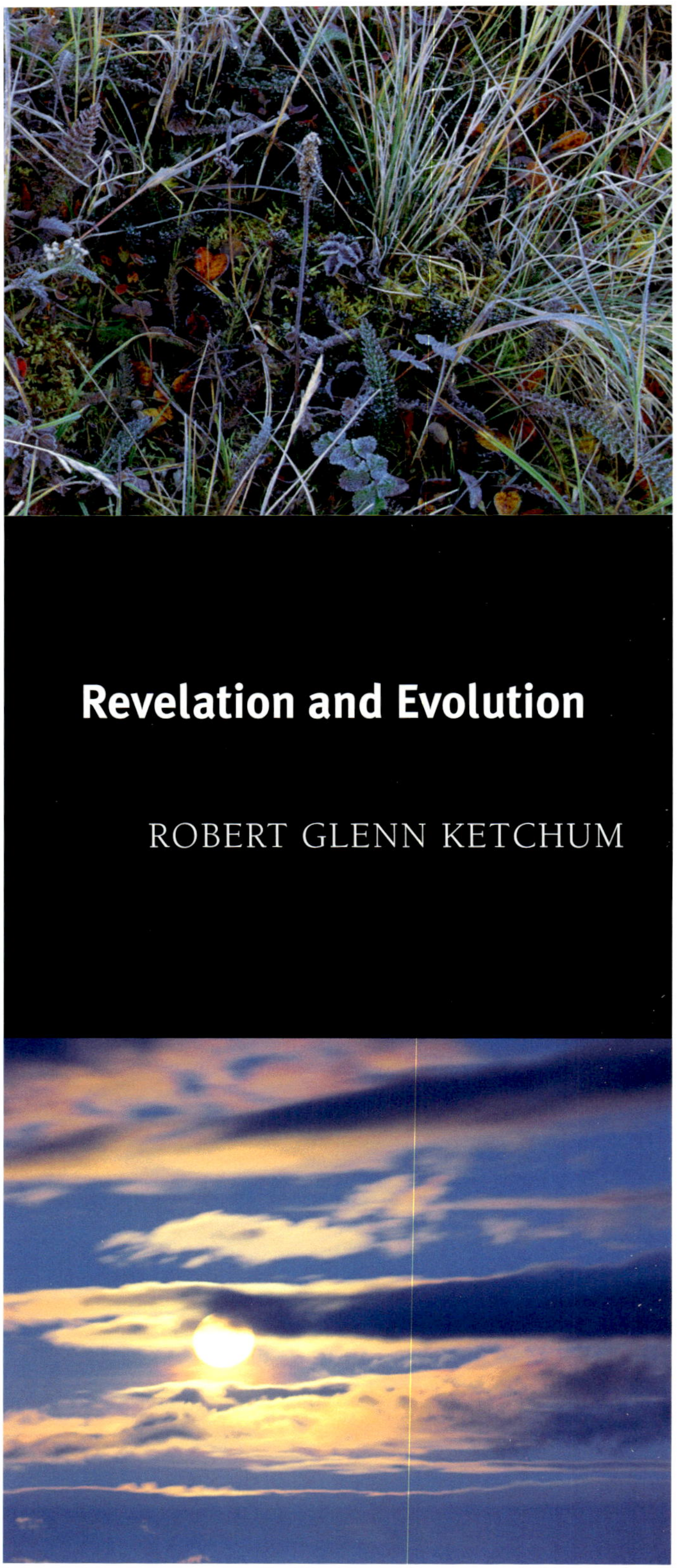

OF THE MANY PHOTOGRAPHERS who have influenced me over the years, Eliot Porter and his work have been most profound, helping to formulate my personal ethic and purpose as well as my artistic discipline.

As a young photographer, I had the pleasure of meeting Eliot several times. The most significant introduction—and the one that left the most lasting impression—occurred sometime in the 1960s, when I was given a copy of the Sierra Club publication *"In Wildness Is the Preservation of the World," Selections & Photographs by Eliot Porter* (1962). This large, beautifully printed book paired quotes from Henry David Thoreau with Eliot's photographs, which resonated with a richness and nuance of color that I had never seen before in print.

The publication awakened a personal environmental activism in me as well. I had recently read Rachel Carson's *Silent Spring* (1962) and Aldo Leopold's *A Sand County Almanac* (1949), and I was broadening my conscious view of the world at the time, becoming increasingly aware of the consequences of my actions. I had also begun to take pictures, mostly in black and white. Seeing *In Wildness* marked the first time I had ever considered color photography apart from its commercial application, and I was seduced by the messaging—the thoughtful, reflective words integrated with the vibrant photographs. The influence of these tandem elements changed my life, working their way into my mind without my fully realizing their power or their impact. I began taking more color pictures. I began taking more pictures of the landscape. I began to participate in various activist endeavors with national environmental groups. I bought other Eliot Porter books. Nothing was ever the same.

The pinnacle of Eliot's work for me is *The Place No One Knew: Glen Canyon on the Colorado* (1963), another Sierra Club publication. The book combines a pointed political argument—preventing additional dams in the Colorado River canyons—with the most colorful

Robert Glenn Ketchum, *Fall Frost at the River's Edge* (detail; p. 92) and *Full Moon Rising, Kanektok* (detail; p. 95)

and abstract of all of his photographs. I had learned to appreciate the sense of the abstract in his compositions of small, textural details, but it was in these photographs of the colorful, narrow slot canyons of the West where his abstract sensibilities merged most effectively with his description of the larger landscape. Many of the images from this body of work appear to be nothing but pure color and form until closer scrutiny suddenly reveals angle, viewpoint, and scale. I found this comprehensive, graphic perspective of the land especially inspiring.

I wrote to Eliot once or twice as I began to do more color photography. I asked about lenses and cameras and film, and he replied, politely, with very succinct information. Finally, my research for the 1978 exhibition *American Photographers and the National Parks* took me quite literally to Eliot's door, as I wanted to include him in this project I was planning for the National Park Foundation. He greeted me warmly at his home in Tesuque, New Mexico, and we spent considerable time together. He showed me his large collection of carefully filed dye transfer prints while we discussed the theme and purpose of the exhibition. It was an amazing morning spent perusing a remarkable archive with one of color photography's most important contributors.

As a young photographer, I was well aware of the prevailing academic resistance to color photography that was finally breaking down, but I was frankly astounded by the attention being lavished on Ansel Adams while Eliot's work was, for the most part, ignored. To me, both his formal imagery and his willingness to explore the medium of color made him as important, if not more so, than Adams. But it was also clear that Eliot was uncomfortable in the spotlight, and he had no desire to assume the outgoing personality that endeared Adams to so many.

During our conversation, Eliot and I discussed print size at some length. He firmly preferred smaller prints that demanded a more intimate observation from the viewer, actually voicing a distinct dislike for the large prints of Adams. I, on the other hand, thought much larger prints were more exciting to view. The images from my series *Order from Chaos* were specifically a reaction to Eliot, some of it honoring his pioneering use of color and graphic composition, some of it mocking characteristics of his style that I found too descriptive and scientifically specific. All eighteen prints in that portfolio were produced in a 30-by-40-inch size, and I never made any other size variations.

Perhaps most importantly, when Eliot and I spoke of his Glen Canyon work his frustration over the politics of the dam and water use in the West was quite clear, and he openly lamented that his book was published after the dam's construction. Hearing him say that awakened a sentiment in me that has resonated through my work ever since. Shortly after our meeting, I promised myself that I would dedicate my life and my photography to issues of evolving environmental concern. I wanted my work to make a difference in political decisions that were in the process of being made. I wanted my photographs to be useful as an activist's tool. This promise has remained the cornerstone of my career.

My face-to-face encounter with Eliot stimulated in me a great range of reflection in the days and weeks that followed our meeting. I soon realized that making pictures exclusively for the sake of carrying on a dialogue about modernism and postmodernism within the narrow realm of the art world no longer addressed or fulfilled my concerns as an artist. I wanted my work to be relevant to my life in more than just esoteric, aesthetic, and artistically philosophical terms. I wanted my photographs to assist and support my activism in the most effective way possible, and that became my overriding consideration. Beginning with my first mildly provocative book, *The Hudson River and the Highlands* (1985), I plunged into the world of making pictures regarding the land for political purposes, and I never looked back.

Many other subtle perspectives filtered into my work from my exchanges with Eliot and from following the evolution of his work, some of which I did not wish to emulate. As he grew older and traveled more widely to remote locations like Antarctica, he occasionally took some pictures with smaller cameras. When published, those photographs from the smaller cameras reproduced poorly when compared to images done in larger formats, and to me the differences were distracting, making the books inconsistent. The imprint of that on my career caused me to consciously struggle with the design of my second publication, *The Tongass: Alaska's Vanishing Rain Forest* (1987), wherein the layout incorporates both 35mm and medium-format imagery. As I struggled to resolve those same problems that I felt compromised Eliot's later books, I learned to work with sequence and text in powerful ways, and these interests continue to be reflected in my work and all of my publications to this day.

Because I held so much respect for Eliot's beautiful, small dye transfer prints, the production of which he carefully oversaw, I was disappointed when, late in his career, he agreed to publish his best-known images as large dye transfers for galleries that represented him. I knew he was doing this at the suggestion of those galleries that now found increasing size fashionable. More importantly, from my experience of printing in dye transfer, I knew working with that material in a large scale was a technical nightmare because of the difficulty of consistently maintaining sharpness and registration of the dye-film layers across the large print surface. I felt this push for marketing was a disservice to Eliot's previous fine print work and was an inadequate representation of his brilliant photographic vision. Again, though, my aversion to his decision in this case has informed my career, and I struggle on a daily basis not to make the same mistake or to otherwise allow my personal vision to be compromised by trends in marketing.

Throughout my education, the study of the history of art has made clear to me that the artists I have most admired were always true to themselves. The focus of their work did not revolve around curatorial acceptance. They followed personal muses and simply did what they felt they had to do, regardless of, and often contrary to, popular opinion. I was most impressed by those who were masters of their craft as well.

As a photographic visionary, Eliot was all of these things. In reflection I realize that embracing and reacting to his work has, over the years, resulted in many epiphanies related to my own career. He was my subliminal mentor. I hope that what I have accomplished reflects upon what I learned from him and contributes not only to furthering the dialogue of art, but to living in a more enlightened world.

Acknowledgments

THIS BOOK is in your hands only through the assistance of many people, first and foremost the two artists whose work is represented here. Eliot Porter generously bequeathed his collection to the Amon Carter Museum in 1990. In making that gift, he graciously encouraged the museum to consider his work a living and complex document open to many interpretations. Robert Glenn Ketchum, who took up Porter's challenge of poetically interpreting landscapes in color, worked closely with us during every stage of this project, helping to secure essential loans and key support from the Advocacy Arts Foundation, Mr. and Mrs. Herb Belkin, Sue and Griff Hopkins, Jack B. Ketchum, Michelle Lund, and Dr. and Mrs. John Uphold.

Michelle Dunn Marsh provided this volume's revelatory design. Stevan Baron oversaw its production with his acute eye and extensive experience. He and Ketchum were on press together to make certain the reproductions in the book satisfied their high standards.

At the Amon Carter Museum, Will Gillham expertly managed all aspects of the publication; he and Mary Jane Crook edited its contents. Miriam Hermann assembled the illustrations. Steven Watson at the Carter and Michael Jones at West Coast Imaging prepared excellent reproduction files for the book's imagery.

Director Rick Stewart and the staff of the Amon Carter Museum provided enthusiastic support for this project from day one. This publication is produced in conjunction with the Anne Burnett Tandy Distinguished Lectures on American Art.

JOHN ROHRBACH
Senior Curator of Photographs
Amon Carter Museum

FOREMOST, I would like to thank the board, staff, and benefactors of the Amon Carter Museum for honoring me with this book and its related exhibition. John Rohrbach's curatorial concept and Will Gillham's attentive oversight have created a beautiful publication that significantly clarifies my artistic practice, but it took the commitment of many others associated with the institution to make this project possible.

I could not have accomplished what I have over my career without the friendship and support of Bobbie and Herb Belkin; Thomas Curran; Robert Heinz and his father, Clifford; Michael Hoffman; Sue and George Klein; Michelle Lund and her father, Bill; Linda and Robert Lytle; Banny and Barney McHenry; Winsome and Michael McIntosh; Robert Redford; William E. Simon; the Gordon Street family; Angela and Rhett Turner; and Judy and Dr. John Uphold. I would be remiss not to acknowledge the master printers with whom I have worked as well: Michael Wilder has printed my Cibachrome for thirty years, and Michael Jones and Terrance Reimer of West Coast Imaging currently manage worldwide reproduction of my digital files. The embroideries have been completed by the dedicated workers of the Suzhou Embroidery Research Institute directed by Zhang Meifang, my insightful collaborator and friend of many years. Michelle Dunn Marsh has produced a striking publication design, and Stevan Baron has assured that the printing of it reflects the tonality and nuance of color that Eliot and I have brought to our visions.

Thank you, Eliot Porter, Robert Heinecken, and Edmund Teske, for your influence on my impressionable youth and for your lifetime of inspiration.

ROBERT GLENN KETCHUM

Selected Chronologies

Eliot Porter

1901 Born December 6 in Winnetka, Illinois; siblings include Fairfield, who later becomes an accomplished painter

1912–19 Receives a Brownie box camera as a Christmas gift from his parents

Photographs around Winnetka and on Great Spruce Head Island, Maine (family's island retreat); takes his first photographs of birds; becomes interested in chemistry while in high school

1920–29 Attends Harvard University and studies chemical engineering; interests broaden to include biology and physiology; graduates in 1924 and enters Harvard Medical School; receives MD in 1929

1928 Marries Marian Brown; Meredith born (exact date unknown)

1929–39 Researches and teaches bacteriology, biochemistry, and biophysics at Harvard Medical School

1930 Resumes photography after purchasing a Leica camera; Meredith dies of meningitis

1931 Eliot Jr. born January 21

1933 Charles Anthony born December 24

1934 Divorces Marian

Meets Alfred Stieglitz in New York City and Ansel Adams in Boston (ca. 1934)

1936 Marries painter Aline Kilham

Exhibition: *Exhibition of Photographs by Eliot Porter* (Delphic Studios, New York)

1938 Jonathan born March 25

Exhibition: *Eliot Porter—Exhibition of Photographs* (An American Place, New York)

1939 Father dies, July 30

Resigns from teaching and research to pursue photography as a career; begins photographing birds in color using Kodachrome film

1941 Stephen born July 23

Receives a Guggenheim Fellowship to photograph birds

1942 Mother dies, May 31

Exhibition: *Photographs by Eliot Porter* (New York Zoological Society)

1942–44 Suspends Guggenheim bird project and moves to Cambridge, Massachusetts, during World War II; works as a job scheduler in the Radiation Laboratory, Massachusetts Institute of Technology

1943 Exhibition: *Birds in Color: Flashlight Photographs by Eliot Porter* (Museum of Modern Art, New York, and other venues through 1944)

1944 Moves back to Winnetka and resumes photographing birds; occasionally makes color photographs of nature and landscape subjects

1946 Patrick born February 4

Moves to Tesuque, New Mexico; renews Guggenheim Fellowship to continue bird project; becomes Photographer-at-Large for *Audubon* magazine

Exhibition: *Leaders in Photography: Eliot Porter* (University of Virginia, Charlottesville, and other venues through 1949)

1951 Exhibition: *Color Photographs by Eliot Porter* (George Eastman House, Rochester, New York)

1952 Begins photographing almost exclusively in color

1953 Exhibition: *Birds in Color: Photographs by Eliot Porter* (American Museum of Natural History, New York, and other venues through 1957)

Book: *Land Birds of America* (New York: McGraw-Hill Book Company)

Portfolio: *American Birds: Ten Photographs in Color* (New York: McGraw-Hill Book Company)

1955 Exhibition: *Photographs by Eliot Porter* (Limelight Gallery, New York)

1957 Exhibition: *Madonnas and Marketplaces: Mexico in Color* (Limelight Gallery, New York)

1959 Exhibition: *The Seasons: A Photographic Essay* (Centerline General Store, Santa Fe, New Mexico, and other venues through 1960); refashioned in 1960 as *The Seasons: Color Photographs by Eliot Porter Accompanied by Quotes from Henry David Thoreau* (George Eastman House, Rochester, New York, and other venues through 1965)

1962 Book: *"In Wildness Is the Preservation of the World," Selections & Photographs by Eliot Porter* (San Francisco: Sierra Club)

1963 Exhibition: *An Exhibition of Photographs: Eliot Porter* (Art Institute of Chicago)

Book: *The Place No One Knew: Glen Canyon on the Colorado* (San Francisco: Sierra Club)

1964 Exhibition: *Eliot Porter Photographs, Aline Porter Paintings, Stephen Porter Sculpture* (Manchester Gallery, Taos, New Mexico)

Portfolio: *The Seasons. Portfolio One* (San Francisco: Sierra Club)

1965 Elected to the Sierra Club board of directors; serves through 1971

Exhibition: *Color Photographs by Eliot Porter* (M. H. deYoung Memorial Museum, San Francisco)

1966 Book: *Forever Wild: The Adirondacks* (Blue Mountain Lake, New York: The Adirondack Museum; New York: Harper & Row)

Book: *Summer Island: Penobscot Country* (San Francisco: Sierra Club)

1967 Receives the Conservation Service Award from the U.S. Department of the Interior

Book: *Baja California and the Geography of Hope* (San Francisco: Sierra Club)

1968 Book: *Galápagos: The Flow of Wildness* (San Francisco: Sierra Club)

1969 Exhibition: *Photographs by Eliot Porter, Paintings by Fairfield Porter* (Colby College Art Museum, Waterville, Maine)

Book: John Wesley Powell, *Down the Colorado: Diary of the First Trip Through the Grand Canyon, 1869* (New York: E. P. Dutton and Company; London: Allen and Unwin)

1970 Exhibition: *Eliot Porter: Nature's Photographer* (Museum of Fine Arts, St. Petersburg, Florida)

Book: *Appalachian Wilderness: The Great Smoky Mountains* (New York: E. P. Dutton and Company)

1971 Becomes a Fellow of the American Academy of Arts and Sciences

Exhibition: *Eliot Porter Photographs of Classical Greece and Asia Minor. Aline Porter Paintings* (St. John's College, Santa Fe, New Mexico)

1972 Books: *Birds of North America: A Personal Selection* (New York: E. P. Dutton and Company); *The Tree Where Man Was Born; Eliot Porter, The African Experience* (New York: E. P. Dutton and Company)

Portfolio: *Iceland.* Portfolio Two (San Francisco: Sierra Club)

1973 Exhibition: *Eliot Porter Retrospective* (University of New Mexico Art Museum, Albuquerque, and other venues through 1975)

1976 Exhibitions: *Eliot Porter Retrospective* (Santa Monica College, Santa Monica, California, and other venues through 1978); *Antarctica* (59th Street Gallery, St. Louis, and other venues through 1979)

1977 Book: *Moments of Discovery: Adventures with American Birds* (New York: E. P. Dutton and Company)

Portfolio: *Birds in Flight* (Santa Fe and New York: Bell Editions)

1978 Exhibition: *Mexican Church Interiors: Color Dye-Transfers by Eliot Porter and Ellen Auerbach* (Sander Gallery, Washington, D.C.)

Book: *Antarctica* (New York: E. P. Dutton and Company)

1979 Exhibition and book: *Intimate Landscapes* (Metropolitan Museum of Art, New York)

Exhibition: *Photographs of Maine by Eliot Porter* (University of Maine, Orono)

Portfolio: *Intimate Landscapes* (New York: Daniel Wolf Press, Inc.)

1980 Exhibitions: *Eliot Porter: Visual Explorations* (Art Center, Amarillo, Texas, and other venues through 1982); *Color Photographs by Marie Cosindas and Eliot Porter* (Art Institute of Chicago)

Book: *The Greek World* (New York: E. P. Dutton and Company)

Portfolio: *Eliot Porter, Glen Canyon* (New York: Daniel Wolf Press, Inc.)

1981 Exhibitions: *1981 Festival of the Arts: Eliot Porter Retrospective* (Sweeney Center, Santa Fe, New Mexico); *American Photographers and the National Parks* (Oakland Museum, Oakland, California, and other venues through 1984)

Book: *American Places* (New York: E. P. Dutton and Company)

Portfolio: *In Wildness* (New York: Daniel Wolf Press, Inc.)

1983 Book: *All Under Heaven: The Chinese World.* Text by Jonathan Porter (New York: Pantheon Books)

1984 Portfolio: *China* (New York: DEP Editions, Inc.)

1985 Exhibition: *Eliot Porter and Richard Misrach: Landscape and Color* (Film in the Cities, St. Paul, Minnesota)

Book: *Eliot Porter's Southwest* (New York: Holt, Rinehart and Winston)

1986 Exhibitions: *Eliot Porter's Southwest* (Museum of Natural History, Albuquerque, New Mexico); *Retrospective: Eliot Porter and Beaumont Newhall* (Photo Gallery International, Tokyo, Japan)

Book: *Maine* (Boston: Little, Brown and Co., A New York Graphic Society Book)

1987 Exhibition: *Eliot Porter* (Amon Carter Museum, Fort Worth, Texas, and other venues through 1988)

Books: *Mexican Churches* (Albuquerque: University of New Mexico Press); *Eliot Porter* (Boston: New York Graphic Society Books and Little, Brown and Co. in association with the Amon Carter Museum)

1988 Book: *The West* (Boston: Little, Brown and Co., A New York Graphic Society Book)

1989 Book: *Iceland* (Boston: Bulfinch Press and Little, Brown and Co.)

1990 Dies in Santa Fe, November 2; estate bequeathed to the Amon Carter Museum, Fort Worth, Texas

Books: *Monuments of Egypt* (Albuquerque: University of New Mexico Press); *Nature's Chaos* (New York: Viking); *Mexican Celebrations* (Albuquerque: University of New Mexico Press)

1992 Book: *The Grand Canyon* (Munich: Prestel; New York: ARTnews)

1996 Book: *Vanishing Songbirds: The Sixth Order: Wood Warblers and Other Passerine Birds* (Boston: Bulfinch Press and Little, Brown and Co.)

1997 Exhibition and book: *A Passion for Birds: Eliot Porter's Photography* (Amon Carter Museum, Fort Worth, Texas)

2001 Book: *Eliot Porter: The Color of Wildness* (Fort Worth: Amon Carter Museum)

2002 Exhibition: *Eliot Porter: The Color of Wildness* (Amon Carter Museum, Fort Worth, Texas, and other venues through 2004)

Robert Glenn Ketchum

1947 Born December 1 in Los Angeles, California

1952–66 Travels widely with his parents; attends Webb School of California

1966–70 Attends University of California, Los Angeles (UCLA); studies with Edmund Teske, Robert Heinecken, and Robert Fichter; publishes first photographs of rock-and-roll bands, including The Doors, Jimi Hendrix, and The Rolling Stones; receives BA in Design

Founds Sun Valley Center for the Arts and Humanities Photography Workshops

1971 Attends Brooks Institute of Photography in Santa Barbara, California

1972–74 Enters the graduate program at California Institute of the Arts, Valencia (CalArts); studies with Leland Rice and Ben Lifson; receives MFA in Photography/Design

1975–76 Joins faculty of CalArts

Elected to Board of Directors of the Los Angeles Center for Photographic Studies (LACPS), also appointed cochair of Exhibition Committee

Discovers historic estate and organizes first comprehensive exhibition of color photographer Paul Outerbridge Jr.

Joins staff of *Powder* magazine as Contributing Photographer

1977 Commissioned by the International Ocean Institute (Malta) to photograph aquaculture around the world

Portfolio: *Silver See* (Los Angeles: Los Angeles Center for Photographic Studies)

1978 Begins relationship with master printer Michael Wilder exploring Cibachrome material

Receives Lila Acheson Wallace Fund grant to research American landscape photographers and related development of the National Park system

1979 Elected President and Executive Director of LACPS; participates in the first photography exhibition ever displayed in the White House

Exhibition: *Seafarm: The Story of Aquaculture* (circulated by the Smithsonian Institution Traveling Exhibition Service, multiple venues through 1985)

Book: *Seafarm: The Story of Aquaculture* (New York: Harry N. Abrams, Inc.)

1980 Organizes James Van Der Zee retrospective

Appointed Curator of Photography for the National Park Foundation, Washington D.C.

Portfolio: *Winters: 1970–1980*

1981 Exhibition: *American Photographers and the National Parks* (Oakland Museum of California, Oakland, California, and other venues through 1984)

Book: *American Photographers and the National Parks* (New York: Viking)

1982 With William Clift and Stephen Shore, commissioned by the Lila Acheson Wallace Fund to photograph the Hudson River Valley

Appointed to the Arts Advisory Board of the University of North Carolina

Portfolio: *Selections from American Photographers and the National Parks*

1983 Completes and publishes the series *Order from Chaos*

Exhibition: *Robert Glenn Ketchum: A 15-Year Perspective* (Municipal Art Gallery, Los Angeles, California, and other venues through 1987)

1985 Commissioned by the Lila Acheson Wallace Fund and the McIntosh Foundation to photograph the Tongass rain forest of Alaska

Receives grant from the New York State Council on the Arts

Exhibition: *The Hudson River and the Highlands* (Albany Institute of History and Art, Albany, New York, and other venues through 1988)

Book: *The Hudson River and the Highlands* (New York: Aperture)

1986 First visit to the Suzhou Embroidery Research Institute of China

Exhibition: *50 Years: Modern Color Photography* (Photokina, Germany)

1987 Commissioned by the Akron Art Museum to photograph the Cuyahoga Valley National Recreation Area

Begins three-year residency program at Sundance Institute in Utah

Exhibition: *Robert Glenn Ketchum: 20 Years* (Gallery MIN, Tokyo, Japan; with complete catalogue)

Book: *The Tongass: Alaska's Vanishing Rain Forest* (New York: Aperture); copies sent to all members of Congress

1988 Receives National Endowment for the Arts and Wisconsin Art Board grants to photograph tallgrass prairie restoration undertaken by the University of Wisconsin

Exhibitions: *The Tongass* (United States Capitol Building, Senate Rotunda, Washington, D.C.); *Chinese Influence on American West Coast Contemporary Art* (Taiwan Museum of Art, Taichung, Taiwan)

1989 Receives Ansel Adams Award for Conservation Photography from the Sierra Club

Exhibition: *All Seasons and Their Change: Photographs of the Cuyahoga Valley by Robert Glenn Ketchum* (Akron Art Museum, Akron, Ohio, and other venues through 1992); additional solo exhibitions in Tokyo and Osaka, Japan

1990 Tongass Timber Reform Bill protecting one million acres of old-growth forest and establishing five new wilderness areas is signed into law

Begins national media campaign to protect the Tatshenshini River corridor

1991 Success of Tongass project prompts invitation to meet with President George H. W. Bush at the White House; receives Global 500 Outstanding Environmental Achievement Award from United Nations Environment Program

Exhibition: *Nature's Changing Legacy: The Photographs of Robert Glenn Ketchum* (Herbert F. Johnson Museum of Art, Cornell University, Ithaca, New York, and other venues through 1996)

Book: *Overlooked in America: The Success and Failure of Federal Land Management* (New York: Aperture)

1992 Commissioned to photograph the Presidio of San Francisco, extreme clear-cut forest activity in the Pacific Northwest, a large land development in California, and desert areas surrounding Saguaro National Monument considered for development

Exhibitions: *Another Perspective: The Photographs of Robert Glenn Ketchum* (National Museum of Fine Arts, Rio de Janeiro, Brazil); show mounted during the United Nations Earth Summit conference, travels to São Paulo and Brasilia; *The Legacy of Wilderness: Photographs by Robert Glenn Ketchum* (The Huntington, San Marino, California); *Between Home and Heaven: Contemporary American Landscapes* (National Museum of American Art, Washington, D.C., and other venues through 1995)

Additional solo exhibitions in New York City; Palm Beach, Florida; Pittsburgh, Pennsylvania; Denver, Colorado; Brazil; Germany; France; and Japan

Portfolio: *COLUMBUS—In Search of a New Tomorrow* (Germany: Edition Michael Domberger)

1993 Receives Award of Excellence in Professional Achievement from UCLA Alumni Association

National media campaign using photographs in support of Saguaro National Monument results in substantial acreage additions and an upgrade to national park status

Joins the Council of Advisors of the American Land Conservancy; becomes Contributing Editor at *Outdoor Photography* magazine

Book: *The Legacy of Wildness: The Photographs of Robert Glenn Ketchum* (New York: Aperture)

Select photographs are used in books as part of environmental campaigns: *Tatshenshini River Wild* (Colorado: Westcliffe Publishers) and *CLEARCUT: The Tragedy of Industrial Forestry* (California: Earth Island Press)

1994 Commissioned by William E. Simon, former secretary of the treasury, to photograph an expedition to the Arctic and through the Northwest Passage

Joins Board of Trustees of the Alaska Conservation Foundation

Exhibition: *The Tongass: Alaska's Magnificent Rain Forest* (National Museum of Natural History, Washington, D.C., and other venues through 2000); organized by Ketchum for Smithsonian Institution Traveling Exhibition Service; opens on Earth Day

Book: *Presidio Gateways* (San Francisco: Golden Gate National Park Association)

1995 Receives the Chevron-Times Mirror Magazines Conservation Award

Awarded honorary master of science degree by Brooks Institute of Photography

1996 Founds Advocacy Arts Foundation

Book: *Northwest Passage* (New York: Aperture)

Portfolio: *images beyond THE NAKED EYE* (Germany: Artists United for Nature)

1999 Commissioned to photograph southwest Alaska

Exhibitions: *Threads of Light: Chinese Embroidery from Suzhou and the Photography of Robert Glenn Ketchum* (UCLA Fowler Museum of Cultural History, Los Angeles, California); *China: Fifty Years Inside the People's Republic* (Smithsonian Institution, Arthur M. Sackler Gallery, Washington, D.C., and international venues through 2004)

Books: *Threads of Light: Chinese Embroidery from Suzhou and the Photography of Robert Glenn Ketchum* (Los Angeles: UCLA Fowler Museum of Cultural History); *China: Fifty Years Inside the People's Republic* (New York: Aperture)

2000 Receives Josephine and Frank Duveneck Humanitarian Award

Commissioned to photograph Wood-Tikchik State Park

Named Outstanding Person of the Year by *Photo Media* magazine; receives certificates of recognition and commendation for advocate work by the Santa Clara Board of Supervisors and the California State Assembly

2001 Named Outstanding Photographer of the Year by North American Nature Photography Association

Receives the Robert O. Easton Award for Environmental Stewardship

Exhibition: *Changing Perspective: The Photographs of Robert Glenn Ketchum* (Galerie Vedovi, Brussels, Belgium, and other venues in four countries)

Book: *Rivers of Life: Southwest Alaska, The Last Great Salmon Fishery* (New York: Aperture)

2002 Receives Lifetime Achievement Award in Photography and Conservation from Aperture Foundation

2003 Commissioned to photograph Piedras Blancas ranch, the private Hearst family property adjacent to San Simeon castle

Exhibition: *The Land Through a Lens: Highlights of the Smithsonian American Art Museums* (Samuel P. Harn Museum of Art, University of Florida, Gainesville, and other venues through 2006)

Book: *Wood-Tikchik: Alaska's Largest State Park* (New York: Aperture)

2005 Photographs assist American Land Conservancy in closing the largest conservation transaction in the history of California, the Hearst Ranch

Exhibition: *Southwest Alaska: A World of Parks and Wildlife Refuges at the Crossroads* (The Hoffman Gallery of Contemporary Art, Lewis and Clark College, Portland, Oregon, and other venues through 2010)

Library of Congress Cataloging-in-Publication Data

Rohrbach, John.
Regarding the land : Robert Glenn Ketchum and the legacy of Eliot Porter / by John Rohrbach with Robert Glenn Ketchum.—1st ed.
112 p., 30.5cm. x 25.4cm.
ISBN-13: 978-0-88360-100-6
ISBN-10: 0-88360-100-1
1. Landscape photography. 2. Nature photography. 3. Ketchum, Robert Glenn. 4. Porter, Eliot, 1901–1990 5. Amon Carter Museum of Western Art—Photograph collections. 6. Photograph collections—Texas—Fort Worth. I. Ketchum, Robert Glenn. II. Title.

TR660.5.R65 2006
779'.36092—dc22
2006001148

AMON CARTER MUSEUM PUBLICATIONS STAFF
Will Gillham, *Director of Publications*
Mary Jane Crook, *Editor*
Miriam Hermann, *Publications Assistant*

Editors: Mary Jane Crook, Will Gillham
Proofreader: Christine Valentine
Designer: Michelle Dunn Marsh
Production Manager: Stevan A. Baron

Unless otherwise noted, reproduction photographs by Michael Jones (West Coast Imaging) and Steven Watson.

This publication is produced in conjunction with the Anne Burnett Tandy Distinguished Lectures on American Art.

The Amon Carter Museum was established through the generosity of Amon G. Carter Sr. (1879–1955) to house his collection of paintings and sculpture by Frederic Remington and Charles M. Russell; to collect, preserve, and exhibit the finest examples of American art; and to serve an educational role through exhibitions, publications, and programs devoted to the study of American art.

Amon Carter Museum
3501 Camp Bowie Boulevard
Fort Worth, Texas 76107-2695
Tel: 817.738.1933
Fax: 817.989.5099

www.cartermuseum.org

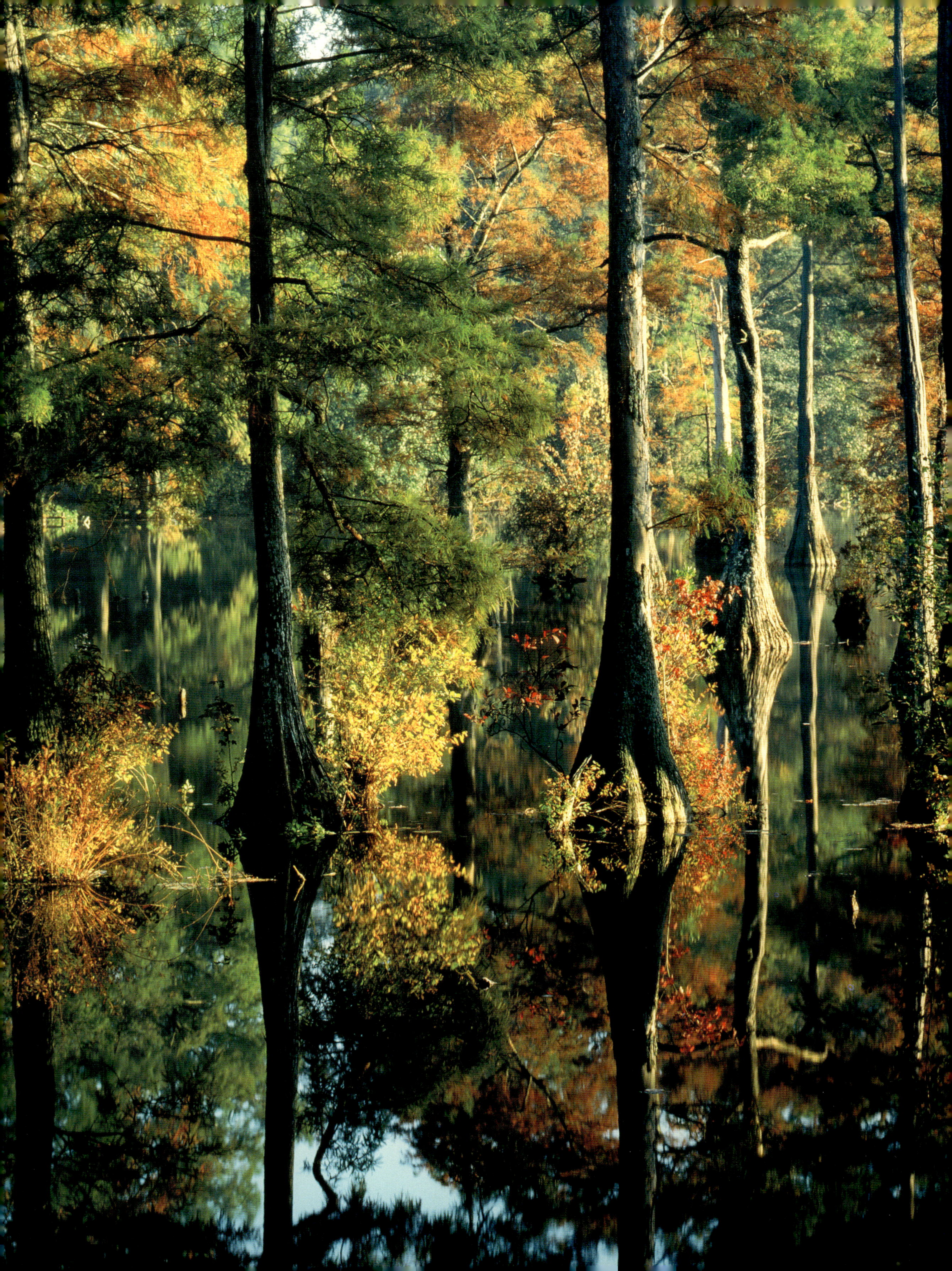

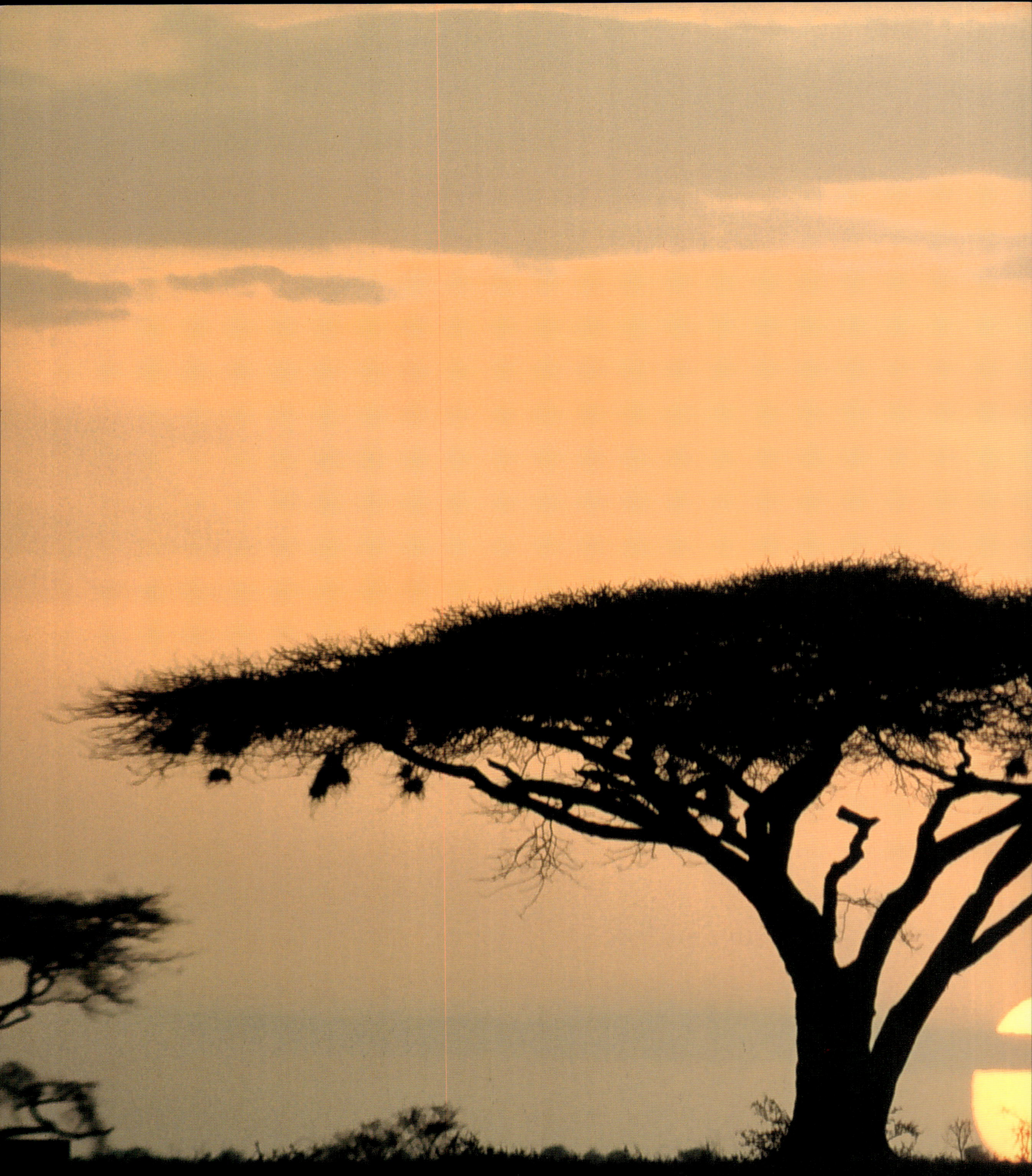

Tom Petherick

Trees

that shape the world

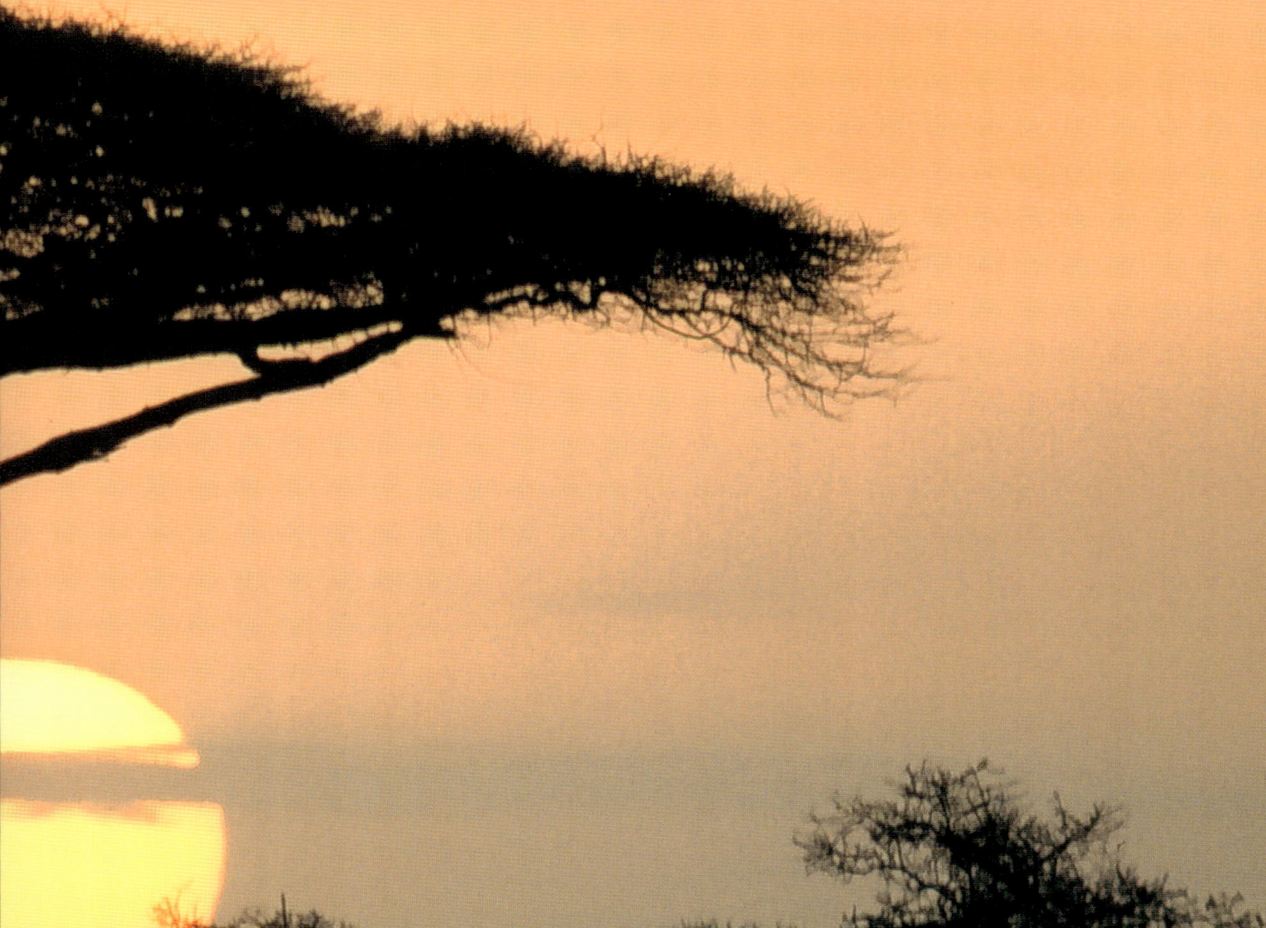

Quadrille

The paper for this book was produced at Oulu Mill in northern Finland by Stora Enso, one of the world's leading forest-product companies. Here the latest technology is combined with a practice of sustainable forest and land management that conserves biodiversity, soil and water resources and safeguards the health and ecology of ecosystems.

First published in 2006 by Quadrille Publishing Limited
Alhambra House, 27-31 Charing Cross Road, London WC2H 0LS

Reprinted in 2006
10 9 8 7 6 5 4 3 2

Project Director	Anne Furniss
Creative Director	Helen Lewis
Designer	Vanessa Courtier
Editor	Carole McGlynn
Picture research	Jess Walton
Picture research assistant	Samantha Rolfe
Production	Bridget Fish, Vincent Smith

British Library Cataloguing-in-Publication Data
A catalogue record for this book is available from the British Library.

ISBN-13: 9781844003174
ISBN-10: 1-84400-317-5

Printed in China

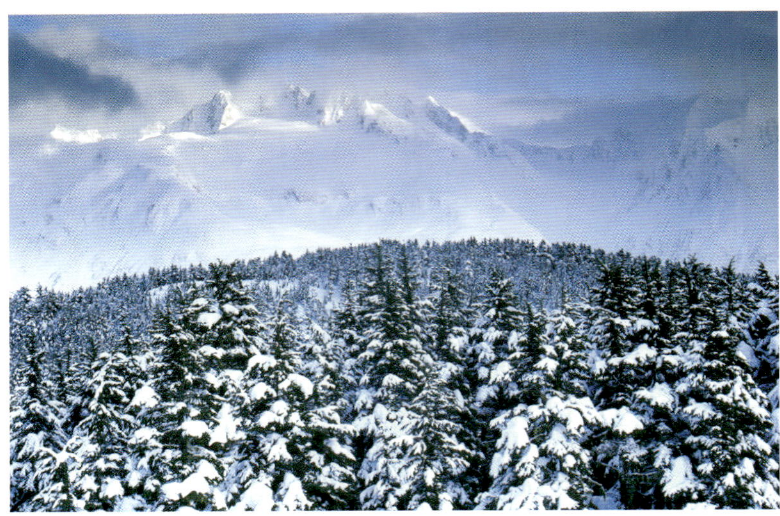

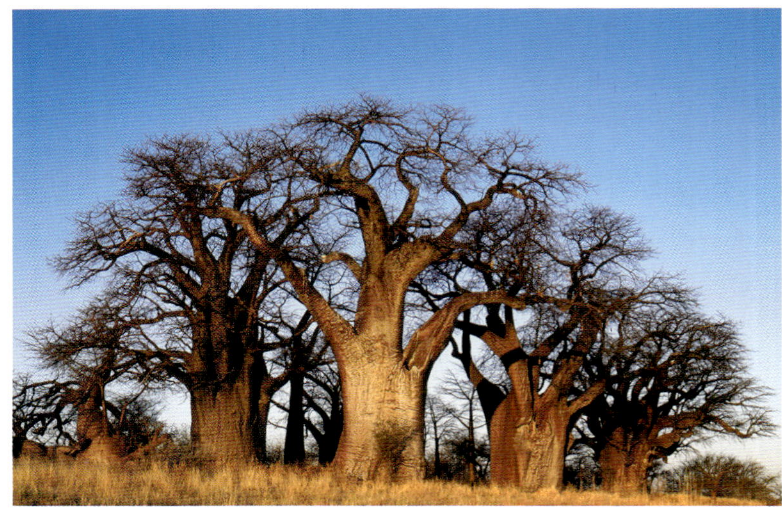

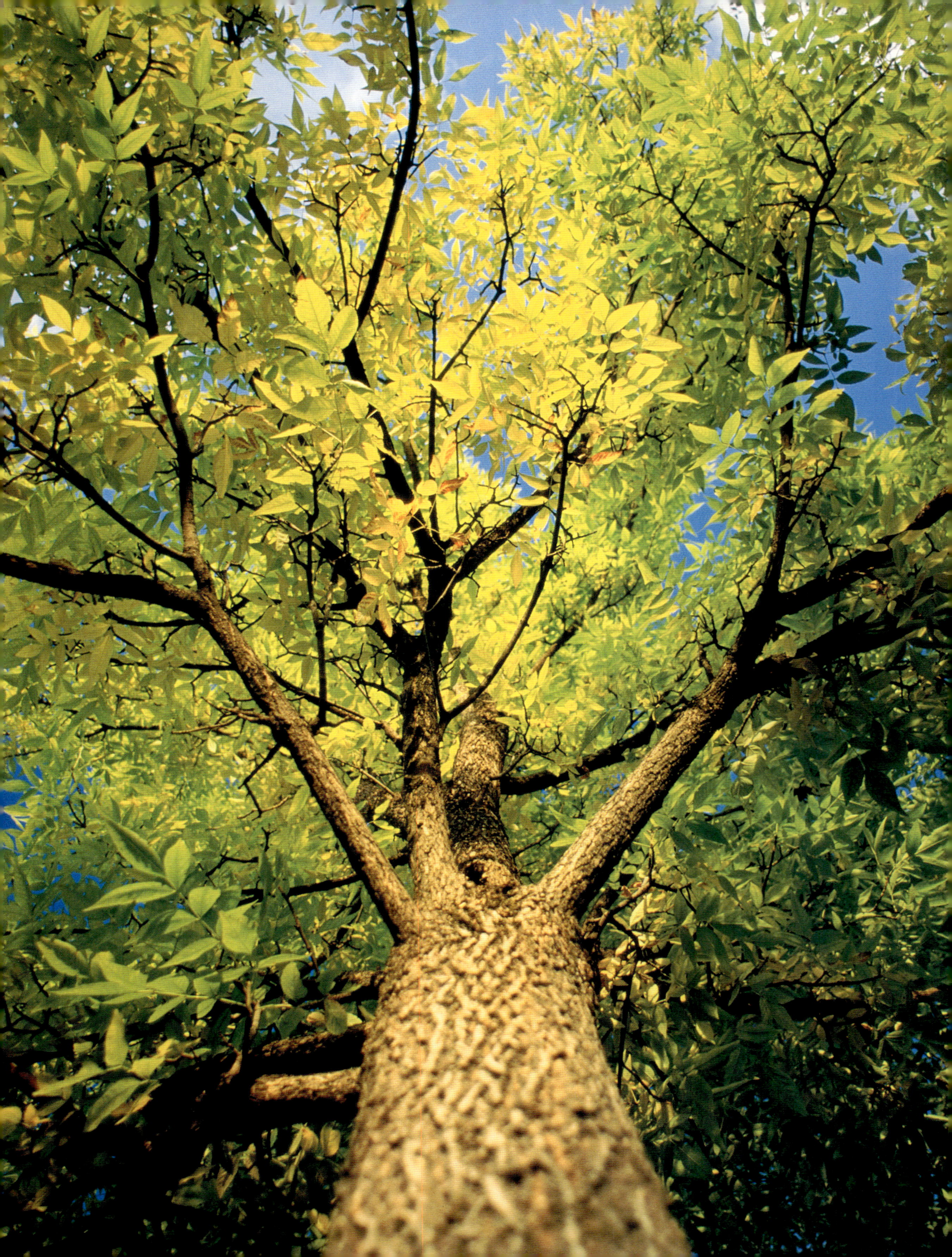

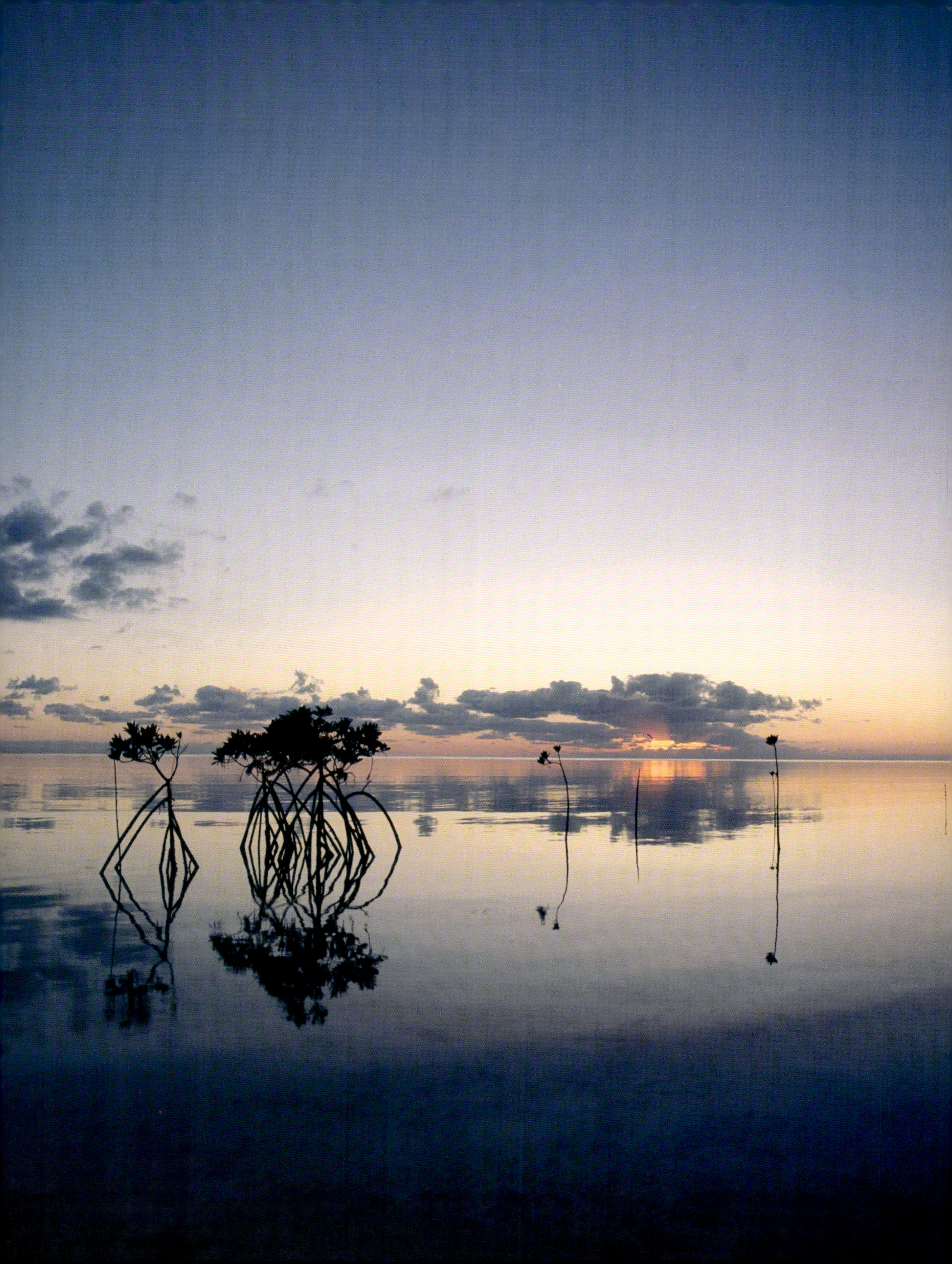

Introduction

Trees are our link between earth and sky; symbolizing strength, protection and longevity, they are vital in maintaining the balance of climate and fragile ecosystems of our planet. Not only are trees the most majestic and the longest lived of plants on earth, they are the most crucial and the most beautiful, their presence as natural and reassuring as the land, the sea and the sky. Surely all of us at some stage of our lives have marvelled at the sight, the sound or simply the smell of a single tree, the beauty of a wood or the stillness of a forest. We are surely at a turning point somewhere between confusion and the realization that we can and will harm our precious environment further if we continue to destroy trees at such alarming rates.

Our whole world is shaped by trees. Nearly every one of us has a connection, perhaps subliminal, with a tree or trees which may have been with us since childhood. For many of us in the 'western world' trees fulfil a decorative role. In our gardens and our public spaces we see them as living monuments of unsurpassed beauty which we hold in great affection. We feel grateful for their shade, their calming presence, their inspiration and their companionship. In the wider landscape we understand their roles as nurturers of the soil, as home to animal and insect life, and as providers for our own practical needs in the way of timber and firewood.

Trees are the most multi-purpose of all plants. From one apple tree comes a supply of fruit, sweet-smelling smoke from the burned wood, blossom to gladden the heart, insects to pollinate other trees, bees to make honey, grass which grows beneath in which animals may forage, mistletoe decorating and windfalls with which to make juice. To examine the role of trees from a global aspect was vital to be able to identify their true worth. Beyond our western world there are trees that serve so many purposes that they are completely indispensable to the communities they serve. Consider the coconut, a tree of which every cell is used in some form or another throughout Asia and the Americas. The fruit offers food and a nutritious drink, the shell is used to make household utensils, the leaves and coir furnish shelter and the trunk provides building materials, to name but a few of its attributes. There are trees in this book from all over the world, with extraordinary and diverse properties. Some heal, such as the gingko, while others soothe spiritually, like the Bo or peepul tree. Many produce wonderful fruit, others fix nitrogen from the air to fertilize the soil below, others, such as the mighty oak, have built cities and ships, and the timber of many trees has produced firewood to warm generations of people. Some will doubtless provide for our future.

Indeed, trees are our future, from the carbon storage that will help to alleviate the effects of greenhouse gases polluting our world to the medicines yet to be discovered in its rainforests. Such a future is one filled with excitement and permanence and the role played by trees is so important that their cultivation goes way beyond the decorative or construction use. The walnut (*Juglans regia*), which originates in both North America and China and grows throughout the temperate biome, has a calorific value far in excess of rice and potatoes and, given optimum conditions, a better yield. The comparison between a majestic tree that may live and yield well for 300 years and a field of annual-grown potatoes or rice with all their pest and disease problems, is pitiful. For the future we must look towards trees.

It was obvious to me, even at a young age, that trees were remarkable living things. As a boy, growing up in London, a gigantic sycamore tree grew in our garden. It was the first tree I came to know and love and was a source of immense pleasure throughout the four seasons of the year. In winter it served as the larger of two goal posts, soon the acid green foliage of spring proclaimed it as the herald to the summer which lay around the corner, and by autumn it came into its own producing pile upon pile of soft brown leaves into which we would leap and disappear. These were the first leaves that I would learn to turn into leaf mould for the borders in the garden and burn to add potash to the vegetable patch.

The book's structure allowed me to look at the planet's six major biomes and see the trees they are home to and what is happening to them in their environment. We begin with the snowy wastes around the roof of the world which we know as the taiga. Moving south over the globe, we come

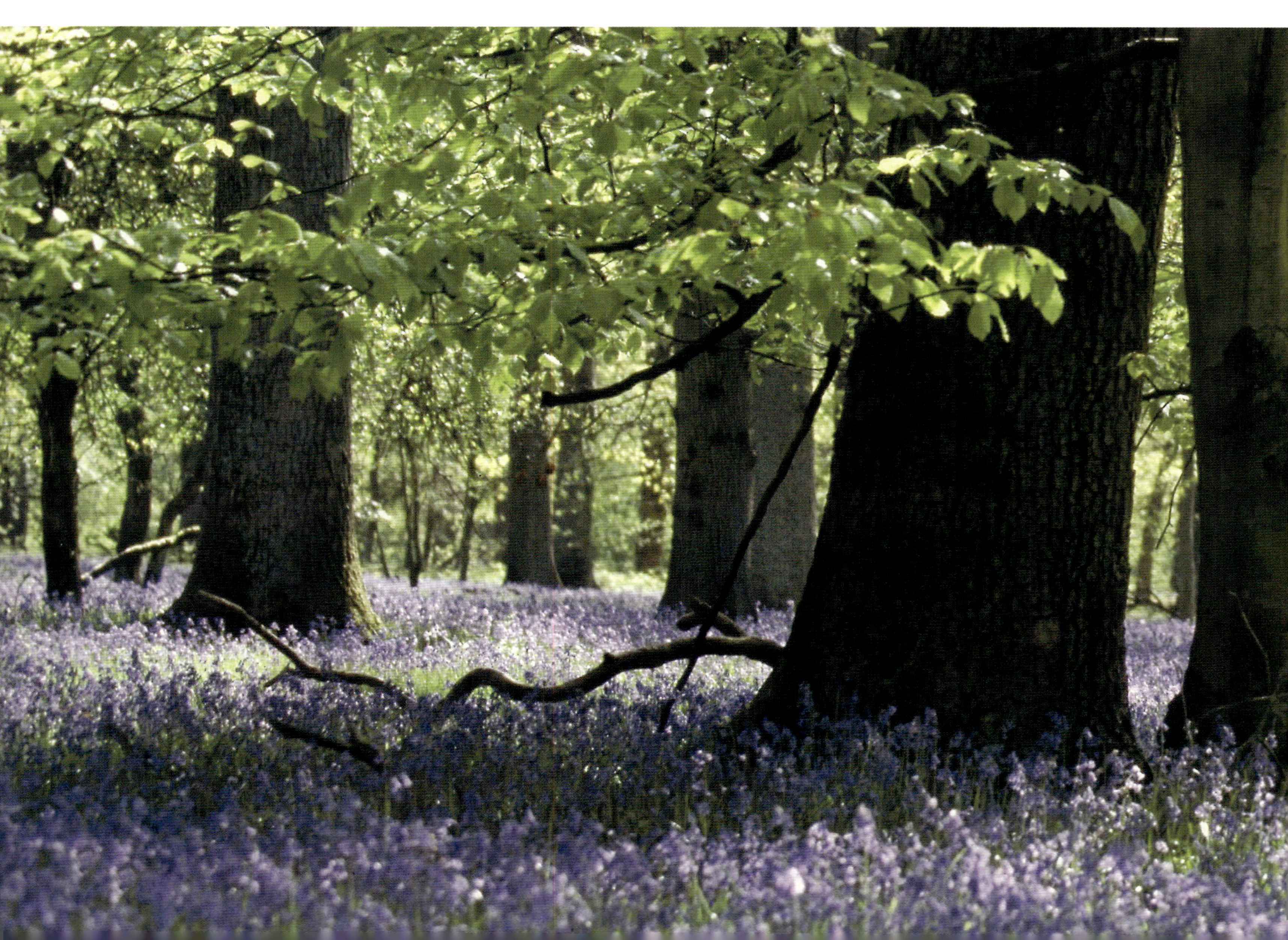

to the temperate biome which feeds further south into the Mediterranean. The monsoon forest, where heavy rains and baking heat make life hard for trees and people alike, covers huge expanses of Africa and Asia and leads on to the tropics, where the mangroves protect the coastline, and the rainforests, which cling to life in their ever-increasing fragility, call out in their hour of need.

Through the course of my life I have sat in, under and against trees that have sheltered generations of travellers and nourished countless hungry souls and I am continually moved by their strength and their calm. Trees help us to a closer understanding and awareness of nature, ecology and the environment and, for the sake of future generations, they have to be protected vigorously. I hope that next time you look at a tree you see in it a plant that shapes our beautiful world.

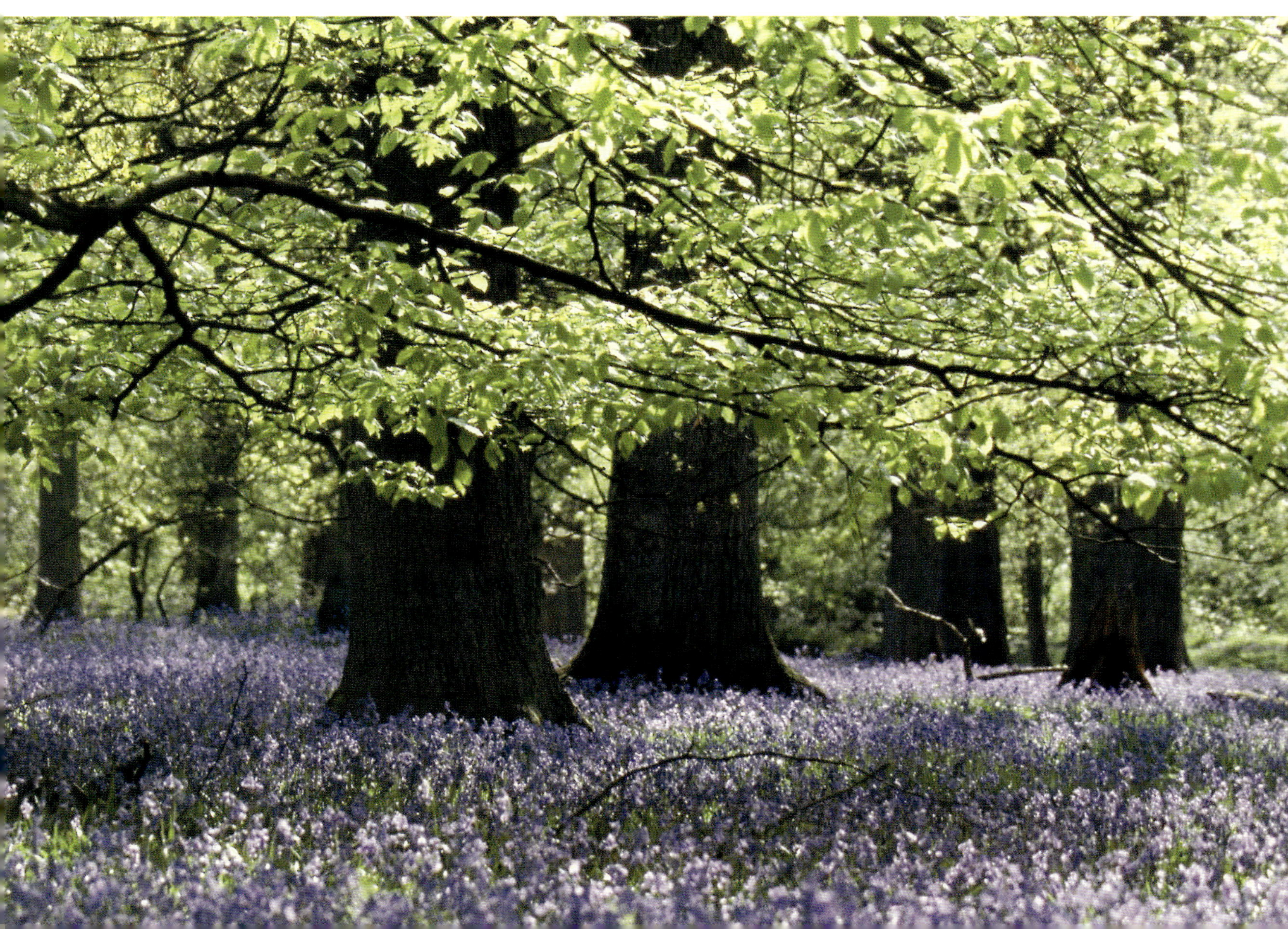

1

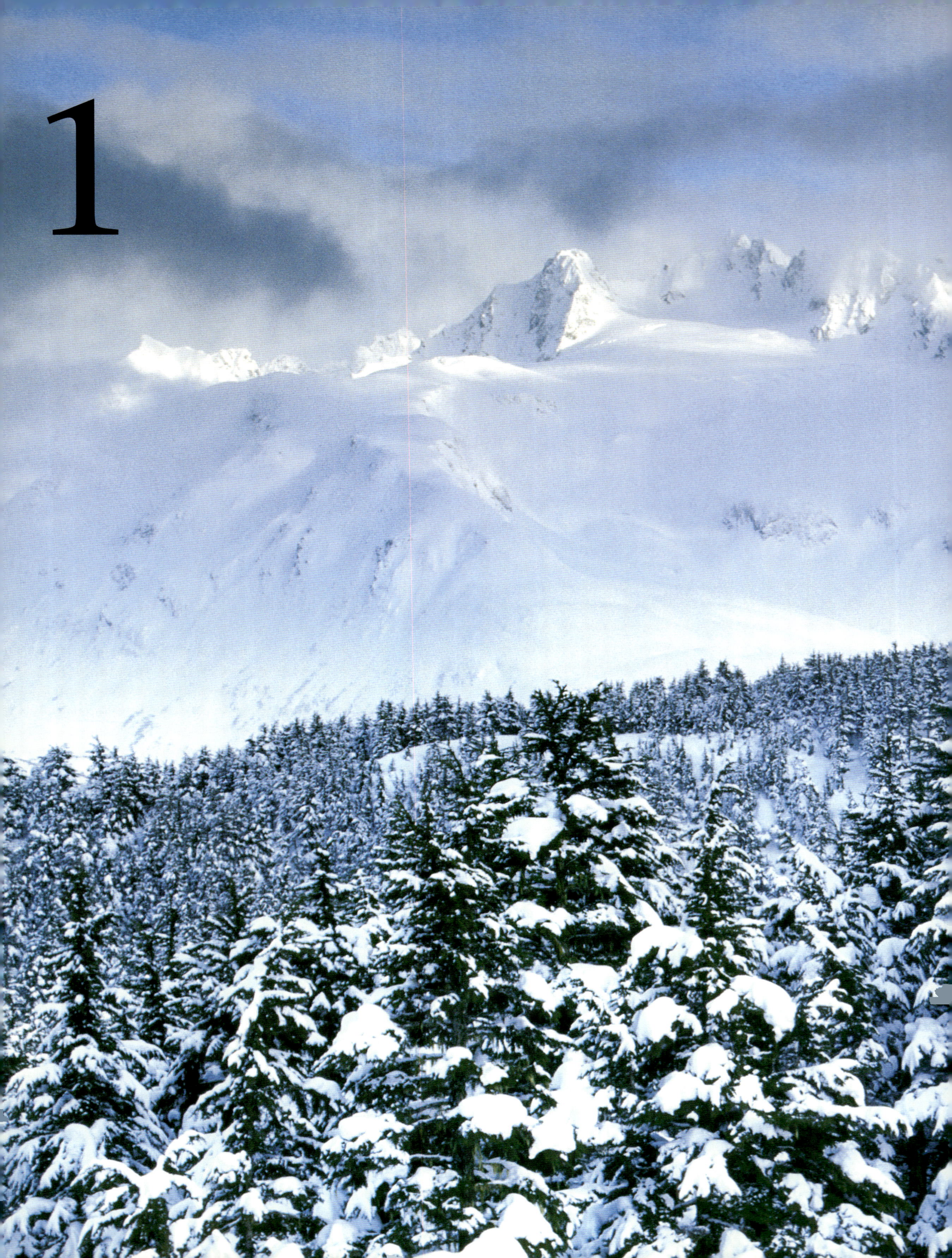

taiga

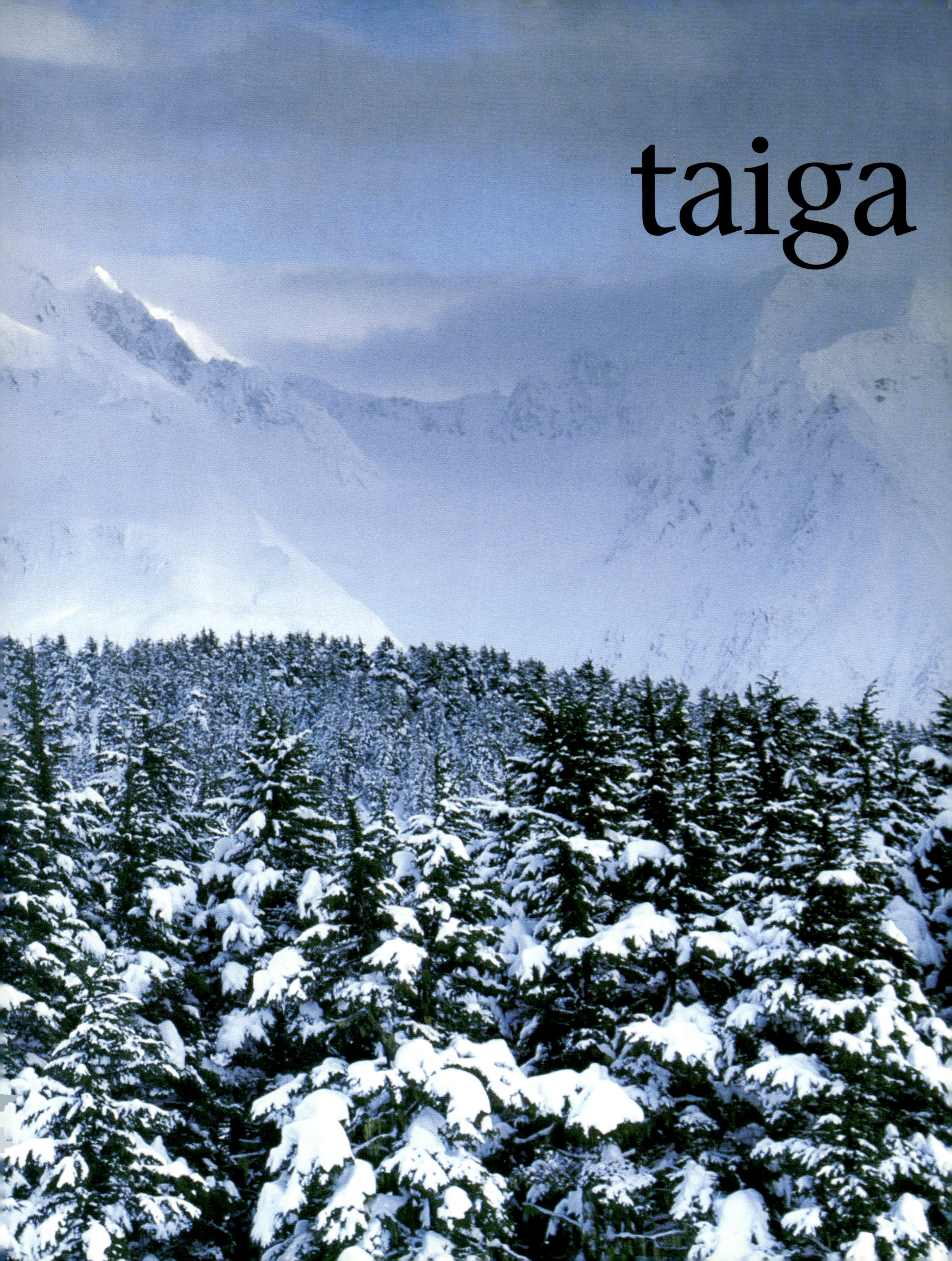

The frozen, snow-clad landscape of the Taiga biome (previous pages) is the harshest environment in which trees can be asked to grow. Freezing winters allow only the toughest of conifers to survive, their resinous trunks and minuscule needles well adapted to the bleak conditions in this biome that skirts the roof of the world.

The world's biggest and most important forest is concentrated in the sub-arctic northern hemisphere, at latitudes of up to 70° N. It is made up largely of conifers such as spruce, fir, pine and larch and covers thousands of kilometres through Asia, northern Europe and North America. Taiga is a Russian word that translates literally as 'a marshy forest in Siberia' (the name is also used in the USA to describe the sub-polar forests). The vast forests of the Russian Taiga alone stretch eastward from Murmansk through Siberia to the Bering Straits, some 6,000 kilometres, in parts 1,000 kilometres deep. A similar distance is covered in North America and Canada and large tracts of Norway, Sweden and Finland come under the blanket of conifers that are the signature trees of this mammoth landscape.

These are the unsung heroes that soak up the carbon dioxide launched into the atmosphere every time we turn the key in the ignition of a car

Why is this impenetrable mass of needle-clad forest so important? Simply because this great ring of trees that meets up around the top of the world plays a vital role in the stabilization of the planet. It is the biggest carbon sink of all, of far greater global significance than the Amazonian or any other rainforest, and it makes the Taiga our most important ally in the fight against global warming. And yet the work is not being done by rainforest giants or undiscovered rarities; it is common-or-garden trees such as the Norway spruce (*Picea abies*), the Scots pine (*Pinus sylvestris*), the common larch (*Larix decidua*) and its Russian cousin *L. sibirica* that are the foot soldiers in the front line of defence.

A polar climate

At its northernmost limit, the Taiga opens out and becomes interspersed with the oft-frozen wastes of the tundra. This is life on the edge, where few humans go, but the conifers that grow here are all well adapted to extreme cold. Temperatures in parts of north-eastern Siberia drop regularly to as low as minus 70° C and still the Siberian larch can withstand the permafrost and thrive. It is astonishing that any life can cope with such conditions, yet tiny tree-dwelling birds such as Arctic tits are as tolerant of the harsh environment as the huge lumbering white-tailed sea eagles that hunt the lakes, rivers and bogs of this vast untamed landscape. In the tundra, the only survivors are mosses, lichens, dwarf vegetation and the few animals and birds that live off the meagre pickings provided by this sparse cover. Beyond lies ice and, ultimately, the North Pole.

*Conifers such as the white spruce (*Picea glauca*) provide a cool., damp microclimate where mosses and ferns can spring to life on the forest floor in a brief summer.*

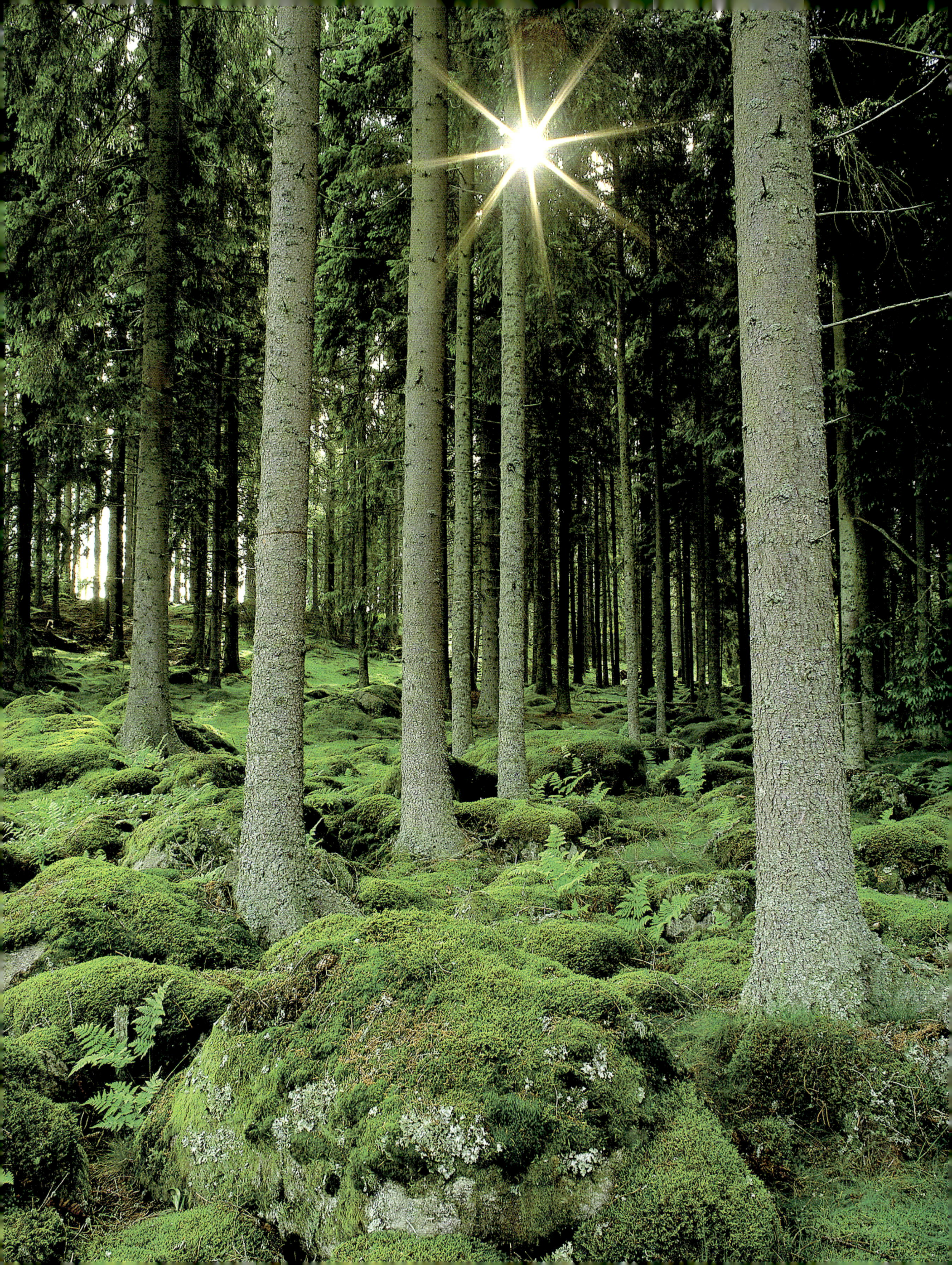

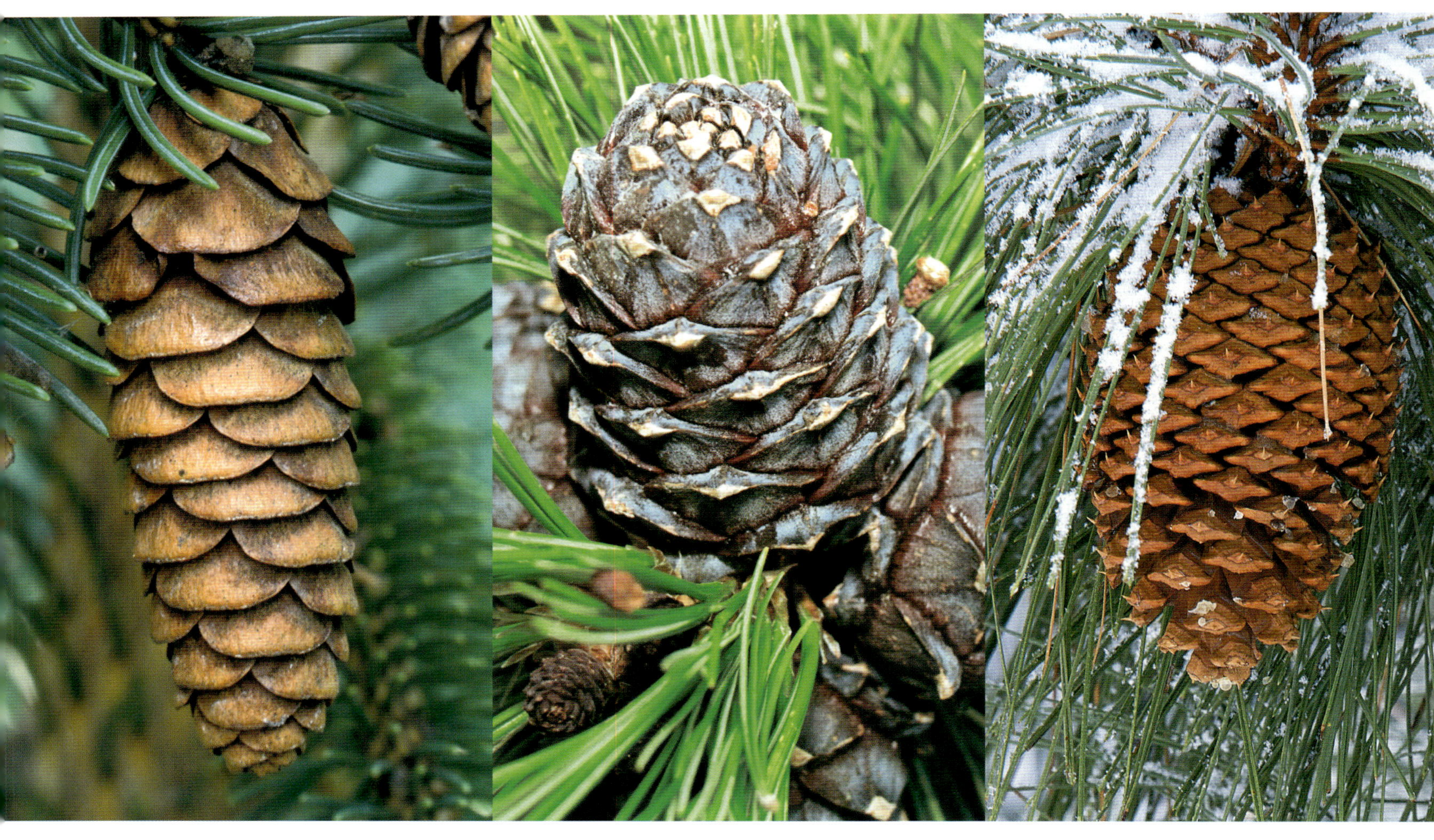

The tree species that survive here are not dull, indeterminate evergreens consigned to a snowy white wilderness. They are sturdy specimens of trees such as the Siberian cembra pine (*Pinus cembra* subsp. *sibirica*), whose pine nuts kept thousands of prisoners alive in the gulags during the dark days of Stalin, and the magnificent white spruce (*Picea glauca*), a towering conical tree which would grace any landscape in a cool temperate climate. Nor is the biome confined to conifers. At lower latitudes are deciduous hardwoods such as quaking aspen (*Populus tremuloides*) and sweetly scented balsam poplar (*P. balsamifera*) which mix with species of birch, willow, rowan and alder.

*Conifers are the dominant trees of the Taiga biome and their cones provide food for humans and animals throughout the harsh winters. Cones include, above left, white spruce (*Picea glauca*) and, centre, cembra pine (*Pinus cembra *subsp.* sibirica*).*

An environment under threat

The Taiga is strongly associated with forestry and that means the production of trees for economic gain. This is the forest that supplies the world with more than half of its roundwood (long logs or poles) and wood for paper pulp; it is in constant production, with the result that carbon is released

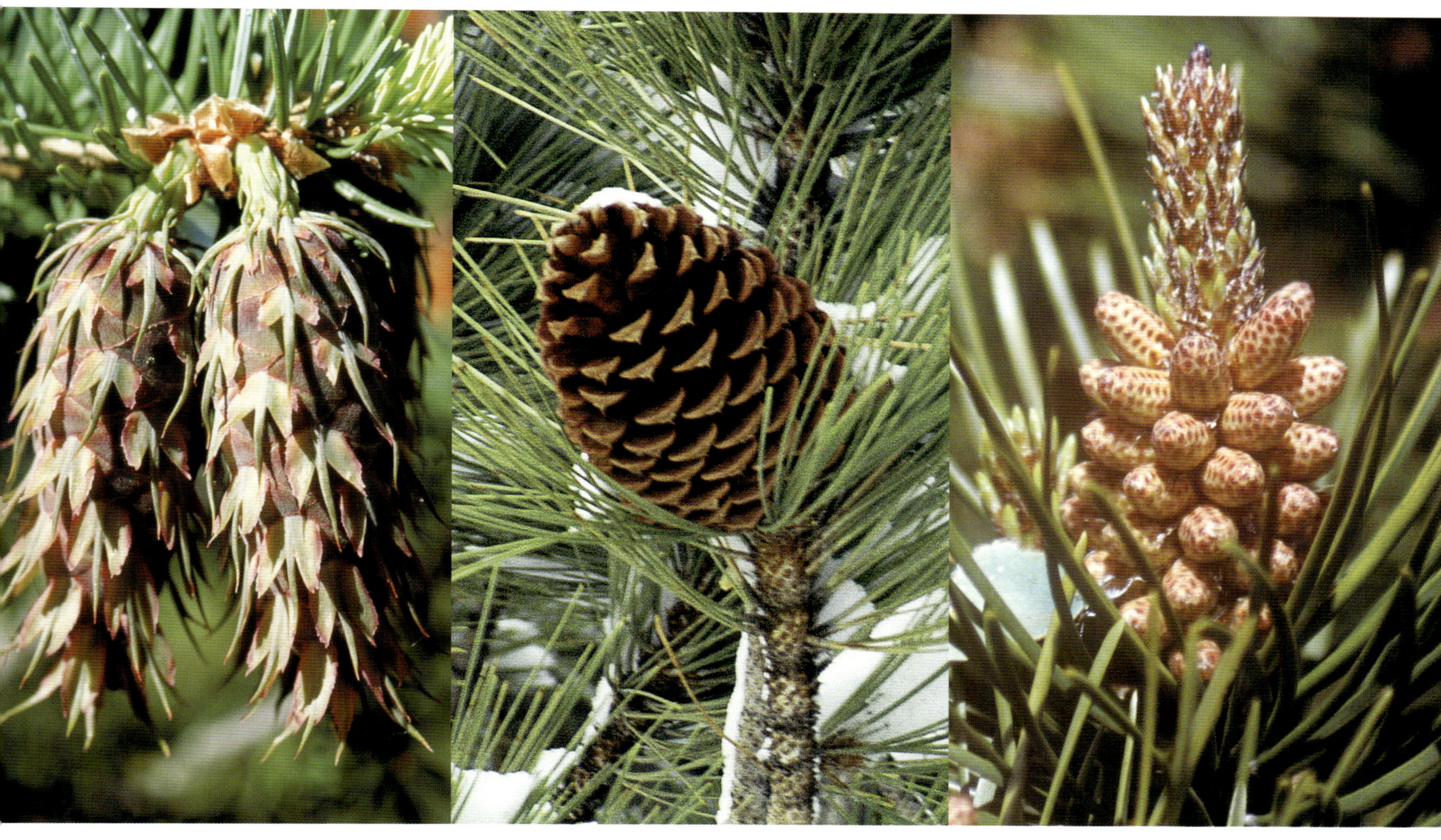

as the forest is cut down. While this is unlikely to change in the next few years, we can all work towards a more sustainable future for the biome by means of education and information. For this precious environment is seriously under threat.

Unsound ecological practices are common throughout the world of trees and the Taiga biome is no exception. Two-thirds of boreal forest is found in Siberia, where unlicensed logging and the extraction of minerals continues to cause wholesale damage. Policing extraction and export is problematic and huge quantities of illegally cut timber are regularly intercepted on their way to China. And such is the world demand for paper and timber that current estimates for the survival of the forests in this biome do not reach beyond 100 years, which would be catastrophic. Protection of the forest must be seen as a priority above commercial gain. On the positive side, President Vladimir Putin now recognizes the fact that the Russian Taiga is, in his words, a 'global ecological shield for the entire planet', which is why Russia finally ratified the 1997 Kyoto Protocol in 2005.

*Above left is the cone of the Douglas fir (*Pseudotsuga menziesii*) and, above right, of the Scots pine (*Pinus sylvestris*).*

In America the US Department of Agriculture's Forest Service is responsible for the national forests and these too are open to commercial forest harvesting. While they are properly managed under the Forestry Management Act, it is probably distance from markets which is the great saviour of the Taiga throughout the country.

In Scandinavia, where more than 90 per cent of the forests are managed, there is an optimistic outlook. Both Finland and Sweden have recent Forestry Acts which promote 'economically, ecologically and socially sustainable management and utilization, as well as conservation of biodiversity in forest ecosystems'. An outstanding example of good forestry practice is the reforestation of the Great Caledonian Forest in Scotland by the charity, Trees for Life. Formed in 1989, its aim is to return an area of 1,500 square kilometres, which was once made up of Scots pine, to natural forest. So far the charity has been responsible for planting more than half a million trees.

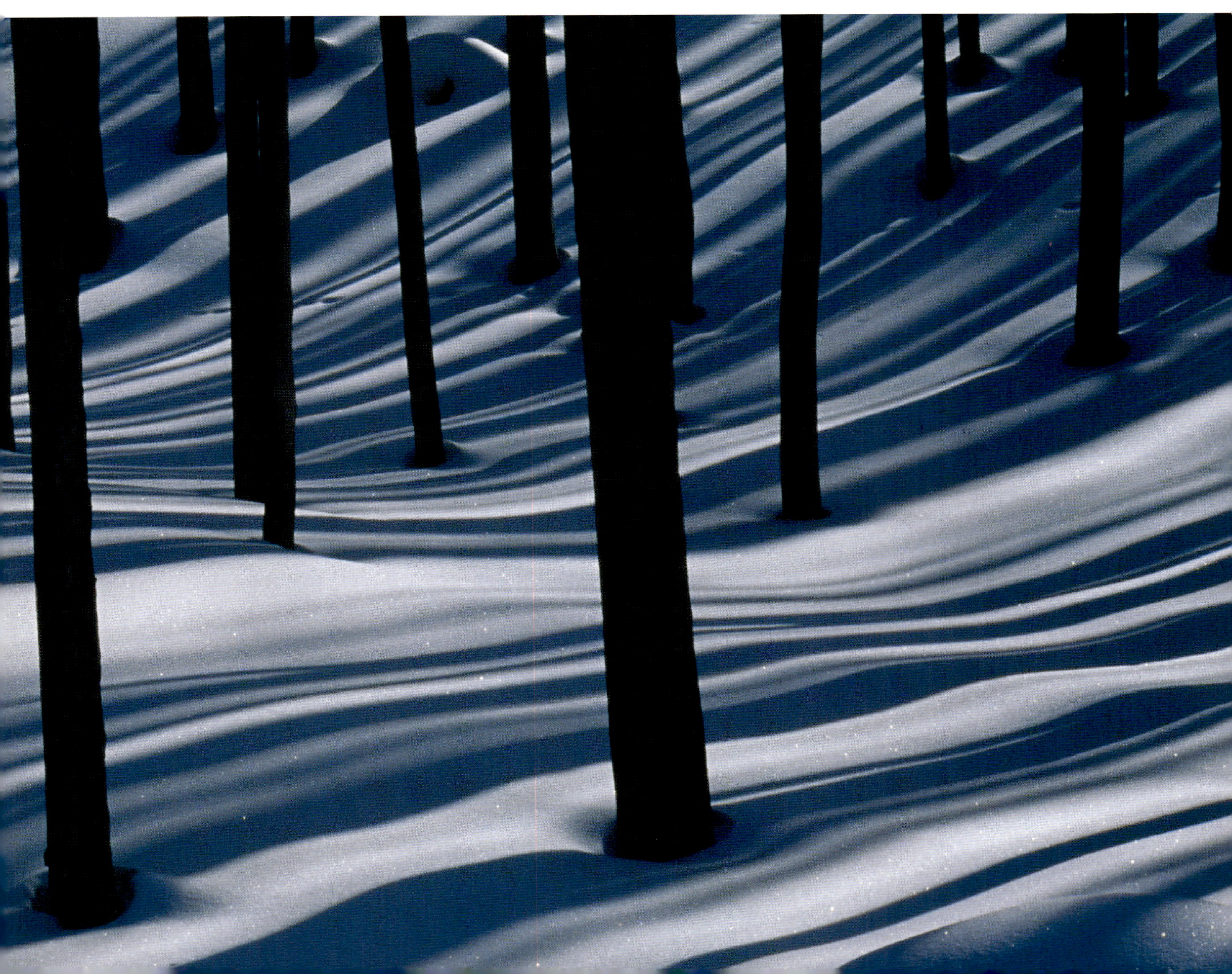

Positive initiatives

One organization promoting change through education is the Taiga Rescue Network who try to bring the ecological needs of the biome into the consciousness of those who work in, and exploit, it. TRN is a non-governmental organization which actively promotes sustainable forest management by encouraging the production of non-timber-based forest products. These include food such as mushrooms, berries and honey, oils for use in health and beauty products and in household items such as cleaning fluids and natural pesticides. These products, all of which are 'a viable and potentially profitable alternative to industrial timber harvesting', provide local communities with medicines, food and the raw materials to make handicrafts. Their promotion brings three vital forms of sustainability to the biome – ecological, social/cultural and economic – and continued development along these paths will help to safeguard its future and deserves our full support. The Taiga is not simply for logging: people, plants and animals live in this biome and they, as well as the trees, need protecting.

Meagre stands of conifers cast their eerie shadows on the white forest floor. In a deafening silence the trees stay deep in dormancy through the long winter, awakening briefly during summer when the sun gains enough strength for photosynthesis to take place.

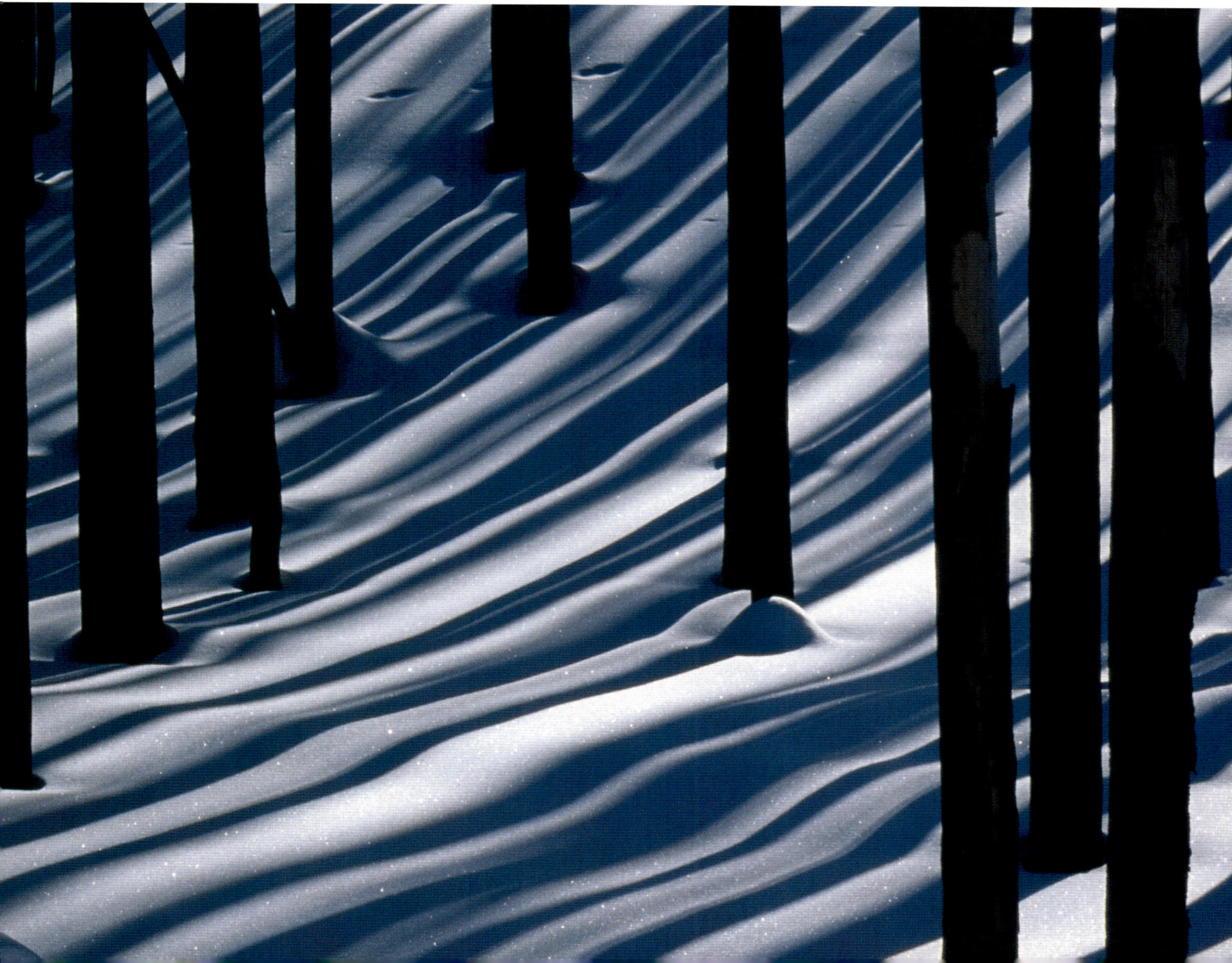

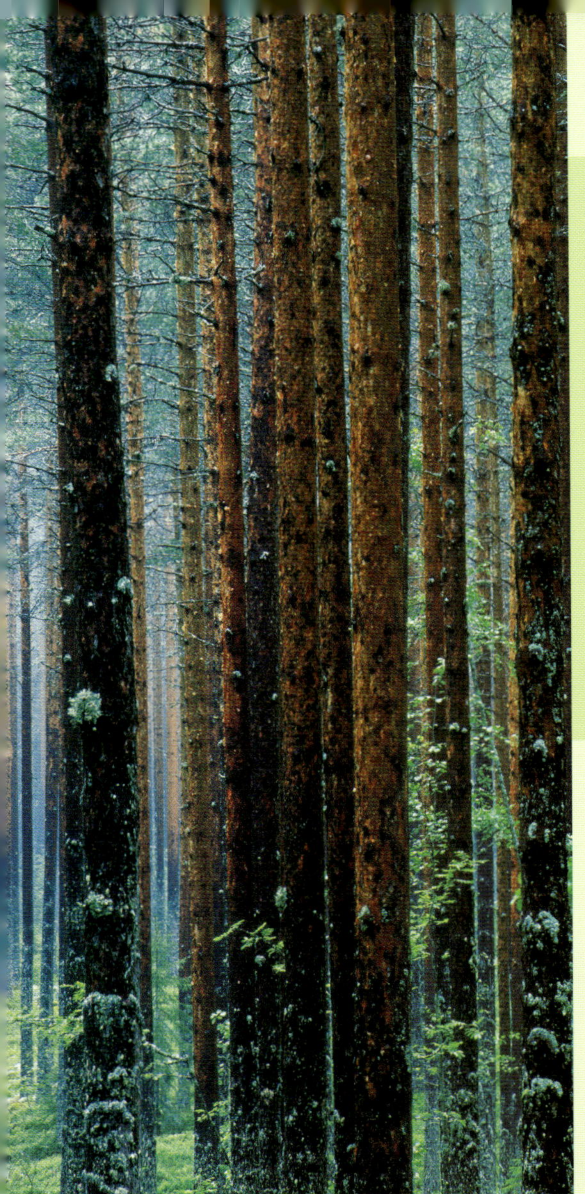

The Norway spruce (*Picea abies*) is the most widespread of all the conifers in northern Europe and the western end of the Taiga. We know this tree best as the Christmas tree and it is grown in plantations for commercial purposes all over the temperate regions of Europe and north Asia, as well as in the colder climates of the Taiga.

This is the major tree grown for timber in Scandinavia and eastward into Russia, just as the white spruce (*Picea glauca*) is in Canada and the United States and the Sitka spruce (*Picea sitchensis*) in parts of central Europe. The Norway spruce is a tall, stately tree with the classic conical coniferous shape; it grows, if allowed, to the great height of 65m. The best timber, which is straight grained and soft, often comes from trees that have been allowed to grow slowly in natural forest, up to an age of one hundred years or more.

A giant of the forest, it holds sway as one of the most important trees in these snowbound regions

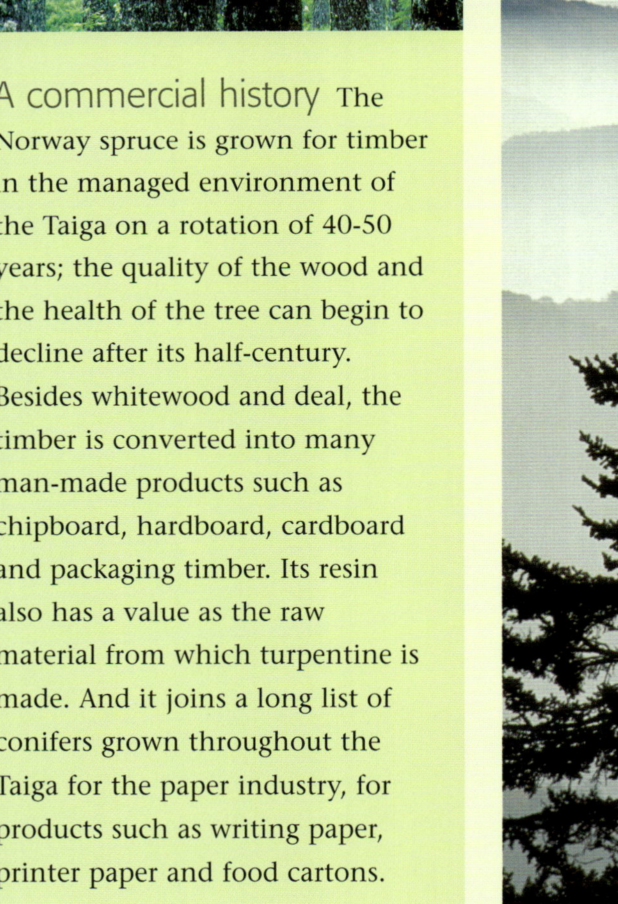

A commercial history The Norway spruce is grown for timber in the managed environment of the Taiga on a rotation of 40-50 years; the quality of the wood and the health of the tree can begin to decline after its half-century. Besides whitewood and deal, the timber is converted into many man-made products such as chipboard, hardboard, cardboard and packaging timber. Its resin also has a value as the raw material from which turpentine is made. And it joins a long list of conifers grown throughout the Taiga for the paper industry, for products such as writing paper, printer paper and food cartons.

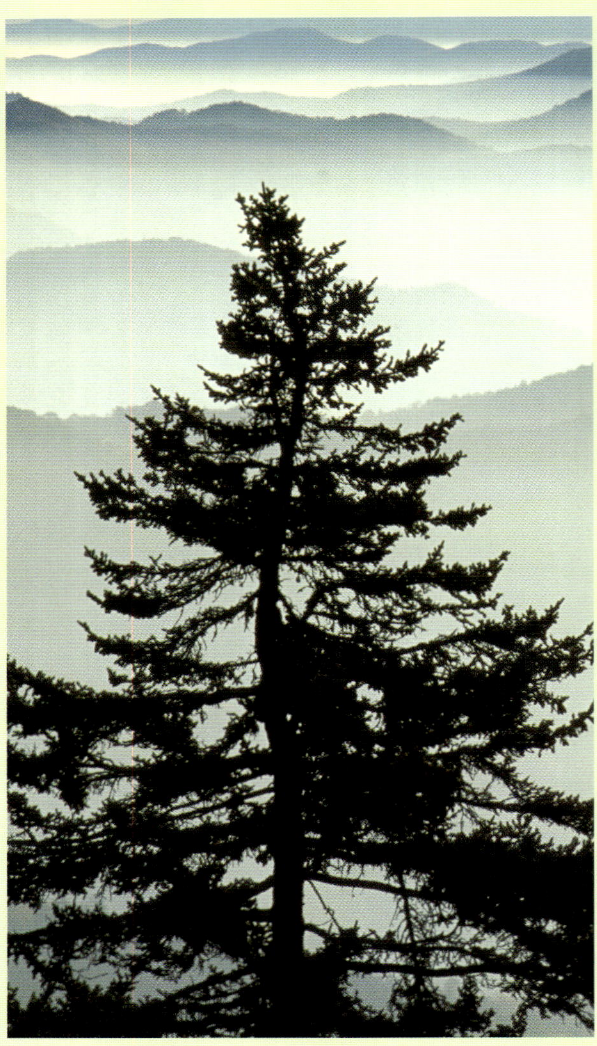

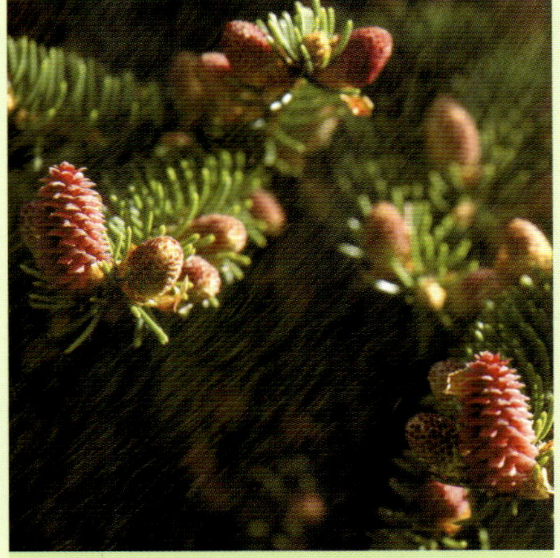

The Christmas tree

The Norway spruce is Europe's tree of choice for the festive season – a curious one considering that it drops its needles readily after a week or so in a warm room. In America it has been outstripped by 'non-drop' Fraser firs. The custom of using the Norway spruce for Christmas was introduced into England from Germany by Prince Albert, Queen Victoria's consort, in 1844, probably as a way of 'Christianizing' the pagan idea that the evergreen tree represents a celebration of birth.

norway spruce

The paper industry

Trees provide the primary raw material for paper, and the statistics concerning their exploitation in some parts of the Taiga make uncomfortable reading. Illegal logging is rife throughout eastern Russia and Siberia, for example, but once the timber is sold and exported it has been effectively laundered and nothing can be done. On the positive side, more than 90 per cent of both Europe and America's forests are new-growth managed plantations and, while this is less desirable than allowing protected virgin forest to grow freely, our desire for paper and timber-associated products is seemingly unquenchable and a source must be found.

Nonetheless, there is hope. Almost half of the worldwide paper industry's raw materials are made up of recovered fibres and, because of the biodegradable and recyclable properties of both the raw and the finished materials, the industry is well placed to work towards sustainable production. The sustainable production of timber for paper used simply to mean growing an adequate supply of wood, but it now incorporates social and environmental issues, such as the effects of production on indigenous populations, wildlife, water and climate. In the light of the role of trees as carbon sinks and creators of balanced ecosystems, as well as providers of fuel, food, water and shelter, it seems absurd that in today's advanced technological society trees remain the primary source of paper. Fibrous crops such as cotton and hemp have been used but wood is still the favourite source because of its year-round constant supply and its renewable properties. We must hope that, under carefully regulated plantation management that prevails across the Taiga forests of Europe and the United States, the sustainable production of timber and non-timber-based products will continue – an encouraging sign for the future.

Genetically modified trees

Unfortunately, that future has a sinister side. Management schemes are looking ever more towards the production of trees which have been genetically modified to contain lower levels of lignin, the glue that holds the fibres of wood together. Lignin is tough to break down and the process requires high-energy input. Lowering the lignin levels might sound laudable because of the lower levels of energy then required in processing the raw material. But there is concern for the consequences of many millions of acres being given over to a single species of a genetically modified tree planted en bloc. The tree in question is aspen (*Populus tremuloides*), a species which occurs naturally all along the southern latitudes of the United States and Canada, whereas the trees traditionally used for paper production throughout the boreal forests have been spruce, pine, fir and larch. We must be perpetually on the lookout for, and avoid buying, all genetically modified timber products, for this type of cultivation has absolutely no future. Because we live in a society with ever-increasing levels of consumption and highly developed but ruthless economies, we know that the paper problem needs addressing at source – that is, by each and every one of us using less paper.

The aspen (overleaf) is one of the most belligerent survivors growing on the lower edges of the Taiga biome. Tough, hardy and very happy in the wet and boggy conditions it finds through all seasons outside of winter, it is one of only a handful of non-coniferous trees that flourish in the Taiga's North American and Canadian stretches. Here it is seen growing in the Rocky Mountains of North America.

...we must learn to consume less, starting by writing on both sides of the next sheet of paper that we use

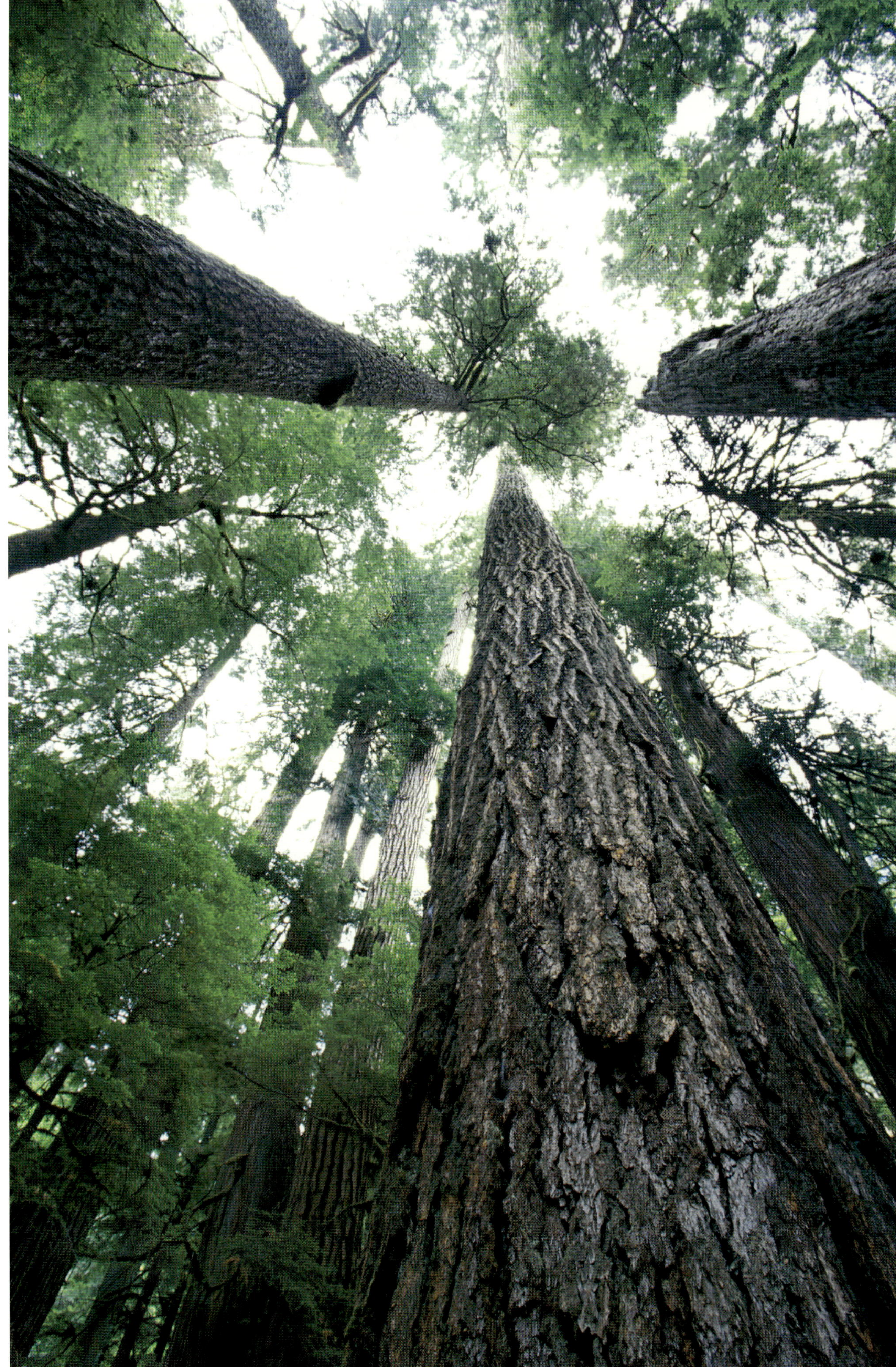

The Douglas fir has traditionally been one of the great trees for the paper industry. Now superseded by fast-growing species such as the Sitka spruce, the find of the great Scottish plant hunter David Douglas still remains a popular ornamental conifer in the parks and gardens of Europe and North America.

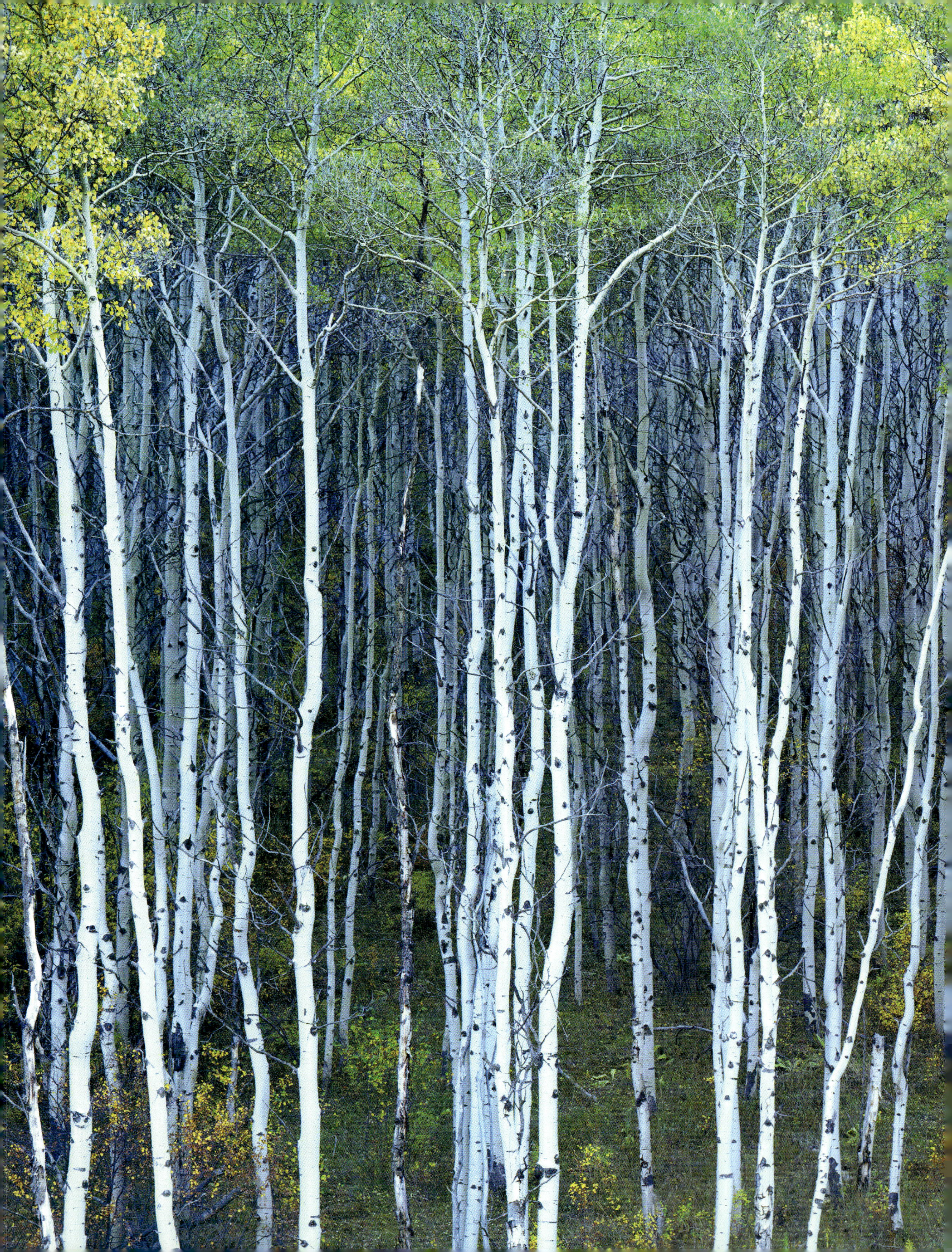

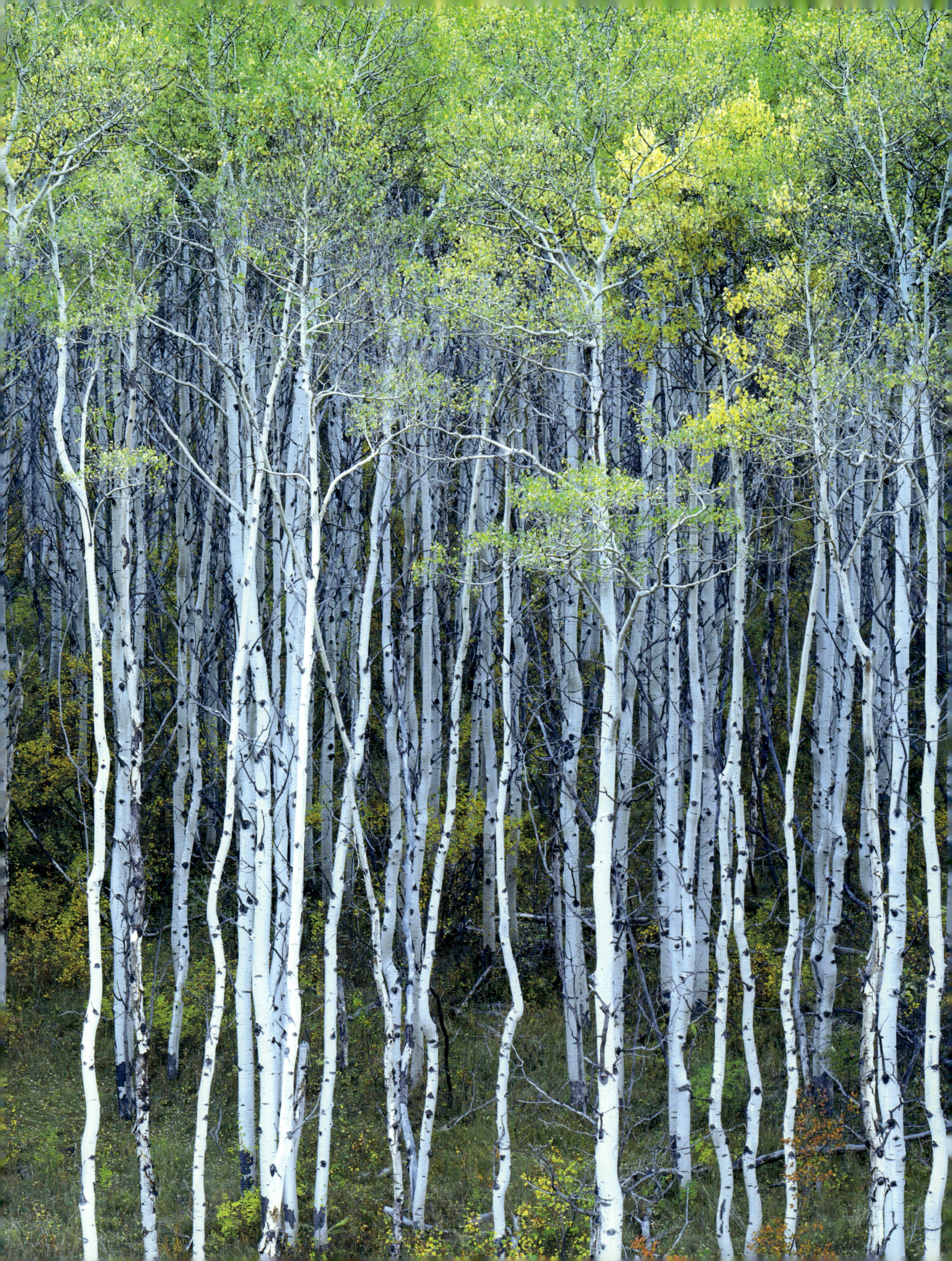

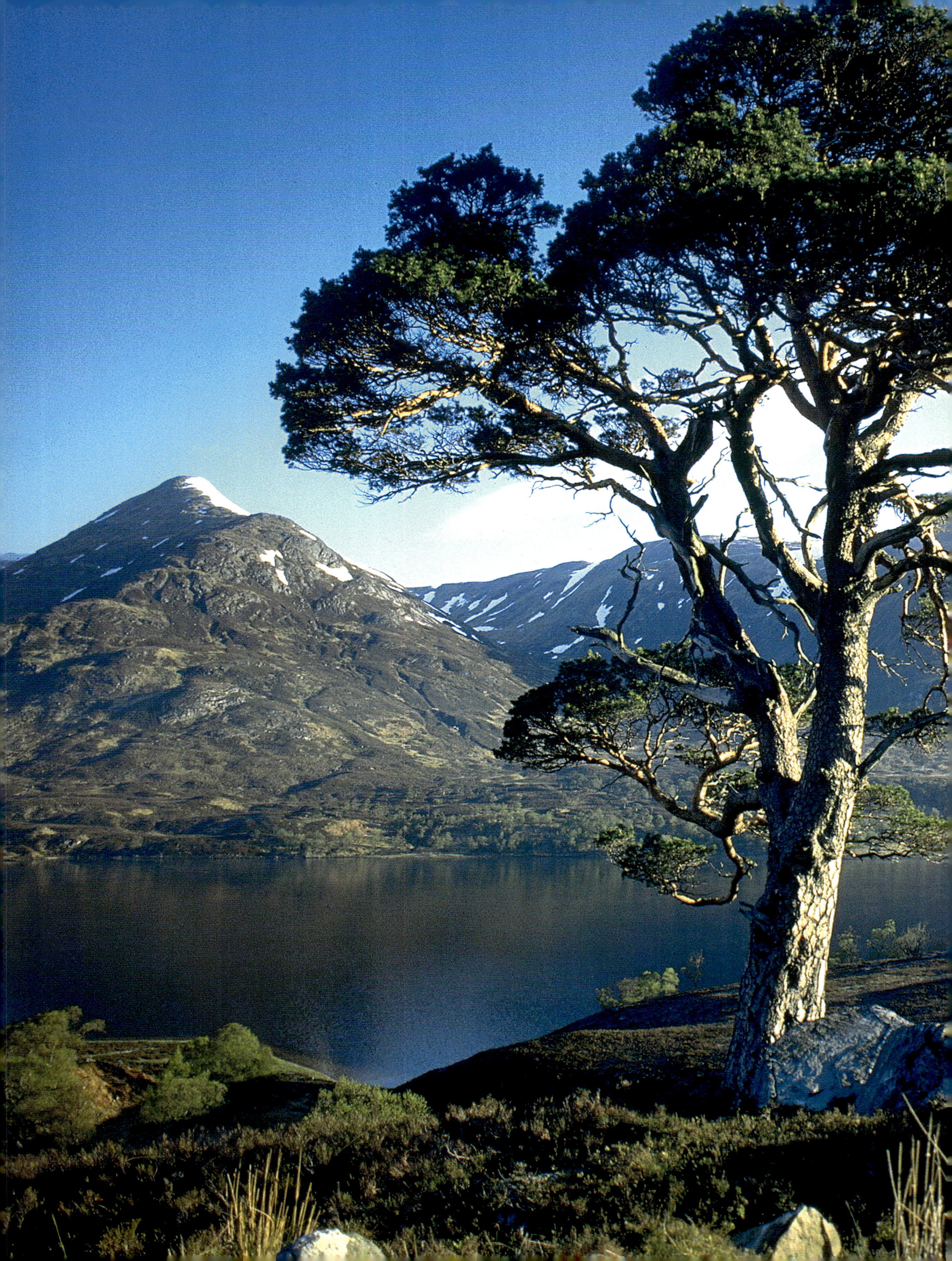

scots pine

The Scots pine is the sole northern European pine to have survived the last Ice Age

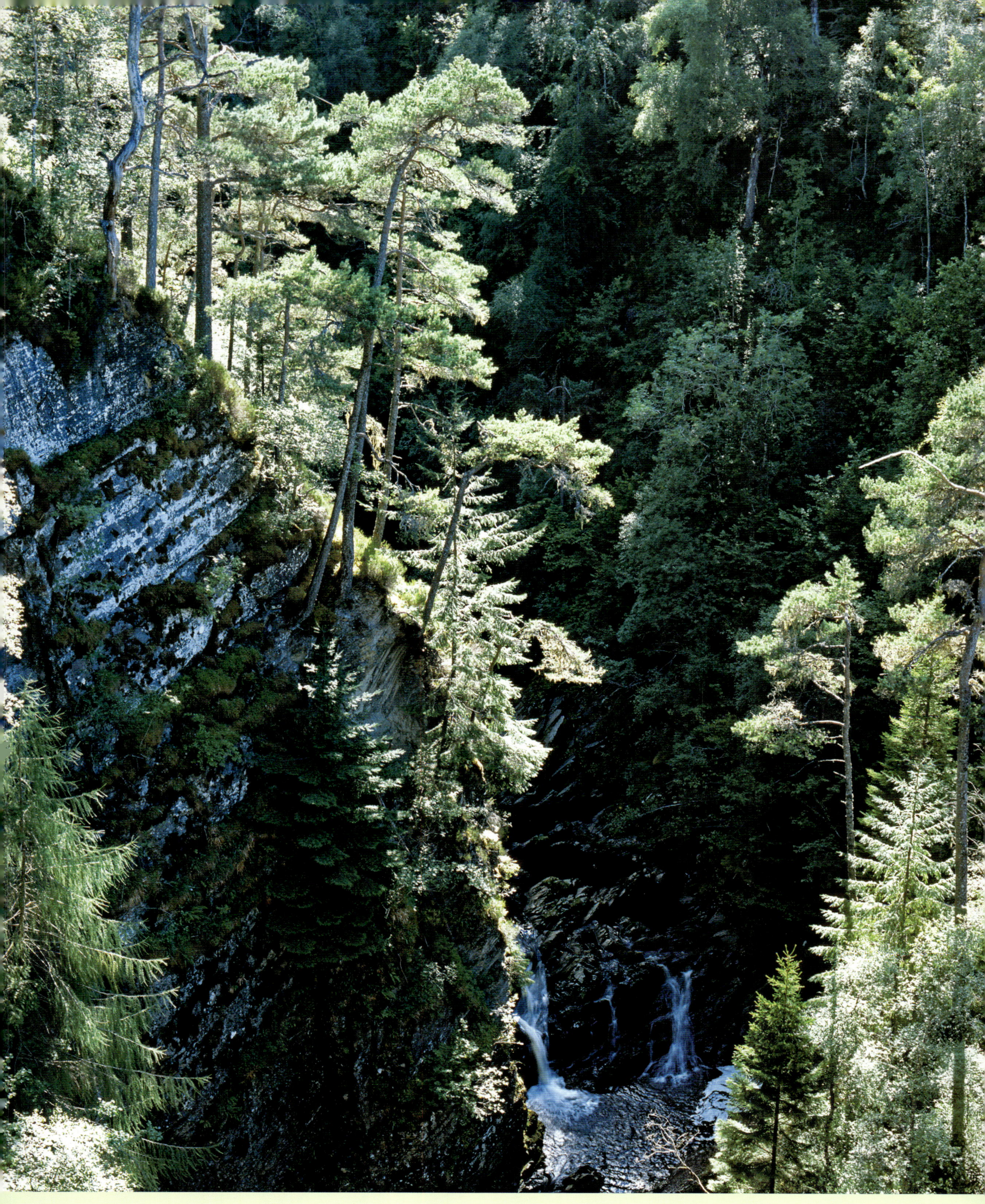

scots pine

The distinctive Scots pine (*Pinus sylvestris*) is found all over the European and Russian areas of the Taiga biome, because of unique characteristics which allow it to cope with the conditions. Hardy and adaptable to all soil types, it puts down a deep tap root which enables it to withstand the high winds of the exposed areas where it is found. The Scots pine is the sole northern European pine to have survived the last Ice Age, which makes it not only a European native but also the only pine tree native to the British Isles. One of the most beautiful of all pines, the Scots pine has a well-defined profile with an engaging growing habit which differs entirely from most of the conical coniferous trees which cover the Taiga biome.

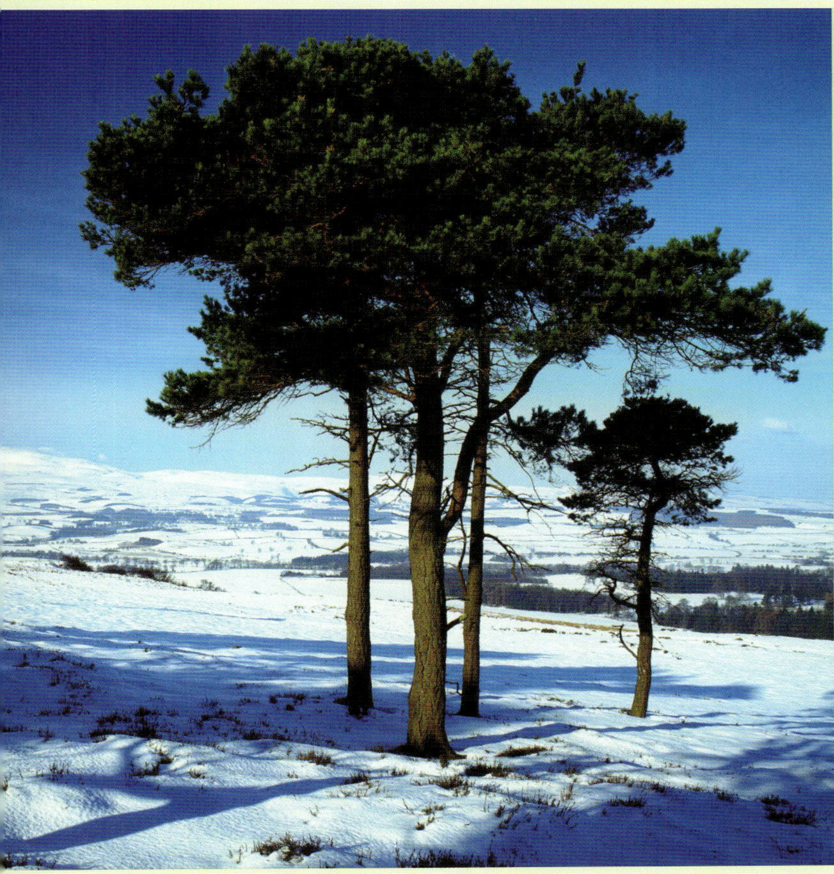

Unlike the spruces and larches of the region, it does not have a conical shape but rather its branches are horizontally layered, spreading out from the main trunk in a non-conformist fashion. The bark is a rich red and the tree is generally unmistakable. As it ages and reaches the considerable height of 25-35m, the lower branches have a tendency to die and drop off, leaving a flat green top and a bare, straight stem which endears the Scots pine to the timber trade.

From its ancient origins to a time when some 80 per cent of northern Europe was covered in forest, the Scots pine has witnessed the devastating effects wreaked by man on the trees that so nobly supported him. European forests have been cleared for agriculture and timber since Neolithic times and served some of the earliest foreign arrivals to northern England and Scotland, the fearsome Vikings. This warlike race, familiar with the tree from their native Scandinavia, felled it for the prows of their longboats and gathered the fly agaric mushroom which grows at the base of the trees to ingest before battle to give them strength.

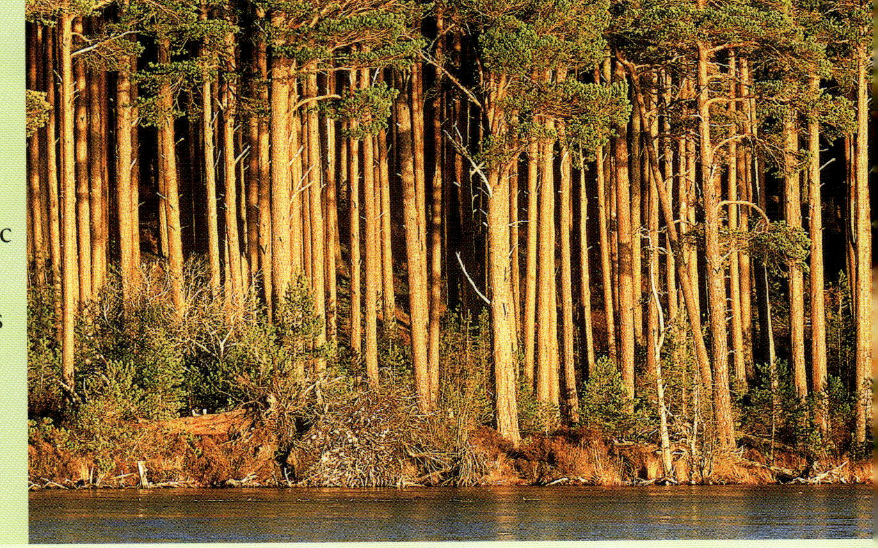

scots pine

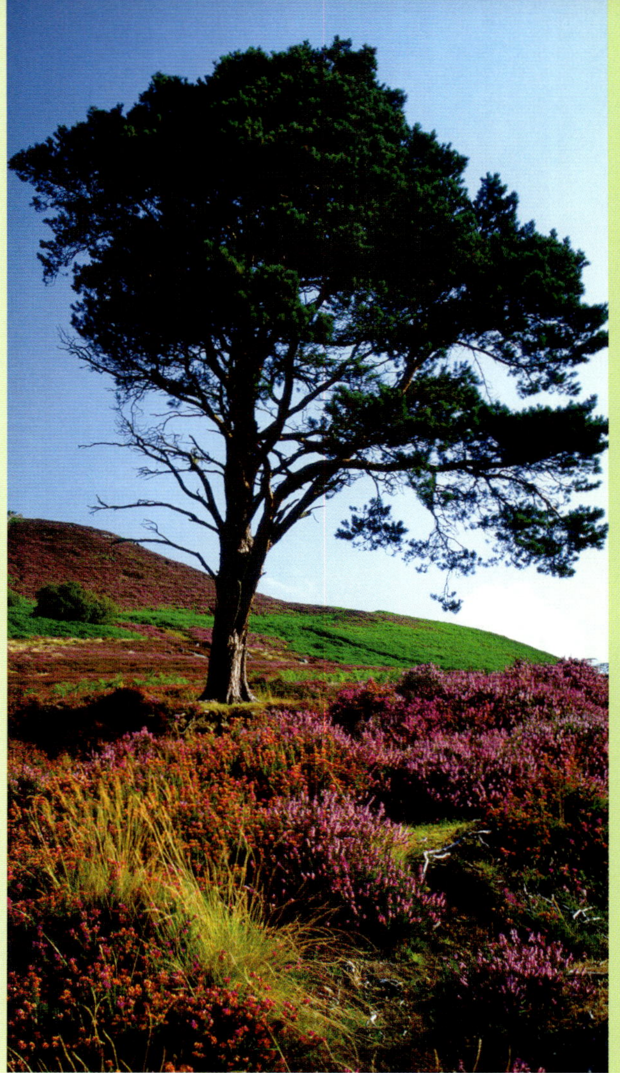

The Scots pine is the subject of one of the most uplifting tree projects currently happening anywhere in the world

Replanting the forest The scheme to replant the native Caledonian Forest of Scotland is a pioneering one in the field of ecological restoration. It is being undertaken by the charity, Trees for Life, based at Findhorn Bay on the Moray Firth coast in north-east Scotland.

The project started in 1989. Considering that native pinewoods are thought to have covered some 1.5 million hectares of the westernmost reaches of Taiga forest in Europe, it is a momentous task. Ever since the Highland Clearances began in 1745, the decline of the forest had been steady and the introduction of sheep put paid to any chance of the forest regenerating itself. The disappearance of predators such as wolves also led to a sharp increase in the number of red deer which, with the sheep, made regrowth almost impossible.

Over the last 30 years, fencing work has been done to keep deer and sheep out of what remains of old-growth forest and, while some regrowth started to take place, the animal numbers grew too high and made the task impossible. The aim of Trees for Life is to link new growth with remaining old forest and to return the chosen areas to wilderness, so that in time the wildlife may also come back.

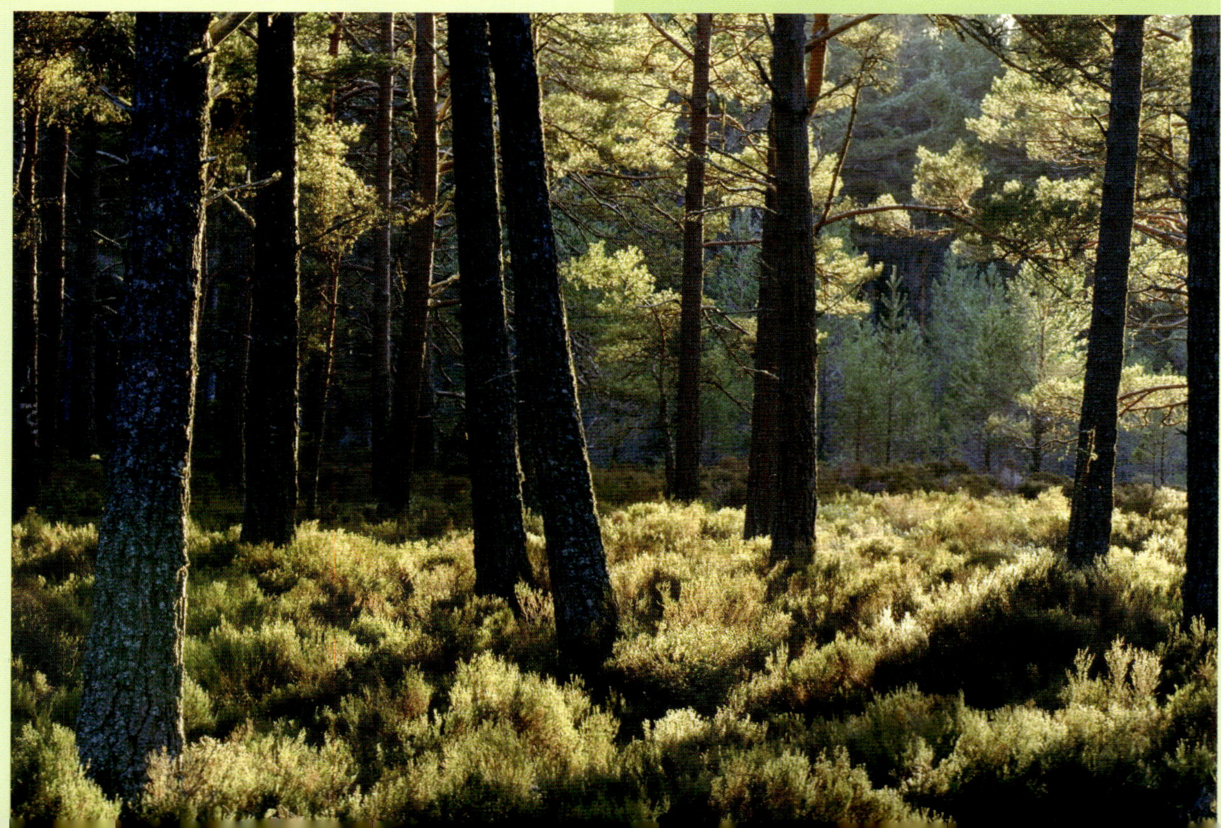

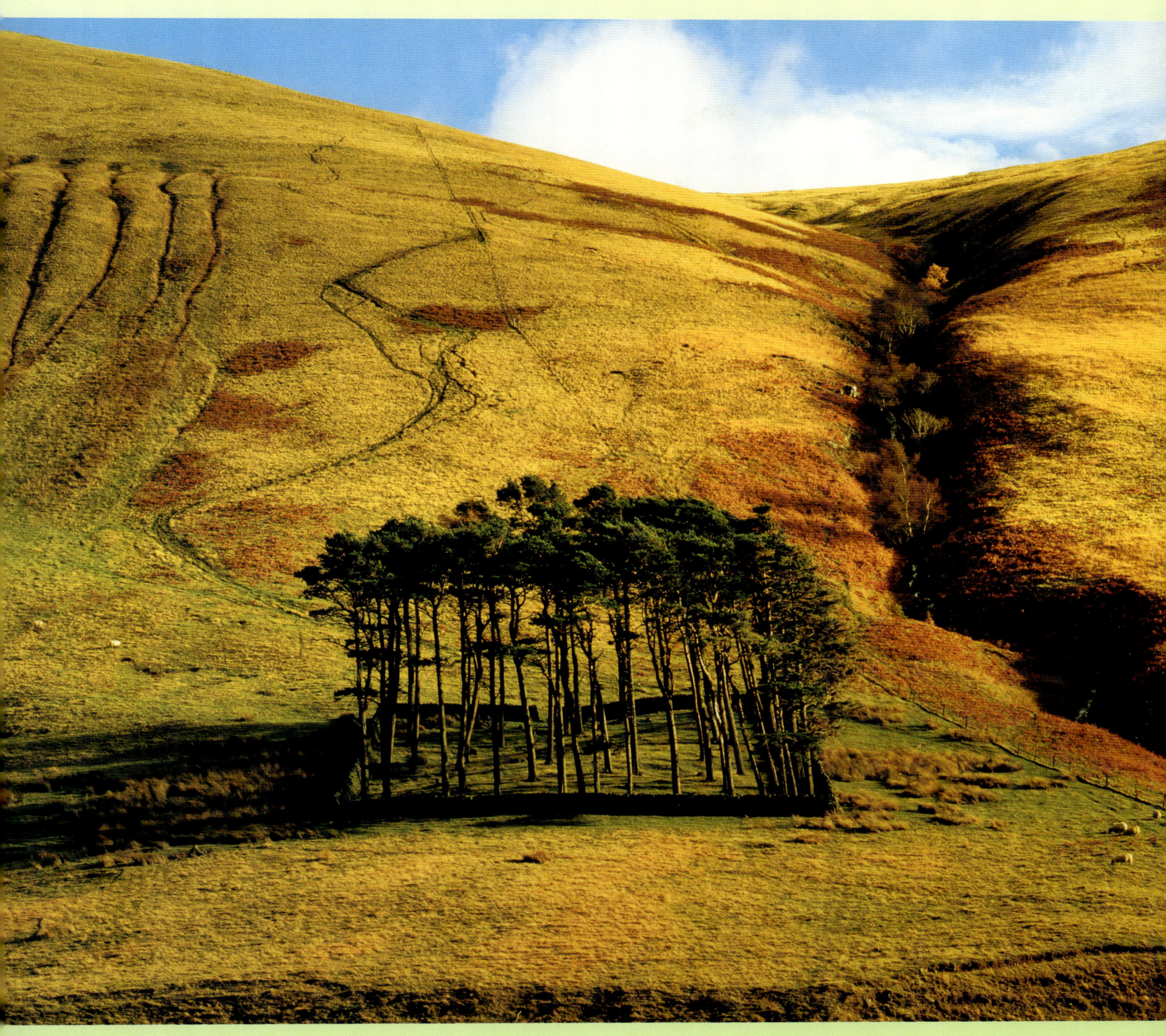

Wildlife The reintroduction of the Scots pine has helped the spread of the crossbill, a small finch with overlapping tips to its beak, which feeds on the pine cones. The seeds in the cones are attractive to the red squirrel too and the Scots pine's reintroduction to Scotland has heralded a significant rise in its population. Forests of Scots pine in the western European zone of the Taiga once supported animals such as lynx, moose, beaver, brown bear, wild boar and wild cat and some of these may once again be glimpsed in Scotland now.

So the threefold strategy for the return of the forest is: to fence out deer and prevent over-grazing; to plant native trees where the forest has disappeared completely; and to remove non-native trees planted underneath old-growth Scots pine forest that are preventing natural regeneration. Ambitious though the project sounds, the Scots pine does well when planted out as a small tree and, once established, grows vigorous and strong. As a testament to its success, in the spring of 2005 Trees for Life planted tree number 5,000,000.

Carbon storage

Larches in their full autumn glory are short-lived (previous pages). The hasty onset of the extremely cold winter will quickly see the golden needles on the ground, soon to be covered by the inevitable white carpet of snow.

As the biome with the greatest area of forest on the planet, the Taiga has a critical role to play as a carbon sink. The need to store carbon is caused by the high levels of the 'greenhouse gas' carbon dioxide present in the atmosphere. Carbon dioxide is by no means the only greenhouse gas – methane, nitrous oxide and the hydrofluorocarbons all trap radiation and in turn are responsible for warming the atmosphere – but it is the most prolific. Like a greenhouse, these gases hold the sun's heat and prevent it from escaping back into space, contributing to the phenomenon we know as global warming. Carbon dioxide is produced by burning fossil fuels such as coal and oil and it is estimated that 50 per cent of all the world's carbon produced by fossil fuel combustion is stored in the Taiga forest.

The role of trees and plants in this cycle of events is crucial because all plants require carbon dioxide to grow. Not only do plants soak up the carbon dioxide, they also release oxygen as they grow, without which life on earth would not exist. Trees, by virtue of their very size, their deep roots, their slow rate of growth and length of life, have the best possible carbon storage facilities. All would be well and in balance were it not for the fact that we burn far too much carbon for the existing plants and oceans on the planet to handle. The surfeit is causing the earth's atmosphere to warm up – which is why we need more trees.

A global responsibility

Logical then, it would seem, to put the preservation of forests, the best of all carbon sinks, and the planting of more, high on the environmental agenda. At the United Nations Kyoto Protocol on Climate Change, signed by more than 100 countries in 1997, the USA, Canada and Russia declared themselves prepared to achieve half of their reduction targets in carbon dioxide emissions by using sinks such as forests. But none of these three countries would consider reducing those emissions at source, that is, by burning less fossil fuels. President George Bush has said that he does not intend to ratify the treaty, on the basis of the damage it would do to the country's economy and because he believes the treaty to be flawed.

The Siberian larch is a rarity among conifers in being deciduous, shedding its leaves in winter to protect itself from the vicious cold of the biome's eastern reaches. When the new growth emerges in the warmer months, this larch is one of the prettiest sights in a landscape lacking much colour.

Huge sections of the forest are under threat. Manitoba, in Canada, is set to cut down 220,000 square kilometres of its forest over the next 60 years, with no replanting programme in sight. The forest is to be clear-felled to make way for agriculture, not tree farming. As well as being held in the wood, carbon builds up in the soil, leaf litter and roots of trees, and whenever trees are disturbed, as happens in a clearing operation, that carbon would be released back into the atmosphere. The replanting of trees in a timber farming system goes some way to redressing the balance but the trees will only reach middle age before they are harvested and processed. This is why the massive northerly old-growth forests have to be protected and, where possible, replanted and left untouched to live out their full life cycle.

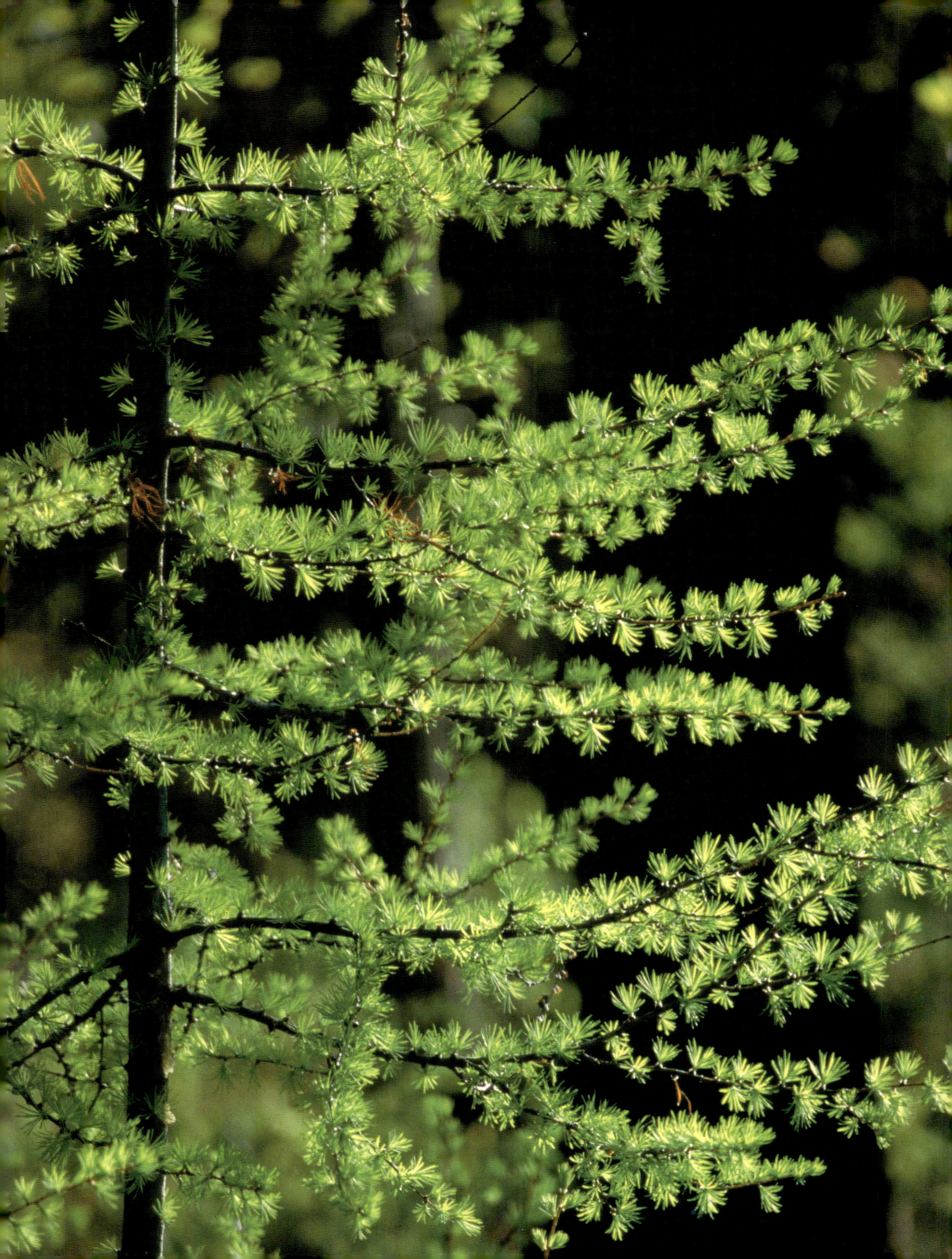

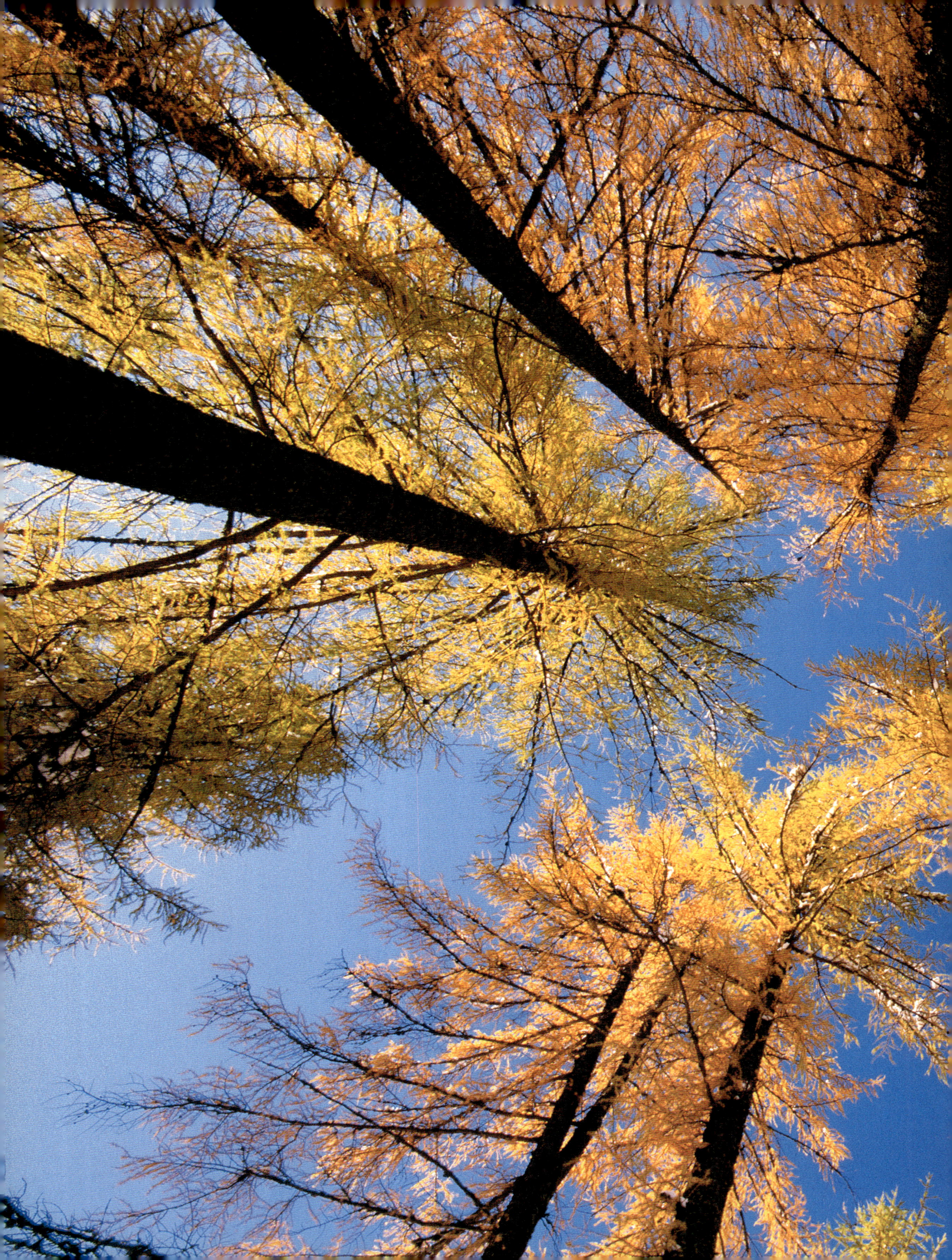

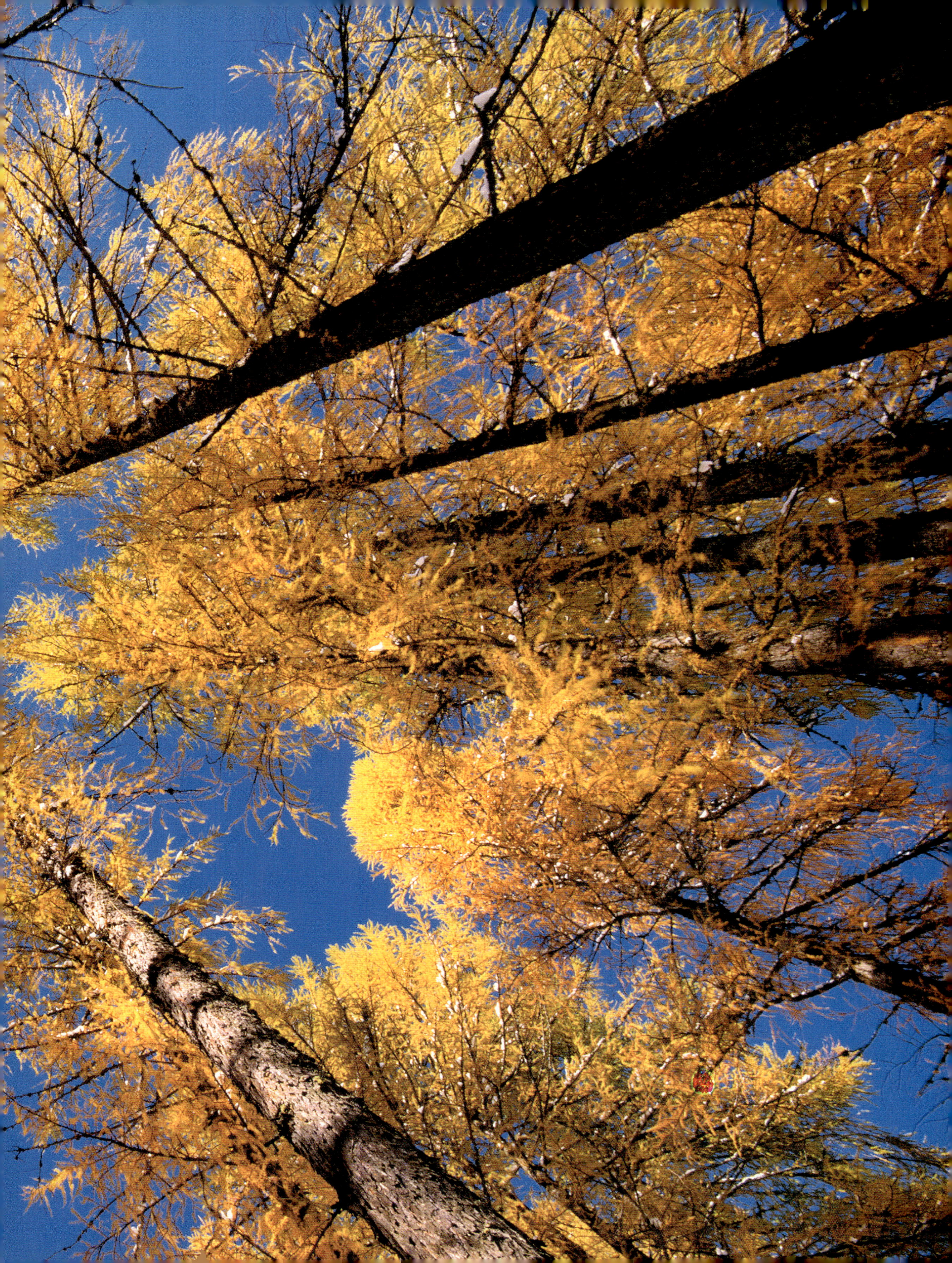

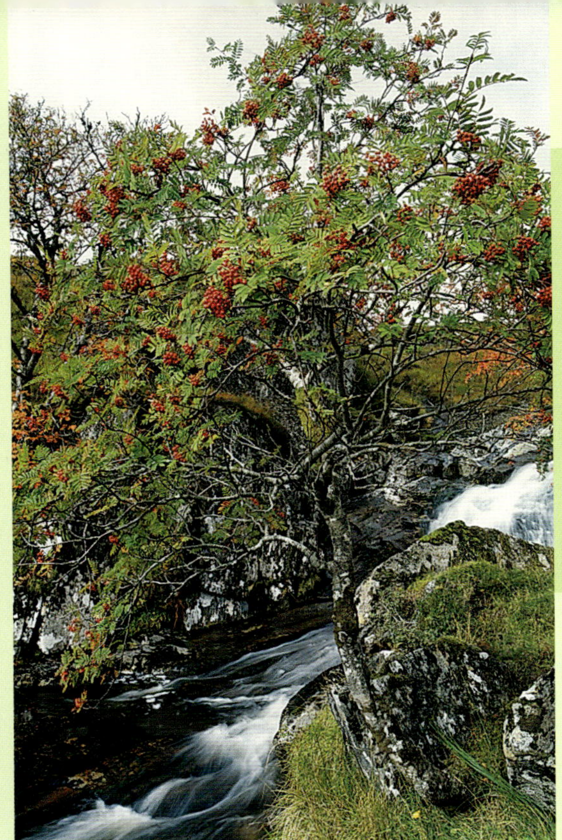

The rowan or mountain ash The Taiga does not consist solely of coniferous trees lying under a heavy blanket of snow: on its southern fringes are belts of deciduous trees which merge ultimately with the coniferous forest. This is a harsh place: the winters long and unforgiving and the summers short. Deciduous trees are restricted to a few species of willow, aspen and birch but one other tree stands out and that is the rowan, once known as the 'famine tree'. This tree (*Sorbus aucuparia*) is native to northern Europe and Asia and widespread throughout the Taiga biome.

The rowan is a hardy tree growing to about 20m high in the acid soil conditions that it favours and which are predominantly found in the Taiga, with its carpet of conifer needles. Its successful colonization of the biome is due to the profuse and attractive red berries produced in summer, which are a magnet for birds. Not only are the seeds removed and spread in the most efficient manner but the tree is fed at the same time by bird droppings, concentrated guano being extremely high in nitrogen. The rowan is very resourceful and is able to grow in tiny pockets of soil in extremely exposed conditions – indeed, its roots can even penetrate solid rock.

The rowan is a favoured homestead tree in Finland today, where a mature tree can produce more than 100kg of berries in a season; most are made into jam or jelly. Even in the far northern reaches of Lapland the tree still grows and brings forth a yield.

The famine tree The rowan is one of only a handful of food-producing trees in the entire biome. While not as great a source of nutrition as its relative the apple, the rowan berry is high in vitamins A and C and has a calorific value only slightly less than potatoes. The berries are too acidic to be eaten raw, but this can be overcome by soaking and/or cooking.

Its life-sustaining qualities gave the rowan important standing, especially as the berries have medicinal qualities and are used as an astringent and an antibiotic. In Neolithic times all red food was deemed suitable for the gods and rowan berries were often found in Neolithic burial sites.

There are several sights in the world of ornithology that are rare and wonderful. An osprey rising from a river clutching a large salmon would be one, and the aeronautical displays of vast flocks of starlings another. Waxwings banqueting on rowan berries belongs in this select group because of the orderly determination and clinical gorging that results in a heavily ladened tree being entirely denuded of all its fruit by this handsome bird. The brown waxwings, with their curled crest and yellow-tipped tail, make no sound and minimal movement, flying to the next tree only when the first is stripped bare. A berry eater par excellence!

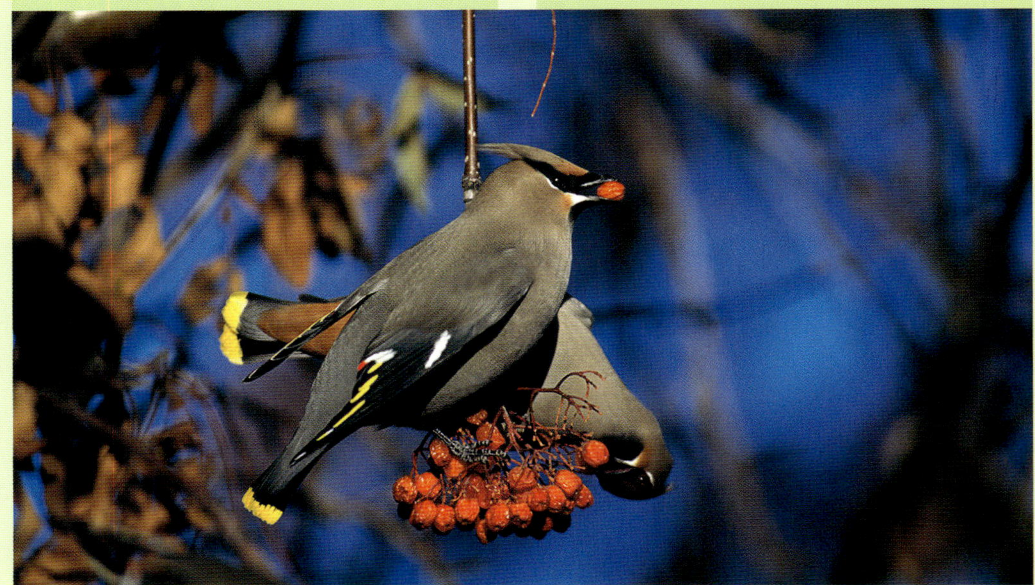

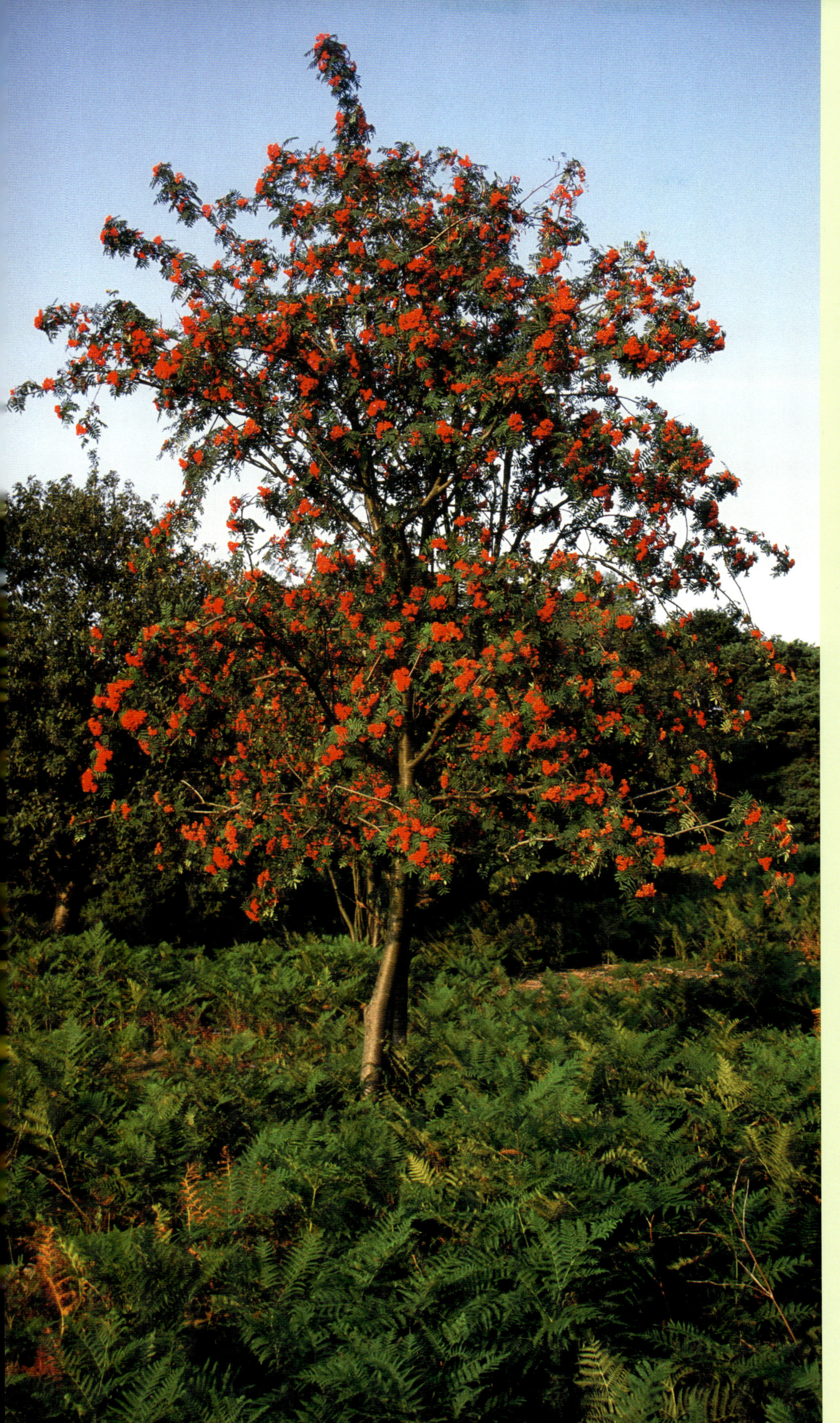

rowan

When, in times of future hardship, we look around and recognize that conventional agriculture has failed us, we will be looking for trees like the rowan to see us through once more.

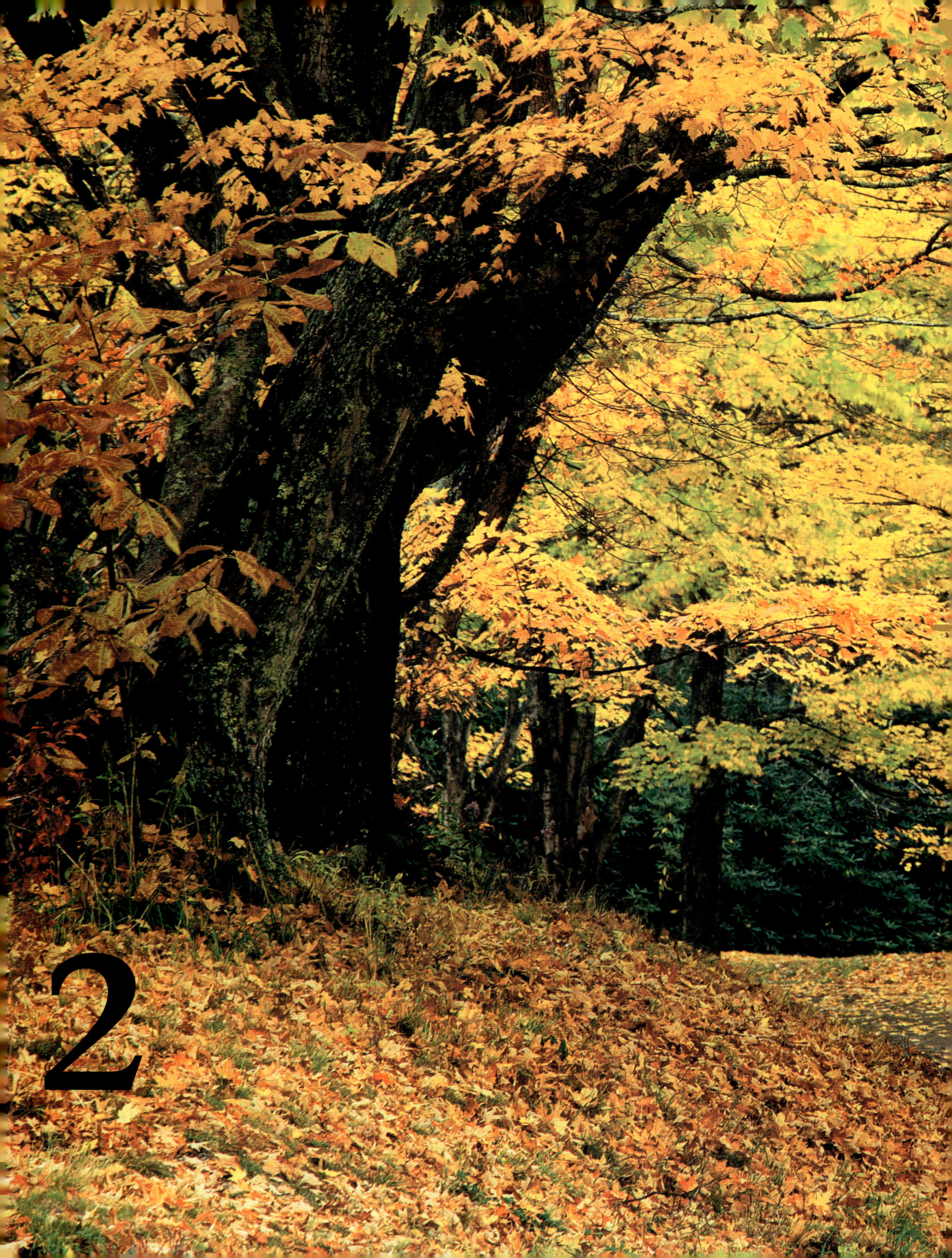

2

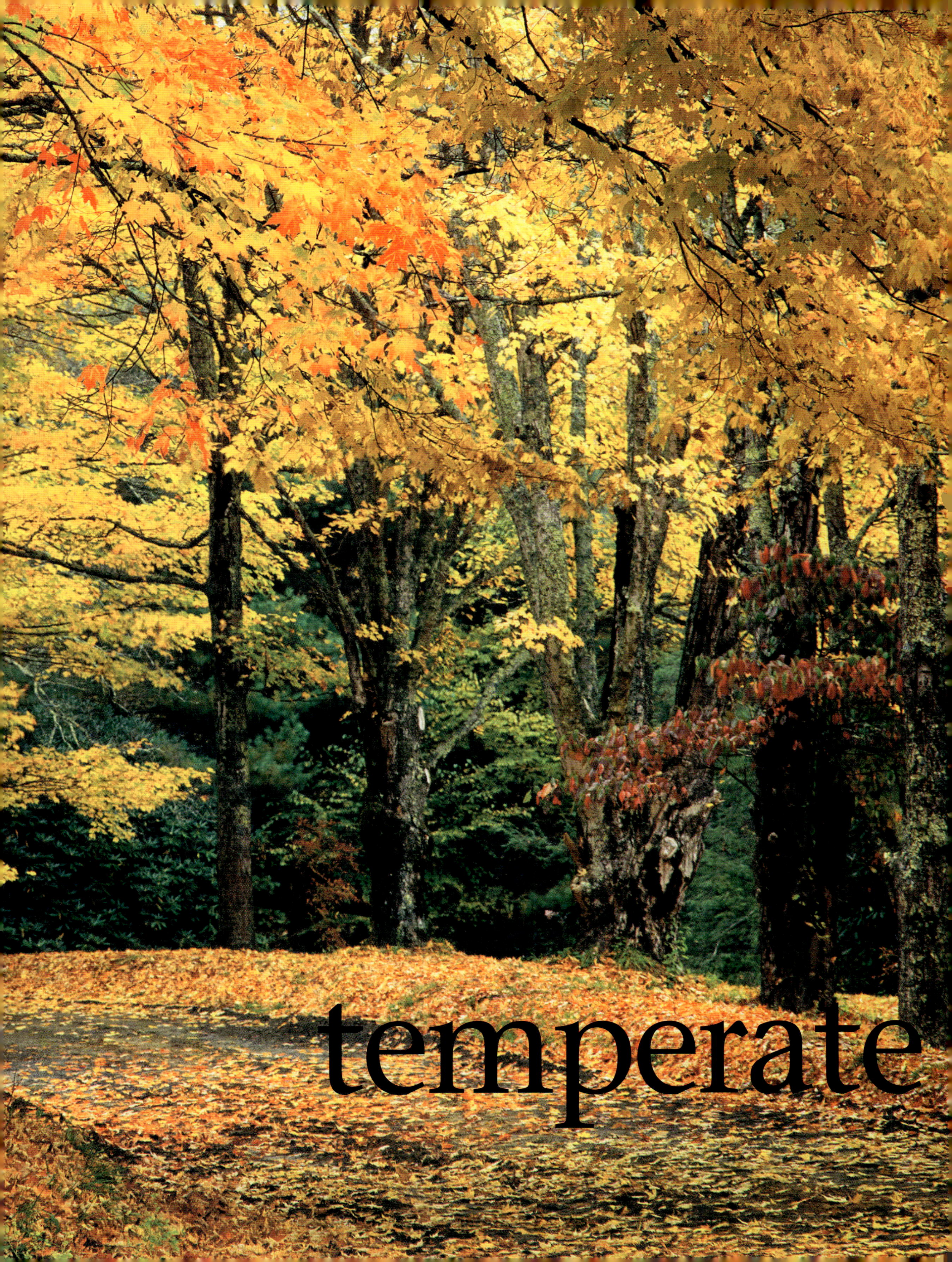

temperate

For stature, presence, antiquity and grandeur, the oak stands clear of the field as one of the greatest of all trees. Each different species holds its place in the landscape of this temperate biome. Oaks have played the biggest part in the creation of the world as we know it, responsible as they are for enormous structures, from cathedrals to battleships.

A broadleaf deciduous forest or wood is one of the most special places on earth. To enter it is to be conscious of utter quiet – there may be birdsong but the overwhelming sense will be one of hushed calm – closely followed by the extraordinary feeling of awe that comes simply from being among trees. Yet listen closely: beyond the quiet is a hum, the hum generated by the mass of life which is so closely linked to the presence of trees.

It is the trees of the temperate broadleaf deciduous biome in the northern hemisphere (and smaller pockets of the southern hemisphere) to which most of us have access. And even though this biome does not cover as great an area as the Taiga biome, which stretches around the roof of the world, or the vast swathes of the forested tropics, it contains more species of tree that are familiar to us and used by us than any other geographical area on the planet. The biome covers central and northern Europe, eastern and some of the north-western states of North America, parts of South America and areas of eastern China, Korea and northern Japan. Each region has its own native species but they share genera; for example, different kinds of oak, beech, maple, apple and cherry may be found throughout the biome.

This is the biome in which the mighty trees that have shaped so much of our civilization originated

The term 'broadleaf' refers to having leaves, rather than the needles of coniferous trees, and the temperate deciduous biome has a predominance of native species that lose their leaves, as well as a number of significant coniferous trees such as the redwoods, yew and certain pines. Some conifers, such as the magnificent redwoods, the Ponderosa pine and the Monterey pine, are native to North America and important trees in their own right. The Ponderosa pine is the second most important timber tree in the USA after the Douglas fir, and the Monterey pine, native to a tiny stretch of the Pacific coast of northen California, is one of the most significant salt-tolerant coastal shelter trees in the biome. The mighty redwood, of course, is California's iconic tree.

There is no greater range of colour among trees than those created by a mature deciduous woodland in autumn. Beeches, chestnuts and maples respond to the cooler temperatures by producing the full spectrum of golden, bronze and deep red leaves to lead the woods into winter, bringing leaf fall and bare wood.

As far apart as areas of the biome may be, their climate governs the fact that many trees within them shed their leaves in winter. The majestic oak, perhaps the biome's defining tree, is the classic example. This tree knows no boundaries and is indifferent to borders, language or custom. Different species of this one extraordinary genus (*Quercus*) cover mountainsides, grace lake shores, fill forests and line the grandest avenues of the oldest cities in Europe, Asia, China and North America.

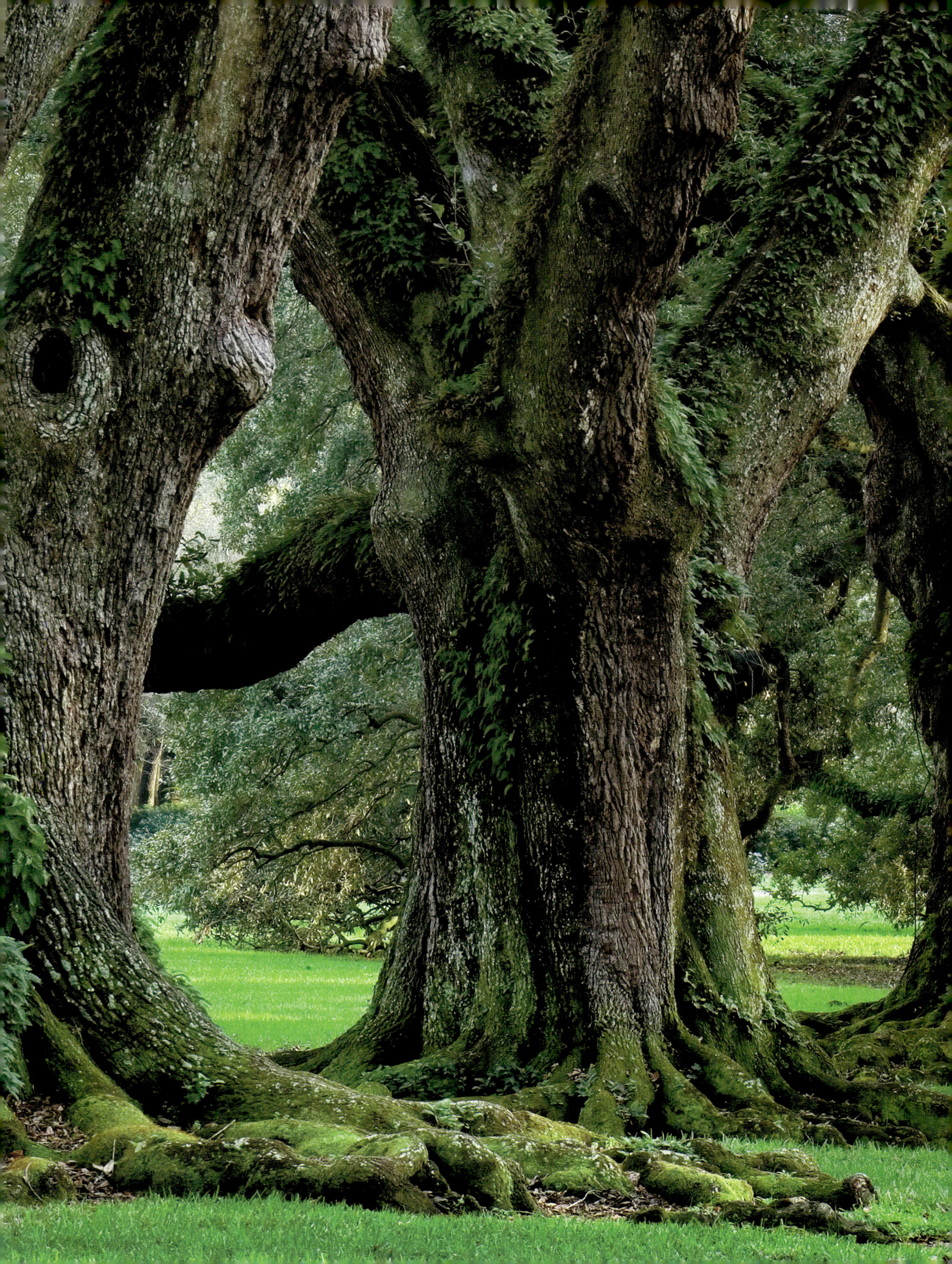

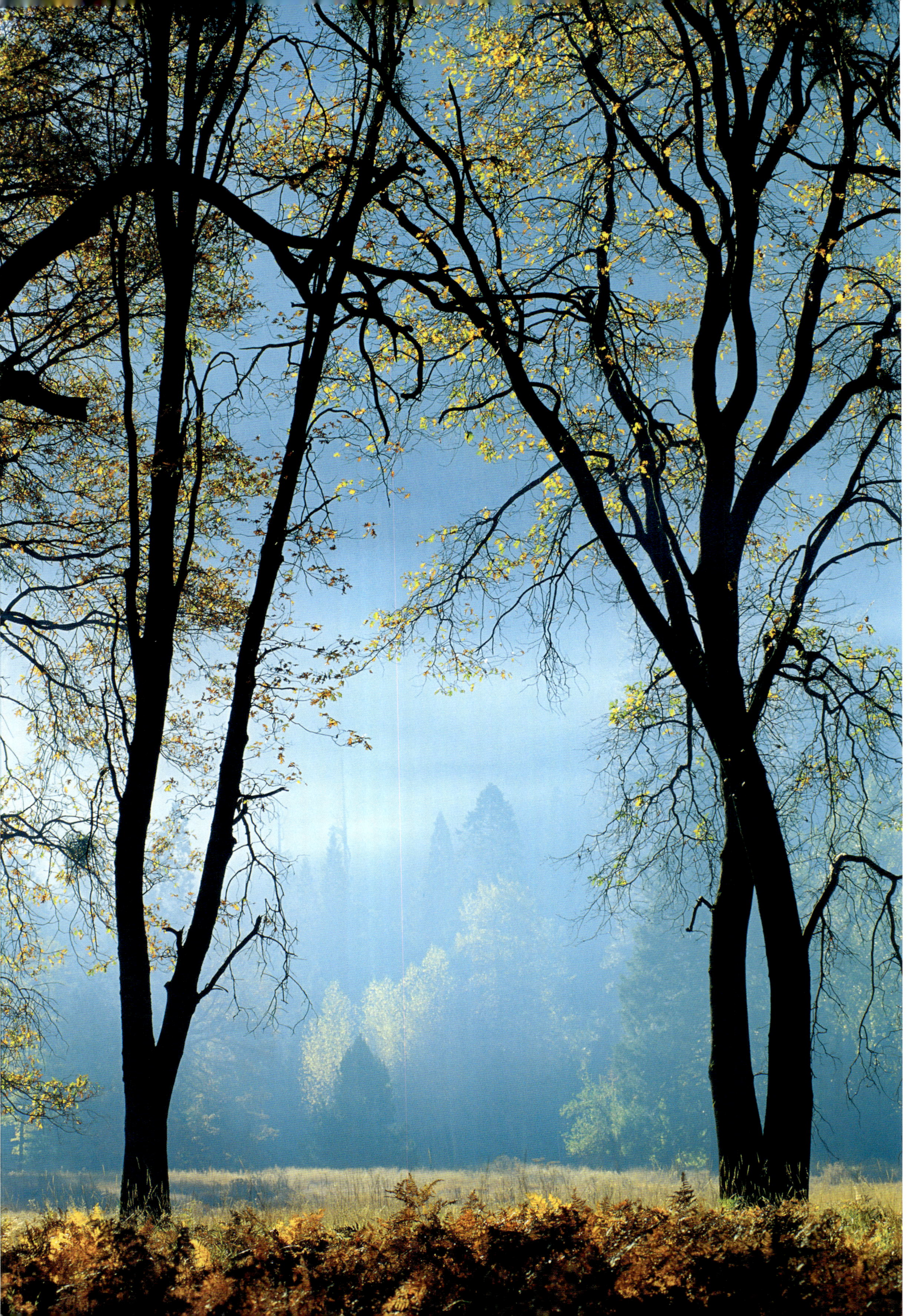

The seasons

A year in the life of a deciduous tree is entirely controlled by the seasons. During spring and summer their leaves take energy from the sun and, using the process of photosynthesis, convert that energy into food. As the days begin to shorten and the temperatures to drop in autumn, the chlorophyll – the green colouring in the leaves – begins to break down. It is this breakdown of the cells that causes some trees, especially maples, to reveal extraordinary bright colours. In order to survive the winter, the deciduous tree must shed its leaves and go dormant so that no rain, snow or ice can penetrate. At the same time the tree creates a concentrated sugar solution to prevent the water in its trunk and branches from freezing. (This shedding of leaves for protection from cold has an opposite purpose for trees in tropical deciduous forests, where leaf loss protects against drought.)

What is interesting now is that the seasons appear to be changing. At the time of writing (December 2005), the autumn has been so mild that many deciduous trees were still in full growth when the first frosts came. The leaves of apple trees in orchards throughout central UK were still attached fast to the branches at the time of what was a very hard frost and the following day were completely browned, as if burned by a blowtorch – but still reluctant to fall and head into dormancy for the winter. Whether this clash of season and climate is cyclical or the result of global warming is the great debate but, whatever the cause, the boundaries between seasons in this temperate biome are becoming increasingly blurred. Warmer and drier winters are now followed by wetter and hotter summers and the two seasons in between are becoming far less distinctive. Milder winters bring spring-like temperatures which trigger associated reactions from plants, birds and animals at unusual times, while autumn is beginning to stretch further into winter.

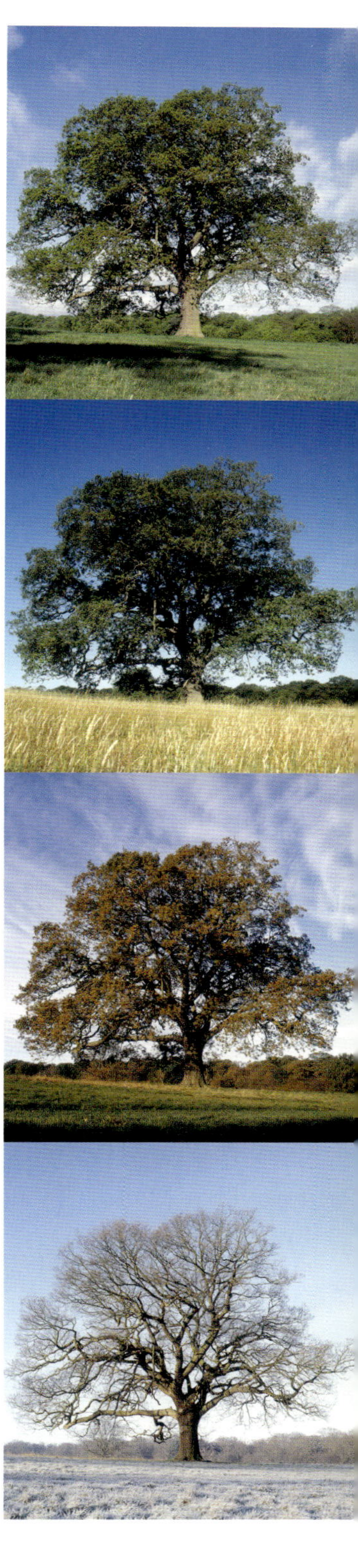

The evocative oak in its four seasons of spring, summer, autumn and winter, each as proud and solid as the other three incarnations.

Temperate trees and man

Unlike 'wilderness' biomes, such as the Taiga or the rainforest, the temperate deciduous biome is characterized by man's interaction with trees. It is the story of social history, both ancient and modern, and the part trees play within it. So how did trees get to this biome and leave us such a fabulous legacy of wonderful trees to admire everywhere, from our back gardens through public parks and into the wild, albeit protected, forests? Three million years ago the majority of North America, Asia and Europe was covered in forests of giant redwoods. Ice Ages all but destroyed them and it was only after the last one withdrew from northern and western Europe, 10,000 years ago, that trees began to return to what would become the temperate deciduous biome. Recolonization of the land was rapid and effective. Tree seeds that had lain dormant under the ice quickly germinated and were carried by wind, water, animal and bird – and where they could grow, they did. To take Britain as one small example, some 2,000 years after the retreat of the Ice Age and the island's separation from the Continent, there were 35 'native' species of tree, including oak, willow, ash, birch and alder. Before man began cutting a swathe through the forests in the second millennium, the vast majority of western Europe was covered in broad-leaved deciduous trees such as oak and beech. Huge tracts of such forest still exist intact in the eastern states of North America, in northern Japan, Korea and eastern China, as well as in parts of mainland Europe and the United Kingdom. Here we find the great trees that have marked history, that have built cities and navies, cathedrals and palaces: the oaks, the maples, the cherries, the willows.

Then came man with his requirements for food and shelter, quickly followed by agriculture and domesticated animals. Since those earliest times, trees have been the great providers and they continue to be absolutely critical for our survival. Through the Middle Ages the requirement for timber and fuel wood grew and grew. While populations increased and timber was cut down for every possible purpose, the more responsible rulers and landowners carried out replanting schemes: orchards for food, avenues and arbours for pleasure, forests for hunting and block upon block of straight-growing timber trees specifically for commercial purposes, such as shipbuilding.

Hunting forests

By 1079 – a mere 13 years after the Norman Conquest of England in 1066 – William the Conqueror had designated the New Forest in Hampshire as the first of the Royal Forests within which all animals and timber were declared Crown Property. Greedy perhaps, but conservationist, certainly. The word 'forest' was in fact a legal term to describe the area of land and the restrictions placed upon it. Commoners were still allowed to graze animals in the forest, a right still in force today regarding pigs (known as pannage), and to collect fallen wood for cooking fires and rushes for roofing and for building.

Royal hunting forests were not confined to England. King Louis XIV of France built the palace at Versailles in 1668, not only to remove himself from the troublesome mobs of Paris but also to be closer to the forests of Fontainebleau where he could hunt. In the Loire Valley, Francis I built the longest wall in Europe around his hunting estate at Chambord in 1542. Still standing today, the 5,500-hectare forest , a mix of oak and pine, is Presidential hunting territory where deer and wild boar are still hunted. The Black Forest in southern Germany, which reaches from Bavaria in the east almost to the French border in the west, has for centuries been a rich hunting ground for deer, wild boar and feathered game, the dense stands of spruce, beech and oak providing ample cover. This is now a state-run forest with a continuous programme of harvesting and replanting; hunting continues to this day.

In the Aosta region in north-west Italy the Gran Paradiso National Park was originally the hunting preserve of the ruling House of Savoy. The pine-forested slopes of the Italian Alps are home to the ibex and, were the area not a National Park, this white mountain goat would now be on the verge of extinction. Likewise, the Kings of Castille created a giant hunting preserve for themselves at Coto Donana in western Andalusia in the thirteenth century. A flat expanse comprising marsh cork oaks and stone pine forests, this was created a National Park in 1969.

King Louis XIV of France built the palace at Versailles in 1668, not only to remove himself from the troublesome mobs of Paris but also to be closer to the forests of Fontainebleau where he could hunt

Of the four main islands of Japan, Hokkaido is the northernmost and here, in the thick lowland forests of magnolian oak (*Quercus magnolica*), the brown bear has traditionally been hunted, although it is protected today. In North Korea, where 80 per cent of the landmass is mountainous, the Siberian tiger population has been reduced to a handful of animals, but in the forests of South Korea, wild boar and Korean roe deer are still hunted among the wooded land of mulberries, chestnuts, ginkgo and black oak.

Although many of the great forests are protected, there are increasing threats to their safety. The hurricanes of 1987 and 1990 removed more than two million trees from the landscape of the United Kingdom alone. Dutch elm disease has resulted in virtually the total loss of species such as the Dutch elm (*Ulmus* x *hollandica*), the English elm (*U. procera*) and most of the American elms, such as *U. americana.* And with the prevalent fungal disease affecting oaks, sudden oak death, it is clear that there is a need for ever-more stringent protection of our trees.

It was not until the Industrial era of the nineteenth century that the heavy use of timber began to take its toll. The worst to suffer from the ravages of population explosion were the forests of western Europe which, by the start of the twentieth century, were seriously denuded and had become species poor. A programme of reforestation began (a Forestry Commission was established in 1919 in the United Kingdom), but such was the demand for materials as the Industrial Age gathered momentum that fast-growing, non-native species were often planted. The temperate broadleaf deciduous forests in eastern North America, however, remain relatively intact. So great is the diversity of the flora and fauna of the Appalachians, for example, that the Great Smoky Mountains have been designated a world biosphere reserve.

Forests were planted in Europe from the eleventh century for the hunting of animals such as deer (overleaf). Many remain protected to this day, planted with native species and allowed to progress in their own way and at their own pace.

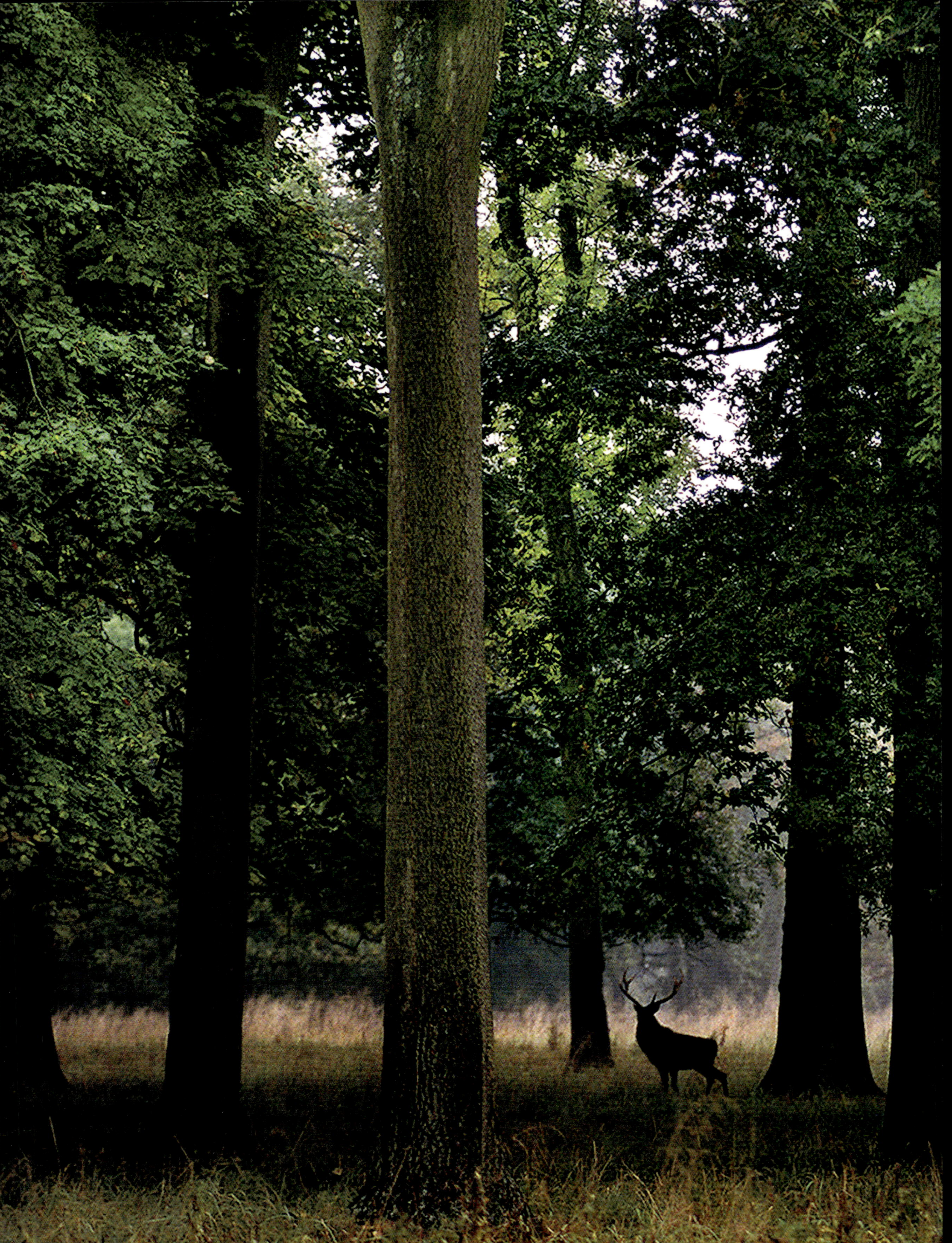

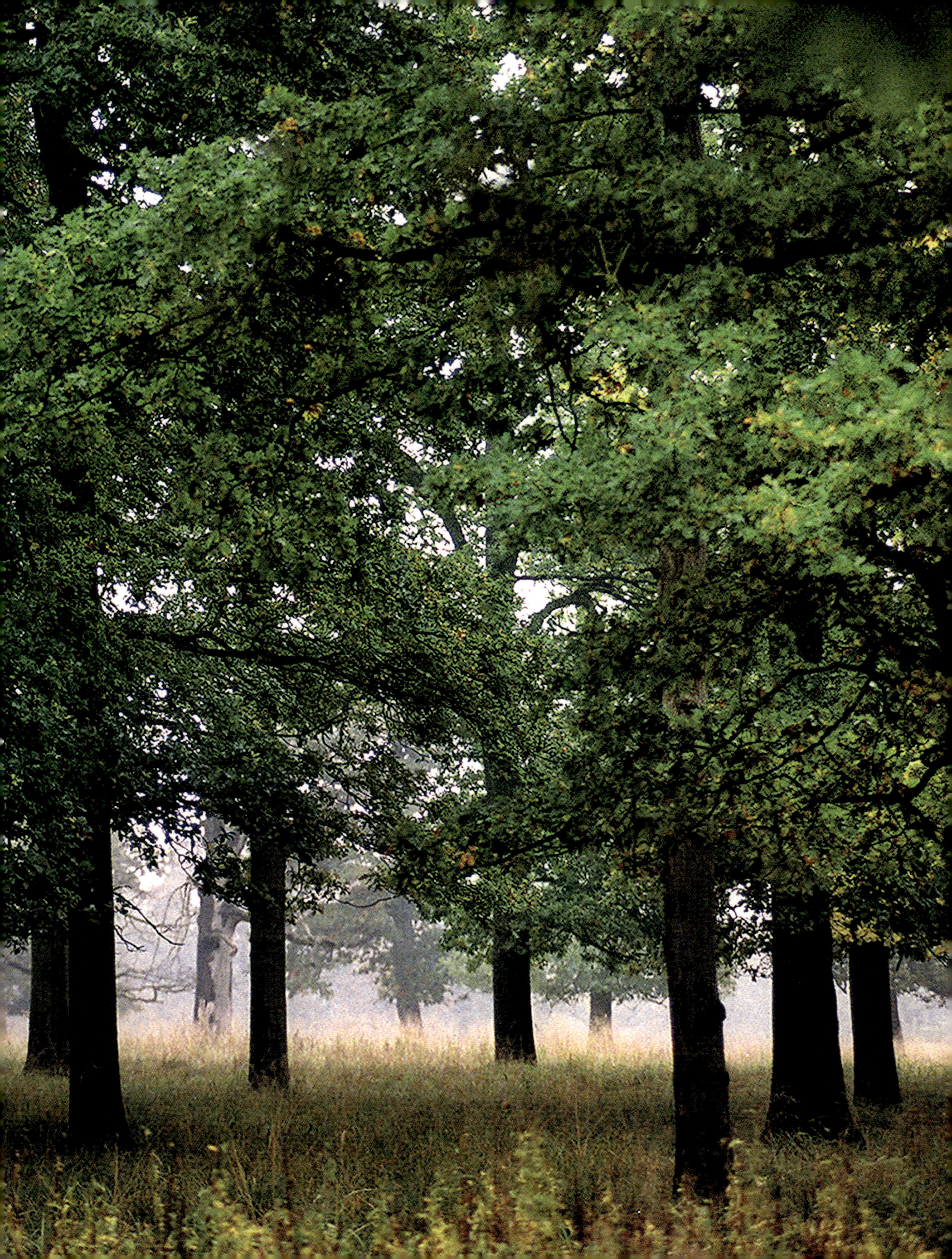

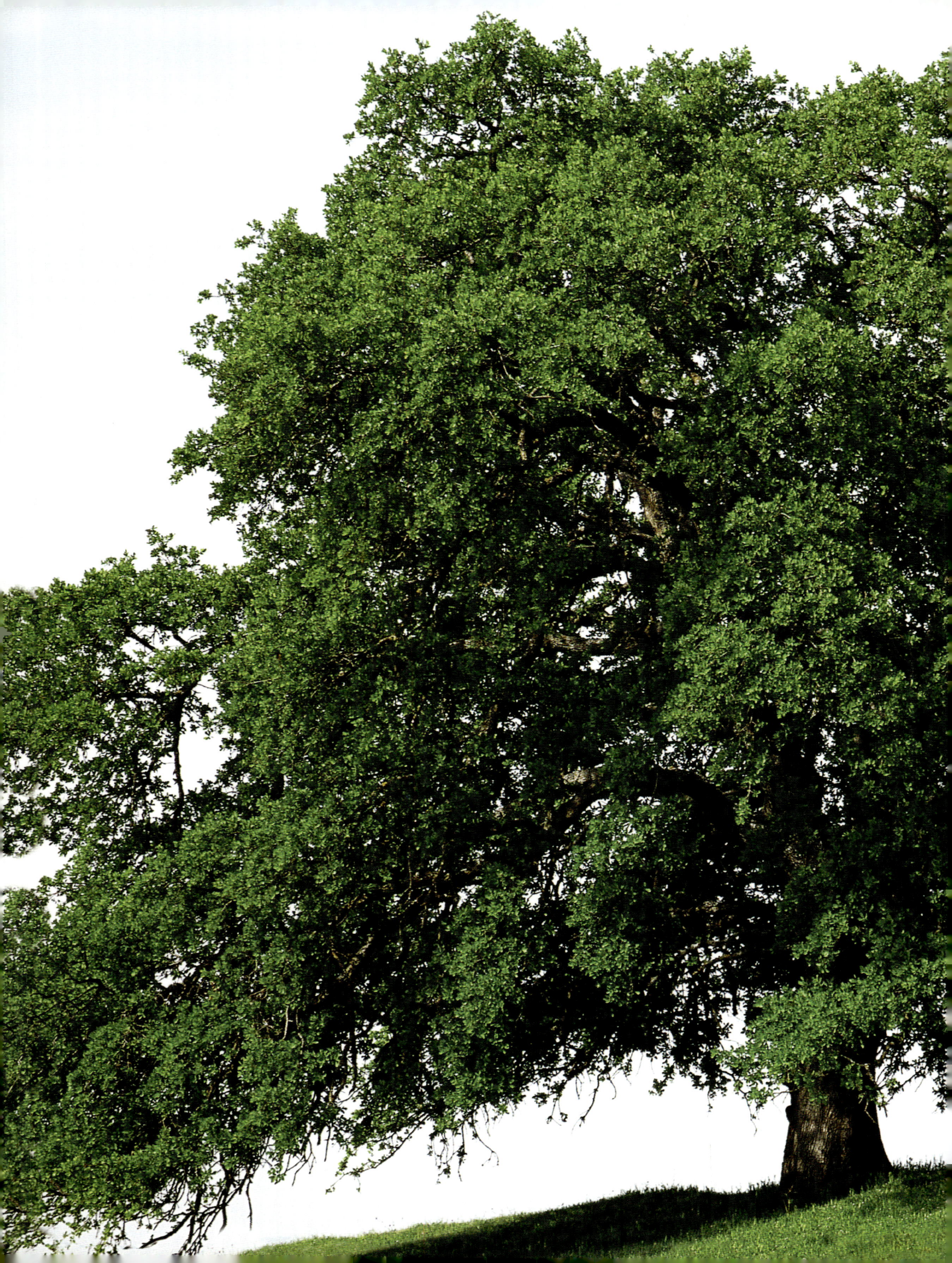

oak

The oak is the crowning glory of this biome and reflects the strength of the earth from which it comes

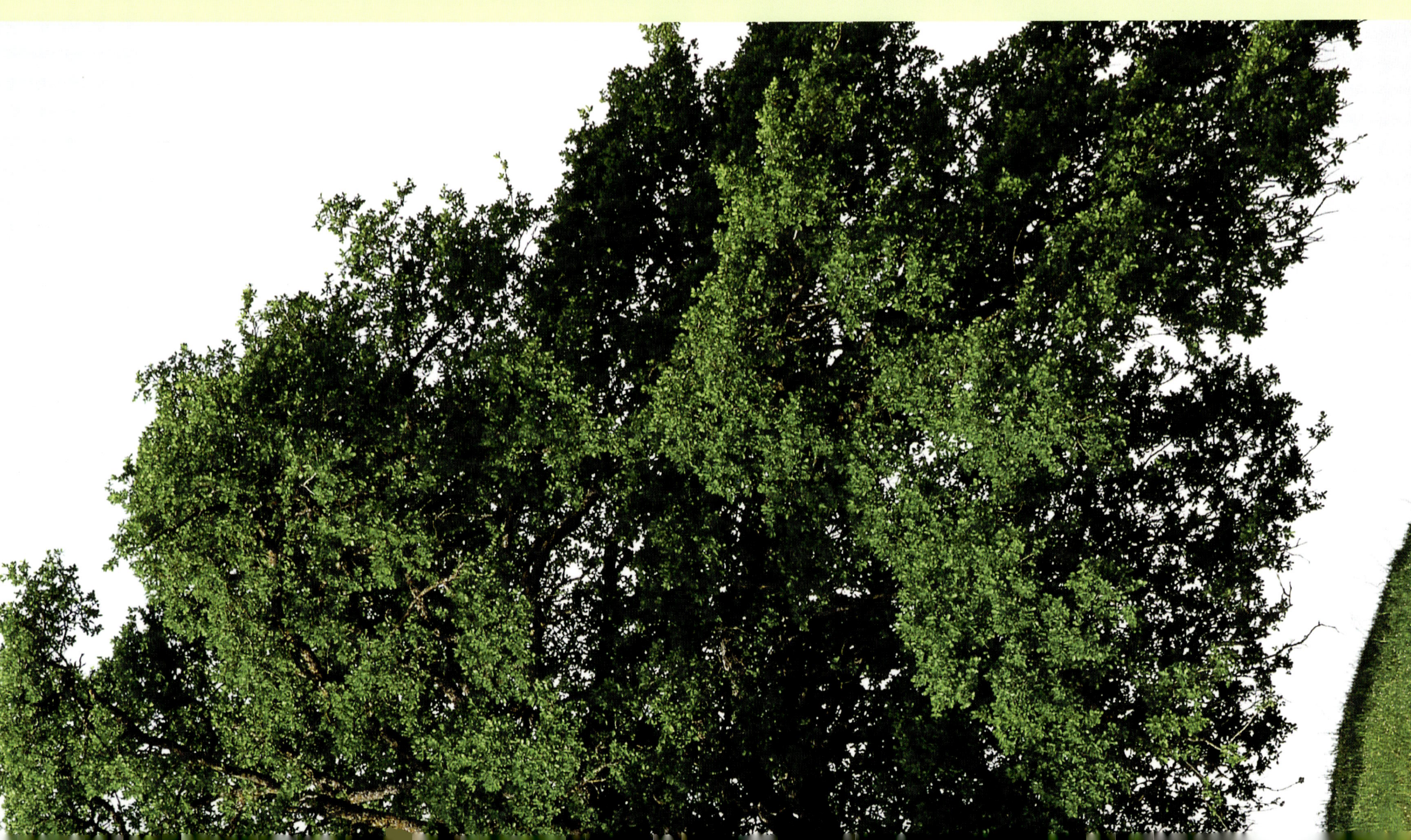

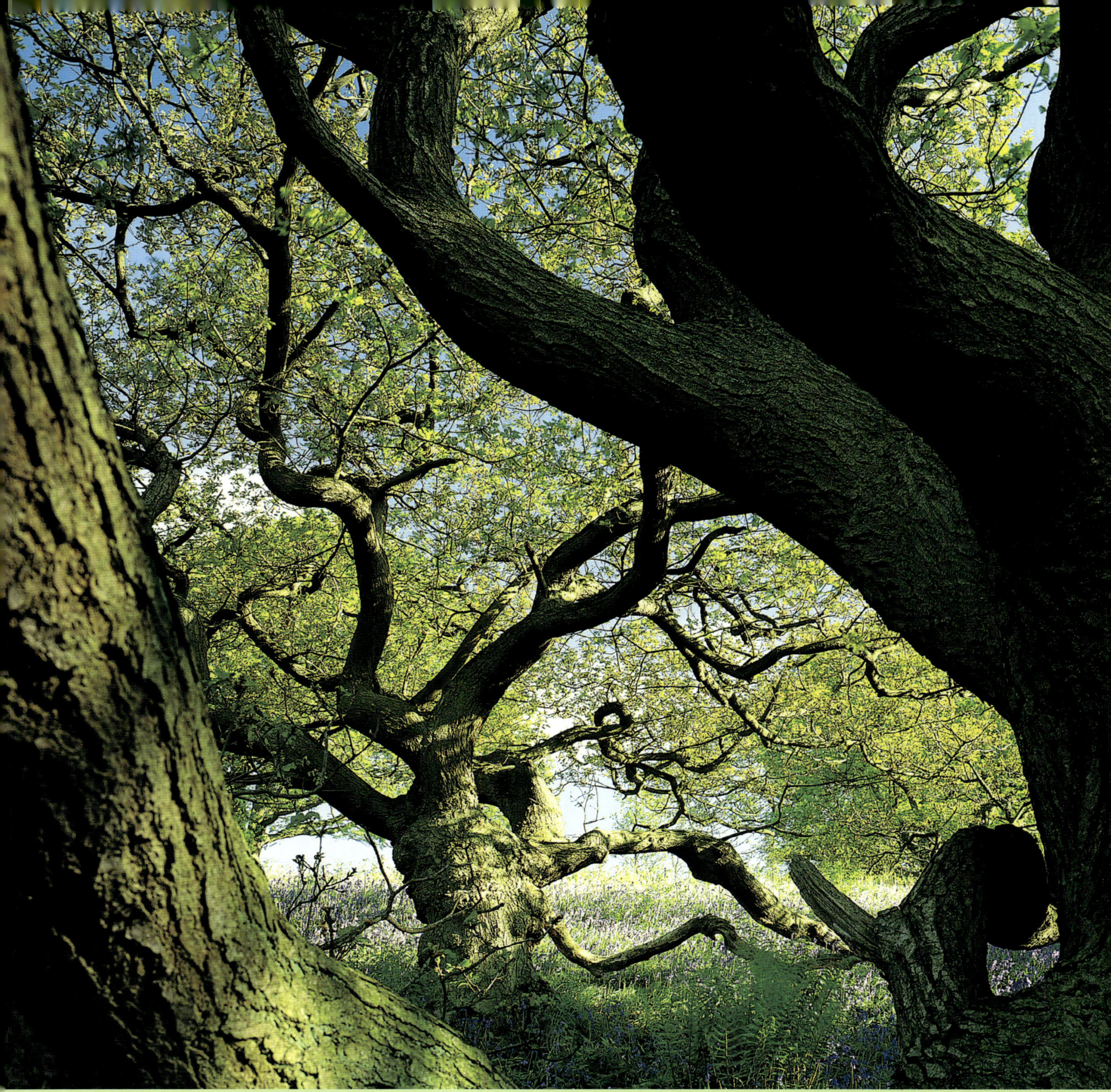

The sheltering oak The oak tree's place in ancient history is firmly cemented with such legends as the Norsemen who met in oak groves to worship Thor and the Druids who used the tree as their link with the dryads or wood nymphs. Just as the Norsemen associated the oak with their thunder god Thor, so the Greek thunder god Zeus is linked with the oak, allegedly because the tree's resistance to electricity is low and it is struck by lightning far more than any other tree. In Christian times, such trees became known as Gospel oaks for the Gospels were preached under their canopy. In British folklore the wizard Merlin worked his magic in a grove of oaks and was never seen without a wand of oak, while King Arthur's Round Table was allegedly made from a single slab of an oak tree. The proliferation of stories surrounding the oak abound because the tree is a giant among trees.

Oak

An oak tree in all its mature glory is one of the finest sights of the natural world. Not only do these magnificent trees mark the landscape, they have shaped countries and civilizations. One of the most widespread of genera native to the northern hemisphere, *Quercus* numbers more than 300 species, including both deciduous and evergreen types. Dominant in western Europe, it reaches throughout North, South and Central America, northern India, Nepal, China, Korea, Japan and Australia. In Europe and the USA in particular, oaks are easily recognized trees and it is here, perhaps more than anywhere, that they enjoy the reverence they deserve. Oaks have a typically rounded crown or canopy which will reach up to 20m in height. Their span can extend beyond this, so they are often wider than they are tall, while the trunk circumference of a fully grown *Quercus robur*, *Q. rubra* or *Q. cerris* can measure more than 3m. Their presence, whether in forest or field, is immense.

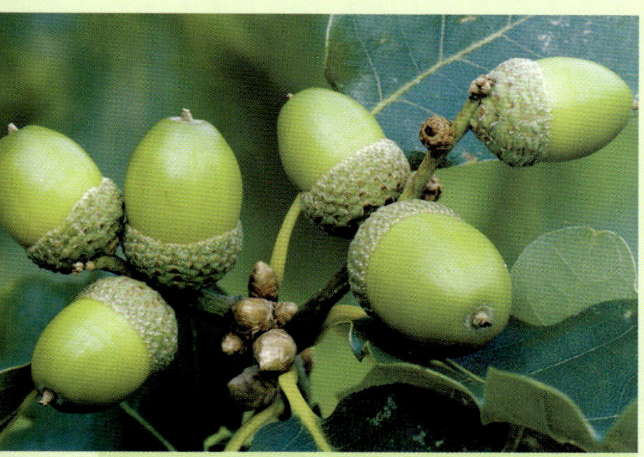

During their lifespan oak trees will produce thousands of tonnes of fruit in the form of acorns to help them in their colonization. Not only do these acorns support manifold species of wildlife, but a single mature oak can provide food and shelter for up to 300 species of living organisms. They also attract the oak's chief propagator, the jay, which is heavily dependent on acorns for winter food. A natural hoarder, the jay buries acorns and returns to the store later, but some acorns are forgotten and a new oak seedling shoots. Acorns also provide food for acorn weevils, Japanese beetles, red oak borers and gall wasps.

Oaks have been growing in the temperate biome since the last Ice Age retreated from the northern hemisphere 10,000 years ago and they once covered most of it, alongside other large, broadleaf deciduous trees such as the beech. They quickly became the timber of choice for so many tasks, not only due to their proliferation and size but also because oak timber has desirable properties not present in many other trees. Oak is a hardwood and very durable as well as beautiful; it is also water resistant and can withstand great heat. So, from the earliest times oak wood fell to the axe and was used to build navies, cities and cathedrals and it has maintained its position as the most sought-after timber tree in this biome ever since. But it is not simply the timber of the oak that is desirable. The tree's place in the landscape is a crucial one as a wildlife habitat, and its deep roots stabilize the soil.

The felling of the mythical giant oak that shaded the earth symbolized the dawn of man and made way for the beginnings of agriculture

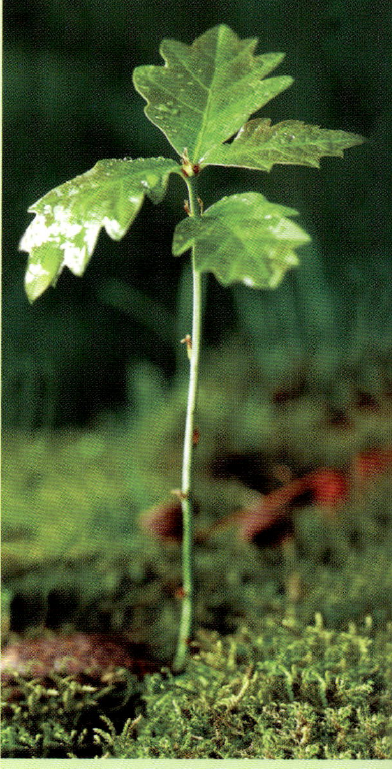

It is quite possible that in the future the oak will be grown for its fruit rather than its timber. An important source of nutrition before the advent of agriculture, the acorn was ground down, added to other cereals and made into dough. The Romans served it roasted at feasts, while for indigenous Indian tribes it was a staple.

Oak

Each 'man o' war' (the ships used by France and England in the Napoleonic naval wars, such as the 1805 Battle of Trafalgar) took the timber of 3,000 oaks

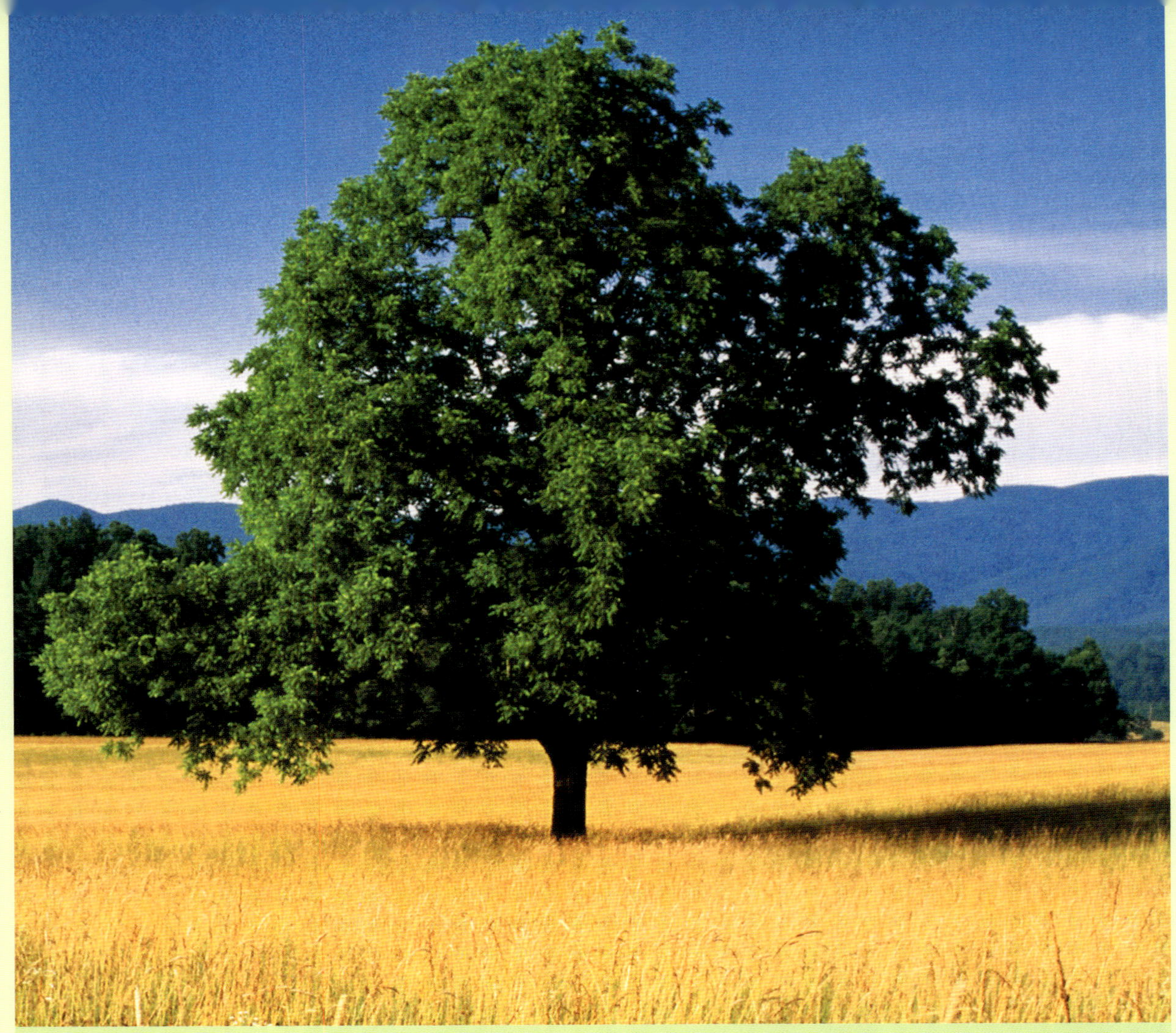

Hearts of oak Besides being used to build every kind of structure from barns to cathedrals, oak timber is used to make barrels to hold alcohol, water or salted meat, as well as to produce the finest veneers. In the great Gothic cathedrals of the Middle Ages, such as Notre Dame in Paris, oak, the strongest wood possible, was used to hold up the roofs, to make the flying buttresses and very often the doors. Vaulted roofs, the design choice of medieval cathedral builders, were also made of oak, because of its fire-resistant properties.

Oak's salt tolerance, a fire resistance greater than that of steel and the tree's proliferation throughout Europe ensured that oak was the tree of choice for shipbuilding. English oak, the most widespread form across Europe, is the species from which *The Mayflower*, which carried the Pilgrim Fathers to America, was built, as well as France and England's fighting 'man o' wars'.

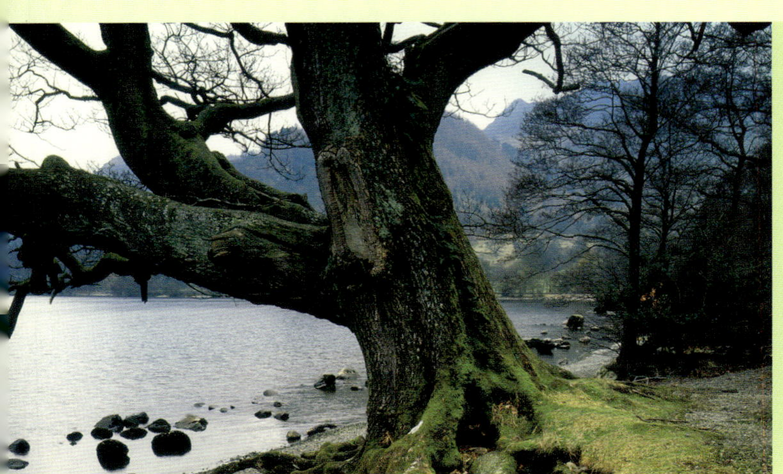

The future The great forests of oak that still stand are largely protected, particularly those which cover vast areas such as the Black Forest in Germany and the New Forest in the UK. The crowning glory of this biome can grow in the thinnest of soils and on the tops of the highest cliffs; it can tolerate salt and still thrive in full sun or deep shade. It will survive and dominate as it has done before, because it has stood the test of time and endured for so long already.

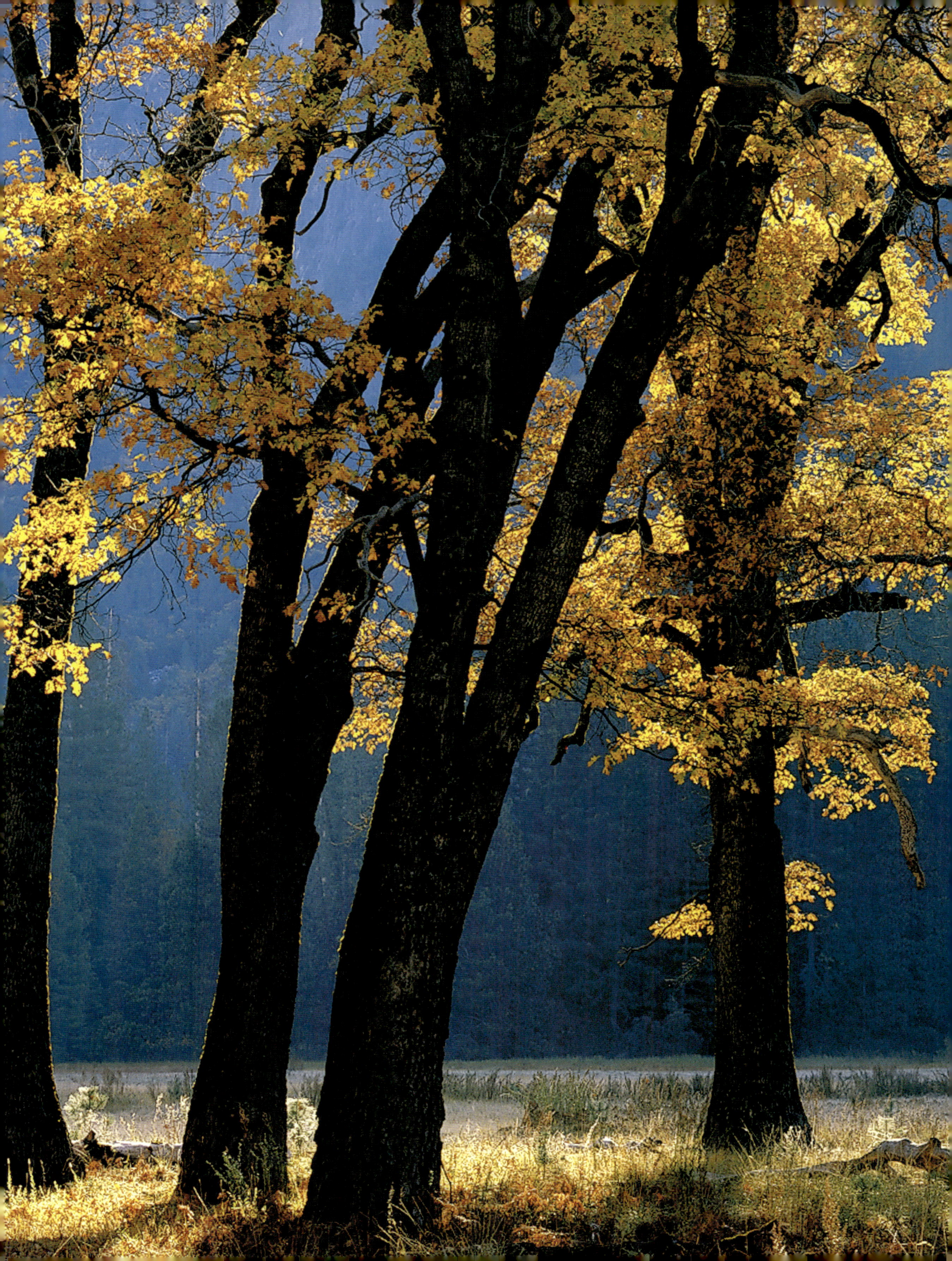

Woodland

Woodland is the most stable and diverse environment on dry land. It differs from forest in that forests have closed canopies, whereas woodland has an open canopy with trees at differing heights that let in more light. The stillness of a wood on a calm day hides a complex, cyclical system of life and death in which the stability attained is directly linked to the life and death cycles of organisms. Plants, animals, birds, insects, fungi, bacteria and other organisms great and small can live and thrive here, to the benefit of one another. But the biggest beneficiary of all is mankind.

Beech woods

Nowhere is this cycle of life more evident than in the broadleaf deciduous woodlands of the temperate biome. Beech woods, which are found all over the biome throughout Europe, Asia and North America, are great examples of this cyclical life and of the yields it can produce. The beech is one of the most stately trees of this biome, a towering grey-barked beauty of sleek strength that looks more human than any other tree, with the European beech (*Fagus sylvatica*) often reaching up to 40m in height, equalled in its grandeur by its American relation (*F. grandifolia*). Beeches are great providers, as anyone who has seen a chipmunk or a squirrel feeding on beech nuts will know.

According to Gandhi and Isomaki in the *Book of Trees*, the vegetable oil produced from beechnuts stays fresher than most, with a high yield of about 20 per cent of the nuts' weight. In Germany, during both World Wars, beechnut oil was produced from nuts (mast) collected by schoolchildren. Today, beechnuts are present in some forms of 'nut butter', a delicious, nutritious and widely available replacement for dairy produce and cheaper forms of margarine, produced from vegetable oil. This is merely one yield from one of the most widespread trees of the temperate deciduous biome and if you add to this the tree's timber, leaves, shade, shelter, play, spiritual food and simply the glory of the tree itself, – all these factors together show the importance of a single species of tree within the woodland system.

Layers of growth

Woodland that has generated naturally has seven storeys or layers of growth, each of which has a place and a purpose. The lowest storey is the root zone where the roots of all plants intermingle. A ground cover layer forms the next storey, which might be made up of ferns or small bulbous plants and the storey after that comprises shrubs. Already we can see how life is building up: in the root zone live earthworms and small mammals, among the ground cover are beetles and spiders and in the shrub layer are those birds that do not inhabit the high branches of the taller trees. The small-tree layer comprises saplings or seedlings canopy trees, or volunteer species of tree that only grow to a certain height and have arrived by accident, perhaps in bird droppings. There is a further intermediate layer before the canopy of the wood is reached. The seventh layer of growth is made up of climbing plants whose natural habit of growth is to wind around or cling to others. An example of this in European woods would be ivy, which makes excellent autumn forage for bees. In the USA it might be a wild grape, poison ivy or Virginia creeper. Epiphytic plants such as orchids and ferns also live on trees in various different layers of a wood but do not constitute a 'layer'.

Woods and woodland, with all the benefits they bring, must never be neglected in the landscape of this biome, for they are the glue that binds all forms of life together

Life cycles and wildlife

A deciduous woodland is habitat-rich and therefore attractive to animals. The combination of nutrients supplied by fallen leaves and animal droppings creates a rich soil which encourages strong plant growth. The more plants there are, the more animals, insects and birds – and the healthier and more robust the system becomes. The specific wildlife supported by the woodland depends on the kind of trees that grow within it. A shining example is in the far northern reaches of Hokkaido in Japan, where the dominant woodland tree is the Konara oak (*Quercus serrata*). These trees are coppiced secondary growth, the original timber having been cut down for commercial purposes, leaving stumps. The coppiced shoots reach some 10-12m in height and, because the growth is on thin shoots rather than older branches, more light reaches the ground, making it a richer habitat for mammals. Grasses and ferns make up the ground cover and the woodland is home to the brown bear, Sika deer and the indigenous Japanese flying squirrel.

The woodlands of eastern North America maintain the greatest diversity of flora and fauna in the temperate deciduous biome. The Catoctin Woods of Maryland, for example, boast impressive populations of oaks, hickories and maples, with an understorey of the beautiful dogwood, *Cornus florida*. The bright berries of this shrub feed cedar waxwings, robins and wood thrushes in the autumn. Mammals abound, including white-tailed deer, chipmunks, squirrels, skunks, raccoons, opossums and even black bears.

In the temperate deciduous biome we are blessed with woodland as a natural feature of the landscape and as a managed environment, and the importance of preserving it cannot be stressed too strongly. Woods are gene banks, carbon sinks, animal and plant refuges and a source of comfort and delight to humans: they stabilize the soil, maintain diversity and offer numerous yields. Thankfully, woodland is now being replanted on a grand scale throughout Europe through grant-led European Union schemes. In North America are organizations such as American Forests, founded in 1875, which helped to create the National Park and National Forest systems which protect so many trees throughout the USA. American Forests plants millions of trees each year through its Global ReLeaf programme.

Differing from forest with its open, rather than closed, canopy, woodland offers more light and more potential for lower-growing species (overleaf). It is no less diverse and adheres to the principles of the seven layers, which range from the root zone up to the tallest canopy tree.

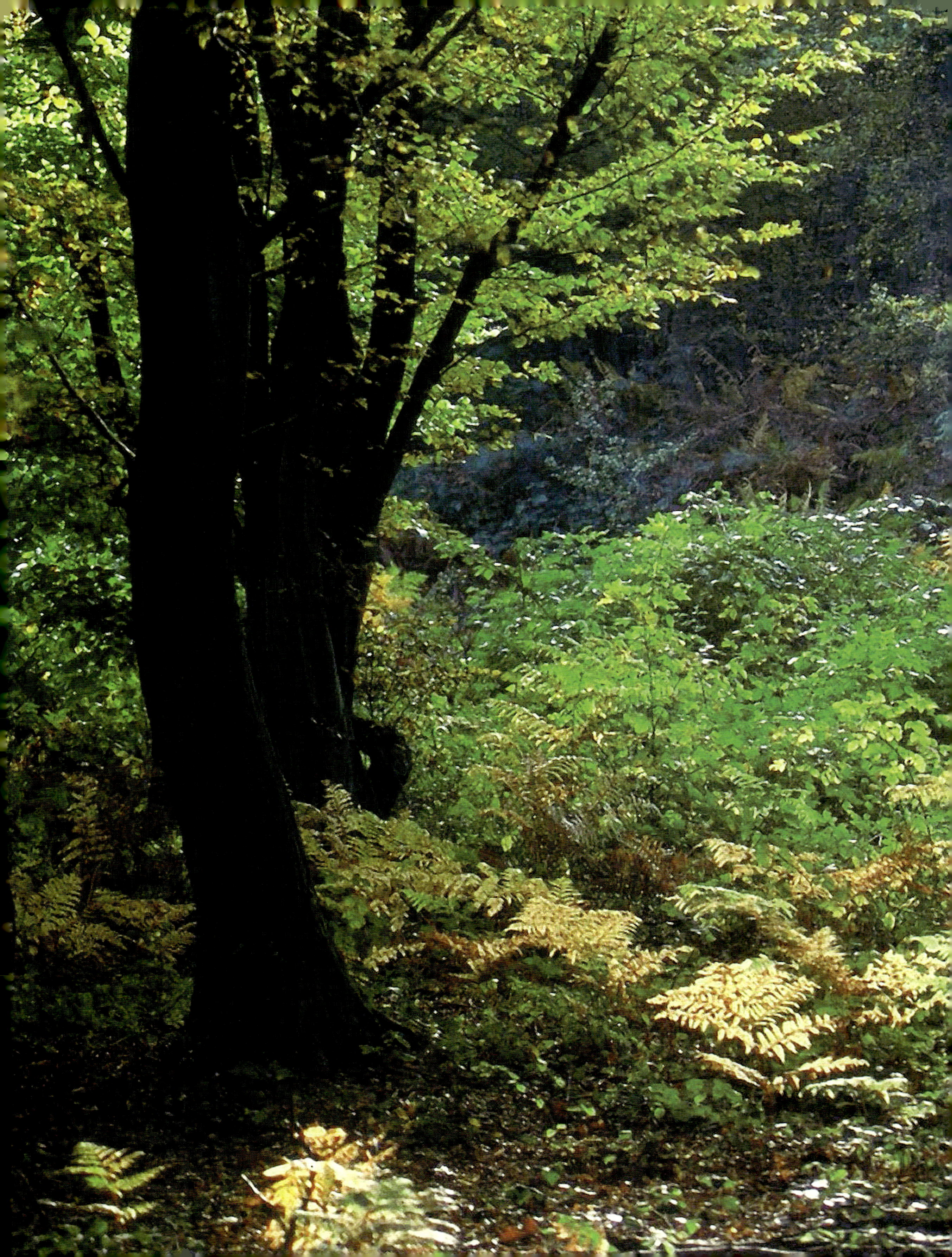

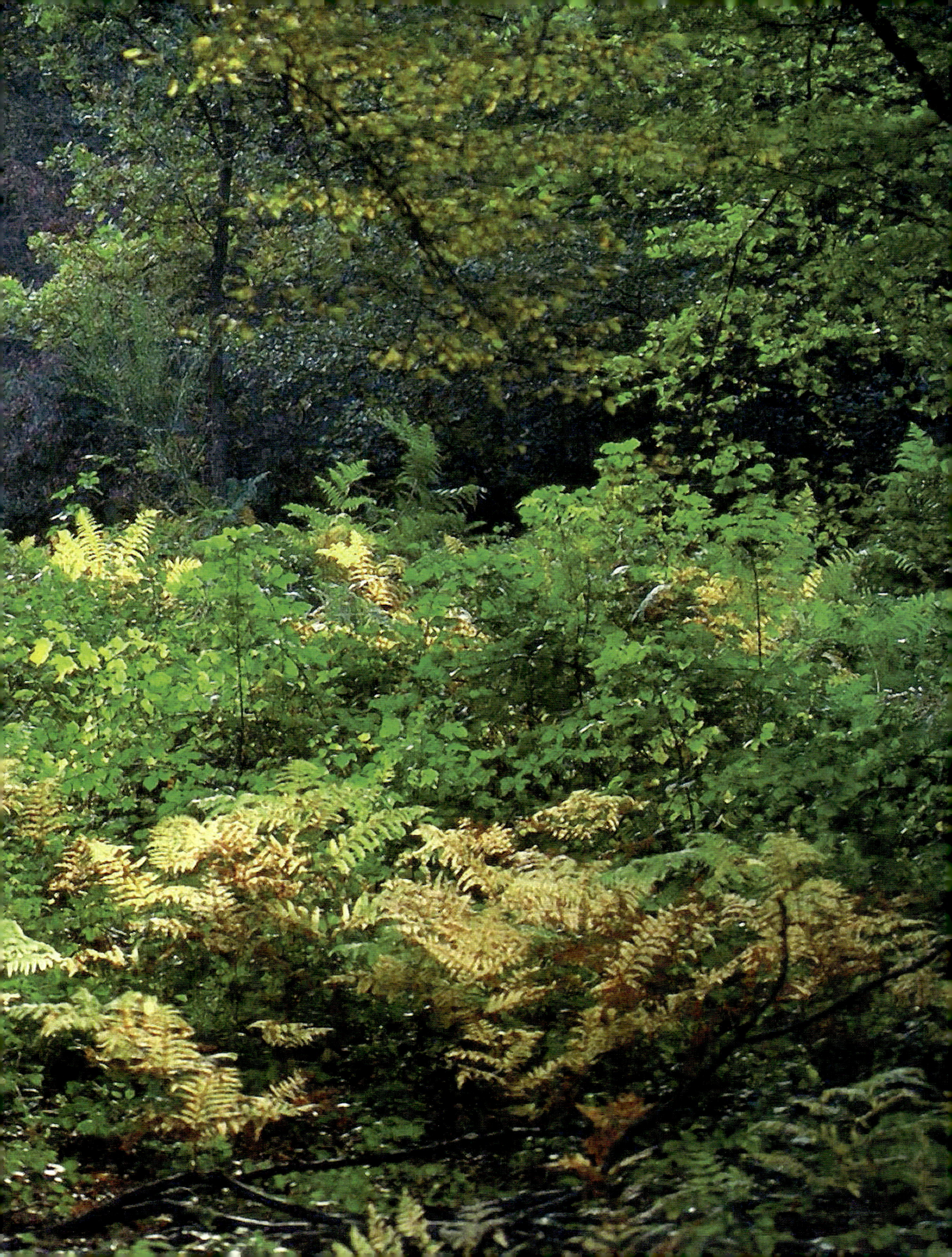

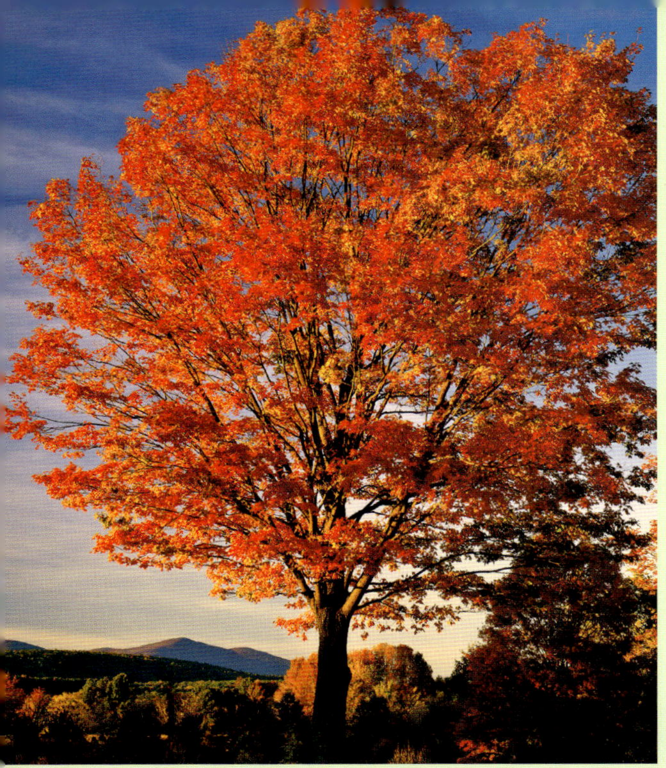

The maple must rank among the finest of trees found in the USA and Canada, every American state having at least one native species. They are such a significant constituent of woods and forests throughout the temperate zones there that 12.5 million hectares of hardwood forest in Michigan, Pennsylvania, Maine, New York and Wisconsin (where the sugar maple is the state tree) is taken up by maples. These two countries are by no means the only homes of this large genus. While the Canadian maple (*Acer rubrum*) and sugar maple (*A. saccharum*) are two of the largest, there are innumerable species. North-east Asia, in particular China, Japan and Korea, has produced many smaller, decorative species and varieties used in gardens today.

Sugar maples, seen above in New York State in their autumn colours, do much more than produce sugar sap. They support hundreds of different birds and insects as well as mammals like squirrel, deer and porcupine. The seeds make early forage for honey bees and are cached by voles and mice for winter. The population of sugar maples in the areas in which it is commercially grown is on the increase as it is fast-growing and the timber can be used for pulp, board, fine joinery and, increasingly, firewood. So hard and resilient is the wood that the tree is a favourite with manufacturers of ten-pin-bowling pins, or skittles.

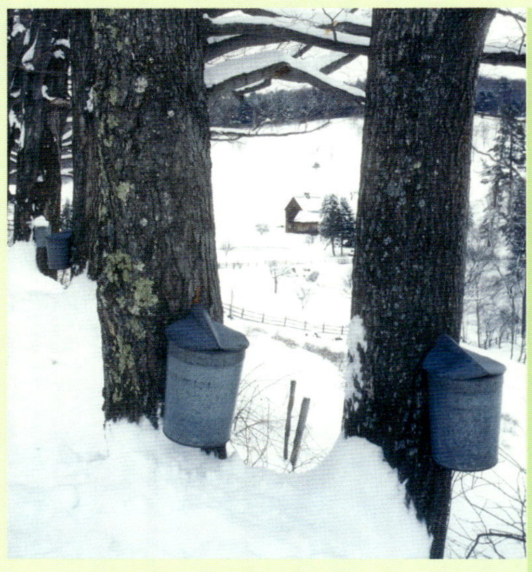

The native Indians were producing syrup well before *The Mayflower* landed in 1620

Maple woods are stable, sustainable environments and the sugar industry is an old one that has been carefully guarded through generations. While the trees tend to grow en bloc, the forest supports several smaller trees and shrubs beneath its canopy. In Canada, where the sugar maple is cultivated on a gigantic commercial scale to produce 85 per cent of the world's supply of maple syrup, there are more than 10,000 producers. It takes 34 gallons of sap to produce one gallon of syrup and a mature tree provides 5-40 gallons per year.

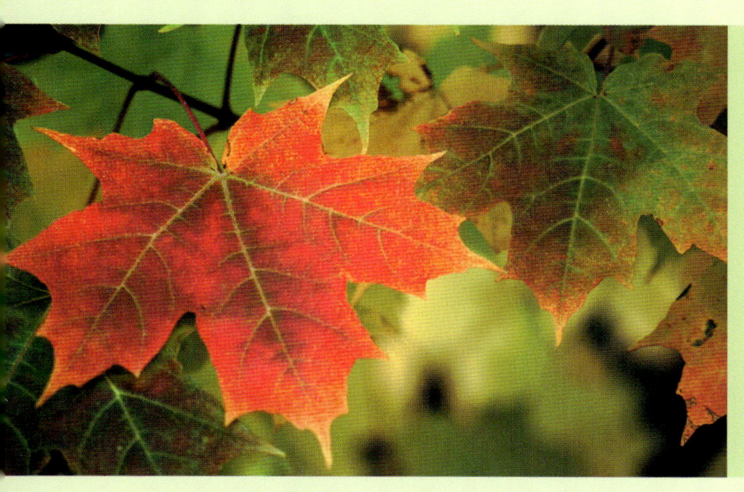

Autumn spectacle For many people, the economic strengths of the *Acer* genus are trifling in comparison to its ornamental qualities. In Japan, 'Hanami', the passion for cherry blossom viewing in spring, is replaced by 'Momiji-gari', maple leaf viewing, in autumn. While not as many maples dominate public parks as do cherry trees, innumerable native species make wonderfully colourful autumn spectacles. *Acer japonicum* and *A. palmatum*, with their numerous named varieties, are two species well represented throughout Japan's – and the world's – public gardens and outdoor spaces.

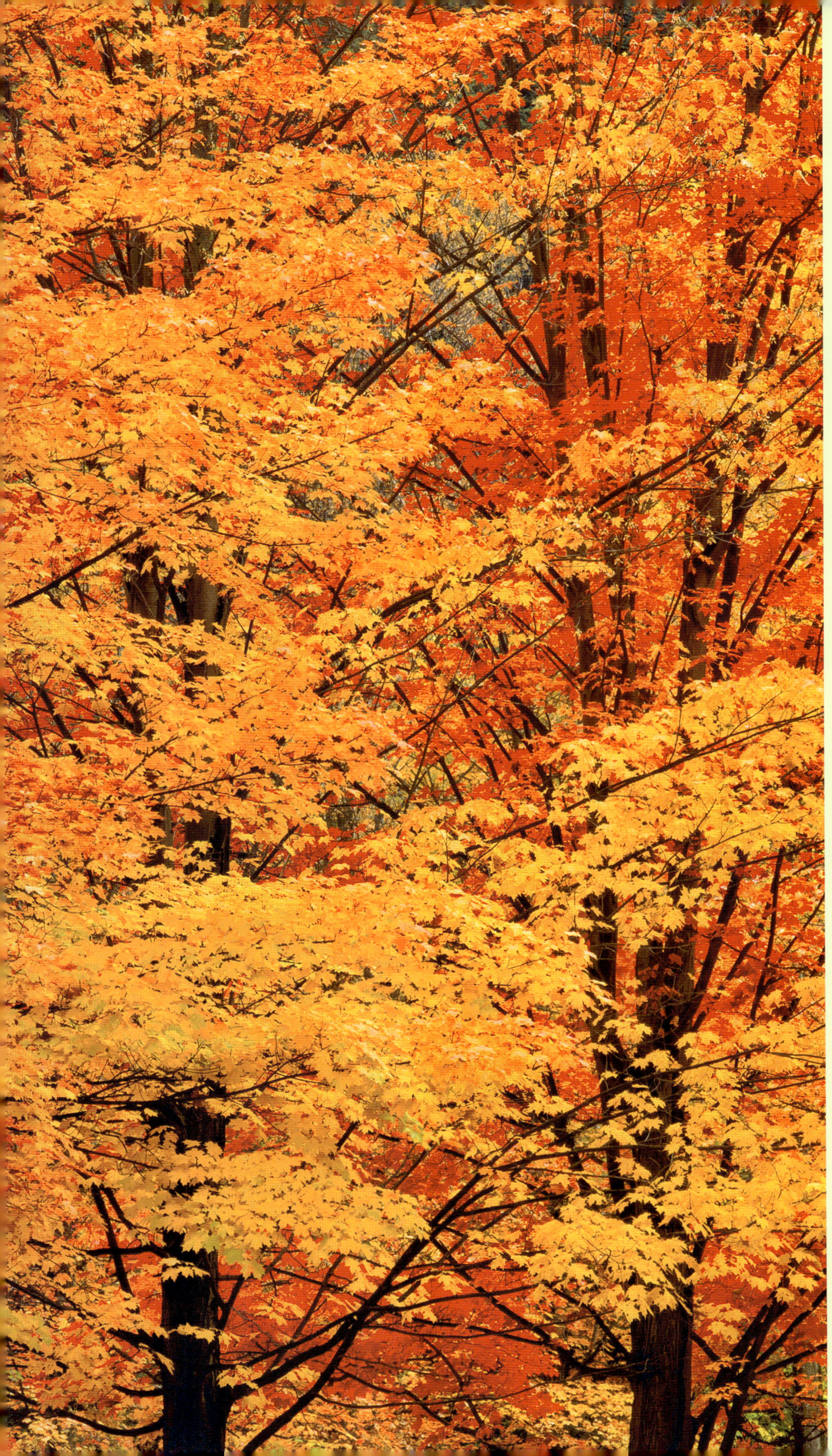

maple

The show of colour produced by maples throughout the temperate biome in autumn would be enough to guarantee the tree a place as a national treasure in any country

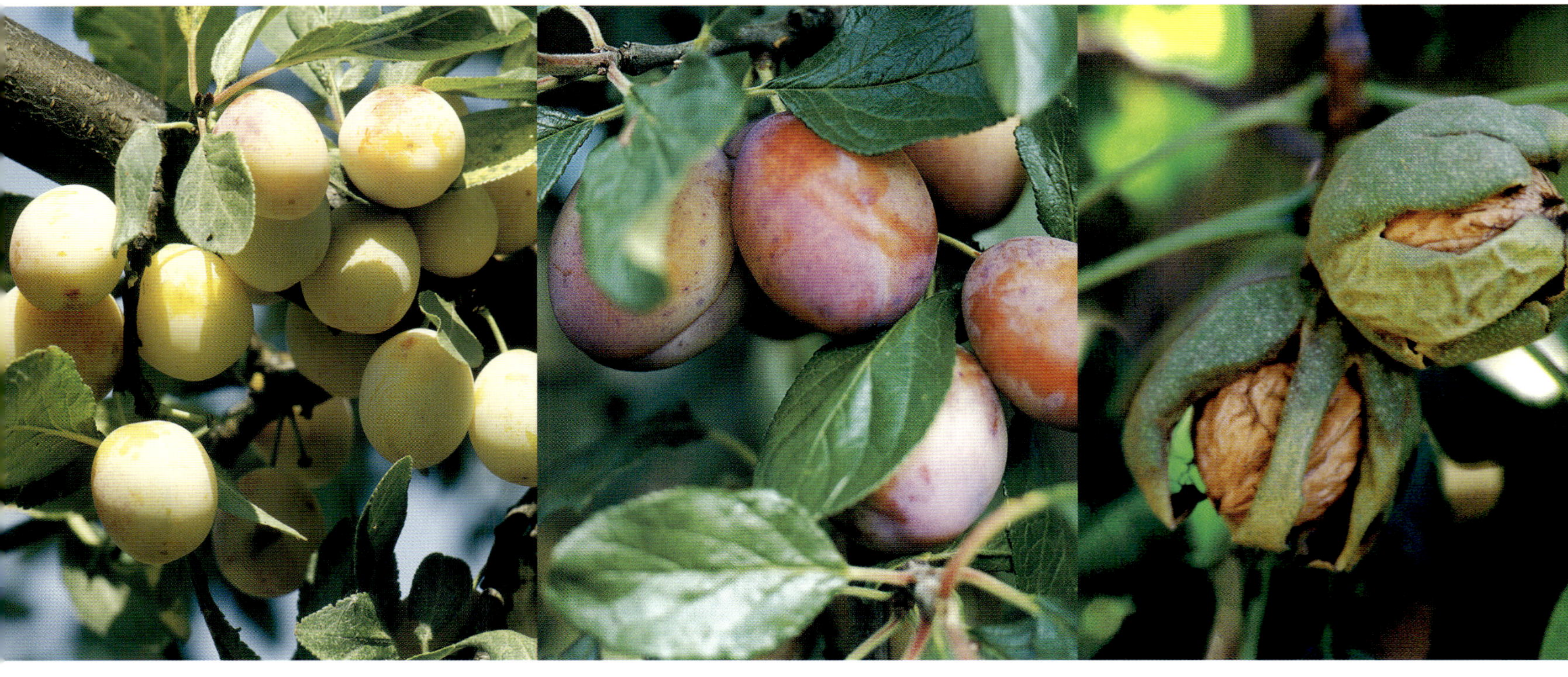

Orchards

There can be few more magical places on earth than an orchard of mature fruit trees. Through all seasons the trees sing their homage to the earth that allows them to bring forth their revered fruit. Whether in the damp of an English winter or amidst the delirium of spring on a Himalayan hillside, when the air is heady with pollen and nectar and the buzz of insects, there is always hope and expectancy in the atmosphere of an orchard. For orchards are special places: they are safe havens for birds, insects and animals and a vital source of food for them and for mankind. They are also a prime source of genetic material for the often ancient varieties of fruit grown in them, which must be preserved at all costs. This comes not from the mono-cropped hectarage of commercial orchards dedicated to overbred varieties of fruit, but from tiny, forgotten orchards all over the world where old fruit trees, gnarled and bent from years of bringing forth crops, hold the secrets of flavour, texture and luxury that made man plant the first orchard in ancient times.

Named varieties of tree fruit are important and must be preserved in small orchards at all costs: above left, Golden greengage 'Mirabelle de Nancy'; above centre, Plum 'Victoria'; above right, English walnuts.

Man's association with fruit has been a long and extremely happy one. From the earliest written times, fruit was seen as a pleasurable luxury, often a sign of great wealth. As early as 5,000 BC the Chinese diplomat Feng Li gave up his high-ranking position in favour of a career grafting fruit on to different rootstocks; he sold the resultant peaches, almonds, persimmons, apples and pears as orchard trees. Other than citrus and bananas, the most popular fruits grown in the world today are the native tree species of the temperate deciduous biome and these include apples, pears, plums and cherries. The cherry (*Prunus avium*) is grown throughout the USA, from Alaska to the Pacific states, as well as all over Europe. It is a big commercial crop in the UK, particularly in the eastern county of Kent whose cherry orchards are famous. There is currently a

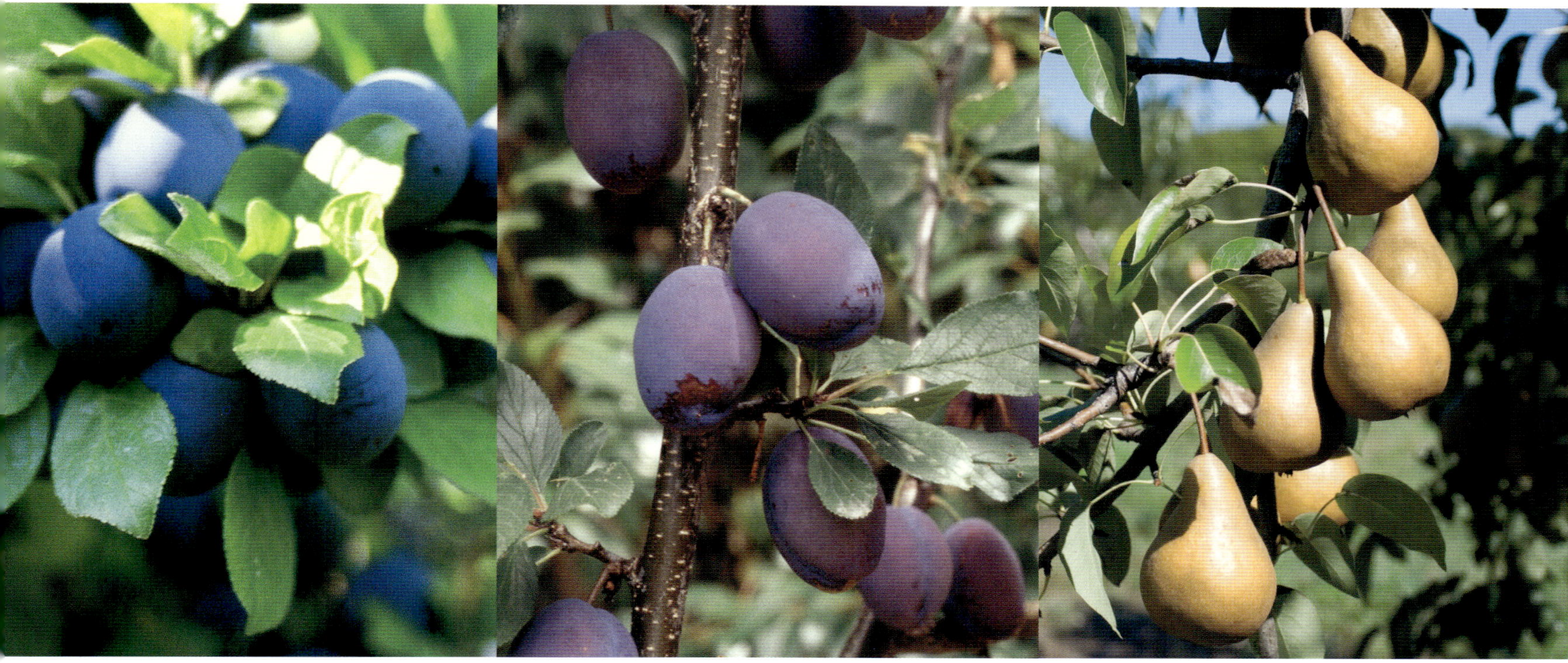

welcome resurgence of the cherry growing industry in Cornwall where, up until the outbreak of the Second World War, the fruit was grown in orchards on the banks of the river Tamar for the early-season London markets. Then there are nut trees, such as walnuts and hazels, which may be grown in orchards too.

Orchards in the temperate biome have suffered badly in modern times in the face of industrial fruit farming. European Community grants were offered to farmers to grub out their orchards in the 1980s, just as they had been for the removal of hedgerows in the 1970s. The UK apple industry has been affected disastrously and may never recover. However, the good news is that a quiet revolution is now taking place as a result of heightened awareness about the quality of our food, the importance of fresh, locally grown produce and sustainable practices of agriculture. Small, homestead orchards are being planted all over Europe and North America, whether they be cherry orchards in Cornwall or walnut orchards in the Dordogne, funded by the same grants that paid for their removal in the first place.

Planting trees in the home environment is probably the single most important act that we can accomplish for the greater good of trees, now and in the future. From watching a fruit tree grow and bear fruit, the next stage is an awareness of the orchard as a place in which to foster self-reliance rather than a dependence on external factors. From excessive 'food miles' to the dominance of the multinational corporations which increasingly control the supply of our food, there currently exists a web of unsustainable practice. But we can play a part in reversing it by petitioning our food retailers to stock locally grown tree fruit; this will help to finance the planting of orchards and to show what food-producing trees can do for the environment.

Small orchards are under threat from cheap imports of regular-shaped but sub-standard fruit produced for the retail giants. Above left, Damson; above centre, Plum 'Czar'; above right, Pear 'Conference'.

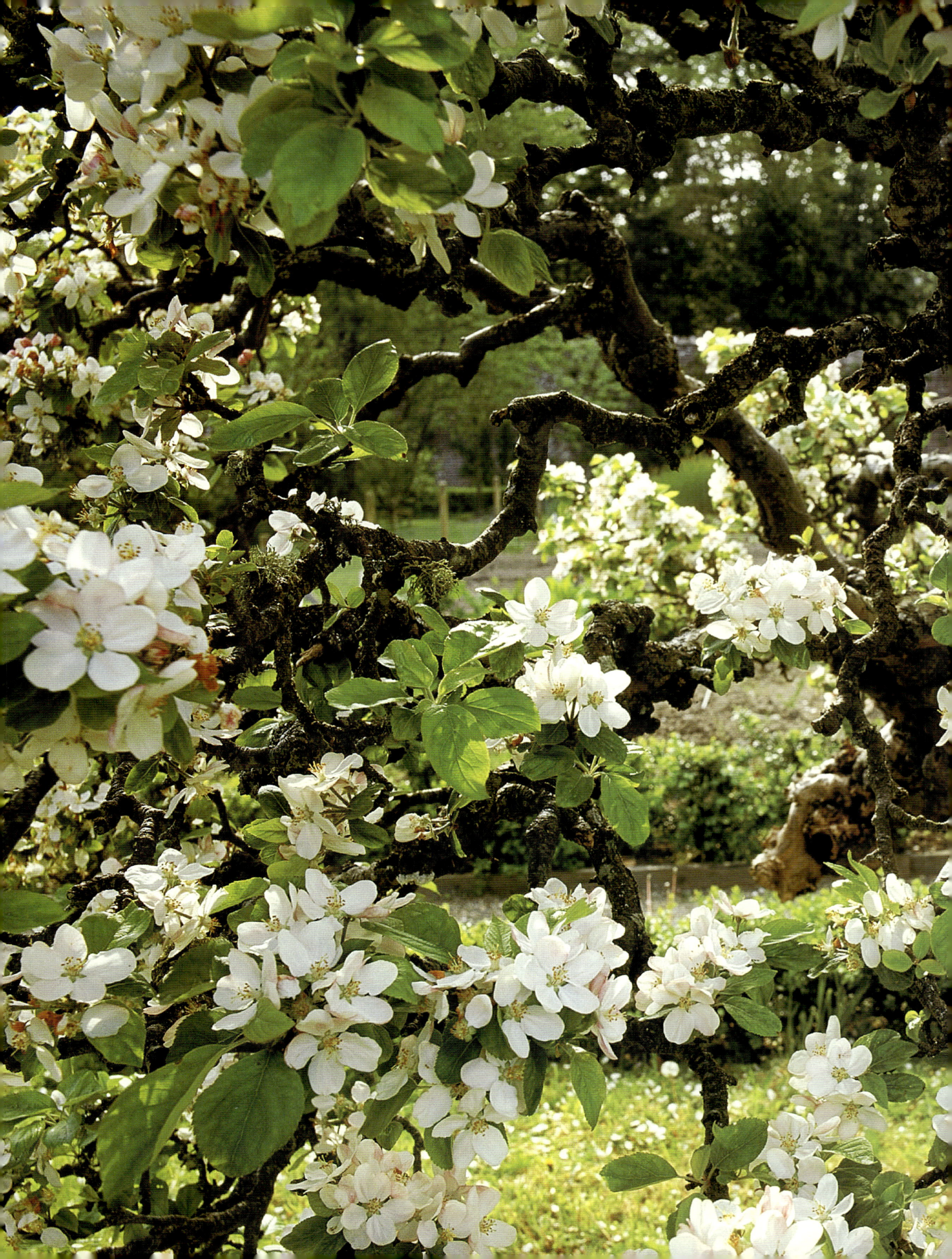

apple

As we shuffle blindly along the path of conservation and ecological recovery, it is something as simple as planting an apple variety with its origins in your area, wherever you happen to live, that will make the difference

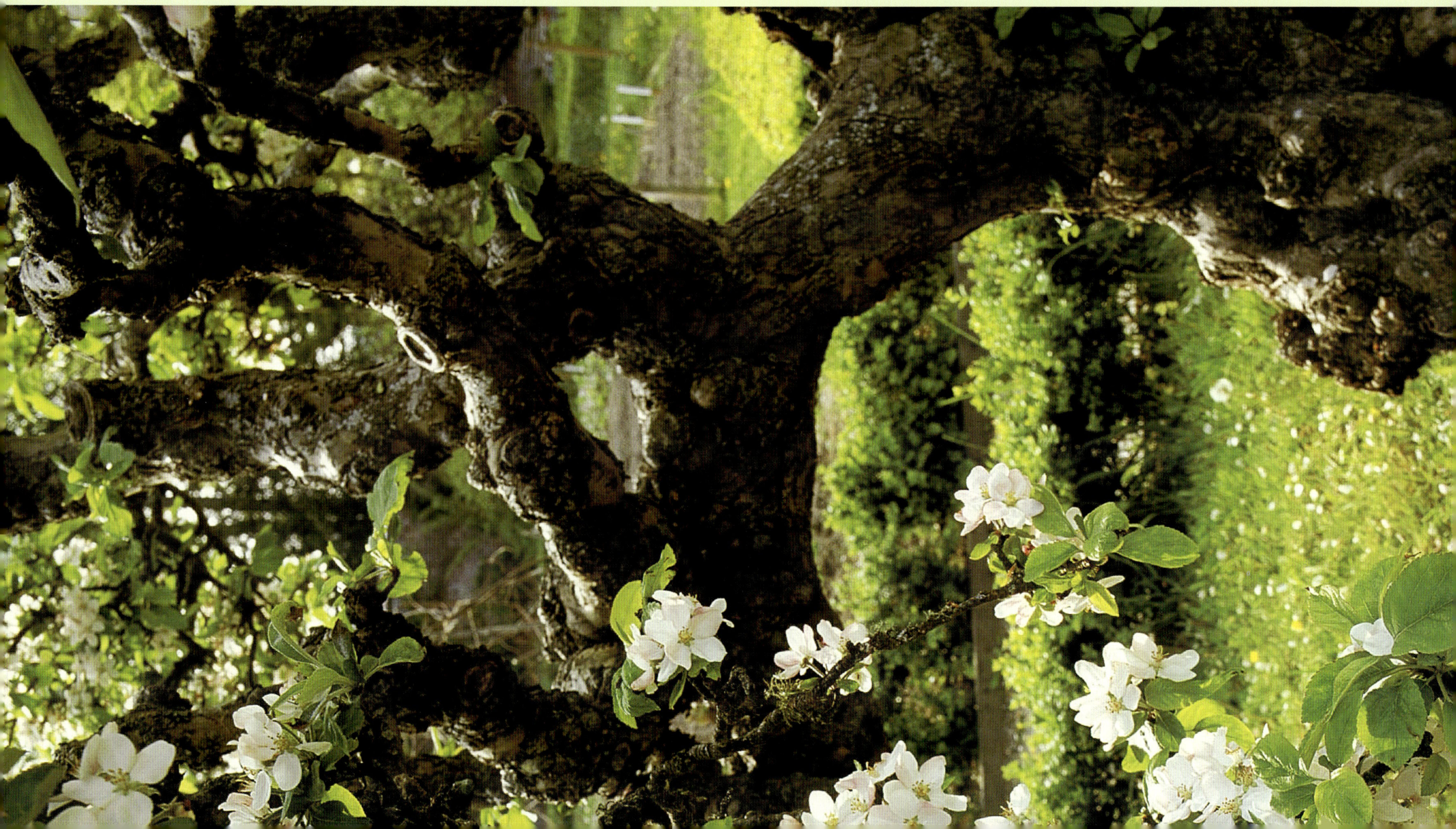

apple

Trees act in many ways for the betterment of the planet and mankind. The apple (*Malus domestica*) does not achieve great height or size, it is not famed as a carbon sink nor is it a great producer of timber. Yet there is so much to an apple tree: the magnificent way in which it curls and loops as it grows, before bending with age as though carrying the weight of the world through its boughs; fragrant pink and white blossom to gladden the heart; the mass of bees and their frantic need for nectar, pollen and pollination; and the groups of blue, great and long-tailed tits which move through the foliage in search of aphids. And then there is the crop itself, rich and scented, tart and sweet, fresh or stored – the range is infinitely varied. Finally, old age, perhaps with mistletoe high in the stooped, gnarled branches; then death and more scent, the scent from the burning apple logs.

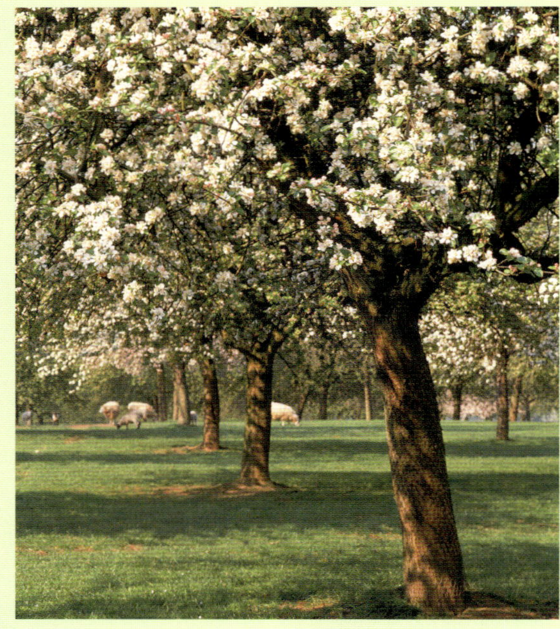

Success story The apple has nourished civilizations since the fruit began its long journey, over 10,000 years ago, from the mountainsides of Kazakhstan where wild fruits grow to this day. Prominent when farming began in the Fertile Crescent 6,500 years ago, the fruit appears throughout history, nourishing armies and kings, inspiring writers and poets. It is known to have fed the armies of Darius of Persia and Alexander the Great 300 years before Christ and, by Roman times, when Pliny listed over 20 varieties in his *Natural History*, the apple's place was assured.

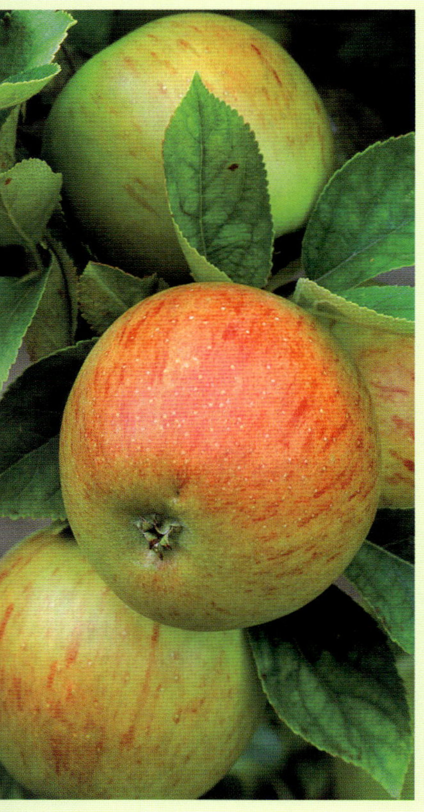

The test of time That the apple took such a hold can be attributed to several factors. The first is that apple varieties do not come true from seed, so varieties were constantly changing, by means of grafting wood on to different rootstocks and improving them to adapt to different climates. Numbers of named cultivars across the world today run into thousands. The second is that the apple is remarkably tolerant of a wide range of temperatures and soil types. Its two basic requirements are a period of cold – a winter – to set fruit buds, and a means of pollinating the flowers to produce fruit, a job which bees and other insects do well. Third, apples hold their vigour and nutritional value in storage like no other fruit; some varieties can last through an entire winter. John Standish, a variety raised in the UK in 1873, is known as the Christmas apple because it needs at least two months in storage, from a mid-autumn picking, to reach full sweetness, during which time it remains crisp and firm. Such qualities ensured that the apple's journey from central Russia to all four corners of the northern hemisphere was a relatively untroubled one. Having withstood the test of time, the apple is now second only to the banana in terms of its commercial value.

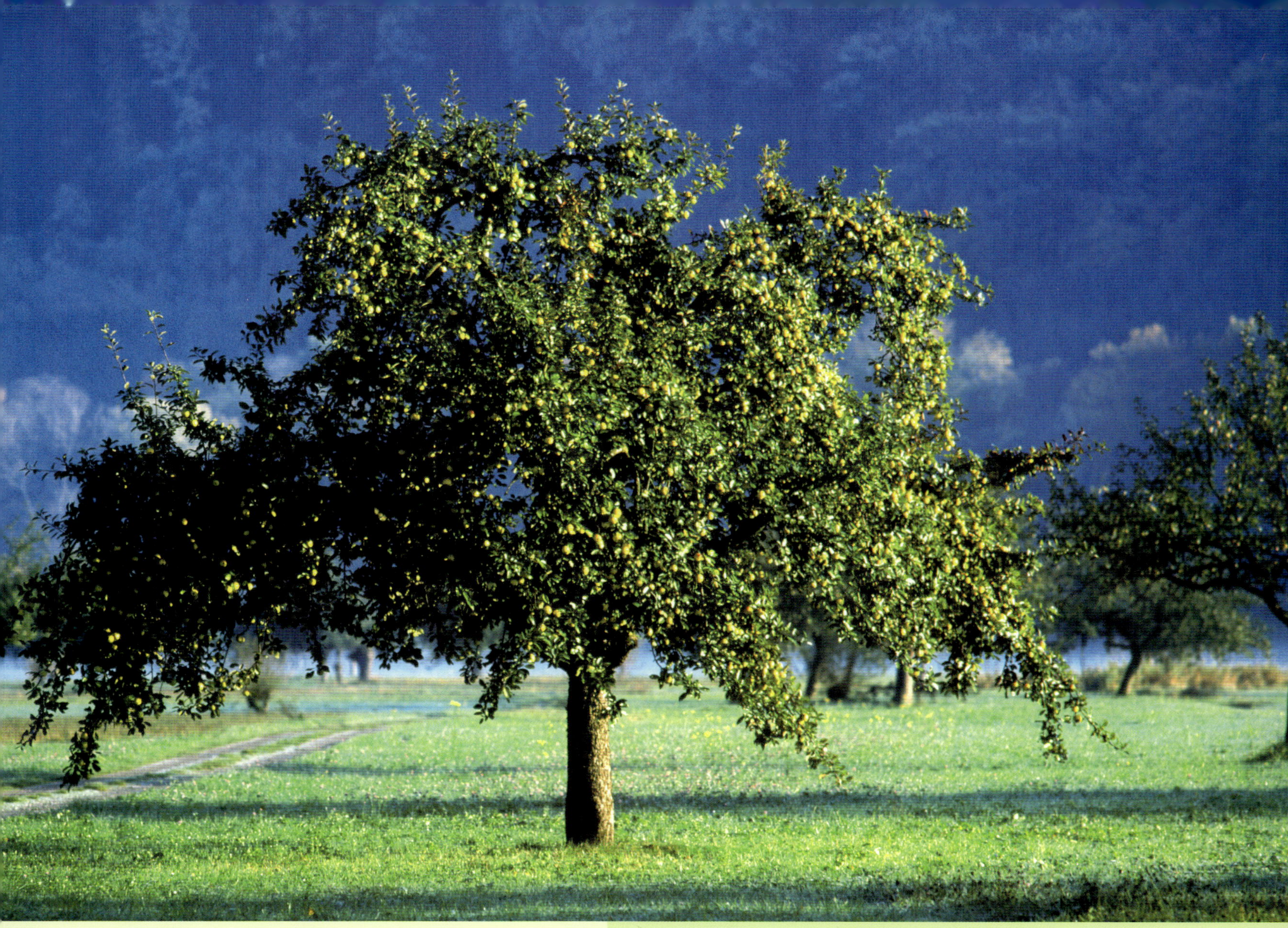

The apple's is a phenomenal success story to which few other trees on the planet have even come close.

A questionable future More than 60 million tonnes of apples are produced worldwide each year, with China alone providing almost half that quantity. The apple's adaptability has served it well: it is eaten raw, cooked and made into any number of drinks, from cider to distilled spirits. There are dessert varieties, cooking varieties, those that do both and specific types that have been bred to produce cider. No other fruit has adapted so well to local conditions through breeding.

But sadly all is not well in today's apple industry. In the UK, for example, orchards of native cultivars are being grubbed out daily in the face of cheap imports which live up to the uniform requirements of the retailing giants. English growers, with their cripplingly expensive spraying regimes, have priced themselves out of the market by failing to change to organic methods and to try new varieties; they must shoulder much of the blame for the decline of a once great fruit. Fewer varieties and a one-size-fits-all mentality might suit the cost-driven policies of the multinational food chains but bode badly for the future of the apple. If we lose the wide range of varieties, we lose not only history but, crucially, genetic diversity. While we know that demand for fresh fruit of local origin exists, it is the way we shop in the first place that has to change. We must support those producers that tend our heritage, campaign for the widest possible number of varieties and support the work of small farmers all over the globe to uphold diversity – for the apple is one of the greatest of all our trees and its fruit a perennial favourite.

Future energy

We are all familiar with solar and wind power as clean forms of energy but there are other, less direct means of accessing power from both of these sources, particularly solar. Humankind has been using 'biomass' since we learned the secret of fire – and burning dried animal waste on cooking fires is still common practice in parts of Asia and Africa today. Biomass is simply the use of plant matter and animal waste for energy; the critical component is the sun, which stimulates plants, and therefore animals, to grow. This is the most basic form of storing the sun's energy. The finite resources that we are now using up, such as oil and coal, were produced in the same way – they too started life as plants and animals.

Renewable sources

Currently, biomass in the USA provides some 30 times more energy than solar and wind power put together. Beyond that, bioenergy resources such as forestry, agricultural crops like sugar beet and various grasses such as species of *Miscanthus*, combined with the wastes and residues from biomass, provide 14 per cent of the world's primary energy supplies. The figures are increasing year on year, and it is all down to the energy of the sun. Under the Kyoto Agreement of 1997, governments are committed to reducing emissions of 'greenhouse' gases, such as carbon dioxide and methane, and have undertaken to ensure that an ever-growing percentage of their electricity requirements are met by renewable energy resources. How astonishing, then, that we still burn coal, a non-renewable, finite resource and one that fills the atmosphere with carbon and other greenhouse gases, to produce electricity.

We are pumping so much more carbon dioxide into the atmosphere from burning fossil fuels that the consequences of global warming are rising

The constituents of the gases are not the problem, in fact, but their action of holding the heat, which warms up the earth and the oceans. Carbon dioxide is an essential element of plant growth but we are pumping so much more into the atmosphere from burning fossil fuels that global warming is rising. And this is why more trees need to be planted.

The role of trees

Trees have an important role to play in the future production of biomass energy. Not only do some species grow extremely fast, they can be cut close to the ground in a practice known as 'coppicing', which stimulates them to regrow. In this manner, trees can be harvested every three to seven years over a 20-30-year period before being replanted. Rotated like this, some crops can reach great heights in between harvests.

Hazel was the tree most closely associated with coppicing through the ages, especially in the UK, primarily for homestead and horticultural uses. Hazel poles are still used to support rows of beans, while the wide, curly tops provided 'pea sticks', for the pea tendrils to cling to. Certain species of willow were also used, and 'pollarded' willows are still a common sight throughout Europe. Pollarding – cutting a mature tree hard back, high up the stem, to force young growth – has been a decorative fashion in mainland Europe for certain trees over the centuries. Particularly in the south of France, plane trees and limes are often seen as bare, headless trunks in the depths of winter and a mass of sprouting shoots in summer.

Growing willows for biomass

The humble willow, which has given us the flexible stems known as osiers, or withies, for baskets, not to mention being the source of the cricket bats which grace the great stadiums of the world, has been singled out as a major player in our energy crisis. Fast-growing species are now being bred specifically for biomass production. It has been joined by certain species of poplar and, in hotter, wetter climates, particularly the south-eastern states of the USA, by sweet gum (*Liquidambar styraciflua*) and in Australia by eucalyptus.

The short-rotation coppicing of willow for biomass gathers steam as farmers explore ways to maximize the potential of their land at a time when food in the western world is over-produced and taxpayers have to pay farmers not to grow crops. Willows are hardy and tolerant of wind; they make good subjects to grow in poor, marginal land and wetlands and, as they are harvested in the winter after leaf fall, allowing nutrients in the leaves to return to the soil, they also make a good upland crop. In areas where fuel is in short supply or expensive, the availability of biofuel energy is of great value.

The fast-growing willow hybrids used for biomass, some of which grow up to 4m a year, are coppiced and harvested on a four-to-six year rotation, producing high per-hectare yields in a short space of time; they also produce valuable wood in their young shoots. Unlike annual crops, there is no need for heavy applications of pesticides and herbicides and, as the trees remain in situ for 20 years or more, a stable environment exists for other forms of life, particularly in the root zone. After the first cut-back in the winter of the first year after planting, they grow swiftly, straight as a die, from the plant's crown or stool. Planted in close proximity, they produce a thick belt of foliage and, at harvest time, when the leaves have dropped, the whole plant is cut to the ground and shipped by road to a processing plant. Here the plants are put through a chipping machine before being burned to produce the chosen form of energy. It seems an ignominious use for such a noble tree, the branches of which the great poet Orpheus was said to have carried with him for inspiration on his journeys through the underworld. But what greater sacrifice could the willow make than to put itself forward for the future?

Willows are being grown for the production of biomass for fuel (overleaf). They have always been pollarded to encourage shoots for manufacturing but now they are burned. Hybrid varieties, specially bred to grow at an astonishingly fast rate, are cut by machine and fed to hungry boilers in the search for cleaner, greener energy.

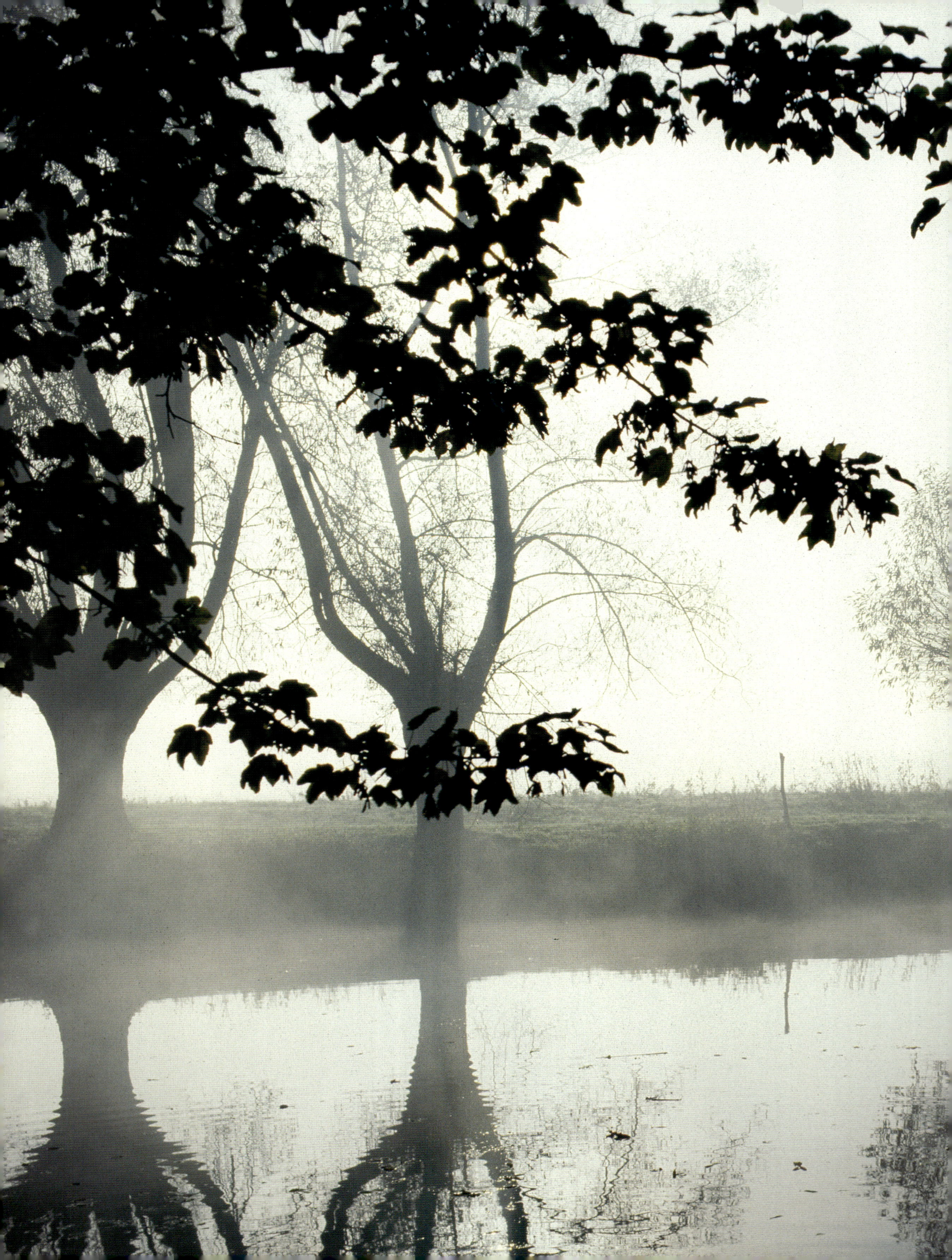

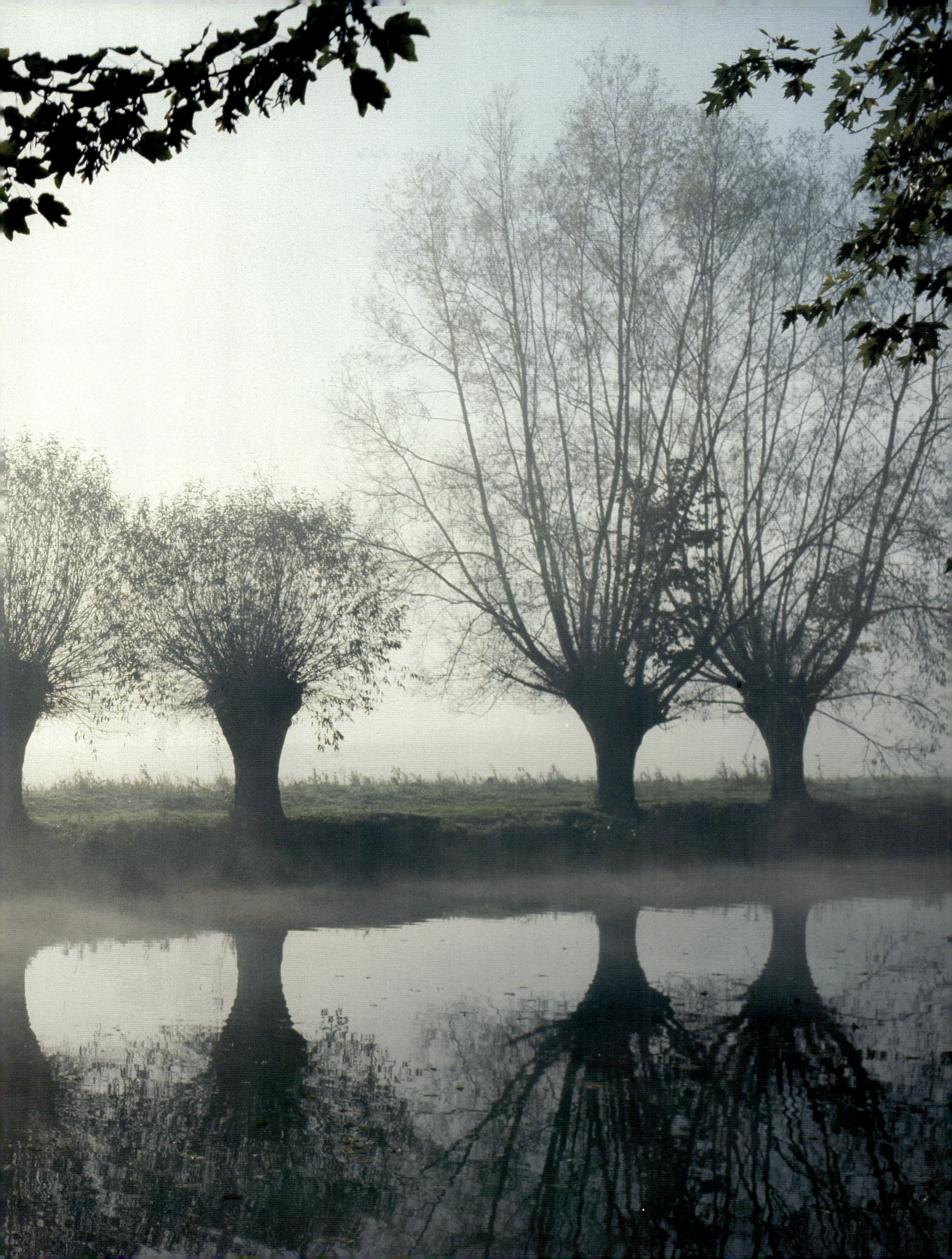

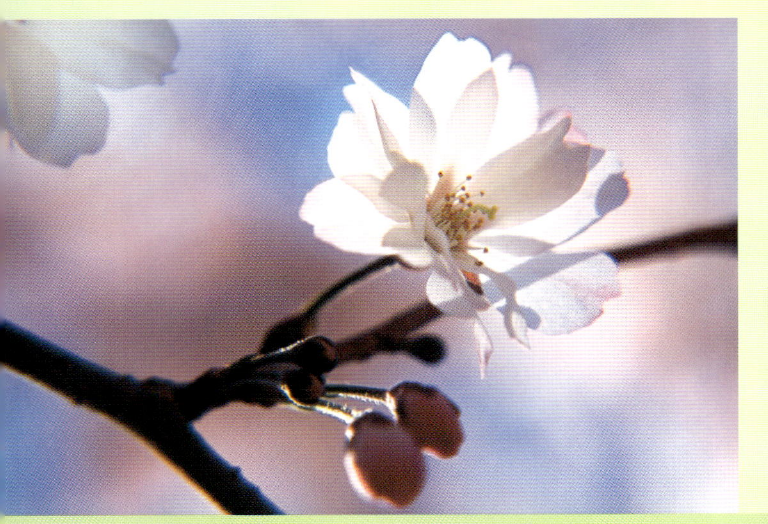

During Japan's feudal period, the cherry blossom became symbolic of Samurai lives – colourful and brief, its brevity like the frailty of life itself. Second World War militarist propaganda claimed that the buds represented the souls of seamen and soldiers and the falling petals the time of their glorious death

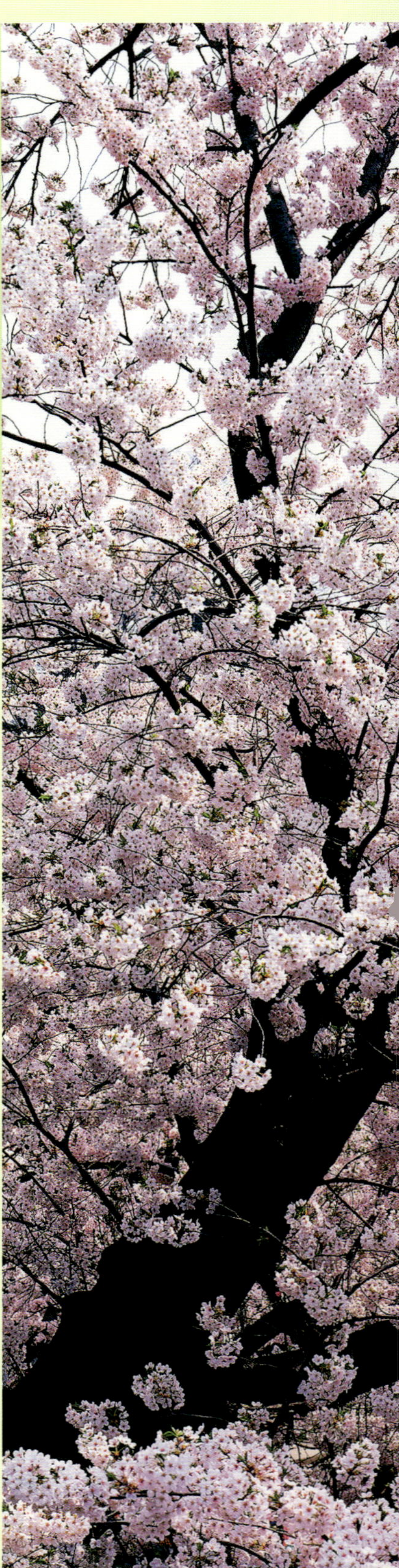

The national flower of Japan is the subject of deep reverence in its country of origin. Like the maple in eastern USA and the oak in England, the Japanese cherry is a true icon – no other race of people pays homage to a tree in the manner of the Japanese to their cherry. *Prunus serrulata* is one species of a large family (Rosaceae) containing some of the finest of flowering trees, particularly with edible fruit, in the temperate biome. While the edible cherry was probably brought to Europe by the Roman General and gourmand Luccullus around 66 BC, the cherry as an ornamental tree was introduced into Europe from China as late as 1822. This wide-spreading, flat-topped tree grows wild in Japan, Korea and China. Its hooped, dotted bark is almost as recognizable as the mass of double white flowers produced each spring on bare wood.

Cultural celebrations The custom of cherry blossom viewing has been in practice in Japan since the seventh century; it is known as 'Hanami' (Hana – flower, mi – to see). Hanami parties and cherry blossom festivals are held all over the country during spring, with merchandise produced especially for the great event. From Okinawa Island in the south to the island of Hokkaido in the north, there is a frantic competition to find out where the first blossom is out and where it is best. Television bulletins and special weather forecasts keep the population up to date with the latest Hanami news. Long queues form in public parks and people jostle to find the best position to hold a party.

The Tokyo cherry 1872 marked the discovery of the hybrid, *P* x *yedoensis*, the Tokyo or Yoshino cherry. This tree, with its scent of almonds and soft white flowers, is unknown in the wild but has become the signature Japanese cherry. It is the most widely planted species throughout the country's public parks. A specimen is planted in front of the White House in Washington and, on a grander scale, 3,700 Yoshino cherries encircle the Jefferson Memorial on the tidal basin at East Potomac Park. A gift from the Japanese in 1912, their great burst of colour signals the start of spring, as it does in Japan, where these magnificent cherries bloom each year.

japanese cherry

To the vast numbers of us who live in cities, green spaces with trees are a lifeline. Not for nothing are trees labelled 'the lungs of the earth'; on account of their ability to exchange carbon dioxide for oxygen, in the cities they may as well be called oxygen masks. In 1950 the combined population of Tokyo/Yokohama, the two great cities of Japan which are joined into one, was eight million people; today it has risen to nearly 29 million. While population growth has slowed since the 1950s in cities such as London and Moscow, and even fell in New York between 1970 and 1984, Tokyo has just carried on growing. Just as well, then, that the people of Tokyo have an unerring respect for nature and the numerous parks of their city. Other parts of the world could learn lessons from Japan and its respect for the tree most dear to the Japanese.

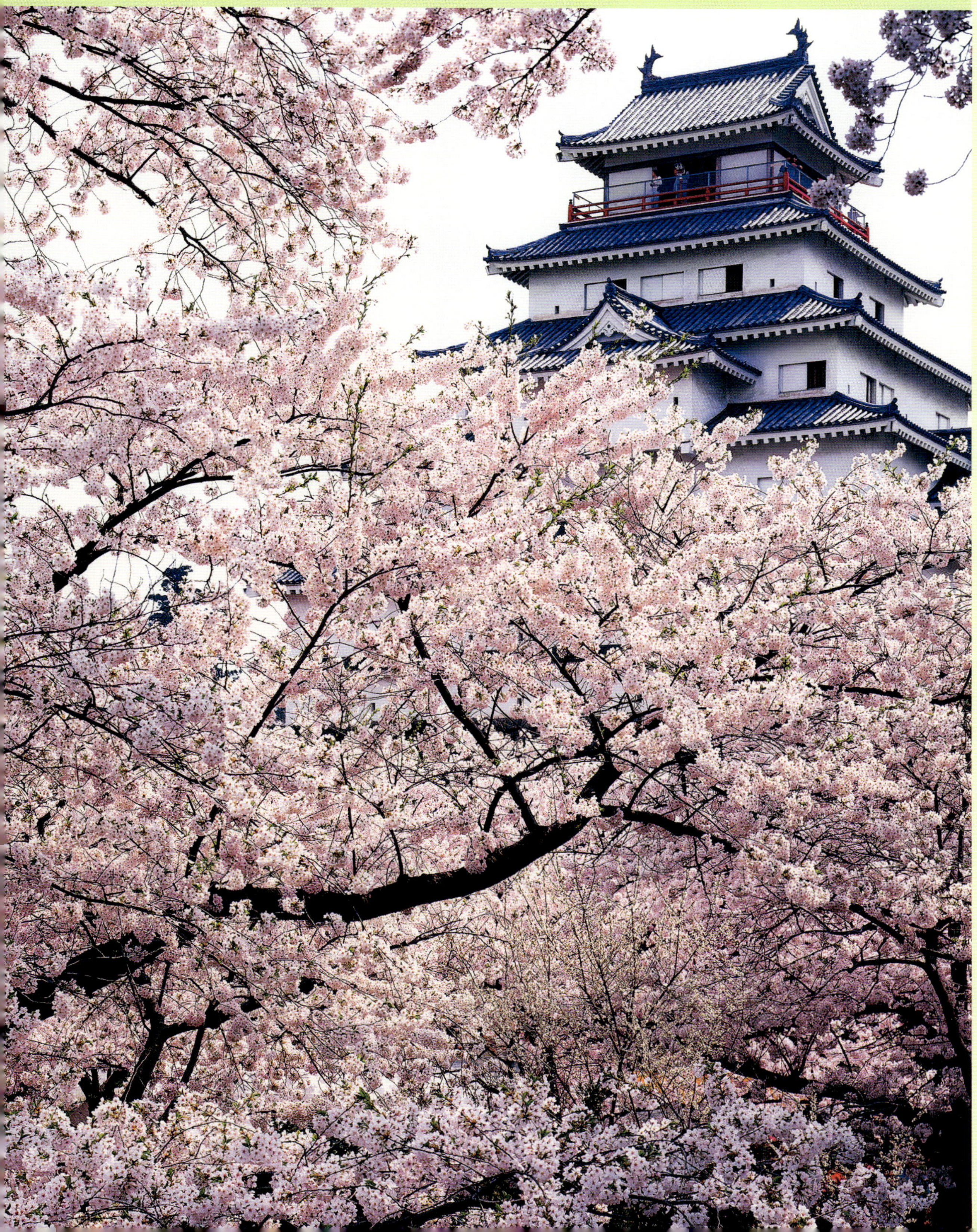

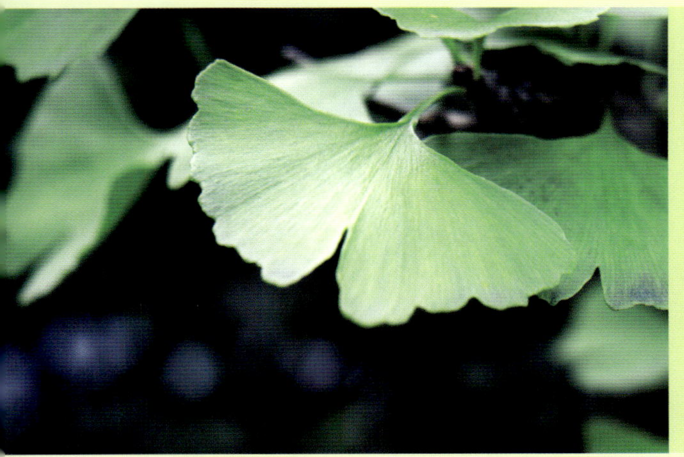

The ginkgo, with its distinctive, notched, fan-shaped leaves, is unchanged since the Jurassic period 150 million years ago. As the only living member of the seed-plants of that ancient era, it is a precious historical link between the realms of the lower and higher orders of plants. To have survived this far gives the ginkgo an excellent chance of continuing to be around in the future, if only because none of its natural predators any longer exist. The maidenhair tree is probably a native of China, although it was discovered by the German scientist Kaempfer in 1690 in Japan, from where it made its way to Europe in the 1730s.

Medicinal properties The Chinese have for centuries used the leaves and seed of the maidenhair tree as a herbal medicine to treat a number of conditions. And today *Ginkgo biloba* is the most widely used herbal medicine in the world and for this reason is grown on a massive scale, particularly in America. In Sumter, South Carolina, more than 10 million trees are cultivated by a French/German partnership in co-operation with the Chinese. *Ginkgo biloba* is administered to help with memory impairment and for dizziness, as well as for other circulatory problems. It also has antioxidant properties, useful in the prevention of many cancers. In Germany it has been approved to treat Alzheimer's disease, and research continues to bring it into use in other countries – an appropriate use for a long-lived tree.

Modern research centres on extract, prepared from only the dried green leaves. Highly concentrated, the extract is more effective in treating health problems than the leaf alone, as it contains a vitamin that strengthens blood vessels and reduces the production of tissue-damaging free radicals. It is fitting that the ginkgo is proving to be one of the most important contemporary medicinal trees, since it must carry some of the earth's ancient secrets in its genes.

The ginkgo is proving to be one of the most important medicinal trees of the modern era

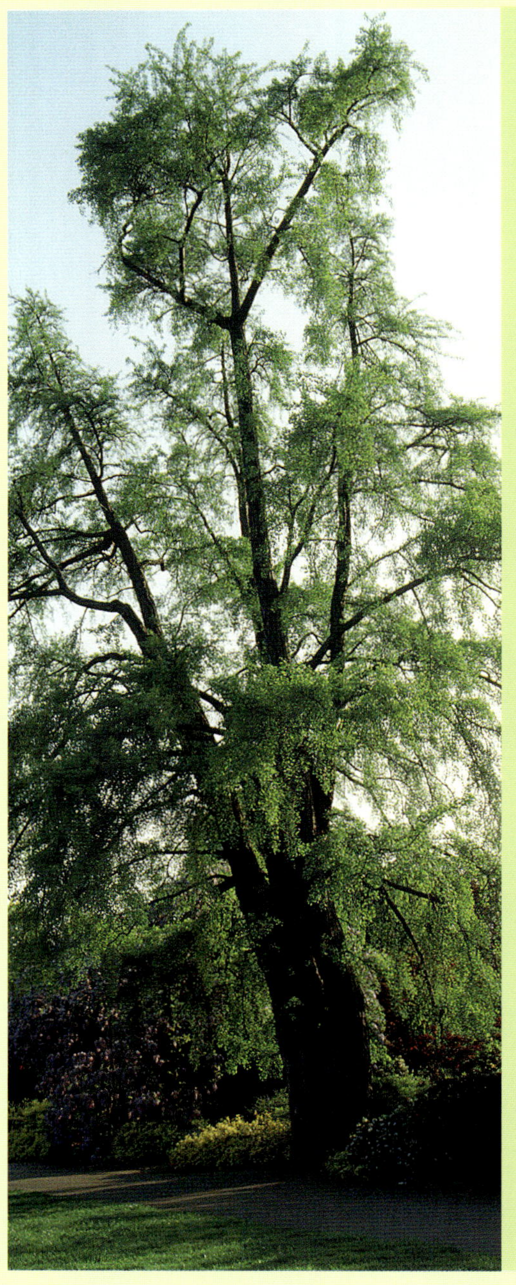

This elegant tree is popular in gardens, parks and open spaces all over the temperate world. The ginkgo grows well in shade as well as full sun and can reach 30m tall, with a spread of some 20m. It is the only one of the gymnosperms to shed its leaves in autumn, after they have turned a glorious shade of butter-yellow. But it is grown not just for its delicate fan-shaped leaves and the good height to which it grows, but because it can withstand terrible punishment from carbon monoxide, the greenhouse gas held in vehicle exhaust fumes. Because of this, it is widely planted as a carbon sink and pollution repellant in urban areas, particularly in China, Japan and North America. It is both fire-resistant and salt-tolerant, making it a great tree for maritime areas.

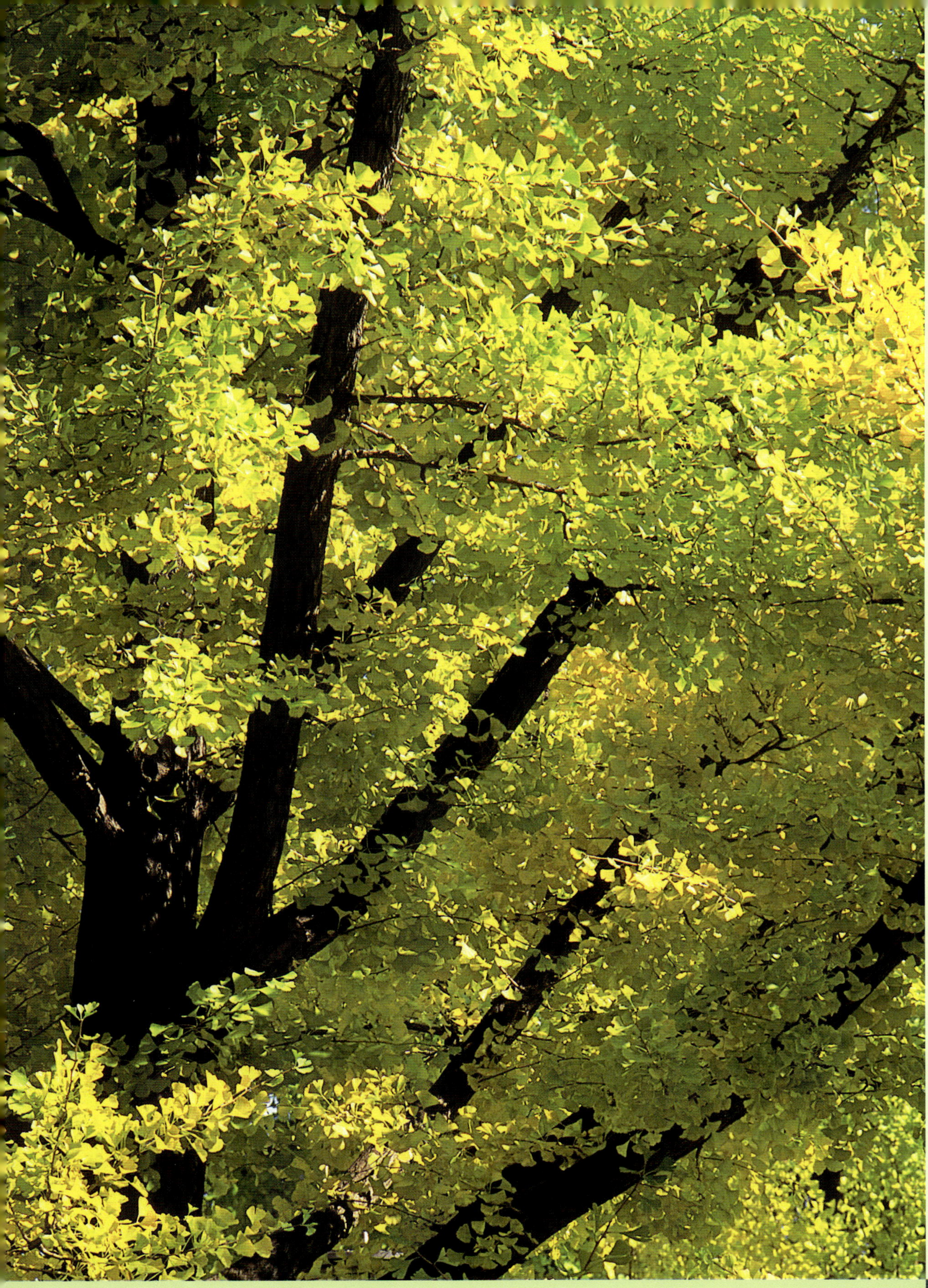

ginkgo

This primitive order of plants was flourishing on the planet some 270 million years ago, long before dinosaurs roamed the earth

Known as the living fossil, the maidenhair tree (*Ginkgo biloba*) is the sole surviving species from a primitive order of plants known as gymnosperms – plants which hold their seed without an ovary, such as pines and spruces. It is the second oldest tree known to man, next to the Wollemi pine, discovered in 1994 growing in an isolated rainforest gorge only 150 kilometres from Sydney, Australia, and which existed over 150 million years ago.

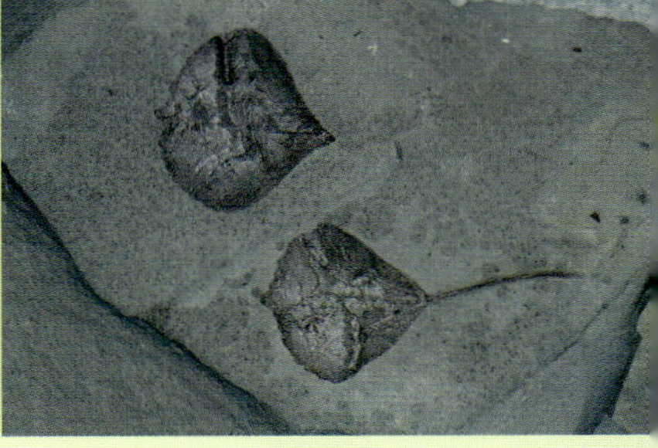

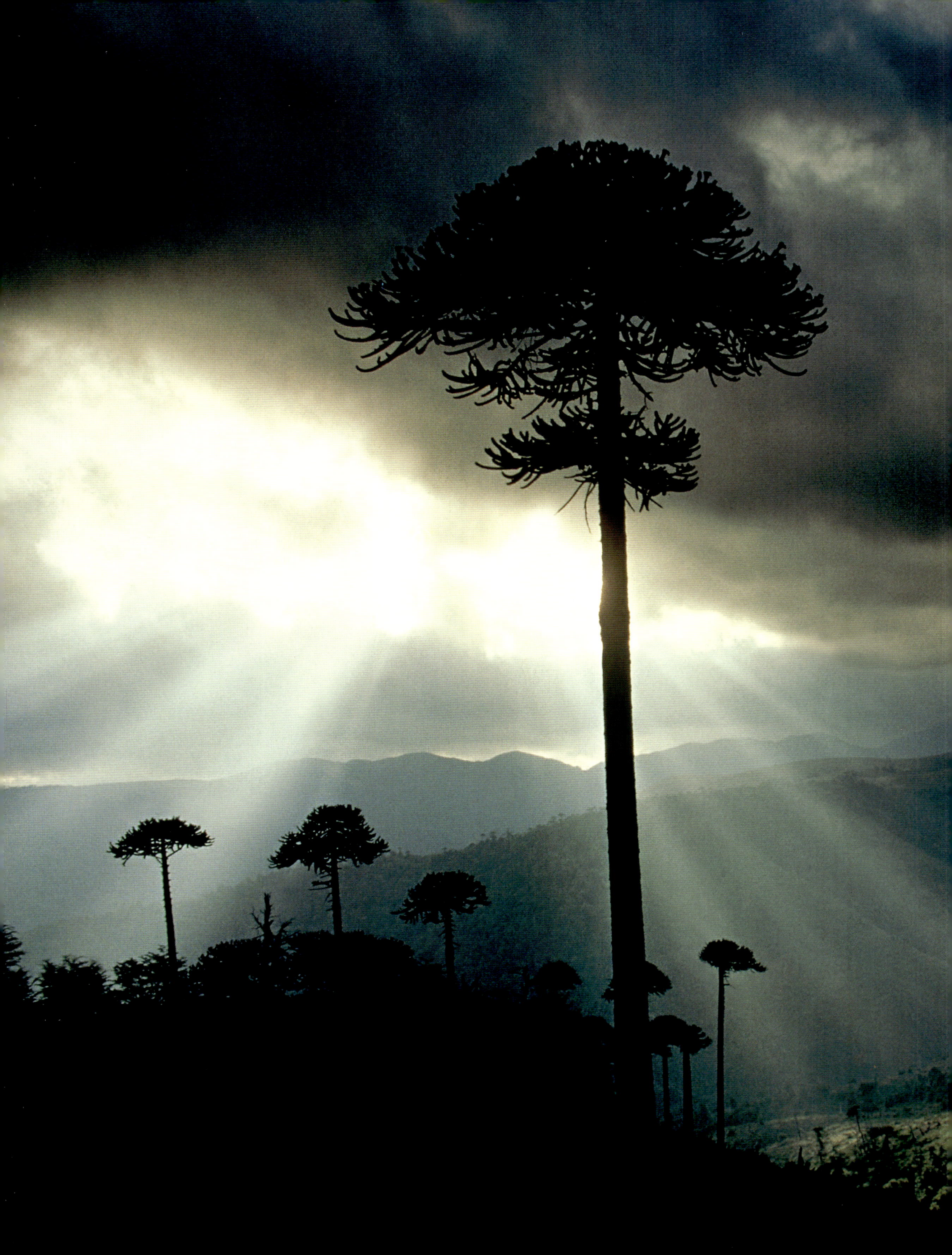

redwoods

Being in the presence of these towering giants is to lose all sense of time, sound and space

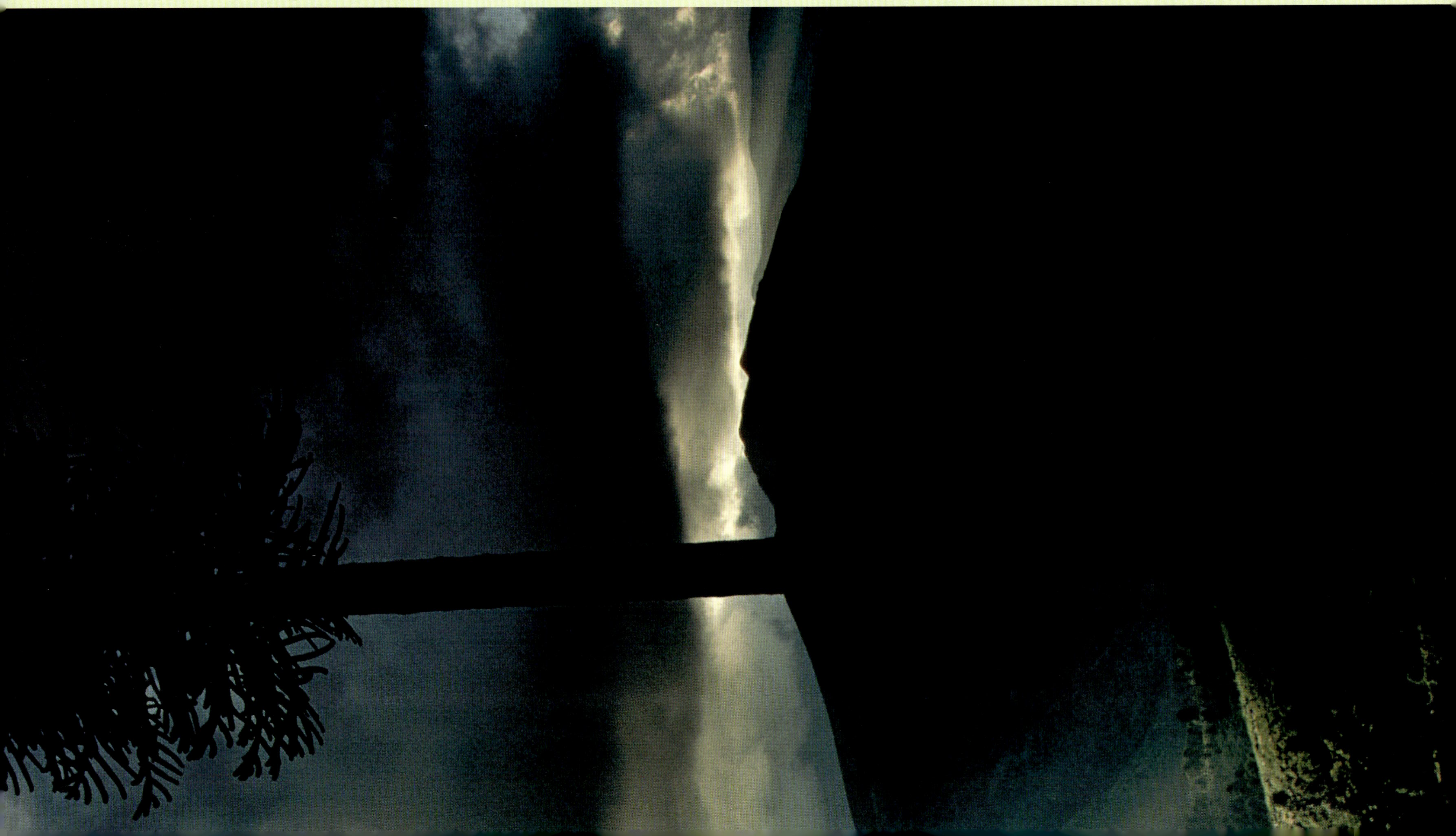

redwoods

Standing in a grove of giant sequoias has been likened to being surrounded by a sense of infinity

A drive up Highway 101 starting in downtown Los Angeles and heading due north up the Californian coast, going through the middle of San Francisco and passing the wine country to the northern extremes of the Golden State, is arguably one of the most scenic journeys in America. And then the landscape changes as the road hits the redwoods – and we are in the country of the ancient giants, the most astonishing trees on the planet.

The coastal redwoods (*Sequoia sempervirens*) are the tallest trees in the world, reaching over 100m in height and 10m across (previous page and these pages). After the Wollemi pine and the ginkgo, they are also the oldest. These monumental examples of the awesome power of nature covered much of the northern hemisphere 20 million years ago and are now limited to a 15km-wide band of the north and central Californian coast and a small stretch of the Oregon coast.

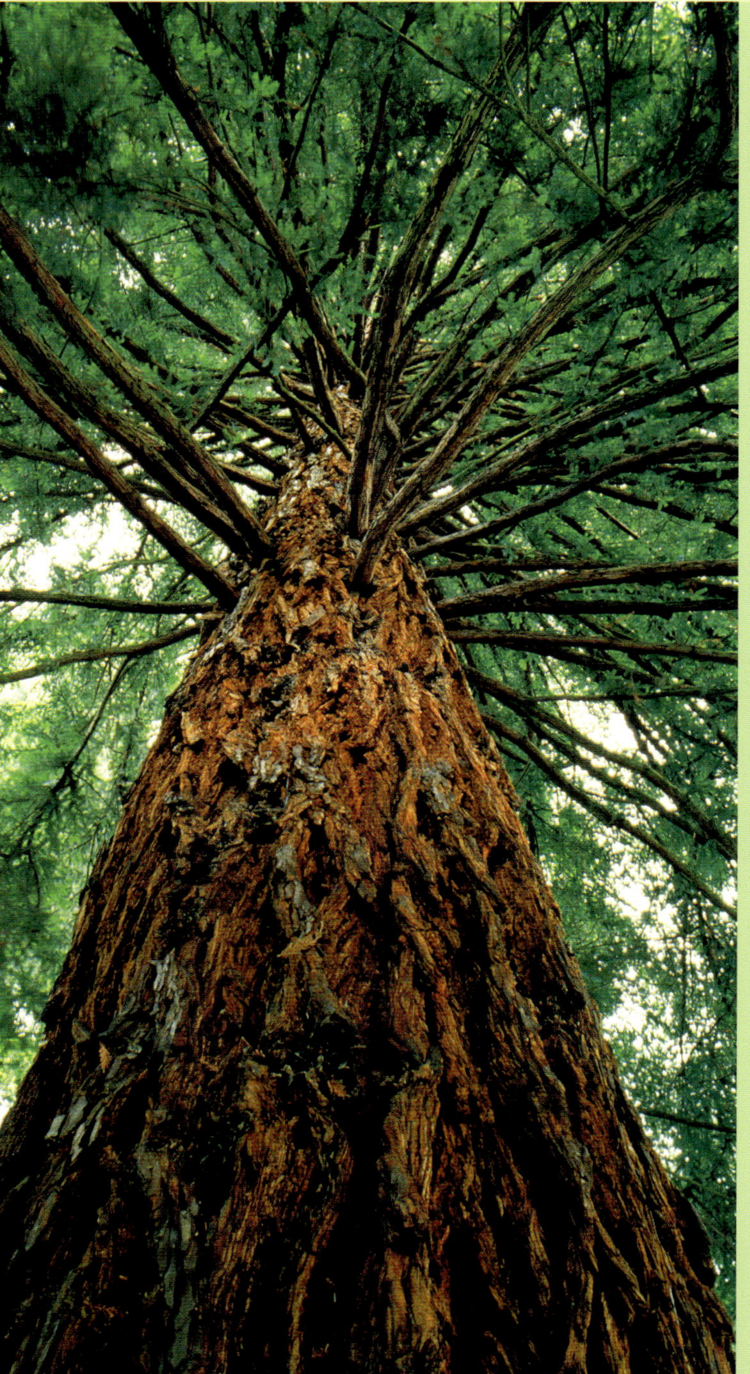

A redwood forest is one of the most silent and tranquil environments on earth; there are few birds and the sunlight slants through in bright green shafts. The mossy, dank, often fog-shrouded coastal redwood forests may include other trees such as the Douglas fir, hemlocks, oaks and strawberry trees (*Arbutus* species). At a lower level the forest floor supports ferns, mushrooms, sorrel and mosses. The mild, moist, humid climate of fog and rain which drifts in from the cold currents of the Pacific Ocean helps the trees grow to amazing sizes and encourages the breakdown of forest-floor litter. Condensation of the fog belt realizes an annual rainfall of 150-200cm, a third of the redwoods' water requirements.

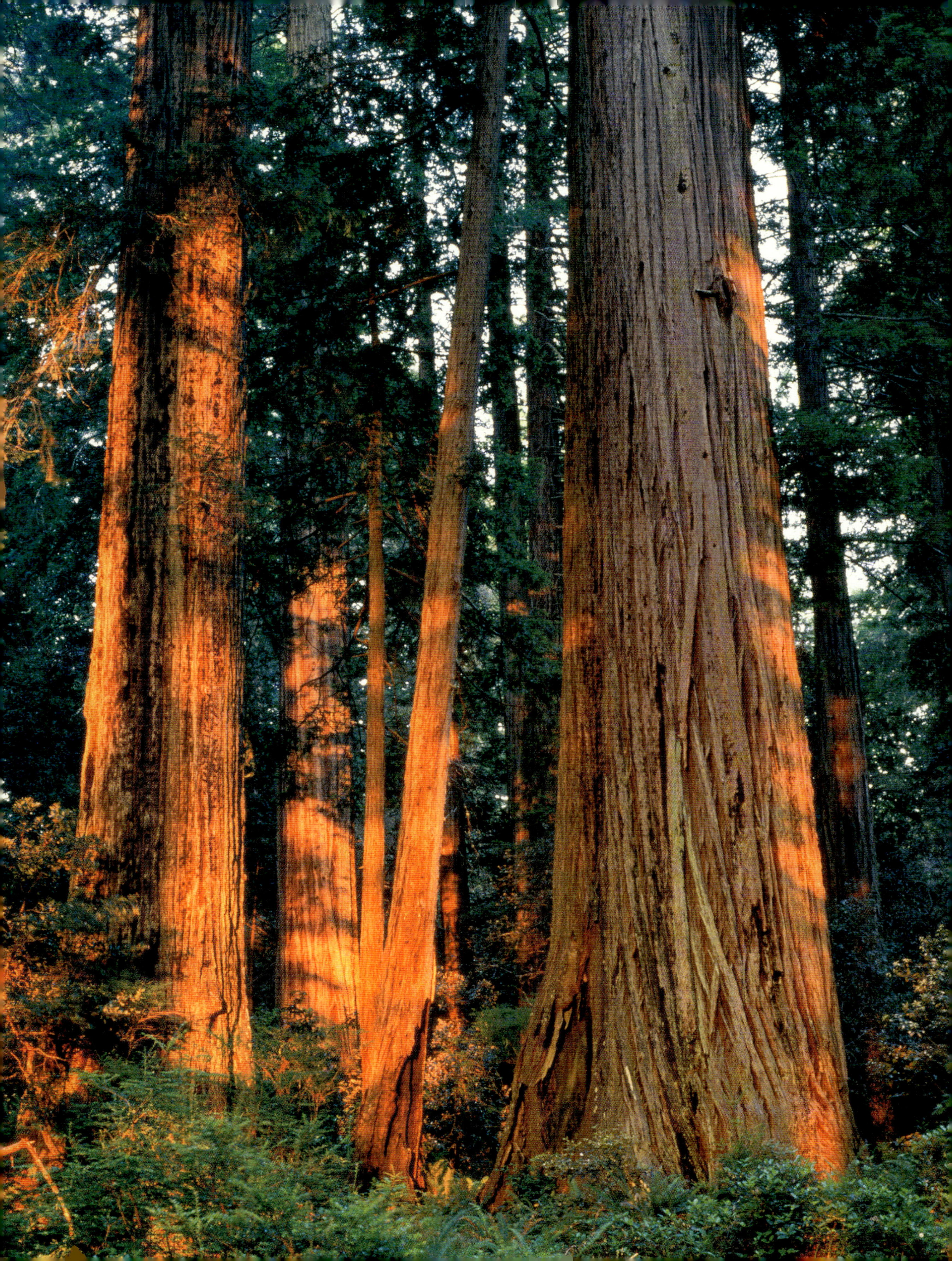

redwoods

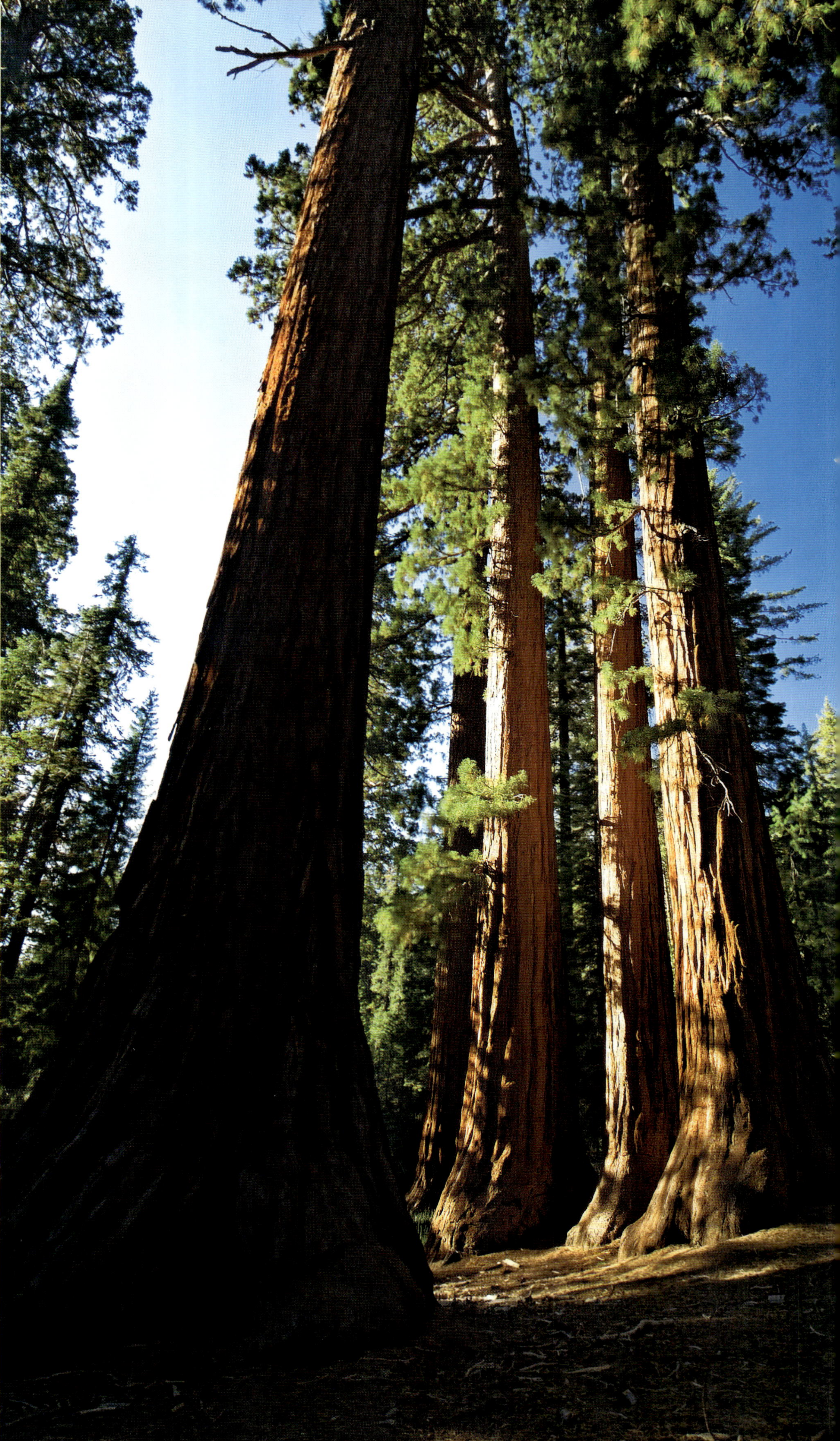

The giant sequoias (*Sequoiadendron giganteum*), which live on the western slopes of California's Sierra Nevada in National Parks such as Yosemite, run their cousins the coastal redwoods close in terms of size, grandeur and antiquity. While the giant sequoias do not grow as tall, they are bigger in girth than the coastal redwoods and can live to twice their age, up to 4,000 years. The two most famous specimens are the General Sherman and the General Grant. Both are in the region of 80m high with girths of 24m; they are not the biggest trees in the 66 groves spread throughout the National Parks but they are the most recognizable and the most impressive.

Survival strategies The redwoods are amazingly resilient. Like the ginkgo, because they have been in existence long before any Ice Age, there are few predators to cause them any worry. Redwoods can also survive their trunks being buried in silt, up to about a metre, by sending up roots, vertically, from buried lateral roots. As standing trees they are resistant to all but the hottest fires and will sprout new stems and roots from latent buds around the base and along the trunk if they have been burnt, cut down or blown over.

A venerable history The genus *Sequoia* is named after Sequoyah (1770-1843), a Cherokee Indian who invented the Cherokee alphabet. The name was quite a long time coming considering that relatives of these giants covered much of the earth's surface over 20 million years ago. At the time of Sequoyah's death there were two million acres of redwoods, but now only 95,000 acres remain. Over the last 200 years 96 per cent of all Californian redwoods have been destroyed by man.

The future The redwoods within the National Parks are fully protected. The Headwaters Forest Reserve in northern California holds one of the most magnificent coastal redwood groves: it is a 1,200-hectare virgin old-growth forest containing some of the world's most spectacular trees. Some are over 2,000 years old and taller than a cathedral spire at 100m high. However, there remains a lot of private land in which the owners may exercise the right to sell their standing timber. The famous 'Avenue of Giants', a 30km stretch of preserved Californian redwoods along the Pacific's Highway One hides a multitude of sins. The trees along the avenue itself are dense, but only metres off the avenue the forest begins to thin out. As we have seen, the reason that old-growth forest is so precious is that it regenerates itself. The high levels of rainfall in this area mean that there will never be enough nutrients to nourish any new trees unless the dead ones are left to rot.

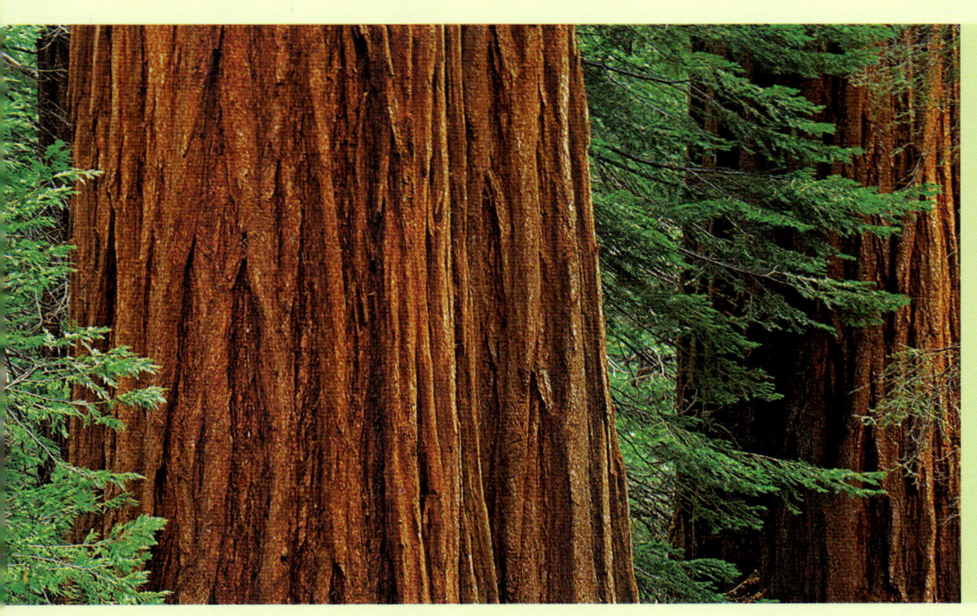

Both coastal redwood and giant sequoia grow well as decorative trees throughout the temperate deciduous biome but it is only in California and a small stretch of the Oregon coast (the coastal redwood) where they are native species. My own first encounter with *S. giganteum* was at school, where an enormous 'Wellingtonia' towered over the large Georgian mansion in which I was taught. It was a comfort, a friend – its bark was soft and malleable, peeling away easily and giving off a strong resinous aroma. Planted in the eighteenth century, it was well over 30 metres tall – yet in relative terms just a baby.

Swamp cypress

As well as owning the great sequoias, the swamp cypress family (Taxodinaceae) boasts two other magnificent tree species. The evergreen montezuma cypress (*Taxodium mucronatum*), native to Guatemala, Mexico and southern Texas, can lay claim to a particularly magnificent specimen known as El Gigante which has been living for 1,000 years in Oaxaca, Mexico. The swamp cypress (*T. distichum*), with its relations the redwoods, is one of the oldest trees on the planet. Like the giants of the Pacific Northwest of the USA, it is a conifer but, curiously, its main home is in the diametrically opposite corner of the country – the Florida Everglades. Here it grows happily in the swamps and, although it is mostly known as the bald cypress, the name swamp cypress is much more appropriate.

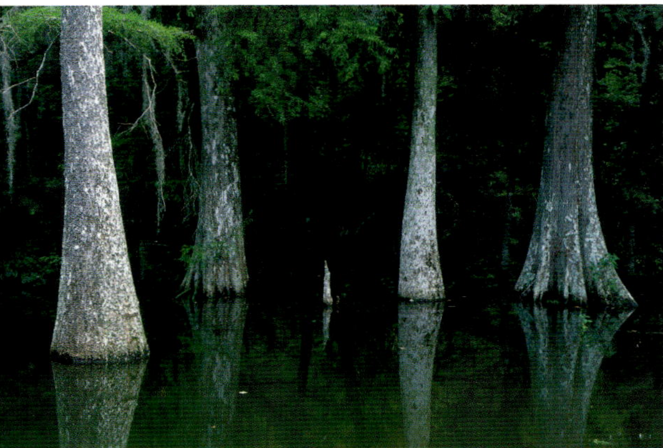

The swamp cypress is distinguished by the presence of 1m-high 'knees' or growths that sprout from roots around its base to project above ground or the water level

In its habitat the swamp cypress is probably the most beautiful of the conifers. To begin with, it is deciduous (a very good trait in a conifer which can be a dull tree by its very evergreen nature) and in the spring it produces the most delicate lime-green feathery foliage of any living tree; this changes to a rich, almost reddish brown in the autumn before the leaves drop in winter. The shape of its branches, some of which stick up almost straight in the air and others which brush the surface of the ground or the water, give the tree a noble demeanour. Its ancient bearing is compounded by the extraordinary 'knees' that are produced by the roots and act like 'ventilator pipes', bringing air and oxygen down to the roots. These stumps project up to a metre off the ground, littering the base of the tree and looking quite other-worldly.

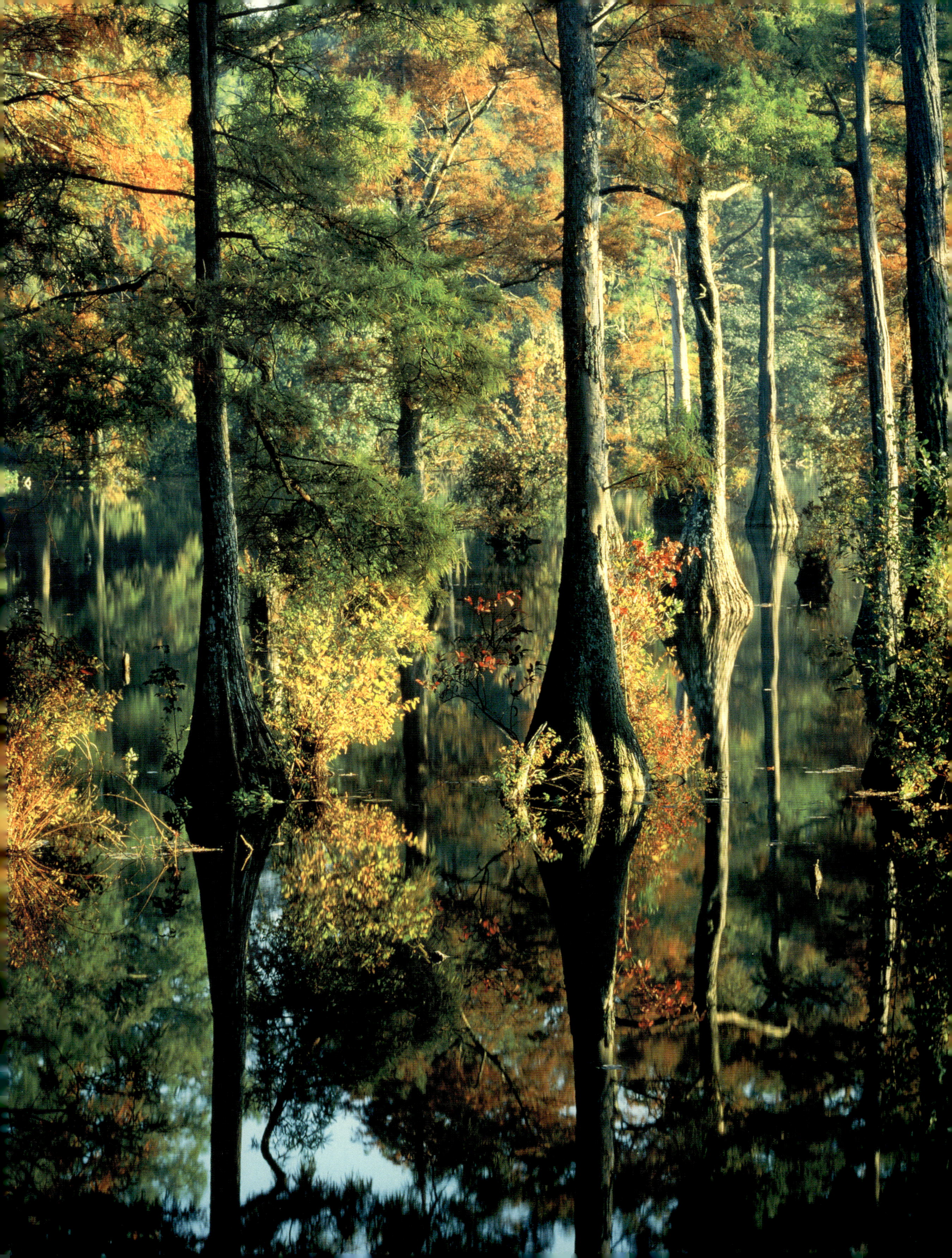

The future

On a simple level our relationship with trees has hardly changed. People in this biome still require trees for building, for shelter and, of course, to soak up carbon dioxide and provide us with oxygen. Trees are required for medicine and to prevent soil erosion as well as for spiritual nourishment and energy, as indeed they are all over the world. But if one looks beyond the obvious, there are two main areas for which we will gravitate seriously towards the trees of this biome for future answers. The first is climate change and the second is food. The second of these may be the most important because, while we have the ability to adapt and to plant new trees to cope with climate change, we may not have the ability to stop change.

Today there is growing awareness that forest and woodland need to be managed in a more sustainable fashion as our need for timber, whether for building or printed paper, is now insatiable. So what exactly can we do if we believe that trees in this temperate deciduous biome hold the key to the survival of the planet? To begin with, let us remember that the vast majority of decorative trees that we see in our gardens, parks

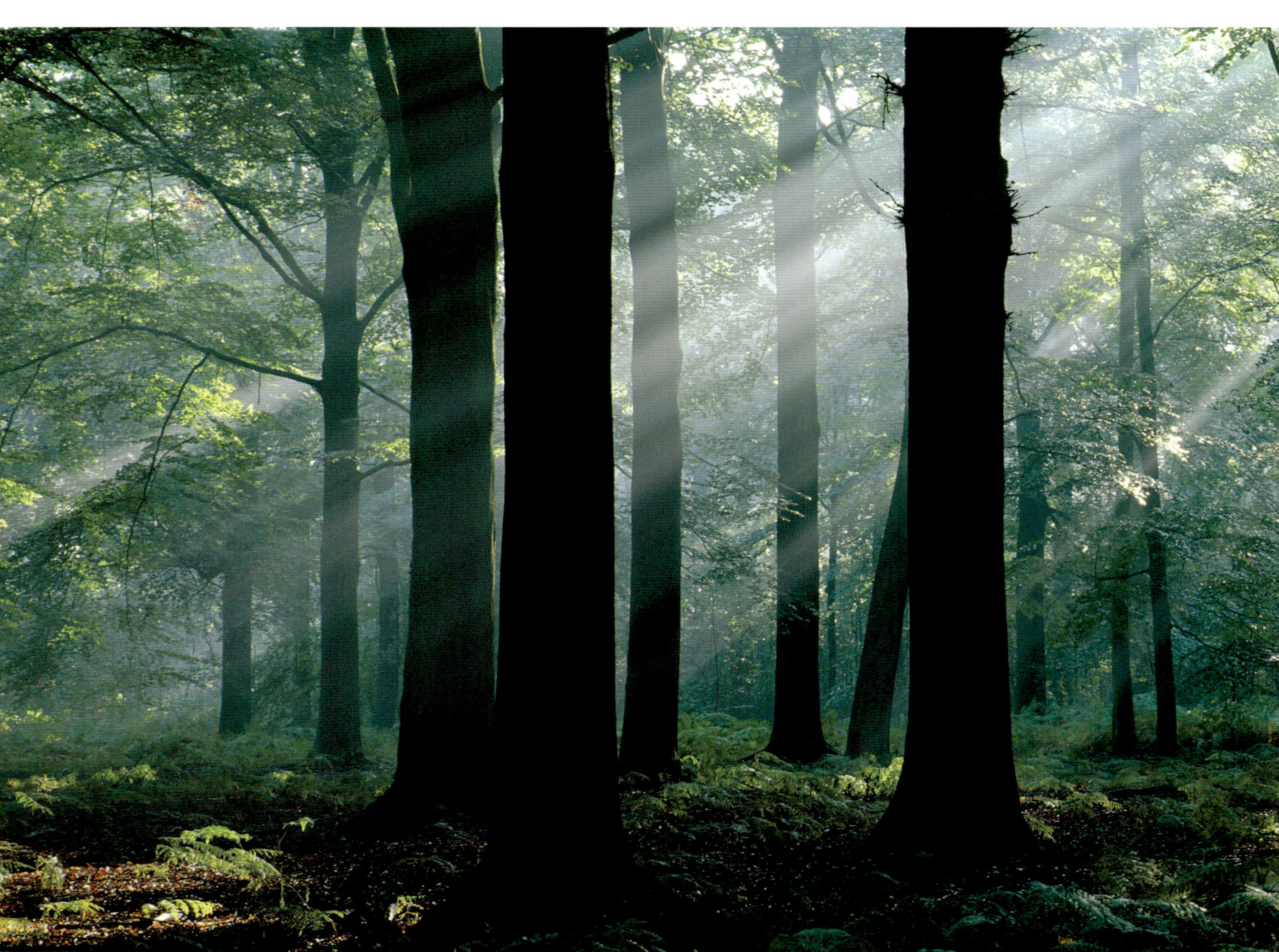

and green spaces come from somewhere within this biome. The horticultural industry, especially in Europe and North America, is dominated by plants that come from those two continents but also from the other main regions of the same climatic biome – northern Japan, Korea, China and the Himalayas. We must continue to grow ornamental trees, not least as a testament to those fearless nineteenth-century plant hunters who gathered plants and moved them across the globe under terrible duress.

We should also continue to lobby for as much green public space as possible, as it is a natural home for trees. We can look as far back as Ancient Rome to a civilization that understood the need for its people to have access to green space but it is now, more than ever, that we need trees in our cities. Allied to this, we must batter down the door of our public service departments and campaign for tree planting schemes to be included wherever there is housing and urban development of any kind. As for our existing great forests and their majestic trees, they must be preserved at all costs.

The splendour of trees, the magic they produce and their enormous solidity is something that we have taken for granted since man first encountered the earth's largest plants. We must cherish them as we cherish our children and acknowledge them for what they have given and will continue to bestow on this earth.

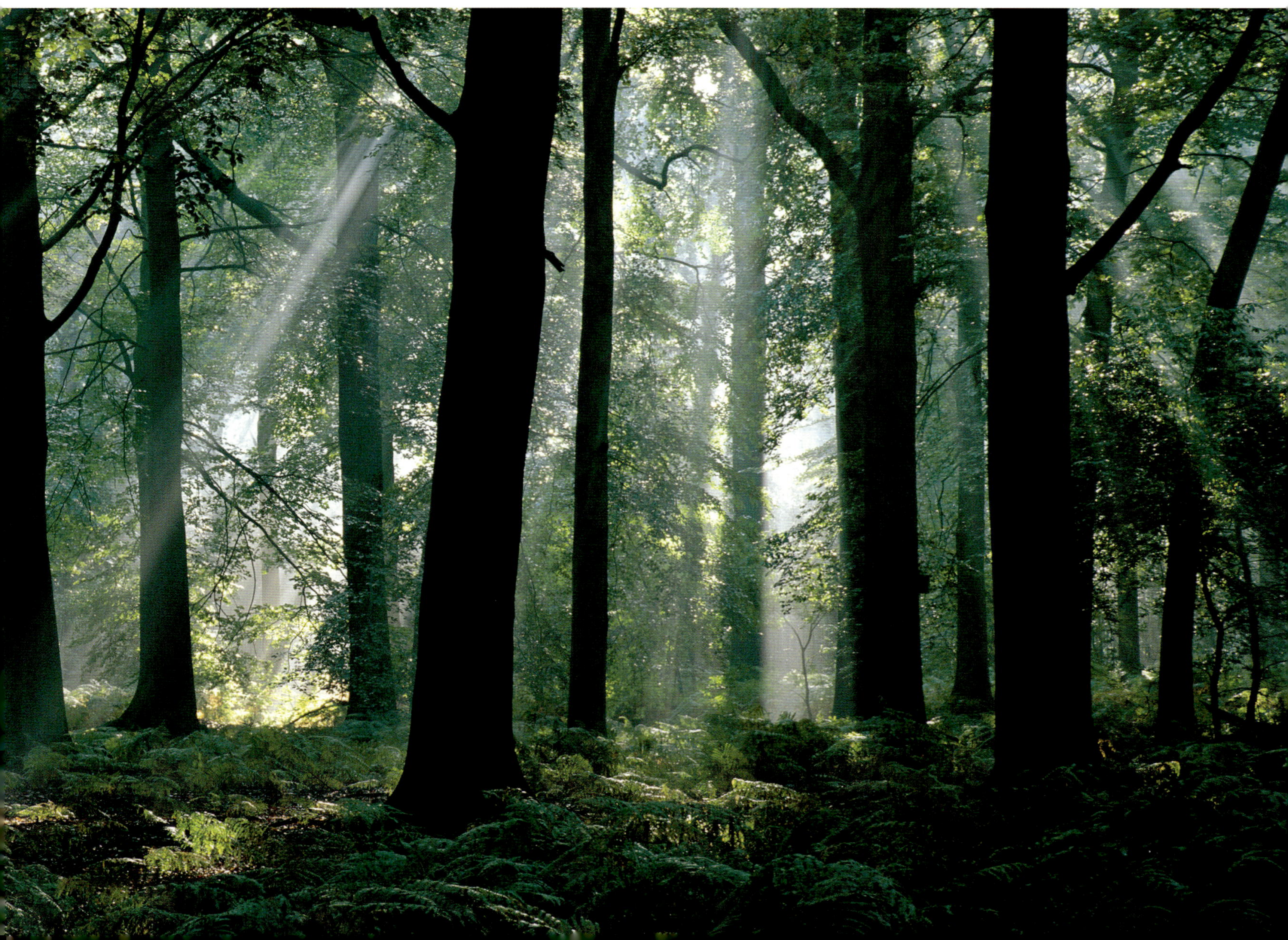

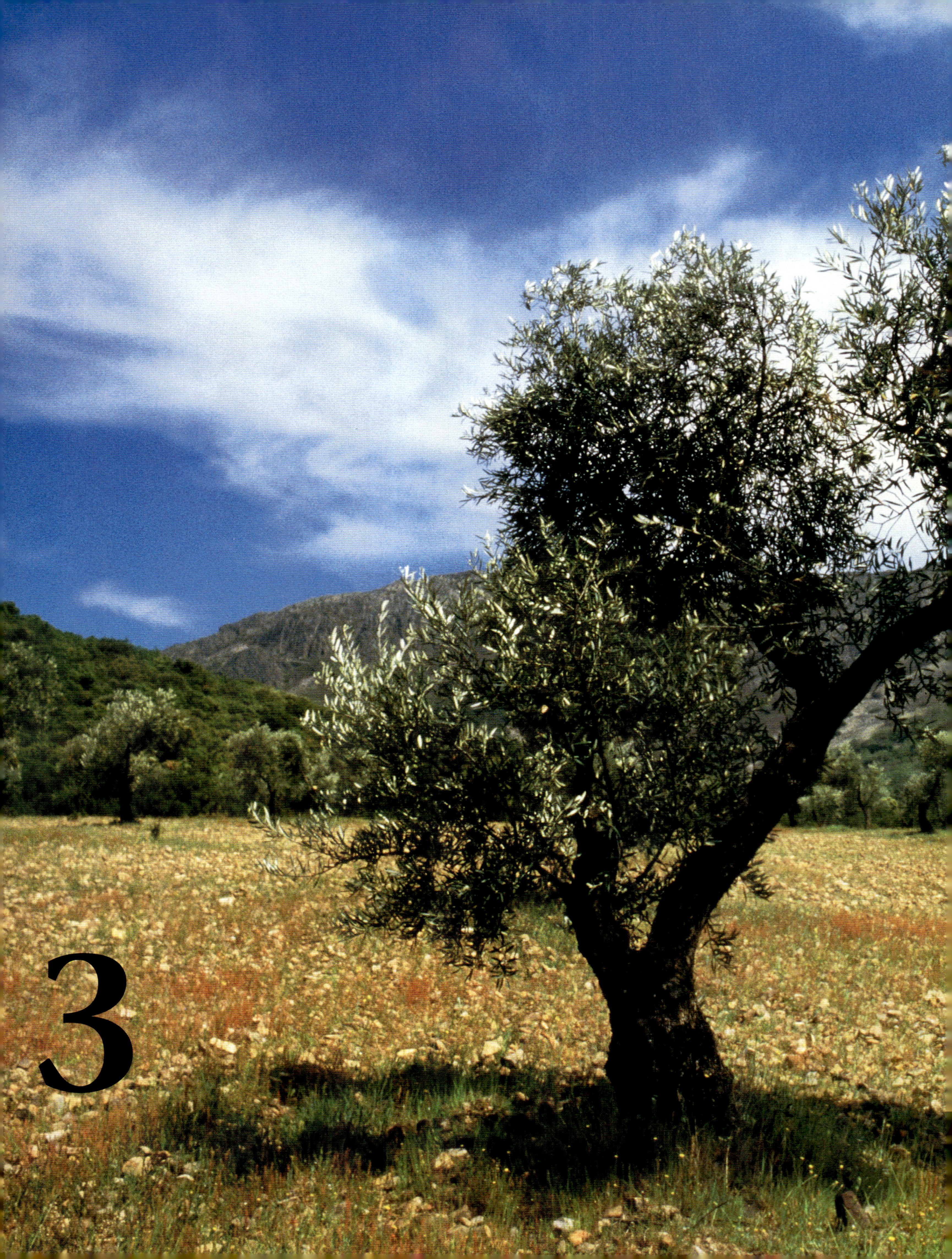

3

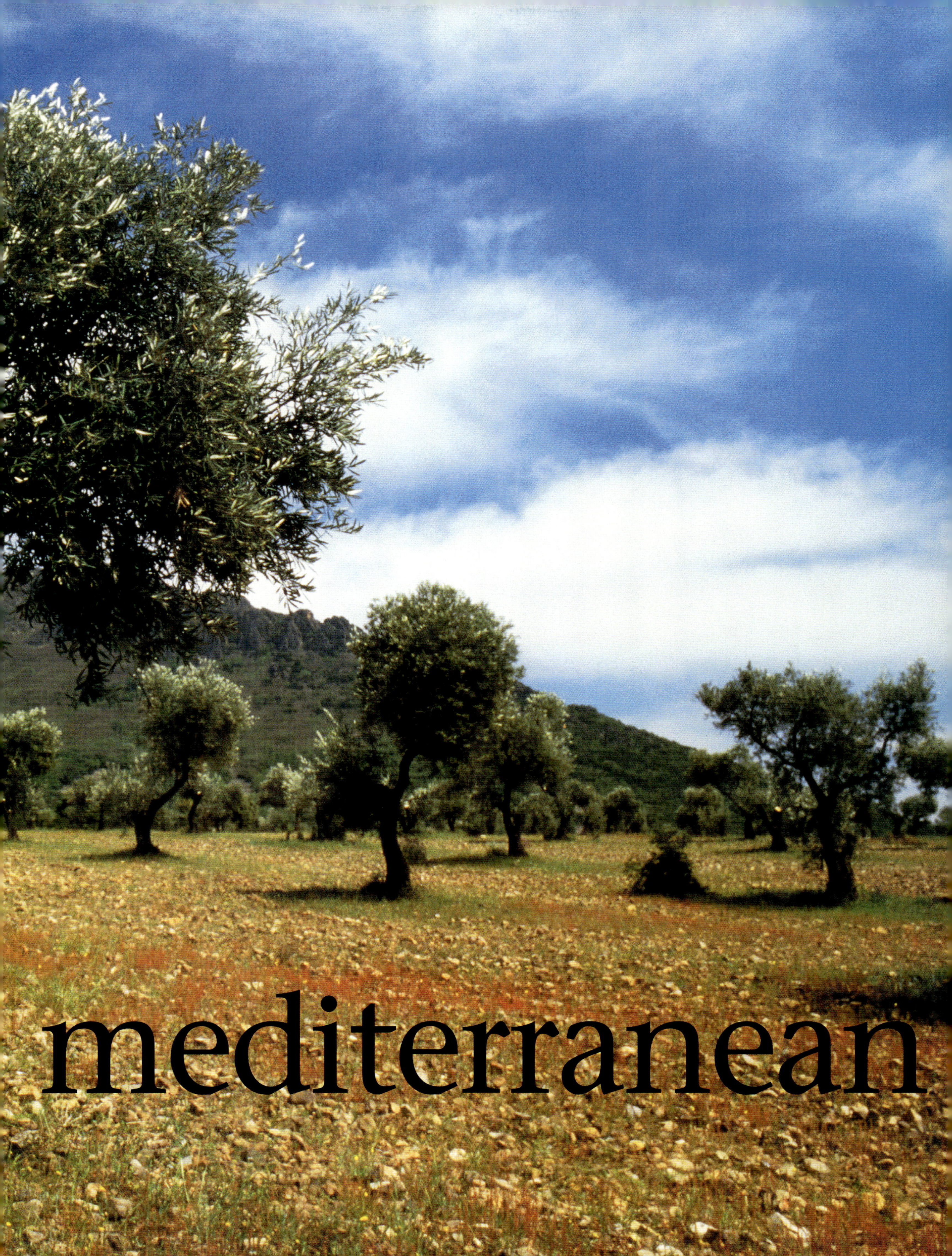

mediterranean

The olive protrudes stubbornly from the landscape and seems to stitch this higgledy-piggledy Mediterranean land together (previous page). Wilfully productive even as an ancient tree, the great old specimens seem to be as old as the land itself.

The Mediterranean biome was once the bread basket of mankind. The lands between the rivers Tigris and Euphrates in modern-day Iraq were the first to support humans by way of advanced agriculture some 10,000 years ago. Today, much of that part of the Middle East is desert and, while it is still on the fringes of the Mediterranean biome, we tend to think of this biome as the areas of southern and eastern Europe and North Africa that connect with the Mediterranean Sea. In reality the biome is more far-reaching than that, since Mediterranean climatic regions are found typically on the west side of continents between 30 and 40 degrees north and south latitude. This brings in California and Baja California in the northern hemisphere and central Chile, the Western Cape region of South Africa and parts of south and south-west Australia in the southern hemisphere. Trees include the southern beeches of Chile, the towering flat-topped cedars of Lebanon dotted through the eastern Mediterranean, the smoky sweet eucalyptus in Australia and dense natural thickets of walnuts in California, while signature trees such as olives and figs help to support large economies.

While the five Mediterranean regions collectively cover only 5 per cent of the earth's surface, crucially they hold 20 per cent of the world's plant species, among them some of the most fascinating trees on the planet

The climate of the biome is dominated by long hot summers and cool, wet winters. Trees and plants here tend to be of a sclerophyllous nature – that is, they have hard, stiff, waxy leaves that can hold moisture and resist drought. Many are evergreen, such as the holm oak and the olive, two broadleaf trees found in the Californian and European zones of the biome. Conifers also abound, with easily recognizable species such as the Italian cypress and the Corsican pine, typically trees which are unable to withstand excessive frost. Many plants in this biome, such as laurels, myrtles and sages, have scented leaves and several have adapted to be able to sprout again from the base if overgrazed by animals or destroyed by fire. Fire is a serious risk in the drought-prone summers: the removal of wood from forests is discouraged, so there is abundant fuel for a forest fire once it starts.

The Corsican pine (opposite) clings to life on the side of a cliff and, like so many trees of this biome, seems untroubled by poor soil and baking hot conditions. Salt-tolerant into the bargain, this is a conifer like those of the Taiga that seem to hold no fear of what the planet can thrust upon them.

The sustainable cultivation of trees, in conjunction with other edible produce – the exact opposite of annual-crop production – is ideal for the Mediterranean zone on account of its poor, often rocky soil, much of which is unsuited to growing annual crops such as grain.

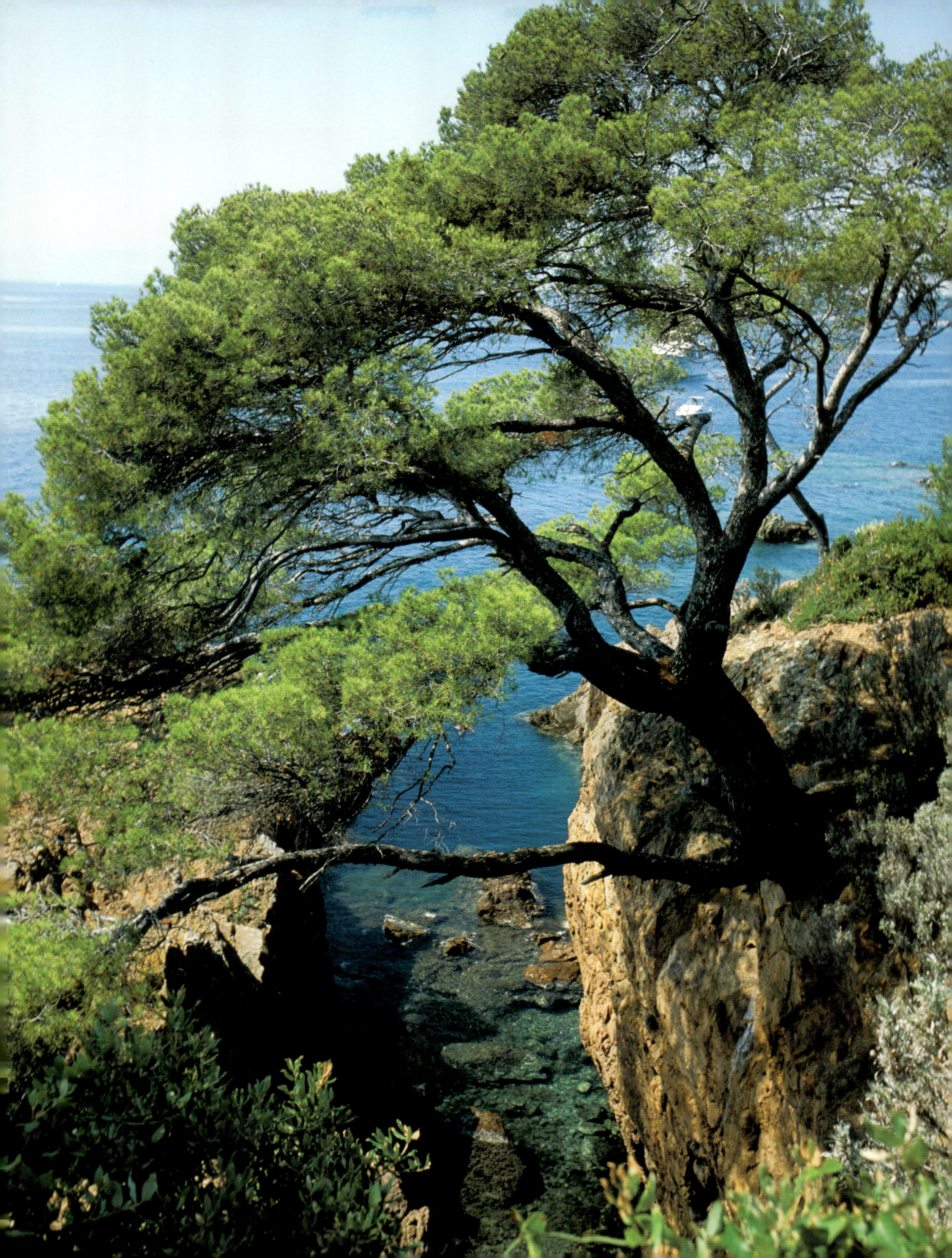

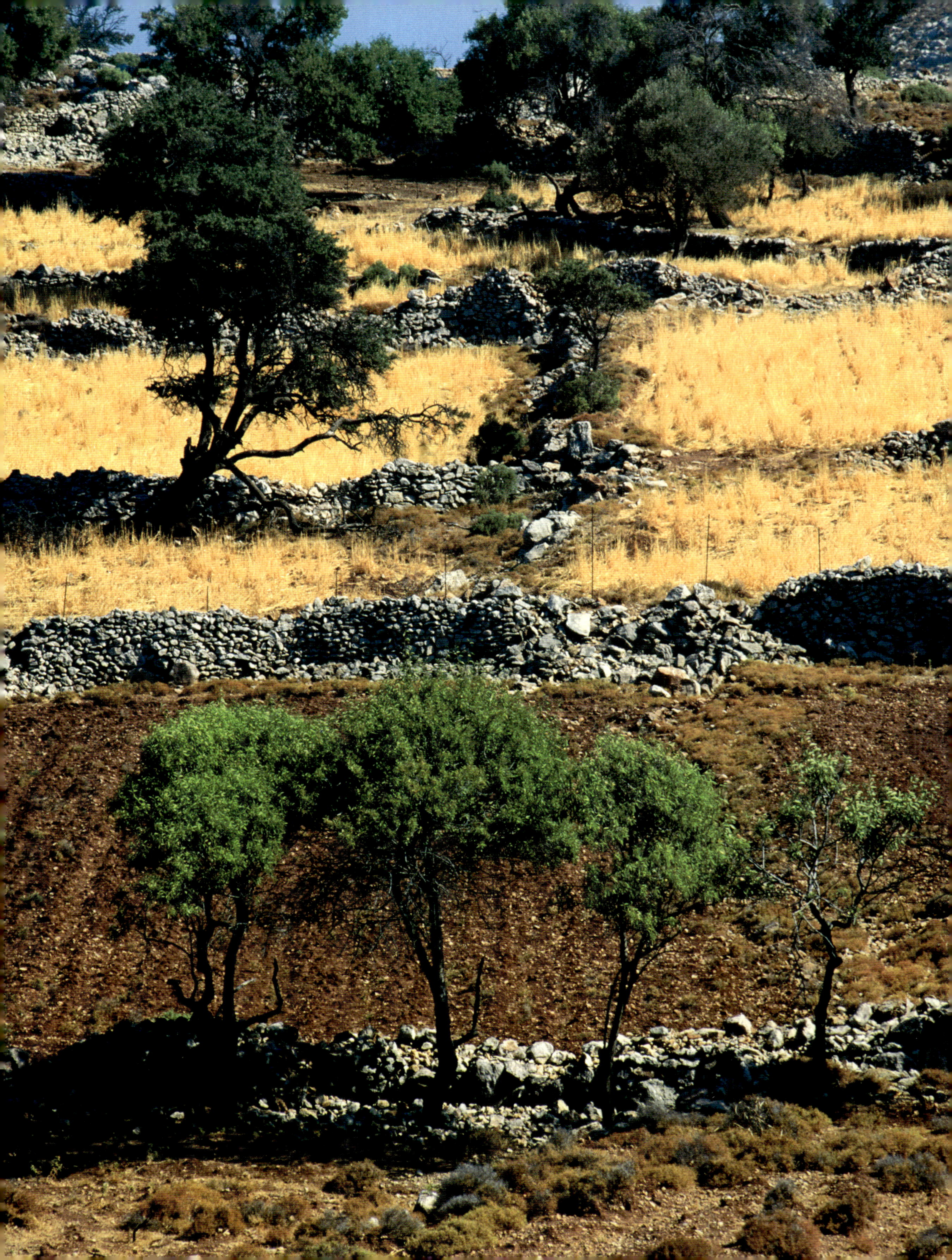

Productive tree cultivation

The Mediterranean biome has in fact been a model of sustainable tree crop production and we would be mad to ignore its lessons: it uses perennial crops (trees), plants them using wide spacings (that is, in the form of a grove rather than the rigid lines of a plantation), does not rely on external high-energy inputs (artificial fertilizers) and integrates animals into the system (insects to fertilize the fruit and animals for yields of meat and milk). Those who inhabit and farm the lands of southern Europe should look back through history to rekindle their knowledge of growing tree crops in natural surroundings. This is a science people once held dear, rather than clearing land to make way for what will inevitably become over-managed, wasteful and unsustainable agricultural systems.

Where damage has already been done, its reversal is not so easy. It is painfully obvious that desirable proximity to the sea in the Mediterranean biome, whether in southern Europe or western Australia, has opened the floodgates for house building and development. Trees have had to be sacrificed and valuable primary resources, such as timber, water and soil, get used up in the process of change. Wholesale land clearance is widespread in some areas, causing severe soil erosion through deforestation. Its extreme weather patterns make this biome fragile and exposed, and the removal of trees and resiting of water courses have dire consequences for its ecosystems.

Maquis vegetation

In all its geographical zones this biome holds forests and woodlands and various different layers of evergreen sclerophyllous vegetation. Local names for this vegetation differ from country to country but the way the plants fit into the landscape is the same. Each is characterized by low scrub woodland and shrubs beneath a canopy of taller trees. The French call it maquis, after the Resistance fighters who hid in the scrub vegetation during the Second World War. In Chile it is called matorral and defined by thickets of low-growing trees with a canopy of taller species such as the Chilean wine palm (*Jubaea chilensis*) and the southern beech (*Nothofagus antarctica*). In the Californian chaparral, oaks mingle with walnuts to create dense, almost impenetrable woodland, while on the Western Cape of South Africa the *fynbos* is characterized by heathers, proteas and reeds.

Despite its small size and widely spread, vastly different geographical locations, the Mediterranean stands proud among the biomes of the planet. It offers up some magnificent trees as well as huge areas of wilderness where both flora and fauna flourish with abandon. This wilderness is precious, firstly because it is an immense green lung which holds high levels of carbon and, secondly, it is self-managing, a complex structure of plants whose purpose and means of survival are interlinked.

Traditional methods of farming in the Mediterranean region have always included fruit trees. Fruit-bearing Rosaceae such as almonds still feature prominently in and among the small fields used for annual crops, their shade welcome and the solidity provided by their roots a saviour in the protection against soil erosion.

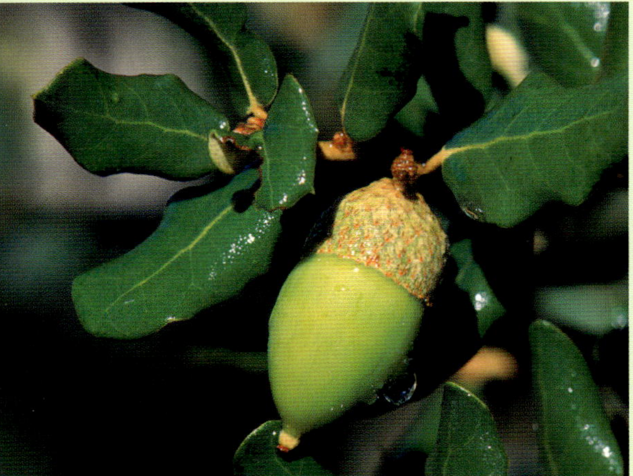

Fruit production As an evergreen which can grow up to 30m tall and live for a thousand years or more, the holm oak provides warmth and dry shelter for innumerable species of small mammal, insect and bird perhaps none more significant than the endangered Spanish imperial eagle. More importantly, it is one of the most productive of all oaks, a mature specimen capable of bearing more than a tonne of acorns in a single season. Holm oak acorns ripen in autumn and the tree is often combined in managed systems with the cork oak (*Q. suber*), whose acorn season is winter. Both trees then provide fodder for sheep, goats and the Iberian black-legged pig, a vital part of the Spanish rural economy and source of delicious hams.

The combination of hardiness, salt tolerance and a powerful ability to flourish in hot, arid conditions, allied with substantial yields of a useful crop which provides for both humans and animals, makes the holm oak a tree of vital importance for the future and one with a key role to play in reforesting this biome. In comparison to the quantities of edible fruit this tree is able to produce, year after year, the inputs required for the production of a similar yield of field-grown corn are absurd.

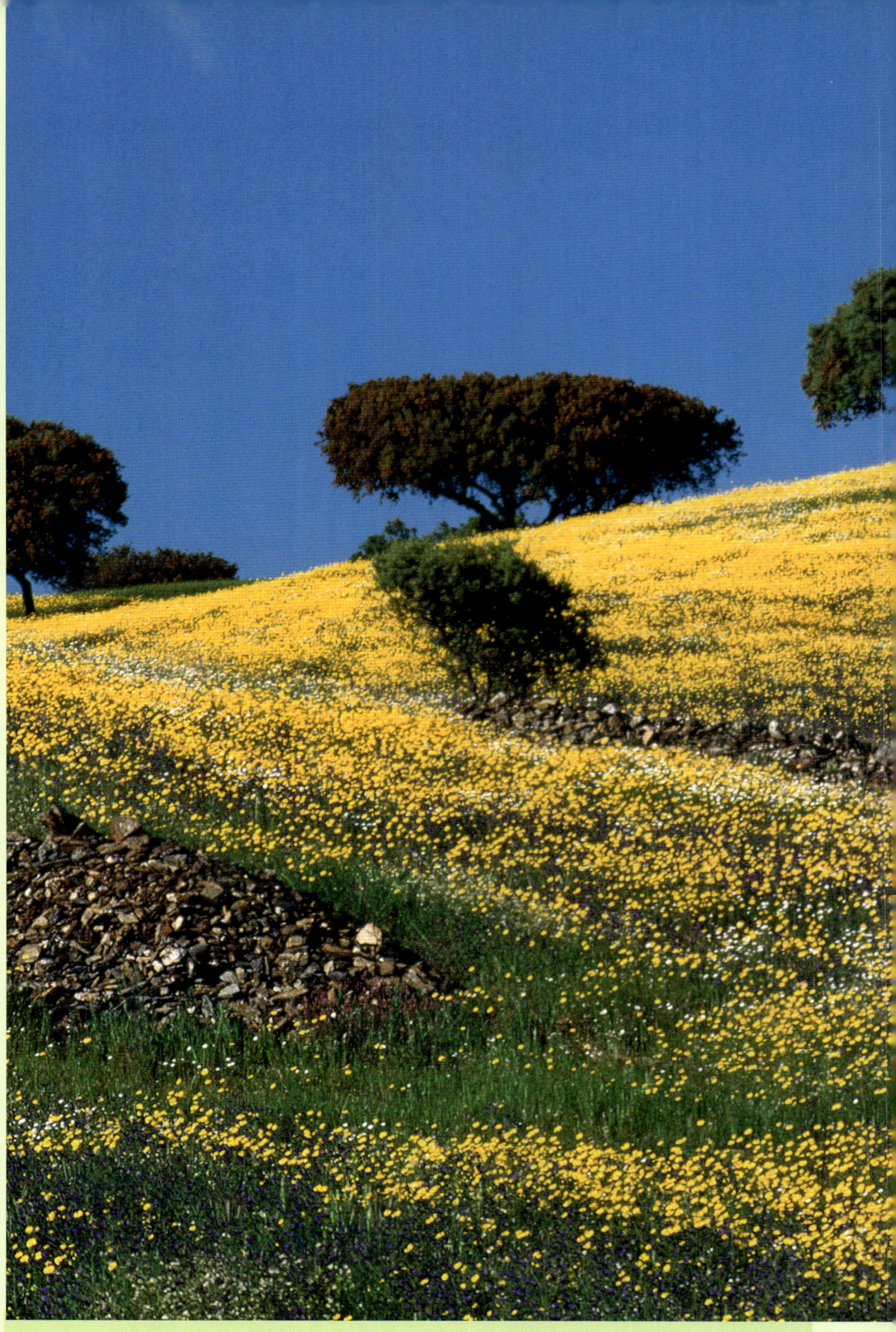

The holm oak (*Quercus ilex*) is one of the most commanding and beautiful of all the 300 and more species of oak that grow throughout the temperate and Mediterranean zones. It takes up the mantle of the common or English oak (*Q. robur*) in the southern climes of Europe and North Africa, for it will not grow where winter temperatures consistently fall to freezing. It occurs naturally from as far east as Cochin on the west coast of India through to Nantes on the Atlantic coast of France, where it is aided by the warm maritime climate found there. It thrives in coastal conditions where no other oak will grow because of its tolerance to salt.

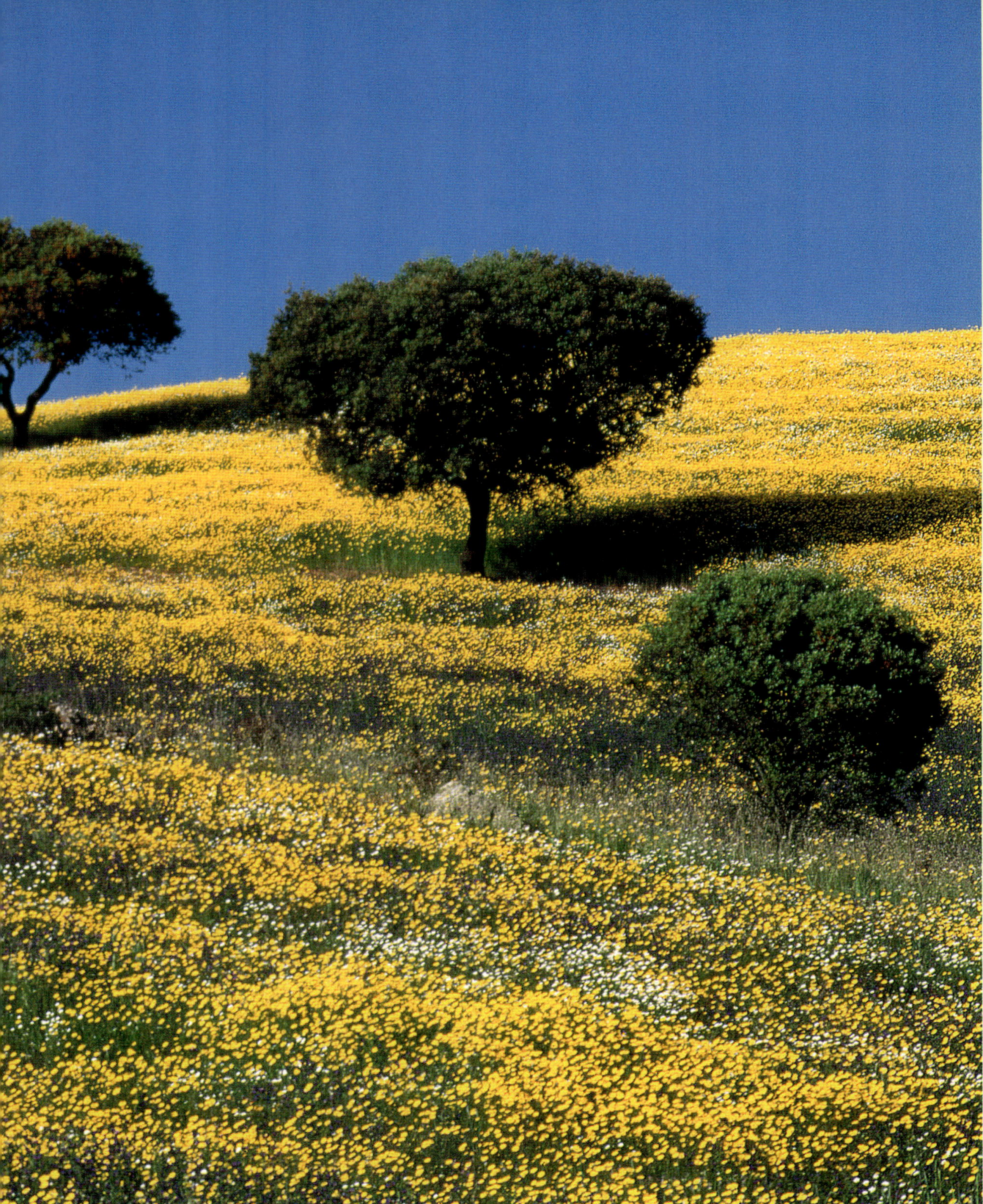

holm oak

Not only does the holm oak mark the landscape, it gives the impression that it is holding the otherwise harsh and arid country together

After the olive, the holm oak is the second most important tree of the biome. It has been called the climax tree of the true Mediterranean forest, a tree that once covered great swathes of Spain from the Aragonese Pyrenees southward to the Sierra Morena in Andalucia. It still covers 25 per cent of the forested area of Spain and can be seen growing all over the eastern side of the country. Interior Catalonia, where the heat is intense and the country as dry as a bone, is a land of broken patches of scrubby forest where the holm oak features prominently. There is not a drop of water to be had during the summer, and dust continuously fills the air on the wind – without the trees, the land would be rocky desert.

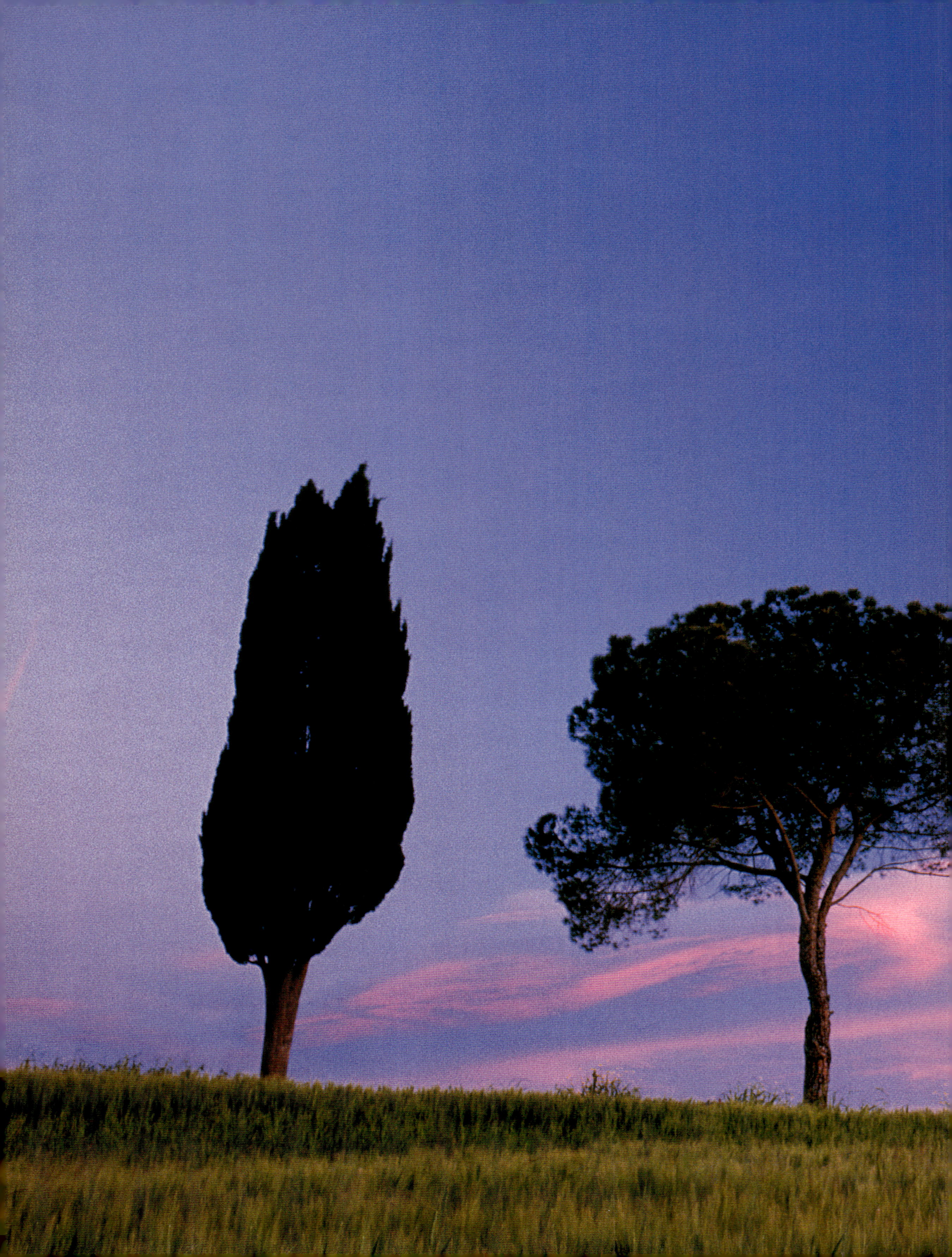

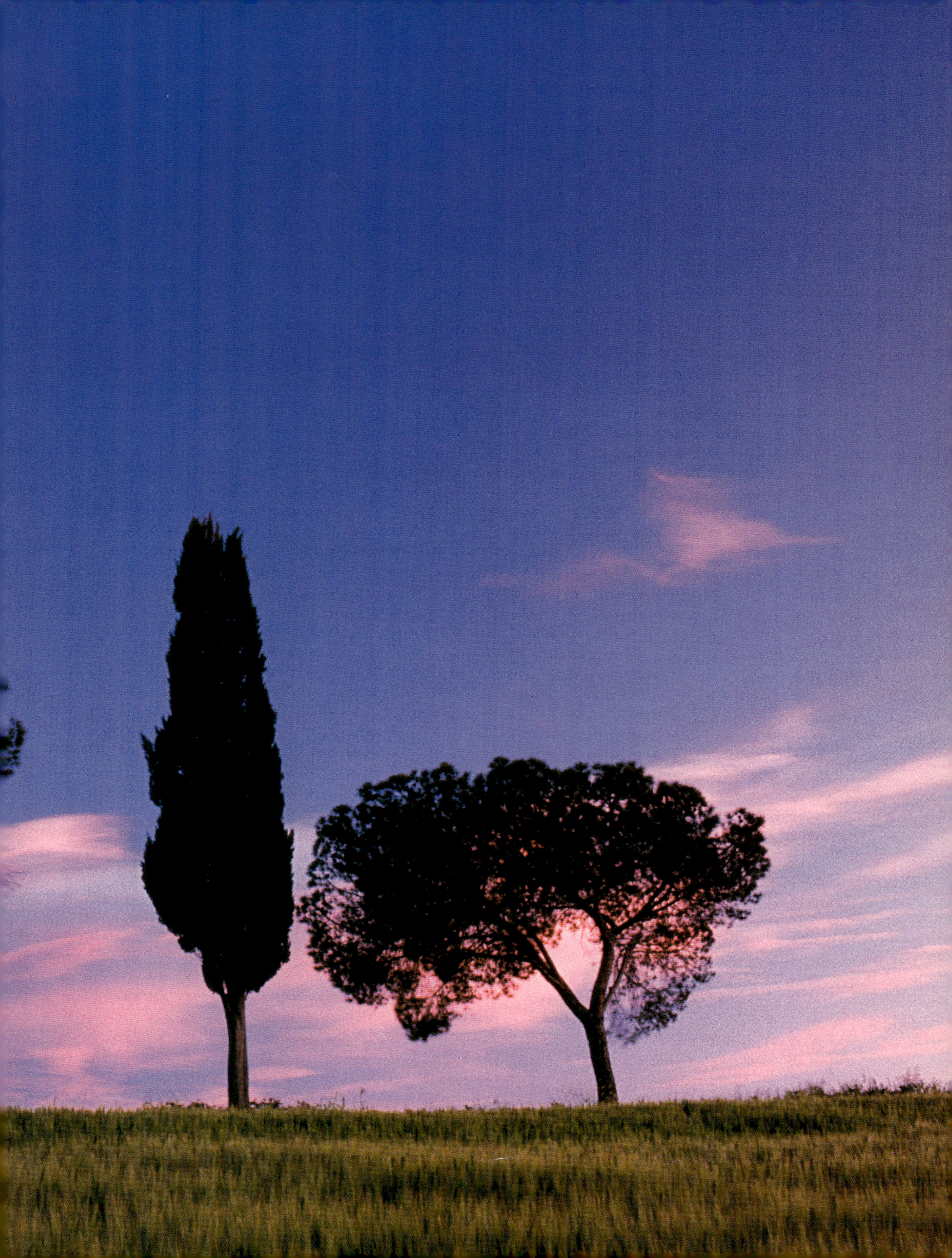

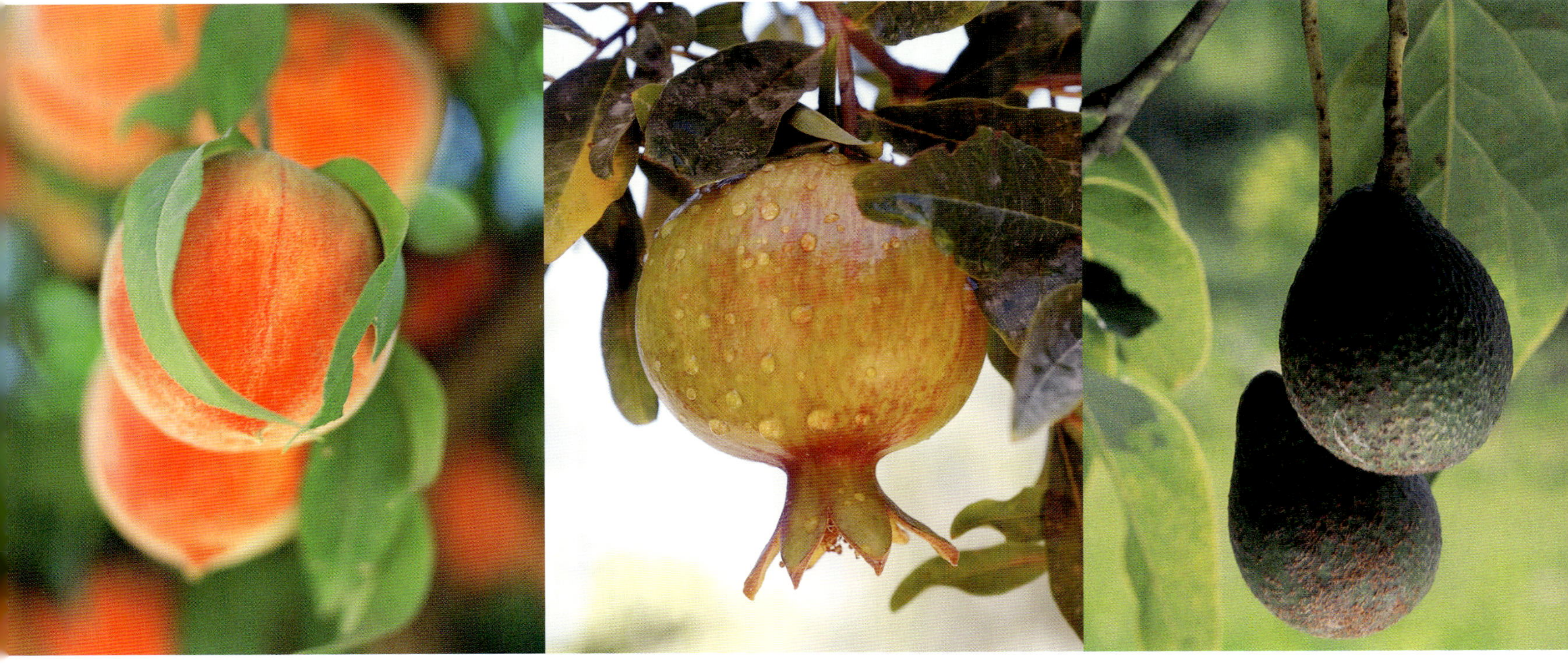

Citrus trees have the compelling attribute of flowering and fruiting

Cypresses have more ornamental connotations than perhaps any other tree of this biome. They produce little and do little but, like the poplars that line the roads of France, they look magnificent and should be treasured. Here they grow alternately with pines (previous pages).

Fruit trees

The Mediterranean biome in southern Europe is home to a wonderful array of fruit trees. One of the most economically important crop-producing trees in the world, the olive combines with citrus, figs and other luxury and high-value fruits and nuts such as pomegranates, peaches, apricots and almonds to make this a key area for food production. The situation is mirrored in California, where massive plantations of citrus stretch as far as the eye can see in a similar maritime climate with short winters and high summer sunshine which provide the good light levels required for the crop. Also found here is the avocado (*Persea americana*), a member of the laurel family with dense evergreen leaves, originating in Mexico. The avocado is a fast-growing tree which can reach more than 20m high in its natural form but has been adapted to grow as a dwarf, or even trained, tree to suit production of the fruit, 95 per cent of which comes from California.

Citrus

Although these handsome evergreen trees are grown commercially across the biome, the Mediterranean countries dominate, with Spain playing the biggest role in production for the fresh fruit market. The most important species is the sweet orange (*Citrus sinensis*) but the smaller fruits such as mandarins, clementines, tangerines and satsumas are all the subject of expanding markets. Lemons, limes and grapefruits make up the rest of this enormous industry which began

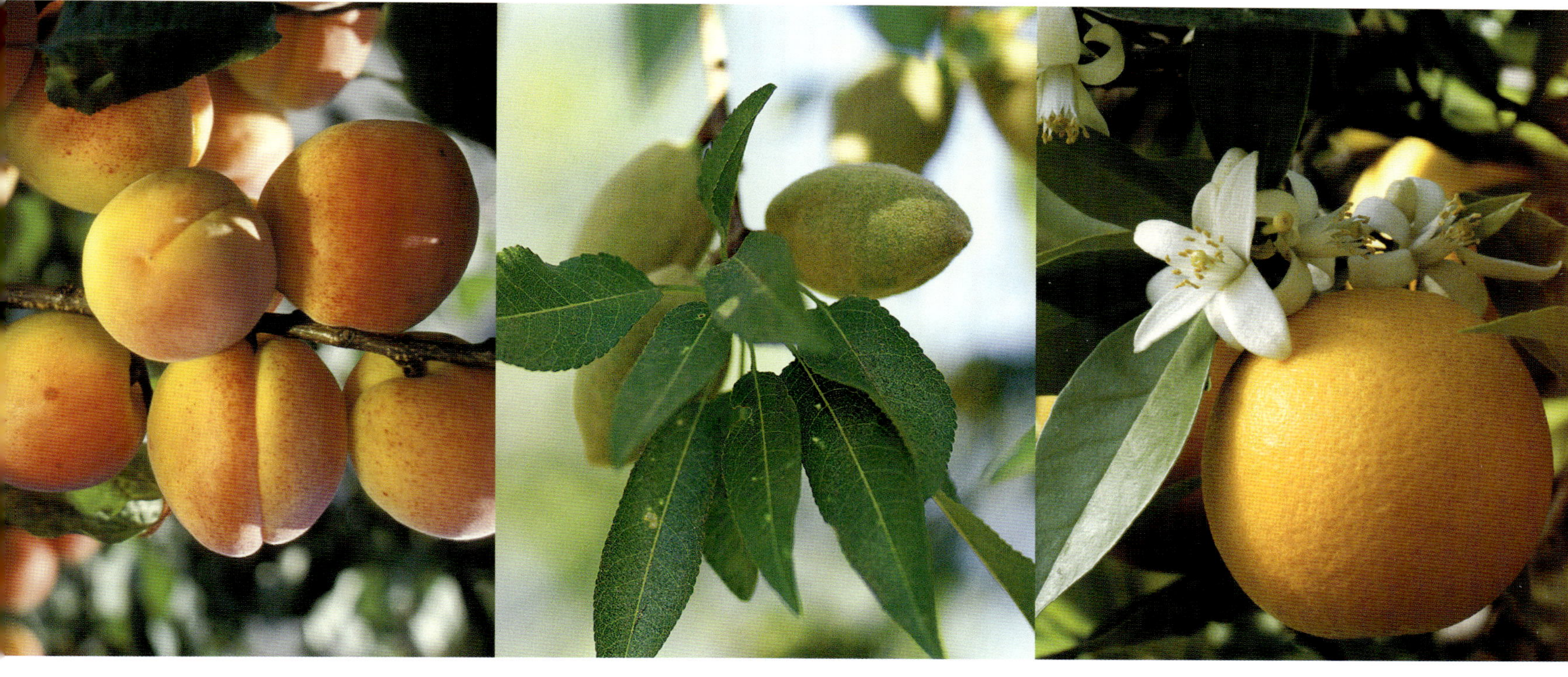

at the same time, the flowers heavily and sweetly scented.

when citrus plants migrated from south-east Asia to North Africa some 4,000 years BC. From there they spread to Europe and by the sixteenth century had made it to America in the hands of the Spanish. Christopher Columbus is known to have carrried seeds with him on his second trip to America. Today, Brazil is the leading producer of juice oranges, followed closely by Florida.

The Mediterranean is the true home of the Garden of Eden, the fruit capital of the world, producing such wonders as, from above left, the peach, the pomegranate, the avocado pear, the apricot, the almond and an array of citrus fruits.

The European groves that provide this sweet, fragrant fruit are concentrated along a 500km stretch of the Mediterreanean coast from Castellon in the west of Spain to Almeira in the south-east. The larger groves are under irrigation, as befits high-level commercial enterprise, because the moisture required for citrus is higher than for olives. But on a smaller scale in the Mediterranean biome, citrus trees, be they oranges, lemons or the famous Seville oranges that produce our marmalade, grow happily alongside olives and other fruit and nut trees in ancient groves on the lowliest of farms.

Uneasy future

Many parts of this biome, especially areas of the Mediterranean basin itself, are uneasily balanced between virgin country and overdeveloped and degraded belts of land given over to urban colonization. And yet there are regions which still count as wilderness and are heavily forested by native species of tree. Of all the biomes, because of its small size and locations spread throughout the world, the Mediterranean is the one which is most under threat and in need of assistance. It is also one of the most important because of what it can teach us about our interaction with trees.

Like olives, lemons and oranges (following pages) grow to a great age and remain productive in the often poor, marginalized land of the small farms of the European Mediterranean. In other parts of the world they are farmed on a massive scale and would be allowed a much shorter lifespan.

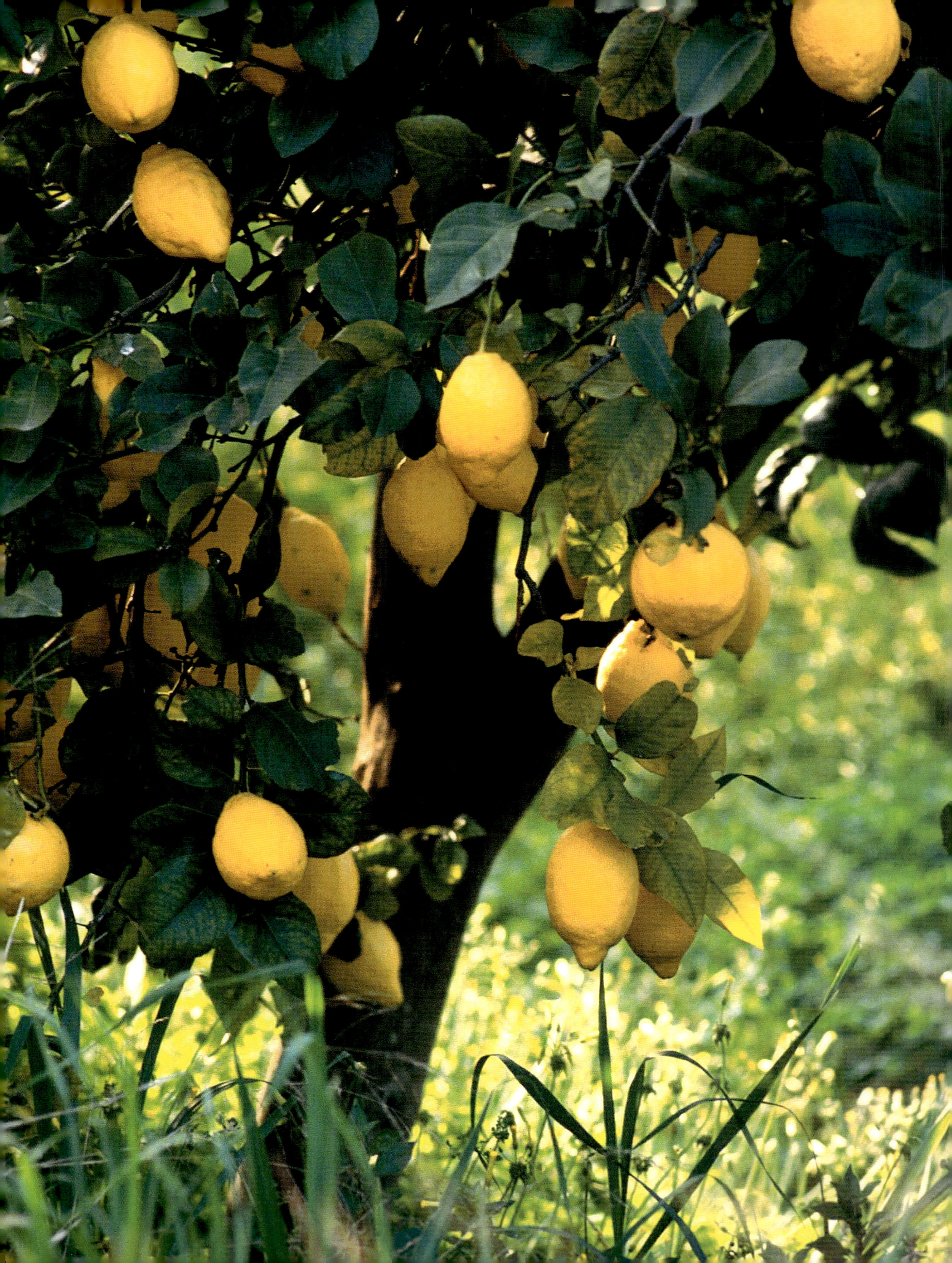

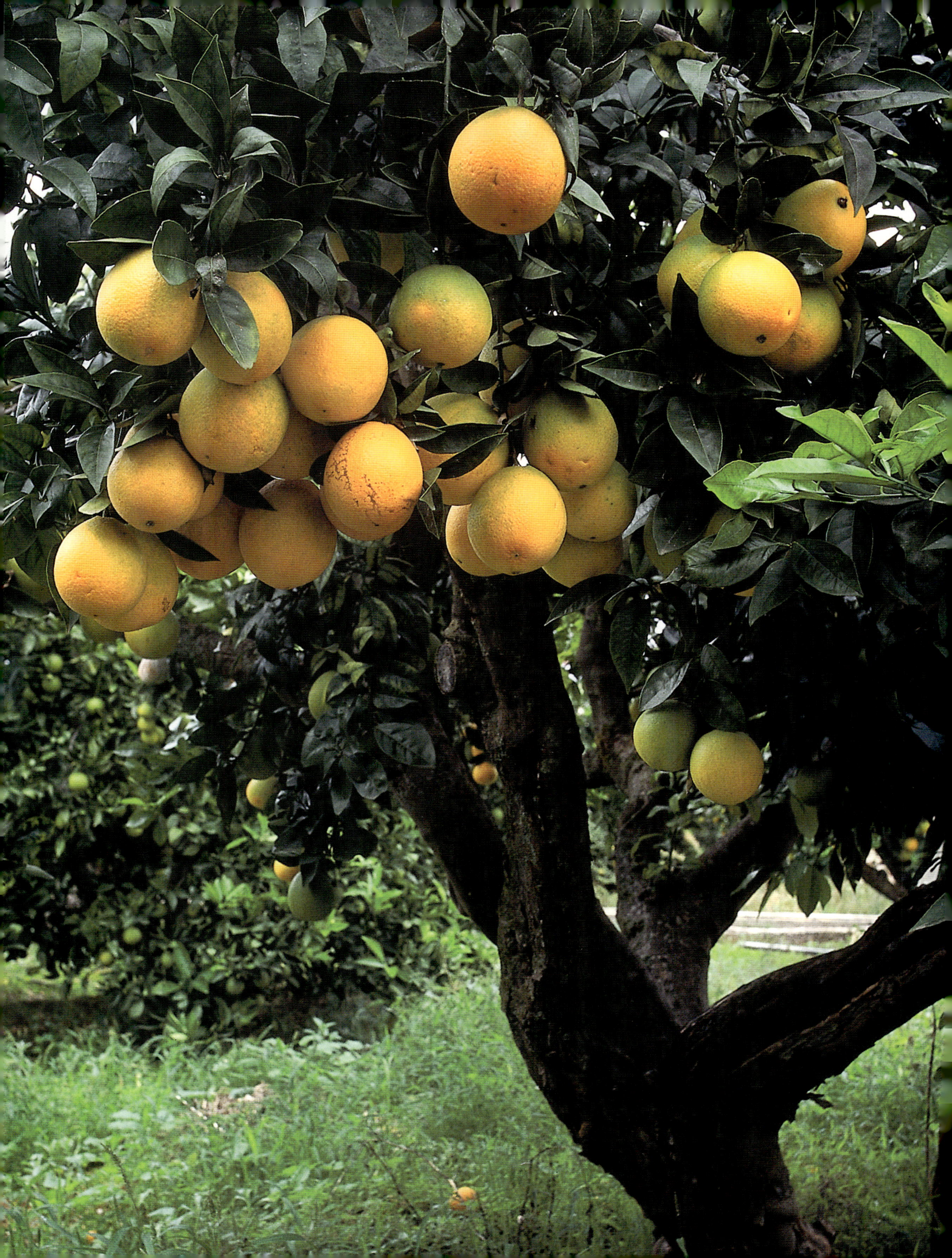

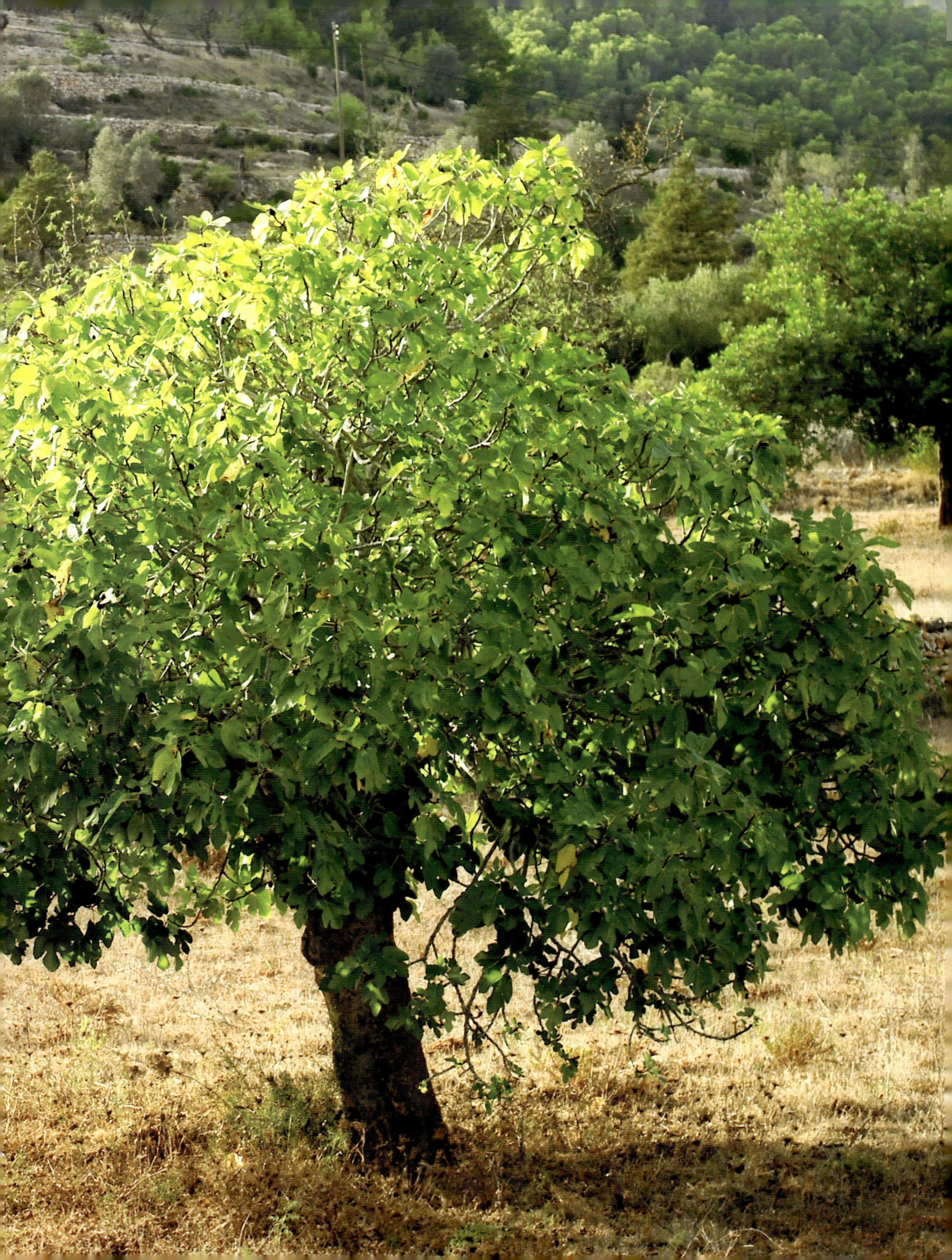

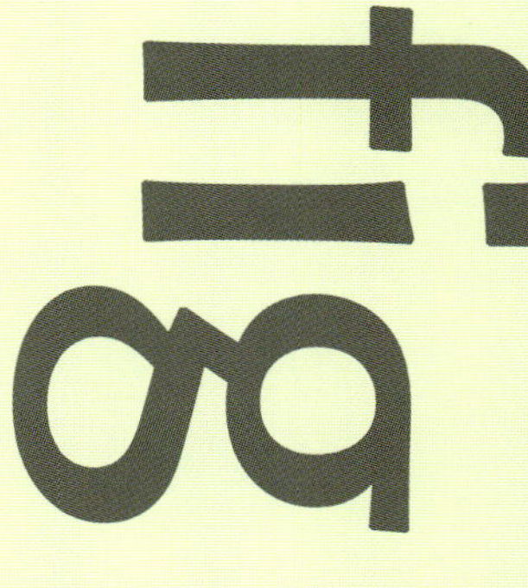

Figs, which have a high carbohydrate content, were said to be used by the Spartans to sustain them in sporting contests, most notably in the Olympic Games

It is as early as the third chapter of Genesis that the fig makes its first appearance in print – not as a fruit-bearing tree but as the provider of the leaves which Adam and Eve, on discovering their nakedness, sewed together to make aprons. There are as many as 750 known species of fig (*Ficus*) worldwide, and over half of these are epiphytic, that is, they grow on other plants, eventually sending roots down to the ground, mainly in the tropics and sub-tropics. But the edible fig (*F. carica*) has been cultivated extensively throughout the Mediterranean biome since pre-Biblical times and, by the time the Romans were at the height of their empire, there were several named varieties. Fig trees are unmistakable for their leathery, tri-lobed, deciduous leaves, almost grey bark and shrub-like growth which skirts the ground to create a mounded shape, with the leaves brushing the surface of the soil.

A native of western Asia and the Mediterranean, where it still grows wild from Afghanistan through the Middle East to southern Europe, the cultivated fig makes another high-profile appearance at an important time in history. After its first mention in the Garden of Eden, it is named as the shade-providing tree under which Romulus and Remus, founders of Rome, were said to be suckled by the she-wolf.

Edible figs grow all over the world. Figs in the Amazonian rainforests, for example, provide a high percentage of food for both humans and animals. In Africa, wild figs abound and breeding programmes have resulted in the production of fig trees able to withstand the harshest of climates. This fig should hold a place in the Mediterranean biome as an attractive, hardy tree with delicious, high-value fruit that might be used more widely in the future. Its wood is durable and water resistant and burns brightly and hot on the fire, if it is not of sufficient quality to be used for construction. But its fruit is still regarded as a luxury and is accordingly expensive.

Food source Pliny, who listed up to 29 varieties in Ancient Rome, said of figs, 'They are restorative, the best food that can be eaten by those who are brought low by long sickness and are on the way to recovery. They increase the strength of young people, preserve the elderly in better health and make them look younger with fewer wrinkles.' Dried figs are still an important product, found all over North Africa and the Middle East. Yet the fresh fig, clearly a valued food source from the time of the earliest organized agricultural systems in the Fertile Crescent 10,000 years ago, has failed to remain a viable economic crop.

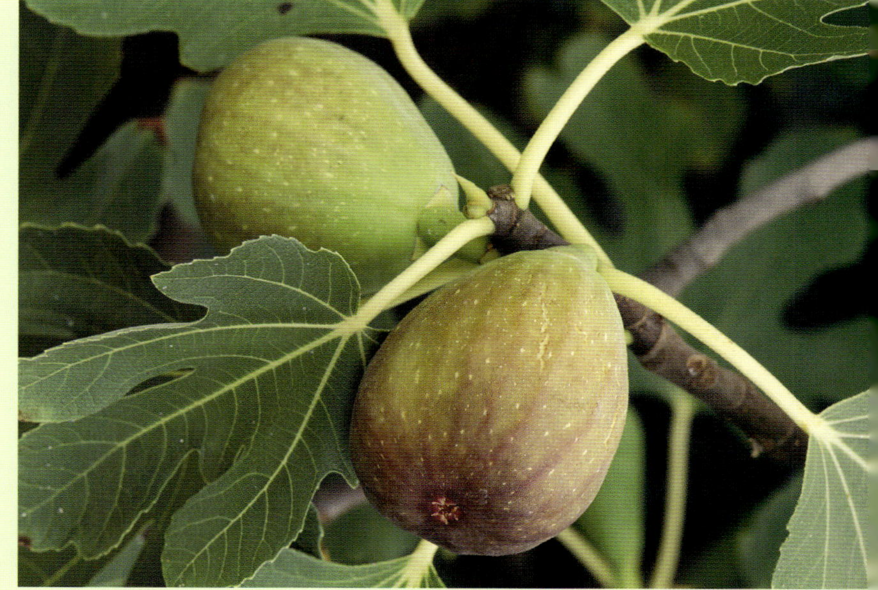

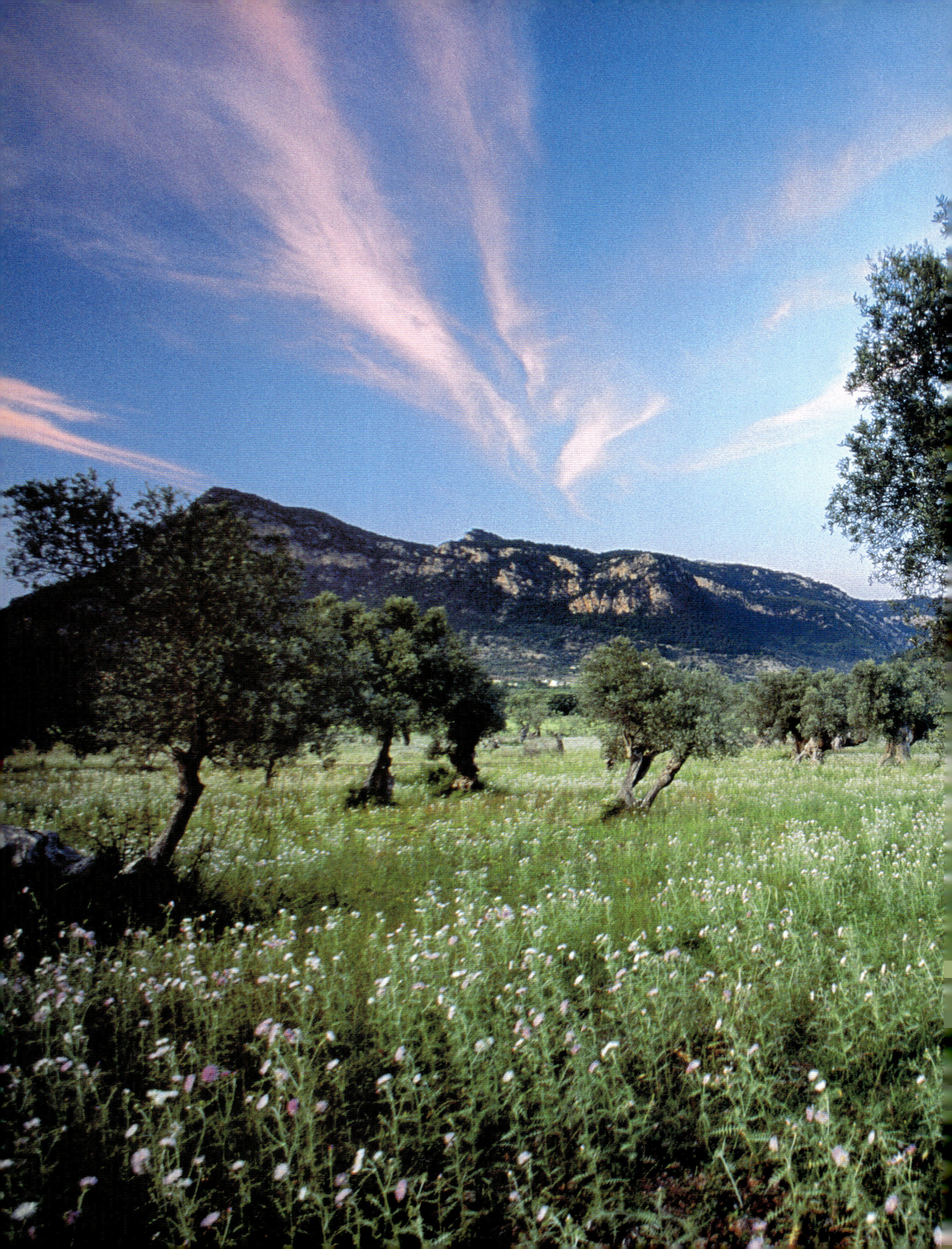

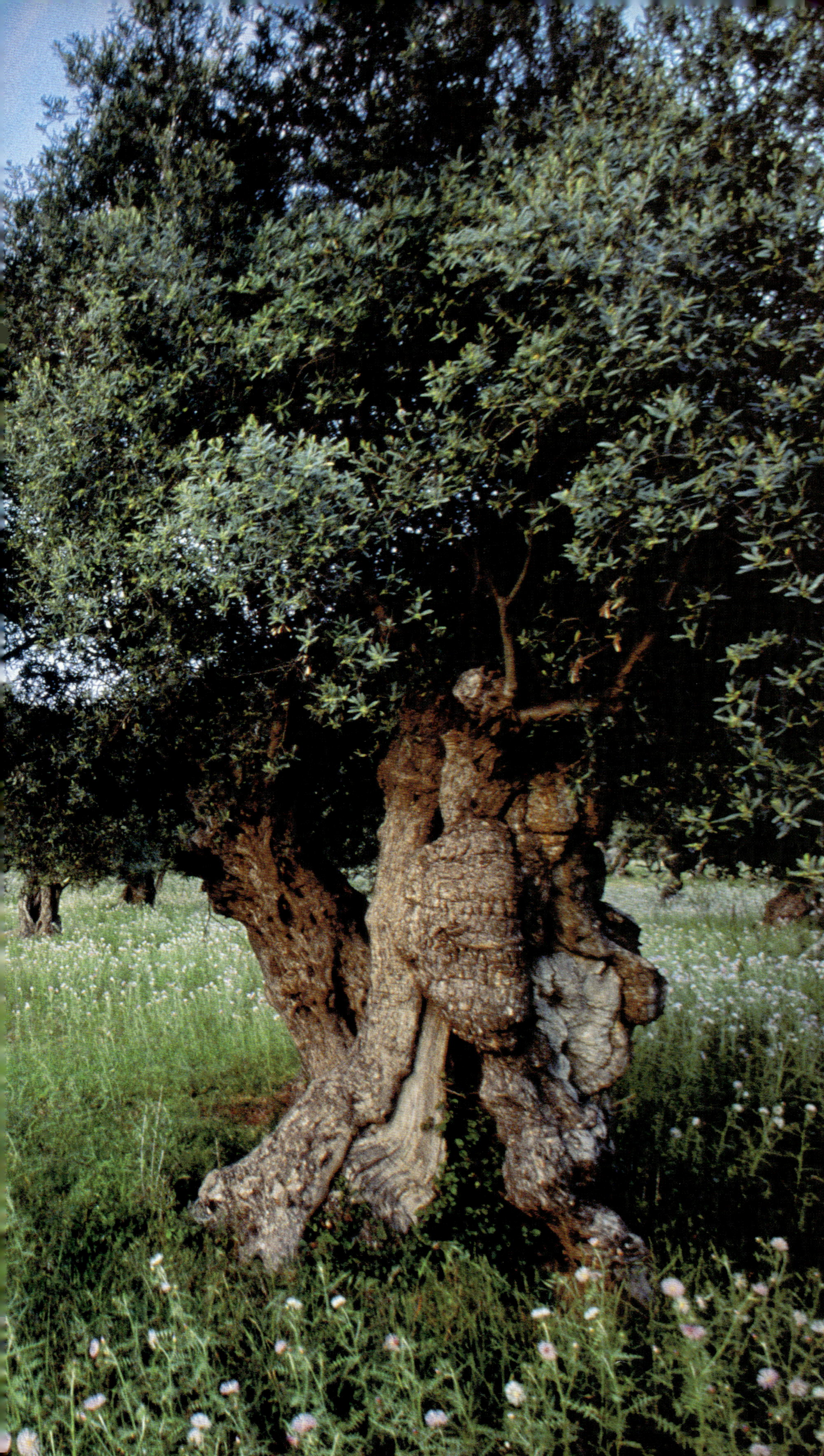

olive

When the dove returned to Noah in the Ark bearing an olive branch, this simple act signified the beginning of a meteoric rise for the humble olive

olive

The olive has been cultivated for 10,000 years. It is a workhorse of a tree, shouldering the burdens of a dry and dusty land where life is hard and the days are hot

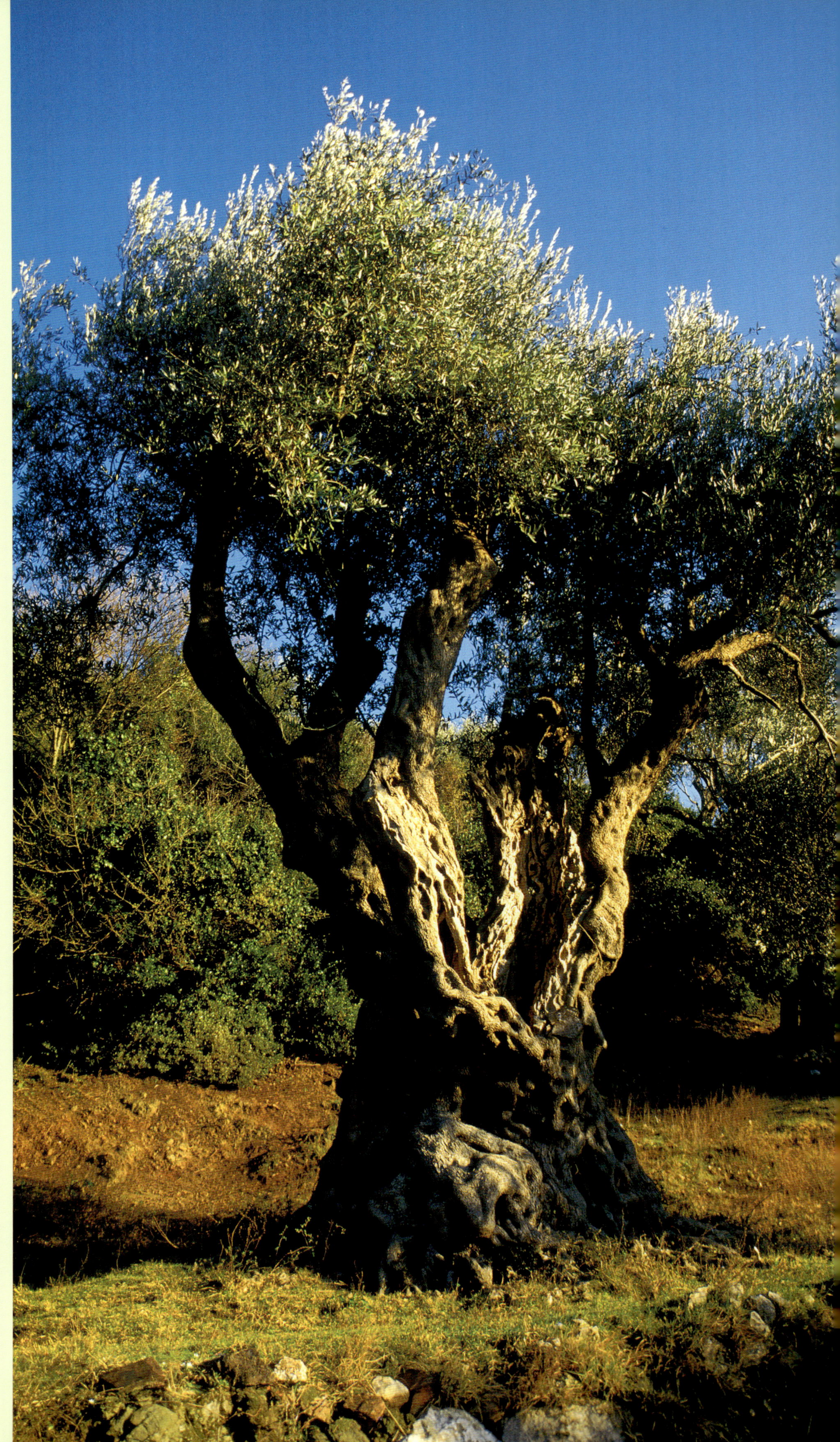

In gardens and on barren land, and from young trees to the gnarled elders of ancient groves, the olive is the economic and spiritual heart of the southern reaches of Europe. It is the defining tree of the Mediterranean biome and no one has summed this up better than Lawrence Durrell in *Prospero's Cell*, 'The entire Mediterranean seems to rise out of the sour pungent taste of black olives between the teeth. A taste older than meat or wine, a taste older than cold water. Only the sea itself seems as ancient a part of the region as the olive and its oil, that like no other products of nature have shaped civilisations from remotest antiquity to the present.'

For all its economic importance, the olive remains one of the most characterful and beautiful of all trees. It has narrow, grey-green leaves and an unmistakable profile; and the older it grows, the more dignified it becomes. Not towering or majestic like the Cedar of Lebanon, it is humble, as befits so many of the plants that inhabit the rocky hillsides of the Holy Land and its neighbouring countries throughout the Mediterranean. A native of this biome, the olive grows at odd angles and in odd places, yet still manages to live to a great age (a thousand years and more) and remain productive on the poorest of soils.

The olive family (Oleaceae) numbers more than 500 species, most of which grow in the northern hemisphere. The common ash (*Fraxinus excelsior*) and the olive are the most widely cultivated. Although its heartland is still the southern European areas of the Mediterranean, and more olives are grown here than anywhere else, olive culture is spreading fast and the tree is now grown all over the world where the climate is suitable: Australia, California and China.

The olive can only be a significant contributor to a safer and healthier planet

A revered history

The olive's place in history has been guaranteed since Zeus decided to award the capital city of Greece to the god who offered the most useful gift to the people. Poseidon offered a horse but when Athena pushed her spear into the soil and an olive tree sprang up Zeus was so impressed that he awarded her the city which now bears her name. She is often shown carrying an olive branch, eternal symbol of peace and plenty. Since Biblical times the tree's oily fruit, the olive, has been revered, the light from its burning oil shining forth from the candelabrum in the Holy Sanctuary.

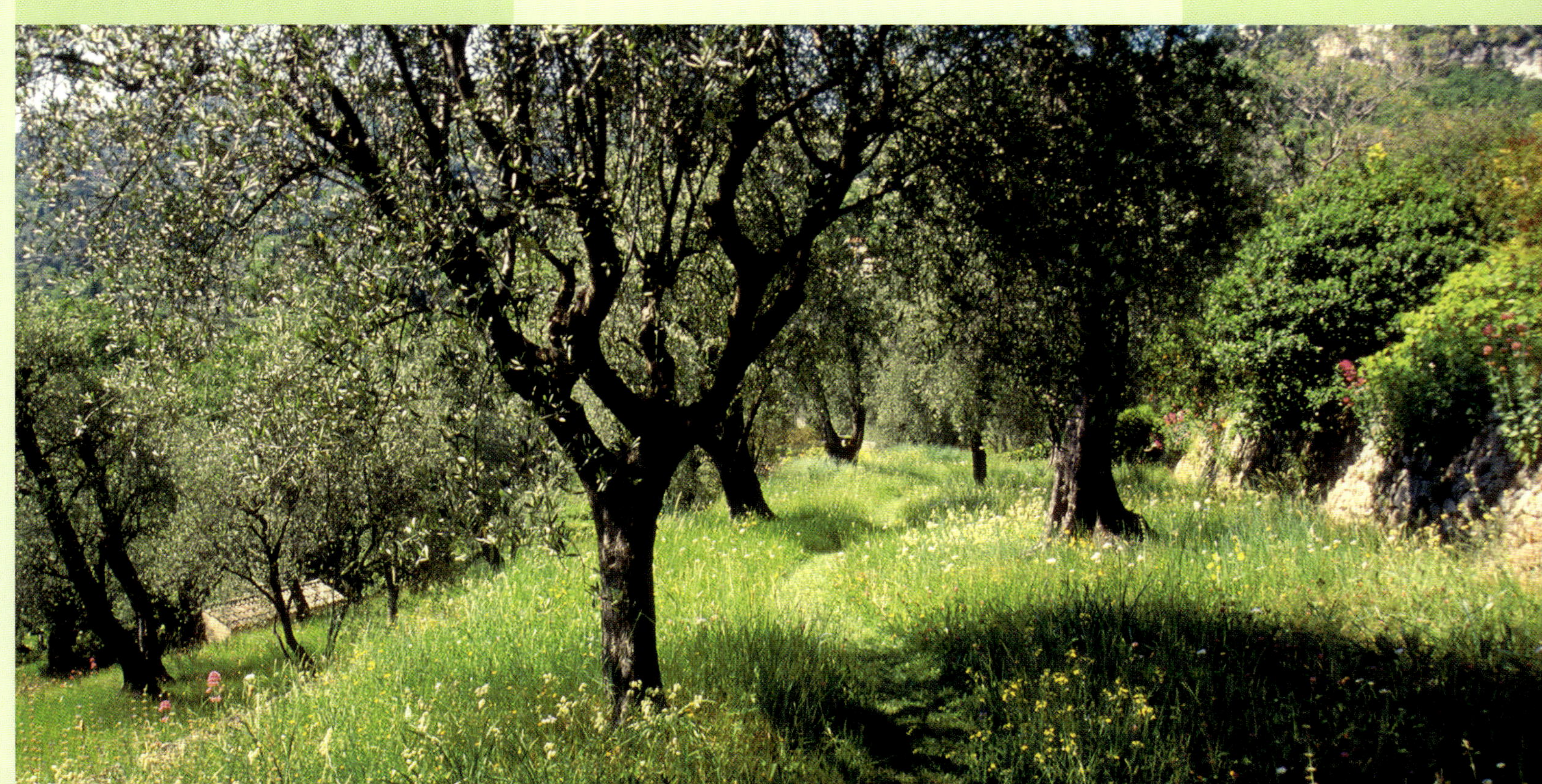

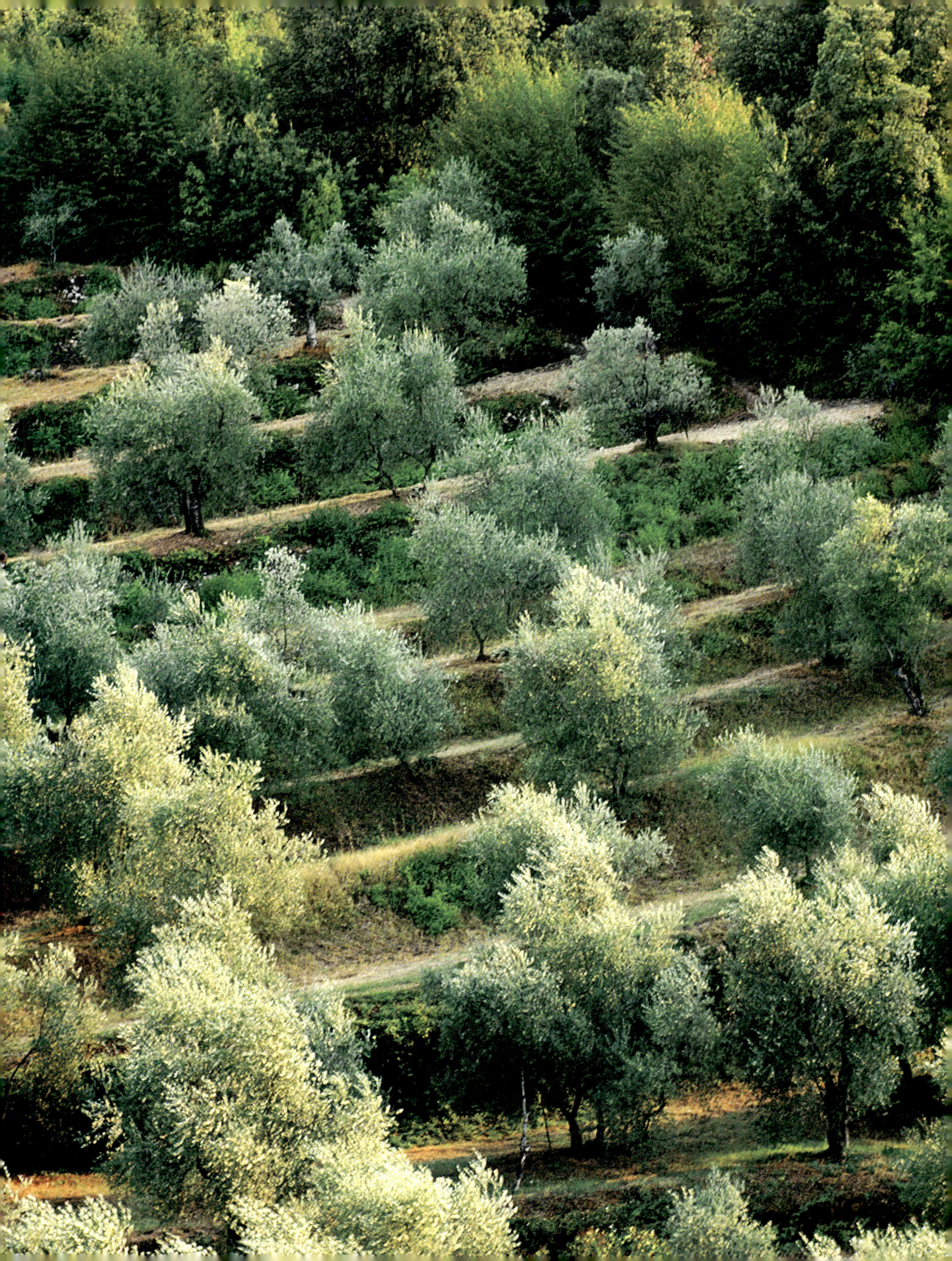

olive

Fruitful groves Just as apple orchards stud the countryside of the temperate biome, groves of olives and citrus trees characterize the Mediterranean landscape, often in a system of tree farming that incorporates other productive species such as the cork oak and the holm oak. The groves in which they grow may be ancient and can range in size from small fields to rambling hectares planted with thousands of trees. Both fruits thrive in the poorest of soils and can be found growing in land that resembles little more than rocky desert, their leaves covered with dust from the fine, dry soil. When planted commercially, the tree spacings may be exact but this precision erodes with time and neither tree nor grower has a great deal of respect for pruning.

The olive is a workhorse of a tree, shouldering the burdens of a dry and dusty land where life is hard and the days are hot. Yet its demeanour is one of strength and purposefulness. The tips of its evergreen leaves are almost spiky and the leaves themselves veer towards abrasive. This is one reason why the harvesters do not climb olive trees to pick the fruit, instead they shake the tree and watch the fruit land on a tarpaulin spread on the ground.

Groves of olives then take on a magical quality that emanates from ancient trees left to grow free. Elderly trees mix haphazardly with new plantings, making these groves the closest thing to a wild landscape. This lies at the centre of the forest farming theory which I touch on throughout the book. This manner of cultivation should be encouraged as a way of protecting diversity and the landscape in general and we should be thankful that, as yet, the terrain in much of this biome is too hostile to allow for anything else. While the inevitable future for the olive lies in straight lines of trees as far as the eye can see in China and California, the truth is that its natural home is in the wilds of an ancient grove sprawling randomly over the Mediterranean country.

With global warming playing into its hands, the productivity of olive trees is likely to increase

'Green gold' Olive oil is the 'green gold' of the agriculturally poor nations of the Mediterranean basin. Three million or more tonnes of olive oil are produced throughout the world each year. The trees grow well in the sun-baked earth of Italy, Greece, southern Spain and the Middle East and new varieties are being bred all the time. Ripe olives are repeatedly pressed to make olive oil, and the first cold pressing is the best quality.

That the olive is reaching new heights of popularity is unsurprising. Its fruits are delicious, as is its oil but, more importantly, that oil is healthy and for the sake of our hearts we should choose olive oil over any other. Because olive oil is a monounsaturated fatty acid it lacks the cholesterol-raising effect of saturated fats. It is also a good source of antioxidants and, unlike seed oil, it remains stable in its chemical structure when exposed to high temperatures, in other words, when used in cooking. Most of the olive oil produced is consumed in the Mediterranean region.

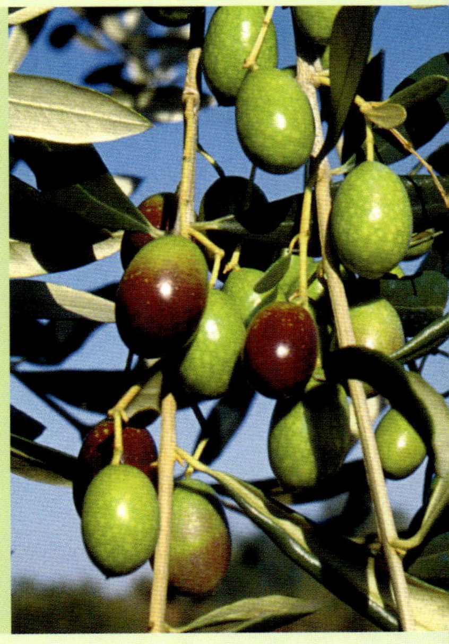

4

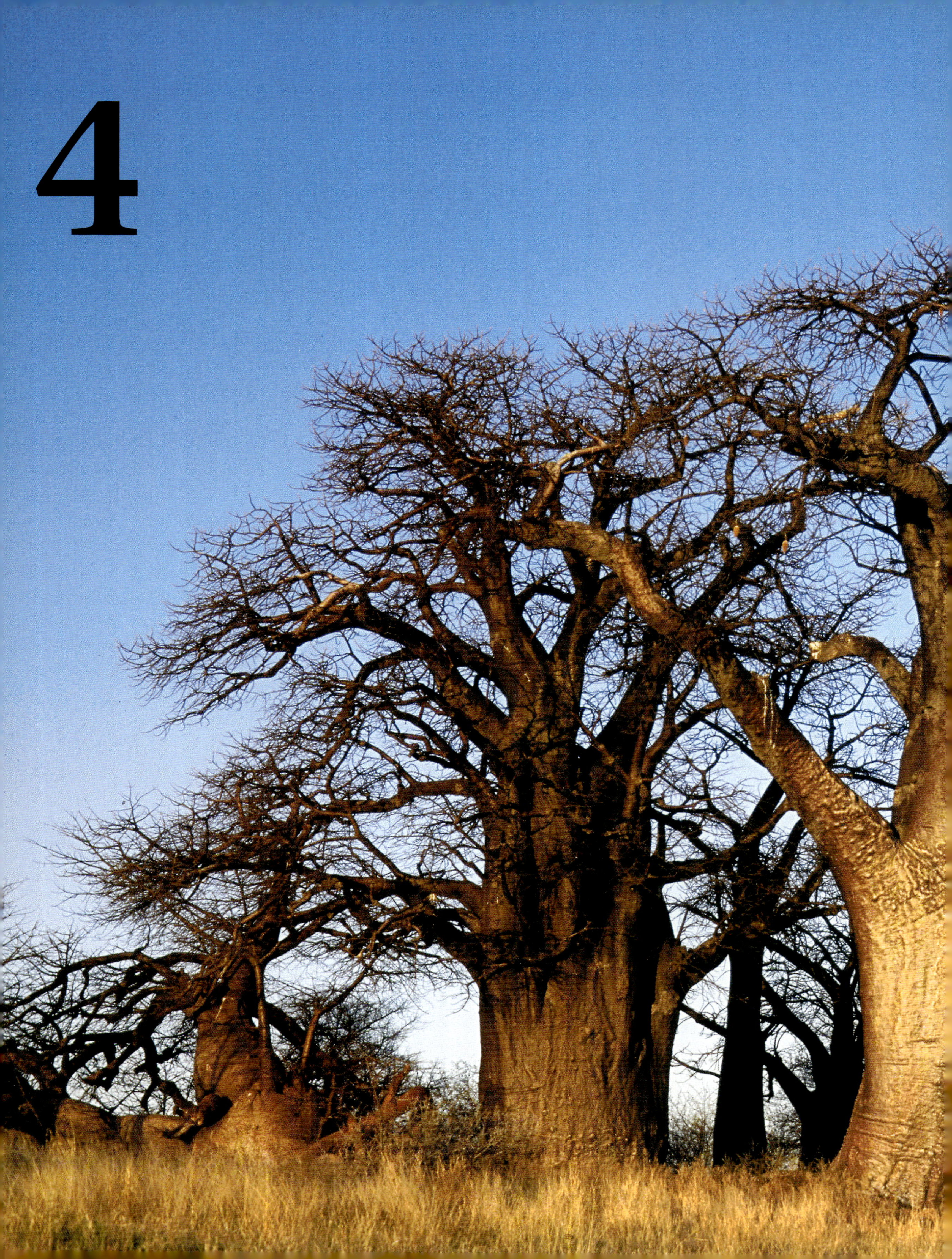

monsoon

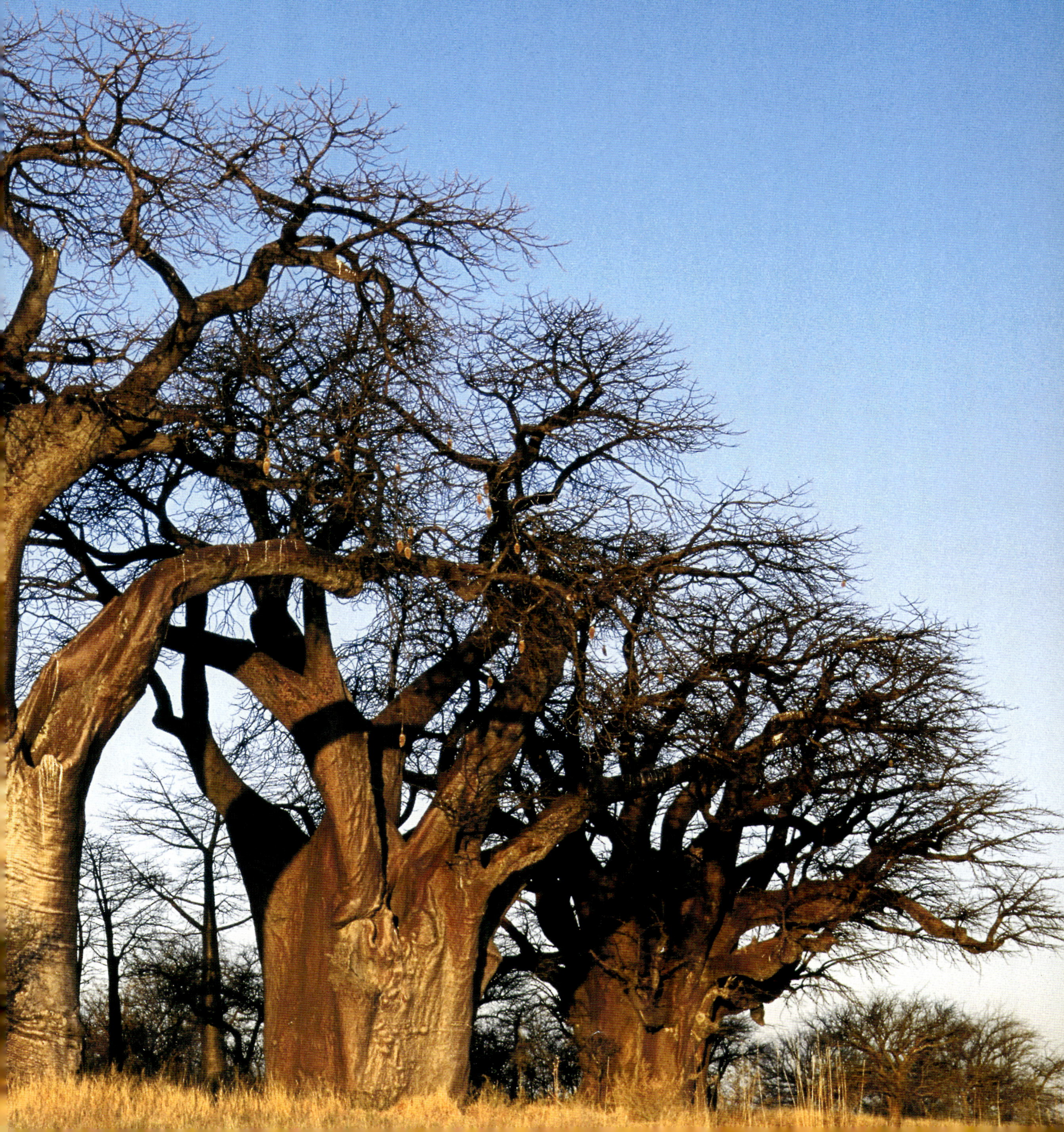

Often found in circles and in groups, baobabs (previous pages) are surely one of the most astonishing trees anywhere on earth. Just as beech trees were planted in Europe on burial mounds, baobabs seem to have found their way into the African landscape to signify a similar deep connection with the earth.

Monsoon forest is the hardest of all the biomes to define, and not only because it covers great swathes of entire continents. The climate that controls the definition differs markedly, both in the length of time the monsoon lasts and in its intensity from place to place. In broad terms, monsoon forest indicates those areas of the tropics where long dry spells are interspersed with periods of heavy rainfall, specifically monsoon. Huge tracts of Asia, Africa and Australia fall within this biome and immediately bring some incredible landscapes and some wonderful trees into play. There are two sides to this area we term the monsoon forest – the forest itself and the wooded and sometimes more open grassland known as savannah. The savannah areas of northern Australia and much of central Africa are scions of monsoon forest where the two climatic zones merge into each other; acacia emerge from out of the forest to grace the plains of Africa. In Australia, the eucalyptus that pockmarks the dry, open landscape alongside the golden wattle has broken out of the forest to find itself in isolation or in small pockets of woodland. On the Indian subcontinent, the dry Deccan plateau of the south-central landmass merges with areas of densely wooded deciduous forest of the Western Ghats and the Nilgiri Hills. This is where the silk cotton tree, often growing alone in an arid landscape, rejoins its companions in the forest where it mixes with ebony and cinnamon trees.

Trees in the monsoon forest have evolved to be deciduous in order for the system to regenerate itself after the ravages of a forest fire, allowing small trees to see the light and catch up – evolution at its most aware

The tall, straight stems of mountain ash are instantly recognizable by their peeling bark and pale trunks. A classic tree of the monsoon forest, seen here in the Dandenong Reserve National Park, Australia, the Eucalyptus *has developed into one of the most important trees of the biome.*

Many of the trees in the monsoon forests of the world are deciduous. They drop their leaves in the dry season to let in the light, allowing other species of plant, as well as other forms of life present in the forest, to flourish. This does not happen in tropical rainforests where the trees are evergreen: for sunlight to hit the ground in rainforest is a rarity rather than a standard occurrence. Since these areas of monsoon forest and savannah are often some of the poorest, wildest and most remote in the world, and trees are under pressure from both humans and animals, it is instructive to examine how native people live and farm in the monsoon biome and how they meet their daily needs from the trees within it.

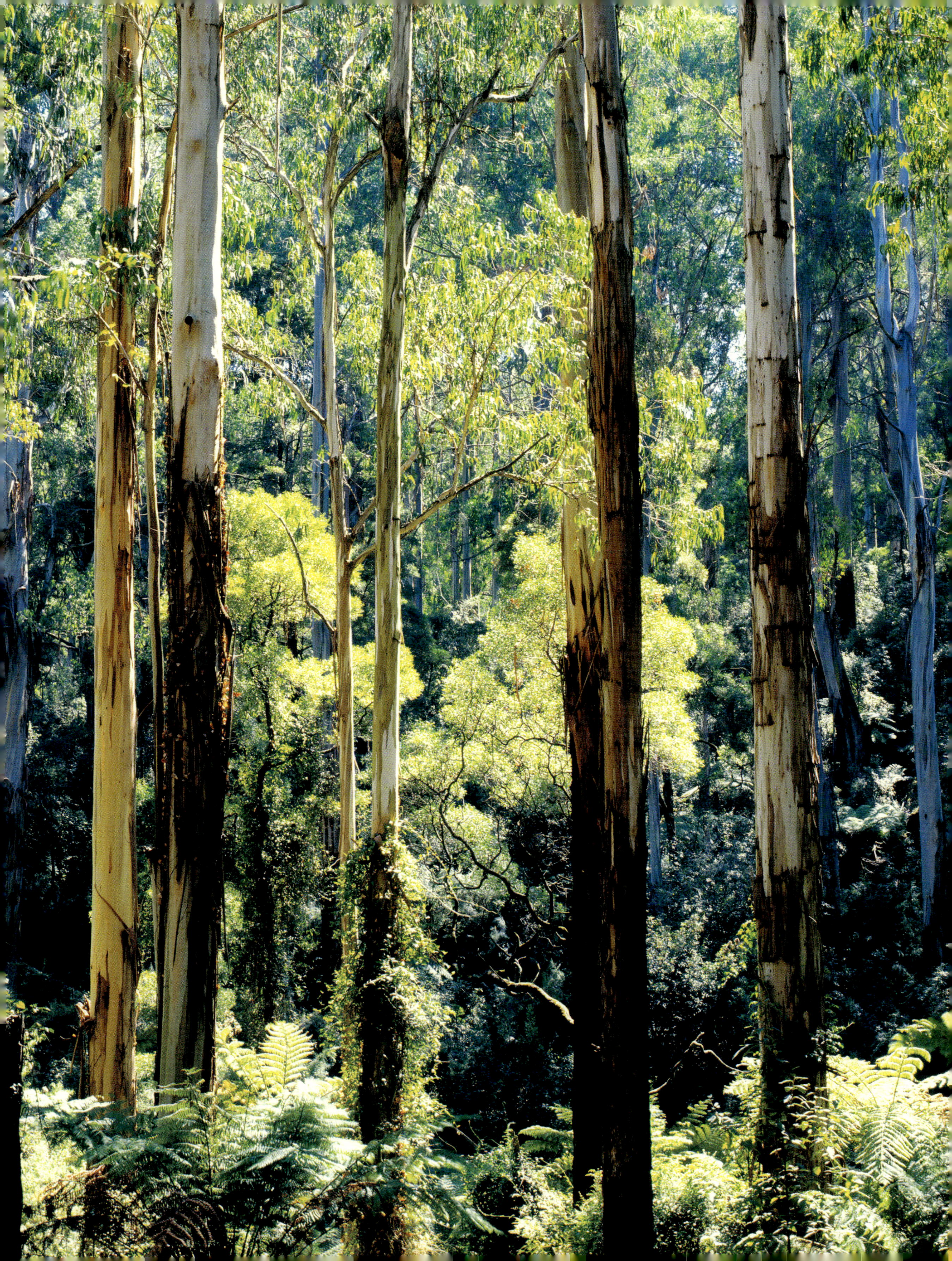

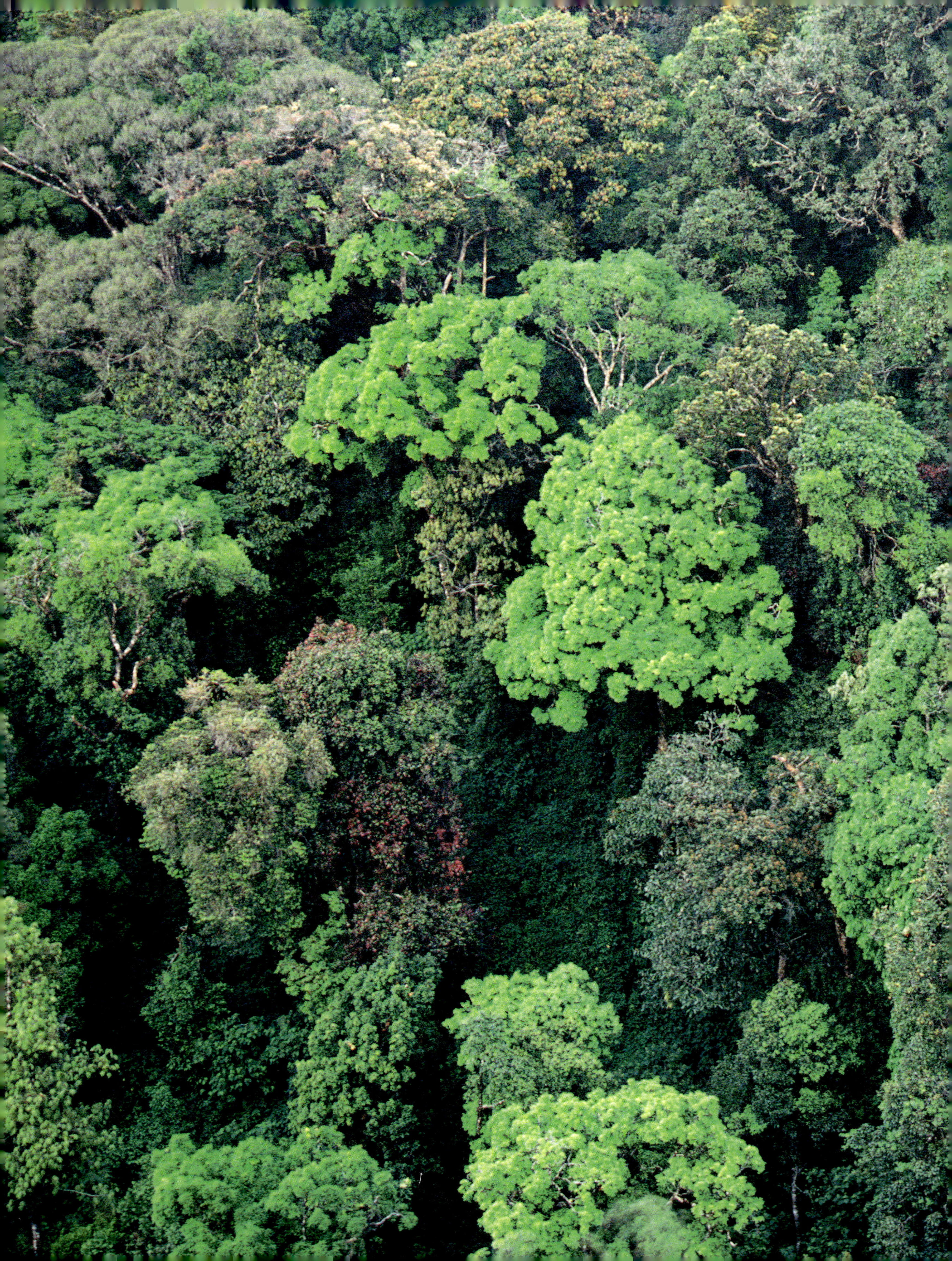

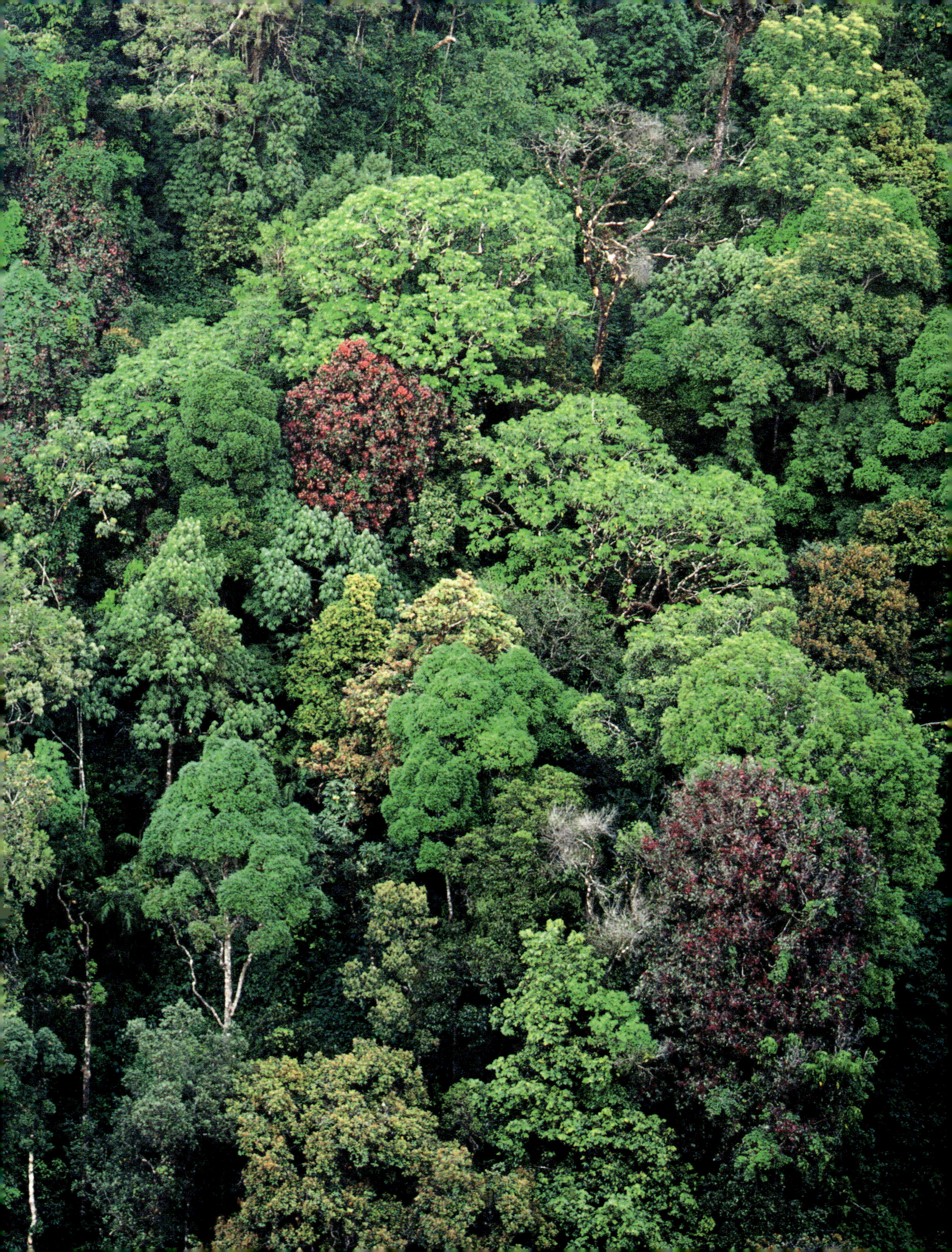

An aerial view of the canopy of a typical stretch of monsoon forest of the Western Ghats in southern India (previous pages). Life inside the forest leans heavily towards the production of valuable commercial crops such as coffee and pepper, both of which are tolerant of shade.

Subsistence living

It is a common misconception that commercial logging is the most dangerous of man's many ways of interacting with trees for his own use. The illegal gathering of firewood can lay claim to this dubious crown by quite some margin. Shortage of firewood is estimated to affect more than two billion people in the world today, and a great many are spread across the monsoon forest biome. Legal commercial logging certainly accounts for the felling of huge quantities of trees but it often leads to reforestation, whereas the illegal felling of trees to garner wood for cooking may not. My abiding memory of the first time I flew into New Delhi, India, at night, is of seeing the glow of hundreds of tiny patches of orange light. It became obvious that this light was shed by cooking fires outside houses, huts and other buildings, spreading all around the city and, I realized, all over the country. No doubt many were fuelled by the dung of domesticated animals such as cattle and water buffalo but the majority were fuelled by wood from trees that were unlikely to be replaced. The rural poor have few options other than to use wood for fuel, yet they make the most of a tree first.

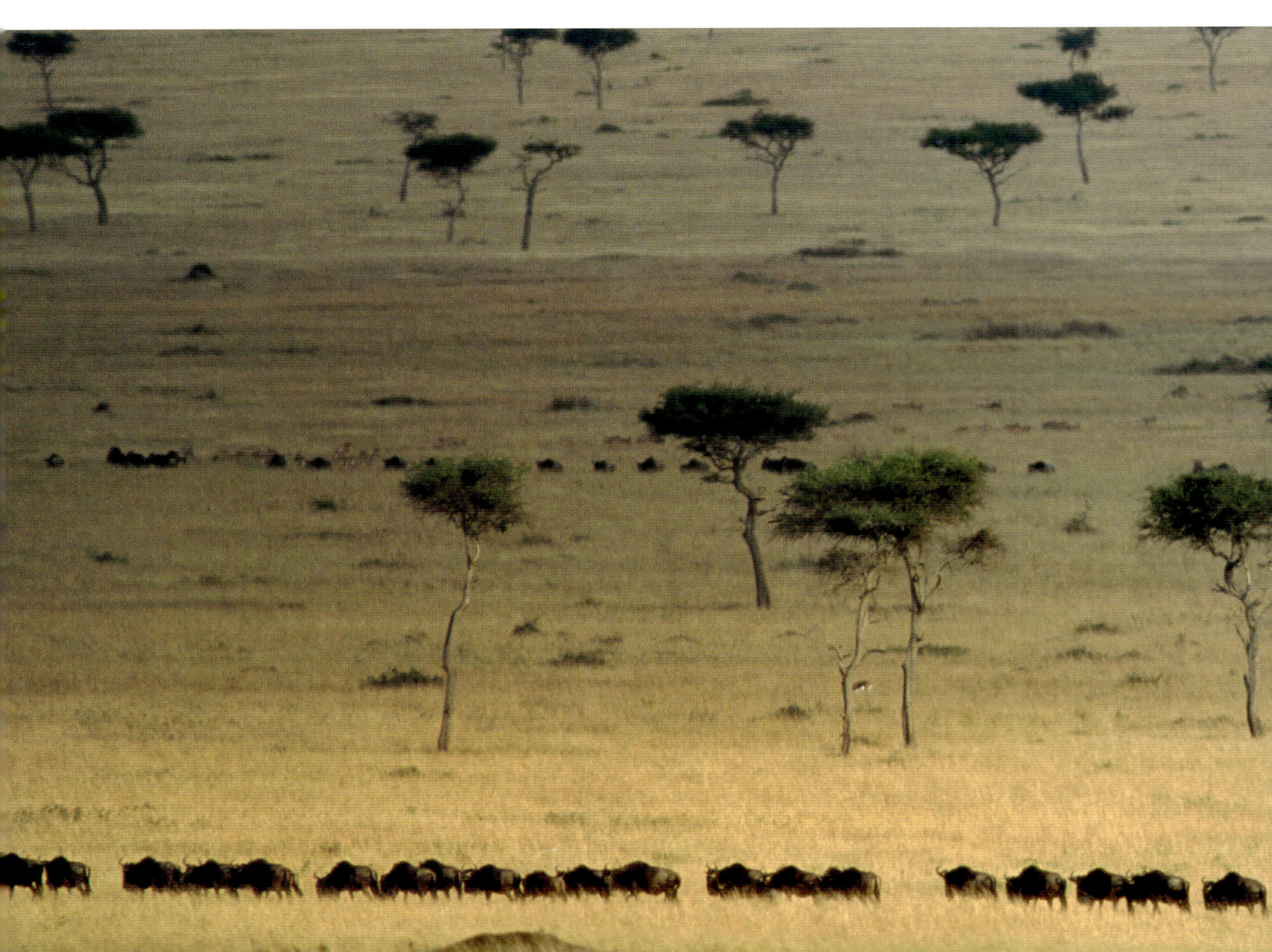

The tamarind, *Tamarindus indica* (see page 114) is an example of a large tree with a multitude of uses. It has spread throughout the central countries of Africa to the west coast and, as its botanical name suggests, is widespread throughout India. A member of the Leguminosae family, the tamarind is a prolific self-seeder, which accounts for its successful spread across continents. Its seeds are held in thick, fleshy pods, as with most members of the bean family, and are easily spread by wind, animals and humans. The flesh of the pods and the seeds are widely processed to make the sour but highly prized tamarind paste, which is in great demand for culinary purposes. The hard, durable wood from this tall, handsome tree is used to build boats, line wells and to make rice pounders, wheels and shafts. The bark is utilized for tanning the hides of animals, and the burned wood makes high-quality charcoal, the ash providing yet another by-product used in the process of de-hairing goat skins. Because this multipurpose tree is so widespread, there is always a danger that, to support a village's economy, it will be cut down for firewood well before it reaches full maturity and is able to have given the best of itself.

The umbrella acacia is a rugged survivor of the African savannah. Heavily grazed at its optimum height by the larger mammals such as elephant and giraffe, it is less troubled by the smaller ones like the wildebeest because of its vicious spines.

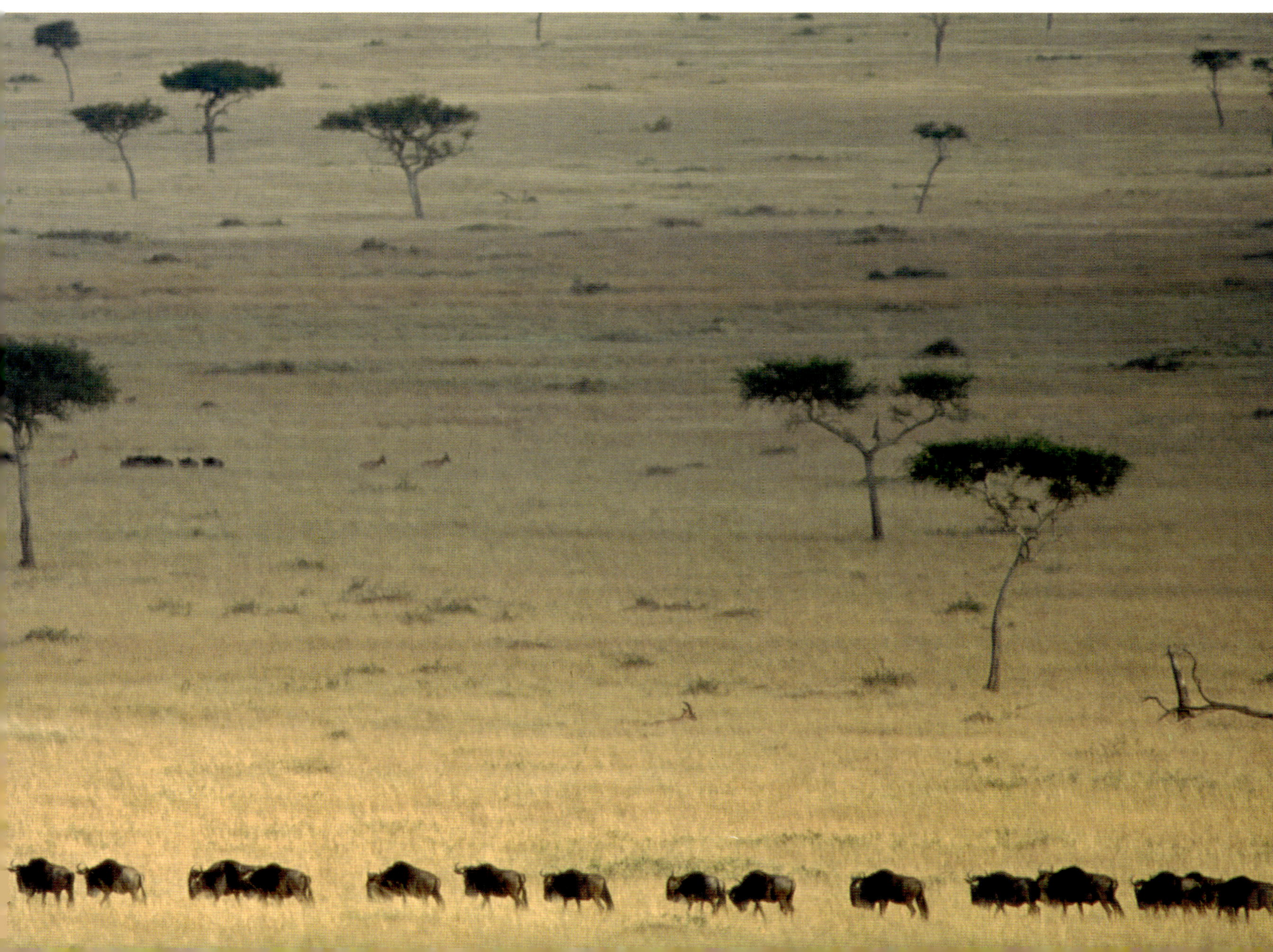

Homestead agroforestry in Bangladesh

What means exist to reverse this cycle of inappropriate tree felling for homestead use? In a series of pamphlets published by the International Council for Research in Agroforestry (ICRAF), researchers Leuschner and Khaleque assessed the prospects of initiating a programme for improving homestead agroforestry systems in Bangladesh.

Bangladesh is a country of 141,000 square kilometres, bordered by the Bay of Bengal to the south and India on all other sides, except for a small south-eastern border with Myanmar. With a population of more than 120 million people and a climate governed by the monsoon, water is the dominant factor and this is restrictive for field-scale agriculture. Nonetheless, agriculture controls the country's economy and its employment, and trees play a huge part in this.

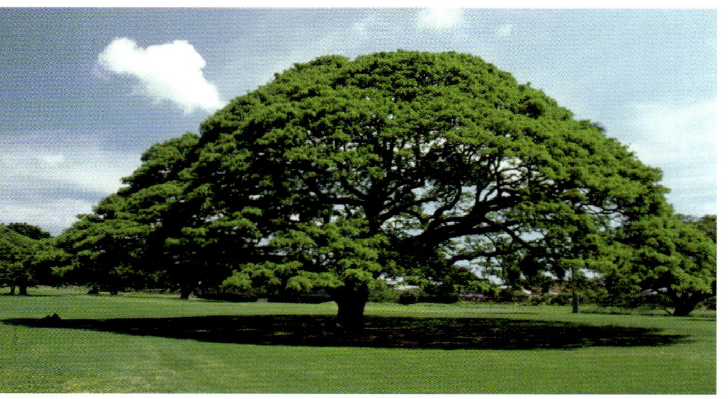

On this wonderful planet of ours the planting, care and nurture of trees always comes down to individual responsibility

The ICRAF research showed the homestead agroforestry system to be key to the country's economy, the variety of trees grown on small farms and in gardens being a major source of fuel wood as well as fodder for animals and timber for building materials. Fuel wood cannot be transported over long distances from the existing forest areas because, to begin with, the gathering is done by women and, secondly, there is often a network of rivers to deal with. And plantation forests, managed for commercial products, are out of bounds for those badly in need of fuel for cooking and heating.

The invaluable tamarind (above) resembles a tree from the temperate deciduous biome, its spreading crown giving it the look of an English oak. Its lower branches are often eaten off by domestic animals such as cattle and goats.

The researchers asked landowners and farmers how they would help deal with the fuel-wood crisis. The farmers responded that they felt there was room for more trees on their land and they had an earnest desire to grow more: an overwhelmingly positive response from the inhabitants of one of the poorest countries on earth. Although the farmers were aware that raising trees was a challenging business, especially in their climate and in soils often denuded of nutrients by rain, they were prepared, with help from government nurseries and expert aid from trained officers, to plant and nurture more trees on their land. On this wonderful planet of ours the planting and nurture of trees always comes down to individual responsibility – whether that responsibility comes from someone high up in government or a non-government agency is immaterial. Searching for answers where I felt they were least likely to be found led to extraordinary revelations and the result of the research in Bangladesh led to investment in trees on the part of aid agencies which continues to the present day.

Ancient knowledge

My travels in Bangladesh some 20 years ago revealed a complex level of knowledge among farmers about farming systems that could only have evolved over thousands of years and survived out of necessity. A prime example is the mound system of tree cultivation: this is highly developed in Bangladesh to cope with the shifting soil caused by the monsoon floodwaters. The entire homestead forest, often no more than a hectare in size, is contained on the mound. These mounds are extraordinary sights: small hill fortresses, practically islands, only a few metres above the level of the river water, heavily bunded (with raised earth banks) against the arrival of the monsoon floods.

This is where the homestead farmer has to produce everything for his family and his livestock. He grows fruit trees such as mango and jackfruit as well as the tamarind tree for spice, fodder and fuel. The mango is widespread in these farming systems across Bangladesh, India and Africa, having considerable economic value. The jackfruit is the pride of any homestead farm, growing to more than 15m in height and producing huge fruits up to a metre long, packed with delicious flesh (the taste is somewhere between a pineapple and a grapefruit) and highly nutritious seeds. The foliage is used for fodder, the wood for building and fuel and the husks of the fruit are fed to livestock: multipurpose trees in a managed system that works for the benefit of the farmer, his family – and the trees.

Cinderella trees

Selective felling is part of a slash and burn agriculture practised by the semi-nomadic Ntumu people of southern Cameroon, northern Gabon and Equatorial Guinea. The ecological effects of this ancestral practice were the subject of research by a scientist on a European Union programme – Future of Tropical Forest Peoples – who discovered that, as well as having its use in the subsistence economy of the culture, selective felling contributed long term to forest regeneration.

The parched Australian outback supports few species of tree that can cope with the harsh conditions asked of them. The eucalyptus (overleaf) ploughs a lone furrow among the grasses and scorched earth of the country's uncompromising interior.

When the Ntumu people clear a plot, roughly a hectare in size, they spare certain trees, usually about 15. This is a deliberate and traditional practice which requires sophisticated knowledge of the environment and the different types of forest tree within it. The Ntumu call these trees 'orphans of the forest' or cinderella trees, and they are spared because they have a high social, cultural, agronomic and ecological value in the long term. They are species of tree that may provide food, medicinal resources, firewood or timber or might represent important hunting grounds. Some, such as the kapok tree (*Bombax ceiba*), also contribute to the fertility of the soil, which the farmers cultivate once the remainder of the vegetation is cleared. The level of humus in the soil is increased through falling leaves, food production will go up and the plants below are shaded from the sun.

Besides having a particular use in the Ntumu's subsistence economy, the cinderella trees are a major force in the regeneration of the forest when the fields are left fallow again. These trees constitute attractive sites for seed-dispersing animals such as birds, bats and monkeys which use them to perch on, or as shelter against predators. The trees isolated in the fields also offer a sheltered microclimate which allows new trees to germinate from seed and grow beneath them. They supply nutrients from leaves, fruit and animal excreta, and the shade cast by the crown of the tree offers increased levels of soil humidity, a valuable commodity in arid conditions.

National parks

In the vast areas of wilderness that are not farmed, perhaps the greatest saviours of trees are the national parks. Every country has them, even lowly Bangladesh, and while some are policed better than others, many remain firmly in the hands of nature. The great savannahs of Africa are renowned for the large and diverse herds of hoofed mammals they support, and these lands are protected as far as is possible considering the huge areas to be covered. Australia contains 24 million hectares of forested wilderness and savannah where eucalyptus groves never see the sight of man and, again, they are entirely protected by the national park system.

*The paperbark tree (*Melaleucca quinquinerva*) was imported from Australia to Florida in 1906, ostensibly to drain the Everglades. Such was its liking for Florida's soil and climate that it was quickly cast as a weed tree. A rampant grower and prolific self-seeder in Florida, it grows in dense clumps but in its native Kakadu it grows happily by the sides of rivers and water courses, troubling no one.*

One such is Kakadu National Park in the Northern Territories. It covers 20,000 square kilometres, which makes it roughly the size of Denmark. Kakadu's landscape is primarily flat savannah woodland mixed with scrubby vegetation, and its climate is dominated by a dry-wet cycle. In the summer it rains continuously and for the rest of the year it is dry and very hot. Apart from one uranium mine, the vast majority of this park is completely wild and the trees within it grow as nature intended, with little or no interference from humans. Kakadu is packed with species of tree typical of the Australian biome such as wattles, coral trees, silver oaks and eucalyptus, including the salmon gum (*E. tintinnans*), whose beautiful peeling white bark is shed to reveal salmon-coloured bark underneath.

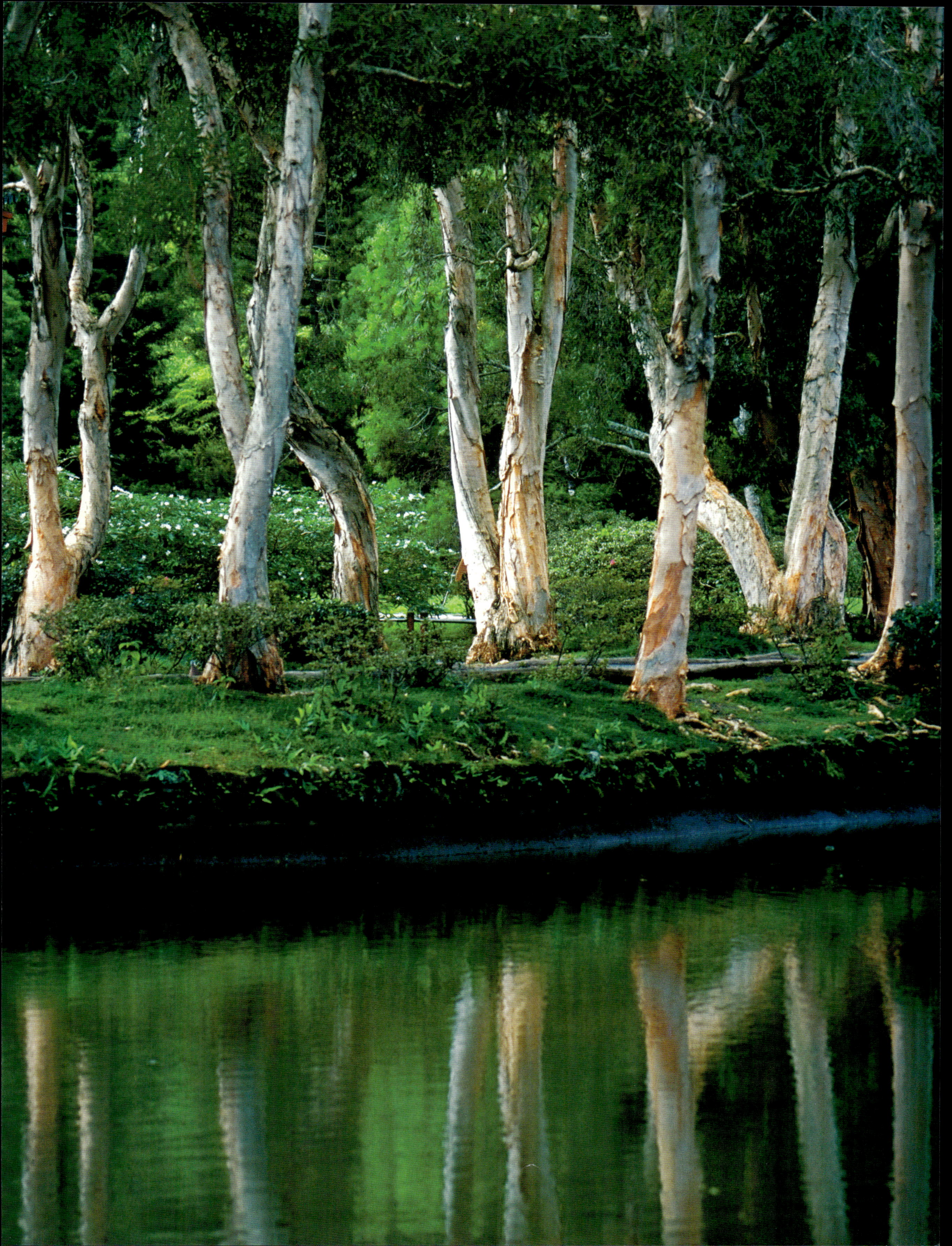

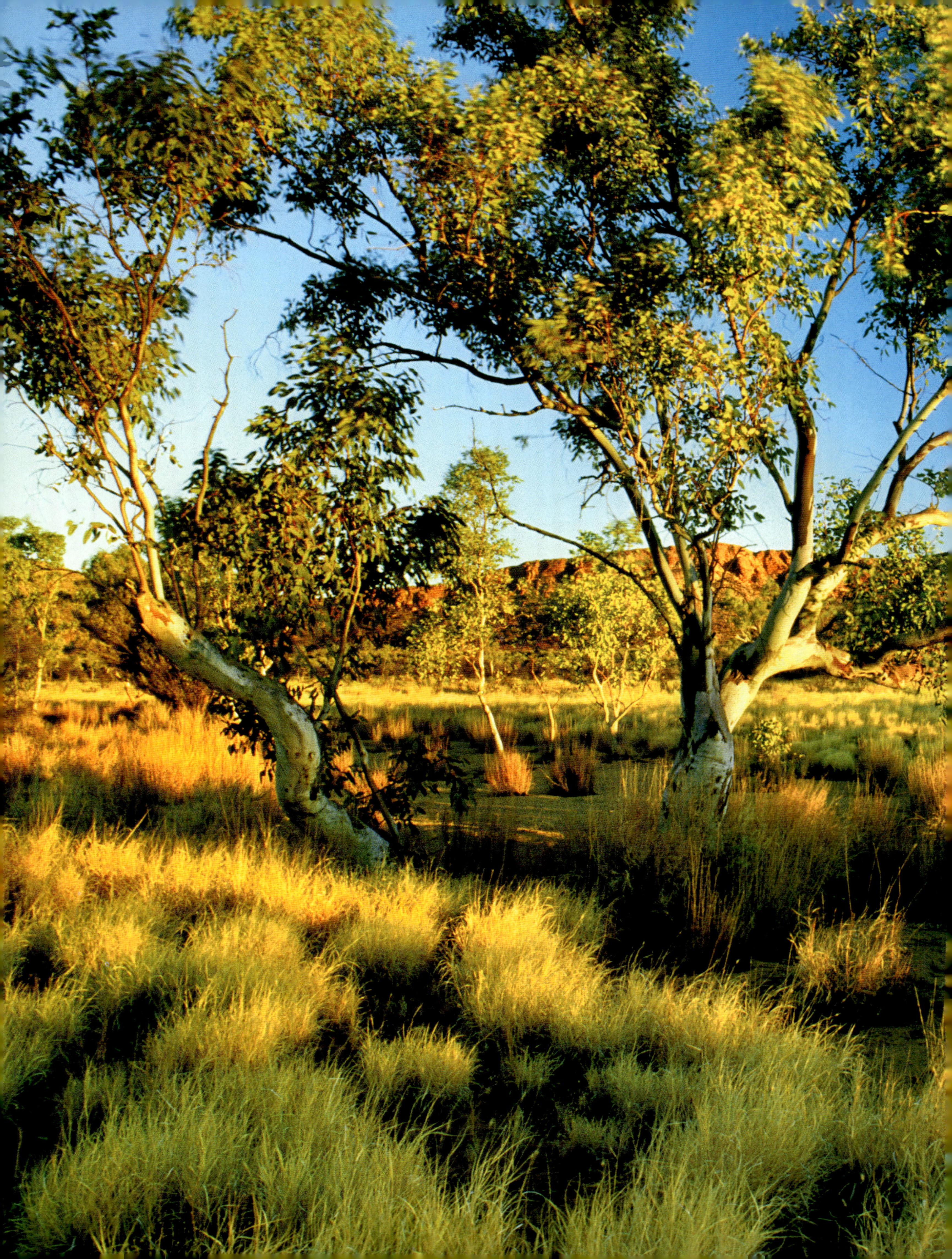

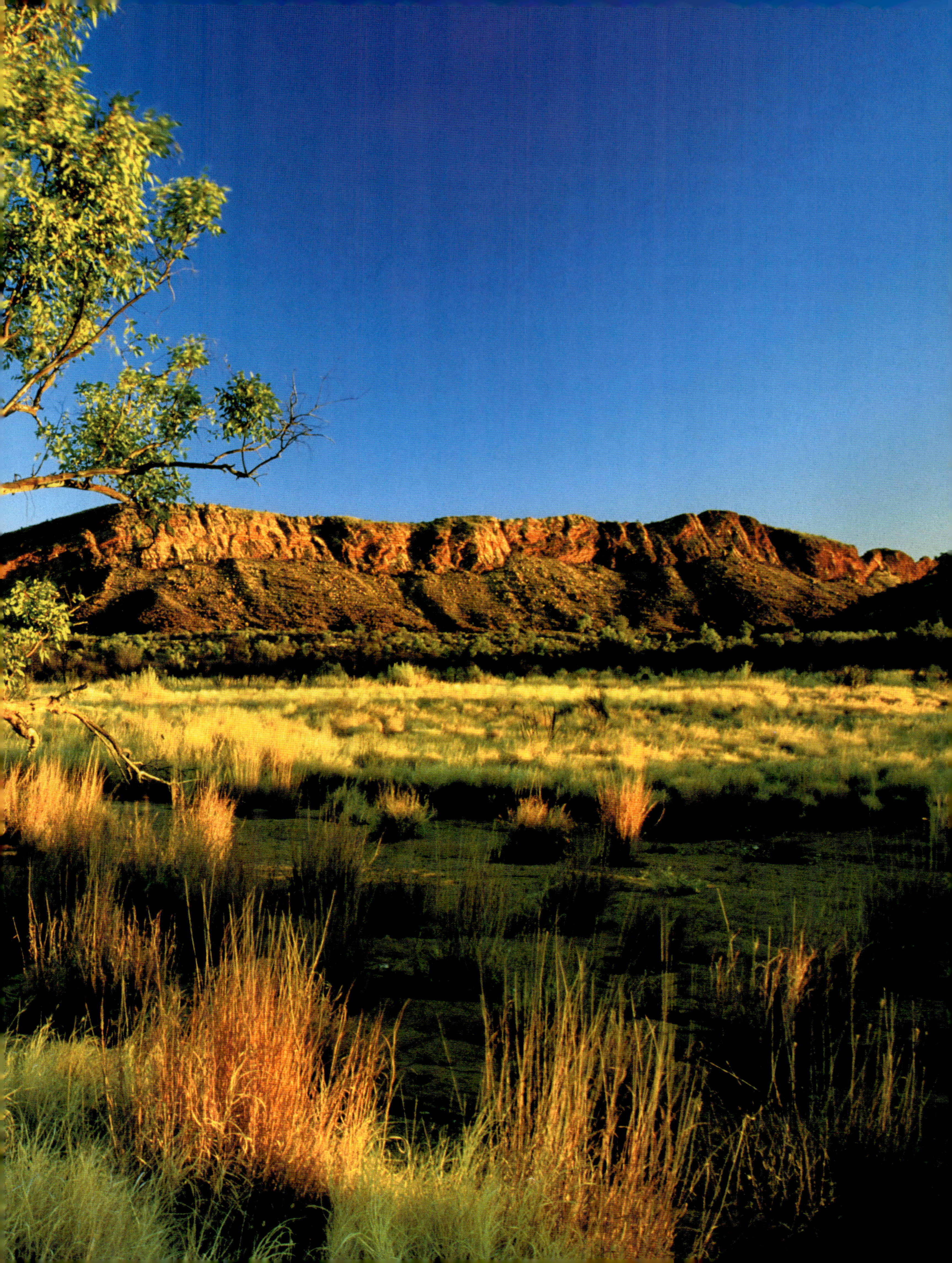

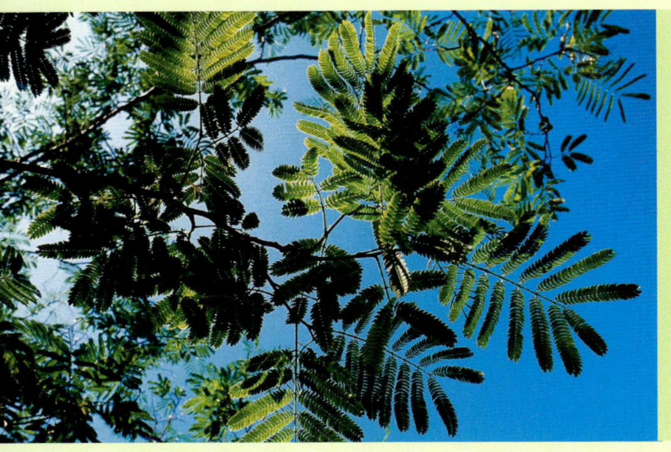

Like the eucalyptus, the golden wattle, which is only one of 900 species of acacia in Australia, is well adapted to poor soil conditions, drought and fire. It has two remarkable features which are that, in very dry conditions it stops growing and, when it rains, the water is directed by its branches straight to the base of the trunk. With most evergreen trees, or deciduous trees when in leaf, rainwater reaches the feeder roots by means of the 'drip line' located on the leaves at the end of the branches. But in the case of the wattle, water is needed for the tap root attached directly to the main trunk.

Survival strategies

Being from the legume family, wattles fix atmospheric nitrogen in bacteria on the root nodules and release it to nourish themselves and other plants, allowing the tree to flourish even in nutrient-poor soils. Birds are attracted to the golden wattle's protein-rich, oily seeds and help in their distribution. In another quirk of nature, these seeds need high temperatures to germinate and this is often provided by fire – a common occurrence in the parched Australian outback – which, in its wake, leaves heat as well as a potash-rich bed of soil, the perfect stimulus for germination.

The differences between the African and Australian acacias offer further insights into this remarkable genus. Seed distribution in Africa's umbrella acacia is carried out by mammals which gather under the trees. In the process they manure the ground beneath the trees with their droppings and this it needs because, although a legume, this tree does not fix nitrogen. Australian acacias are legumes and do fix nitrogen, so they have no requirement for animal manure – and therefore do not attract any animals.

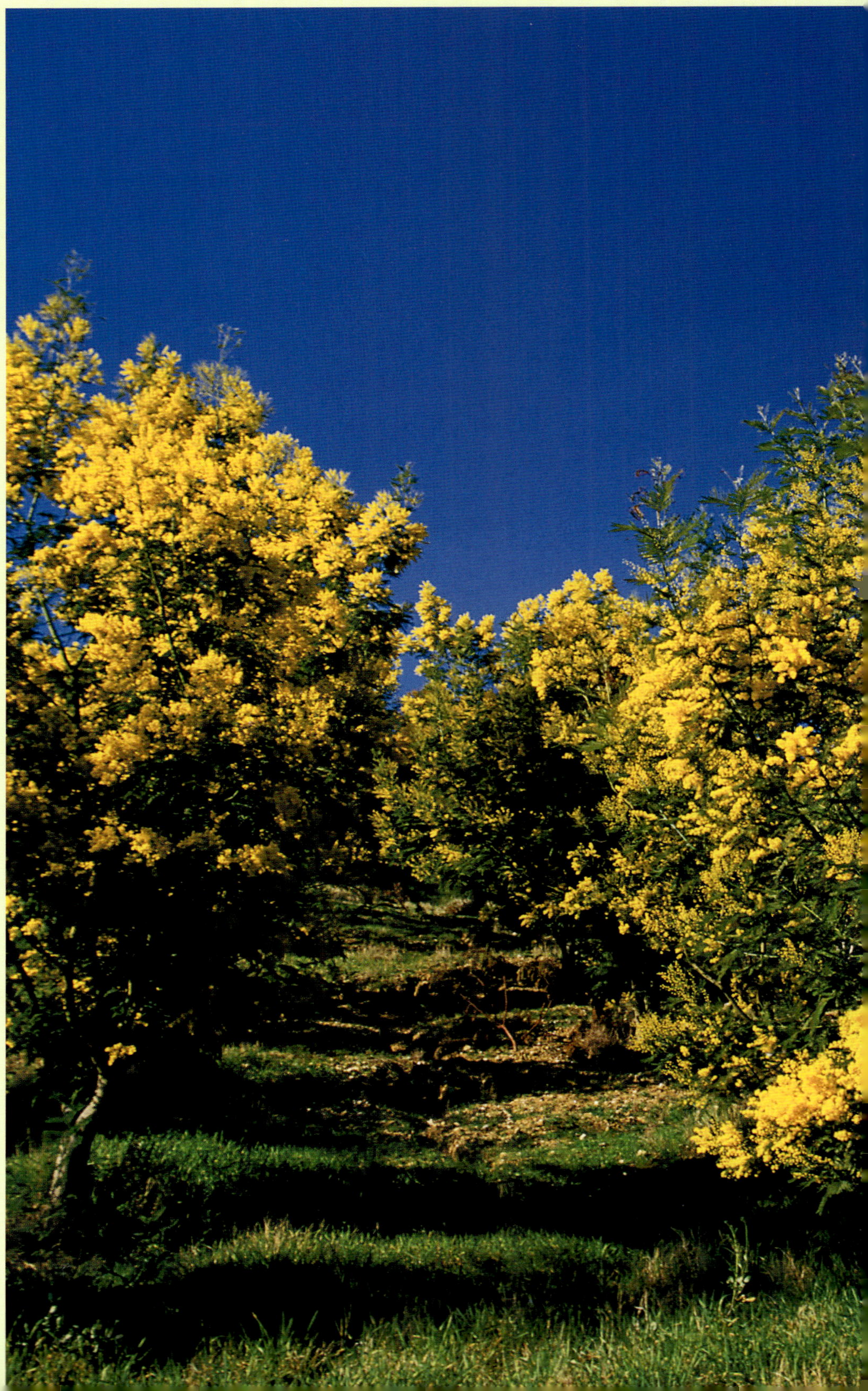

golden wattle

Its fluffy flowerheads have made it the pride of the forest and the open woodland

The golden wattle is the national floral symbol of Australia and one of the most beautiful flowering trees in the country. Though it grows only 4-8m in height, its golden-yellow flowerheads hold up to 80 minute and sweetly scented flowers, and have made it the pride of the forest and the open woodland where it grows. Its hardiness, stunning appearance and ability to grow in a wide range of soils have also made *Acacia pycnantha* a popular garden plant and it is exported all over the world.

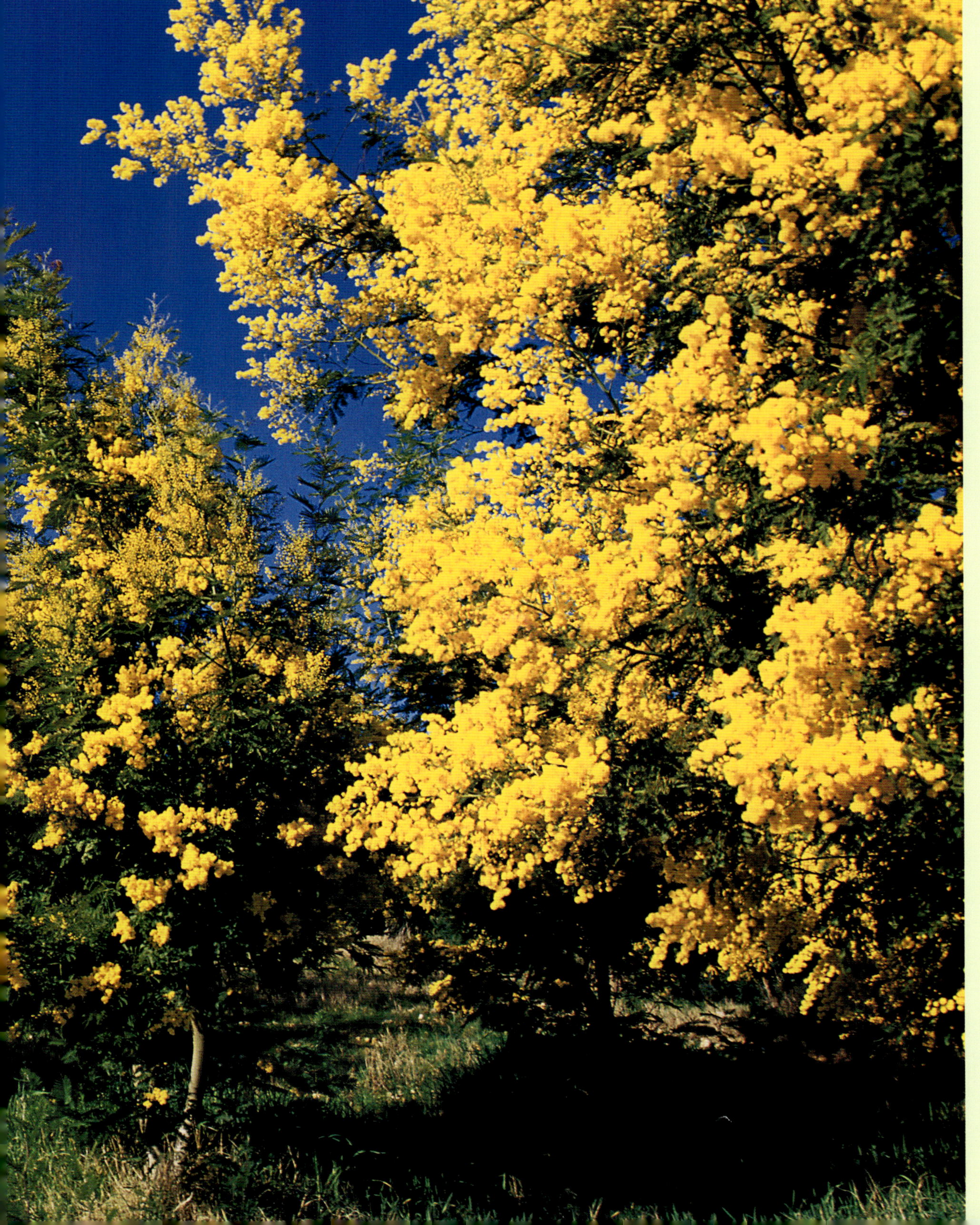

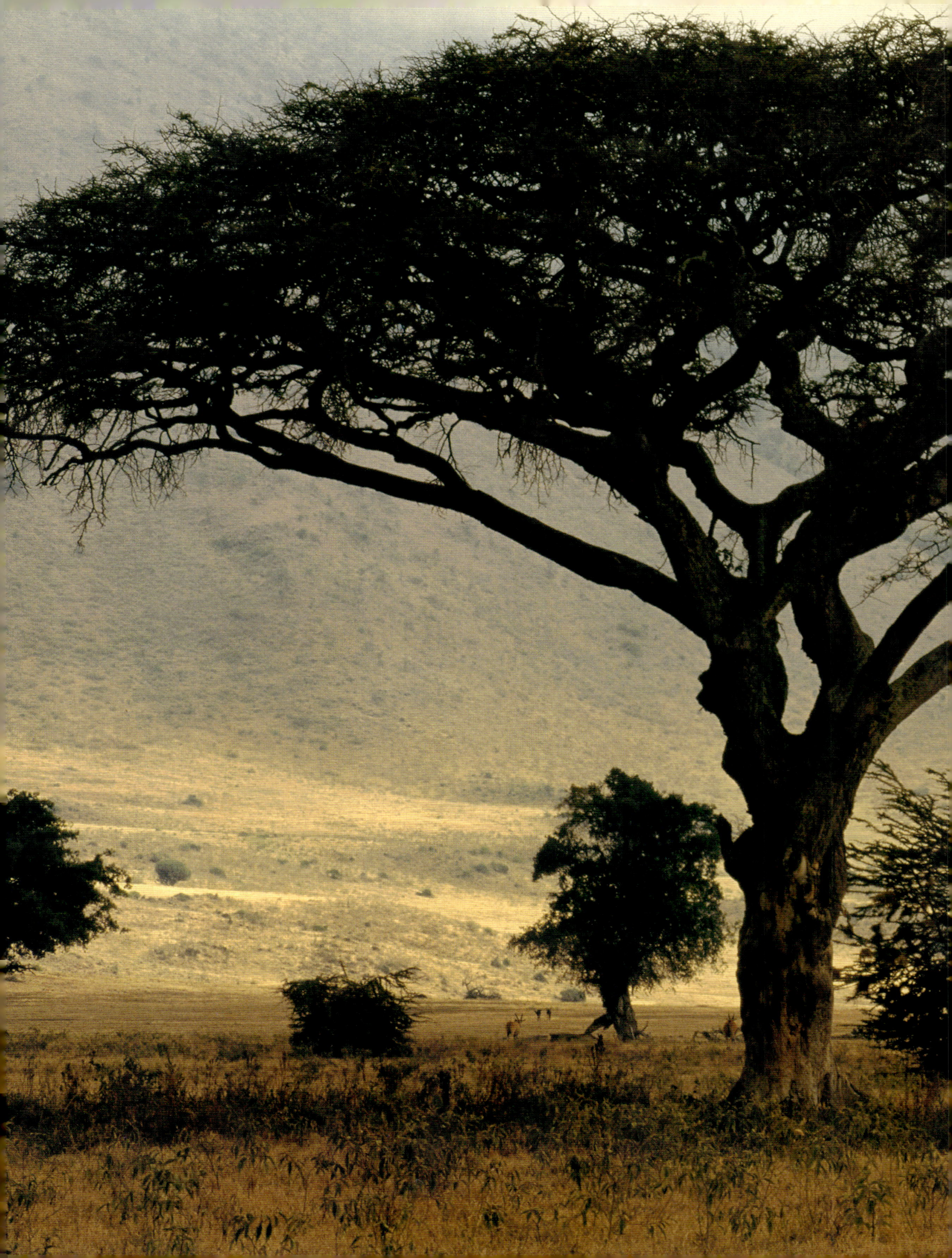

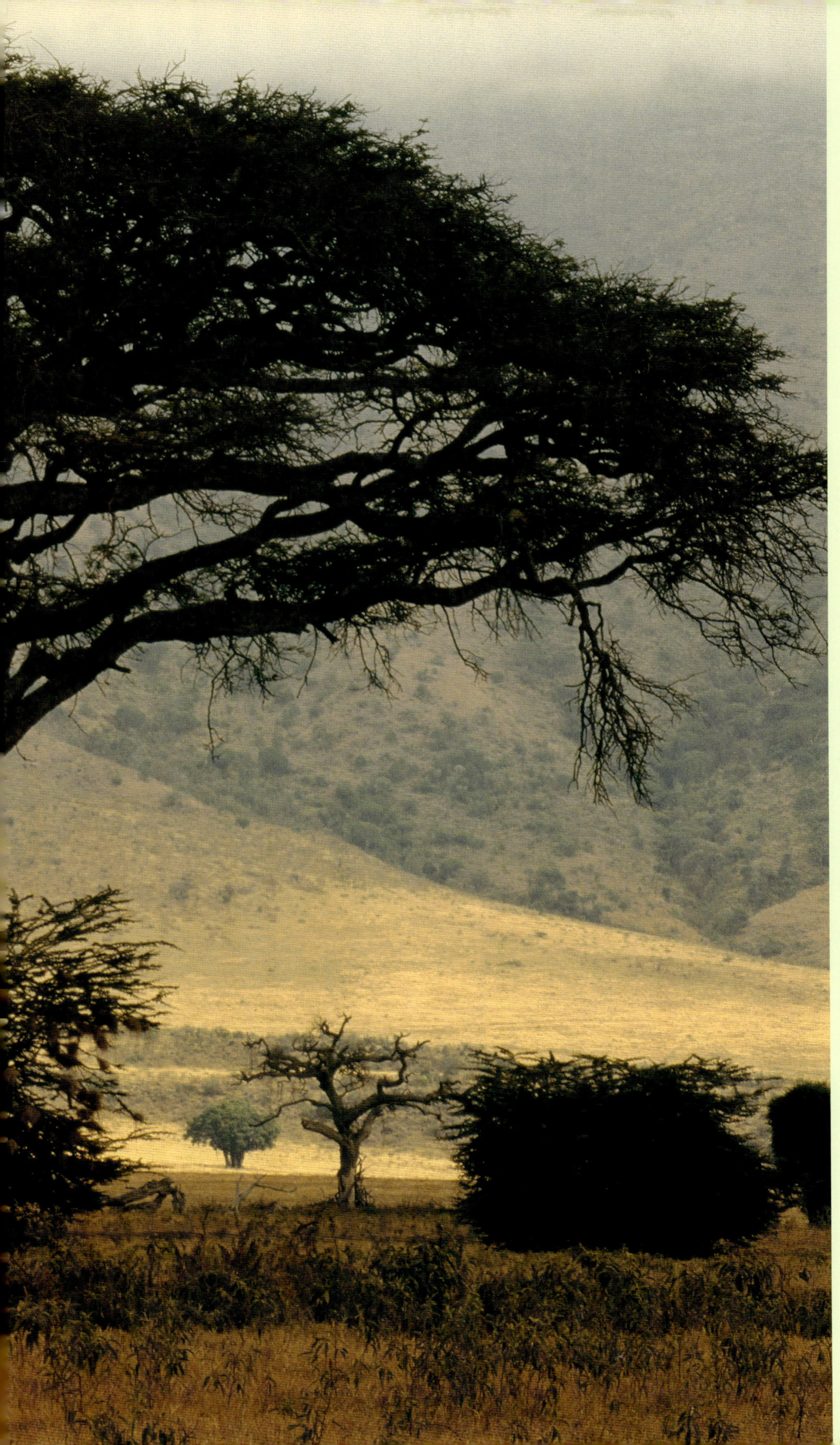

umbrella acacia

umbrella acacia

The umbrella acacia (*Acacia tortilis*) is one of the most widespread and recognizable of trees found on the African savannah. The flat-topped crown, typical of so many types of thorn tree, is an absolutely unmistakable feature of the landscape in Africa's seasonally dry areas. It is only one of over 900 species of acacia growing throughout the world but is by far the most important on the continent of Africa.

This thorny tree, which produces seedpods that are highly palatable to both humans and animals, is distinguishable from all other acacias by the length of its thorns. Their role is to prevent the tree from being overgrazed by domesticated herbivores such as goats and camels, as well as wild ones such as kudu and gazelle. Two more built-in means of survival – its drought tolerance and the fact that its seeds are spread by animals and birds – allow for its dominance from Senegal to Somalia and down into South Africa. This is the tree that often encroaches further than any other into the Sahara Desert.

The flat-topped crown, typical of so many types of thorn tree, is an absolutely unmistakable feature of the landscape in Africa's seasonally dry areas

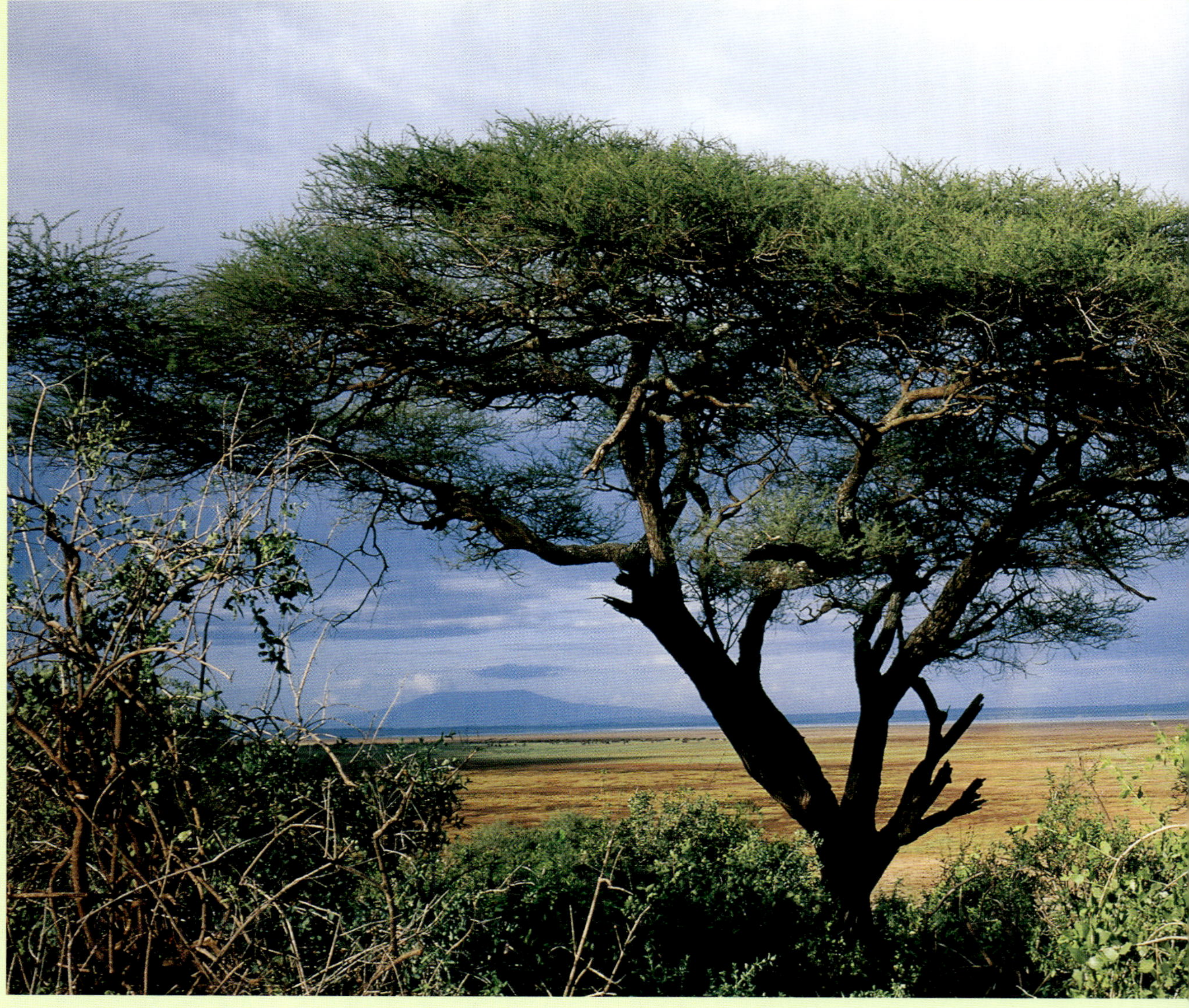

I can only find admiration for trees that manage to survive in conditions so inhospitable that no others will grow in their place, and the umbrella acacia is such a tree. Largely on account of its ability to withstand drought, it is used in the reclamation of land where human life is barely sustainable, such as the Sahara Desert. Its role as a crucial tree of this biome is all the more remarkable when one considers that its natural home is the land much further to the south, where there is considerably more rainfall. As further proof of its versatility, *Acacia tortilis* is also being grown in Rajasthan in western India to reclaim the Thar Desert. In being used to shore up badly eroded soils, it creates microclimates for other trees to grow, a practice that is common in marginal lands. In its capacity as a nurse tree the umbrella acacia acts as a windbreak, sheltering young species from the sand-laden winds that are such a feature of desert areas, while its fierce thorns keep foragers at bay. It is truly an inspirational tree.

A pioneer species Because of its stubbornness in the face of overwhelming odds, the umbrella acacia can be called a pioneer species of tree. This term is applied to trees that have the ability to establish themselves by their own means, often by successfully spreading seed. This is a remarkable achievement considering how much the protein-rich pods and seed are valued. Besides being eaten by animals, the seeds are gathered by humans and taken off to market.

This tree has had to develop strong survival tactics to protect itself

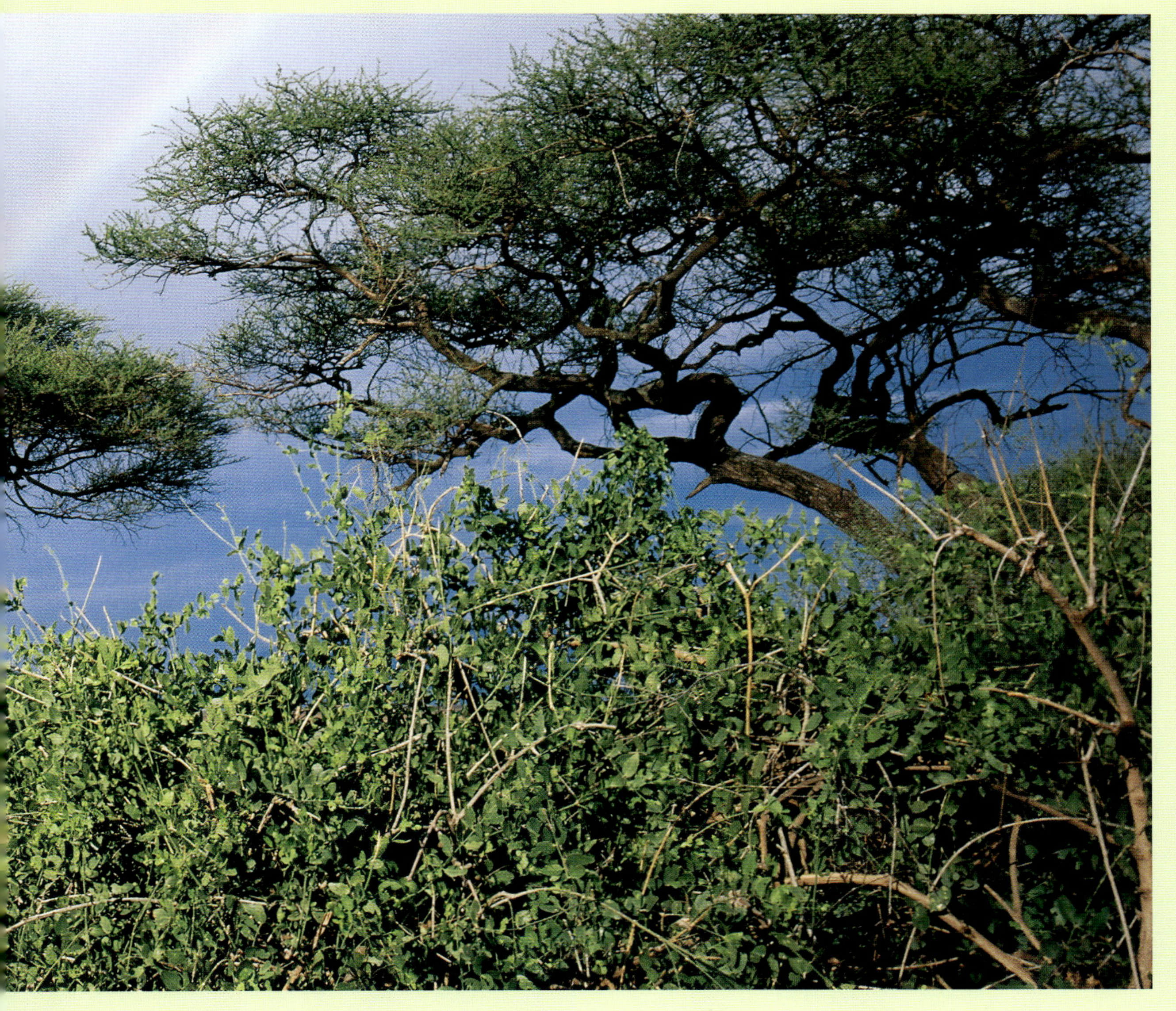

The umbrella acacia is not a tall tree, generally reaching 3-5 metres. It can grow up to 20 metres if not overgrazed when young, but this is rare; being so widespread makes it vulnerable. Like many thorn trees, it is slow growing and this does not improve its chances of survival. This acacia is a popular tree for fuel wood and, because of the density of the timber, it is in constant demand for fence posts, furniture and for making wheels. But when the umbrella acacia reaches its full glory it is a magnificent tree, gracefully shaped and imperious, quite the opposite to its African companion, the baobab.

Forest farming

The forest is perhaps the most stable life-supporting system on the planet. If land is cleared and left to its own devices, it will revert to forest and quickly organize itself in such a way that the indigenous species of the ecosystem can coexist. This is nature's way. Each species – be it tree, shrub, climbing plant or ground cover – has a place within the system. The correct levels of diversity and fertility required to support the relevant species of plant, animal, insect and other organisms is attained in an entirely natural manner, without human intervention. Any model that can mimic the system of a forest will be a sustainable one as it evolves around trees and what they produce beyond timber (fruit, flowers, seeds) – therefore it must have their best interests at the heart of it.

Forest farming, which has the planting of trees at its core, has a huge part to play in the protection of our environment and of the trees on the planet

The forest has several layers of growth and, through time, man has adapted these to suit his own requirements in a system that has loosely become known as forest farming. As the idea hangs on the principle of working with, rather than against, nature, it has been lauded by those who advocate organic or chemical-free farming. Two of the practice's most serious promoters, Robert Hart and James Sholto Douglas, have put forward the forest farming system as a means of 'adopting multiple-usage methods and of fostering the integration of forestry with farming to form one pattern of agri-silviculture'. An intermingling of perennial tree crops and annually cultivated plants can be seen all over the monsoon forest biome, whether in the agroforestry systems or homestead forest gardening, to give it two more names, of Bangladesh, the Kandyan gardens of Sri Lanka, or farms on the dry Deccan Plateau of South India. While it is now entering the European system of agriculture, the system has in fact been practised in parts of Asia and South America since before conventional agriculture began.

The forest layers are clearly visible as the sunlight filters through (overleaf). As well as the three different layers of trees, the ground cover and the climbing layer show through. The productivity of natural monsoon forest is astonishing, from timber, fruit, spices, fodder for domestic animals or natural habitats for wild animals.

Forest farming in southern India

Three of the southern states of India – Tamil Nadu, Karnataka and Kerala – have strong traditions of forest farming practices, particularly in the homestead environment and very often over areas of ground of less than a hectare in size. It has been estimated that more than 50 per cent of the cultivated area of Kerala is under this system and within it grow some of the world's most important and valuable spices. The heavily forested hill country of the Western Ghats probably hold more secrets of responsible farming and sustainable tree care than anywhere else throughout this biome. Working on the restoration of a redundant coffee estate in the Palni Hills of Tamil Nadu allowed me a close look at the workings of the system. The farming system is modelled on the seven storeys of forest growth which comprise: a canopy layer, smaller trees, shrubs, herbaceous plants, ground cover plants, the root zone and the climbers. In India the varieties of arabica and robusta coffee must be grown in partial shade to produce their best, thus a canopy layer has to be in place. In the Palni Hills region one of the most common trees making up the canopy layer is Indian rosewood (*Dalbergia latifolia*). Rosewood is a tall, straight-growing tree with rich red bark and timber that is considered harder than teak, another important shade tree of the region and indeed the biome. Up the trunks of shade trees climb the vines that hold the 'king of spices', black pepper. Already we can see the interdependence between one crop and another. Even in the canopy layer, a single tree has become multi-functional. The rosewood is a nitrogen-fixing member of the legume family and so makes nitrogen available to itself and other plants. In addition it creates shade for the coffee, supports the pepper vine and will produce the finest timber in the forest for all manner of uses, from house building (its resistance to white ants makes it particularly valuable) and fine cabinet making. It also holds the ground against soil erosion as well as being a habitat for animals, birds and insects.

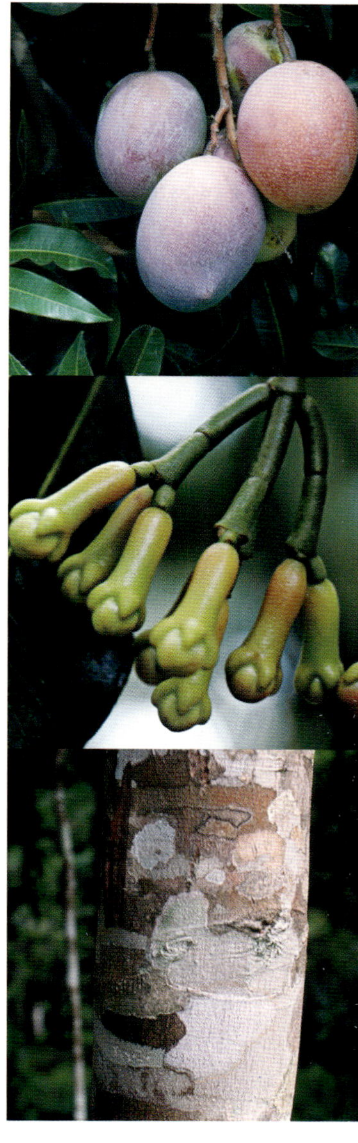

Three giants of the forest farming systems of south India are the mango (top), the clove (middle) and the cinnamon tree (below). The mango and the two spices bring vital income to the often subsistence-level farming communities that surive on tiny acreages yet play host to these world-renowned fruits and spices.

The second layer is likely to be a commercial fruit crop such as mango, citrus or avocado. The mango (*Mangifera indica*), a fruit tree of extreme importance throughout Asia and Africa, lives to a great age, all the while producing heavy crops of delicious fruit with little tending. It is a vital fruit tree of the forest farming system in this biome because, despite the high economic value of the fruit for export – mangoes account for as much as 50 per cent of the world's tropical fruit production, half of which is produced in India – most of the crop is consumed domestically and sold locally.

This secondary layer may equally be a spice tree such as cinnamon (*Cinnamomum zeylanicum*), the inner bark of which is dried as 'quills' and sent to markets all over the world, or the most valuable spice of all, the clove (*Syzygium aromaticum*). The picking of the unopened flower buds of the clove, which are then dried, takes an inordinate amount of time and makes the crop as valuable as cardamom, which also grows in the shade of the forest gardens, and twice as valuable as their nearest rival, another spice tree, the nutmeg (*Myristica fragrans*) which yields both its large seeds (the nutmegs themselves) and their 'aril' or outer coating (mace).

Then come the shrubs in the form of coffee or pomegranate (*Punica granatum*) and below that the herbaceous layer which may comprise the cardamom. The ground cover layer is made up of annual crops such as trailing gourds or squashes, and at the root zone are two more highly prized spices which are sold in the form of rhizomes (thick roots) – ginger and turmeric. This is forest farming at its best – a multilayered and productive environment in which every tree has a specific purpose. One or more will produce a crop while another 'nurses' that crop by providing shade or support or by preventing soil erosion.

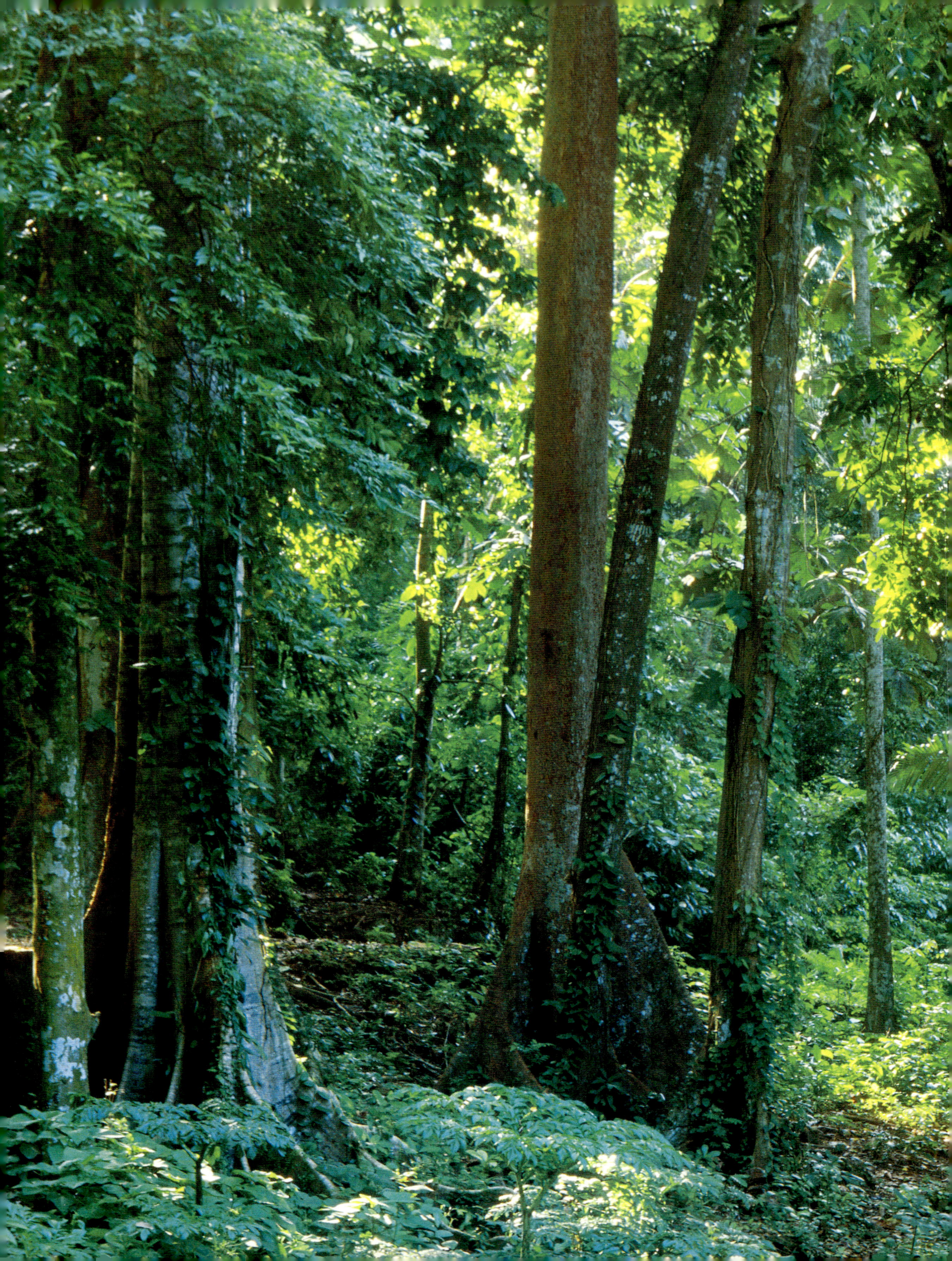

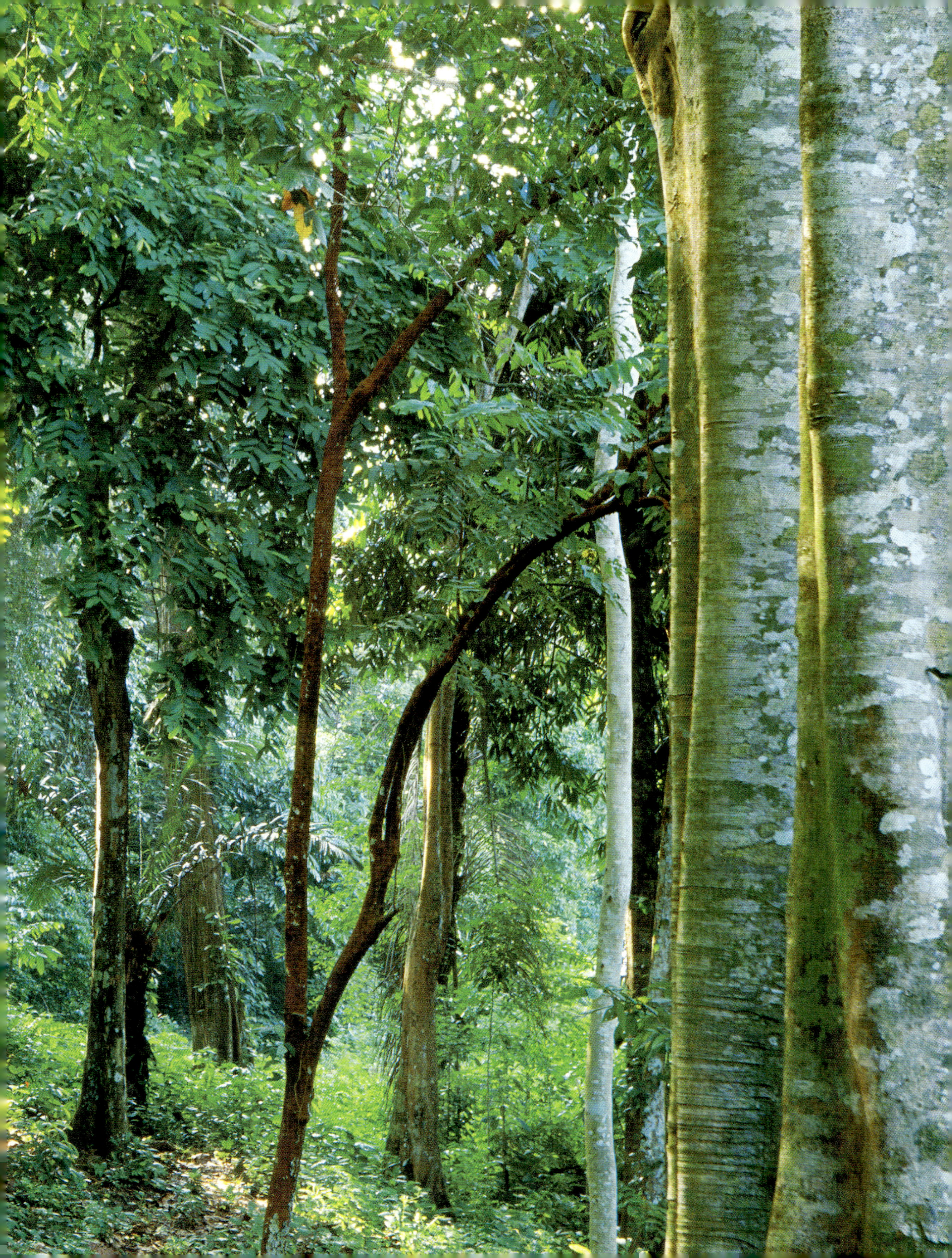

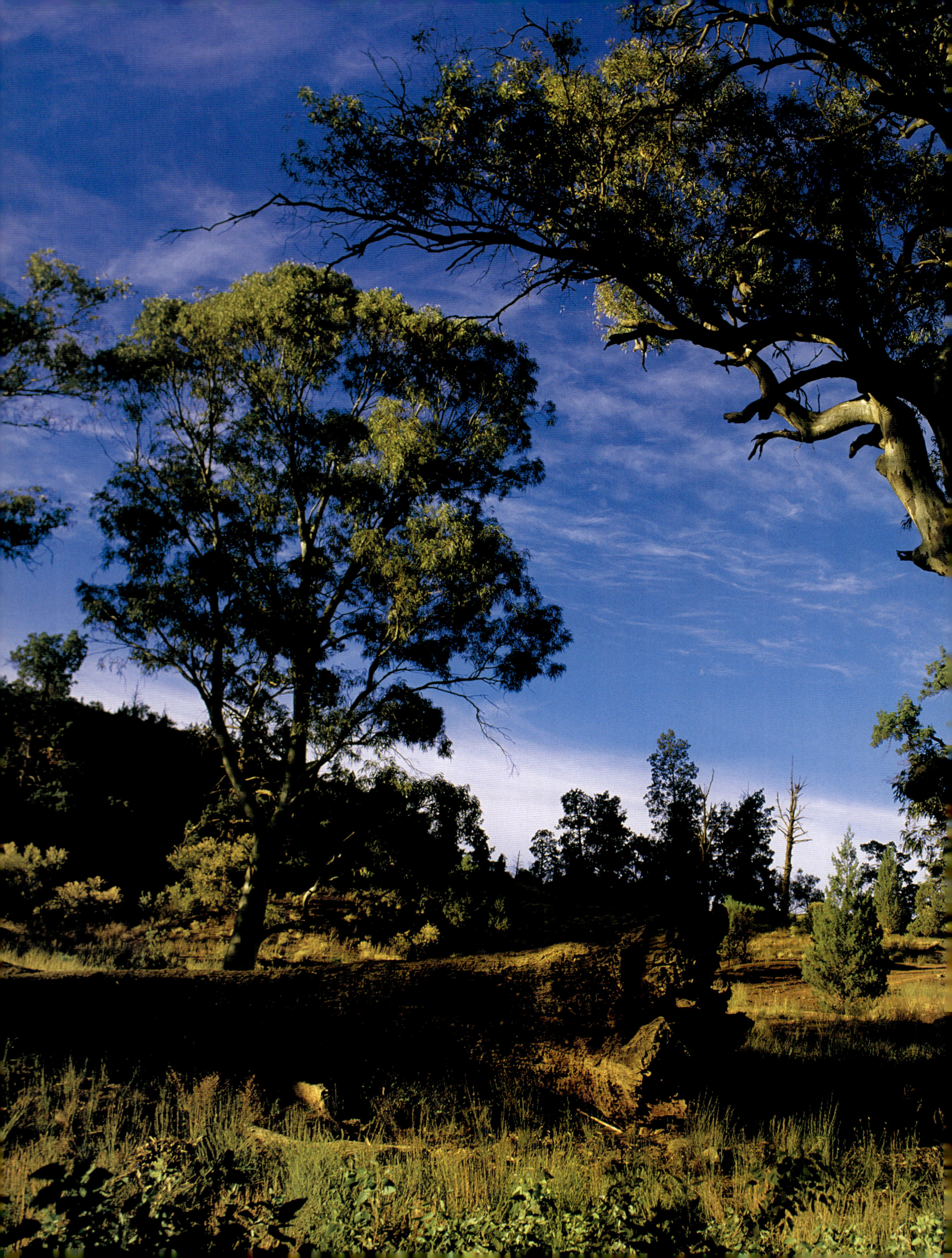

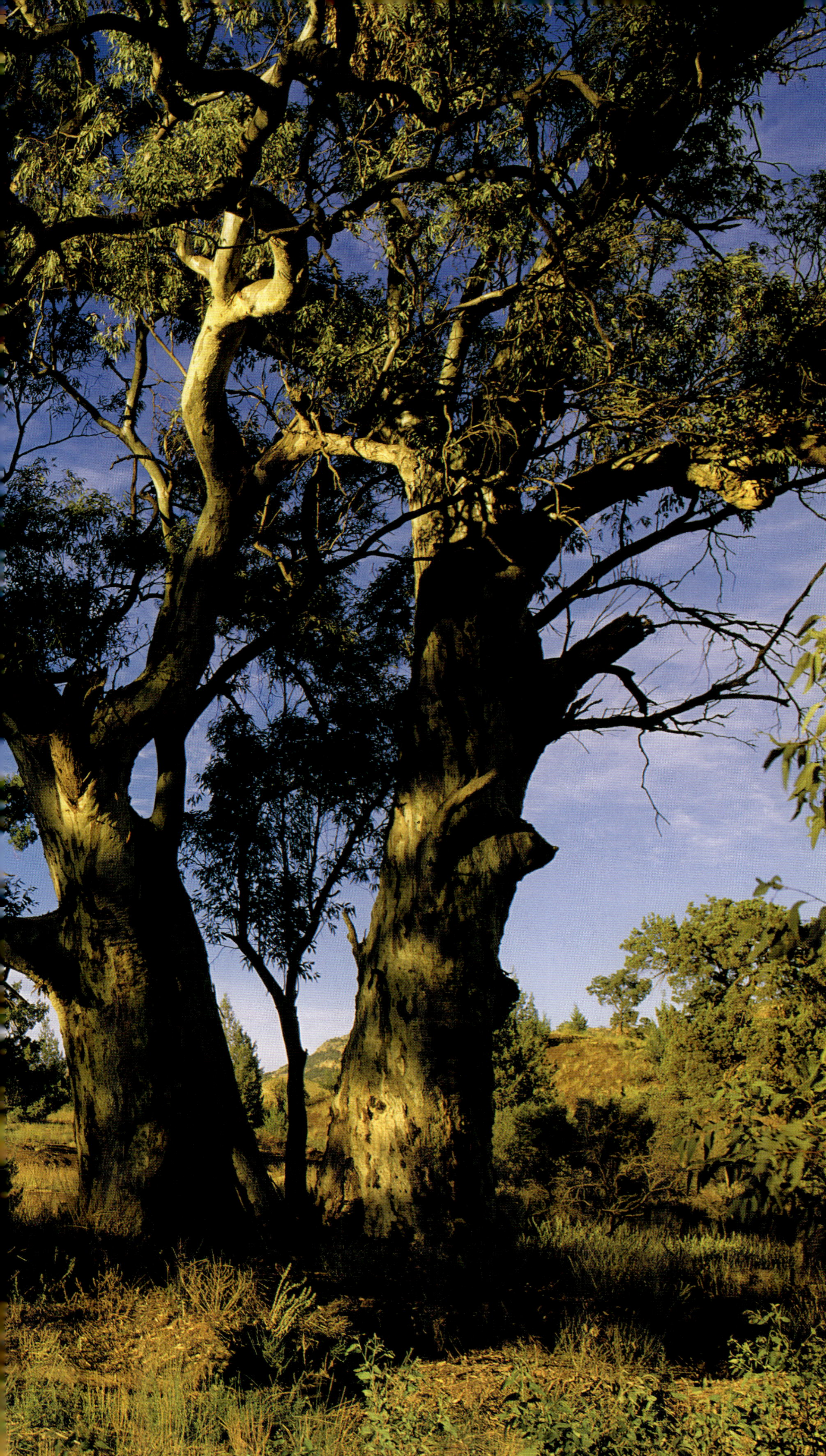

eucalyptus

The eucalyptus, which existed 35 million years ago, has seen everything that has happened to Australia and its people

eucalyptus

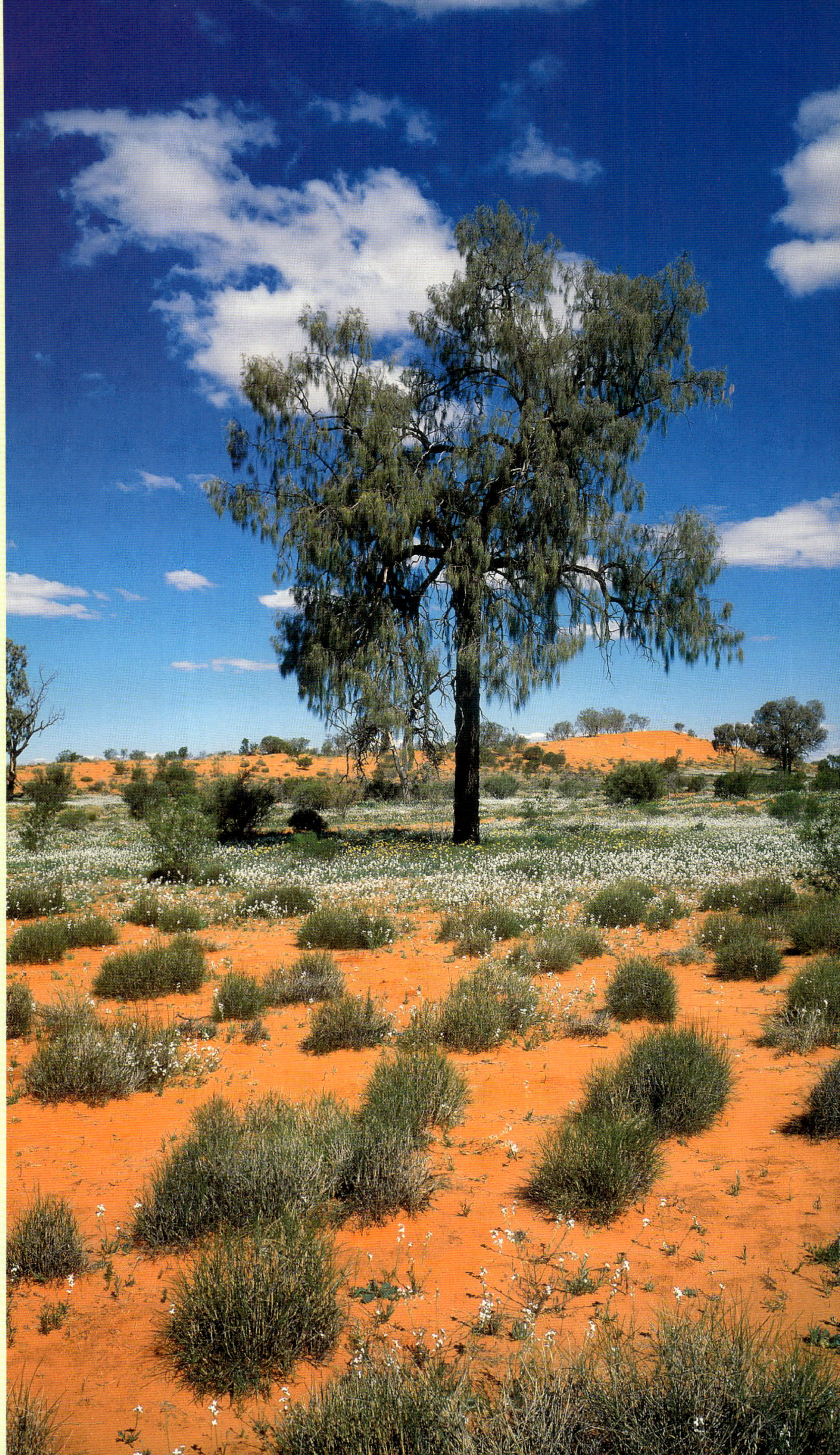

Approximately the same size as continental USA and the sixth largest country in the world, Australia is the only country that occupies a complete continent. With a population of 20 million people, it is the least densely populated country in the 'first' world and has a diverse and varied range of ecosystems. Throughout the whole country, however, the dominant tree is the eucalyptus. The name derives from two Greek words, 'eu' meaning well and 'kalyptus', covered: this description refers to the unusual flower buds, closed over by a hood. When the hood comes off at bud break, a mass of vivid red stamens unfurl and burst forth.

Termed the 'gum tree' by early European botanists because of its gum-like sap, *Eucalyptus* has more than 700 species to its name, most of which are endemic in Australia. The trees dominate most landscapes of this continent, barring the highest alpine sites and the extremely arid interior, and they have evolved to tolerate a wide range of environmental conditions, from bush fires and drought to poor soil.

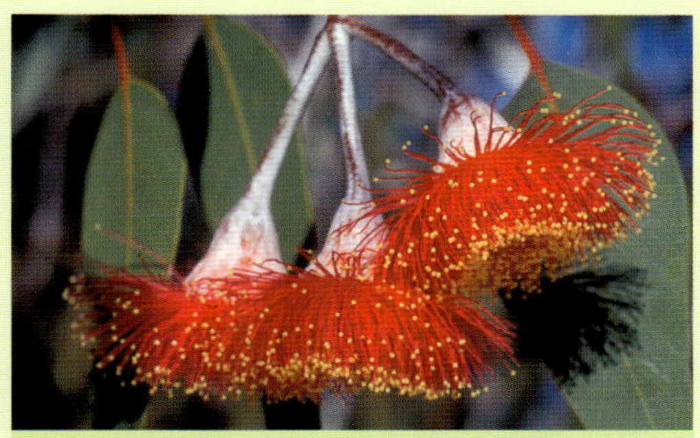

A protected genus Despite devastating levels of deforestation by early settlers, the wild population of eucalypts in Australia is no longer under threat. The trees are well protected in the surroundings of National Parks and those that are used for commercial purposes are grown in managed plantations. The indigenous people of Australia, the Aboriginals, have a deep understanding of the importance of eucalyptus trees to both the landscape and the history of their country and have played a big part in their survival.

Because of their adaptability to different climates and soils, eucalyptus have been adopted as good subjects for plantation trees. This has led to them being cast as villains, particularly as they have often replaced natural forest and deprived local populations of their source of firewood and timber. Since the nineteenth century, eucalyptus plantations have been established in places as far apart as Brazil and South Africa, to build railways and fuel trains.

Survival against all odds

Perhaps the greatest and best recognized of all gum trees is *Eucalyptus regnans*, the mountain ash. Life is tough for plants in Australia's dry climatic conditions and it is a testament to the tree's survival skills that this species has been recorded as growing to over 100m tall. Soils are generally poor, and for half the year the ground is totally parched.

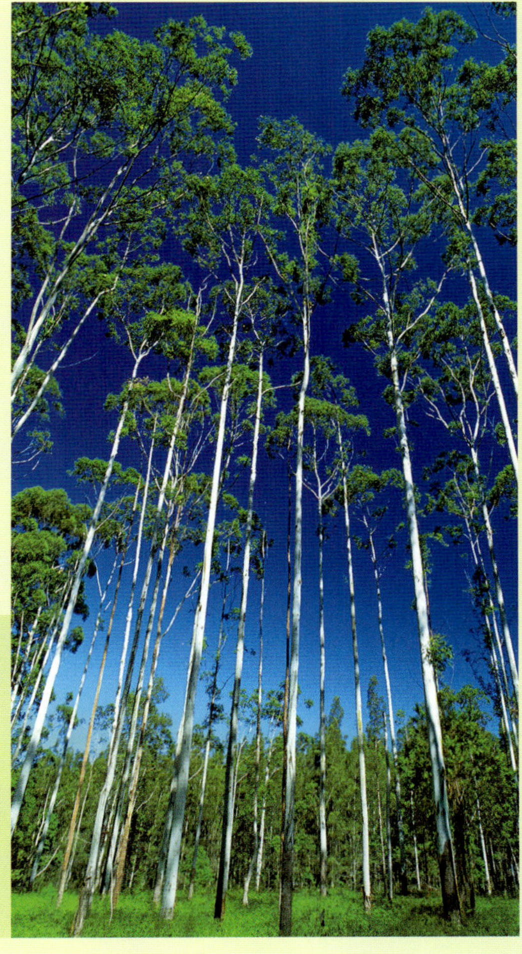

Eucalyptus send down deep tap roots which, besides bringing up valuable nutrients from the subsoil, allow the trees to attain great heights while standing firm. This is entirely the opposite strategy to tall-growing trees in tropical rainforests whose roots spread out over the surface of the soil where their main source of nutrients are found. The eucalyptus' ability to heal scars from fire damage matches its considerable resprouting abilities and seed production.

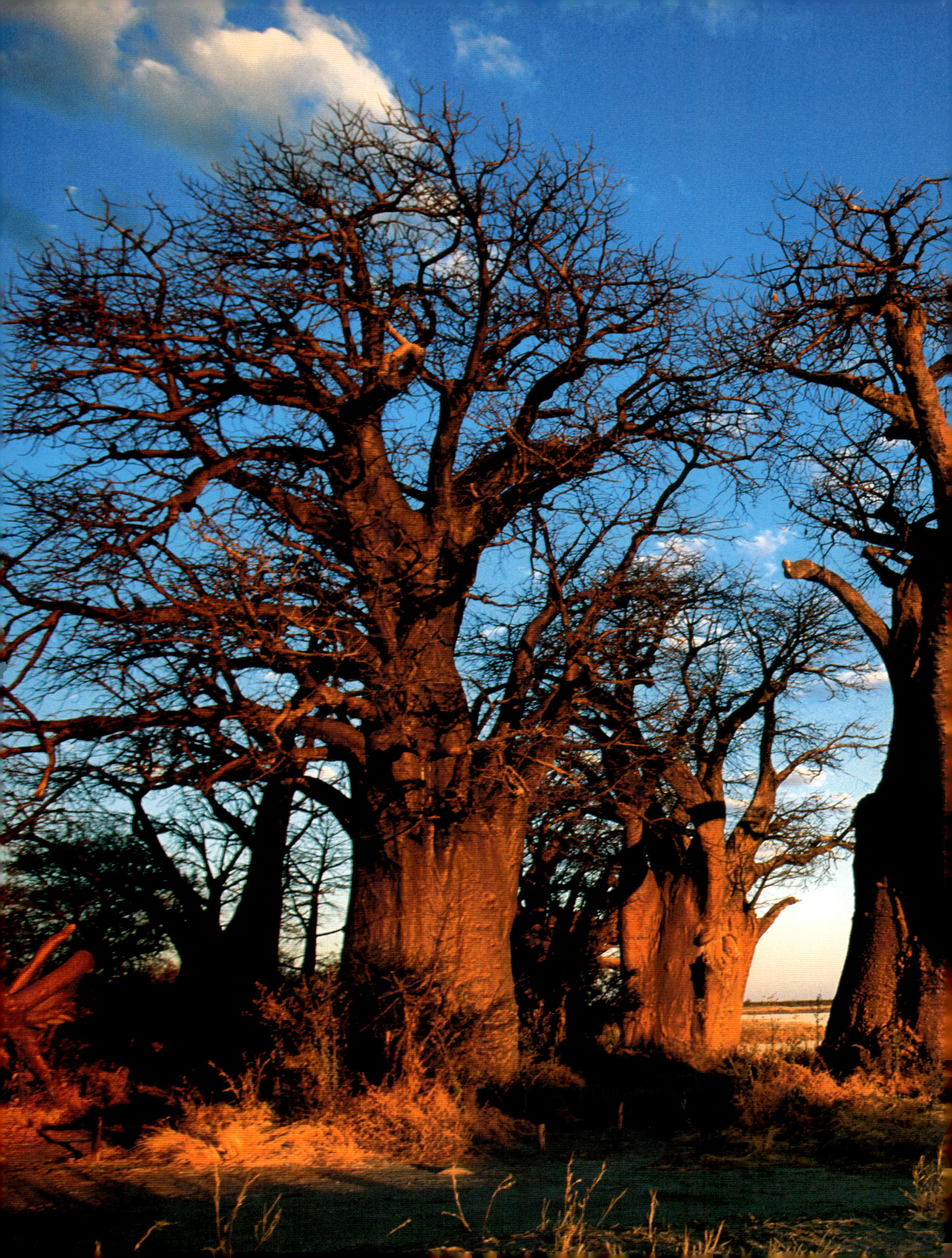

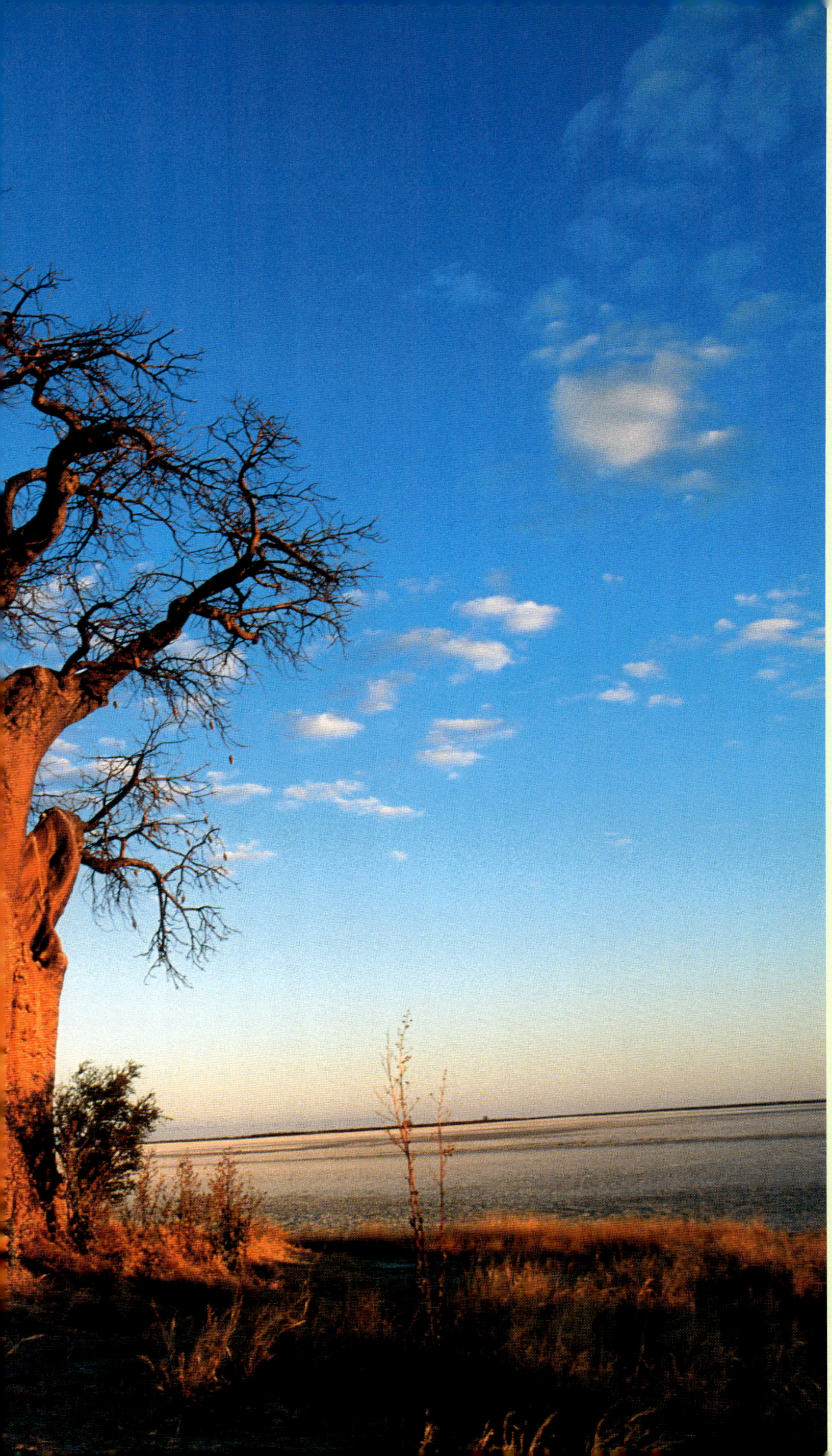

baobab

Legend has it that a displeased god cast the baobab from heaven and it landed the wrong way up

baobab

It is thought that the baobabs originated in Madagascar, from where some seeds floated to Africa and to India where, given optimum conditions, it can live for thousands of years. The tree loses its leaves in the dry season for nine months of the year and in the wet months stores water in its mammoth trunk for the dry season ahead. In wild specimens the trunk hollows out as it ages, making it impossible to age the trees with any degree of accuracy because of the lack of complete rings. Carbon dating indicates that baobabs may live to be 3,000 years old and one ancient specimen in Zimbabwe is said to be able to fit some 40 people in its hollow trunk. In some villages the hollow trunk, which may hold more than a thousand litres of water, is filled with water and used as a local reservoir.

Perhaps one reason for the baobab's longevity is simply that it is difficult to kill. Strip the tree of its bark and it regrows, burn it and it recovers. It takes the might of an African elephant to bring the baobab to its knees and, in their search for water during the dry season, these beasts have been known to eat entire trees. But it is not only the larger mammals that use this tree: birds find shelter among its high branches, monkeys eat the fruit (it is also known as the monkey bread tree), bush babies and fruit bats pollinate the flowers and drink the nectar, and this huge space is home to a wealth of insects and smaller organisms.

Besides being dotted throughout the savannahs of Africa and India, baobabs are also planted around villages for their many uses. How amazing to have a clump of inspiring baobabs on your village green. In Zimbabwe a cooperative called Phytotrade Africa is marketing products from the baobab tree as part of an initiative to use native plants for the benefit of the local economy, a local initiative in a poorer area.

As befits a widespread tree of such gargantuan size and grandeur, the baobab has attained a level of respect which few others can match. Myths abound about its appearance, particularly in relation to its resemblance to an upside-down tree, once it has shed its leaves, with its roots sticking up into the air. Legend has it that a displeased god cast it from heaven and it landed the wrong way up. Other stories say that the devil plucked the tree up and thrust its branches into the earth in a fit of pique.

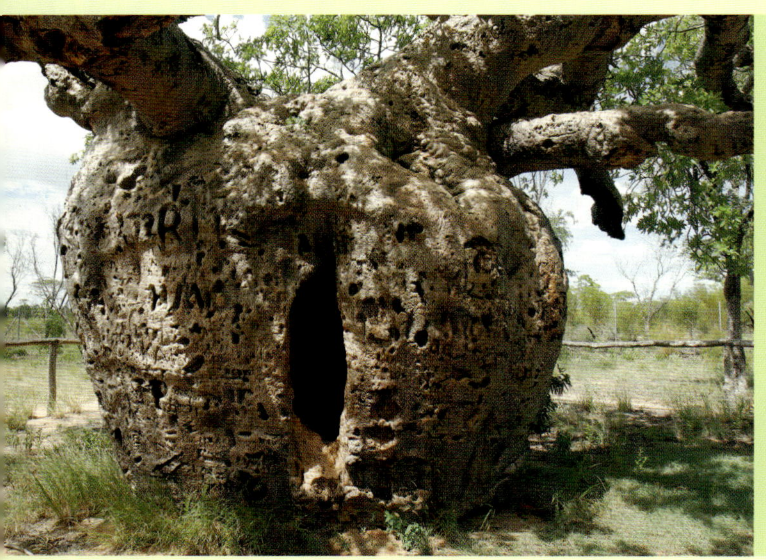

Many uses It is astonishing that the baobab has so many uses while it is still living, whereas most trees have to be cut down to realize their full potential. Of the inexhaustible list of uses, the main one is the manufacture of rope from the fibres of the inner bark; this rope, according to a spokesperson for the Indian Agricultural Service, is indestructible. Aside from rope, other fibrous products are produced, such as netting and mats. The white, gourd-like fruits are used as floats for fishing nets and the woody shells, rich in protein, go to feed livestock in Africa; and in India, monks use them as water carriers. The seeds provide valuable oil and potters use them to smooth earthenware.

A defining tree of the savannahs of Africa, stretching from south of the Sahara to the low veldt of South Africa, the baobab almost defies description. *Adansonia digitata*, to give the baobab its full botanical name, is distorted and out of proportion and yet it is imposing, monumental and completely compelling. In addition to its outrageous physical appearance and its massive presence on the African continent, it has been suggested that the baobab will one day become the most important species of tree in the world on account of its ability to absorb carbon dioxide.

The baobab comes from the bombax family and is related to the kapok (*Malatarica*) and the silk cotton tree (*Bombax malabaricum*). It grows quickly, up to 20m in height, and from the top emerges a crown of twisted branches which look more like roots. Like the silk cotton tree, the most captivating and engrossing aspect of the baobab is its overall shape and this is completely dominated by the trunk. This is used to store water and swells in what seems an unstoppable manner until it reaches 40m or so in girth (10m diameter).

It has been suggested that the baobab will one day become the most important species of tree in the world on account of its ability to absorb carbon dioxide

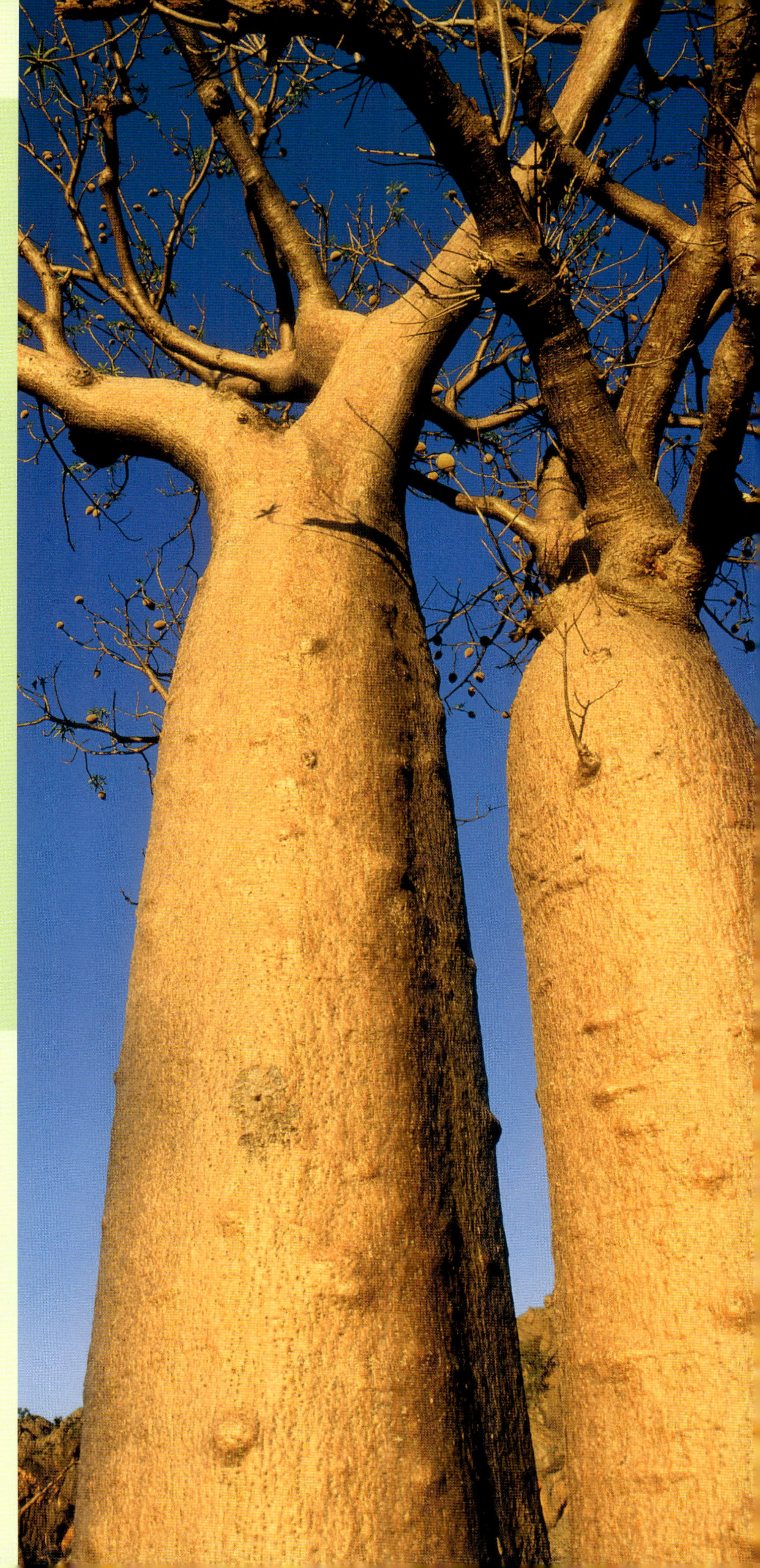

The teak tree (*Tectona grandis*) arrived at its name from the Greek word 'tekton' meaning carpenter, while 'grandis' refers to its large size.

Unsurprisingly, this tree has remained a favourite for making fine furniture since Ancient Greek times. Its native range is from the Indian subcontinent down through Myanmar, peninsular Malaysia and parts of South-East Asia where it inhabits the monsoon forest, happy in long dry spells followed by a period of rainfall. Because of its popularity for timber it has spread, as a plantation tree, all over the world and is now grown in Africa, the Caribbean and South America (especially Brazil) as well as Asia. It is a true hardwood in that the wood is dense and long lasting and is able to withstand extreme treatment, whether from salt water or white ants. In a plantation system the deciduous teak tree obligingly grows straight and tall and will produce a clear stem of 30m within 50-60 years. In India this slow-growing tree is traditionally harvested on an 80-year cycle.

The towering teak tree belongs to the forest, not to machinery and farms. This slender beauty reaches for the heavens in its natural state: 'grandis' is so very appropriate

Is the story really as cut and dried as this? It sounds as though the teak tree has been reduced to a subject now grown only in plantations for the purposes of hardwood production. Nothing could be further from the truth. Thousands of hectares of natural teak forest remain all over India, Thailand, Laos and Myanmar and they will continue to regenerate because the teak tree is adept at this. By 1998 the total area of teak worldwide was estimated at 28 million hectares – the majority of which was still in natural forest. Teak trees are also popular ornamentally and can be seen by roads and in gardens all over India. Traditionally, they have always had medicinal uses among the people of India and Thailand. The bark has been used for centuries to counteract stomach ache. In plantations they are the subject of research projects into genetics, tissue culture and the control of pests and diseases.

Despite the great aura that surrounds it, the prosaic truth is that the teak tree has become probably the most important subject of clinically managed timber farms. When statistics are quoted claiming that only 3 per cent of all tropical trees used for paper and timber are farmed, this means that the rest are being cut down from natural forests. This is all the more reason why the sustainable production of teak should be applauded. In support of the farming of teak it must be stressed that only such timber with a certificate indicating its sustainable credentials should ever be purchased.

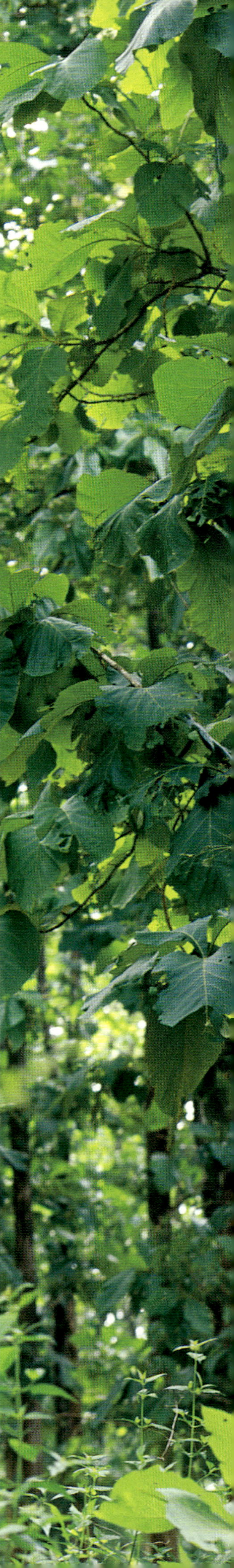

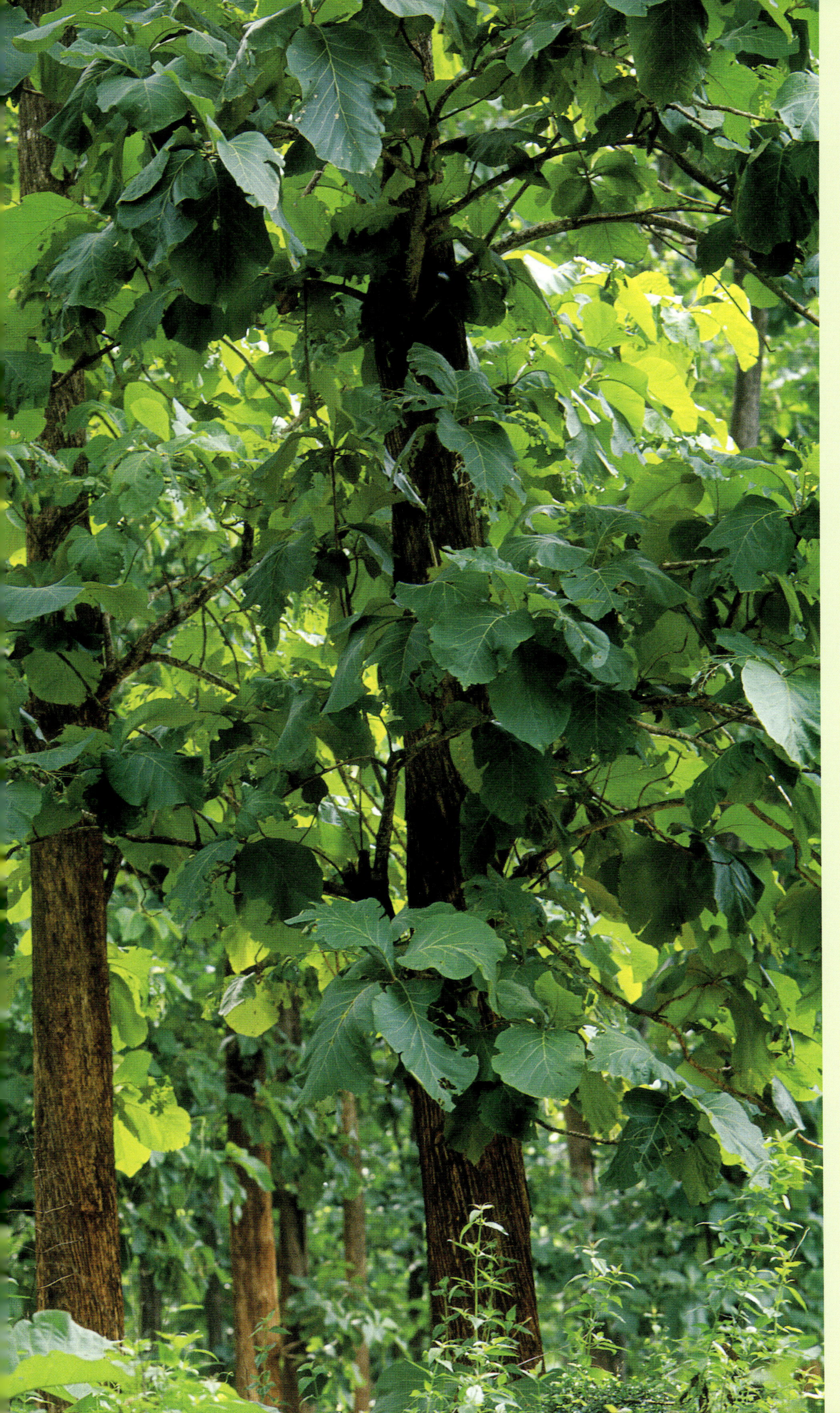

teak

In a plantation system the deciduous teak tree obligingly grows straight and quickly and will produce a clear stem of 30m within 50-60 years

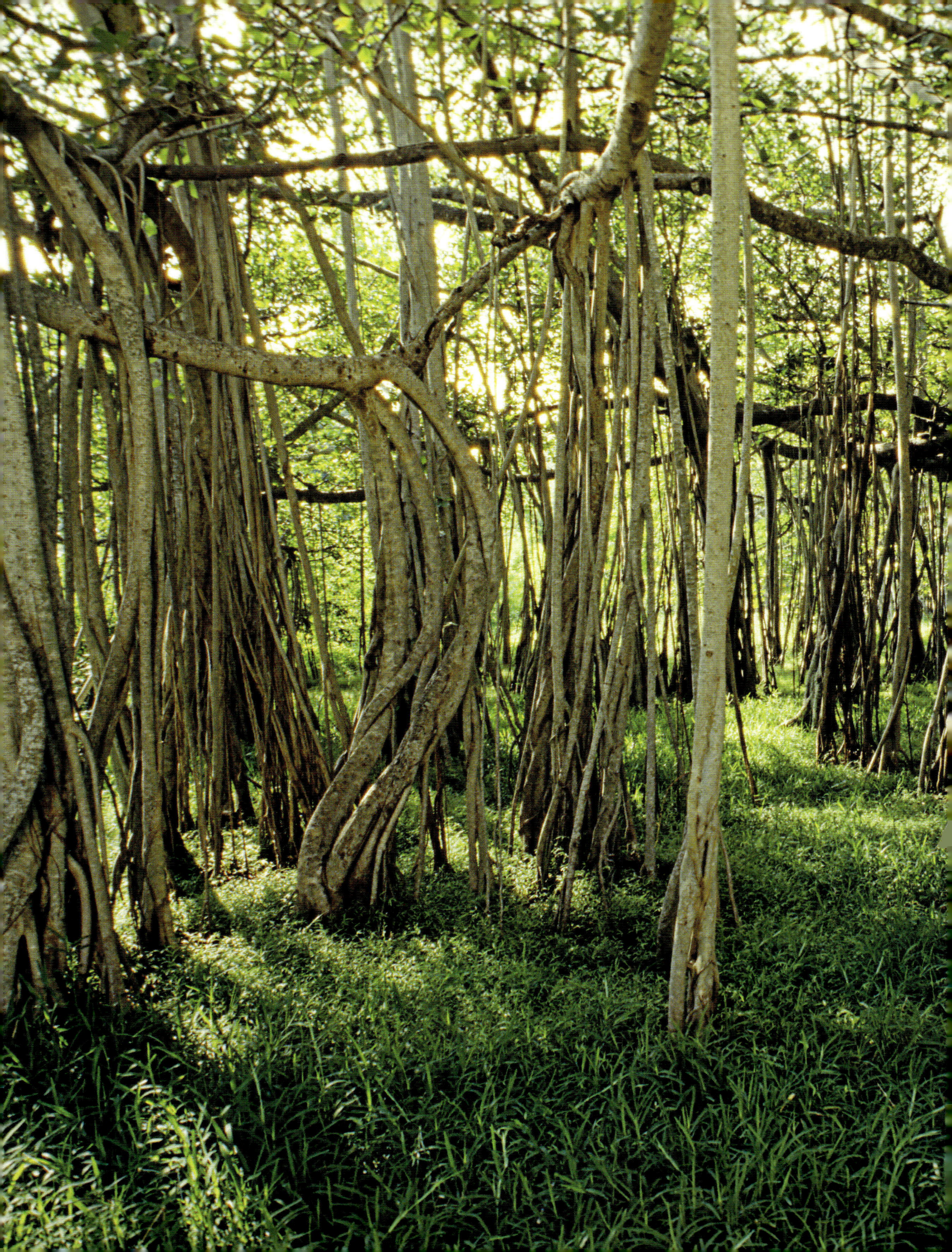

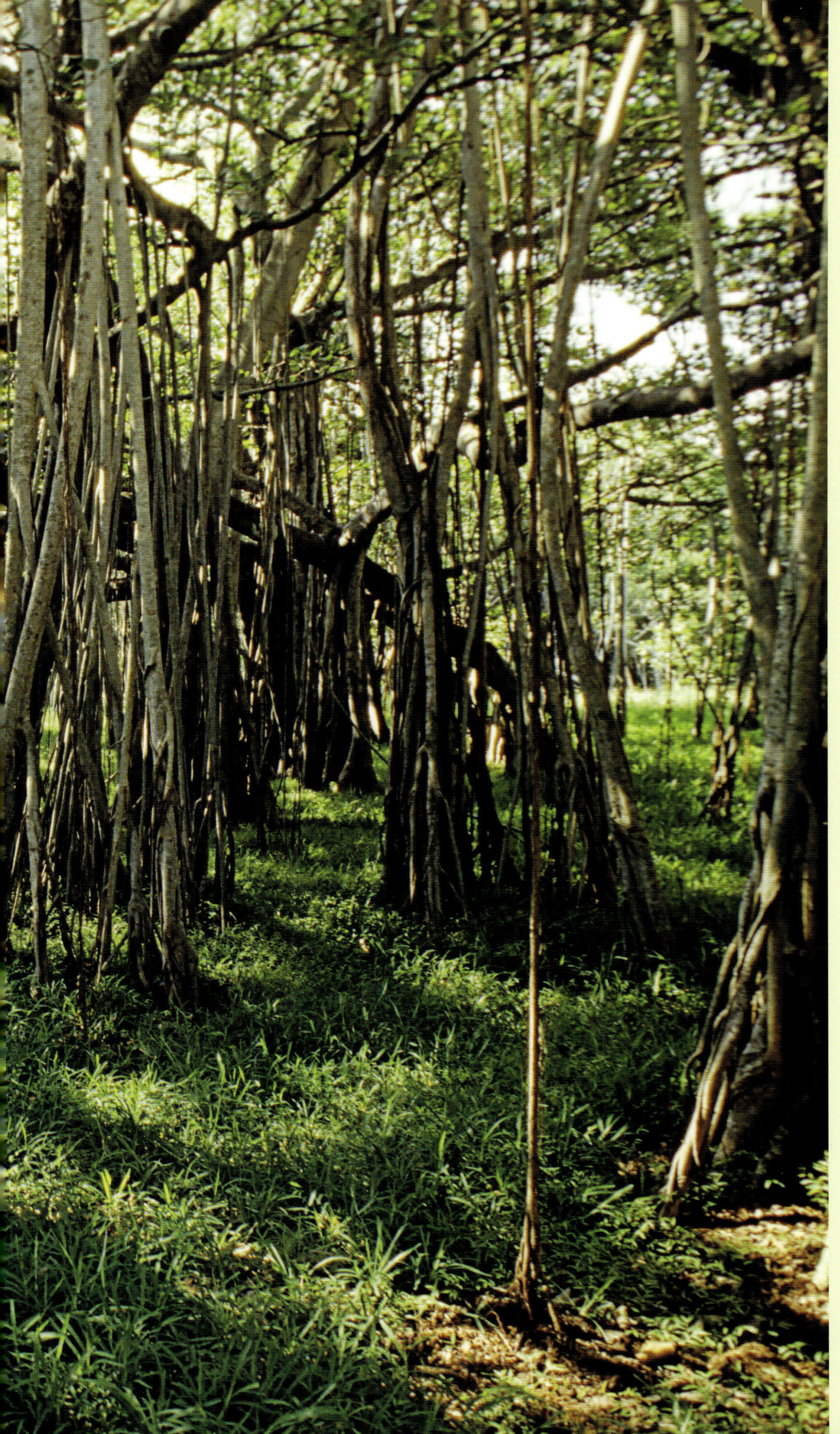

ficus

They live to a great age, but then that is hardly surprising considering the prayers that are offered to and through them

ficus

The traveller who rests under the peepul tree will not weary on his journey but find fresh reserves of energy instilled from the great fig tree

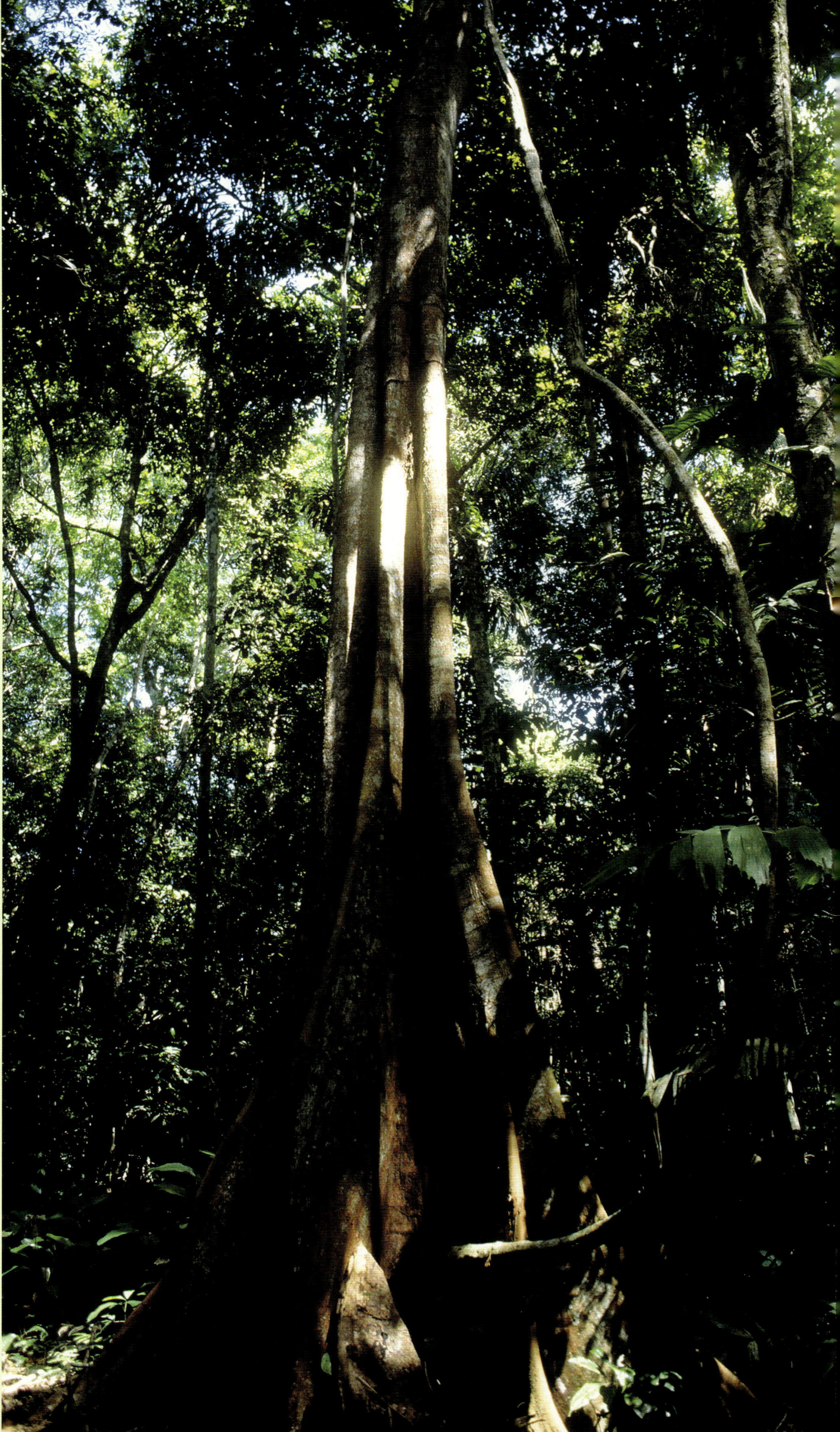

Religious significance can work wonders for the health of trees, particularly if it prevents them from being cut down. The two sacred figs – the banyan tree (*Ficus benghalensis*) and the peepul tree (*Ficus religiosa*) – are found throughout India, Pakistan and Bangladesh. Along with the cow, they are sacred to Hindus and therefore vigorously protected and prolific in number. While the fig family is huge and very productive, it is perhaps significant that these two highly revered species do not have fruit of edible quality for humans. In contrast, the family includes some other important fruit trees such as mulberries, jackfruit and breadfruit, as well as the edible fig of the Mediterranean biome (*F. carica*).

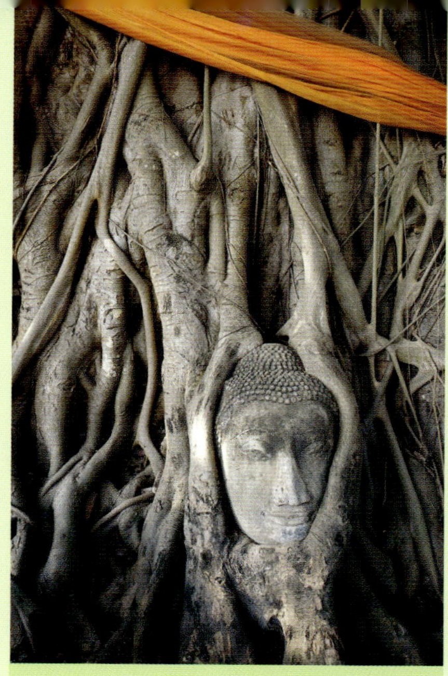

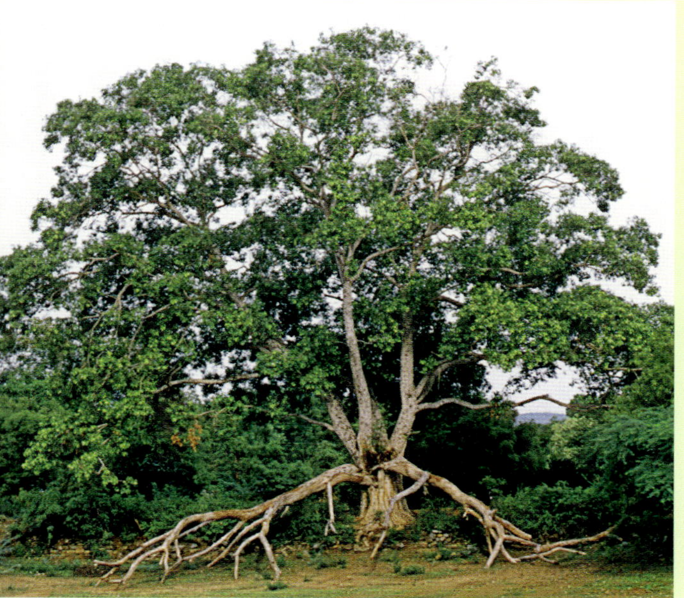

Ficus religiosa The deciduous peepul or Bo tree grows to a great height of 15m or more, with a wide-spreading canopy. It is the tree under which Prince Siddartha (Buddha) found the enlightenment that led to the tradition of Buddhism some time in the sixth century BC. It is therefore sacred to Buddhists as well as to Hindus. To ordinary mortals this remains a magnificent tree of considerable size and particular strength; its wood is never used for firewood though the leaves are often cut for fodder. Because of its religious profile, the peepul is planted in prominent and auspicious sites in towns, villages or by roadsides where it is often decorated or garlanded and acts as a conduit between man and God.

Ficus benghalensis

Slightly more rotund than its relation the peepul and not quite as tall, the banyan tree (opposite) is found throughout the Indian subcontinent. It is easily recognizable by the extraordinary rope-like aerial roots that hang down from its branches, eventually forming multiple trunks. The biggest known specimen, in the Botanic Gardens of Calcutta, is reputed to have a girth of a quarter of a mile in circumference, while its hundreds of trunks connect overhead to form a colonnade.

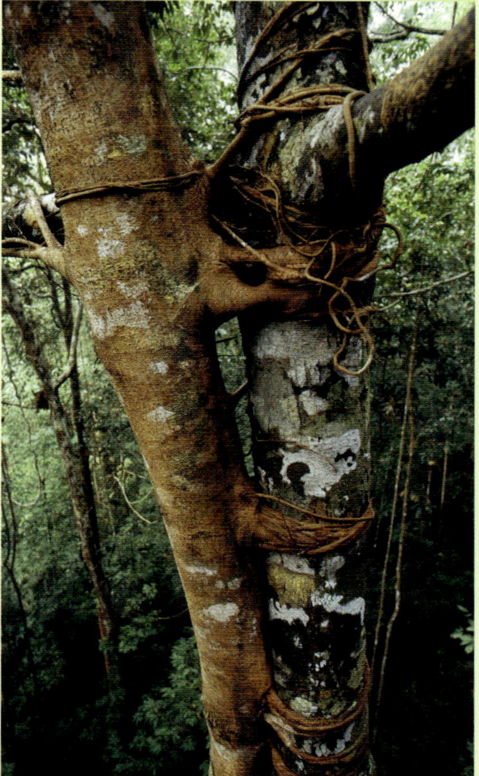

I once undertook a two-week solitary walk from Pokhara to Kathmandu through the middle-range hills of the tiny Hindu Kingdom of Nepal. The climatic zone is one where monsoon forest meets deciduous forest, and at up to 1,000 metres the crossover in species makes for some fascinating tree spotting. There are no roads through this terrain, only paths, and everything has to be carried on foot. The hills are steep, the tracks narrow and the going tough, especially for those carrying heavy loads. Time and time again, when I was suffering complete exhaustion, a small village would appear as if by magic with, at its centre, a peepul tree. In Nepal the trees have a two-tiered stone framework, 'a chautara', built around their base so that porters may rest their loads and take a break from their arduous journey.

5

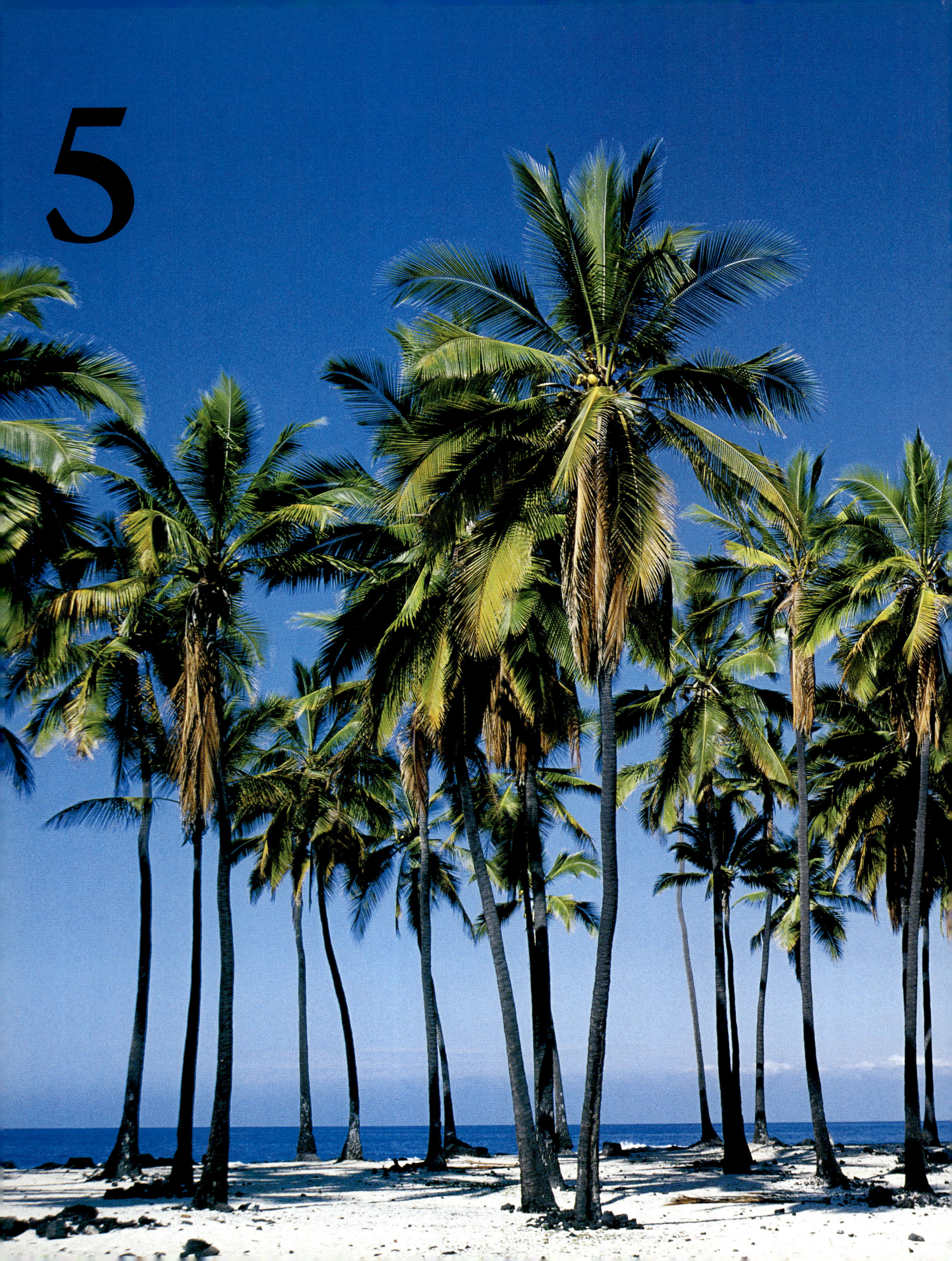

tropical coasts

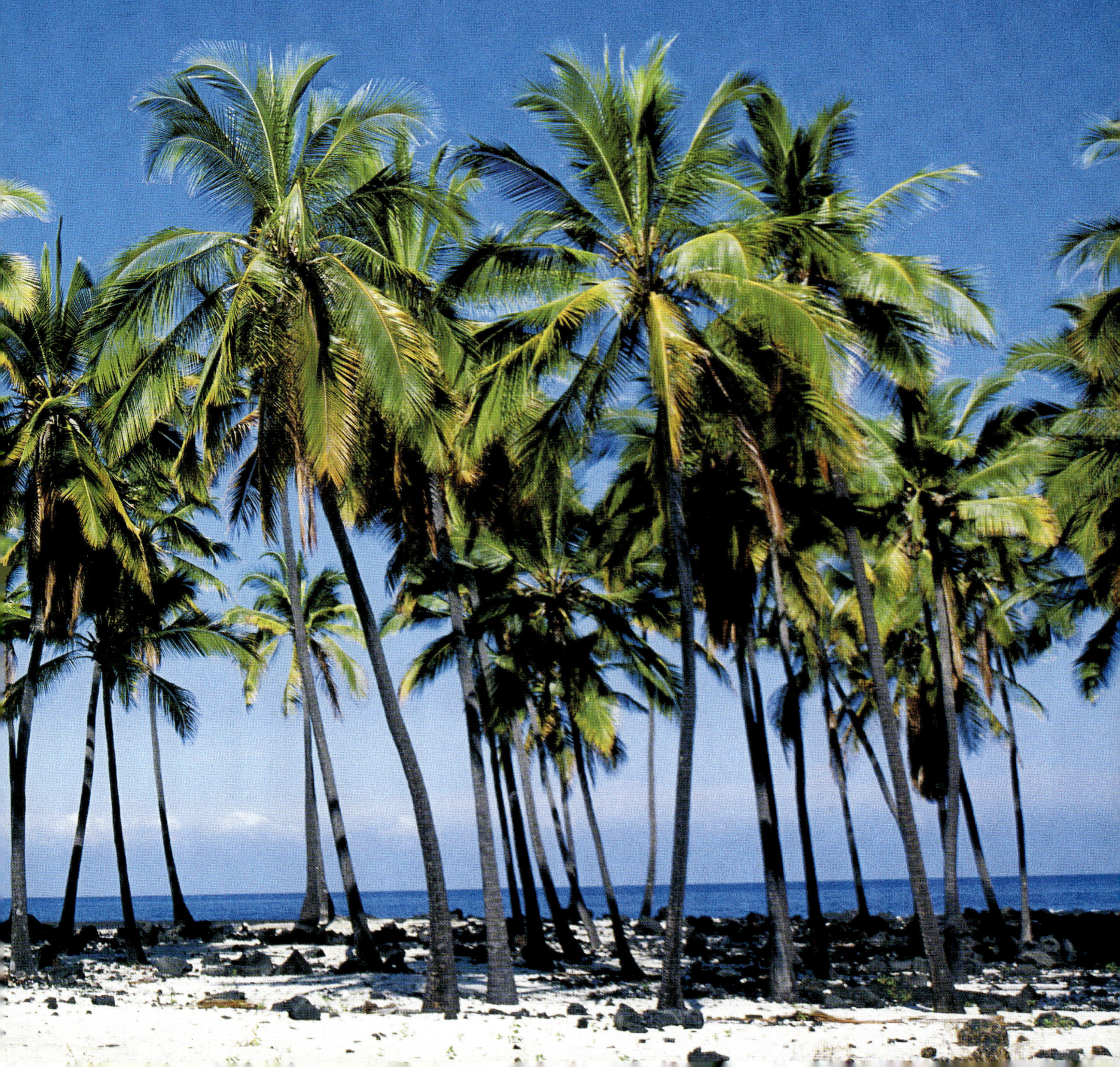

The coconut belies its image as a beach-front layabout (previous pages). This tree is the first line of defence for many tropical coastlines, able to withstand the often brutal onslaughts of salt-laden storms, and grow happily in the pure, almost nutrient-free sand.

The tropical coastline that skirts 80 or so countries around the world is somewhat different from the palm-fringed, sun-drenched paradise that we might imagine it to be. Here we see, with increasing frequency, the devastating power of nature. Thirty degrees in both a northerly and southerly direction from the equator there are vast stretches of tropical forest lying just behind the coast which are protected by sand dunes and trees that grow even closer to, and sometimes in, the sea. Those in the front line matter more than any others because, without them, no other trees would survive.

These are the trees that stand in the way of everything that nature can throw at them, be it tropical storms, hurricanes from the air or giant, salt-laden sea waves

It is because of their geographical position that coastal forests are, for many people, a first line of defence against the ravages of nature. This was brought very close to home in the dreadful aftermath of the tsunami in December 2004. Following the loss of life in Thailand, Sri Lanka, India and other parts of south-east Asia came the post mortems on the appalling disaster. They focused on early warning systems, barricades and evacuations but ignored, to many people's astonishment, the role of the natural defence system, the mangrove swamps that covered some 6 million hectares of the coasts of affected countries. While nothing can stand in the way of a tsunami in full flow or a violent tropical storm, there is enough evidence to suggest that forested coastline was subjected to far less damage and the inhabitants to much less suffering and death during the 2004 tsunami than those areas of coast where forest had been removed. Similarly in Louisiana in 2005, the wrath of Hurricane Katrina was felt with much more intensity where the wetlands have been severely degraded. We must be ever more conscious of the importance of the trees that inhabit the coastline and, with this awareness, we can take steps to protect them.

The willingness of the mangrove to survive in the face of the sometimes overwhelming forces of nature but also to spread and propagate itself is one of the great miracles of the plant world. Its tolerance of salt and the ability of its stilt roots to grow in saline water are testament to this.

The changing face of the world gives rise to constant debate about our influence upon it. All around us we see populations growing and standards of living rising and, as a consequence, enormous pressure increasing on natural resources. Our astonishing levels of consumption are quite clearly unsustainable. From time to time we come face to face with appalling natural disasters, some of which, such as earthquakes or volcanic eruptions, we are powerless to do anything about. All we

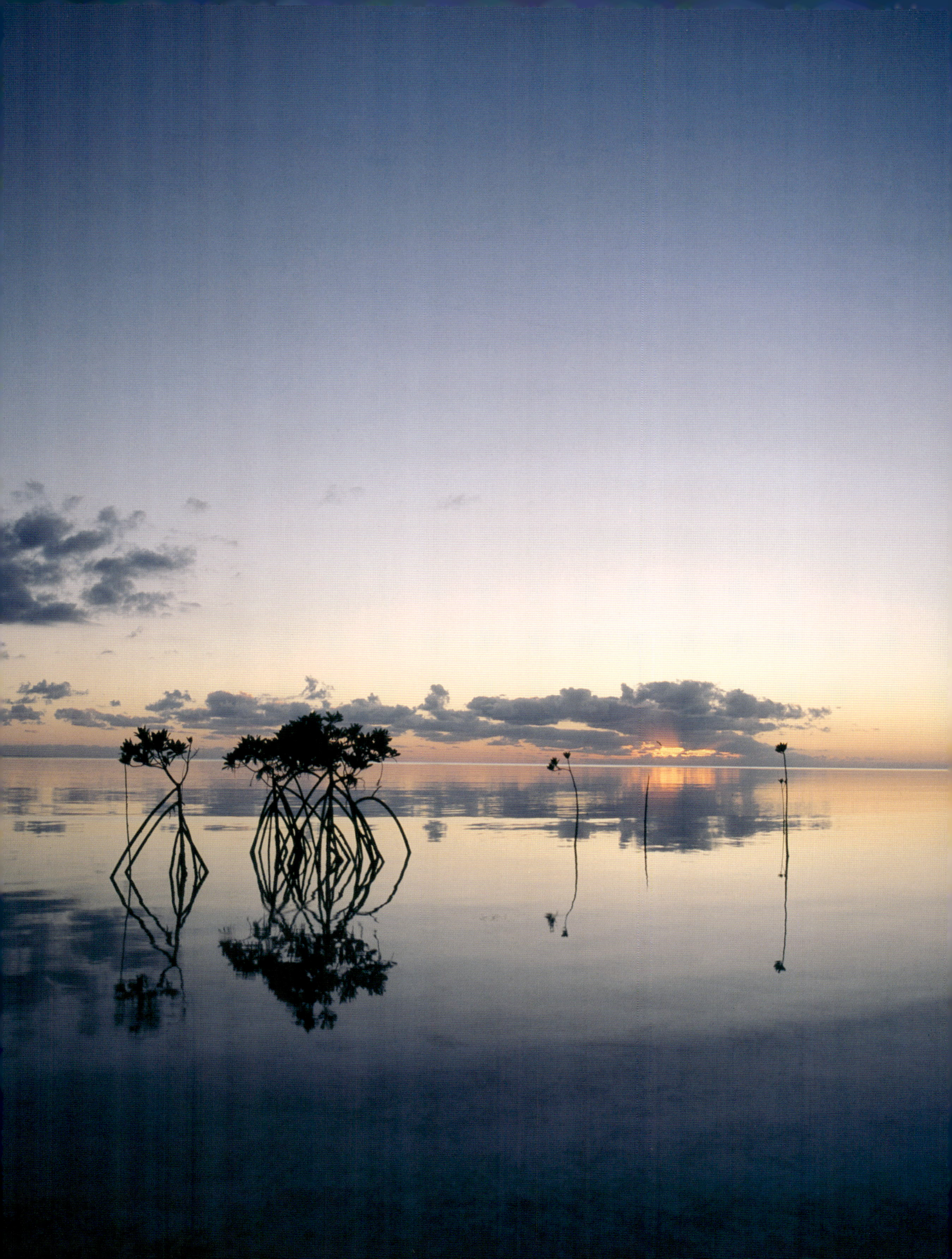

The nipa palm is one of a small number of trees which, like the mangrove, can stand salinated water; it flourishes in the brackish waters of the Ganges delta in Bangladesh. Similar to the coconut, it is a multi-purpose tree, all parts of which are used to feed cattle and cover buildings.

can do is be ready for their arrival and hopefully cope better with the consequences. Tropical storms, hurricanes, typhoons and tsunamis (large waves caused by underwater earthquakes) are similar acts of nature that, at their most fierce, can be extremely destructive, causing wholesale loss of life. In the coastal forest around the equator, the natural landscape and vegetation is equipped to deal with these extremes of weather and we must look at this model to see what we can do to lessen the impact of such events in the future.

The current fears about global warming and the rise of sea levels are felt strongly in coastal regions where the sea is recognized as being an all-powerful force. Much of the coastline of countries such as Guyana, for example, is already below sea level and this is forecast to get worse. When a disaster like the 2004 tsunami occurs, those fears increase considerably – and small wonder in the light of the devastation this type of weather pattern releases. What can be done to minimize the risks for people living on the fringes who are exposed and at risk?

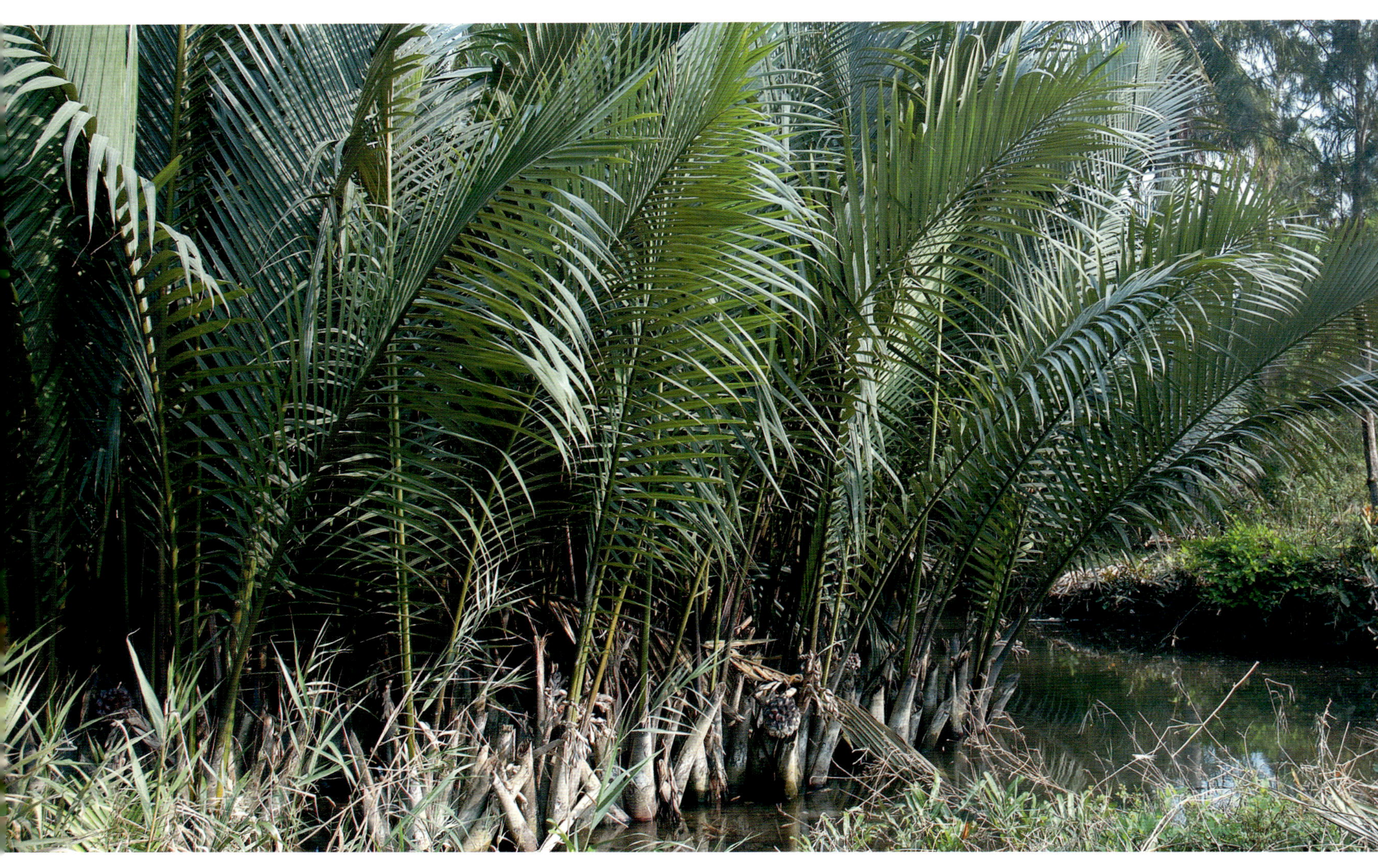

Shrimp farming

There are many shocking facts and figures attached to this coastal defence story but perhaps one of the most damning involves the latest 'get rich quick' scam to hit the Third World: shrimp farming. In 1991, thousands of people were killed by a tsunami in an area of Bangladesh where shrimp farms had replaced all the mangrove trees. Yet in 1960, when a tsunami of similar magnitude hit the coast, there was not a single fatality. Taking away the trees that make up the natural coastal defence system is akin to the removal of trees anywhere – the inevitable result is soil erosion. Just as cutting down trees on mountainsides will lead to landslides, so will coastlines be battered if the trees are removed. These trees have evolved for a reason, they are part of a forest and we remove them at our peril – and the peril of all who live in and around them. They must be replaced, in the knowledge that they are a critical part of the natural scheme of things.

Before the advent of the shrimp farming boom, local communities were dependent on the mangrove forests for food, fuel and timber – as well as protection. Industrial-scale shrimp farming, with its toxicants and clear felling, throws the whole food chain into disarray and displaces indigenous people. For the safety of the coastline and its people all over Asia and South America, the shrimp industry, currently worth some 8 billion US dollars worldwide, needs to be reconsidered.

A report in the journal *Science* in 2005 showed that areas buffered by coastal forest made up of such trees as mangroves were strikingly less damaged by the 2004 tsunami than areas without tree cover. Using satellite photographs of Cuddalore District in Tamil Nadu, south-east India, the researchers had a straightforward task trying to gauge the level of damage. The coast is straight and it was obvious which patches of coastline were forested and which were not. Most of the coastal villages were badly ravaged – but those that had the protection of the natural coastal defences were not. Less than a kilometre from the high-tide mark, the 6,000 villagers of the Pichavaram mangrove reserves were unharmed. The report concluded that a population density of 30 trees per 100 square metres could reduce the maximum flow of another tsunami by up to 90 per cent.

So what chance is there for a reversal in the fortunes of coastal forests? The bad news is that they are among the most threatened habitats in the world. This is attributable to the usual collection of unstoppable forces which dominate in such regions: population growth, unsustainable economic development, high levels of pollution and shrimp farming. It is tragic that the suffering should reach such astonishing levels before anyone takes notice. In October 1999 a 'super cyclone' hit the coast of the state of Orissa on the east side of India, below West Bengal and Bangladesh, killing 10,000 people and making over 7 million homeless. Amid the shocking chaos, only the villagers of the Bhitarkarmika Mangrove Sanctuary, the country's second largest mangrove swamp, were unharmed.

Low tide in the mangrove swamp. The high-tide mark is clearly visible and the depth between high and low water suggests the swamp is close to the sea in a tidal estuary. The roots support a mass of sea life and the whole health of the tropical deltas depends heavily on the mangrove forest.

Improvement schemes

This appalling super-cyclone tragedy happened in the middle of a seven-year Joint Management Mangrove project funded by the Canadian International Development Agency. During this time the project has restored 1,447 hectares of degraded mangrove forest on three levels: replanting the trees themselves, transferring salt-tolerant genes to various agricultural crops such as rice and mustard, and creating safe fishing zones, all the while raising awareness of impending storms and teaching people what to do before and during the event. The second point is perhaps the most interesting one – the genetic modification of crops for the purpose of inducing salt tolerance is an issue that has raised serious moral and ethical dilemmas. But those who live in areas where there is a permanent risk of tropical storms – and the Bay of Bengal is certainly such a place – might argue strongly in favour of a process that can preserve the essential characteristics of their most basic

These amazing mangrove trees have evolved for a reason, they

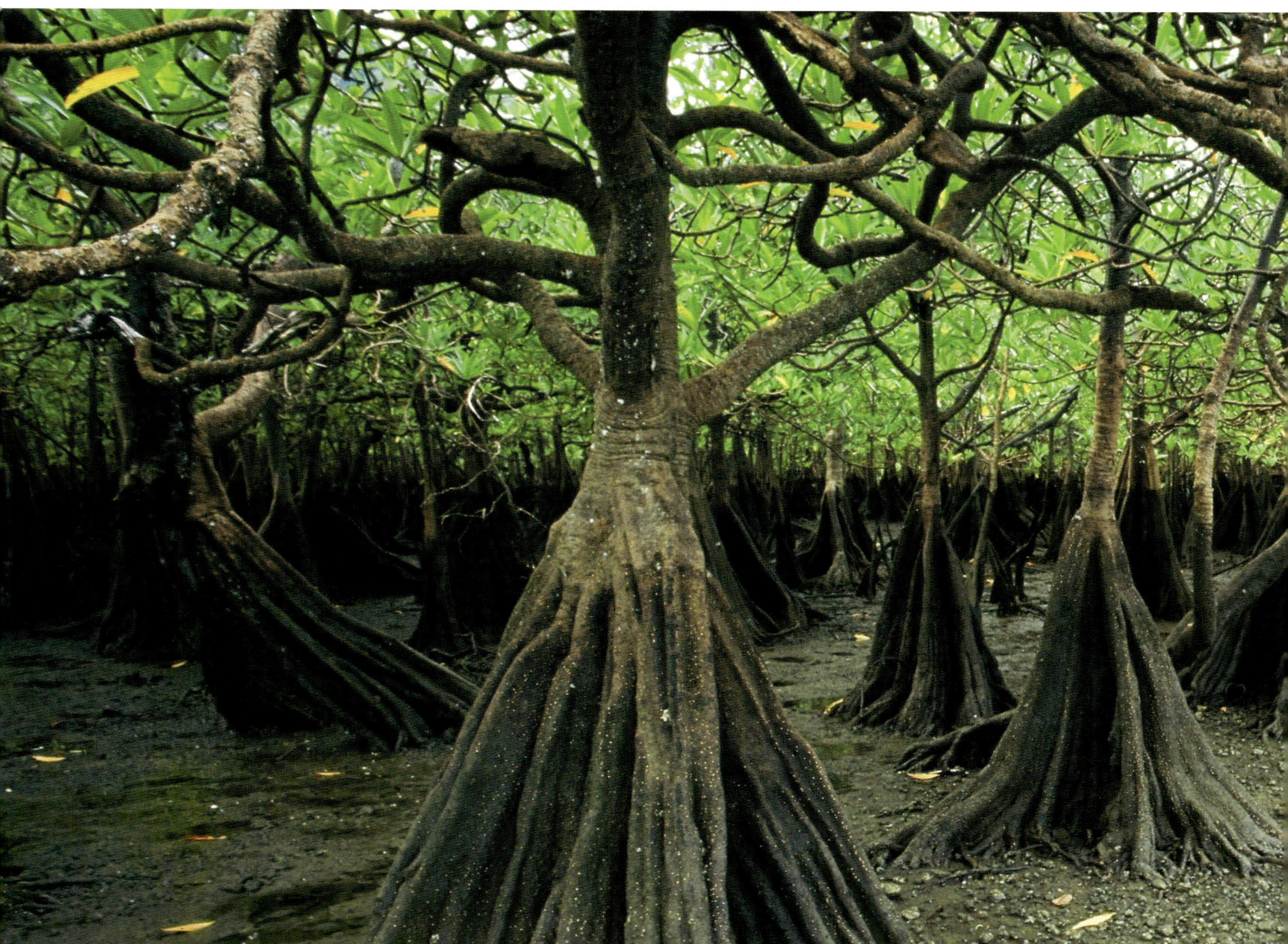

staple crops while at the same time making them less vulnerable to potential natural disasters such as typhoons, cyclones and tsunamis.

While it may appear extreme to look at genetic modification as a means of overcoming associated problems, there are fewer and fewer options available. North Vietnam is a country that suffers badly from the effects of typhoons, of which they have usually four per year. Their action is similar to hurricanes, devastating to land, property, livestock and humans. The Government decided to build a wall stretching for 3,000 kilometres in the hope of keeping the sea at bay. The annual cost of keeping the wall intact had reached the absurd sum of 7.5 million US dollars because it was continuously breached by typhoons. Finally, after undertaking some research, the Government initiated a mangrove planting scheme which ran to 12,000 hectares, and now the wall is rarely breached.

The mangrove forest guides the river to the open sea (overleaf). The natural barrier formed by these trees is Nature's way of protecting the tropical coastline from the devastating effects of flooding, storms and the eroding qualities of salt that is carried with them.

are part of a forest and we remove them at our peril

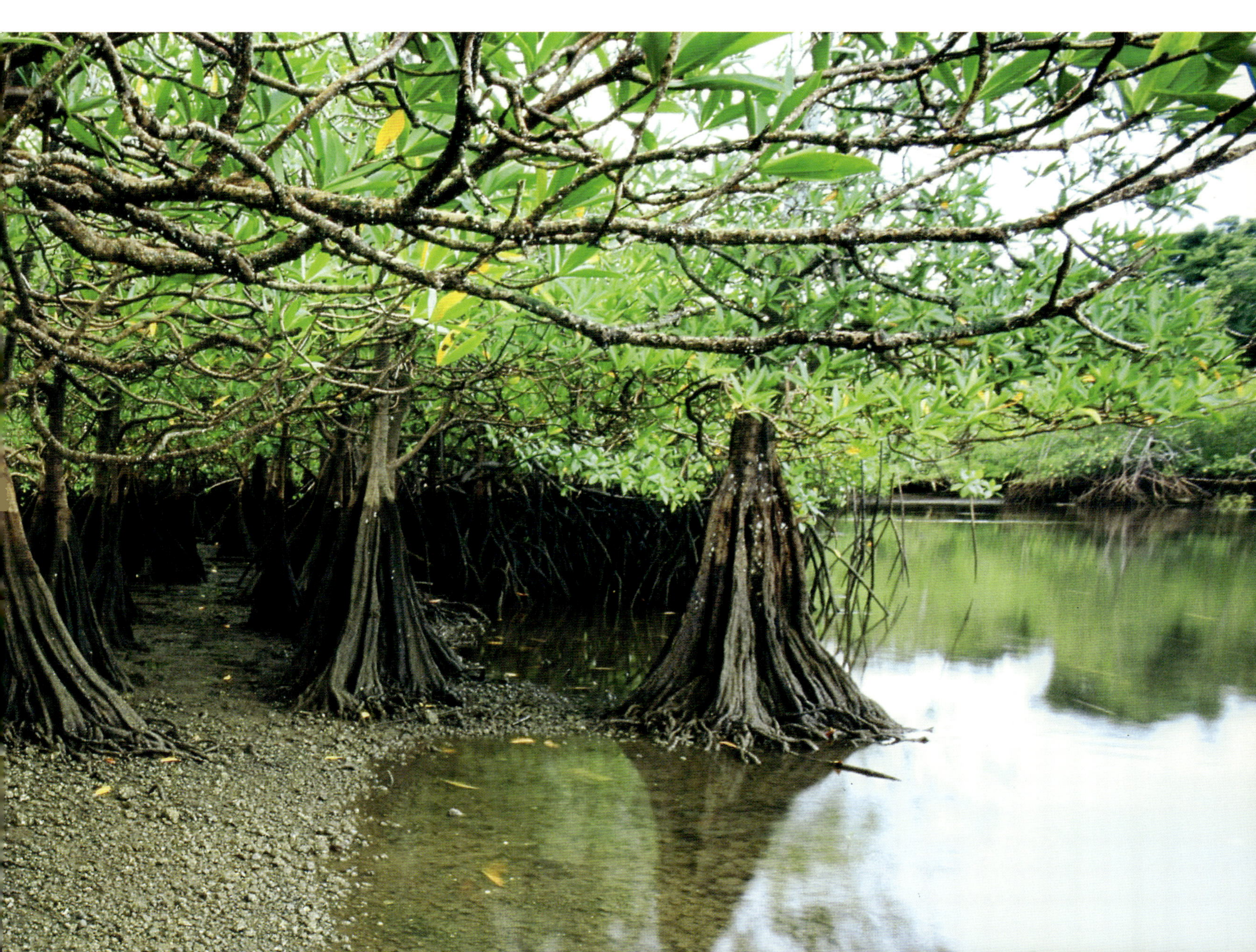

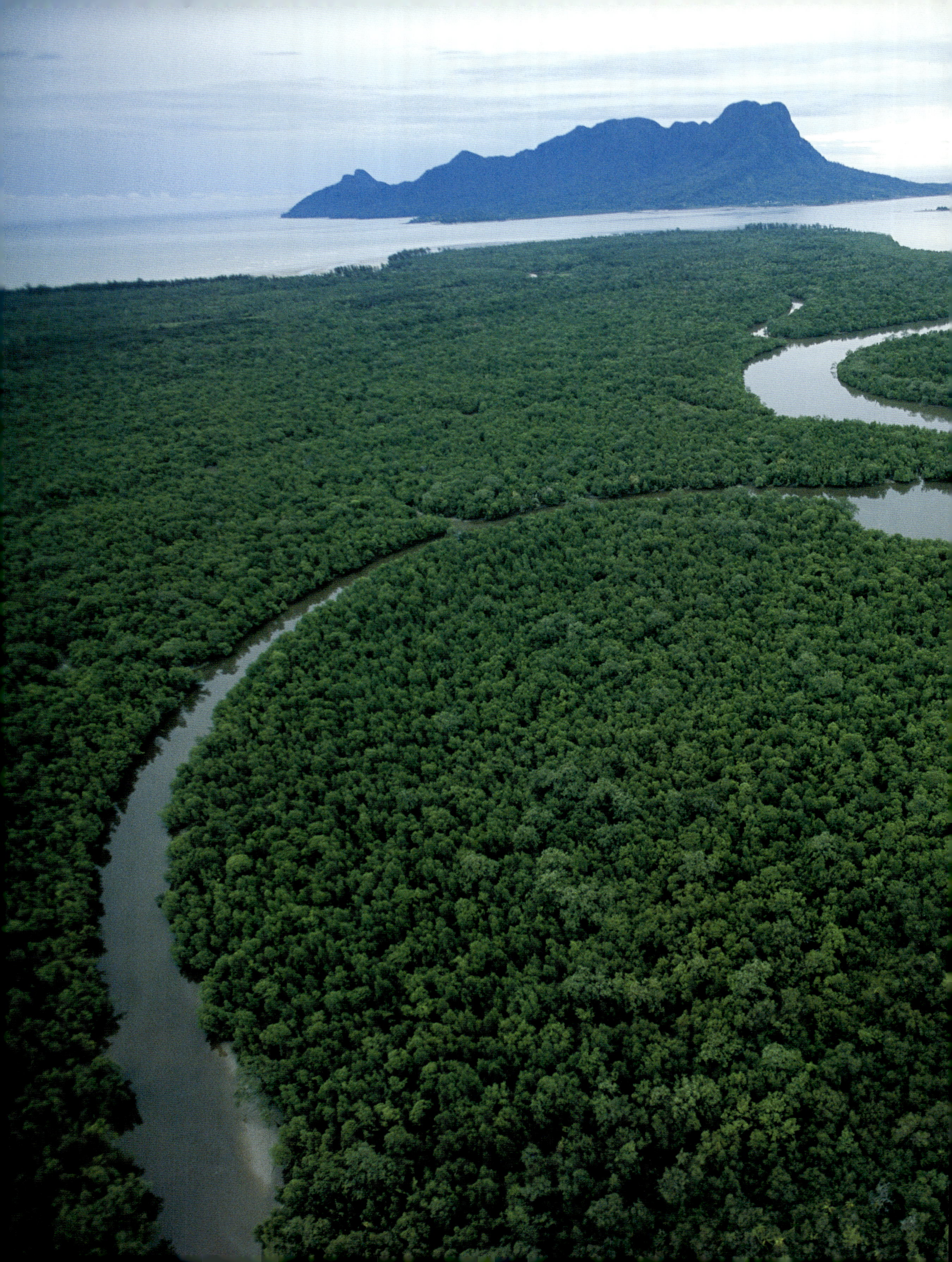

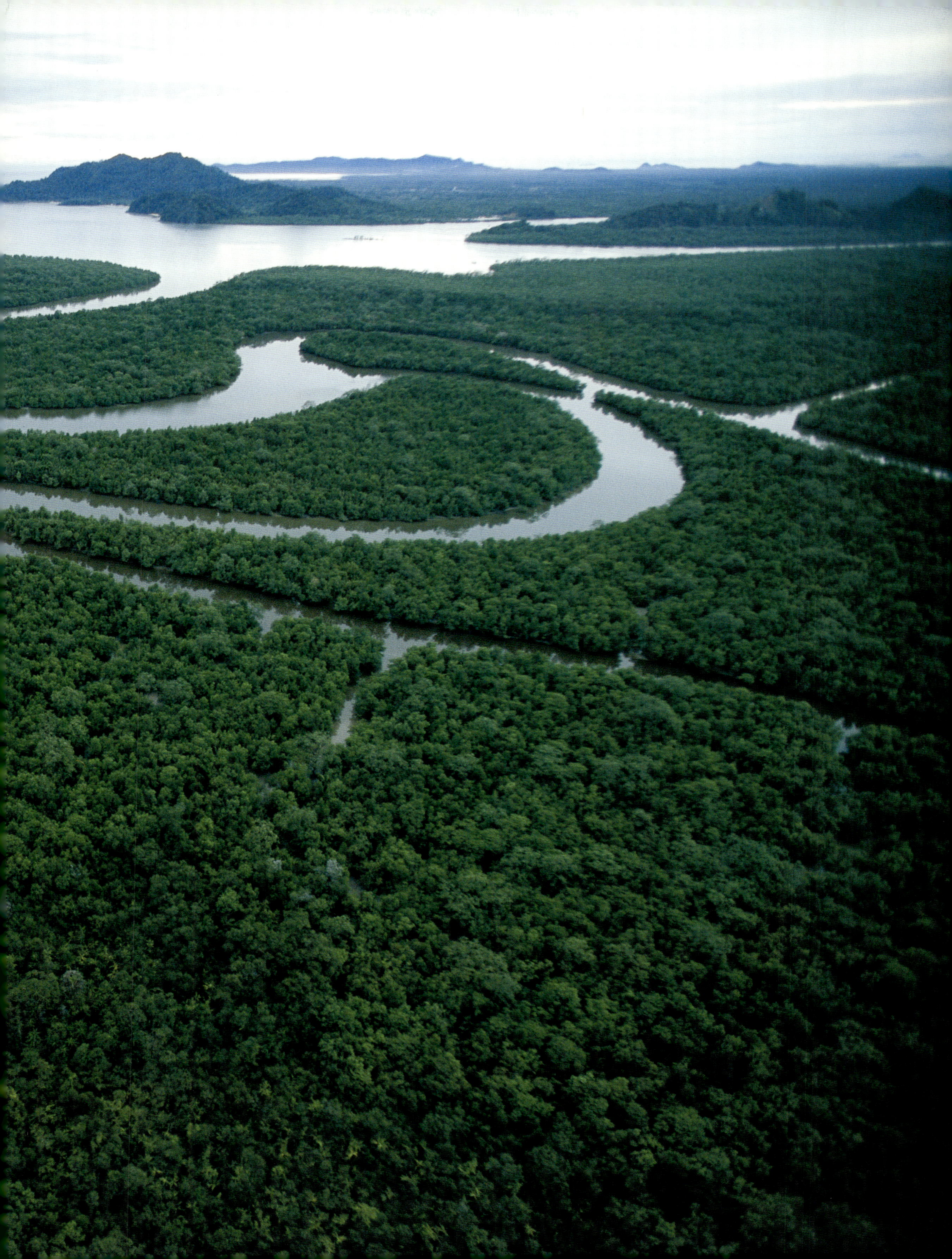

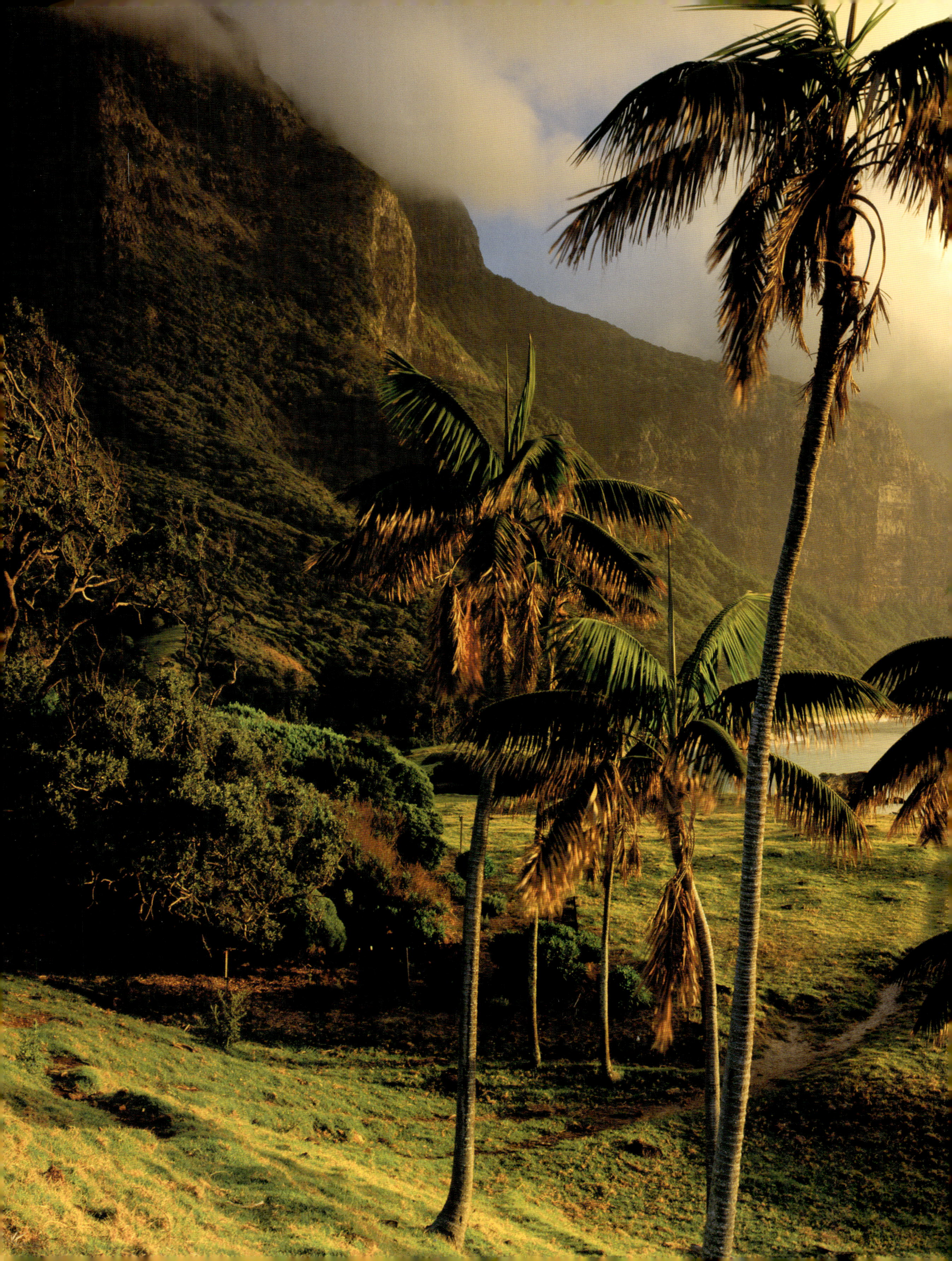

coconut

This is the ultimate multipurpose tree: it is known as the tree which provides all the necessities of life and it thoroughly deserves this accolade

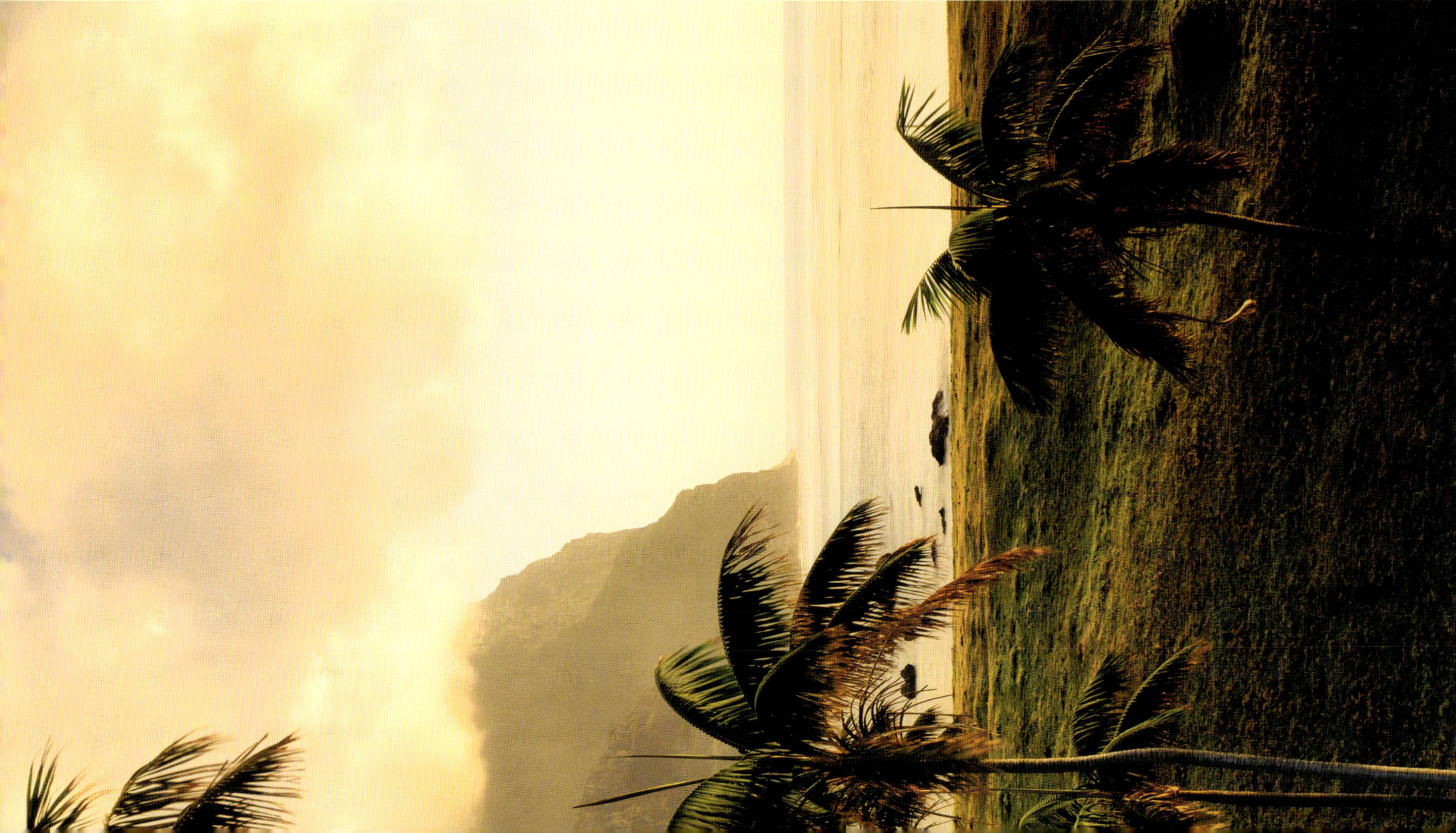

coconut

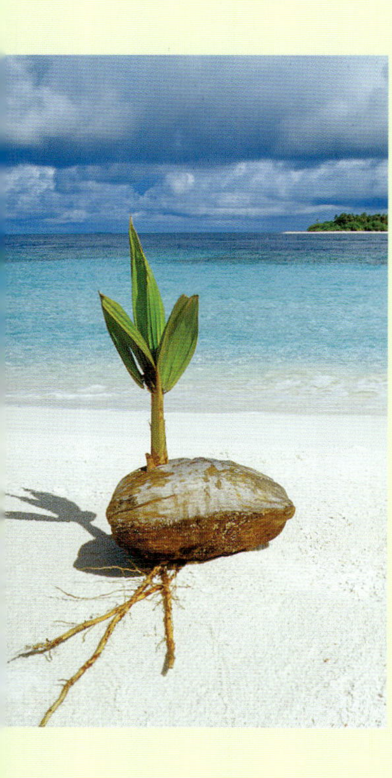

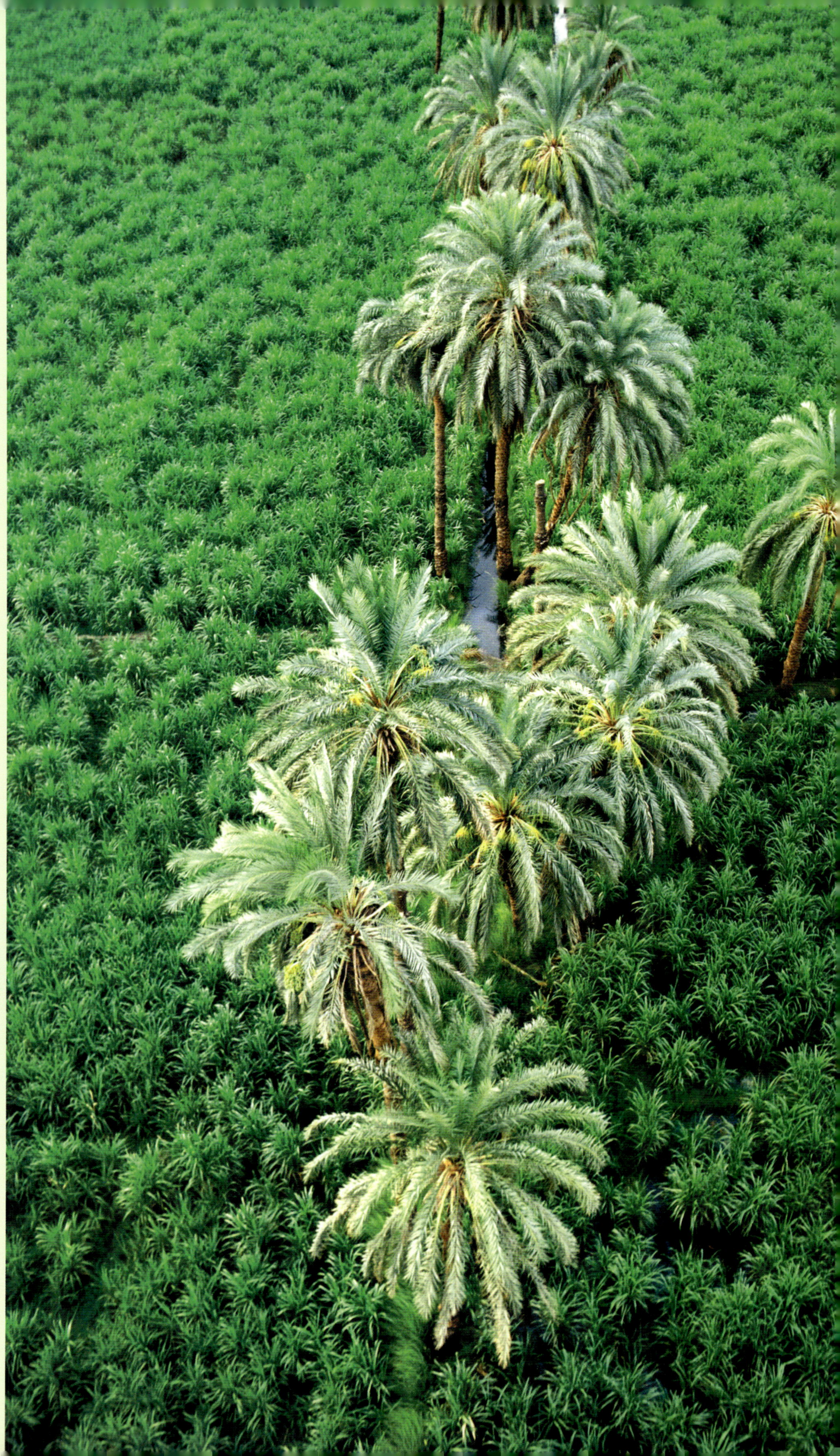

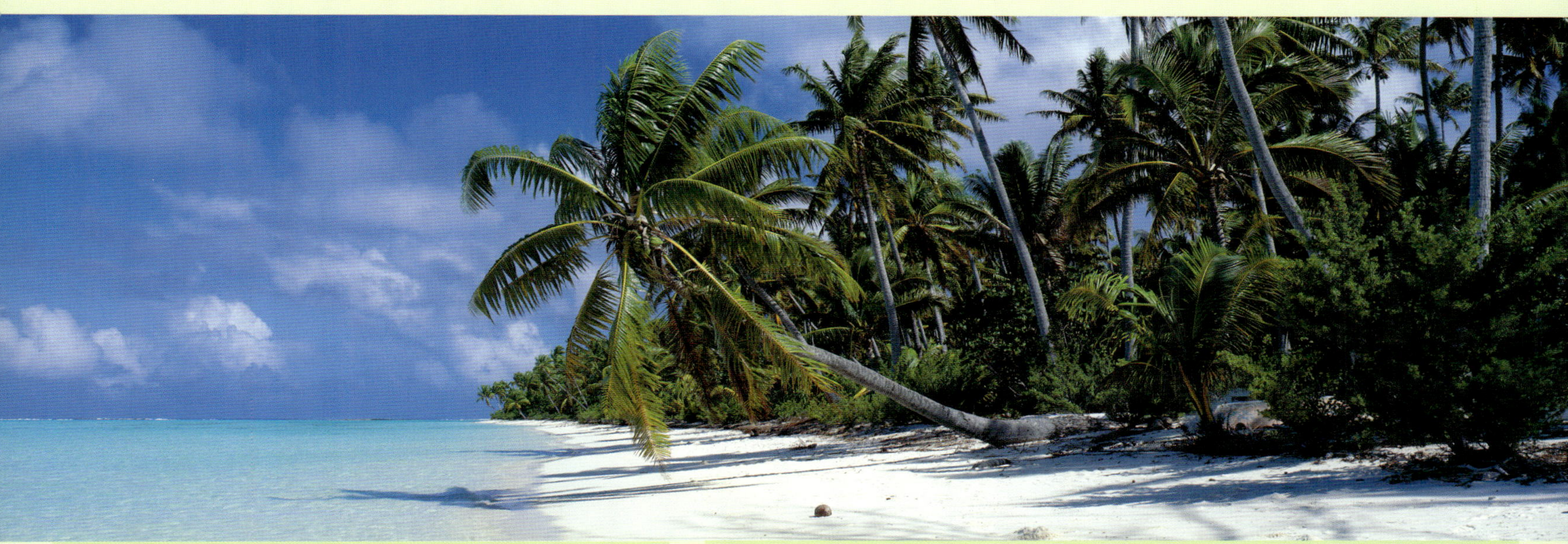

Growing to 30 metres tall and above, and almost devoid of branches, the coconut tree has a striking presence. It has a long, thin trunk, which does not increase in diameter with age, with fruit and fronds clustered together at the top. Instead of branches it has fronds, the primary use of which is to provide materials for household purposes, such as roofing and mats. This is a species of tree that seems to know its function, whether shoring up fragile stretches of coastline behind mangrove swamps or standing tall to protect the rice paddies of inland farms from typhoons. Together with the strong, durable and salt tolerant timber, which provides their structure, it is not unusual to see entire houses built from coconut trees along tropical coasts.

There is a slight sense of the absurd about the fact that the coconut (*Cocos nucifera*) is one of the most important trees in the world. Our vision of a coconut palm is not one of a tree with gravitas, such as the oak or the teak tree. Yet its ubiquitous presence on postcards from beauty spots all over the tropics belies its status as a tree with serious economic implications. It has earned respect for being one of only a handful of trees that can cope with its natural environment here in the tropical coastal forest biome. Several members of the palm family are well adapted to growing in sand but not many can withstand the levels of salt and the high winds faced by the coconut on tropical coastlines around the world. Curiously, its origin is unknown and theories as to its homeland vary from Asia to South America. But it has been carried all over the tropics by man and has spread itself through the buoyancy and the salt tolerance of its seed, which may live for up to a year floating in the sea.

The fruit A mature coconut tree has fruit in twelve stages of development at any one time, from open flower to ripe fruit. Usually the fruit is left to drop as a means of harvest because it has a hard outer shell. But in parts of Thailand, monkeys are trained to climb and pick the fruit and it is also not unusual to see men and boys shinning their way up the trees. Once harvested, the inner fruit has great culinary value in many forms, from coconut milk to desiccated coconut; and, when dried, is the source of an oil widely employed for cooking and other domestic uses. The water, drained out before the nut is cracked, has a high nutritional content too and is so pure that it was used in the Second World War as a sterile solution for wounded soldiers.

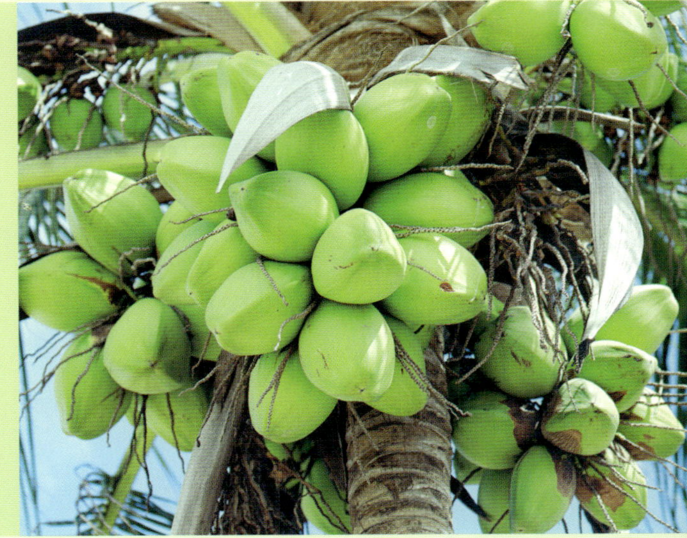

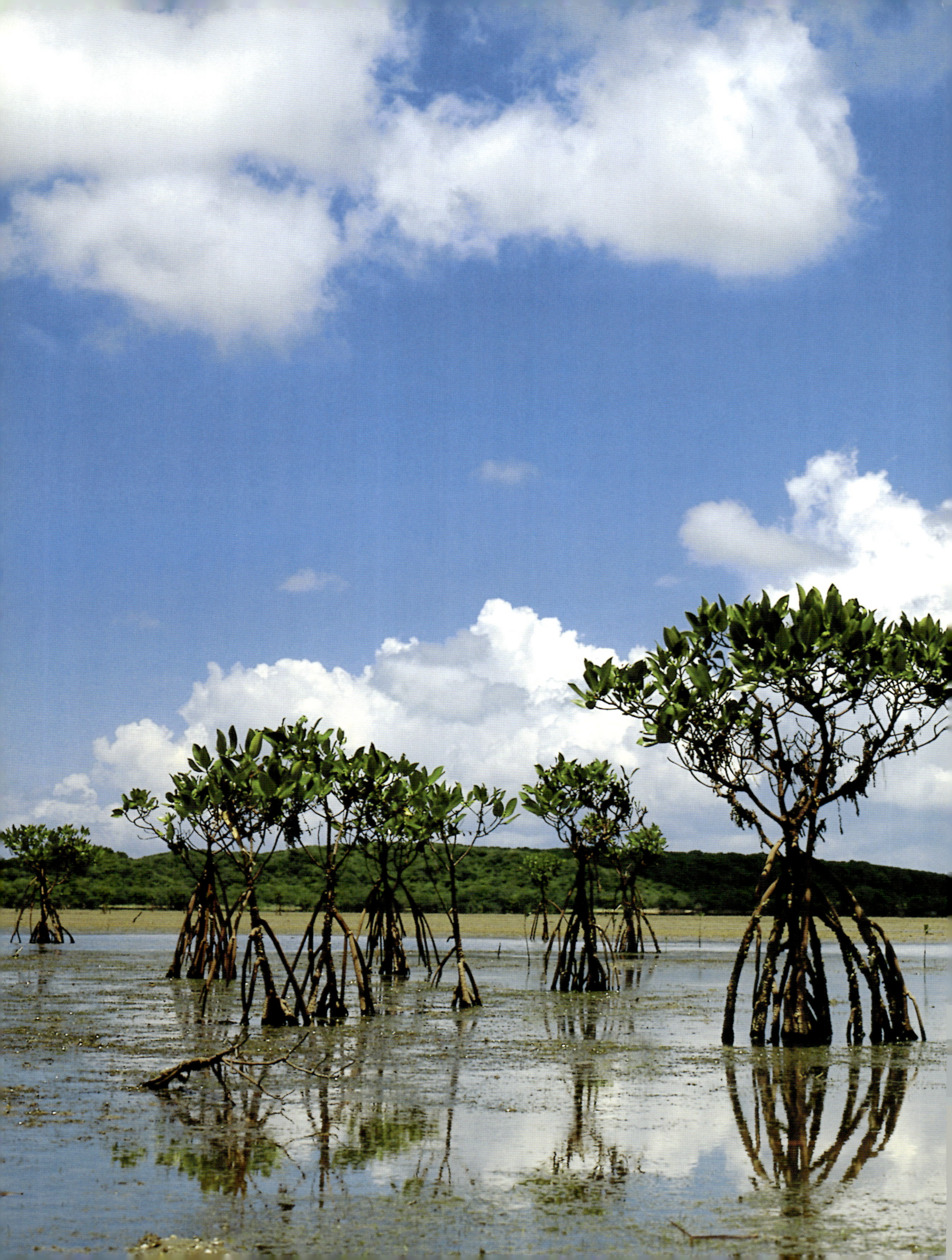

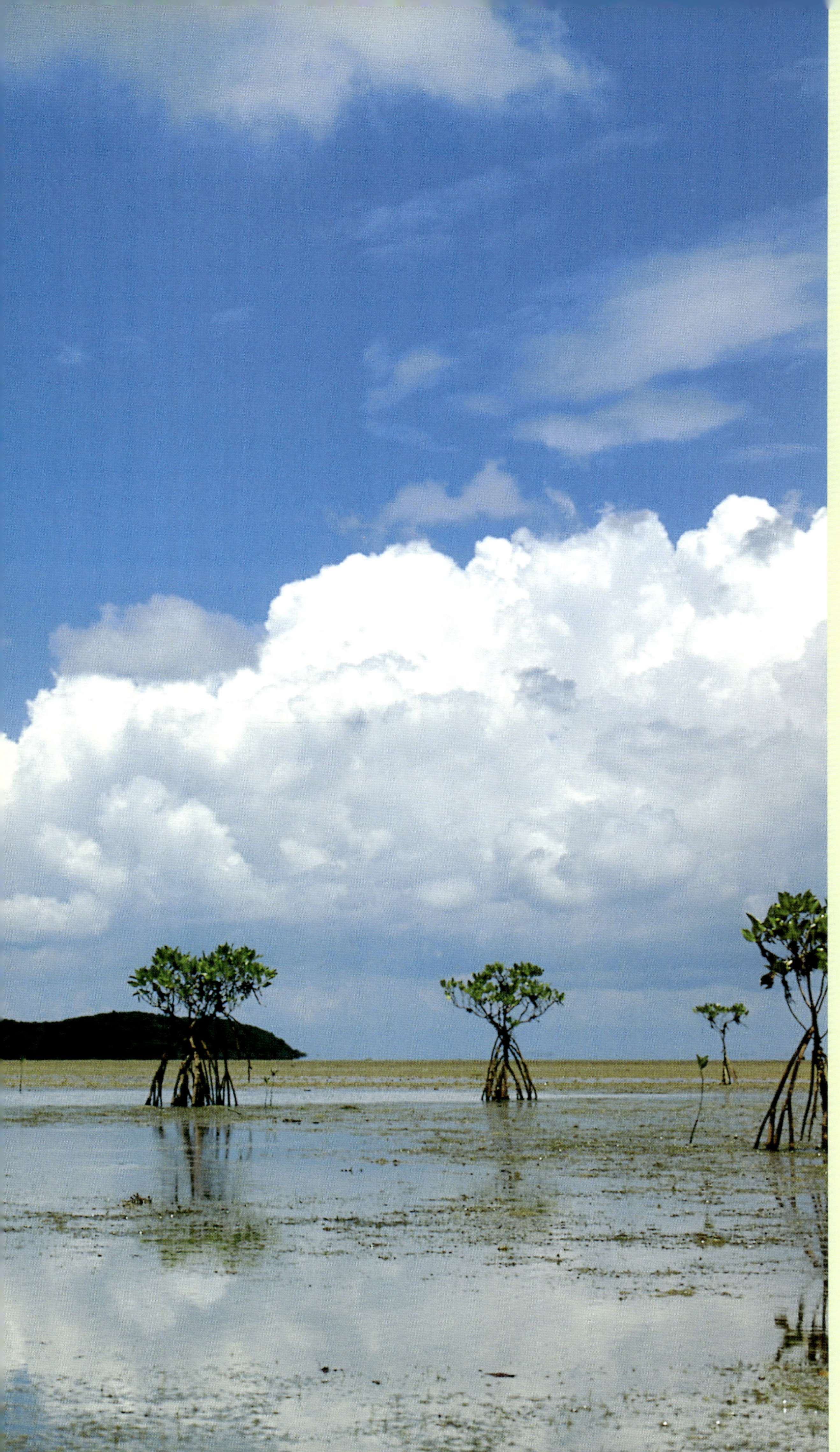

mangrove

Mangroves grow as swamps and forests and are the most stable natural system on the planet

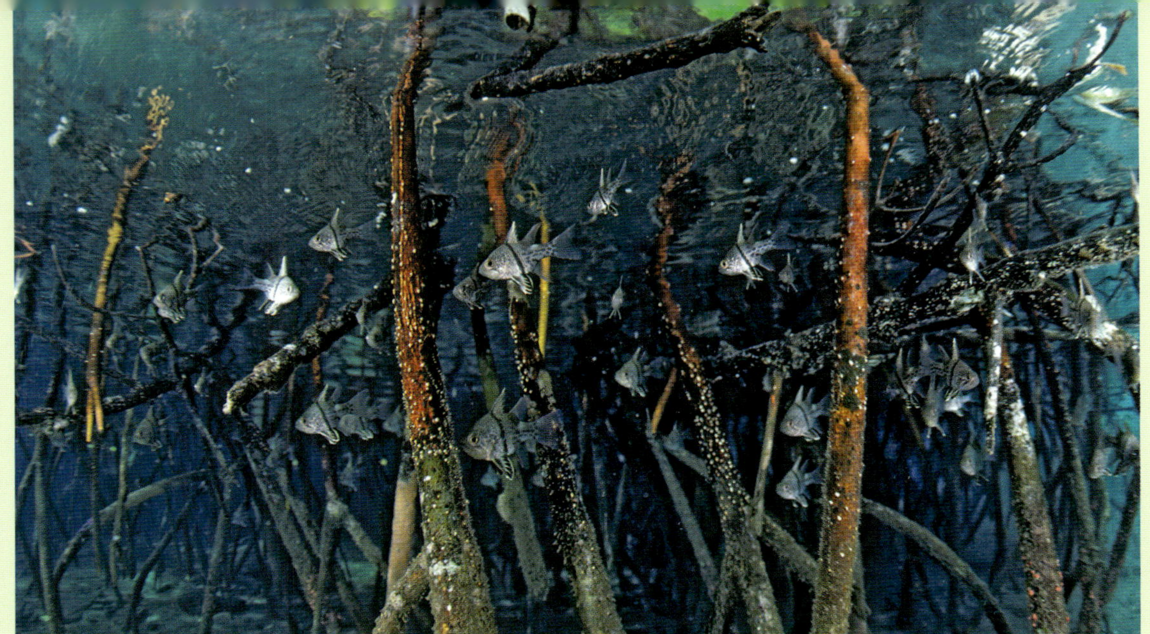

Mangroves grow as swamps and forests and are the most stable natural systems on the planet, supporting huge networks of wildlife and effectively linking the food webs of land and sea. This life exists in a multitude of forms among the mangroves: from the tiniest of fish that swim in the perennially muddy waters, through to the Gangetic dolphin and salt- and fresh-water crocodiles, all the way up to grazing cattle and the mighty Royal Bengal tigers that prey on them. These areas are almost uninhabitable to humans because the land is constantly shifting as monsoon water courses powerfully through the channels.

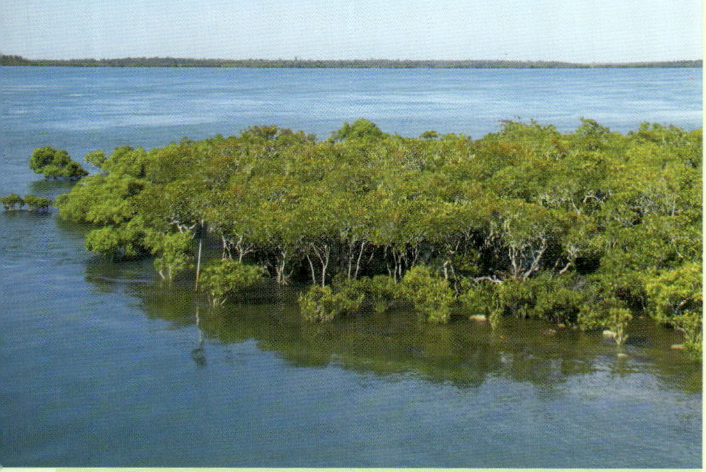

The Bay of Bengal, the world's biggest delta, is a giant swamp made up almost entirely of one tree species, the mangrove (*Rhizophora mucronata*). Here, where the mouth of the sacred river Ganges meets the Bay of Bengal in India's West Bengal and its neighbouring country Bangladesh, the mangrove is the centrepiece of a unique ecosystem that prevents these low-lying coastal regions from being washed away.

Mangrove forest is a community of trees and shrubs which grow in the tidal zones of sheltered tropical coasts on both sides of the Equator, where mangrove 'swamps' act as a buffer zone between land and sea. These forests occupy only 180,000 square kilometres of the earth's surface and extend only a few kilometres inland, but the trees have evolved unique features to withstand the hardships of their habitat, including stilt roots and salt-excreting leaves. Mangroves are the most important of the 80 species that have adapted to live in the intertidal zone of coasts.

Mangrove swamps

The natural world is filled with examples of plant and animal species finding the means to adapt and survive, sometimes in the face of overwhelming odds. The mangrove is perhaps the most extreme example. This is a tree whose extraordinary roots are able to grow and flourish in salt water, to convert the saline solution to pure water and find the ability to propagate itself, by seed, or entirely unaided through a system of underwater roots and rhizomes that can grow in salt water. Mangroves occupy the fringes of tropical coastal waters to protect the inshore environment from the dangers it faces. The roots of mangrove trees effectively breathe, the force of the tides acting like inflating lungs.

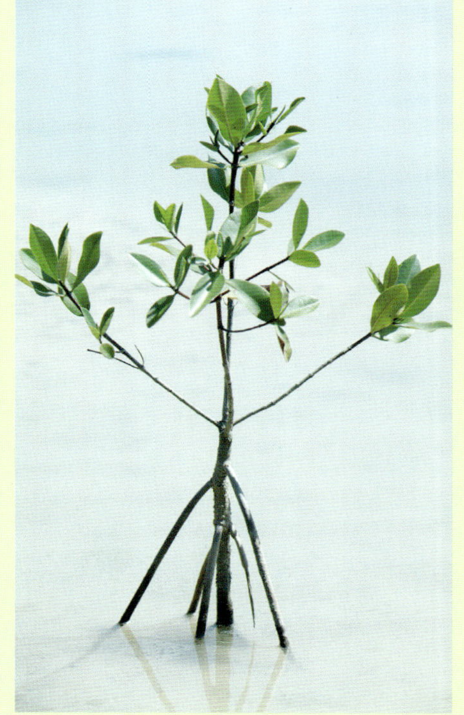

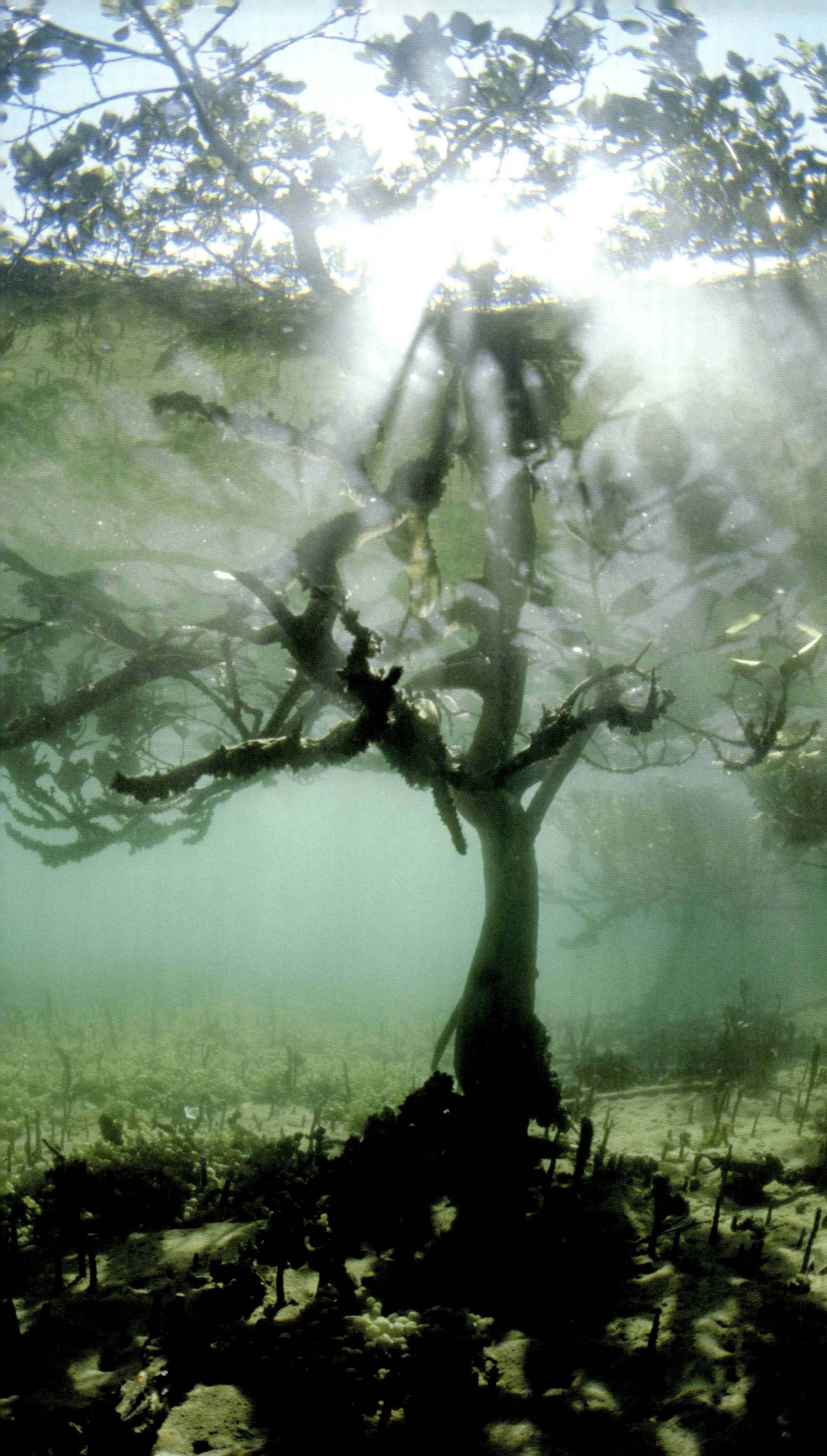

mangrove

This is a tree whose extraordinary roots are able to grow and flourish in salt water

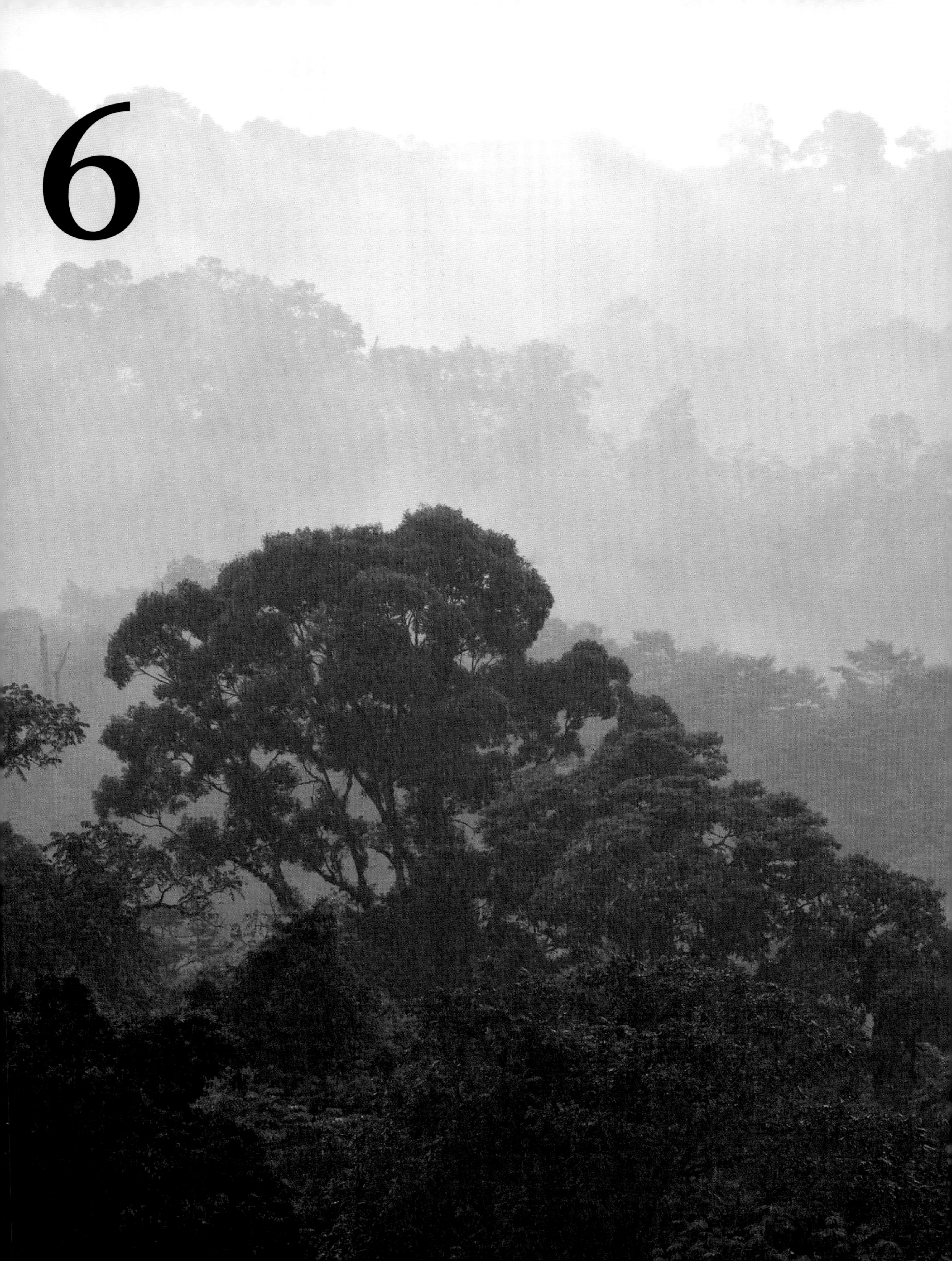
6

rainforest

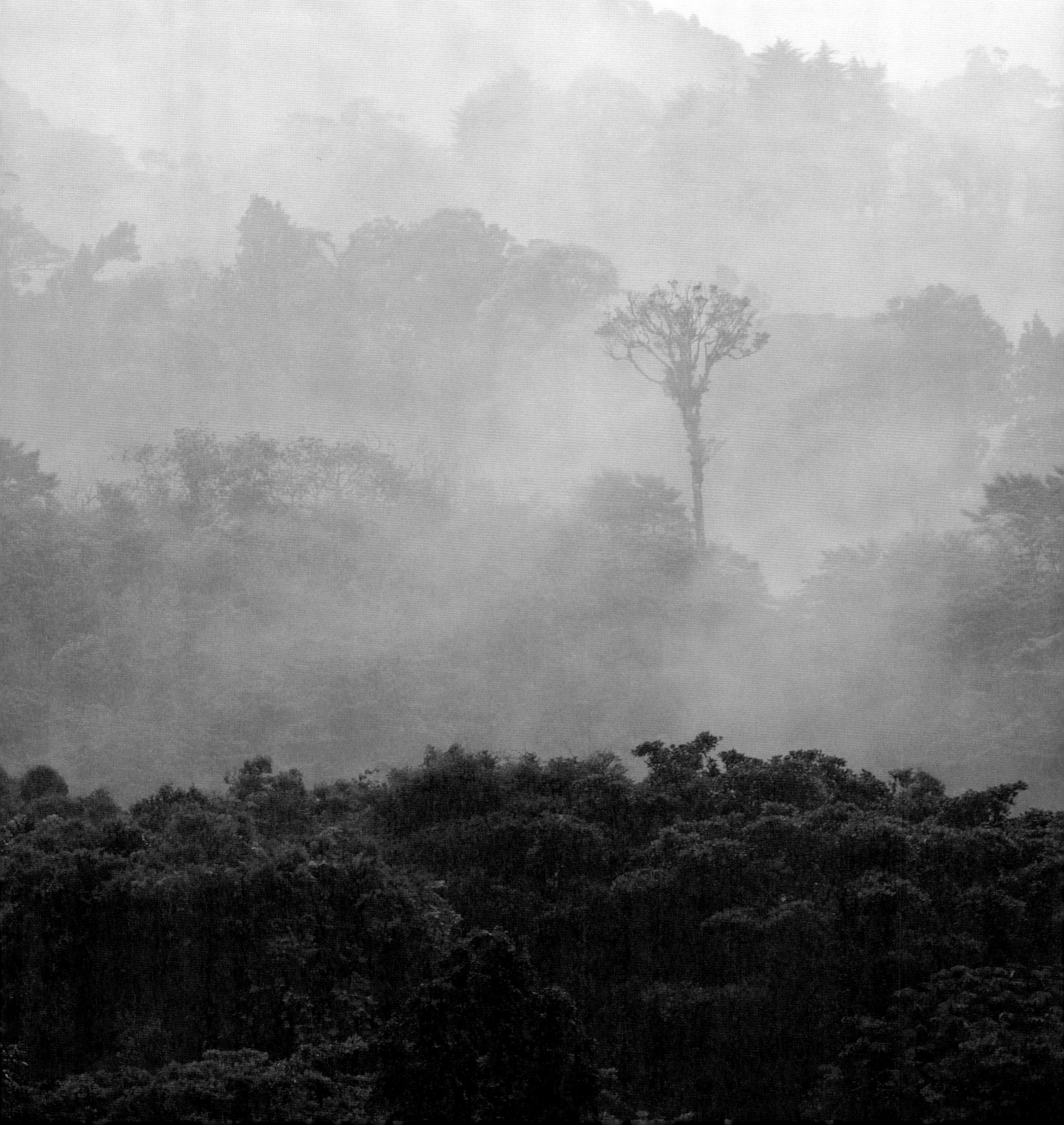

The rainforest is rich in diversity beyond the wildest dreams of any other ecosystem on the planet (previous pages). New species of plant, animal and insect are still being discovered in parts of this world where few humans tread. Trees remain unclimbed and what truly happens in the canopy layer of large tracts of rainforest remains uncharted.

Perhaps closer to western hearts than any other type of forest, the rainforest is probably the forest we know least about. The rainforests of the world cover a massive area, awe-inspiring in their scope and crucially important in its implications for the future, in which new species of plant, animal and insect are constantly being discovered. For the visitor, there is no place on earth quite as astonishing as a rainforest. Perhaps it is the coming together of so much life working in precise order for the greater good of the whole – all the way down to the tiniest single organism – that leaves us in a state of bewilderment. There may be birds and animals singing and screeching at eardrum-splitting levels, the constant piping of cicadas and the extraordinary hum of life and death in all its glory, but underneath there is the silence of deep peace, mutual respect and confidence that everything is as it should be. How could this possibly be when, outside, all that is dominated by humankind appears to be in bedlam? It may be the shade cast by trees both large and small, it may

The rainforest enviroment is entirely beholden to the trees that populate it and it is upon them that everything in the system depends

be that most humans are completely out of place in this environment and therefore feel unsafe and somewhat helpless, or it may simply be that the rainforest is the most primeval of all the biomes on the planet that makes it a place of such overpowering magic. What is without doubt is that the rainforest is a self-sustaining and complete body of life and the most stable and important collection of trees on earth.

Some trees burst through the canopy of the rainforest in their desperate search for light, like this one in Sabeh, Borneo (opposite). Many trees survive with nothing more than filtered sunlight in the depths of the interior, while others grow with only their tops in the light. Either way, each different species manages to extract its individual needs through sheer determination to survive and out-compete its fellow trees.

Tropical rainforests are found all over the globe between the Tropics of Cancer and Capricorn on either side of the Equator. This brings in Central and South America, Western Africa, the Congo basin in central Africa, much of the island of Madagascar where 80 per cent of the plant life grows nowhere else, and huge tracts of south-east Asia, notably Malaysia. Indonesia, in the shape of Borneo, Irian Jaya and Papua New Guinea, also features significantly, while there are still smaller pockets in East Africa, northern Australia, Tasmania and in the Pacific north-west USA. Many different types of rainforest exist, including subtropical forest and cloud forest, depending on the elevation and the amount of rainfall. In addition to the wet, evergreen forests of the tropics, isolated examples of subtropical forest are found in the foothills of the Himalayas, the east coast of South Africa, southern Brazil, northern Argentina and the east coast of Australia. All have differing aspects and

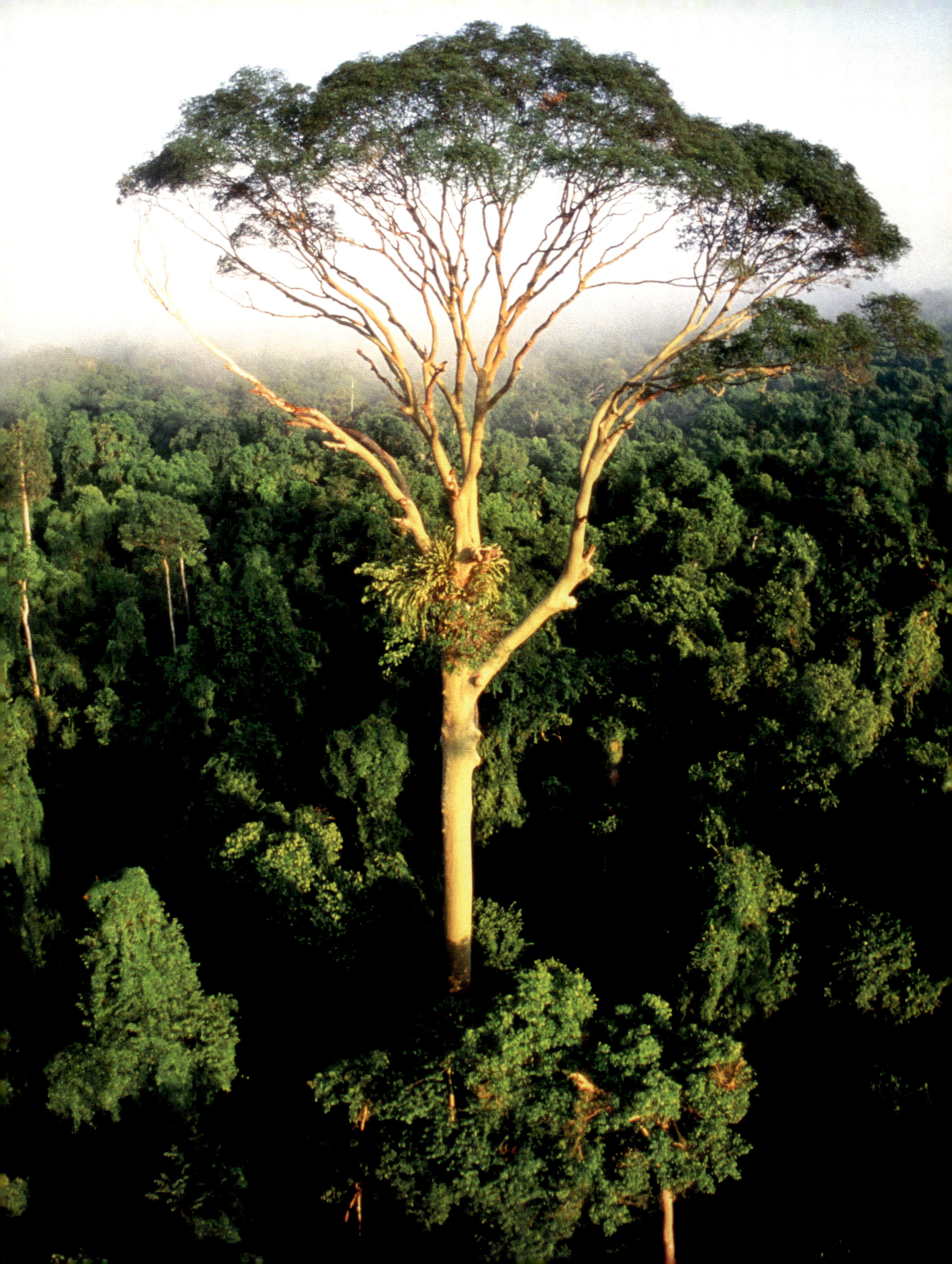

species of tree but the unifying factors are steady levels of rainfall and warm temperatures. The trees have to compete hard for light and nutrients and so have developed straight, branchless trunks and buttress roots to help in their survival.

South India

For a while I lived on the fringes of the rainforest in Tamil Nadu, South India. The area was heavily forested for coffee growing, with native trees such as the silk cotton (*Bombax malabarica*), Indian rosewood (*Dalbergia latifolia*) and teak (*Tectona grandis*) – but these were forest trees. In the rainforest things were different; here the native trees were absolutely enormous, one after the other stretching hundreds of metres in the air. I remember being astonished at the change from the forested hillsides to the rainforest because the difference in the vegetation and atmosphere was extraordinary in every possible way – it was like walking into a different world from another time.

The rainforest is the most primeval of all the biomes on the planet and that makes it a place of overpowering magic

That small area of rainforest in India is the last patch on the subcontinent and, were it not for the Palni Hills Conservation Council who have set up tree nurseries for replanting purposes, this too would now be eradicated. Encouraging the local community to raise trees has helped to meet the native population's needs for fuel, fodder and timber and so deterred them from cutting down trees in the forest. When it comes to stopping the destruction of the entire Amazon basin, which is more than a million square kilometres in size and which, if it were a country, would be the ninth largest in the world, things are different.

*Three rainforest giants (opposite). Top: the capok tree (*Bombax ceiba*), the tallest tree in the canopy of the Lowland Corcovado National Park, Costa Rica; centre: the sal tree (*Shorea robusta*) in the Bandavgarh National Park in Madyar Pradesh, India; bottom: a dipterocarp, a large tree which forms the main component of sal forest of central and Northrn India, valuable for timber, resin and seeds as well as its leaves.*

A threatened environment

The aura that surrounds the rainforests as they are subjugated to hideous levels of destruction has allowed their reputation to reach almost mythical proportions. All predictions say that the destruction of the rainforests will continue unabated at the hands of those countries which have heavy requirements for the hardwoods in which the rainforests abound. Where else do they go for them? The single most important reason that the forests are being cut down is that the world needs the wood. The secondary use comes in the form of cattle rearing and soya bean production, rather than the replanting of trees. The USA has cut down 90 per cent of its natural forest and almost all of what we see there today is planted and managed. China has lost all of its rainforest, India has sacrificed all but the last tiny piece, Bangladesh and Japan are empty and Malaysia is fast running out. Indonesia is high up in the league of foul play when it comes to logging in its rainforests and will quickly go the same way. Some estimates give the world's rainforests only 40 years to live at the current rate of destruction. Both timber and cleared land are in serious demand and the damage being caused is irreversible.

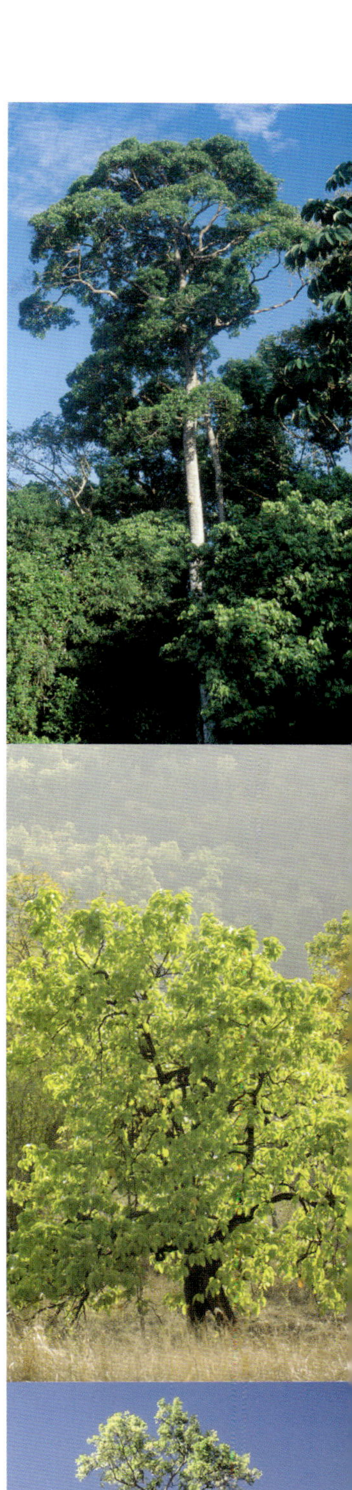

How can we take these statements seriously when rainforests cover huge areas of so many countries? The trees hold the answers. The Dipterocarpaceae family, for example, has more than 500 species which are spread across all the major areas of rainforest in the world, from America through Africa to Asia. Most of these species, including the sal tree (*Shorea robusta*), are hardwoods that are found in both the emergent layer (above the canopy) of the rainforest and the canopy itself. Growing straight and tall, they are targeted as prime candidates for cutting and they dominate the international market in tropical timber, often marketed as 'meranti'. The timber is used for any number of purposes, from building to paper pulp, and there appears to be no stopping the seemingly insatiable appetites of the giant corporations involved.

It is astounding that this state of affairs should still prevail when it is so obvious that the destruction of the rainforests and trees such as the dipterocarps can only be disastrous. This will occur because of the removal of a vital source of carbon storage, in both the trees and the litter layer on the forest floor, the lack of oxygen that will result and the inevitable soil erosion that follows on from deforestation. We argue that the displacement of indigenous peoples is scandalous and we have come to believe that corporate greed and, ultimately, our own level of consumerism is at fault.

Biodiversity

Increasingly – and this may be an important factor in the process of halting such appalling levels of destruction – we are beginning to realize that the biodiversity of the rainforest is way beyond our comprehension. The statistics are staggering: rainforests are home to more species of animal and plant than the rest of the world and the oceans put together but, tragically, only 4 per cent of them are protected because the rainforest is in private hands in South America and the Amazonian rainforest is under no ownership at all. New species of plants, trees and organisms large and small are being discovered all the time; and to imagine that the world will allow the removal of the rainforests before we know what they contain is surely unthinkable. Dozens of new plants have recently been discovered on the slopes of the Mount Foja range in New Guinea by a team of scientists from Indonesia, America and Australia. The discoveries were made at altitudes of up to

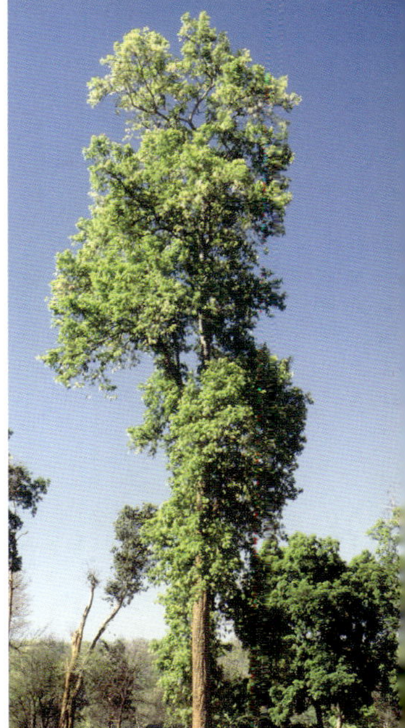

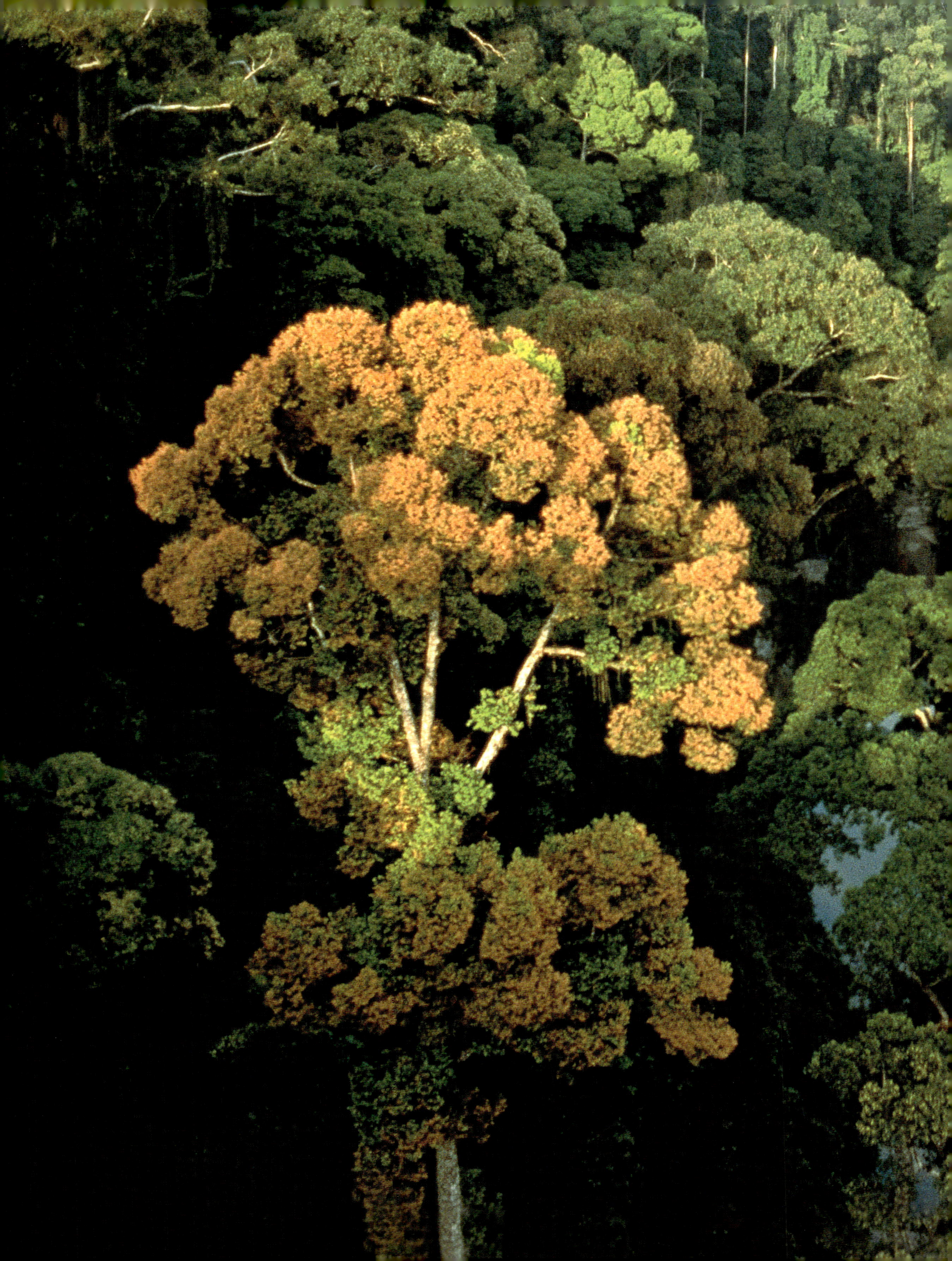

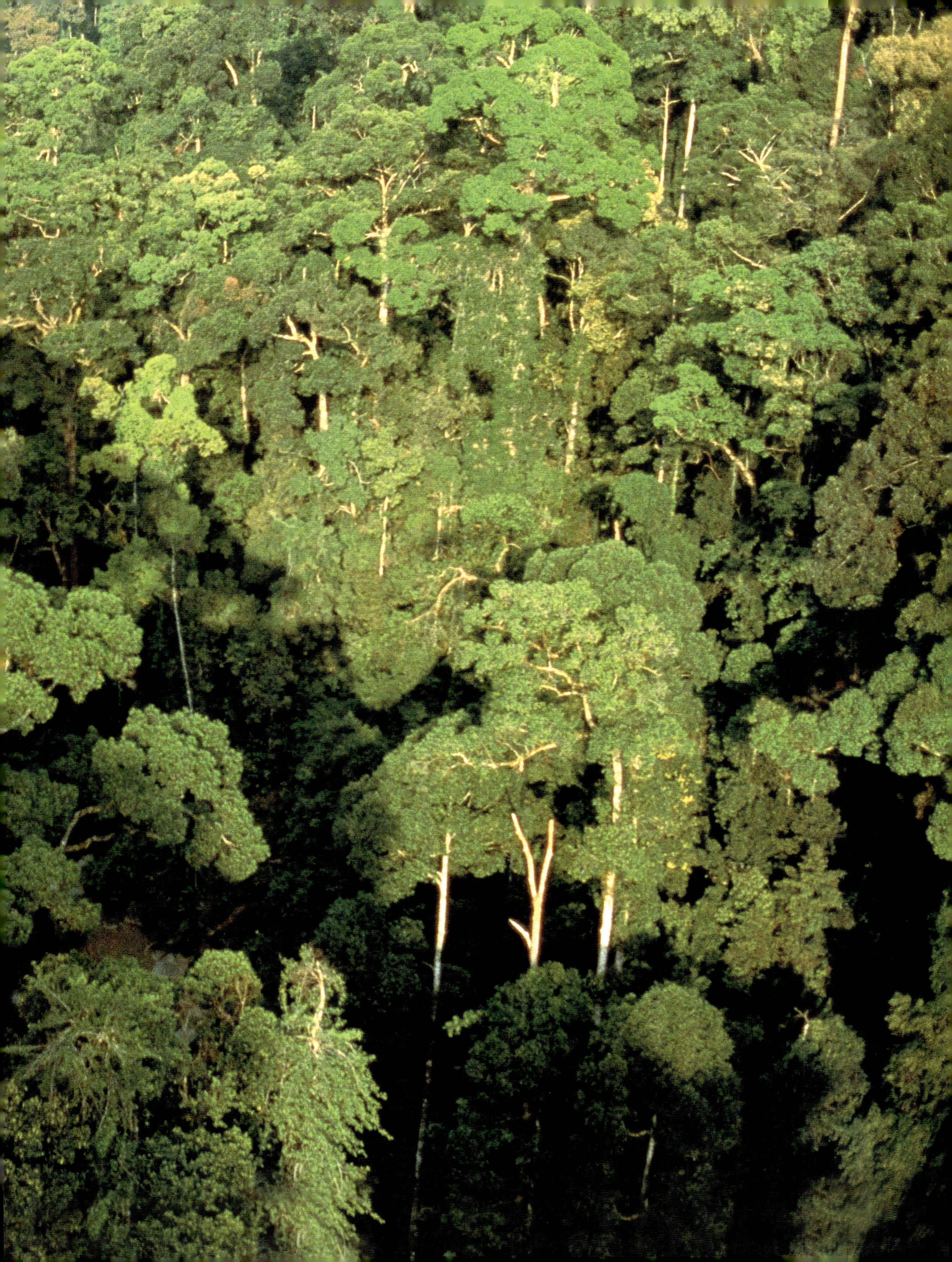

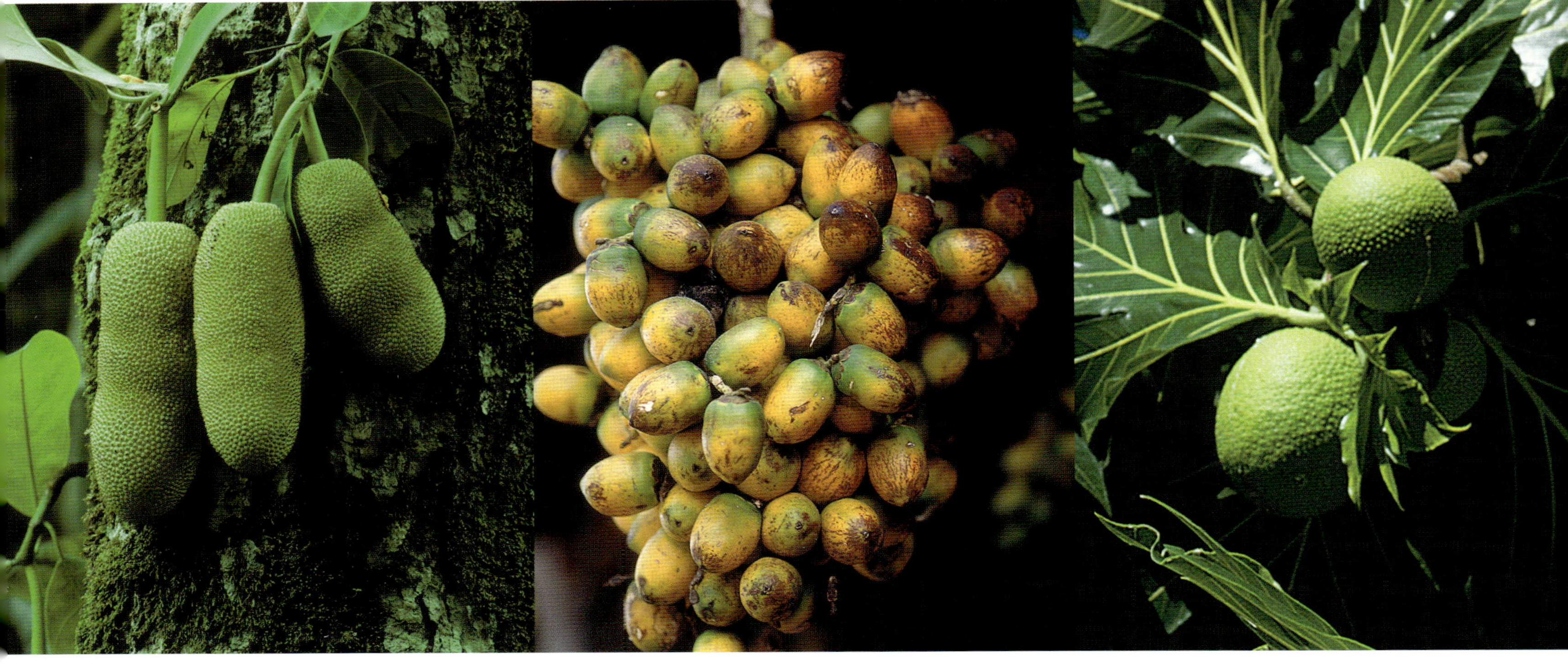

The rainforests are a huge resource pool: the way the plants and

1,600 metres in what is now the largest surviving untouched area of jungle in the Asia-Pacific region. They include previously unkown species of vireya rhododendron and an undescribed species of palm (*Pholidocarpus* sp.). The scientists also identified 20 new types of frog, four new butterflies, a previously unknown honeyeater bird and a golden-mantled tree kangaroo. The depth of diversity revealed in these recent discoveries only adds substantial weight to the argument that the rainforests must be protected at all costs, not only for the treasures they hold but for the stability of the entire natural world.

From above left: jackfruit, pupunha fruit, breadfruit, star fruit, cashew nuts and banana. Some have enormous yields for rainforest commercial crops and the breadfruit and jackfruit require considerable climbing skills to harvest safely. The large, heavy fruits are considered delicacies but often there is tough competition from monkeys, who know as well as humans when the fruit are ripe for the taking.

A quarter of drugs used in the pharmaceutical world derive from rainforest plants, yet less than 5 per cent of forest plants have been tested for their potential medicinal value. According to the Rainforest Action Network, the World Health Organization gives a figure of 80 per cent of people in developing countries still relying on traditional medicine for primary health care (largely because they have no access to any other medicine), and this gives a glimpse into how much knowledge is hidden away in the humidity of the forest. Some of it has been tapped: the cinchona tree (*Cinchona officinalis*), the source of quinine, is a plant that has been saving lives from malaria for two centuries and the rosy periwinkle (*Catharanthus roseus*) from Madagascar, whose properties provide a 99 per cent chance of remission from lymphocytic leukaemia, generates sales of 160 million US dollars per annum. But here we are only scratching the surface of the world's greatest treasures and time is fast running out.

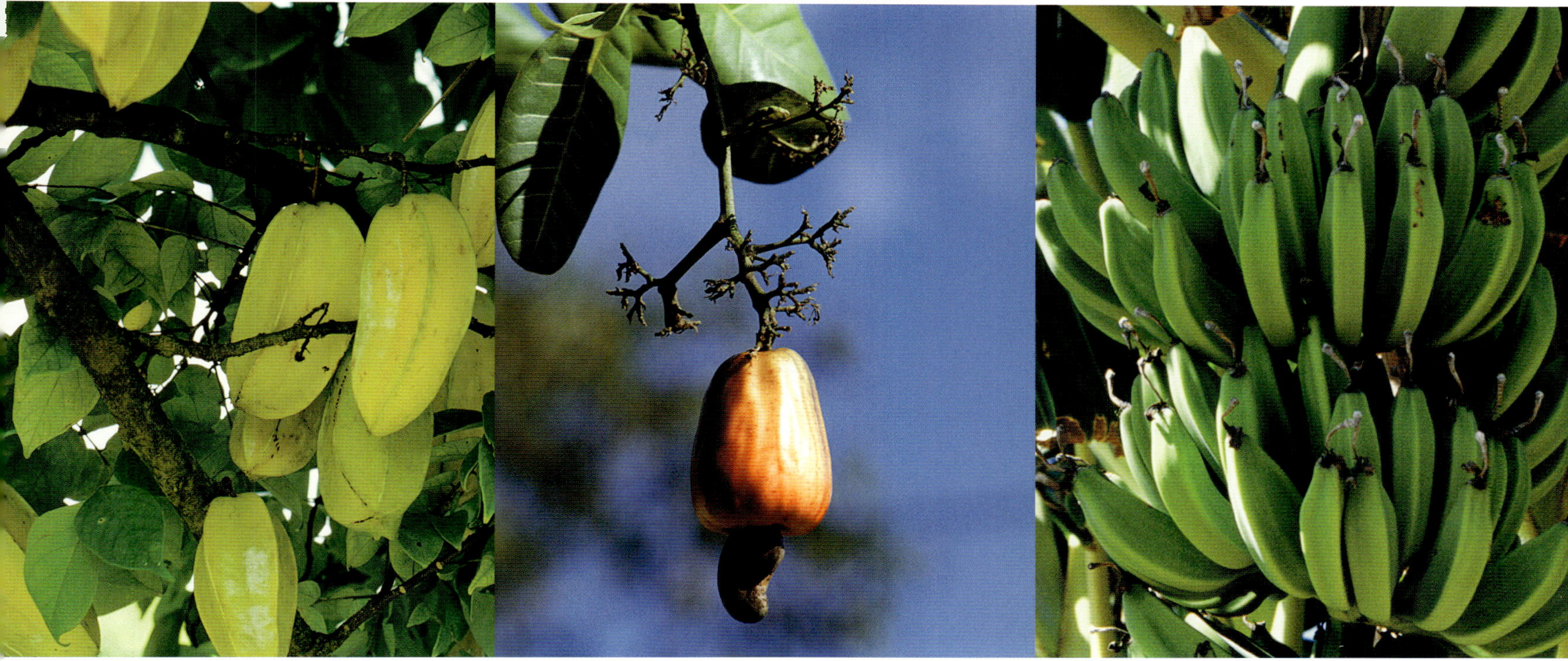

animals mix and interact is how the rainforest retains its health

Biodiversity is what allows the forest to survive by its own means. The rainforests are a huge resource pool critical for their own and our survival, and the way the plants and animals mix and interact is how it retains its health. The dipterocarp and the wild kapok tree (*Bombax valetonii*) are good examples. In the aerial photograph of the rainforest (page 165) there are emergent trees that stick up through the canopy layer at wider spacings than those trees that make up the canopy. This is not by chance – it is controlled natural selection designed to avoid stands of the same species growing too close to one another. This way, some trees will avoid the plague of a particular pest or the ravages of certain diseases. Their means of self-protection has been in place for millions of years.

Native peoples

Native rainforest people are the true guardians of the forest, and all over the tropical biomes of the world these indigenous people understand how to make the most of their precious resources. It is, after all, absurd to think that people can manage by hunting and gathering alone, and 'shifting cultivation' is the means by which most survive today. Simply put, an area is chosen and selected trees are cut and burned to produce ash which provides nutrients for plant growth. In order to live this way, portions of forest have to be cleared but, as in the monsoon forests of Africa and India, the native people know what to clear and what to leave. They know the essential properties of each individual tree and what it can give them in terms of food, medicine and other materials. Shifting

Once the rainforest is cut down, the whole ecosystem is then destroyed and it will take thousands of years to put it back

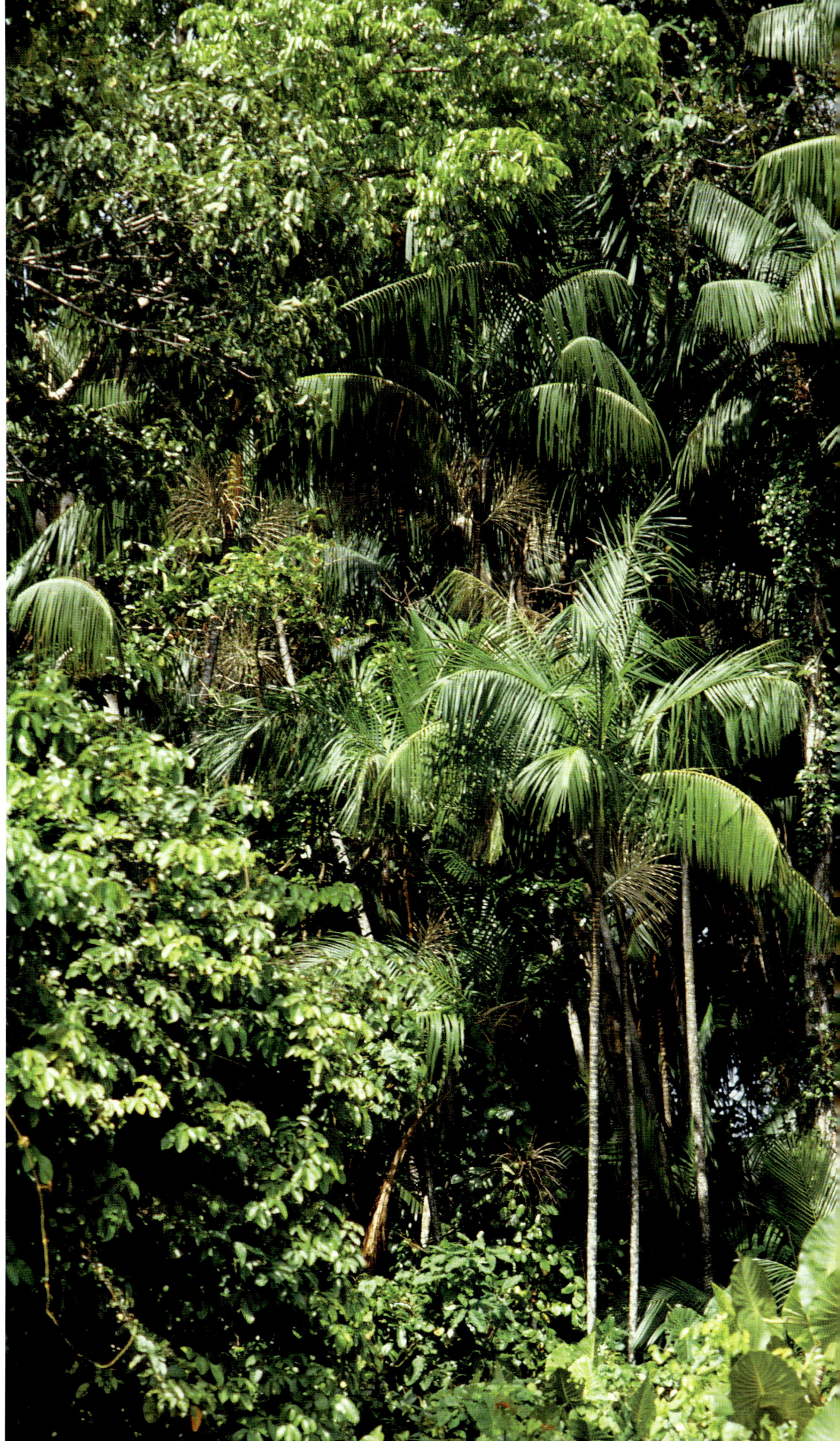

The richness and diversity of plant life in a tiny area of rainforest is astonishing. With plants come animals, and with animals fertility and the spreading of seed. As with any other forest, the continuous cycle of life and death makes for a vibrant and rich system that is entirely self-sustaining: the natural order of life in progress.

cultivation is not a haphazard form of clear felling such as might take place when forest is cleared for logging or agricultural purposes; it is a carefully planned operation which has been practised since farming began in these regions thousands of years ago. What is more, it is the only method of cultivation which allows the rainforest to recover. It is a slow but effective process because it takes into account the needs of both people and forest. The types of crops grown on the cleared land are often annuals, like rice and maize, but also fruit trees such as bananas, mangoes and avocados. After a few years the nutritional value of the soil is reduced to low levels again and the site will be temporarily abandoned, although the productive trees will remain because, in time, the people will be back to renew their connection with the land and the trees that they have left behind.

Shifting cultivation has always been part of native people's means of survival but there is change afoot and it is important that the indigenous people are not implicated in the problems that are occurring at the lowest level. Once roads have been made into the forests by logging firms, some subsistence farmers are heading into the forest and clearing it for the purposes of agriculture. If they do not have land to farm and on which to grow food, they starve. There has been an unwritten form of squatter's rights in the rainforest, particularly in the Amazon, where settlers can lay claim to areas of land to clear and farm. But therein lies the problem. For the indigenous rainforest peoples there has been a rotation period for patches of forest that have been cleared – and this might be anything up to one hundred years. Today these periods have been reduced to even as little as three years in the hands of the new wave of subsistence (slash and burn) farmers. This is simply not enough time to allow the land to reinvigorate itself; and the only things that will flourish in this short space of time are pernicious weeds such as coarse grasses.

The future

So what can be done to stop the destruction? The rainforests are disappearing at several square kilometres per second and all the statistics make depressing reading. We can join activist groups such as the tireless Rainforest Action Network and campaign on behalf of the forests, or we can simply boycott any sort of product that comes from the rainforest that does not have watertight sustainable credentials. Any uncertificated hardwood such as teak should be ignored and every hamburger from cattle reared on cleared land should be avoided. We can try to learn from the examples set by those who manage rainforests and, in the process, protect them; one such example is the Monte Verde community managed rainforest in Costa Rica, a giant reserve run by the Santa Elena High School. We can admire those who have set up butterfly farms in Papua New Guinea, a type of farming guaranteed not to threaten the environment, and we should support products that come from sustainable growing systems that produce cashew nuts, brazil nuts and wild fruits.

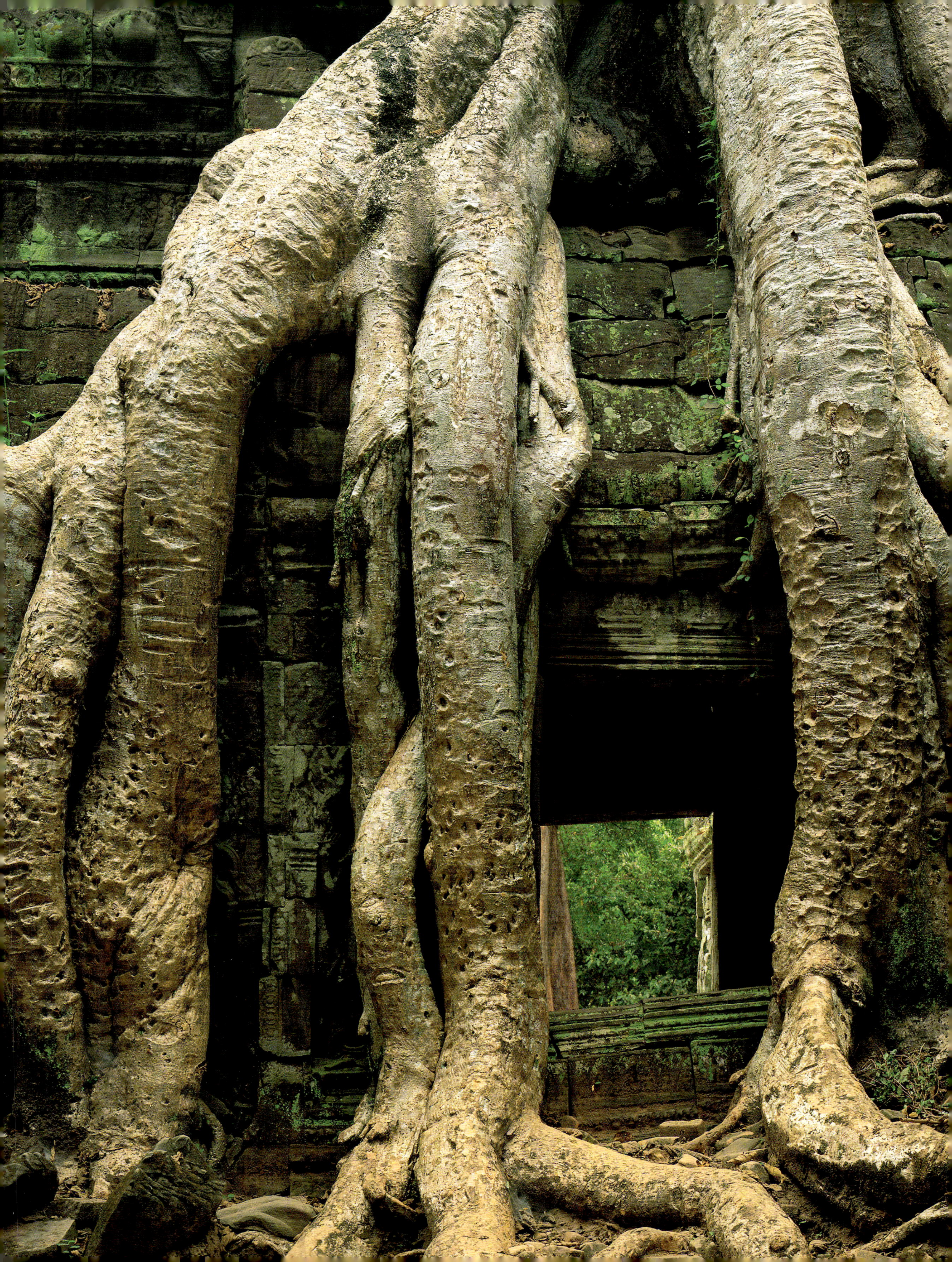

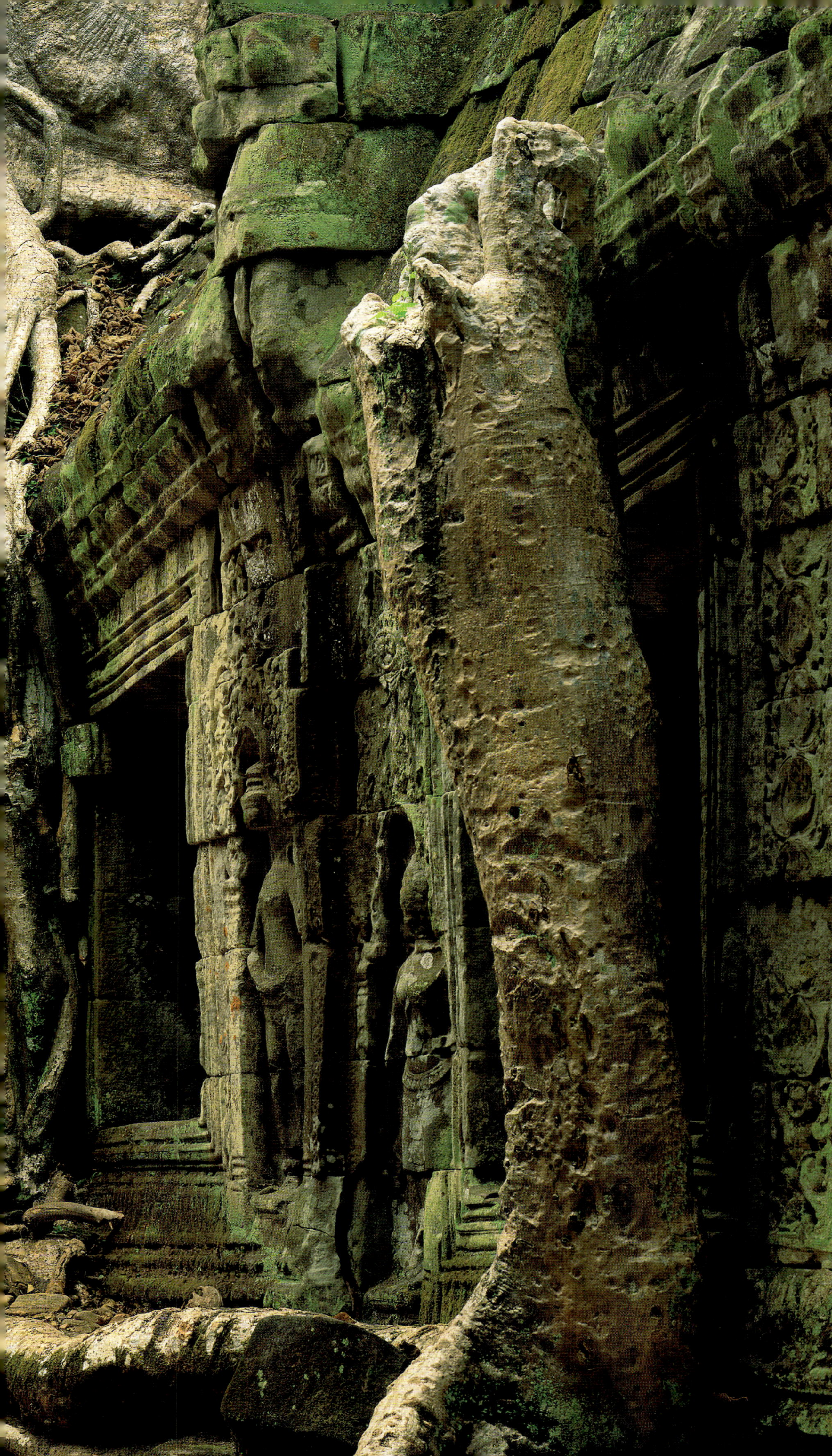

strangler fig

strangler fig

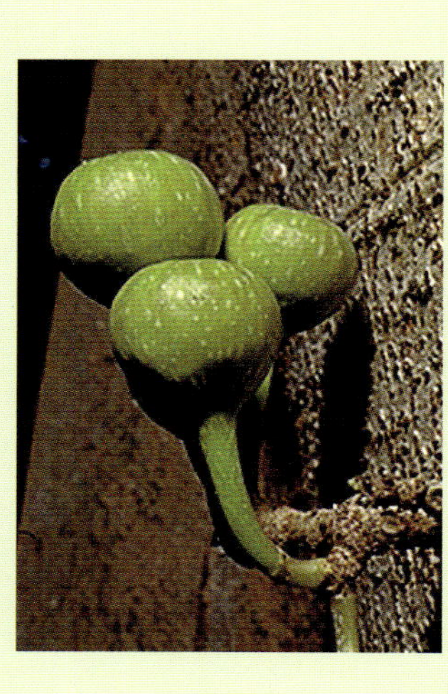

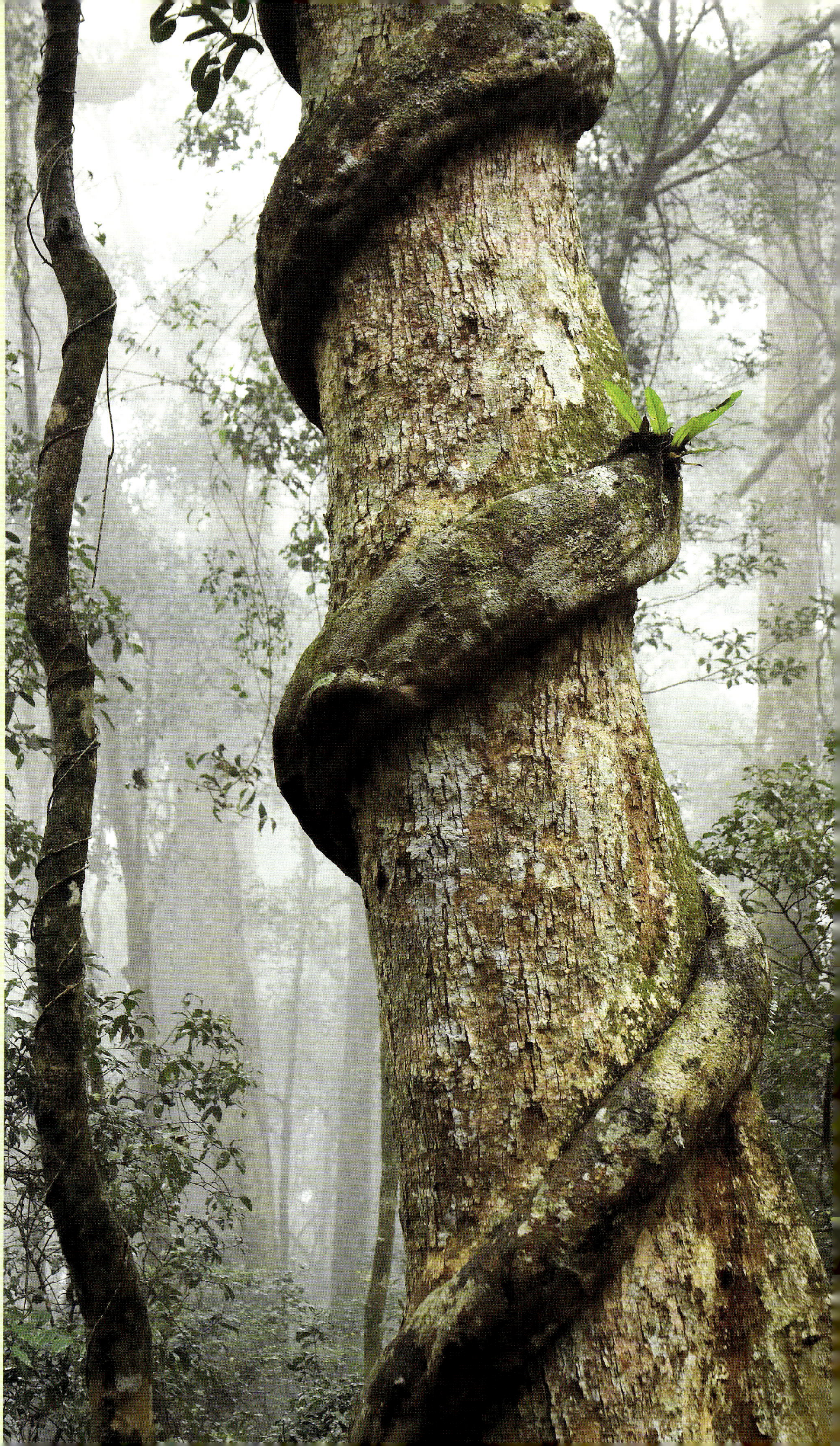

The fig is a species of tree to have gained 'iconic' status more than once in this book. *Ficus carica* is a major tree of the Mediterranean biome and its two sacred species, *F. benghalensis* and *F. religiosa*, feature strongly in the monsoon forest, particularly in Asia. In the rainforest the fig comes into its own again, revealing its extraordinary ability to colonize and provide for a multitude of animal species as well as humans. The fig is the dominant member of the Moraceae family which includes other important tropical fruits such as the breadfruit and the jackfruit as well as the mulberry, a fruit of the temperate biome. There are more than a thousand different species in the Ficus genus itself and this is one of only a tiny number of genera whose members can tolerate the full range of temperatures and conditions.

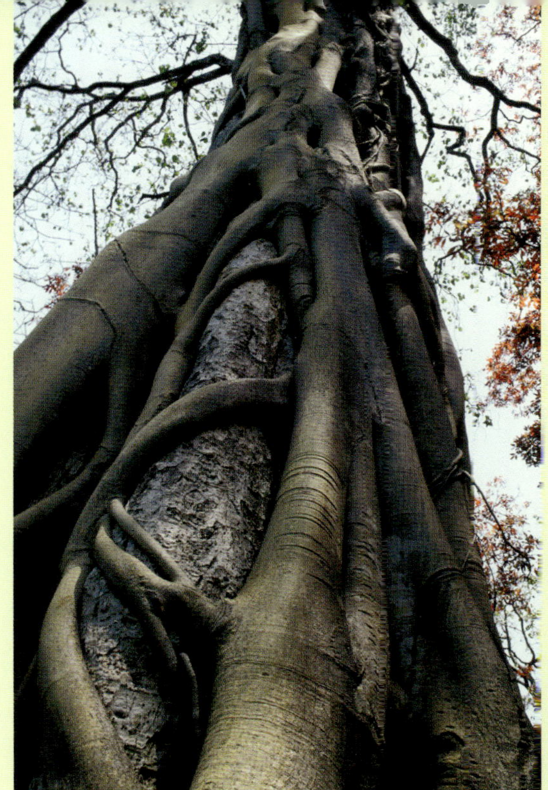

There is a sinister side to rainforest figs. I first encountered the fig in its alter ego on a visit to the Andaman Islands off eastern India. Almost touching the Equator, this small archipelago is hot, steamy and tropical. I visited Ross Island, a short boat ride to the capital, Port Blair. At first glance from the sea, the island looked heavily forested: where only 40 years previously there had been gardens and colonial buildings now lay thick jungle, ruined buildings smothered in strangler fig's roots.

For a tree that provides 70 per cent of all the dietary requirements of large primates throughout tropical Africa, this fig is a deserving case

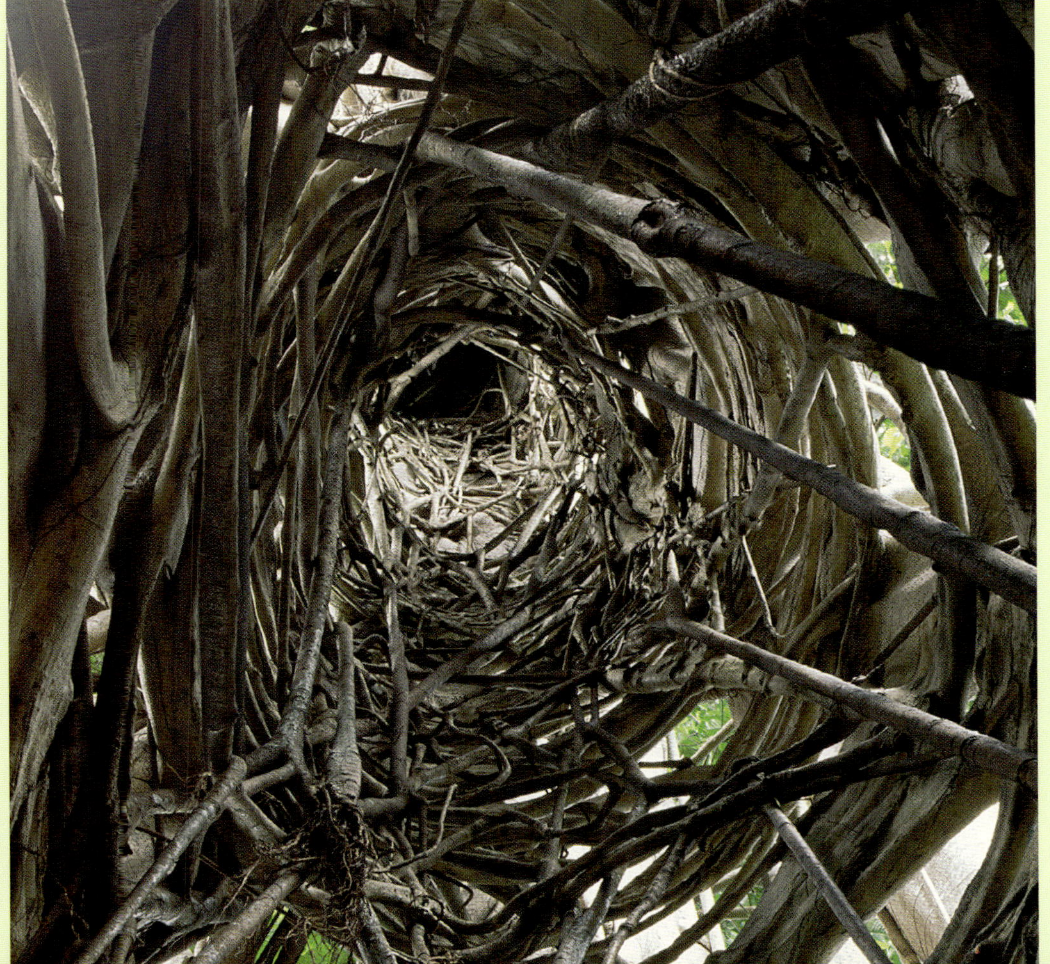

A unique habit of growth

The strangler fig is an epiphyte which means that it is not parasitic, but merely uses the other plant as a means of support. In the process it squeezes the life out of the support plant. Despite ample moisture and steady temperatures, the rainforest is not an easy environment for plant establishment. Light levels on the forest floor are poor and there is severe competition for moisture and nutrients. The strangler fig has adapted itself to a different style of growth. Because the fruit is eaten by animals and birds, the seed is deposited randomly but seeds that come to rest in the crooks of a tree branch find more light, moisture and nutrients. Germination quickly follows and the young fig plant sends its roots down the side of the tree or, further away, as aerial roots. By the time the roots reach the ground the new tree is desperate to grow and immediately begins to compete with the host tree for water and nutrients.

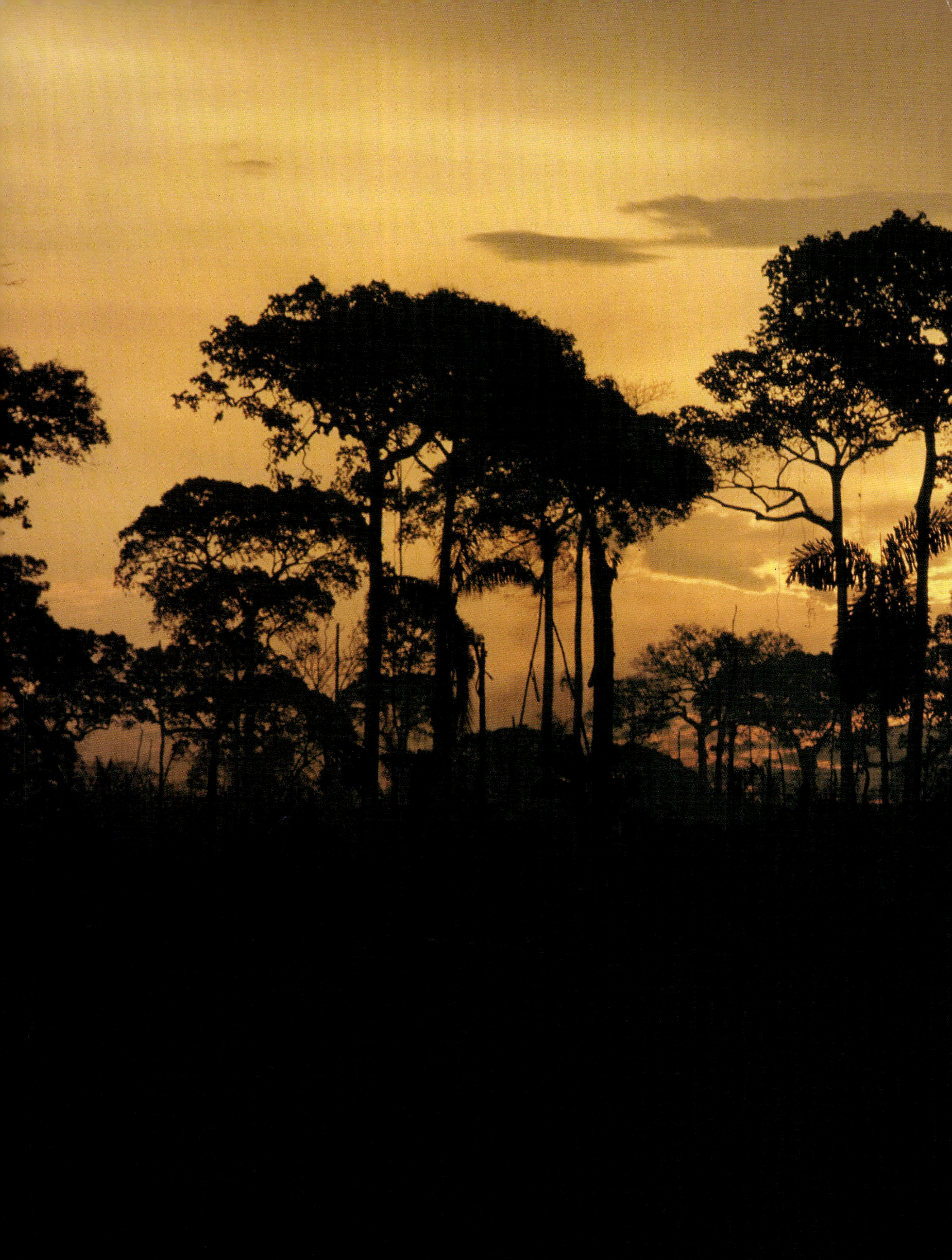

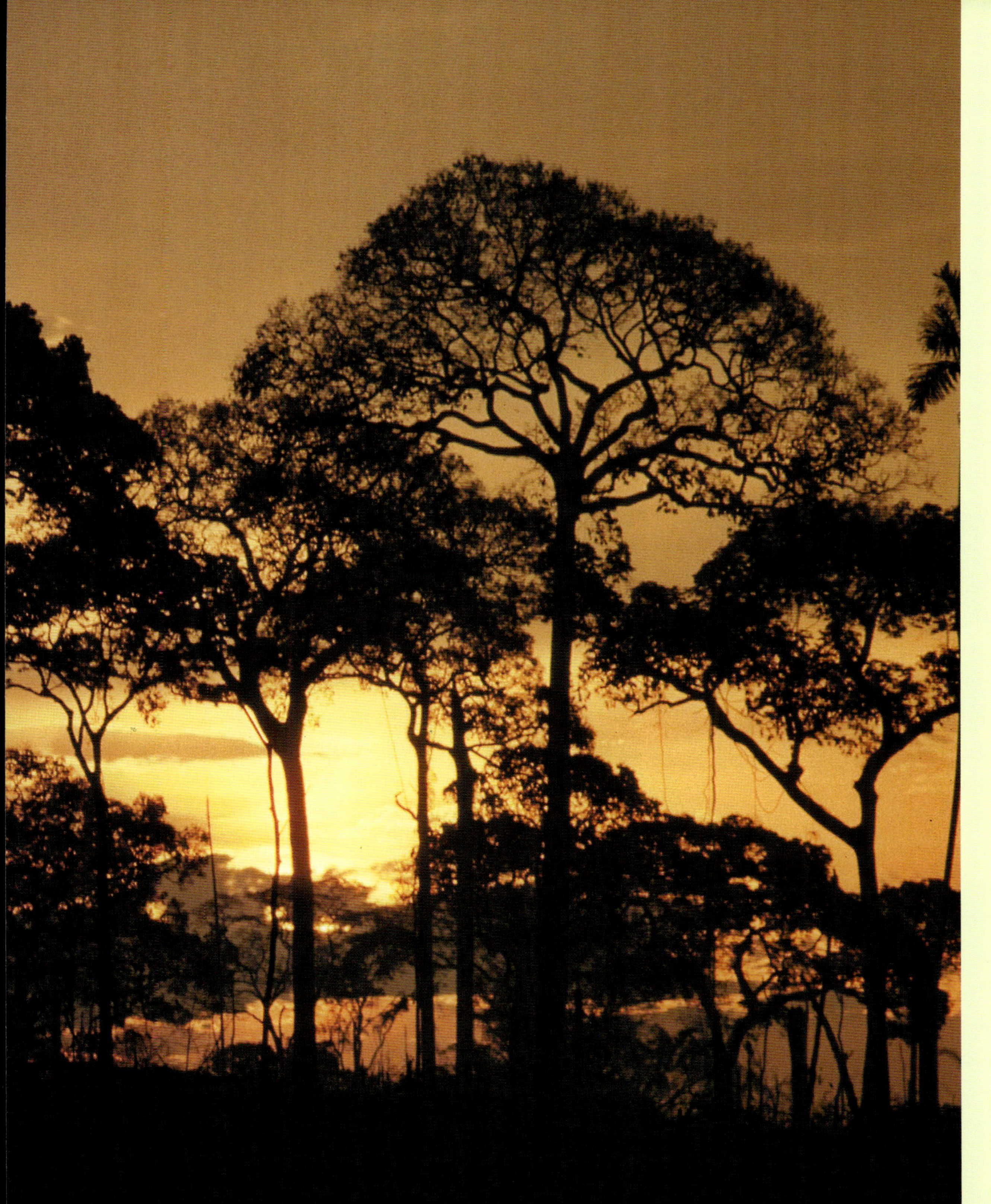

brazil nut

Without the three elements of pollinator, spreader and tree itself, there would be no Brazil nuts to nourish us

brazil nut

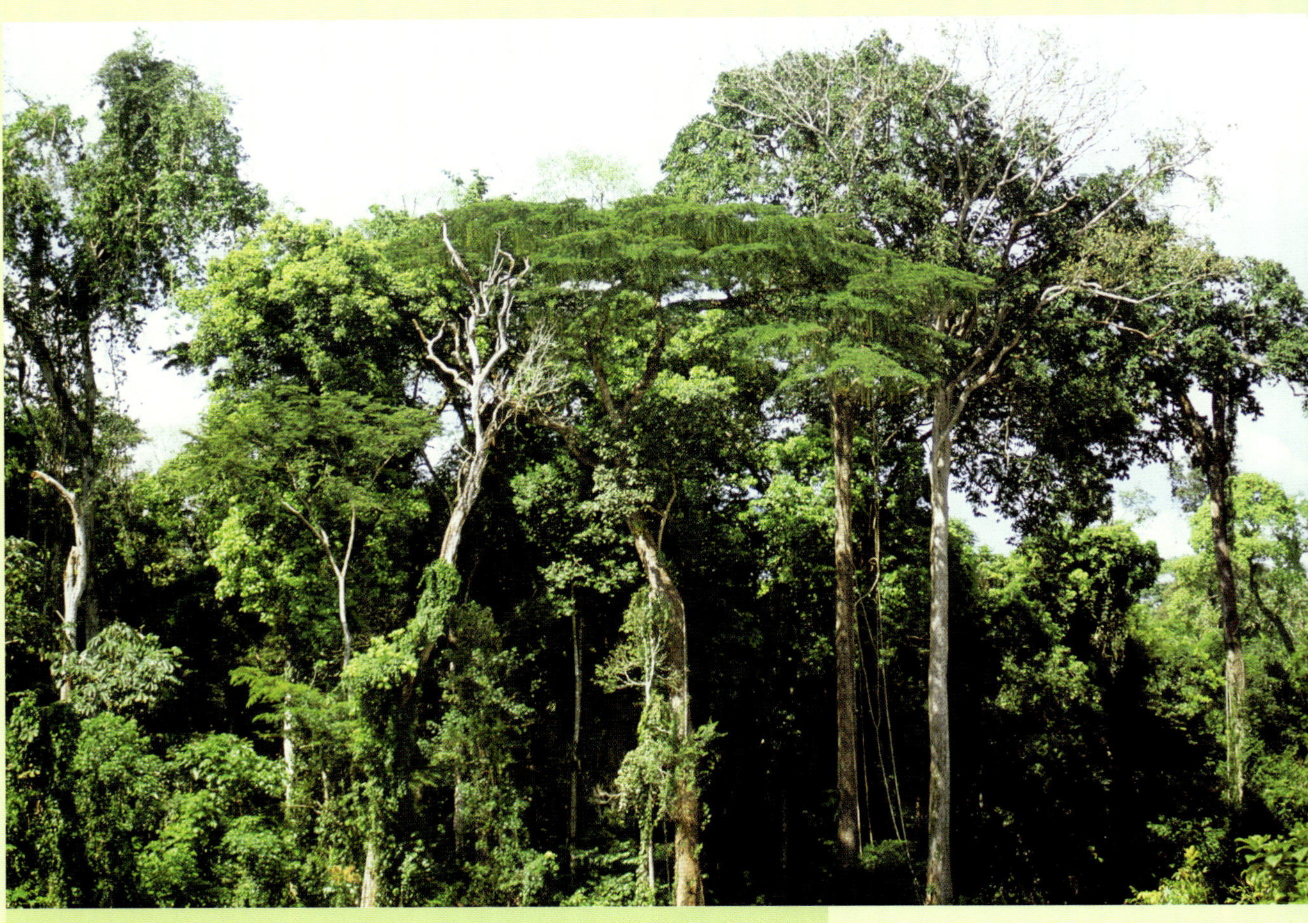

After rubber, the Brazil nut is the most valuable export from the Amazon rainforest. Almost all the fruit is harvested from trees that grow wild in the rainforests throughout Brazil, Peru, Colombia, Ecuador and Venezuela. For a trade that began with the Dutch in the seventeenth century it is strange to think that the Brazil nut cannot be bred 'in captivity'. Removed from its native place, it will not be found by its pollinator, a small bee, and therefore will not fruit. When areas of the forest are cleared, the land to be sown is often found to be dotted by isolated Brazil nut trees.

Because of the value of its nuts, the Brazil nut tree is on a shortlist of Amazonian trees which it is forbidden to fell

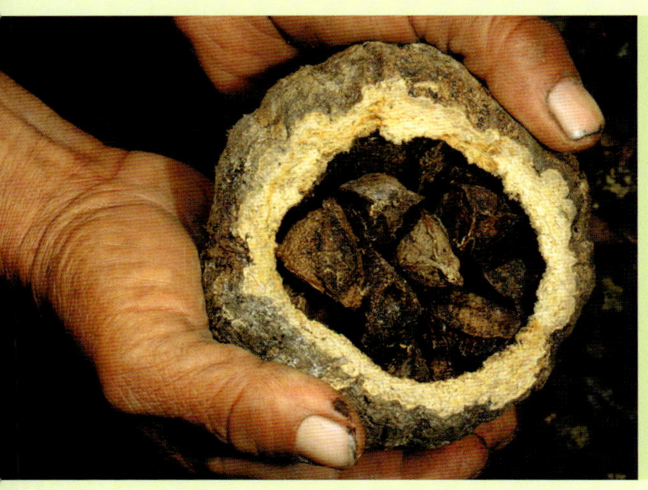

In the wild the tree is dangerous to be around, especially when the fruit, which is the size of a large coconut and can weigh more than 2kg when fully ripe, is ready to drop from the tree. The pod, which contains 12-25 hard nuts, tightly packed in the case, can only be opened in the wild by a large rat-like creature called an agouti, a long-legged relative of the guinea pig. The animal's razor-like teeth find the pod's weak spot and, once it is opened, the agouti will spread the nuts through the forest, where they will take 12-18 months to germinate.This is sophisticated nature at work, doing all it can to ensure the tree's survival.

The Brazil nut tree (*Bertholettia excelsa*), like the strangler fig, exemplifies the rainforest at its most diverse and nature at its most advanced. This monumental tree, which can grow to a height of more than 50 metres, is known as an emergent species, growing half as tall again as most canopy trees. It provides us with a nut that we once opened with a pair of nutcrackers, especially at Christmas, though now we are more likely to eat it ready-shelled directly from a plastic packet and take it entirely for granted as an excellent source of protein, fat and the trace element selenium. In the Amazonian rainforest, tribal people also eat the nuts raw but they grate them and mix them with the flour of the staple root crop manioc, which is high in carbohydrates. Though tall, the tree is not especially long-lived, being susceptible to fire; the tallest are probably less than 300 years old.

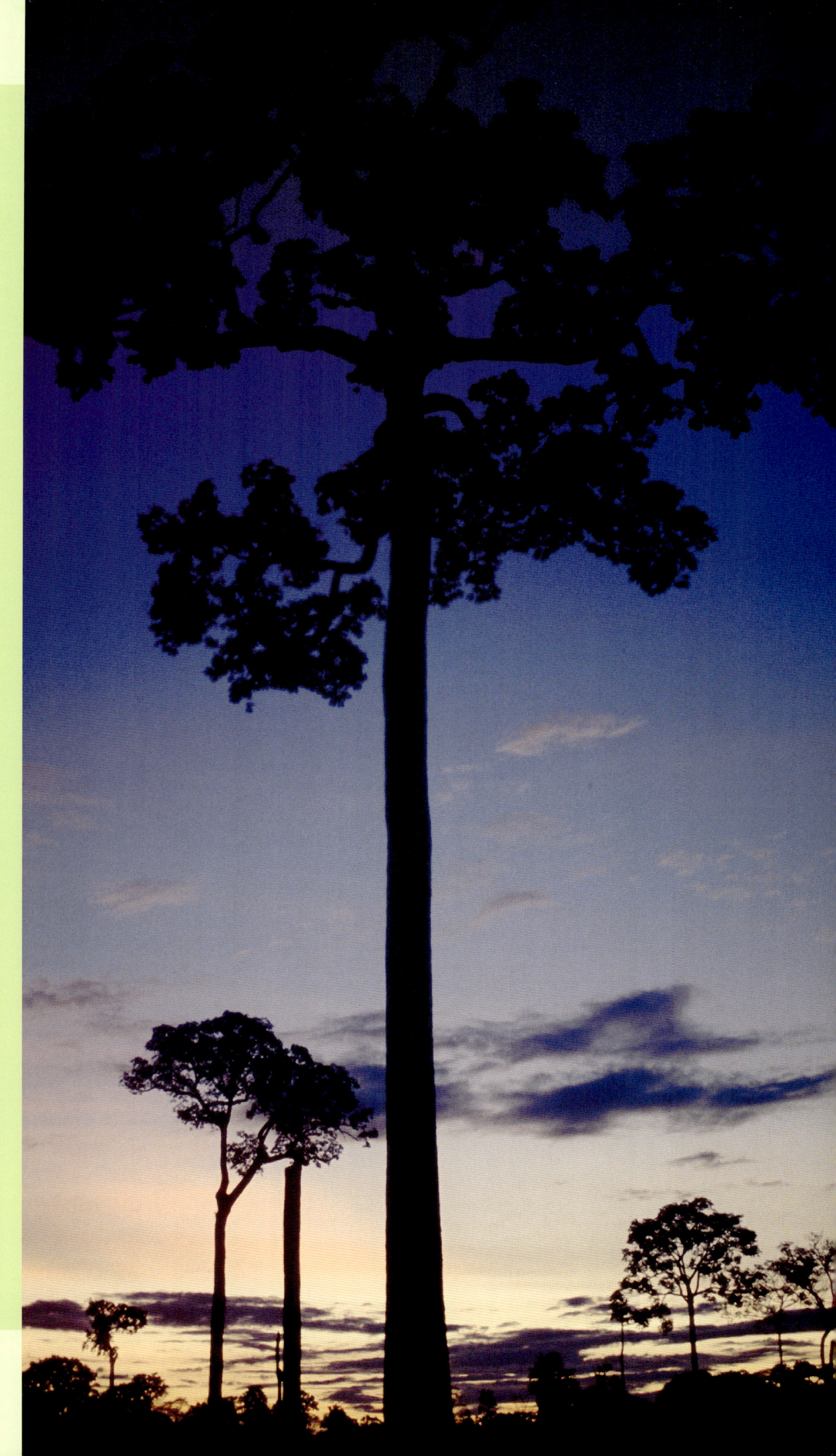

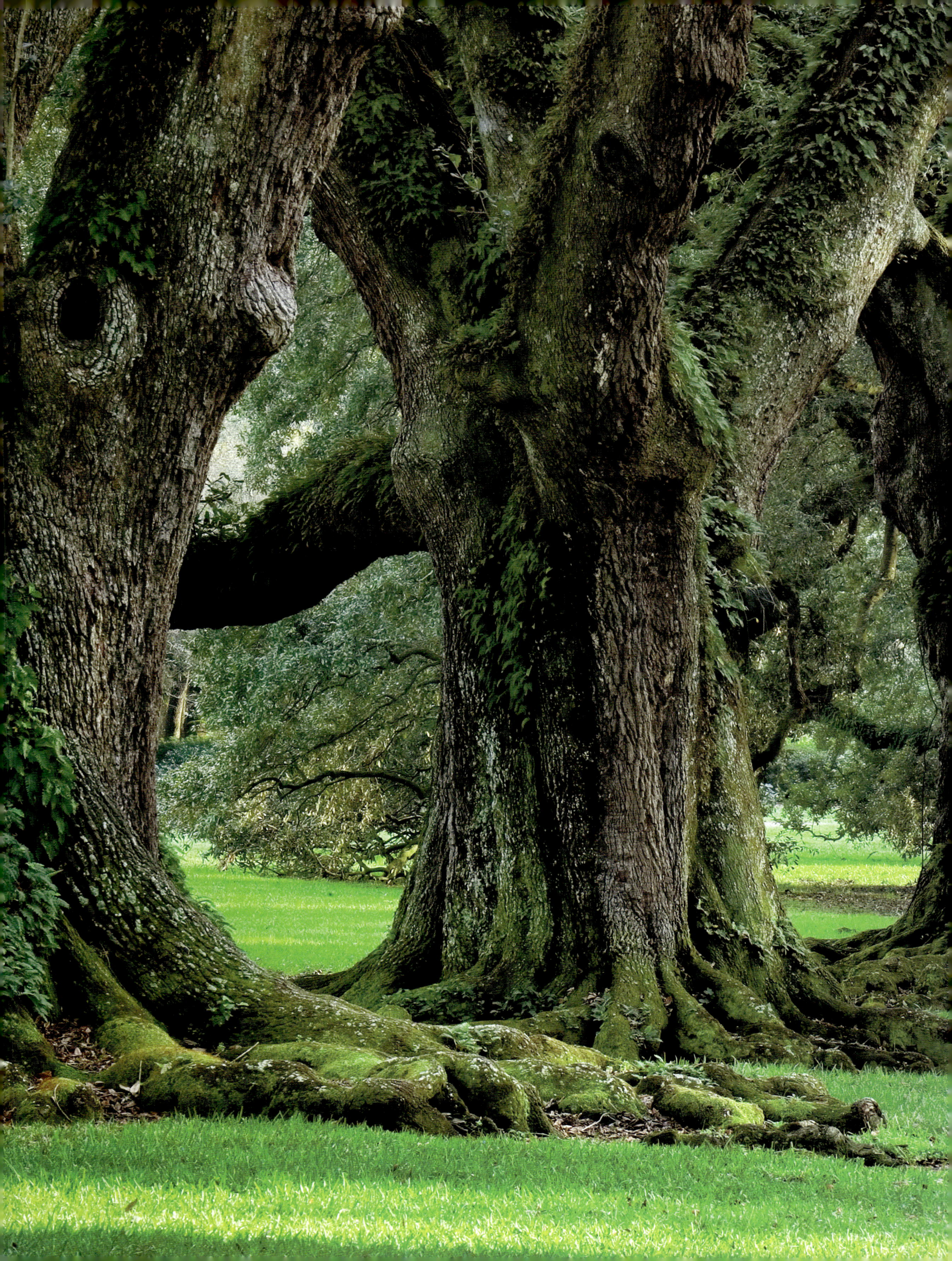

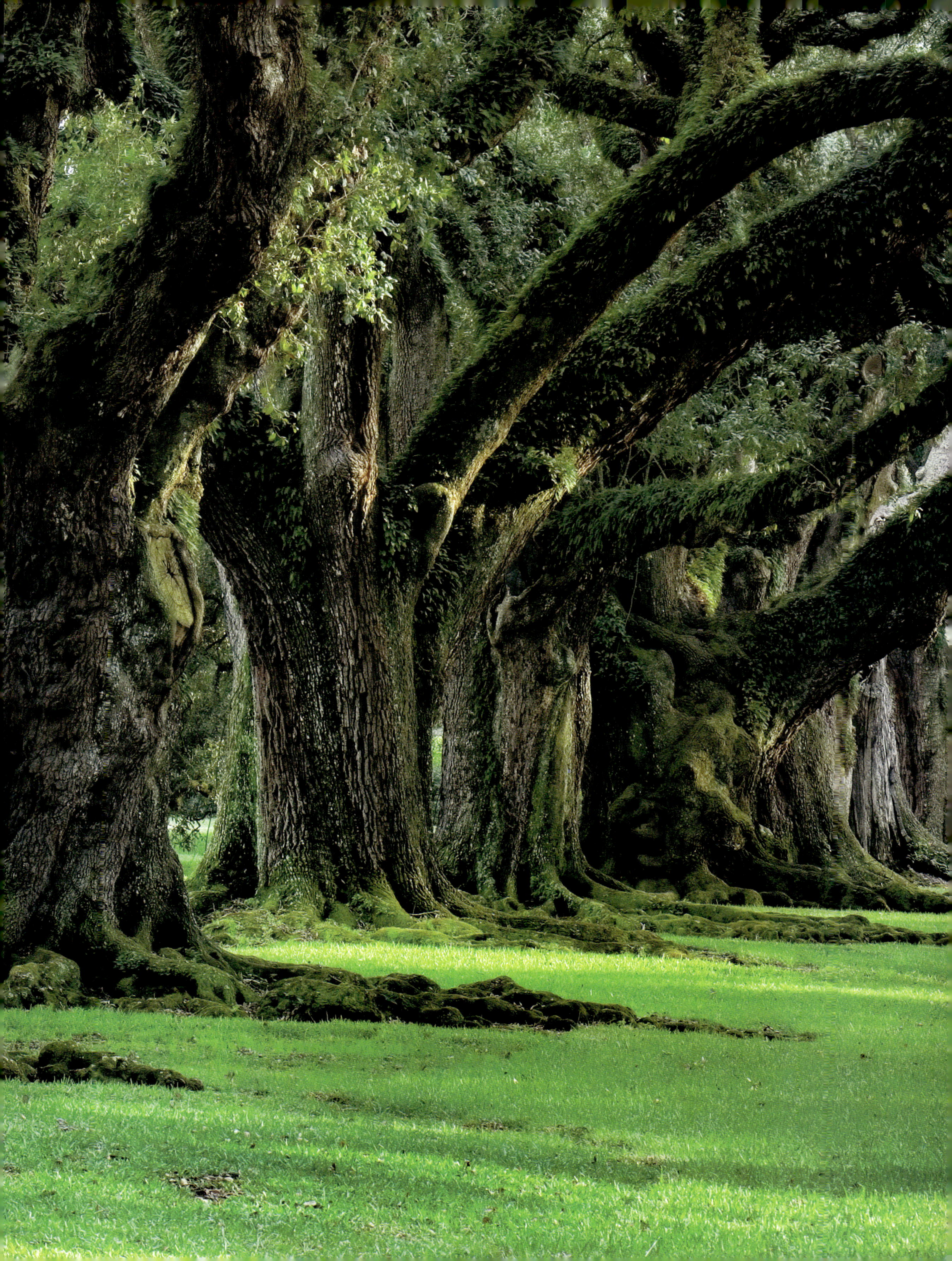

useful addresses

Agroforestry Research Trust
www.agroforestry.co.uk
Hunter's Moon
Dartington
Totnes
Devon
TQ9 6JT

BTCV
(British Trust for Conservation Volunteers)
36 St Mary's Street
Wallingford
Oxon OX10 EVU
Tel. 01491 839766
This Trust works on many projects throughout the UK restoring land and planting trees.

BTCV Trees
Plaskett Wood
Rose Hill
Isfield
Uckfield
E. Sussex
TN22 5UQ
An excellent source of native trees suitable for planting in the UK.

Common Ground
www.commonground.org.uk
Gold Hill House
21 High Street
Shaftesbury
Dorset
SP7 8JE
Tel. 01747 850820
info@commonground.org.uk
A charity which investigates the common wealth of landscape and nature; it has done much for orchards in the UK.

Dendrologist Tree Group Federation
PO Box 341
Chesham
Buckinghamshire
HP5 2RD*nature; it has done much for orchards in the UK.*

The Eden Project
Bodelva
St Austell
Cornwall
UK PL 24 2SG
Tel. 01726 811911
www.edenproject.com
The giant biomes of the Eden Project in Cornwall, England, are a world-recognized landmark. They house the finest collection of plants native to the humid tropics found anywhere under cover and the project organizers work closely with NGOs for the welfare of trees.

Forest Restoration Information Service
www.unep-wcmc.org
219 Huntingdon Road
Cambridge
CB3 ODL
Tel. 01223 277314
This UN site is an information resource about forest restoration around the world.

Friends of the Earth International
www.foei.org
Secretariat PO Box 19199
1000gd Amsterdam
The Netherlands
Tel. 00 31 20 622 1369
The world-renowned direct action network with regularly updated news about key global issues and events.

Greenpeace
www.greenpeace.org
Greenpeace International
Ottho Heldringstraat 5
1066 AZ Amsterdam
The Netherlands
Tel. +31 20 7182000
The premier organization, with Friends of the Earth, for 'green' activism.

Mangrove Action Project
www.earthisland.org/map//index.htm
This action group works with mangrove community dwellers, non-goverment organizations, researchers and local governments to conserve and restore mangrove forests.

National Small Woods Association
www.smallwoods.org.uk
The Cabins
Malehurst Estate
Minsterley
Shropshire
SY5 OEQ
Tel. 01743 792644
This organization supports and promotes the work done by the owners of small woodlands in the UK.

The Living Rainforest Project
www.livingrainforest.org
The Living Rainforest
Hampstead Norreys
Berkshire
UK RG18 OTN
Tel. 01635 202444
This is a growing rainforest under glass in southern England. Educational and inspirational, it can be visited online at enquiries@livingrainforest.org

Paradise Forest
www.paradiseforest.org
This site is concerned with the rainforests of Papua New Guinea and the Solomon Islands.
Contact via Greenpeace as above

The Permaculture Association
www.permaculture.co.uk
BCM Permaculture Association
London WC1N 3XX
Tel. 0845 4581805
'Permaculture' is a specific design system for sustainable living and encourages all those interested to plant trees. It combines all the key elements of organic cultivation, multi-usage trees and energy efficiency with economics, building and life. For anyone interested in planting trees and finding out their true potential, an investigation into permaculture is a great place to start.

Plants for a Future
www.pfaf.org
The Field
Penpol
Lostwithiel
Cornwall
Tel. 01208-873554
This excellent organization has done more than perhaps any other to encourage and promote the ideas behind forest farming and the cultivation of perennial crops, especially trees.

Rainforest Action Network
www.ran.org
221 Pine Street
5th Floor
San Francisco
CA 94104
USA
Detailed website concerning up-to-the-moment rainforest actions in progress.

Rainforest Concern
www.rainforestconcern.org
27 Lansdowne Crescent
London W11 2NS
www.guidedtour.rainforestconcern.org
This charity produces an excellent quarterly magazine with up-to-date rainforest news. It also has a volunteers programme. For more information call 0207 229 2093 or subscribe at info@rainforestconcern.org
Rainforest Concern has also produced a computer-based education program for children.

Reforesting Scotland
www.reforestingscotland.org
62-66 Newhaven Road
Edinburgh
Scotland
Tel. 0131 554 4321
This organization is raising awareness of the ecological damage which has resulted in the deforestation of 98% of Scotland's forests.

Save-the-Redwoods League
www.savetheredwoods.org
114 Sansome Street
Room 1200
San Francisco
CA 94104 - 3823
USA
Tel. +415 3622352
The League has been active since 1918. Its website contains all relevant information about conserving the redwoods of north-west America.

Taiga Rescue Network
www.taigarescue.org
TRN International Coordination Centre
Box 116 Ajtte
SE-96223 Jokkmokk
Sweden
Tel. +46 971 17039
TRN campaigns tirelessly for the boreal forest known as the Taiga and holds useful information about what can be done to preserve the taiga as well as direct action links. It also promotes non-timber forest products.

Tinker's Bubble
Little Norton
nr Yeovil
Somerset
erika@ofek.com
Tinker's Bubble is a woodland community concerned with low-impact living. Most of its resource base is trees.

Trees for Life
www.treesforlife.org.uk
The Park
Findhorn Bay
Forres
Scotland IV36 3TZ
Tel. 01309 691292
trees@findhorn.org
Trees for life is a pioneering project actively involved in restoring the Great Caledonian Forest in the north of Scotland.

Wildworks
c.hockey@virgin.net
Tel. 01773 880329
This company explores everything to do with willow and can be contacted by e-mail.

Woodland Trust
www.woodlandtrust.org
The trust is dedicated to the protection of the UK's woodland.

World Wide Fund for Nature
Forest for Life Campaign
www.panda.org
WWF International Gland (CH)
Avenue du Mont Blanc 1196
Gland, Switzerland
Tel. +41 22 364 9111
This is a campaign for the world's forests and includes details of global loss of forests and effects of the international timber trade.

Some further reading

Risto Isomaki and Maneka Gandhi **The Book of Trees**
Other India Press 2004

J F Dastur **Useful Plants of India and Pakistan**
DB Taraporevala Sons & Co Private Ltd 1964

Nathaniel Altman **Sacred Trees**
Sterling 2000

Bill Mollison **Permaculture**
Tagari 1979

Adrian and Jimmie Storrs **Discovering Trees in Nepal**
Sahayogi Press 1984

J Sholto Douglas and Robert A de J Hart **Forest Farming**
Intermediate Technology Publications 1973

Coen Reijntjes, Bertus Haverkort and Ann Waters-Bayer
Farming for the Future
ILEIA/Macmillan 1992

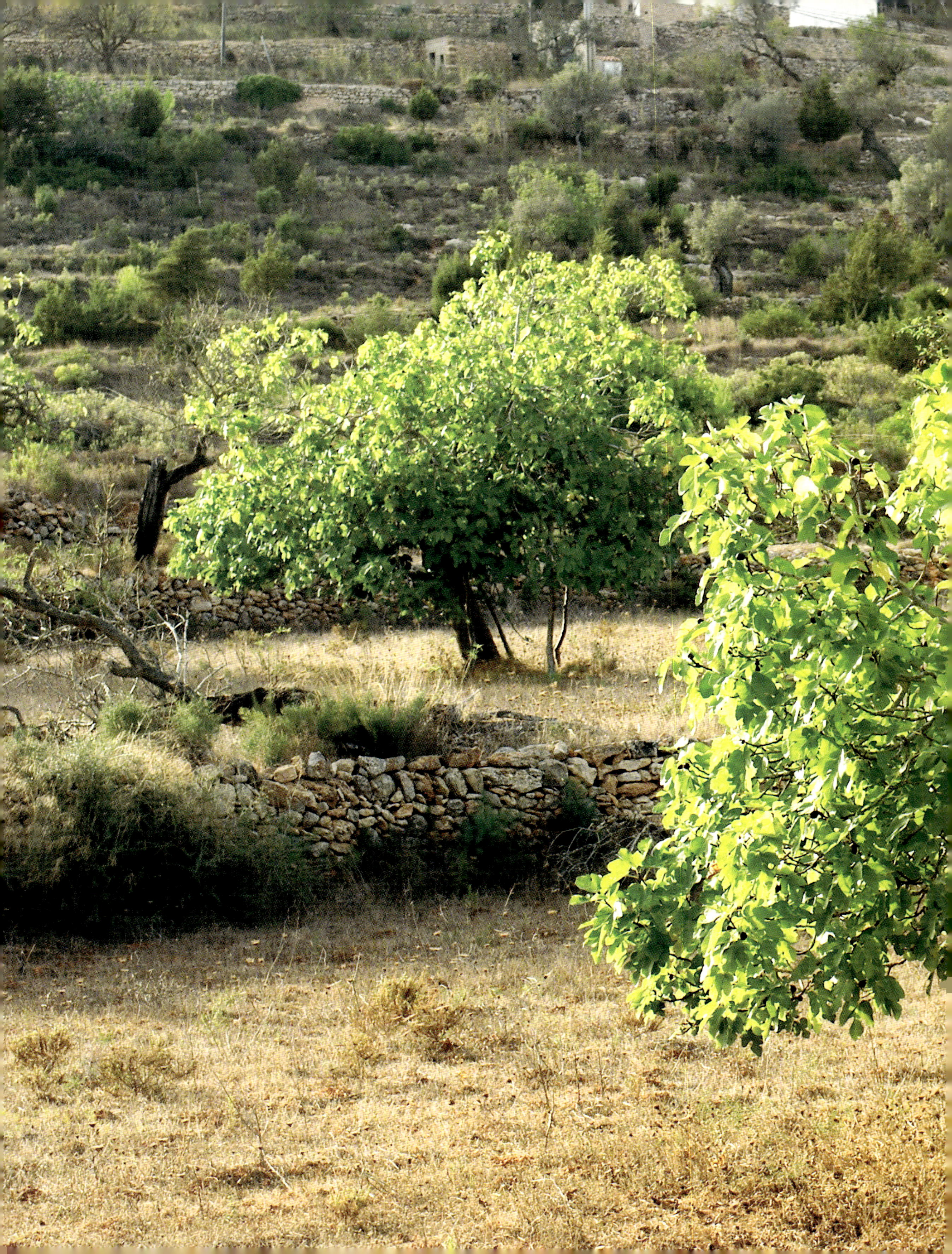

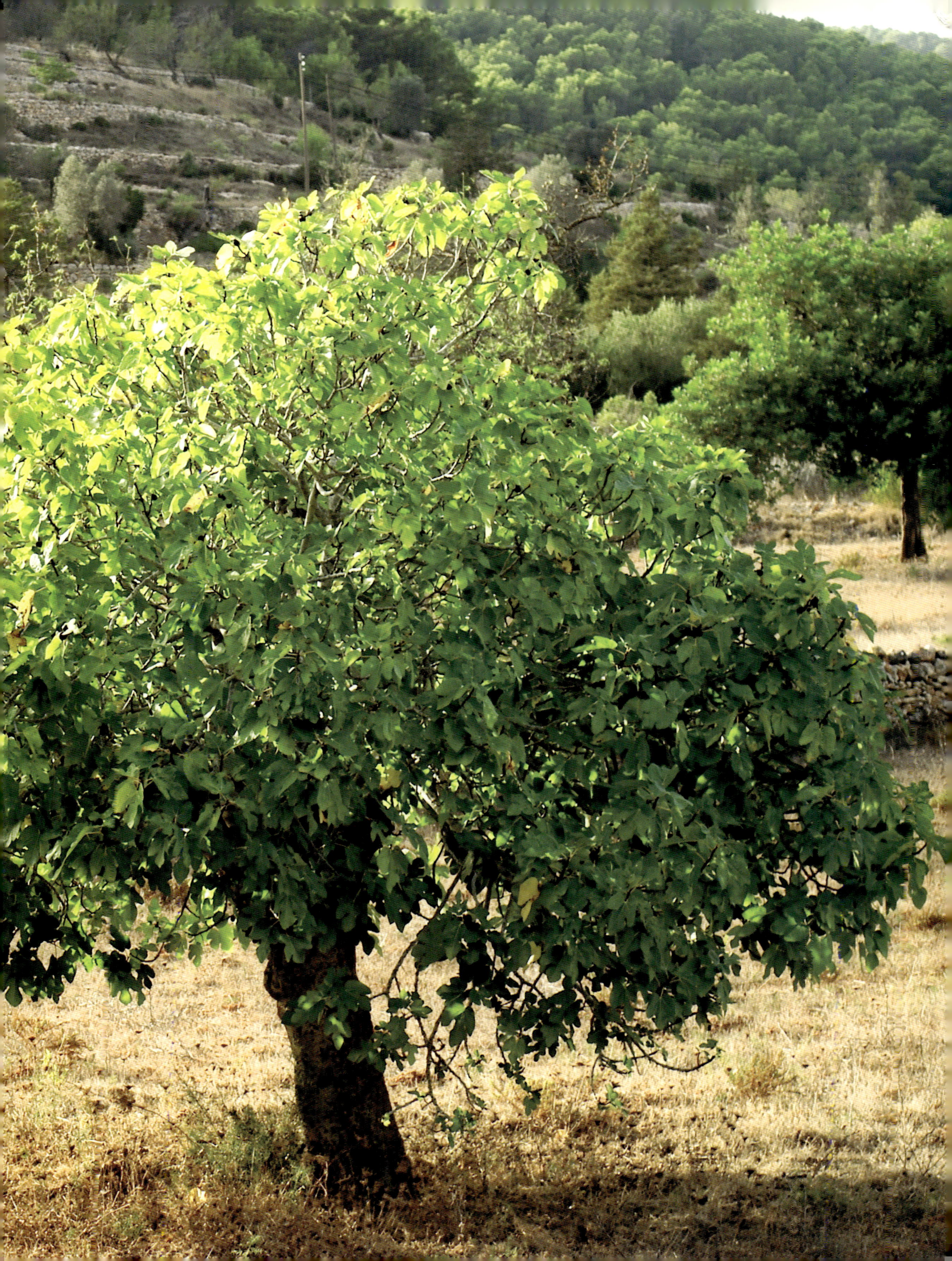

index

Figures in *italics* refer to captions

photographic acknowledgements

The publisher would like to thank the following photographers and agencies for their permission to reproduce the photographs in this book:

P.1 David Muench/Stone/Gettyimages
P.2 Boyd Norton/Evergreen Photo Alliance
P.4-5 Ron Niebrugge/Alamy
Adam Jones Charlie Waite/Stone/Gettyimages
Hilary Pooley/Photolibrary
Vaughn Greg/Pacific Stock/Photolibrary
Ron Niebrugge
P.6 Mitch York/Stone/Gettyimages
P.7 Ian Cumming/Axiom
P.10-11 John Downer/Photolibrary
P.12-13 Ron Niebrugge/Alamy;
P.15 ImageState/Alamy;
P.16L ©Bruce Coleman Inc/Alamy;
P.16C ©Pavel Filatov/Alamy
P.16R ©ImageState/Alamy
P.17L Gary Braasch/Gettyimages
P.17C ©Brand X Pictures/Alamy
P.17R ©Colin Leslie/Alamy
P.18-9 ©Brand X Pictures/Alamy
P.20L Photolibrary
P.20 C Tim Seaver
P.20 R Photolibrary
P.21 Photolibrary
P.23 ©Brad Mitchell/Alamy
P.24-25 ©nagelestock.com/Alamy
P.26-27 ©Alan Watson/Forest Light
P.28 ©Benjamin Micklem/Alamy
P.29L ©Don Brownlow/Alamy
P.29R Mark Hamblin/Photolibrary
P.30 A ©Don Brownlow/Alamy
P.30B Mark Hamblin/Photolibrary
P.3 Graeme Norways/Gettyimages
P.33 ©imagebroker/Alamy
P.34-35 Martin Ruegner/Gettyimages
P.36L ©Alan Watson/Forest Light
P.36R HowieGarber/Wanderlustimages.com
P.37 ©geogphotos/Alamy
P.38-9 Adam Jones
P.41 Adam Jones
P.42 Galen Rowell/MountainLight/IPNStock.com
P.43 Andrew Olney/Gettyimages
P.46-47 Timothy Allen/Axiom
P.48-9 ImageState/Alamy
P.50 Joe Cornish/Digital Vision/Photolibrary
P.51L ©NTPL/Naturepl.com/Duncan McEwan
P.51R ImageState/Alamy
P.52A Adam Jones
P.52B Jon Sparks/Corbis
P.53 Carr Clifton
P.56-7 © Lapoirie/Agence Images
P.58AL Tom Till
P.58C Andre Jenny/Alamy
P.58B © LeighSmithImages /Alamy
P.59 Tom Till/Alamy
P.60L Michele Lamontagne/Photolibrary
P.60C Ewa Ahlin/Photolibrary
P.60R Mardis/Alamy
P.61L Penny Cash/Photolibrary
P.61C Alamy
P.61R Enigma/Alamy
P.62-3 ©NTPL/Ian Shaw
P.64L John Glover
P.64R © Robert Harding Picture Library Ltd/Alamy P.65 © archivberlin Fotoagentur GmbH /Alamy
P.68-9 Jane Gifford/NHPA/Photoshot
P.70AL Robert Wojtowicz/Alamy
P.70-1 ©Royalty-Free/Corbis
P.72L Alamy
P.72R Heather Angel/Natural Visions
P.73L ©Bohemian Nomad Picturemakers/Corbis
P.73R Phototake Inc/Photolibrary
P.74-5 Edward Parker/Photolibrary
P.76 Michael Orton/Stone/Gettyiamges
P.77 Gary Braasch/Stone/Gettyimages
P.78 ©Mike Dobel/Alamy
P.79 Adam Jones
P.80 f1online/Alamy
P.81 David Muench/Stone/Gettyimages
P.82-3 Bernard Castelein/Naturepl.com
P.84-5 Charlie Waite/Stone/Gettyimages
P.87 Palomba/Agence Images/Alamy
P.88Rob Reichenfeld/Dorling Kindersley/Gettyimages
P.90L Nature Picture Library/Alamy
P.90-91 Winfred Wisniewski;Frank Lane Picture Agency/Corbis
P.92-93 Martin Ruegner/Photographer's Choice/Gettyimages
P.94L Botanica/Photolibrary
P.94C Vladimir Godnik/Alamy
P.94R ImageState/Alamy
P.95L Alamy
P.95C Botanica/Photolibrary
P.95R Botanica/Photolibrary
P.96 Robert Harding Picture Library Ltd/Alamy
P.97 John Miller/Dorling Kindersley/Gettyimages
P.98 ©imagebroker/Alamy
P.99 The Garden Picture Library/Alamy
P.100-1 William J Hebert/Stone/Gettyimages
P.102 ©Diomedia/Alamy
P.103 Alamy
P.104 Photodisc Blue/Gettyimages
P.105 Terry Williams/Photographer's Choice/Gettyimages
P.106-7 Hilary Pooley/Photolibrary
P.109 Eva Mainka/Alamy
P.110-1 Elio Della Ferrera/Naturepl.com
P.112-3 Michael Gore/FLPA/Corbis
P.114 Douglas Peebles/Corbis
P.117 Wolfgang Kaehler/Corbis
P.118-9 Gary Bell/OceanwideImages.com
P.120AL A.Riedmiller/Still Pictures
P.120-1 Agence Images/Alamy
P.122-3 FotoNatura/FLPA
P.124-5 Brita Lomba
P.127A Holt Studios International Ltd/Alamy
P.127C Fred Bruemmer/Still Pictures
P.127B Nik Wheeler/Corbis
P.128-9 Edward Parker/Alamy
P.130-1 Howie Garber/Wanderlustimages.com
P.132 Ted Mead/Still Pictures
P.133L Daniel L. Geiger/SNAP/Alamy
P.133R Gary Bell/OceanwideImages.com
P.134- Martin Harvey/Alamy
P.13 Martyn Vickery/Alamy
P.13 AM Corporation/Alamy
P.138-9 Edward Parker/Alamy
P.140-1 Dinodia
P.142 Sue Cunningham Photographic
P.143L Dinodia
P.143C Tim Laman/NGS/Gettyimages
P.143R image 100/Alamy
P.144-5 Vaughn Greg/Pacfic Stock/Photolibrary
P.147 Ian Cumming/Axiom
P.148 Kevin Lang/Alamy
P.150-1Oxford Scientific/Photolibrary
P.152-3 Tim Laman/National Geographic Image Collection
P.154-5 Tom Till
P.156L Yuri Afanasiev/Alamy
P.156R James Sparshatt/Axiom
P.157A Douglas Peebles/Panoramic Images/NGSImages.com
P.157B Botanica/Photolibrary
P.158- Aqua Image/Alamy
P.160A Bob Halstead/Oceanwideimages.com
P.160B David Wall/Alamy
P.160BR FotoNatura/FLPA
P.161 Tobias Bernhard/Photolibrary
P.162-3 Ron Niebrugge
P.165 Frans Lanting/Minden Pictures/
P.167A Woodfall Wild Images/Alamy
P.167C Chris Gomersall/Alamy
P.167B Ephotocorp/Alamy
P.168-9 Frans Lanting/Minden Pictures/FLPA
P.170L Heather Angel/Natural Visions
P.170C Lena Trindale/Brazil Photo
P.170R Heather Angel/Natural Visions
P.171L Brian Rogers/Natural Visions
P.171C Sue Cunningham Photographic
P.171R Sue Cunningham Photographic
P.172 Sue Cunningham Photographic
P.174-5Tom Till/Alamy
P.176L Foto Natura/FLPA
P.176R David Wall/Alamy
P.177L Foto Natura/FLPA
P.177R John Waters/Naturepl.com
P.178-9 Edward Parker/Photolibrary
P.180-1A Sue Cunningham Photographic
P.180B Pete Oxford/Naturepl.com
P.181 Claus Meyer/Typa/Brazil Photos
P.182-3 Adam Jones
P.186-7 © imagebroker/Alamy

author's acknowledgements

This has been a wonderful book to write and my thanks must go to Anne Furniss, whose idea it was, for commissioning it. Her feeling for trees and their importance were strong enough to make this book happen and I am hugely grateful. Jess Walton has found the most stunning pictures, some of which will always be mind-blowing images, and Vanessa Courtier has designed a beautiful book. Carole McGlynn has sifted through and sorted out all my text with tremendous patience and I cannot thank her enough. Finally, the trees of this planet deserve the biggest acknowledgment of all – it is they and their inspiration that I must truly thank for giving so much.